Special Physical Education

NINTH EDITION

JOHN M. DUNN
Western Michigan University

■

CAROL A. LEITSCHUH
University of Minnesota

Kendall Hunt
publishing company

Book Team

Chairman and Chief Executive Officer **Mark C. Falb**
President and Chief Operating Officer **Chad M. Chandlee**
Vice President, Higher Education **David L. Tart**
Director of National Book Program **Paul B. Carty**
Editorial Manager **Georgia Botsford**
Editor **Denise M. LaBudda**
Vice President, Operations **Timothy J. Beitzel**
Assistant Vice President, Production Services **Christine E. O'Brien**
Senior Production Editor **Carrie Maro**
Permissions Editor **Renae Horstman**
Cover Designer **Marilyn Kupferschmidt**

Cover images: Down Syndrome Child © 2010 R. Gino Santa Maria. Used under license from Shutterstock, Inc.
Child in Wheelchair © 2010 Muelle K. Used under license from Shutterstock, Inc.
Blind Man © 2010 Jupiter Images Corporation.

Kendall Hunt
publishing company

www.kendallhunt.com
Send all inquiries to:
4050 Westmark Drive
Dubuque, IA 52004-1840

Dedication

Patricia Carroll Leitschuh, the mother of Carol, passed away June 6, 2006. We are dedicating this ninth edition of our textbook to her memory. Although Carol notes, she would be terribly embarrassed at being singled out for this, my honor, our honor, with all gratitude I recognize her love of our little family of seven and the importance she gave to being an educated person. Following the early death of my father (when I was five years of age; there were five younger than I (twins)), she raised six children on her nurse's salary. The summer before my freshman year at Oregon State University, with an undeclared major miserably looming over me, she insisted ". . . no one can take education away from you." After I received my PhD and completed a postdoctoral study, I told her I got a little carried away with her words of wisdom!

She lived to be 86 years old and saw all her children highly educated: three medical doctors, one engineer, a surgical nurse, and myself, the only PhD of the last three generations. Even though we grew up poor, we never knew it because our house was always full of delicious foods and endless celebrations of the seasonal events, be it birthdays, the summer beach vacations, Christmas music and liturgies, chamber music concerts, films during school breaks, or St. Patrick's Day! The family table always had room for another plate. Our backyard picnic table never sat empty during a summer evening meal, and when we were older, we stayed there long after to talk.

Of course, she also gave us a love of physical activity. She started us out at the local parks playing endlessly on the equipment and finishing the time with rolling down the "big hills." Our family features many accomplished people: marathon runners, ballerinas, downhill racers and skiers, swimmers, tennis players, windsurfers, bicyclists, hikers, Pacific-Ocean-wave-jumpers, pick-up football and basketball players, hide-n-seekers, bocce ball enthusiasts, international travel-walkers, and great social dancers. (Curiously, the next generation moves with very similar ways!)

So, it is in memory of Carol's wonderful mother that we dedicate this book, acknowledging her influence on those qualities of life that both of us, and our respective families, are privileged to live and work each day.

We also dedicate this textbook to our other colleagues, particularly to Dr. Allen Burton, whose legacy continues to influence our work at every level. We recognize Dr. Jeff McCubbin at Oregon State University, who has dedicated his life to educating doctoral and masters degree professionals to achieve the expertise to teach, conduct research, and care about people with disabilities. We also recognize the influential work of Drs. Lauren Lieberman and Cathy Houston-Wilson of New York University, Brockport, who continue to articulate the applied field of physical education for people with disabilities. Other colleagues who have helped to inform the profession, as well as ourselves, include: Hester Henderson, Laurie Zittel, Manny Felix, Georgia Frey, Paul Maguire, Joe Huber, Barry Lavay, Dale Ulrich, Dave Poretta, and many others whom space does not permit us to identify. We would like to dedicate this textbook to Dr. Steve Skaggs, who died just one year after receiving his doctorate from Oregon State University. We cannot think of him without feeling the joy he felt for his work with individuals with disabilities.

As in previous editions, we dedicate this textbook to the memory of Dr. Hollis Fait, who began the work of a textbook in special physical education more than four decades ago.

We each thank our family and friends for their support, because without them the project would not been completed. Dr. Dunn extends appreciation to his family for their support and patience. He continues to extend special gratitude to his wife, Linda, for her encouragement, cooperation, and sacrifice. He thanks his children, Matthew, Michael, and Kerry, for their affection, humor, and example. He also acknowledges the contributions and inspiration of his mother, Arah May Dunn Belbas, and to the positive role models provided by his brother, Gerald (Jerry) Dunn, his sister, Frances Schmitz, as well as his aunts and uncles who contributed to his development as if he was their child. His mother's work ethic and pride in her children's accomplishments strengthened his resolve to give to others and to bring projects to completion. He extends his love, pride, and gratitude to these individuals, with the understanding that "... no man is an island. No man stands alone."

Dr. Leitschuh expresses her gratitude to her uncle, Robert Lincoln, Professor Emeritus, Rutgers University; her aunt, Professor Jeanne Lincoln, New Jersey City University; her brothers Paul Leitschuh, MD, orthopaedic surgeon, Mark Leitschuh, MD, cardiologist, and her sister Mary Leitschuh Whitely, MD, anesthesiologist (direct advisors in the text); and her sister Jeanne Leitschuh, RN, and brother Nick Leitschuh, engineer; and her numerous in-laws and energetic nieces and nephews! She would also like to express gratitude to her colleagues and friends Jill Campbell, Judith Hylton, Doug McKinney and Aaron Brown; and the monastic communities of the Camaldolese Benedictines in Big Sur, California, and the Trappist monks of Lafayette, Oregon. Finally, Dr. Leitschuh would like to posthumously thank her father Linus Leitschuh, MD, who died at a young age but left behind a legacy for his family: Take good care of each other and all those in need of your love.

John M. Dunn
Carol A. Leitschuh
January 2009

Brief Contents

Contents

Preface

We can say with all assuredness that there has been growth since the first edition of this textbook! When PL 94-142, the Education of All Handicapped Children Act of 1975, first was implemented, the Bureau of Education for the Handicapped awarded grants to create training programs for special educators, including grants for physical education. The universities, colleges, and community professionals receiving awards *created* the curriculum to train a new genre of professionals for a very great need in American society: educating children with disabilities. Along with training professionals to do the work of PL 94-142, an enormous amount of energy, creativity, and thought went into developing the curriculum *for the children with special needs* in their day-to-day educational life. We had very few resources when we started and now, despite the reality that our field is relatively small, we have definitely "arrived" with numerous textbooks, various special resource books, and a number of journals. Our professionals can be trained at the highest academic levels and are competitive with grants for research in both the applied and basic fields. In fact, it is time to prune the content in our textbooks! The early pioneers in the field are people who are now retired or have left this world. Today in 2009–2010, the training programs and the research they conducted have influenced our discipline. In addition, their ideals and their students have grown the field of kinesiology and the subdiscipline of adapted physical activity. In most cases, it is time to prune the texts because so much new material has developed since the early editions in adapted activity. The old has been subsumed into the new and also transformed to meet today's needs. And, much like any other disciplines, we have actually discarded material.

The newest edition of *Special Physical Education* is now a hard copy textbook with a companion CD. We have begun the pruning. We believe this approach helps the transportability of the book as well as the transmission of the newest knowledge. This edition expands on the eighth edition with additional information on autism, IDEA 2004, Americans with Disabilities 2008, learning disabilities, and an exceptional chapter on healthy nutrition for children. This chapter was co-authored by a young and highly recognized new researcher at the University of Minnesota, Dr. Holly Willis, who is a registered dietitian and licensed nutritionist. In creating this chapter, we presented critical information on growth and development that will help physical educators understand children's nutrition and allow the educator to then do the work of creating an environment of success in physical activity. In this epidemic time of obesity in America, this chapter will be a fresh wind of information for any teacher or parent of any child. Our information and recommendations address the needs of the child with and without disability.

We believe that as we move into the current educational times, the physical educator will be one of the most valuable educators on the faculty. Yet, we know that this has not been a national sentiment. But we have hope that as we continue to train young people to carry on the important work of adapted physical education, their young energy and dedication will overwhelm the misunderstanding that physical education is not a necessary academic area. It cannot be tossed off in tough economic times in America or globally. Engaging in physical activity is health.

We have a lot of work to do and our textbooks are the beginnings of the journey to a profession. We know so much about creating supportive environments where children can move and enjoy their life in health from their birth to their old age. Our profession has changed dramatically from 1975 and yet it remains the same. Let us remember what was stated over many revisions of this text: "... *it is the desire to be of service to those who frequently are in greatest need of the skills and talents that we offer.*" Yes, let us remember and let us go forth again ... in this, the ninth edition!

Resources

Resources for obtaining information about IDEA 2004 regulations will be posted on professional advocacy websites such as the Council for Exceptional Children (CEC) (www.cec.org), as well as government resources (www.ed.gov).

Acknowledgments

The writing of a textbook requires the support and assistance of many individuals. Special gratitude is extended to the numerous professionals and colleagues who shared their expertise and offered advice and assistance.

The special talent of those individuals who helped to revise chapters for this edition is particularly appreciated: Dr. Paul Leitschuh, orthopedic surgeon, United States Army, Savannah, GA, for revising *Cerebral Palsy* and *Orthopedic Disabilities;* Dr. Mark Leitschuh, cardiologist, North Shore Cardiology, Milwaukee, WI, for his assistance with *Cardiovascular Conditions;* Dr. Lauren Lieberman, State University of New York at Brockport, for continued sharing of her extensive knowledge and background in the rewriting of the chapter on *Sensory Impairments;* Dr. Jeanne Lojovich, University of Minnesota, *Assistive Devices;* Dr. Jean Ann Summers, University of Kansas, *Understanding Individuals with Disabilities;* Dr. Stan Deno, University of Minnesota, *Learning Disabilities and Attention Deficit Hyperaction Disorder;* and Dr. Georgia Frey, Indiana University, *Physical Fitness.* Several graduate students provided thoughtful comments about services and programs for individuals with disabilities that added to the content of this edition. These individuals include: Barbara Schnizlein and Carrie Shaw at the University of Minnesota. Special note is accorded to professionals who were so generous in sharing of resources: Dr. Barry Laray, California State University in Long Beach; and Patricia Krebs, Special Olympics.

Dr. Holly Willis is recognized for her enormous contribution in co-authoring the chapter *Nutrition for Healthy Children.* There is no chapter like this in any textbook on physical activity for children with disabilities. Dr. Willis is a registered dietitian and a licensed nutritionist. Her particular doctoral research and up-coming publications are cutting edge in the science of fiber in nutrition. In addition, her knowledge about the growth and development of young children with and without disabilities comes from her extensive clinical training and experience. The authors believe this information has been needed for many years in our discipline of adapted physical activity and are proud to present it in this newest edition of our text.

We are indebted, in particular, to the following people who reviewed the manuscript and offered valuable suggestions regarding this and earlier revisions: Virginia Atkins, California State University at Fresno; Paul Bishop, University of Nebraska at Kearney; Gail Dummer, Michigan State University; Leon Johnson, University of Missouri at Columbia; Luke Kelly, University of Virginia; and Michael Loovis, Cleveland State University.

To the individuals, schools, organizations, and publications that loaned photographs, illustrations, and materials go sincere thanks for their courtesy in making these items available. Deep appreciation is extended to Dr. Jeff McCubbin, Rena Thayer, and the families of IMPACT (Individualized Movement and Physical Activity for Children Today) at Oregon State University; Sue Lungren and Kathy Healy, Minneapolis Public Schools; and Jill Campbell, graphic artist, Portland, OR. Thanks is also extended to the National Ability Center, Park City, UT.

Tributes in this section could not end without acknowledging Ruth Bowman Overgaard, who contributed pictures and ideas to earlier editions. Ruth was one of Dr. Dunn's first graduate students; a bright and generous individual who made many contributions to her profession, including helping to establish the Portland Public School Motor Development Team. Ruth's life was much shorter than planned, but her contributions were enormous and will be remembered by the authors and the many others who were touched by her.

A work of this magnitude would not be possible without the support of our respective families. Your support and encouragement made the creative moments special and the down times bearable. You know who you are!

About the Authors

John M. Dunn

John M. Dunn is President of Western Michigan University. Prior to this he was Provost and Vice Chancellor at Southern Illinois University Carbondale. Dr. Dunn has also held teaching, research, and administrative appointments at the University of Utah, Oregon State University, and the University of Connecticut.

Dr. Dunn is internationally recognized for his efforts to enhance the lives of individuals with disabilities, specifically their long-term health. He has published over 50 scholarly papers and chapters, developed innovative graduate programs, secured external grants and contracts, and established a clinic to serve children and youth with special needs. Dr. Dunn is president of the American Academy of Kinesiology and Physical Education (AAKPE) and has been invited to speak throughout the United States and several international countries. In recognition of his efforts, Dunn has received numerous awards for his scholarship, teaching, and leadership and has held offices in several professional organizations. He is a Past President of the Research Consortium of the American Alliance for Health Physical Education, Recreation and Dance, past Editor of *Quest,* a scholarly publication for kinesiology scholars, and Secretary for AAKPE.

In addition to his professional responsibilities, Dunn has been an active participant in community affairs. He served as a member and Chair of the Corvallis, Oregon School Board for 13 years and played a key role in issues related to diversity, governance, and curriculum. His service efforts have been recognized at the local level by the Association for Retarded Citizens, National Association for the Advancement of Colored People, and Occupational and Physical Therapy Associations.

John Dunn and his wife, Linda, are the parents of three adult children: Matthew, Michael, and Kerry. In his free time, Dunn enjoys the outdoors, running, working in the yard, and reading. Dunn is a native of Illinois (Pinckneyville). He received his bachelors (1967) and masters (1969) from Northern Illinois University and was recognized by the NIU Alumni Association in 2000. Dunn received a doctorate from Brigham Young University in 1972.

Carol A. Leitschuh

Carol Leitschuh, PhD, is a recent recepient of a Fulbright Award for the Czech Republic. At the University of Minnesota she is a Research Associate in the School of Kinesiology, Coordinator with the Center on Early Education and Development (CEED), and an Affiliate Member of the Center for Neurobehavioral Development. In the School of Kinesiology, Dr. Leitschuh coordinates and instructs the Masters in Education in Applied Kinesiology, Developmental and Adapted Physical Education (DAPE), teaches motor development for both doctoral and masters students in kinesiology, as well as undergraduate students in early childhood education and special education. Dr. Leitschuh is an avid traveler and has conducted teaching and research in Italy, Greece, Singapore, and the Czech Republic. In 2000, Dr. Leitschuh was the recipient of an Initial Career Award from the Office of Special Education and Rehabilitative Services (OSERS, U.S. Department of Education). This grant developed and validated a functional movement skill assessment for infants, toddlers, and preschool children with and without disabilities. This assessment tool is under investigation as an early indicator of cerebral palsy. Dr. Leitschuh was a Research Fellow with the Early Childhood Research Institute on Measuring Growth and Development (ECRI-MGD, 1996–2000) with Principal Investigators Drs. McConnell and McEvoy at the University of Minnesota, a three-university consortium (Minnesota, Oregon, and Kansas), and a five-year project funded by the Office of Special Education Programs (U.S. Department of Education) to develop and evaluate individual growth and development indicators for infants, toddlers, and children up to age eight with disabilities. For CEED, Dr. Leitschuh provides expertise in early childhood special education/developmental adapted physical education; movement assessment for infants, toddlers, and preschool children; and consultation to school districts. Dr. Leitschuh has presented in the United States on movement assessment and development in early childhood, and has collaborated with the University of Rome in Italy, the University of Athens in Greece and the Center for American Education in Singapore on assessment of functional movement skill for infants, toddlers, and young children. Dr. Leitschuh received her PhD in 1996 from Oregon State University in Human Performance with funding from the United States Department of Education focusing on Movement Studies in Disability.

Fundamentals

This initial section delineates the role of physical education in providing a special education service through presentation of certain basic information about the historical background, the general patterns of growth and development, the nature of motor learning, and the psychology of the person with a disability.

OBJECTIVES

The section is designed to help the reader to:
- Understand and appreciate the influences that have shaped present-day physical education for students with disabilities.
- Recognize and apply the developmental patterns of motor movement as they relate to the performance of the basic skills.
- Apply motor learning concepts to the development of appropriate physical education experiences for special students.
- Accept students with disabilities as unique individuals with physical, emotional, and social needs.

Historical Background

CHAPTER OBJECTIVES

After studying this chapter, the reader should be able to:

1 Understand the evolution of programs and services for individuals with disabilities.
2 Recognize various terms that are used to refer to special populations and use these terms appropriately.
3 Analyze selected terms that have been developed to refer to physical activity programs for individuals with disabilities.
4 Identify factors that have contributed to a more positive understanding of persons with disabilities.
5 Analyze the role that governmental agencies have played in expanding services for individuals with disabilities.
6 Identify and explain the significance of federal legislation and the impact of this legislation on physical education and sport programs for individuals with disabilities.
7 Recognize significant events and people that have been instrumental in the evolution of physical education for those with disabilities.
8 Identify professional organizations that promote physical education and sport for individuals with disabilities and the role these organizations play in helping professionals.

Since the beginning of time there has been an interest in and fascination with human development and individual differences. This is reflected in the writings of the early religious prophets and documented as well by the actions of the kings and emperors of ancient time. The early attitude was one of describing differences that existed between individuals considered to be normal compared to those identified as atypical. Nowhere is this fascination with individual differences more real than when applied to those who possess some type of disability. Fortunately in the United States, with the passage of enlightened educational legislation such as Public Law 105-17, the Individuals with Disabilities Education Act (IDEA '97), a concerted effort has been made to recognize not only differences but to accentuate as well similarities between individuals with and without disabilities. Within this chapter, information will be presented to assist readers in understanding the changing perspective that is occurring in society concerning those individuals with disabilities and the importance of physical education in contributing to the

lives of individuals with special needs. To help the reader understand this chapter and the rest of the book, selected terms will be defined before undertaking a discussion of the role of those with disabilities in society.

Initially, when referring to an individual with a disability, the term "handicapped" was used in both civil law (e.g., Public Law (PL) 93-12, Vocational Rehabilitation Act of 1973, which was enacted to protect the rights of individuals with disabilities) and in educational law (e.g., PL 94-142, The Education of All Handicapped Children Act of 1975, which mandated services to individuals in need of special education). In 1990, the term "disability" was substituted for handicapped in the enactment of both civil law under PL 101-336, Americans with Disabilities Act (ADA), and educational law under PL 101-476, Individuals with Disabilities Education Act (IDEA). The shift in terminology was due in part to a growing awareness of the detrimental effects of labeling a person as "handicapped" and the resulting demeaning status of that individual. The shift in terminology recognized that an individual might have "differences" owing to a condition (a disability, an impairment, or a disorder) but ultimately was valued similarly to those individuals without disabilities. Person-first language was then employed whereby the person is addressed first and then, if necessary, the condition. For example, an inappropriate address for an instructor would be "my severe and profounds' swimming class," whereas an appropriate description would be "Sara has a severe physical disability and is in my swimming class." If it is not necessary to describe the disability, then the statement would be: "Sara is in my swimming class."

In educational law, the shift away from the term "handicap" was concomitant with the shift away from special education service delivery based on an individual's medical diagnosis. In the early years of federal educational law, the medical doctor, the diagnosis, or both was at the top of the hierarchy of the decision-making process in the education setting. Given a decade or more of this model, advocacy gained momentum across the United States for placement and service delivery to be separated from the pure medical diagnosis and be driven by a broader understanding of the uniqueness of individuals with disabilities, their family concerns, and the educational resources available for them.

The World Health Organization (WHO) further influenced the change in terminology from handicap to disability. According to WHO's International Classification of Functioning, Disability and Health (ICF, 2002), *health-related domains* are classified in terms of body functions which are ". . . all body functions, activities, and participation," and *disability* is the term for ". . . impairments, activity limitations and participation restrictions." As with federal educational law, the ICF recognizes that the unique characteristics of individuals and their environment interact with both function and disability. It is important to realize that, in WHO's terminology, an individual may have a disability that limits function, but that limitation may be imposed by the body itself, by the individual, or by society in general. For example, an individual who is blind may have a Ph.D., be employed as a teacher, be married with children, and participate in competitive athletics. The disability is blindness, which requires certain modifications in such areas as reading, but the individual is not necessarily limited in the roles of an educator, spouse, parent, or athlete. Instead, these limitations may be more quickly attributed to this person by society. In addition, WHO supports the reality that medical diagnosis is not a predictor of service needs, extent of care, functional ability, or the degree of social integration.

The term "disabled" is used in the most current federal educational law, the Individuals with Disabilities Education Improvement Act (IDEA, 2004). Individuals who are disabled are specified under IDEA 2004 are seen in table 1.1. For children ages three to nine years, the term "child with a disability"

may, at the discretion of the state, include a child who is experiencing developmental delays as defined by the state. The authors accept the definitions under federal education law and will address each of these disabilities and their implications for developing movement skills. In addition, this book will include information about individuals with other disorders who require special considerations in physical education, such as those who are obese, low-fit, and awkward.

Regarding physical education, a number of different names are given to the special educational provisions made in the physical education curriculum for those unable to benefit from the offerings made to the general student body under general physical education. In its 2004 position statement, the Adapted Physical Activity Council of the American Alliance for Physical Education, Health, Recreation, and Dance (AAHPERD, 2004) states:

> A strong preference within IDEA is that children with disabilities are educated in neighborhood schools and general classrooms (including physical education) whenever appropriate. Consequently, the general physical education class should be considered the first placement option. Appropriate placement within the general physical education class will require consideration of environment, equipment modifications, and support personnel involved.

According to Block (2000), the term "general physical education" is used rather than "regular physical education" to acknowledge the educational trend away from placing students separated into "regular" and "special" education classes. As noted previously, inclusion of students with disabilities in the general education curriculum is considered appropriate when supports and services are in place in the general curriculum for student academic success. In addition, terms such as "individualized," "therapeutic," "developmental," "remedial," and "adapted" are used in the delivery of service in physical education to students with special needs. The choice of names is determined largely by the emphasis and approach of the special program. The basic intent of all the programs is the same: the development of total well-being, with specific emphasis upon the improvement of motor fitness and physical fitness through movement activity.

- *Individualized* physical education refers to programs that respond to the unique needs of each individual. It does not imply one on one instructional time, but rather means providing individuals with disabilities with involvement in movement programs that respond to the physical, mental, and emotional needs of the person through structured, success-oriented learning experiences.
- *Therapeutic* physical education strives to rehabilitate through prescribed exercises those who have temporary disabilities.

TABLE 1.1   Categories of Disability under IDEA 2004

There are 14 specific primary terms included in IDEA under the lead definition of "child with a disability." These federal terms and definitions guide how states define disability and who is eligible for a free appropriate public education under special education law. The definitions of these specific terms from the IDEA regulations are shown beneath each term listed. In order to fully meet the definition (and eligibility for special education and related services) as a "child with a disability," a child's educational performance *must be adversely affected* due to the disability.

The webpage used here is listed for ease of clicking on one of the linked terms that will take you to NICHCY's fact sheet for that particular disability and to other related information.

1. **Autism** means a developmental disability significantly affecting verbal and nonverbal communication and social interaction, generally evident before age three that adversely affects educational performance. Characteristics often associated with autism are engaging in repetitive activities and stereotyped movements, resistance to changes in daily routines or the environment, and unusual responses to sensory experiences. The term "autism" does not apply if the child's educational performance is adversely affected primarily because the child has emotional disturbance, as defined in #5.

   A child who shows the characteristics of autism after age three could be diagnosed as having autism if the previous criteria are satisfied.

2. **Deaf-Blindness** means concomitant [simultaneous] hearing and visual impairments, the combination of which causes such severe communication and other developmental and educational needs that they cannot be accommodated in special education programs solely for children with deafness or children with blindness.

3. **Deafness** means a hearing impairment so severe that a child is impaired in processing linguistic information through hearing, with or without amplification, that adversely affects a child's educational performance.

4. **Developmental Delay** for children from birth to age three (under IDEA Part C) and children from ages three through nine (under IDEA Part B), the term "developmental delay," as defined by each state, means a delay in one or more of the following areas: physical development; cognitive development; communication; social

or emotional development; or adaptive [behavioral] development.

5. **Emotional Disturbance** means a condition exhibiting one or more of the following characteristics over a long period of time and to a marked degree that adversely affects a child's educational performance:

   (a) An inability to learn that cannot be explained by intellectual, sensory, or health factors.

   (b) An inability to build or maintain satisfactory interpersonal relationships with peers and teachers.

   (c) Inappropriate types of behavior or feelings under normal circumstances.

   (d) A general pervasive mood of unhappiness or depression.

   (e) A tendency to develop physical symptoms or fears associated with personal or school problems.

   The term includes schizophrenia. The term does not apply to children who are socially maladjusted, unless it is determined that they have an emotional disturbance.

6. **Hearing Impairment** means an impairment in hearing, whether permanent or fluctuating, that adversely affects a child's educational performance but is not included under the definition of "deafness."

7. **Mental Retardation** means significantly sub-average general intellectual functioning, existing concurrently [at the same time] with deficits in adaptive behavior and manifested during the developmental period, that adversely affects a child's educational performance.

   (Note: "Mental retardation" is the term found in the law since passage of the original legislation in 1975. In 2008, the American Association on Intellectual and Developmental Disabilities (AAIDD) (formerly the American Association on Mental Retardation, AAMR) and members of the community recommended use of the term "intellectual disability." For changes in language to be made in the regulations, Congress must first change it in the legislation. Until such action occurs, we provide the existing language from IDEA.)

8. **Multiple Disabilities** means concomitant [simultaneous] impairments (such as mental retardation-blindness, mental retardation-orthopedic impairment, etc.), the combination of which causes such severe educational needs that they cannot be accommodated in a special education program solely for one of the impairments. The term does not include deaf-blindness.

TABLE 1.1 (Continued)

9. **Orthopedic Impairment** means a severe orthopedic impairment that adversely affects a child's educational performance. The term includes impairments caused by a congenital anomaly (e.g., clubfoot, absence of some member, etc.), impairments caused by disease (e.g., poliomyelitis, bone tuberculosis, etc.), and impairments from other causes (e.g., cerebral palsy, amputations, and fractures or burns that cause contractures).

10. **Other Health Impairment** means having limited strength, vitality, or alertness, including a heightened alertness to environmental stimuli, that results in limited alertness with respect to the educational environment, that—

    (a) is due to chronic or acute health problems such as asthma, attention deficit disorder or attention deficit hyperactivity disorder, diabetes, epilepsy, a heart condition, hemophilia, lead poisoning, leukemia, nephritis, rheumatic fever, sickle cell anemia, and Tourette syndrome; and

    (b) adversely affects a child's educational performance.

11. **Specific Learning Disability** means a disorder in one or more of the basic psychological processes involved in understanding or in using language, spoken or written, that may manifest itself in an imperfect ability to listen, think, speak, read, write, spell, or to do mathematical calculations. The term includes such conditions as perceptual disabilities, brain injury, minimal brain dysfunction, dyslexia, and developmental aphasia. The term does not include learning problems that are primarily the result of visual, hearing, or motor disabilities; of mental retardation; of emotional disturbance; or of environmental, cultural, or economic disadvantage.

12. **Speech or Language Impairment** means a communication disorder such as stuttering, impaired articulation, a language impairment, or a voice impairment that adversely affects a child's educational performance.

13. **Traumatic Brain Injury** means an acquired injury to the brain caused by an external physical force, resulting in total or partial functional disability or psychosocial impairment, or both, that adversely affects a child's educational performance. The term applies to open or closed head injuries resulting in impairments in one or more areas, such as cognition; language; memory; attention; reasoning; abstract thinking; judgment; problem solving; sensory, perceptual, and motor abilities; psychosocial behavior; physical functions; information processing; and speech. The term does not include brain injuries that are congenital or degenerative, or brain injuries induced by birth trauma.

14. **Visual Impairment Including Blindness** means an impairment in vision that, even with correction, adversely affects a child's educational performance. The term includes both partial sight and blindness.

Source: **Nation Dissemination Center for Children with Disabilities (NDCD and NICHCY)** http://www.nichcy.org/Disabilities/Categories/Pages/Default.aspx

- *Developmental* physical education stresses that learning movement skills and physical fitness for those below the desired level is mastered in a progression of developmental levels beginning with the more elemental level and moving to more mature levels. This approach is also sensitive to the chronological age of the individual and the consequent implications for curriculum offerings.

- *Remedial* physical education consists of programs designed to correct faulty movement patterns through selected activities.

- *Adapted* physical education programs are those that have the same objectives as the regular physical education program, but in which adjustments are made in the regular offerings to meet the needs and abilities of exceptional students.

The term "adapted" physical education has been widely used as a general term for all the programs directed toward students with deficiencies and disabilities. The authors prefer the umbrella term "special physical education," a term first promoted by Hollis Fait, that has won wide acceptance in the United States and abroad. In addition, federal educational law refers to "specially designed" physical education. Special physical education consists of programs designed to enhance the physical and motor fitness of persons with disabilities and is aimed at successful participation through modified and developmentally sequenced movement experiences, including sports and games. Whatever terms are used, they should communicate to a specific community or agency that the program has received attention to facilitating well the engagement of children, youth and young adults in successful physical activity programs (figure 1.1).

Figure 1.1 Special physical education emphasizes experiences that are adapted, developmentally sequenced, and individualized for each participant.

Role of Those with Disabilities in Society

Education for all is a basic tenet of our democratic faith, and the opportunity for each individual to develop optimum potential is a guiding principle of our educational system. In the progress toward equalized educational opportunities for all, individuals with disabilities have not always received due consideration. The development of special programs and methods of instruction and the integration of special students into the general school programs have had to wait largely upon enlightened public opinion regarding students with disabilities and their special needs.

The first real public awareness in the United States of the problems of those who have disabilities came in the early years of the 20th century, growing out of the tragic consequences of disease and war. In 1916 our country experienced an epidemic of infantile paralysis, and within the next few years the wounded returned from World War I. An aroused public's desire to help those with paralysis and veterans who were disabled forged a new attitude toward those with disabilities that spurred legislative and educational assistance.

Early Attitudes

To appreciate fully the new attitude and its ramifications, one must leaf back through the pages of history and appraise the prevailing attitude toward those perceived as disabled, as those perceptions are atypical in other times and places. In primitive societies, children born with defects generally perished at an early age as a consequence of their inability to withstand the rigors of primitive man's strenuous existence. Even in the civilized societies of early Greece, the Spartan father of a child with a disabling condition was expected to carry the babe to the hills to be left to perish, whereas the Athenians, whom we generally consider to be more humanitarian than their Spartan neighbors, permitted such babies to die of neglect. During the days of the Roman Empire, babies with birth defects suffered a like fate.

Although some individuals with disabilities found social acceptance as court jesters during the Middle Ages, the prevailing attitude was one of superstition and fear. Physical and mental disabilities were believed to have been caused by Satan, and the afflicted were held to be sinful and evil. Hence, those with disabilities were either harshly treated or carefully avoided.

The humanistic philosophy that flowered in the period of the Renaissance undoubtedly softened the general attitude toward those with physical disabilities, but the gain in understanding of their problems did not extend to include treatment, care, and education. Some legislation to prevent conditions that might produce crippling injuries was passed during the Industrial Revolution, but beyond this, society lost sight of the conditions of those with disabilities in the tremendous technical advancement of the age.

The effort to improve the lives of individuals with developmental disabilities in the 1800s is traced to the work of French physician Jean Itard who believed that Victor, also known as the Wild Boy of Aveyron, could be cured of his lack of language and social skills and become normal (Morris & Morris, 1999). Although Victor never became "normal," Itard's work in Paris influenced the writing, research, and treatment practices of others, who in turn directly influenced the construction of institutions in the United States. In 1848, the Perkins Institution for the Blind was, in part, dedicated to caring for individuals with mental retardation, as well as those with developmental disabilities, and was the first such facility in the United States. Other institutions followed across the United States. Their aim was never to be primarily state custodial residences, but in fact they were exactly that (e.g., Wolfensberger, 1972).

Thus, it was not until the 1900s that social awareness of the problems of those with disabilities gained momentum in this country. This awareness resulted in the organization of conferences on the welfare of the child with a disability and in the opening of schools for children with orthopedic impairments and clinics and centers for their treatment.

World Wars I and II gave impetus to the development of the techniques of orthopedic surgery, which had already made important gains through the treatment of children with disabilities. From the treatment of war casualties, care was gradually expanded to include civilians with physical disabilities. Accompanying the physical reconditioning of seriously injured soldiers and civilians came a movement to rehabilitate those with disabilities, to help them become useful, self-sufficient citizens again.

There developed after World War I what were known at the time as curative workshops, in which individuals were taught purposeful activities for their therapeutic value. This type of program is now known as occupational therapy, and it has as its goal the rehabilitation of individuals through the teaching of skills by which they may become either partially, or fully, self-sustaining. Today there are also programs of physical therapy, therapeutic recreation, corrective therapy, and art, dance, and music therapies that endeavor to help those with disabilities reach maximum potential.

Funds for most early efforts to provide rehabilitation services for those with disabilities came from charity and fraternal organizations, private philanthropy, and community service organizations. A great deal was accomplished through the efforts of these groups, not the least of which was helping to arouse public concern for the needs and rights of those with serious disabilities including the blind, the deaf, and the otherwise disabled. As a result, states began to pass the legislation needed for a more complete program of care and rehabilitation of a heretofore largely neglected segment of our population. Today, states own and support hospitals and institutions at which adults and children can secure the kind of professional care and treatment their disabilities require. The states also assume a share of the responsibility for the educational and vocational needs of those with disabilities.

Governmental Assistance

Federal legislation was enacted following World War I to provide certain benefits to veterans with disabilities; these were supplemented by further legislation in 1943 to increase the scope of aid to the veterans of World War II. The legislation provided for the rehabilitation of soldiers with war disabilities under the supervision of the Veterans Administration.

The first law providing for assistance to civilians with disabling injuries was passed in 1920. Under its provisions, civilians injured in industrial accidents or due to certain other causes were entitled to vocational rehabilitation; they were to be returned to employment whenever possible. A subsequent law in 1943 provided for physical restoration as well as for vocational rehabilitation.

From the 1940s to the present there has been a steady growth of services to individuals with disabilities as the result of private, state, and federal assistance. Examples of the expanded services include

- research into the cause and cure of mental and physical diseases;
- better facilities and increased knowledge in detecting, diagnosing, and treating disabling conditions;
- vocational rehabilitation and training;
- job placement or replacement;
- in the case of veterans and the industrially disabled, compensation or disability allowances and pensions.

Also during this time special hospitals and schools for certain types of individuals with disabilities were established throughout the country. These included hospitals or special homes for the physically disabled, convalescent, and aged; institutions for the mentally ill and emotionally disturbed; and schools for the blind, deaf, and mentally retarded. In the late 1970s, the movement of deinstitutionalization began, whereby individuals were removed from institutions to begin normal lives (normalization movement) in their communities. In 1977, 149,892 people with disabilities resided in large state-operated institutions whereas by 1999, 51,485 remained in such facilities (Prouty & Lakin, 1999). Heated debate ensued following the federal deinstitutionalization mandates in the 1970s. According to mental health clinicians, educators, and advocates of people with disabilities, the resources needed to facilitate transitioning and humane treatment outside the institutions were not in place. Even today professionals claim that states are still unable to handle vital placement issues.

Following deinstitutionalization, efforts were also made to de-emphasize the role of state institutions by providing training for parents, thus enabling many to care for their children at home. Some states also provided funds to initiate group homes, creating living environments within the community for older adults who need assistance but not total care. A service of a different kind, but nonetheless important, was the legislative mandate that all new and remodeled public buildings must be made accessible to those with disabilities. Individuals with disabilities were able to function much more independently with features such as ramps and elevators to replace stairs and corridors, and toilet facilities large enough to accommodate wheelchairs.

It is important to note that during the 1960s federal support occurred for measures to improve education for children with disabilities. During this time, in the United States Department of Education, the Bureau of Education for the Handicapped (BEH) was created and was of singular importance. With BEH, for the first time there existed at the federal level an agency with the sole purpose of administering programs and projects related to the education of students with disabilities. Another milestone of the period was the passage of an amendment to the Elementary and Secondary Education Act that provided funds to support research and demonstration projects in physical education and recreation for those with disabilities. (BEH is now known as the Office of Special Education and Rehabilitation Service (OSERS)).

The 1970s saw the development of a different emphasis from that of the 1960s, one that focused on restatement by the courts of the scope of the rights of all individuals with disabilities. Although deinstitutionalization began in the 1970s, various civil and human rights long denied people with disabilities were sought in state and district courts across the country. An example is the "right of treatment," desperately needed on behalf of individuals in institutions for the mentally ill and mentally retarded, where a humane physical and psychological living environment is often lacking. By and large, the courts upheld the plaintiffs' quest to ensure equality under the law for those with disabilities in all areas of human endeavor.

Federal Legislation

The legislative process has affirmed that individuals with disabilities may not be denied equal access to or services under any program that receives federal financial assistance. Major laws protecting the rights of individuals with disabilities are Section 504 of the Vocational Rehabilitation Act of 1973, the Individuals with Disabilities Education Improvement Act of 2004 (mandated as PL 94-142 of 1975 was referred to as IDEA '97), and the Americans with Disabilities Act of 1990 (ADA). The rights of those with disabilities were firmly established with the passage of the Rehabilitation Act of 1973, Public Law 93-112. This law, popularly known as the Civil Rights Act for the Handicapped, is very broad, encompassing all aspects of the disabled person's life. The major concept of Public Law 93-112 may be summarized by explaining that individuals may not be discriminated against because of their disability.

Section 504 of The Vocational Rehabilitation Act of 1973 reinforces the right of students with disabilities to participate in physical education by stating, "A recipient that offers physical education courses or that operates or sponsors intercollegiate, club, or intramural athletics shall provide to qualified handicapped students equal opportunities for comparable participation in these activities." This statement extends the concept of equal physical education opportunities beyond classroom instruction into the areas of intramurals and athletics. As will be discussed in chapter 18, *Competitive Sport for Athletes with Disabilities*, this means that those with disabilities who are qualified may not be denied equal opportunity to participate on regular teams or comparable special teams.

To ensure that all children are secure in their right to quality education, Congress in the fall of 1975 approved passage of Public Law 94-142, The Education for All Handicapped Children Act. This law has been reauthorized over the years and, consequently, amended several times. It is now known as PL 105-17, The Individuals with Disabilities Education Act of 1997 (IDEA '97). The law includes several provisions that are designed to enable students with disabilities to receive a free appropriate public education (FAPE). An Individualized Education Program (IEP) must be written by a team specifically for the student with a disability ages 3 to 21 years, and an Individualized Family Service Plan (IFSP) is written for infants and toddlers. Under IDEA '97, the IEP team is composed of the parents or legal guardians, the student's general education teacher, the special education teacher or supervisor of special education and, when appropriate, the student and other personnel as needed (e.g., occupational therapist, speech-language pathologist). The IEP team is also responsible for placing the student with a disability in educational programs that are as conducive to the individual's educational growth and, to the extent possible and appropriate, mainstreamed with nondisabled peers. This is referred to as the least restrictive environment (LRE). The IEP team must document that the student cannot succeed in general education and, therefore, is in need of special education. In addition, the law also requires that a continuum of placements be available. For some students with disabilities, this can include placement in general education with few supports and services. Other students may require more assistance and thus part- or full-time placement in special programs (figure 1.2).

Since the passage of PL 94-142 in 1975 and through the continued reauthorization of that law and the resulting amendments, educational law has emphasized that, for each student with a disability, the environment that is least restrictive to the student's growth is the appropriate educational placement. In addition, when considering special education for students with disabilities and access to specialized physical education programs, the law *was* very clear: **physical education is an academic area under the law**.

Individuals with Disabilities Education Improvement Act of 2004 (IDEA, 2004)

In 2004, the Bush Administration amended IDEA '97. Under this amendment, the federal education law is now entitled the *Individuals with Disabilities Education Improvement Act, 2004*. But, it has been stipulated that in referring to this law, IDEA 2004 will suffice rather than IDEIA 2004. Of course, the official name of the law contains the added word "improvement." For physical education there originally were no changes observed in the amendments of IDEA 2004 until the regulations were published in 2008. At this time, it was a shock to many that the regulations changed and added stipulations into the implementation of IDEA 2004 regarding special physical education.

Figure 1.2 Physical education for students with disabilities is an identified service under federal educational law.

Physical Education in IDEA 2004

IDEA 2004 was amended to be more in line with No Child Left Behind (NCLB, 2001) (Turnbull, Huerta, & Stowe, 2009). The focus in NCLB is on the academic areas of reading and mathematics. As it currently stands in IDEA 2004, physical education is moved from a required academic area under the law for qualifying special education students. Yet, the definition of physical education in federal education law has remained the same since the seminal Education of All Handicapped Children Act of 1975. *Physical education means* (adapted from Federal Register, section 300.39 (2)):

> The development of physical and motor fitness; fundamental motor skills and patterns; and skills in aquatics, dance, and individual and group games and sports (including intramural and lifetime sports); and includes special physical education, adapted physical education, movement education, and motor development. *Specially designed instruction* means adapting, as appropriate to the needs of an eligible child under this path the content, methodology or delivery of instruction.

Thus, physical education remained in IDEA 2004 but an astonishing regulation was that special physical education would not be offered to students with special needs unless physical education was offered to other students in the schools. According to the Federal Register for IDEA 2004, Section 300.108:

> *General.* Physical education services, specially designed if necessary must be made available to every child with a disability receiving FAPE, unless the public agency enrolls children without disabilities and does not provide physical education to children without disabilities in the same grades.

And, the Register continues with a seemingly contradictory statement:

> *Special physical education.* If specially designed physical education is prescribed in a child's IEP, the public agency responsible for the education of that child must provide the services directly or make arrangements for those services to be provided through other public or private programs.

Thus, the interpretation for states and the local school districts is challenging. At first read, it appears that the burden of implementation of an existing Individualized Education Program (IEP) in motor will fall to the parents of the child or to adapted physical educators involved in that child's education. And, these same individuals will also be advocating for assessment that leads to an IEP in motor. Fortunately for some states, their state rules mandate special physical education (e.g., Minnesota Rules—DAPE criteria 3525.1352). This would supersede federal education law. Unfortunately for other states, battles will be taking place around the "spirit of the law" that clearly indicates that, if a child with a disability needs modification or adaptation to be successful in the education setting, the school must use its resources to make reasonable accommodations for the child to succeed.

IEP Team

The IEP Team is referenced in IDEA 2004 as the Non-Discriminatory Evaluation Team (NDE Team). Yet, in practicality the NDE Team members are often the same as the IEP Team. These individuals, including the parents, meet to determine the presence of a disability requiring special services and the appropriate educational plan.

Evidenced-Based Practice

In keeping in line with NCLB 2001, the amendments In IDEA 2004 require teachers to use evidence-based practice in the classrooms. The Council for Exceptional Children (CEC, www.cec.sped.org) readily admits that in special education the criteria have not been established for evidenced-based practice. To refer to a practice as evidence-based, the practice must be backed up by scientific investigation. The What Works Clearing House (WWC, ies.ed.gov/ncee/wwc) circulates information on research that has validated a practice in serving children in educational settings. The WWC is an initiative of the U.S. Department of Education's Institute of Education Sciences. CEC works closely with WWC and the U.S. Department of Education's Office of Special Education. Although WWC targets all children, the evidence-based literature on special education is very limited. Part of the problem is that children with disabilities are not a homogeneous group and, within disability areas, the same hold true: A child with cerebral palsy (CP) is unique, and finding a group of children with CP for group-designed research is realistically not possible. Instead, single-case design research is a prominent tool for validating practices and interventions. Yet, it will be a while before larger bodies like the WWC are able to circulate findings given single-case design although efforts have always been in discussion.

In special physical education, single-case design research is more prominent, as a look through the Adapted Physical Activity Quarterly (APAQ) will attest. Also, when research is conducted on children with disabilities, the sample size is usually very small, thus leading to difficulties with generalizing to educational settings. What many researchers in physical education for children with disabilities will admit is that while the research may lag, the physical education classes will still be held—in fact, they must be held. What is relied on is "best practice," whereby the field of adapted physical education has adopted practices (e.g., teaching strategies, checklists for modifications and adaptations) that the discipline knows are effective. They are valid for many children across many different disciplines. In time, with greater funding available at the national level, there could be a point when research will be able to validate many of the practices we hold appropriate and effective.

Technology to Reduce Paperwork: Goals and No Objectives

IDEA 2004 also addresses the overwhelming concern that special educators have been increasingly burdened with paperwork to the detriment of the education of students with special needs. To respond to a reality that high numbers of special educators have been leaving the field because of this, IDEA 2004 stressed the use of technology to ease paperwork. More importantly, IDEA 2004 requires that only goals are written in the IEPs and not goals and objectives. Since 2004, more districts are using software that has automated IEPs. Although the learning curve is slow at first with this automation, the time saved has been a boon for some educators. Realistically, many school districts have retained objectives as a way to evaluate progress toward IEP goals.

Early Intervening Services

Strengthened in IDEA 2004 is the allowance of special education monies to be spent on "Early Intervening Services." This addresses students who are not formally classified under IDEA but who need "additional academic and behavioral support to succeed in a general education environment"

(Section 1413(f), Turnbull et al, 2009). This means that a student who is lagging educationally, but who is not formally entered into the special education system, can be identified for extra academic assistance. If that assistance is successful, in many cases, special education is not warranted. One term given to this assistance is Response to Intervention (RTI). Here educators can plan educational interventions and set a timetable for evaluating the success of the plan. If the student shows success, then referral for assessment for special education services is not needed. Teachers receive special training to use RTI appropriately. Speculation is some states is that using RTI will lower the referrals for special education (Associated Press, 2008). In fact, RTI holds promise for assisting children who need more assistance in the classroom but for whom special education services are not needed. The Council for Exceptional Children (CEC) has issued a position paper on RTI (www.cec.sped.org > Policy & Advocacy>CEC Professional Policies). They emphasize that RTI is a schoolwide initiative that works with families to identify needs of learners early, even in preschool; and does not delay the referral of a child who is suspected of having a disability from a comprehensive evaluation. Their policy statement includes guidelines for interventions, team roles, resources, and professional knowledge and skills.

Under IDEA '97 and IDEA 2004, the term "special education" continues to mean ". . . specially designed instruction, at no cost to the parent, to meet the unique needs of a handicapped child, including classroom instruction, instruction in physical education, home instruction, and instruction in hospitals and institutions." Physical education means "the development of physical and motor fitness; fundamental motor skills and patterns; and skills in aquatics, dance, and individual and group games and sports, including intramural and lifetime sports." Specially designed physical education services may be necessary for some students, and public schools must either provide this service or make arrangements for special programs through other public or private agencies.

Students with disabilities ages 5 through 21 years were served under PL 94-142, The Education of All Handicapped Children Act of 1975. In 1986, Congress amended PL 94-142 thus creating Public Law 99-457, The Education of the Handicapped Act Amendments. This law reaffirmed the provisions of PL 94-142 and mandated special education services to include preschool students with disabilities ages three through five years. The intent of the law was to ensure the availability of intervention programs and services at the earliest ages for children with disabilities. To do so, the law also offered financial assistance to states to develop statewide systems of early intervention for infants and toddlers ages birth through three years. These youngest children (infants and toddlers) have an IFSP that is constructed by the child's educational team similarly to the IEP team but with a special emphasis on the necessity of family involvement in understanding the disability and the intervention program, as well as the transition needs, as the child moves into preschool programs. Former Senator Lowell Weicker of Connecticut, the primary architect of Public Law 99-457, recognized that children with disabilities cannot wait until the school year to begin the process of developing skills necessary to function effectively within the mainstream of society.

The emphasis that PL 99-457, The Education of All Handicapped Children Act of 1986, places on the importance of early intervention services has been recognized by authorities in various fields as essential to ensure that persons with disabilities are provided optimal opportunity to achieve at the highest possible level. Most notably, the National Academy of Science report (Shonkoff & Phillips, 2000) on early brain development states that when delay in development is detected, it is imperative that intervention begin as soon as possible to stave off negative developmental trajectories. Other scientists have long reported the cumulative developmental risk that develops if delay is not detected early and intervention begun (Sameroff & Chandler, 1975).

The nature of the preschool child with a disability and the importance of physical and motor development requires the expertise of specialists including physical educators with specialized training. Information concerning the motor development needs of the preschool child will be discussed in chapter 2. The recent educational law, The No Child Left Behind Act of 2001 (NCLB), PL 107-110, impacts children with disabilities. This law replaces the Elementary and Secondary Education Act of 1965 and mandates that all students reach a "proficient" level on state educational tests by 2013–14. According to current census, this affects 6.6 million special education students (Olson, 2004), and states are currently defining how students with disabilities can be assessed using the standard state assessments and when it is appropriate to use alternative assessments to measure educational progress (Thurlow, Elliott, & Ysseldyke, 2003). Further review of NCLB related to assessment of progress in physical education will be addressed in chapter 6.

Americans with Disabilities Act Amendments Act, 2008 (ADAAA, 2008)

President Barack Obama, as senator, was co-sponsor of the legislation that amended the Americans with Disabilities Act (ADA, 1990). After the signing he issued a statement: "With nearly fifty-four million Americans living with disabilities today . . . [ADAAA] will reverse judicial decisions that permit discrimination against person with disabilities."

(www.adabill.com) ADA 1990 was the seminal civil rights law for individuals with disabilities.

> The ADA prohibits discrimination on the basis of disability in employment, State and local government, public accommodations, commercial facilities, transportation, and telecommunications. It also applies to the United States Congress.

> To be protected by the ADA, one must have a disability or have a relationship or association with an individual with a disability. An individual with a disability is defined by the ADA as a person who has a physical or mental impairment that substantially limits one or more major life activities, a person who has a history or record of such an impairment, or a person who is perceived by others as having such an impairment. The ADA does not specifically name all of the impairments that are covered. (www.ada.gov)

A student who needs reasonable accommodation in the general education setting, but who does not need special education, can file for this accommodation under ADA and Section 504 of the Rehabilitation Act Amendments, 1973. These laws prohibit discrimination against students with disabilities in educational systems under two civil rights purposes: not to be discriminated based solely on their disabilities, and the right to reasonable accommodations in education (Turnbull et al., 2009). In some states, students have a disability but do not qualify in their state for special education because they may not meet the state criteria. For example, qualifying for developmental adapted physical education (DAPE) in Minnesota using standardized tests of psychomotor skills have a cutoff at seven percent. Those performing at greater than seven percent do not, unless otherwise ruled by the IEP Team, qualify for special physical education services. But some children who have a disability desperately need modifications in order to be successful in their physical education activities. Being served under 504 or ADA can facilitate the assistance that a child would need. In reality, it is helpful for parents, children, and physical education teachers that 505 and ADA have an impact on these children who are outside of IDEA reach. All children need to be physically active. In the long run, those who are physically active, happy, and healthy save monies for families, government, and education districts. For all involved, it is most important ethically.

In the foregoing paragraphs we have attempted to understand individuals with disabilities and their position in society. We have seen how society's perception of those with disabilities has grown from the ancient practices of isolation, ridicule, and, in some cases, elimination of those who

Figure 1.3 President Obama, as senator, co-sponsored legislation that amended the Americans with Disabilities Act (ADA 1990).

appeared different to the current acceptance of the right of all to a life that is as normal as possible. For those with disabilities, this means the right to receive an education, find employment, and live in a community, giving and sharing in all civic and governmental activities similar to all citizens. To achieve the highest level of self-realization possible is the ultimate goal for the highly motivated, regardless of whether one is disabled or not. Society's challenge for the future is to accept those who are different not as people with disabilities but as individuals who differ from others only to the extent of their disability.

Evolution of Special Physical Education

Although special physical education is a relatively recent developed service for individuals with disabilities, it is interesting to note that an integral part of the program—the improvement of motor functions of the body through exercise—is an ancient one. Pictures and records dating back 3,000 years before Christ have been found in China depicting the therapeutic use of gymnastics. In more recent times a system of medical gymnastics was developed in Sweden, by

Per Henrick Ling, which was introduced in this country in 1884 and was widely in vogue. It was a system of calisthenics of precise, definite movements designed to produce a healthier body and improve posture. Because it was believed that exercise of this nature would be highly beneficial to school children, programs of calisthenics were widely introduced in the public schools of that period.

Adapted Physical Education

A department of corrective physical education was first established by Dudley Sargent at Harvard in 1879 with the objective of correcting certain pathological conditions. The idea of physical education as corrective exercise for bad postural habits and for the general improvement of health persisted until about the time of World War I. Then, following the development of successful physical therapy techniques for paralyzed and convalescent soldiers, the idea of corrective exercises for students with physical handicaps took hold. Soon, a number of colleges had established corrective classes for students who were unable to participate in the regular physical education program. Corrective physical education for the improvement of posture was de-emphasized generally, but a few schools continued to stress corrective exercises in their physical education classes.

Adapted physical education developed from the early corrective classes that were established specifically for those with disabilities. Gradually, over the years following World War I, the practice grew of assigning students with disabilities to corrective courses in order to protect their conditions from possible aggravation. As yet little consideration was given to the idea that students with disabilities could be taught to play modified forms of sports or games or that they could be integrated into regular classes for part of their instruction.

During the 1940s fundamental changes were initiated in physical education for students with disabilities in some universities and colleges. A recognition of the value of play as an educational tool to implement social, mental, and physical development became the philosophical basis of course offerings to those with disabilities. Calisthenics, gymnastics, and corrective exercises were supplanted in the course content by games, sports, and rhythmic activities modified to meet the individual needs of the students. In some schools special classes of adapted activities were developed for students with special needs; in other schools those who could participate with safety in some activities of the general physical education classes began to receive as much instruction as their cases warranted in these general classes.

Programs for Those with Physical and Mental Disabilities

Although physical education programs for those with disabilities were limited in number during the years from 1940 to 1960, a slow but steady increase was discernible. Almost all of the programs developed at this time were for those with physical disabilities. Students with mental disabilities and with abnormal behavior problems were generally not provided for unless they were in one of the few institutions that recognized the residents' need for a special kind of physical education program. Even in these institutions physical education was directed primarily toward those with adequate motor skills for sports participation.

Physical education for students with mental retardation began to receive attention early in the 1960s. The publication of the first textbook to discuss the need of students with mental retardation for adapted physical education, Fait's *Adapted Physical Education,* although not responsible for the upsurge of interest in providing for the physical and motor fitness needs of students with mental retardation, did chart the direction for the future development of such programs. Interest in the movement was fostered by the attention focused on it by the family of President John F. Kennedy; their concern was expressed by their active support of a number of projects to enhance the motor experiences of individuals with mental retardation.

The greatest impetus to the movement to provide quality physical education to serve the needs of those with disabilities came from the establishment of federal funding for the promotion of research and training in physical education in colleges and universities. These monies were directly related to the federal educational laws discussed earlier in this chapter. The seminal PL 94-142, The Education of All Handicapped Children Act of 1975, mandated a free, appropriate, public education for all (FAPE). Physical education was identified under this law as an academic area for eligible students. The availability of federal research and training monies for physical education is political and, therefore, has resulted in a changing availability of funds over the years since 1975. Even in the mid-1990s (Bokee, 1995), more than 40 institutions of higher learning received grants either for research and demonstration projects related to the physical and motor needs of those with disabilities or for programs to prepare personnel to work with those with disabilities in physical education or recreation.

The effect of increased knowledge and understanding that has resulted from these programs has been a commendable expansion in the number and quality of public school physical education programs for students with disabilities. New and more sophisticated methods and procedures for evaluating, planning, and teaching students with disabilities are replacing the "watered down" adaptations of physical education programs of the past. Students with disabilities who have had the advantage of a good physical education experience, one that served their special needs, have reaped benefits that supply the best possible indication of the importance and value of the federally funded programs.

Further evidence of the growth occurring in the field of physical education for those with disabilities is found in the number of specialized journals that have originated. The *Adapted Physical Activity Quarterly* (APAQ) is an excellent reference published by Human Kinetics (www.humankinetics.com), which prints current research findings and articles of general interest on various topics related to special populations. A journal begun in 1983 that offers many excellent activity suggestions is *Palestra* (www.palaestra.com). *Sports 'N Spokes,* begun in 1975, is a valuable resource that provides helpful information on programs and activities for individuals with spinal cord injuries. *Sports 'N Spokes* is published by Paralyzed Veterans of America (www.sportsnspokes.com). *Challenge* is published by Disabled Sports USA (www.dsusa.org). Other journals addressing physical activity in general, including articles relevant to adapted physical activity, are *Journal of Health, Physical Education, Recreation, and Dance* (JOPHERD) and *Strategies* both published by American Alliance for Health, Physical Education, Recreation and Dance (AAHPERD) (www.aahperd.org).

Individualized Programming

Although educators of children with disabilities have long recognized the need to develop instructional programs that respond to individual needs, the movement to individualize instruction gathered momentum in the 1970s. The increased number of highly trained professionals in special physical education contributed to the growing awareness that movement experiences for students with disabilities must be personalized to maximize learning. Efforts to focus on individual needs received a boost in 1975 with the passage of PL 94-142 and its requirement that Individualized Educational Programs (IEPs) be developed for students with disabilities. Despite the fact that the logic of individualized instruction is obvious, in the past some physical educators dismissed this concept as an unrealistic goal. This response may be attributed in part to the common misconception that to individualize requires a pupil-teacher ratio of one to one. Although it is true that those with more severe disabilities might need one-to-one instruction, it is generally recognized today that many students with disabilities can receive individualized instruction in small and large groups.

Currently, many schools operate with an inclusive philosophy of education, whereby children with disabilities primarily received their education within the general curriculum. This move has required a broader understanding of individualization.

Individualizing instruction for special students has required that physical educators attain some skills that have not traditionally been stressed in professional preparation programs. In addition to the skill of writing goals and objectives for the Individualized Education Program (IEP) and the Individualized Family Service Plan (IFSP) the physical education instructor working with special students should be able to task-analyze (break skills down into smaller parts), manage behavior, evaluate student progress, train volunteers, work with parents, and serve as an interdisciplinary team member. Within the following chapters, these and many other skills will be presented to help physical educators provide effective individualized instruction for special students. Of course, many of these skills will also be helpful in working with all students regardless of ability level.

Fortunately, since the early 1970s, many resources have been developed to assist physical educators in responding to the activity needs of children with disabilities. These range from material found in several excellent adapted physical education texts to specific curricula that have been published. Resources that can be used to teach students with disabilities will be described in greater detail in chapter 5, *Teaching Special Physical Education.*

Individualized instruction builds upon the original concept of adapted physical education to produce special learning environments. Thus, the term "special physical education" is a contemporary title that emphasizes the value of adapting activities while stressing that modifications must be individualized and thus personalized to the needs of those with disabilities. It is in this way that physical education becomes special.

Professional Organizations and Physical Education for Individuals with Disabilities

Professional organizations have played an important role in helping physical educators serve students with disabilities. The type of assistance offered varies according to the organization but includes many possibilities, such as publishing journals and resource material; conducting annual meetings, workshops, and continuing education courses; certifying professionals; organizing legislative efforts; and serving as a catalyst to continually upgrade the general status of the profession and its professionals. Included within this sec-

tion is a discussion of some of the more visible organizations that have been developed to promote physical education for students with disabilities. The address of each association is found in Appendix I on the CD.

American Alliance for Health, Physical Education, Recreation, and Dance

The American Alliance for Health, Physical Education, Recreation, and Dance (AAHPERD) is a 35,000-member organization of professionals concerned with the physical activity, health, and leisure needs of citizens within the United States. AAHPERD's commitment to those with disabilities is long-standing as evidenced by its formation in 1952 of the Therapeutics Council. The Council focused its early concerns on the rehabilitative needs of those with disabilities but broadened its mission in later years to include physical activity services for all disabled populations including the elderly. Perhaps the single most important effort by AAHPERD to promote services for those with disabilities occurred in 1965 when the Project on Recreation and Fitness for the Mentally Retarded was initiated through a grant by the Joseph P. Kennedy, Jr., Foundation. This project led to the development of AAHPERD's Unit on Programs for the Handicapped in 1968. Under its director, Dr. Julian Stein, the Unit on Programs for the Handicapped expanded its focus to include all special populations and developed numerous publications and resource materials. In 1975 a third organization, The Adapted Physical Education Academy, was formed by AAHPERD to focus primarily on school-age children with disabilities and their special physical education needs.

Although the Therapeutics Council, the Unit on Programs for the Handicapped, and the Adapted Physical Education Academy were successful in coordinating programs for the AAHPERD annual convention and in cooperating to develop guidelines for the preparation of specialists in adapted physical education, it became apparent to the leaders of the organizations that much duplication existed among the three groups. Therefore, representatives of the organizations proposed in 1985 that one organization be formed by AAHPERD to provide programs and services to assist professionals in responding to the physical activity needs of those with disabilities. Thus, the Adapted Physical Activity Council was formed in 1985. This organization, housed within the Association for Active Lifestyles and Fitness of AAHPERD, has accepted as its primary purpose ". . . to advocate, promote, stimulate, and encourage programs for physical activity for special populations." The council provides AAHPERD and its members a unified base for cooperative interdisciplinary services for individuals with special needs.

For additional information on AAHPERD visit www.aahperd.org.

National Consortium on Physical Education and Recreation for Individuals with Disabilities

In 1973, a small group of college and university adapted physical educators and therapeutic recreators met in Minneapolis, Minnesota, to discuss the feasibility of developing a new organization that would have as its sole purpose the promotion of physical education and recreation for those with disabilities. From this meeting the National Advisory Council on Physical Education and Recreation for Handicapped Children and Youth was formed. This organization was the forerunner to the present National Consortium on Physical Education and Recreation for Individuals with Disabilities (NCPERID). The Consortium is an organization of individuals with extensive backgrounds in the fields of adapted physical education and therapeutic recreation who agree with NCPERID's efforts to promote professional preparation programs and research in physical education and recreation for those with disabilities. In addition to conducting an annual meeting, NCPERID publishes a quarterly newsletter called *The Advocate* and supports legislative efforts on behalf of those with disabilities.

Related Therapy Organizations

The psychomotor needs of those with disabilities are so varied and intense that professionals from many fields can be called upon to assist physical educators in enhancing the performance capabilities of those with disabilities. Professionals from the fields of physical therapy and occupational therapy, for instance, are frequently employed by school districts to work with specialists in special physical education either as a member of an interdisciplinary motor development team, or as specialized motor experts. Other professionals who are concerned with movement deficiencies include dance therapists and recreational therapists.

The various forms of therapy, with some exceptions such as dance therapy, can trace their origins to World Wars I and II, when individuals were trained to rehabilitate and prepare injured soldiers for new occupations, and to help them make the transition from hospital to home. The types of therapeutic services offered have changed dramatically over the years. Today, physical therapists can specialize in educational pediatrics to work extensively with individuals with disabilities in the schools. By federal education law, physical therapists and occupational therapists focus on assisting with movement concerns that would impact students' learning across the varied educational settings in a given day.

Each of the therapies identified in this section has an active professional organization with a code of ethics and procedures for certifying and registering qualified therapists.

Most of the therapy associations also have a professional journal that reports the latest research or motor treatment procedures for individuals with disabilities. The American Occupational Therapy Association (www.aota.org) is an example of a professional organization and its professional journals include: *American Journal of Occupational Therapy* (OTJR): *Occupation, Participation and Health,* and the *Canadian Journal of Occupational Therapy.* The professional organization for physical therapists is the American Physical Therapy Association (www.apta.org) and professional journals in this field include *Physical Therapy* and *Pediatric Physical Therapy.*

Specialists in physical education for those with disabilities realize that effective services for students with disabilities require cooperation and consultation on a regular basis with other experts in the field of motor development. In addition, an increasing number of physical educators are attending professional meetings sponsored by therapy organizations to pick up new ideas concerning procedures for working with students with disabilities. Therapists, too, have found meetings sponsored by physical educators helpful in enhancing their ability to provide effective services. Neither physical educators nor therapists desire to perform the professional responsibilities of their colleagues, but both groups are interested in improving the total services available to students and young children with disabilities. This effort can be accelerated by therapists and special physical educators who have the foresight to collaborate at the school level, to attend professional meetings together, and to read and discuss each others' professional literature.

Council for Exceptional Children

The national organization with which most special educators affiliate is the Council for Exceptional Children (CEC). Although the historical origin of the CEC can be traced to 1922, it was not until 1958 that the organization officially adopted its present name. The CEC is a large professional organization dedicated to improving the education of students with disabilities as well as gifted students. Because of this, CEC provides services to its membership that are linked closely to the ongoing understanding and implementation of federal educational laws serving individuals with disabilities. According to its website, "CEC advocates for appropriate governmental policies, sets professional standards, provides continual professional development, advocates for newly and historically underserved individuals with exceptionalities, and helps professionals obtain conditions and resources necessary for effective professional practice" (www.cec.sped.org). CEC conducts an annual conference, sponsors institutes, disseminates information, and publishes journals, including *Exceptional Children* and *Teaching*

Exceptional Children. The primary focus of the CEC is the promotion of quality special education programs for exceptional students, including the talented and gifted.

In recent years, many physical educators have joined the CEC, leading to an increased awareness on the part of special educators and physical educators as to the contribution each profession can offer to students with disabilities. The Council for Exceptional Children has included more information about physical activity in its publications and at its conferences. The Division of Physical and Health Disabilities (DPHD) advocates for quality education for individuals with physical and multiple disabilities, and those with special health care needs.

Office of Special Education and Rehabilitative Services

The federal agency responsible for initiating, expanding, and monitoring educational services for students with disabilities is the Office of Special Education and Rehabilitative Services (OSERS). Prior to President Carter's creation of the Department of Education in 1980, OSERS was known from its inception in 1968 as the Bureau of Education for the Handicapped (BEH). Although OSERS is not a professional organization per se, it does sponsor many meetings and, consequently, opportunities for professionals from various disciplines to meet and share ideas about special education. One of OSERS's primary responsibilities through its Division of Personnel Preparation is to provide grants to colleges and universities for the training of professionals in special education and related services to work with students with disabilities. Funds for the training of physical educators to teach those with

disabilities have increased since 1968. Monies have been allocated yearly to train teachers in special physical education and to help general physical education personnel teach students with special needs. The Office of Special Education and Rehabilitative Services has significantly enhanced the quantity and quality of special physical education services across the United States (www.ed.gov/about/offices/list/osers).

Related Sport Organizations

Supported by the provisions of the Rehabilitation Act of 1973 and its emphasis on nondiscrimination in all facets of life, individuals with disabilities are striving to achieve success and recognition in all fields of endeavor, including sports. In 1970 specialized sport organizations such as the United States Association for Blind Athletes and the United States Cerebral Palsy Athletic Association were founded to provide and expand athletic experiences for participants with disabilities. These groups, with the assistance of organizations formed earlier such as the Special Olympics (1968) and the Wheelchair Sports USA, founded in 1959 as the National Wheelchair Athletics Association, have been instrumental in enhancing the quality of training and coaching for athletes with disabilities. The spinoff of this effort has been to increase public awareness of the ability level of athletes with disabilities and to assist other service providers, including physical educators, in utilizing thesvaluable training materials generated by these specialized organizations. Chapter 18, *Competitive Sport for Athletes with Disabilities,* will provide information about these organizations and the exciting challenges created by segregated and integrated competition sport experiences for participants with special needs.

Summary

Within this chapter, a review of the origin of services for individuals with disabilities was provided from ancient times to the present. Careful review of the meaning of selected terms such as "handicapped," "disabled," and "impaired" were presented. Terms specific to physical education for individuals with disabilities, such as "adapted" and "special physical education," were discussed, with the term "special physical education" proposed as the appropriate term to describe physical and motor fitness programs for students with disabilities.

Society and its view of those with disabilities was described. The favorable changes that are occurring in services and programs for those with disabilities and the important role the federal government plays in helping

to make this possible were emphasized. Significant federal legislation, including IDEA '97, Section 504 of the Rehabilitation Act, and the Americans with Disabilities Act, and the relationship to physical education for students with disabilities were discussed.

Finally, the evolution of special physical education was traced from its beginning as primarily therapeutic and corrective exercises to its present status as an integral part of the services available to a large number of individuals with disabilities with a wide variety of disabilities.

Major professional organizations and the services they offer to physical educators interested in programs for those with disabilities were identified and described.

Enhancing Activities

1. Interview a person with a disabling condition or a parent of a child with disabilities. Try to determine whether the individual feels that society's perception of those with disabilities has changed in recent years.

2. Review your state law to determine if services, including physical education programs, are provided for the preschool child with disabilities.

3. Explore with students or professionals from other fields (such as physical and occupational therapy) their views regarding physical education and its contributions to the development of children with disabilities.

4. Develop a list of prominent people including entertainers, athletes, and politicians who have a disabling condition. Select one and attempt to find information about how the disability has affected the person's life.

5. Review the local newspaper and assess its coverage of items related to persons with disabilities and programs. Is the reporting positive or negative in its views of those with disabilities?

6. Review your institution's library holdings to determine if journals such as *Adapted Physical Activity Quarterly* and *Palaestra* are included.

7. Obtain a copy of one of the issues of the Federal Register that describes one of the pieces of legislation discussed in this chapter.

8. Review the website of one of the professional organizations discussed in this chapter to obtain information about the organization, including services to professionals.

Selected Readings

Block, M. E. (2000). *A teacher's guide to including students with disabilities in general physical education* (2nd ed.). Baltimore: Brooks.

Bokee, M. B. (1995). Fiscal year 1982 through 1995 adapted physical education and therapeutic recreation program analysis. Unpublished report. Office of Special Education and Rehabilitative Services: U.S. Dept. of Education.

Colarusso, R., & O'Rourke, C. (2003). *Special education for all teachers.* Dubuque, IA: Kendall/Hunt.

Dunn, J. M., Morehouse, J. W., & Fredericks, H. D. (1986). *Physical education for the severely handicapped.* Austin, TX: Pro-Ed.

IDEA '97. Individuals with Disabilities Education Act of 1997. Federal Register. Retrieved June 16, 2004, from: www.ed.gov/legislation/FedRegister/finrule/1999-2/062499a.pdf.

Morris R. J., & Morris, Y. P. (1999). Developmental disabilities. In M. C. Eisenberg, R. L. Glueckauf, & H. H. Zaretsky (Eds.), *Medical aspects of disability* (pp. 287–311). New York: Springer.

Olson, L. (2004, Jan. 8). Special needs, common goals. *Education Week, 23*(17).

Prouty, R., & Lakin, C. (Eds.). (1999). *Residential services for persons with developmental disabilities: Status and trends through 1998.* Minneapolis: Research and Training Center, Institute on Community Integration.

Sameroff, A. J., & Chandler, M. J. (1975). Reproductive risk and the continuum of caretaking casuality. In F. D. Horowitz, M. Hertherington, S. Scarr-Salapatec, & C. Siegel (Eds.), *Review of child development research* (pp. 187–244). Chicago: University of Chicago.

Sherrill, C. (2004). *Adapted physical education, recreation and sport* (6th ed.). Dubuque, IA: McGraw Hill.

Sherrill, C., & DePauw, K. P. (1997). Adapted physical activity and education. In J. D. Massengale & R. A. Swanson (Eds.), *The history of exercise and sport science* (pp. 39–108). Champaign, IL: Human Kinetics.

Shonkoff, J. P., & Phillips, D. A. (Eds.). (2000). *From neurons to neighborhoods: The science of early childhood development.* National Research Council/Institute of Medicine. Washington DC: National Academy Press.

Silverman, J. (2008, March 12). CES *email on developments in special education.* Retrieved July 23, 2005 from www.cec.sped.org.

Thurlow, M., Elliott, J., & Ysseldyke, J. (2003). *Testing students with disabilities: Practical strategies for complying with district and state requirements.* Thousand Oaks, CA: Corwin.

Turnbull, H. R., & Turnbull, A. (2000). *Free appropriate public education: The law and children with disabilities* (6th ed.). Denver: Love.

Turnbull, R., Huerta, N., & Stowe, M. (2009). *The Individuals with Disabilities Education Act as Amended in 2004,* (2nd ed.). Boston, MA: Pearson.

Wolfensberger, W. (1972). *The principle of normalization in human services.* Toronto: National Institute on Mental Retardation.

World Health Organization (WHO). (2001). *International classification of functioning, disability, and health* (ICF). Geneva, Switzerland: Author.

CHAPTER

2

Developmental Patterns

CHAPTER OBJECTIVES

After studying this chapter, the reader should be able to:

1 Identify the importance of the Principles of Motor Development and Principles of Physical Growth as factors that help to explain the developmental patterns observed in children.
2 Recognize the developmental patterns associated with the periods of infancy, early childhood, and later childhood.
3 Appreciate the close and significant relationship among physical growth, motor development, and the social, emotional, and cognitive development of children.
4 Identify common reflexes observed in infants, their time of onset and integration, and their importance as early indicators of potential neurological problems.
5 Analyze the common movement patterns, forms of locomotion, and manipulative patterns associated with various ages and levels of performance.
6 Appreciate the wide range of individual difference found among children of similar ages.

Knowledge of the patterns of development is critical for those engaged in providing services in physical activity for individuals with disabilities. The authors refer to typical development, with the understanding that the unique characteristics of the individual, the environment, and the task being asked of the performer will influence the movement performance of the individual (Davis & Burton, 1991). Historically, the difference in the execution of movement skills at early ages was attributed to the maturation of the central nervous system (CNS) and was used to identify stages of development (e.g., Gesell, 1928). Now current scholarship considers the contribution made by the ecology of the developing child (e.g., Bronfenbrenner & Crouter, 1983) in accurately describing both the current levels of motor development and, when developmental lag is detected, what interventions may be most appropriate. Instead of using a theoretical approach based solely on the maturation of the CNS, research has been conducted using a dynamic systems approach (e.g., Thelen & Smith, 1994), whereby developmental patterns are analyzed, taking into consideration the task being asked of the performer, the environment in which the task is performed, and the identification of the unique characteristics of the

individual performer. The current assessment tools in early childhood often reflect a marriage of both dynamic systems theory and the neuromatural theoretical approach (e.g., Miller & Roid, 1994; Piper & Darrah, 1994).

A further extension of the ecological perspective is the tenet of individual differences, whereby each individual is unique. If two individuals have a similar motor impairment (e.g., spastic cerebral palsy), then the manner in which they engage in physical activity and their level of performance at a certain age is not predictable based on their motor impairment (e.g., Sherrill, 2004). Rather, it is understood by the contribution made by such realities as the child's particular life experiences, the family setting, and cultural values (e.g., Bronfenbrenner & Crouter, 1983). It is also important to realize that in the early ages of development, the domains are considered intertwined (e.g., Piaget, 1952), so much so that it is unrealistic to attribute delayed developmental status to just one variable or to believe that only one domain is affected by an intervention.

Within the study of motor development, the most rapid rate of development takes place in the first few years of the child's life (Gabbard, 2004; Haywood & Getchell, 2005).

Overall, in the growth of children from infancy to adolescence, certain discernible patterns of development occur roughly at each year of age. Consequently, at a certain chronological age, a large majority of children demonstrate much the same physical development and similar intellectual and social traits. An understanding of the patterns of physical, intellectual, and social developments that are characteristic of each age group is extremely useful to teachers of children from nursery school to secondary school. During the early years, definite patterns in development are readily observed, and awareness of them will help the teacher serve the individual student more effectively; this is particularly true if the student has a disability. In adolescence, development becomes more highly individualized so that patterns characteristic of specific age groups are no longer easily identifiable. Teachers of children from preschool to secondary school find this knowledge extremely useful in understanding patterns of physical, intellectual, and social development that are characteristic of each age group.

As discussed in chapter 1, the need to provide early intervention services to infants and toddlers with suspected or diagnosed disabilities is the intent of current federal educational law. Public Law 94-142 has been amended since 1975 and is currently referred to as Individuals with Disabilities Education Improvement Act of 2004. This law continues to highlight that preschool children and infants and toddlers with disabilities will benefit from early intervention services if the child is ". . . experiencing developmental delay . . . in one or more of the following areas: physical development, cognitive development, communication development, social or emotional development, or adaptive development." Federal laws do not specify the types of services to be provided, but leave the decisions to the state, and more important, to the child's IEP or IFSP team, of which the parent or guardian is a member.

Many professionals recognize that motor development activities should play an integral part in services for preschool children, including infants and toddlers (McCall & Craft, 2000; Pangrazzi, 2001; Saunders, 2002; Wessel & Zittel, 1995, 1998). In addition, professional organizations are publishing new guidelines to support developmentally appropriate practice in facilitating and teaching young children's movement skills. For example, the Council on Physical Education for Children (COPEC) of the National Association for Sport and Physical Education (NASPE) published a position statement, *Appropriate Practices in Movement Programs for Young Children Ages 3–5* (2000; www.aahperd.org/nasped) containing information such as the premises of quality movement programs, developing movement skills and concepts, and facilitating maximum participation. In addition, NASPE published *ACTIVE START: A Statement of Physical Activity Guidelines for Children Birth to Five Years* (2002; www.aahperd,org/naspe) and the National Association for the Education of Young Children (NEAYC) has published *Active for Life: Developmentally Appropriate Movement Programs for Young Children* (Saunders, 2002). New curricula have also been developed to facilitate movement skills in young children, such as the *I Can Primary Skills K-3* (Wessel & Zittel, 1998) and the *Smart Start: Preschool Movement Curriculum Designed for All Abilities* (Wessel & Zittel, 1995). And to address the unique equipment needs of very young children, texts such as *Make It Take It!* (Cox & Lubbers, 1999), written by experts in early childhood adapted physical education, is a solid resource for teachers, therapists, and families.

Given the importance of the early years of development (e.g., Shonkoff & Phillips, 2000), this chapter provides a basic overview of developmental patterns and the relationship between early and later movement experiences and successes. The patterns of development common to various age periods are a very important piece that can be used by the teacher as criteria to evaluate the degree to which a disabling condition is affecting normal growth and development. For some children, the disability will be seen to have interfered with the development of certain motor skills that most other children of the same age have developed; or it may be determined by a comparison with the pattern of social development typical of the age group that a child's social growth has been retarded by his or her attitude toward the disabling condition.

It should be noted at this point that significant differences in development can be expected where children are approximately the same age. Although children of a given age can follow the same general developmental patterns, some progress at a faster or slower rate. It is also usually true, but not always, that the rate of intellectual and social development parallels physical development. The exceptions can be found among children with and without disabilities. Therefore, the account must be taken of the existence of the possible differences in rate of development when evaluating the effects of a disability upon development. If it is determined that a disabling condition is negatively influencing development, special steps can be taken to help the child improve. These might include activities to promote physical development, or if help is needed to overcome poor social development, attention can be directed toward instruction to increase the opportunities for social interaction in group play. These are only two examples of the numerous ways in which the teacher can meet the special needs of students whose development has not kept pace with that of their peers. Other strategies will be explored more fully in later chapters.

Familiarity with the developmental patterns provides the teacher with a means of assessing progress toward achieving the degree of development for a given age period. This is particularly helpful with very young children who are difficult to test with standardized tools of evaluation and may not perform on the day required or have the interest in the test items (Neisworth & Bagnato, 1996). When this happens, the teacher may receive inaccurate information about the child. Although the comparison of a child's status of development with patterns that are generally characteristic of the age group is highly subjective and open to errors in interpretation, it is nevertheless a useful means of determining if and how much improvement has been made.

It is often difficult to determine if a child with disabilities is ready to learn a new skill. Readiness is that state of development in which the child has acquired the physical, mental, and emotional capacity to comprehend the requirements of a task and to execute them. Because a disabling condition may so alter the responses of the child as to cause misdiagnosis of his or her readiness for new learning experiences, teachers need other means of making the determination. The patterns of development can provide one of the means, because they indicate the abilities and potentialities usually evident in those of the same age group, abilities that may well be present in the student with a disability as well.

When studying the developmental patterns presented on the following pages, it should be kept in mind that no single description of the characteristics for various age periods will fit every child of that age group. It is not likely that very many children will exhibit all of the patterns ascribed to their age group; it is possible that very few will evidence a particular pattern. Each child does, after all, grow and develop at his own individual rate, a rate that is influenced by factors such as inheritance, socioeconomic background, and educational environment.

Care should also be exercised to recognize that biology and environment play a significant role in the development of infants and children (Berman, 1993). Biology, to a large extent, is controlled by genetic factors. In the past, genetics has been recognized as an important, but little understood field. This is changing dramatically. Scientists have gone from mapping just a few human genes into mapping more than 1,900 genes (Kunau, 2003, Van Dyke & Lin-Dyken, 1993). The implications of this for infants with disabilities is profound. What was once viewed as genetic and largely unknown is becoming more widely understood with the promise of major changes in the diagnosis, management, and possible treatment of children with developmental disabilities.

The environment in which infants and young children are raised is also becoming more widely understood and appreciated as to its importance in development. Included in environment are factors such as family relationships, cultural perspectives and child-rearing practices, poverty, and the availability of community resources.

Principles of Development

Investigators from several fields, including physical education, child development, medical sociology, and psychology, have identified some rather consistent, predictable developmental trends in children. Many of these trends will be discussed in this chapter. General principles have also been defined that help to explain some of these trends. The following principles will help professionals comprehend the process of motor development and guide them in developing appropriate movement experiences for youngsters with and without disabilities. The term "developmentally appropriate practice (DAP)" is a cornerstone guiding early childhood programs (e.g., www.naeyc.org; www.cec.org) and is concomitant with understanding the developmentally appropriate skills that a child can be practicing and learning. Conversely, it is unfortunate when the wrong developmental level is identified for a child and the child, quite naturally, fails at the skill performance. And logically, when the appropriate level is identified, the child typically experiences success with a skill. Thus, the child learns the new skill and can continue to develop other skills while experiencing fun and success. The following discussion will facilitate the understanding and implementation of the principles needed for teachers to facilitate motor development. This discussion will be grouped into two sections: *Principles of Motor Development* and *Principles of Physical Growth*.

Principles of Motor Development

Each of the following principles has implications for how a teacher understands the motor development of a child, particularly one who is very young. The teacher can use these principles to ascertain where the child's developmental level stands and any apparent delays warranting intervention. The following chapters will elaborate on these principles. Without these principles, it is easy to miss the appropriate developmental level, resulting in difficulty targeting accurate motor interventions. In general, it is nearly impossible to expect that a child can perform a motor skill or participate in a game if that child is not at the maturation level necessary for the activity. The following information will assist in determining the appropriateness of physical activity for a given child.

Maturation

Early developmental patterns are dependent in part upon maturation. This means that certain physical and behavioral changes can be attributed to the innate process of growth.

The maturational concept suggests, therefore, that certain changes occur as growth proceeds. Characteristics subject to the maturational process, such as early infant reflex patterns, will occur at broadly predictable periods of time in normal children. Close supervision of the child's development may detect significant delays in the maturational process, thus indicating a need for intervention.

Cephalocaudal (Head to Tail)

Development is not haphazard. In physical and motor development, two directional sequences have been noted. The first of these implies that muscular control and coordination advances in an orderly sequence from head to foot. In the initial stages of motor development, children gain control of the muscles that support the head and upper body before they gain control of the lower musculature. The progression in muscle control proceeds from the neck, to the back, lower back, upper leg, lower leg, and foot. Therefore, if babies are lying prone on their stomach, they will voluntarily lift their head up off the ground before their feet.

Proximodistal (Point of Origin to End)

The second of the directional sequences suggests that controlling body parts proceeds from the center or torso of the body to the periphery in a proximodistal fashion (proximate location on the body to distant location). Efforts to control the torso and shoulder, therefore, precede controlled movement of the elbow, wrist, and finger. In the lower half of the body, control of the hips precedes efforts to control the legs, feet, and toes. Therefore, babies will be more proficient in moving their trunk and shoulders before they are voluntarily able to use their fingers.

It is important to note that developmental principles of cephalocaudal and proximodistal, while generally recognized and accepted, have been challenged by some researchers (Allen & Capute, 1990). Some speculate, for instance, that head control may be functional first because it does not rely on the development of other body segments (Damiano, 1993).

Mass to Specific

An understanding of the proximodistal principle also suggests that motor function progresses from mass to specific. Therefore, control of gross motor movements will occur before fine motor movements. Skills that are simple and involve large muscles will be learned sooner than those that are refined and require the use of fine muscle movements. A very young child drawing with a crayon is performing a fine motor task that follows his controlled movement of the shoulder, wrist, and hand.

Bilateral to Unilateral

After the age of four, children normally exhibit preference for conducting activities using one side of the body. This is referred to as dominance. Thus, a child may eat and draw with the right hand, kick a ball with the right foot, and use the right eye to look through a kaleidoscope. Until this preference is established, the child will do various activities with either the right or left hand or foot. A recent concern of many specialists is that children be given the opportunity to explore activities bilaterally (i.e., kick with the left *and* right foot) and that they not be forced into unilateral preference (using only the left *or* right hand or foot). Fortunately, parents and teachers have become more sensitive to the needs of left-handed children and are providing them with greater opportunities to exhibit their preference in a right-handed culture. Some children take longer to develop preference, or dominance, and some are ambidexterous. As adults they may be able to write with their left hand and perform a physical task such as throwing with their right hand. Some activities encourage bilateral coordination (see figure 2.1).

Phylogenetic versus Ontogenetic

Traditionally, changes in behavior that occur rather automatically as the individual grows are referred to as phylogenetic behavior (developmental changes over time). Grasping, reaching, and crawling are examples of behavior that fit into this category. Behavioral changes that depend primarily on learning and environmental influences are called ontogenetic behavior. Unlike phylogenetic behaviors, ontogenetic responses do not occur automatically but are taught. Behaviors that are ontogenetic include such activities as throwing, catching, and riding a bicycle. This principle underscores the need for early childhood movement skill and game instruction. The access to free play (recess) for

Figure 2.1 Riding a tricycle helps develop bilateral coordination.

preschoolers does not support the learning of motor skills, particularly when children are delayed (McCall & Craft, 2000).

Individual Development

A discussion of developmental patterns is incomplete without an emphasis on the uniqueness of each individual. Although there may be patterns that apply to the whole species, each child is different and thus the rate and speed at which certain movement patterns appear varies. These differences may be attributed to the combination of heredity and the environment in which the young child develops. The style in which children learn, whether auditory, kinesthetic, or visual, varies and is inclined to be genetically based. Awareness of the individual difference principle will help teachers recognize that all children are not ready for the same experiences at the same age.

Dynamic Systems Theory

Dynamic systems theory is one of the newest perspectives currently being applied to the understanding of movement performance. The dynamic systems theorists believe that the role of the central nervous system (CNS) in the control of coordinated movement should be deemphasized with greater attention placed on information in the environment and the dynamic properties of the body and limbs.

The key to understanding this approach is to accept the important connection between the person, the task, and the environment. While this relationship is generally recognized and supported by most developmental theorists, proponents of the dynamic systems theory argue that too much attention has been placed on the control center (CNS) and not enough on the importance of the interaction between the environment, the task, and the person.

This, of course, has significant implications for motor programs for children with special needs. For example, proponents of the dynamic motor systems theory would argue that under traditional views of motor development, the inability to inhibit certain reflexes in a youngster with cerebral palsy would delay the development of motor activity programs. Using a dynamic system perspective, movement patterns are not prescribed but emerge from interaction among body, task, and environment with little central input (Whitehall, 1988). The implication of this, of course, is to suggest that the traditional strict reliance on a neuromaturational theory of development may be a disservice to infants and toddlers with developmental disabilities. This is not to suggest, however, that the traditional principles of development are unimportant, but it does mean that professionals should continually be open to new ideas and, most importantly, recognize the specific needs of the infant

and the relationship of the task, the environmental stimuli and the self-initiated movement of the young child (Adolph, 1997). For older students with special needs, this approach is profound in the impact it can have on both assessing, as well as teaching, skills. For example, Davis and Burton (1991) reported that "body scaling" was important when asking children to throw a ball. If the ball chosen for the execution of the skill of throw was scaled to the size of the child's hand, then his or her accuracy was increased. The ball selection is accomplished by looking at the size of the hand in relationship to the ball: The assessor should give the performer a number of balls of different sizes. The one chosen is typically better scaled to the size of the student's hand. If not, the teacher can coax/suggest a different ball size. Burton, Greer, and Wiese-Bjornstal (1992, 1993) reported variations in grasping patterns in children, as well as the resulting changes in overhand throwing patterns, as a function of ball size. In another study, children were accurate when researchers analyzed the size of the child scaled to the distance the researchers felt the child could perform a horizontal jump.

It is important to remember that all the answers to the best approaches to the developmental needs of individuals with disabilities and the appropriate remedial practices are not known. Thus, professionals will need to seek and be open to new ideas and suggestions for working with this population. Chapter 15 will provide additional suggestions and activities that have been found to be helpful in working with infants and toddlers. A more thorough discussion of dynamic systems theory will be found in chapter 3.

Infant (Zero to Two Years)

The best practice in the field of physical activity for very young children is to allow for time in a given day devoted to physical activity (NASPE, 2002). Not only is it important to the current level of health, it is felt to be a foundation to enjoyment of a happy, physically active life. Within this section, the development of the individual during the first two critical years of life, the infant period, will be discussed.

Physical Growth

The average full-term baby weighs 7½ pounds and is approximately 20 inches long. One fourth of the baby's length is attributed to the head, with the trunk size accounting for slightly more of the remaining length than the lower extremities. As the baby grows during the first six months of life, these proportions remain constant. After approximately six months of age, however, the relationship of body proportions begins to change: the growth of the head slows and a rapid increase occurs in the growth of the extremities, with the rate of development of the trunk remaining constant. As the infant approaches two years of age, the relationship of the lower limbs and trunk are approximately equal. This adjustment in growth equips the two-year-old with the body size and proportion needed to successfully undertake the various locomotor skills.

Infant Reflexes

The earliest movements that can be observed in the infant are reflexes. These actions are involuntary behaviors elicited by various types of external stimuli. In typical development, infant reflexes appear and disappear at specific months of age. For educators working with young students with disabilities, familiarity with some of the more common infant reflexes is essential because the absent reflex, or one that persists for too long, may be an indication of neurological impairment. Thus, observing infant reflexes becomes a method of assessing the child's nervous system (Brazelton & Nugent, 1995). In specific disability areas such as cerebral palsy, these primitive reflexes do persist, and discussion of this is found in chapter 8. Haywood and Getchell (2005) point out that responses seen in reflexes are atypical if:

1. the reflex is exhibited when it should have disappeared; and
2. a reflex is not exhibited and it should be present.

Norberg (2001) would add that when an expected symmetrical reflex is asymmetric, such asymmetry is atypical.

According to developmental psychologists Lamb, Bornstein, and Teti (2002), infant reflexes are thought to be biologically meaningful as survival and adaptive skills. Such reflexes are defined as ". . . simple unlearned stimulus-responses common to all members of a species" (p. 122). Infant reflexes are traditionally divided as follows: approach reflexes (e.g., rooting, sucking, swallowing, breathing), avoidance reflexes (e.g., coughing, sneezing, blinking), and other reflexive responses that continue now but were important in the earlier development of humans (e.g., the palmer grasp, Babinski toe fanning, Moro responses). Clearly some reflexes diminish early in infancy, whereas others are sustained throughout a normal, healthy life.

The diminishing of reflexes that were important to the development of the species but now hold no apparent value have ". . . origins in the deepest and most primitive parts of the central nervous system. So long as these neurological structures dominate function, the reflexes endure. As higher cortical processes come into play . . . they appear to inhibit subcortical structures and thus prevent the expression of reflexes" (Lamb et al., 2002, p. 123).

To obtain accurate information about infants, it is important to obtain input from the infant's primary care provider, not only to validate the assessment outcomes but also to obtain additional information. It is critical to note whether the infant tested is alert or drowsy, and to recognize that infants can quickly change from one state to another. Also, differences can exist between behavioral data collected by eliciting the behavior or by observing the infant's spontaneous behavior (Lamb et al., 2002).

Moro Reflex

The Moro reflex can be elicited in infants by lifting the infant's head up in relation to the trunk, and then letting the head drop into the examiner's hand (Norberg, 2001). This response can also be elicited if infants are exposed to a loud noise or change of light. In the Moro reflex, the infant is typically in a relaxed position (figure 2.2A). Then if either the baby's head is dropped, or there is a sudden loud noise or change of light, then the infant's response will be that his/her arms and legs will extend in symmetric adduction (away from the midline) and the fingers and toes will spread out (figure 2.2B). Typically the infant cries in distress with his/her arms and legs outstretched, and then will bring the arms to midline as if to catch a caregiver. The Moro's vestigial origins are thought to have been a response to the baby being dropped. The Moro reflex is normally present at birth and is evident during the first 6 months of life. If the Moro reflex persists much past this age, it may be an early warning sign of neurologic problems.

Rooting and Sucking Reflex

The rooting and sucking reflexes are present in all normal newborns. The search reflex may be initiated by stimulating the infant's cheek and observing as the infant turns her head

Figure 2.2 The (A) infant in a relaxed position and (B) Moro reflex extension phase.

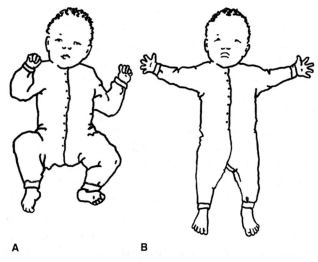

A   B

toward the source of stimulation, opens her mouth, and searches to suck. This allows the infant to ingest food and obtain nutrition. The sucking reflex persists well past the first year of life. In some newborns the suck is not fully developed and intervention must be directed toward stimulating this reflex.

Symmetrical Tonic Neck Reflex (STNR)

This reflex is elicited by extension and flexion of the neck and is characterized by two distinct patterns. When the neck is flexed, the arms go into flexion and the legs into extension (figure 2.3A). When the head and neck is flexed back beyond the midline, the arms go into extension and the legs into flexion (figure 2.3B). The symmetrical tonic neck reflex is present at birth and its primary function is to help the infant develop extension patterns. Normally, the reflex is suppressed by the seventh month. Therapists often use the terms STNR to refer to symmetrical tonic neck reflex, or the symmetrical response that occurs when both sides of the body (arms and legs) respond in the same pattern. This is to distinguish the reflex from the asymmetrical response described in the following text. Again, these reflexes are seen in older individuals with certain types of cerebral palsy and will be addressed in chapter 8.

Asymmetrical Tonic Neck Reflex (ATNR)

The apparent purpose of this reflex is to aid in the development of extension patterns. The primitive interpretation of this reflex is often associated with protection of the eyes by the baby or in early reaching for a desired or needed object. The reflex is often referred to as the fencing reflex, which mimics a fencer's stance with the arm extended with sword in hand and the other arm extended in the other direction and flexed upward. The ATNR reflex is elicited from a

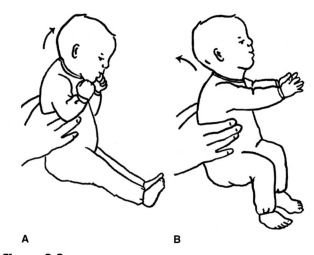

Figure 2.3 Symmetrical Tonic Neck Reflex (STNR)

relaxed position of the infant (figure 2.4A) by rotation of the head to either side. When the head is turned, the arm and leg on the side of the body to which the face is turned are extended and the limbs on the opposite side are flexed (figure 2.4B). Usually the ATNR disappears by six months after birth.

Palmar or Grasp Reflex

Pressing against or stroking the infant's palm elicits a grasp reflex. The classic action is for an adult to place his/her finger horizontally at the base of the infant's fingers. Involuntarily the baby will hold onto the finger with a strong grasp. Attempts to remove the finger will produce a stronger grasp! The palmar reflex response becomes weaker by the sixth month of life. Delays in motor development may be apparent if this reflex persists or is asymmetrical (strong on one side and not the other).

Figure 2.4 Asymmetric Tonic Reflex (ATNR)

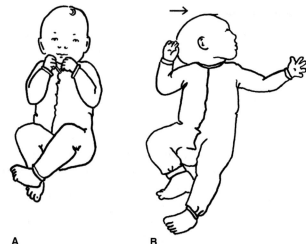

Infant Reflexes Involuntary

- Moro Reflex
- Rooting and Sucking Reflex
- Symmetrical Tonic Neck Reflex (STNR)
- Asymmetrical Tonic Neck Reflex (ATNR)
- Palmar or Grasp Reflex
- Babinski and Plantar Grasp Reflexes
- Labyrinthine Righting Reflex
- Parachute Reflex
- Righting Reflexes of the Head and Body
- Crawling Reflex
- Stepping Reflex
- Positive Support Reflex

Babinski and Plantar Grasp Reflexes

The Babinski reflex is elicited by stroking the sole of the foot of the newborn. The pressure causes an extension of the toes and they fan out. This reflex persists through the first year of life.

The plantar grasp reflex is elicited by pressing against the infant's foot directly below the toes (figure 2.5). The pressure causes the toes to contract. The plantar grasp reflex is usually present about the fourth month and persists to approximately the twelfth month. Persistence of the plantar grasp reflex beyond this point may interfere with the infant's early attempts at standing and walking.

Labyrinthine Righting Reflex

The labyrinthine righting reflex is important in helping the infant assume an upright head and body posture. This reflex can be initiated by holding the infant upright, then tipping the body forward. The infant's head will go back in an attempt to maintain an upright position. Angling/swaying the infant to the right or left will also initiate this response. The head will tend to move so as to maintain an upright position. The reflex may first appear at two months and becomes increasingly stronger until the fifth or sixth month. It is abnormal if this response fails to develop or is asymmetric.

Parachute Reflex

The parachute reaction may be elicited in several ways and is an effort by the infant to protect against sudden shifts in directions. As noted in figure 2.6, the infant, when gently tilted forward from a held position, extends the arms as a protective mechanism. The infant's lower limbs also extend, are tense, and abduct. The parachute reflex tends to persist beyond the first year and plays an important role in assisting the infant in learning to walk.

Righting Reflexes of the Head and Body

Within the first year of life, the infant has two involuntary reactions that help it to maintain a comfortable position in the crib. The first of these, the neck-righting reflex, is elicited by turning the head as the infant is on its back. The trunk will reflexively turn in the same direction. Likewise, if the

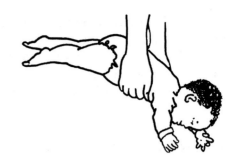

Figure 2.6 Parachute Reflex

hips are turned while the infant is in a prone position, the head will follow in the same direction.

Crawling Reflex

The crawling reflex can be observed by placing the infant in a prone position on the floor and applying pressure to the sole of one foot (figure 2.7A). The infant will return the pressure by pushing with the affected foot while doing an extensor thrust with the nonaffected leg. Reflexive movement will occur, which resembles that of crawling. The crawling reflex is generally present at birth and disappears around the third or fourth month. The delay between reflexive crawling and voluntary crawling is approximately four months with most infants crawling around the seventh month. This reflex is interesting because it is one in a group of reflexes wherein newborns seem capable of activities that are not possible until later in their infant life. These movements of the newborn are involuntary as opposed to the voluntary movement such as crawling seen in later infant life (Haywood & Getchell, 2009). This reflex is often of great interest to caregivers.

Stepping Reflex

Another involuntary reflexive movement that interests parents and caregivers is defined as moving from point A to B and is when they see their one-month-old baby make a response that looks very much like the taking of steps. This action is very normal and can be elicited in infants as young as two weeks by holding the baby in an upright position with the feet touching a level horizontal surface (figure 2.7B). The walking pattern is very immature and involves only the action of the legs and knees. The stepping reflex normally disappears by the end of the fourth month.

Figure 2.5 Plantar Grasp Reflex

Figure 2.7A Crawling Reflex

Figure 2.7B Stepping Reflex

Positive Support Reflex

With the positive support reflex, when the infant is held over a surface and the balls of the feet come into contact with the surface, the infant extends the legs (figures 2.8*A* and *B*). This reflex persists throughout the first year of life. For the child with cerebral palsy, the extension of the legs becomes very rigid with increased tone, and thus interferes with the development of standing and walking.

Early Voluntary Movement Patterns

Zero to two Years of Age

The precise process by which reflex actions are phased out and replaced by voluntary movements is not clearly understood. This is due, in part, to the differences found within individuals as well as to the lack of definitive timeliness indi-

Figure 2.8 Positive Support Reflex

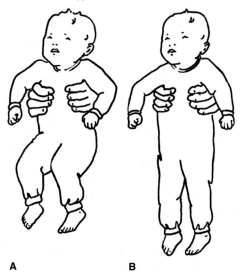

A   B

cating when reflexes will normally appear and disappear. Nevertheless, professionals interested in the motor performance of those with disabilities find it helpful to study the relationship between reflex action and voluntary movement. For instance, familiarity with the walking reflex will help movement specialists explain to parents that although it appears their child with developmental disabilities is ready to walk, the necessary *voluntary* responses may not be present. Also, for those working with children with developmental disabilities, it is useful to understand the relationship between the failure of infant reflexes to disappear in those who have cerebral palsy and the motor problems these individuals experience. (For further discussion, see chapter 8.)

Within this section, six voluntary movement patterns developing before the age of two will be discussed. According to Burton and Miller (1998), the term "early movement milestones" denotes locomotor and object control skills attained by the child before standing or bipedal locomotion. The transition from infancy into toddlerhood is noted by the acquisition of walking and is the first *fundamental movement skill*. As a word of caution it is important to emphasize that although we expect children at 24 months to have developed in a similar manner, differences in the rate of change and the quality of movement will be seen in young children and can be considered within the range of normal development.

Postural control and locomotion are two movement challenges that the newborn must resolve. Postural control refers to the ability of the infant to develop head control, sit without support, and pull to a standing position. Locomotion is defined as moving from point A to B and includes the pre-walking skills of rolling, crawling, and creeping as well as the notable achievement of walking alone.

In figure 2.9, progressions of change in postural control are reported for head control, sitting alone, and standing. The progressions are based on the normative data by Frankenburg and Dodds (1991) with the Denver Developmental Screening Test-II (DDST-II). The DDST-II describes

Examples of Voluntary Movement Patterns Zero–Two years of age:

- Locomotion
  - Rolling over
  - Sitting
  - Crawling
  - Walking
- Reach and Grasp
- Striking

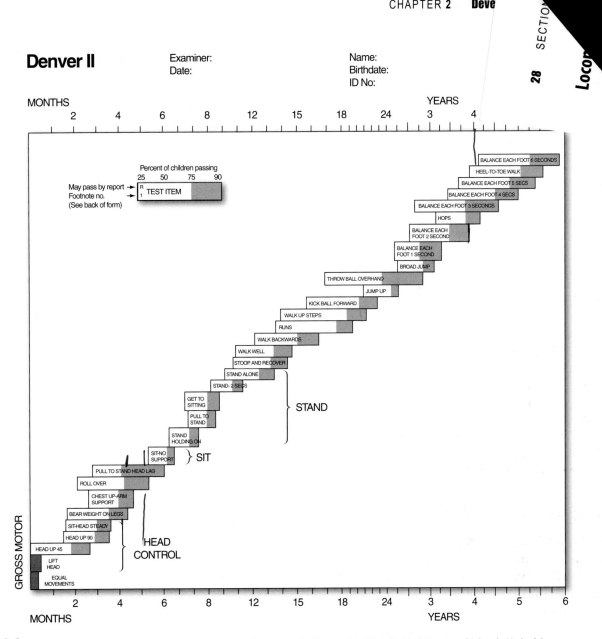

Figure 2.9 Progression of change: postural control (Adapted from William K. Frankenburg and Josiah B. Dodds, University of Colorado Medical Center, Boulder, Colorado.)

developmental progressions and indicates where 25, 50, 75 and 90 percent of the normative sample achieved the skills. The descriptions that follow herein are based on the 50 percent normative sample. As noted in figure 2.9, head control, or the ability to keep the head steady, without support while being moved is achieved at approximately two months. Improvements in head control may also be noted when the infant's head does not lag while being pulled up from a supine position. The movement behavior of sitting without support is generally achieved by five months, which indicates a basic control of head and trunk although only in a stationary position. As infants progress they develop the movement capability of getting to a sitting position from a supine or prone position. This means that by seven months

the infant can change body position rather than being limited to the sitting position in which he/she is placed. As the ability to sit with no support is developed, the infant learns to do other things, including manipulating objects while seated.

The third progression in postural control is for the infant to pull to a standing position. As noted in figure 2.9, this is generally achieved by approximately nine months of age. In developing this movement behavior, infants combine the skills of sitting without support, reaching, and pulling. As the infant becomes more and more accustomed to standing with support (by holding onto furniture, etc.) the necessary postural control emerges to stand alone. The ability to stand alone, normally seen at approximately 11 months, prepares the infant for walking.

motion

ring the first six months of life, infant development is rich but not very mobile. A typical newborn moves arms, legs, and head a great deal but full understanding of all this movement is not known. Initially, when placed prone or supine, the infant will remain in that position with little change in direction or location. This begins to change at approximately four months of age when the infant learns to move from the side to the back and back to side. Rolling over is the first progression of change in locomotion and is achieved at three and one-half months of age for 50 percent of DDST-II sample (figure 2.10). This voluntary movement is believed to be triggered by a sequence of reflex actions. The infant lying supine in the crib focuses on and follows an object with the eyes. Thus, the head turns, initiating the body righting reflex. The body turns in the same direction as the head, resulting in a roll over.

Crawling

The infant begins at approximately seven months of age to move forward from a prone position which resembles a "combat crawl." (In professional movement terminology this is referred to as crawl and the later movement is referred to as creep; however, in the more classical parent and caregiver world, a creep is a crawl.) "Crawling" is the term used to indicate this early movement response. Crawling usually occurs spontaneously when infants are placed in front-lying positions for increasing periods of time.

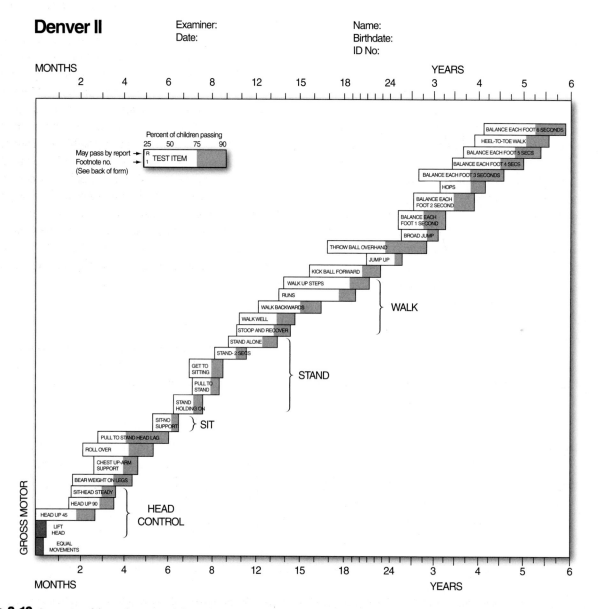

Figure 2.10 Progression of change: locomotion (Adapted from William K. Frankenburg and Josiah B. Dodds, University of Colorado Medical Center, Boulder, Colorado.)

From this position it is natural for the infant to look up and eventually reach for items. Movement occurs when both arms are used to reach for an item. When this happens, the head and chest will fall toward the floor, with the infant sliding forward. From this primitive beginning a more concerted effort is developed to use the arms systematically as an aid in crawling.

The rate at which children learn to crawl is highly dependent on individual development. Most, however, crawl at about the seventh month.

Crawling, a more sophisticated form of locomotion than creeping, requires that the infant use the hands and knees for support. From this position, the mature crawl pattern requires that the infant move the arms and legs in a contralateral pattern. Thus, as the left arm moves forward so does the right leg. Early efforts to crawl are not always this efficient. Some infants move only one limb at a time followed by a hesitation before the next limb is moved. Approximately 20 percent of all infants move the same side arm and knee forward when crawling. Burton (1999) reported a quadrupedal gait of infants walking on hands and feet. These infants are not yet walking independently. It is also observed that some infants use a three-point crawl and never proceed to a four-point crawl. Some children use a "scoot," whereby they move forward on their bottoms as a primary mode of locomotion (Burton & Miller, 1998) and never really use a crawl before progressing to a walk. The infant who crawls using a unilateral rather than a contralateral (opposite leg and arm move in motion) pattern may or may not experience future problems. As the child develops, further observations should be made to determine if other opposition problems exist. Development of crawling skills occurs at 10 to 11 months of age. According to Haywood and Getchell "... atypical development is not indicated if an infant doesn't creep [crawl]" (2009, p. 120).

Walking

There is a great deal of variation among infants as to the age at which independent walking begins. Some infants walk as early as nine months, whereas others may not walk until 18 months. Both early and late responses may be normal, depending on the individual's experiences and level of maturation. Figure 2.11 notes progressions in direction and skill with walking in the early years.

The development of the locomotor skill of walking is generally believed to follow from crawling and creeping. As proficiency in these skills increases, efforts to gain an upright posture will become more evident as the infant moves around the environment, using objects such as tables and chairs for aids in standing. The first attempts at walking involve the child standing and moving along a surface using one handhold to another. This is referred to as cruising. Many children use a table or chair as their support. Early attempts to step away from the adult handhold are frequently unsuccessful. This explains why some infants revert to creeping when learning to walk, because it is a more efficient form of locomotion. Infants soon discover, however, the numerous advantages of walking.

There are various stages through which young children progress as they move from an immature pattern to an integrated, efficient walking motion. Initially, the infant walks with a wide base of support in a flat-footed manner with the toes turned out. In addition, the arms tend to be held in a high-guard position. Little evidence of extension in the hip, leg, and ankle of the new walker is noted. A graphic representation of the walking pattern of an infant is presented in figure 2.11.

The walking pattern of young children becomes more refined as they become stronger and gain additional practice. When this occurs, the individual assumes a narrower gait, with the feet placed straight ahead and with a heel-to-toe step. The arms also swing forward and backward in opposition to the legs. The walking gait generally matures in infants between 11 and 18 months of age.

Reach and Grasp

The development of hand control is very important in the early months of life. In the first weeks of life infants' hands are in a fist with their fingers together. When touched, the

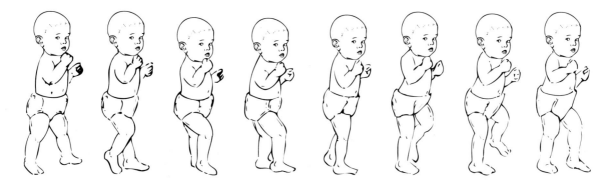

Figure 2.11 Early walking pattern of a 14½-month-old infant. Note the high arm position, flat foot contact, and general tentative nature of the walking pattern. (Adapted from Wickstrom, Ralph L.: *Fundamental Motor Patterns*, 3rd ed., Philadelphia, Lea & Febiger, 1983.)

infant will close the fist tighter, similar to a grasp. This is followed by a period in which the hands are open much of the time. In the second month of life infants develop the ability to put the hands together. The first successful reach and grasp of an object occurs at approximately three to four months, when the infant reaches for and picks up a small cube. The first grasp of the cube is normally awkward with the infant holding the cube in the palm using the fingers. It is not until five to six months that the infant progresses to thumb opposition, where the thumb opposes the fingers to pick up an object. As the infant develops, the ability to pick up smaller objects is facilitated by the thumb working in opposition to the fingers. This refined form of opposition, known as the neat pincer grasp, is normally seen at nine to ten months. Development of the neat pincer grasp is important because it allows the fingers and thumb to work together in the manipulation of small and large objects.

The release of an object, normally seen at eight months, is another important landmark in being able to successfully manipulate objects. The initial release is crude in that the hand is opened and the object dropped. From this beginning, however, the important manual dexterity tasks, such as placing items in containers, begin to develop. Infants learn by the second year of life to make horizontal and vertical lines, color on paper, turn the pages of a book, and stack six to eight cubes.

Striking

Striking in its earliest form develops from an overarm action that occurs in the anteroposterior (front-to-back) plane. The infant uses his/her hand as an implement to strike at suspended objects; this strike is usually restricted to a push rather than an actual hit. By 22 months, the child may still utilize an overarm striking pattern with an implement such as a small lightweight paddle. The striking action is still confined to extension of the forearm, and the child may exhibit one step forward. Mature striking movements do not occur until after the age of six or seven years.

Social Development

Interaction with the caregiver and the world begins at birth. Each newborn is unique in the need for sleep and alertness as well as the capacity for interaction. Brazelton, a leading pediatrician from Harvard University, developed the Brazelton Neonatal Behavioral Assessment Scale (1979) to rate the state and interaction capacity of the infant. Based on his work, it is clear that some infants initiate chance interactions with their caregiver. For some newborns, the interaction will be more subdued due to a greater need to control stimulation and temperament of the infant (see M. A. Rothbart for reviews of temperament in early childhood). Caregivers

need to be cognizant of the wide range of infant behavior and note that an infant does not always respond to adult initiated interaction.

For motor development specialists, the primary development during the infant period is in the motor domain, yet evidence of social growth and change is also an important and documented domain. Some of the earliest forms of social expression are the facial gestures seen in infants. Imitative smiling in response to a familiar face may occur as early as the first month of life.

Early forms of social interaction may also be observed in the play behavior of infants. For instance, most young children have enjoyed the games of pat-a-cake and peek-a-boo by 10 months of age. However, parallel play, in which two children do the same thing at the same time, but not in direct contact with one another, is the preferred play pattern of the very young.

Early Childhood (Two to Six Years)

The early childhood period, ages two to six, is another exciting time in the developmental process of the young. During this time frame, children build upon and expand their walking ability into a variety of other locomotor activities. The foundation for the later refinement of manipulative skills, throwing, catching, and striking, is also established in the early childhood years. Social interaction becomes more complex, with the preschool child engaging in a variety of simple games. Within this section, the physical growth, locomotor activity, and social development of the young child will be presented.

Physical Growth

The rapid gains in weight and height associated with the period of infancy taper off and slow down during the period of early childhood. From ages two to six a relatively uniform process of growth is observed, with the rate of gain in height nearly double that in weight. Body proportions also change, with the lower limbs growing rapidly in proportion to the trunk length. Thus, the young child loses the round, stocky body build characteristic of the infant and becomes more rectilinear in appearance. Few differences in growth between the sexes are noted during this time. Boys tend to be somewhat taller and heavier, but the proportional rate of growth remains similar for both sexes during this time.

Brain growth is about 75 percent complete by age three and nearly 90 percent by age six. The increase in myelin, a fatty substance around the neurons, permits the transmis-

Figure 2.12 Young children with developmental disabilities require special activities to help them develop basic movement patterns.

Examples of Voluntary Movement Patterns
Two–Six years of age:

- Locomotion
  - Running
  - Climbing
  - Jumping
  - Hopping
  - Galloping and Skipping
- Throwing
- Catching
- Kicking
- Striking

sion of nerve impulses. It is important to note that in addition to experience with myelination (the development of myelin), children will perform at higher levels both motorically and cognitively.

Similar to the brain, the sensory apparatus is still developing during early childhood. The eyeball does not reach its full size until age twelve with the macula being incomplete in its development until age six. This accounts for the hyperopia (farsightedness) generally associated with young children.

Locomotor Activity

As children become more proficient in their walking ability, they will begin to explore other forms of locomotion, such as walking sideways and, eventually, backward. Children will also learn that they can walk quickly and, as they gain additional strength, will initiate other exciting movement patterns, including running, climbing, jumping, hopping, galloping and skipping. These patterns of locomotion are discussed in the following paragraphs.

Running

The initial running pattern of young children is characterized by unstable and uncoordinated movements. As the young become more proficient in their walking ability, they tend to walk faster. At first, the increased rate creates a problem because of insufficient balance and experience. For this reason, many young children move from a mature walking pattern to a somewhat immature running pattern, in which the feet are turned out and the arms are held away from the body. The "flight phase" distinguishes a run from a walk. This is the period where both feet are off the ground. From ages two to six, observable changes take place in the running pattern. Some of the more observable changes (figure 2.13) include the following:

1. The stride lengthens as the amount of time in the flight phase increases.
2. The trailing foot is higher in the recovery phase and is swung forward faster and higher.
3. The arms are held higher and used more effectively as they move in opposition to the legs.
4. The amount of forward lean increases (Gallahue & Ozmun, 2005).

Climbing   *easier to go up*

Once an independent walking pattern has been established, a young child may attempt to climb stairs in an upright position. Ascending a flight of stairs is negotiated sooner than the upright descent. A child will successfully ascend a flight of stairs, with alternate foot placement, between 29 and 41 months. Descending stairs proficiently may occur between 48 and 55 months. *than down (perception)*

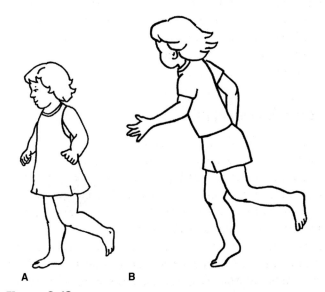

Figure 2.13 Obeservable changes in running pattern from ages two to six years. The arm and leg action of (b) is more mature than (a).

Jumping

A jump is the act of propelling the body off the ground by extending one or both legs followed by a landing on one or both feet. This form of locomotion requires greater strength, coordination, and balance than are needed for running or walking. For this reason, jumping is viewed as a more difficult skill but is a locomotor pattern that most young children can master. Jumping is usually perceived as a very exciting skill by preschool children. The various types-of jumps—vertical, horizontal, from objects, to objects, and over objects—all present different challenges to the young.

Although it is beyond the scope of this chapter to analyze the developmental phases of the various jumps, valuable information can be presented concerning the progressive difficulty of different forms of the jump. This information will help teachers of children with disabilities properly sequence instruction for students who have difficulty with jumping. From an analysis of table 2.1, it becomes clear that for many children jumping down is easier than jumping up. For example, jumping off a step is developmentally easier than jumping up to a step. Likewise, a jump down from one foot is an easier skill than a jump up from one foot. Jumping in the vertical plane up/down is less difficult than horizontal jumping (jumping out).

Most children will master the sequence in table 2.1 by five years of age. Further improvement in jumping performance will thus be found in the height and distance of the jump.

Hopping

Hopping is a locomotor skill similar to jumping but more difficult in that it requires a one-foot takeoff and landing on the same foot. Children do not hop successfully until they have gained sufficient strength and the necessary balance skills. By age four, however, most children can hop from four to six steps on their preferred foot. Rapid gains in the ability to hop greater distances and at faster rates of speed are made between the ages of four and six. Girls generally become more proficient hoppers at an earlier age than boys do, although there is wide variation in the ability to perform this skill within both sexes.

Galloping and Skipping

The skills of galloping and skipping are more advanced movement patterns that usually appear after children have learned to run, jump, and hop. Although galloping and skipping include variations of locomotor skills already learned, they are more difficult because of the balance and the movement sequences that must be learned.

Galloping, which includes the skills of walking and leaping, is a popular skill among children as young as four years. Proficiency in this pattern, however, is usually not observed until children reach the age of six. Skipping, a movement that includes a step and a hop on one foot followed by the same pattern on the opposite side, appears a little later than galloping. It is not until the age of six that children can accomplish this task with some degree of proficiency. Even at this age the variation in performance among children is great.

Manipulative Patterns

During infancy and the early childhood years, considerable energy is exerted by the young to explore their environment. At first, these efforts are restricted to simply observing. With increasing age, however, children become more mobile and quickly learn to interact with various objects. As infants develop the ability to reach, grasp, and release, they learn to play with blocks, rattles, and many other toys. Voluntary control of these basic manipulative abilities leads to refined patterns enabling children to throw, catch, kick, and strike.

Throwing

Any activity that requires using one or two arms to thrust an object into space falls into the general category of throwing. Although this definition is very broad and includes all of the major forms of throwing, only the developmental pattern of the overarm motion, the most commonly used motion, will be discussed here.

Sufficient evidence is available to document that children's throwing ability improves from infancy through childhood. Changes have been noted in the accuracy, distance, and form used by children of various ages. As distance and accuracy are dependent on the form used, the pattern of development of the throwing action is of primary importance. In 1938, Monica R. Wild conducted a thorough investigation of the developmental pattern of throwing. Although her

---

TABLE 2.1　　**Jumping**

Types of Jumps Achieved by Children in Terms of Progressive Difficulty

Jump down from one foot to the other foot.
Jump up from two feet to two feet.
Jump down from one foot to two feet.
Jump down from two feet to two feet.
Jump forward from two feet to two feet.
Jump over object from two feet to two feet.
Jump from one foot to same foot rhythmically.

(Adapted from Wickstrom, 1983)

work is dated, the developmental stages proposed by Wild are generally accepted today. The four stages she identified are summarized as follows:

Stage I. Children ages two and three years throw primarily with a forearm motion with no rotation of the body. The feet remain stationary throughout the throw but there is a slight forward body sway.

Stage II. As children become older, three and one-half to five years of age, several important changes occur in their throwing pattern. These changes include rotation of the body first to the right as the ball is brought backward and then to the left as the ball is delivered by the right hand. In preparation for the throw, the ball is brought backward further and held with a cocked wrist. The throwing arm also swings forward in an oblique horizontal plane. Similar to Stage I, the feet remain stationary.

Stage III. This stage, normally observed in children five and six years of age, is marked because of the addition of a forward step with the leg on the same side of the body as the throwing arm. Forward form is added to the throw by the shifting of weight that occurs during the step.

Stage IV. The final stage, the mature throw, is normally achieved by boys six and one-half years of age, with girls generally acquiring this pattern slightly later, unless they have had as much opportunity to observe and practice as the boys have, in which case they develop the pattern at the same age. In this stage the arm and trunk rotate backward in preparation for the throw. A contralateral step is then taken moving the body weight forward followed by rotation of the hips, trunk, and shoulder. The addition of opposition, coupled with the wider base of support, permits the throw to be completed with greater force.

Burton and colleagues (1992) documented that proficient throwing patterns were influenced by attending to the ratio of the hand size to the ball used for the throw. It should also be noted that developmentally, larger balls tossed at a close distance are easier for a child to catch and smaller balls (relative to hand size) are easier for young children to throw.

Catching

Stopping the momentum of and controlling a thrown object using the arms and hands is referred to as catching. This skill, similar to those previously discussed, follows a developmental trend. As children become older, they become more proficient catchers. Children experience three stages as they learn to catch.

In the initial stage, children less than three and one-half years of age frequently avoid the thrown ball by turning the head or holding the arms in extension. Young children also tend to hold the palms up and try to trap the ball against the chest (see figure 2.14). During the second stage, the elementary level, children of approximately four years of age learn

to follow the ball with the eyes. The earlier tendency to avoid the ball also disappears in this stage, although they tend to close the eyes only when the ball is about to make contact with the hands. Other changes include the position of the palms, which are held perpendicular rather than up as in the first stage. A mature catching pattern, the third stage, is achieved by many children at approximately six years of age. During this stage children track the ball from the time of release to when it is caught. The arms are held in a ready position, with the elbows flexed and the hands in a cupped position. As the ball is caught the arms give to help absorb the ball's momentum. These stages are presented in figure 2.14.

Kicking

Kicking is a manipulative pattern in which the foot is used to impart force to a ball. Although children as young as 24 months can kick, there have been few efforts to analyze the development of the kicking pattern. Gallahue and Ozmun (2002) have reviewed the available information and identified three progressive stages young children exhibit as they learn to kick.

In stage one, the ball is kicked with a straight leg action with little arm and trunk action. Little force is imparted to the ball because there is no backward movement of the kicking leg prior to the kick and the follow-through is limited. During the elementary stage, the arms are held outward for stability. The straight-leg kicking action observed in the first stage is replaced by a flexed knee position with the leg "uncocking" and extending forward to hit the ball. The beginning of a follow-through is also present during this stage. During the last stage, the mature kicking pattern emerges. In general, more total body action is found in this stage. The arms swing in opposition to each other during the kick. Length of the leg swing increases with a larger backswing and a higher follow-through. During the follow-through, the trunk flexes at the waist with the support foot raising to its toes. These stages are presented in figure 2.15 on page 35.

Striking

In general, well-defined sidearm striking patterns will be utilized by children beginning at approximately three years of age. Legs and lower body portion are used in a mature striking pattern after the age of six or seven.

Social Development

The early childhood period is a time of rapid change in the social development of the young. From ages three to six, children move from a preference for parallel play to an interest in small group activities and games with simple rules. Changes are also noted in social behavior. Whereas two- and three-year-olds are very possessive of their play items and

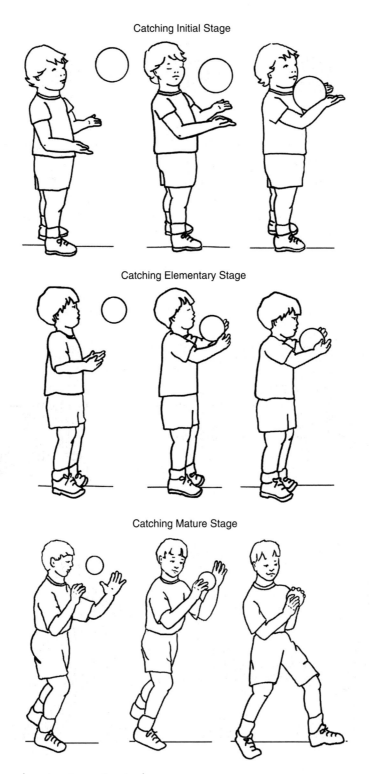

Figure 2.14 Catching (initial stage, elementary stage, mature stage).

KICKING
Initial Stage

KICKING
Elementary Stage

KICKING
Mature Stage

Figure 2.15 Kicking (initial stage, elementary stage, mature stage).

intolerant of others who intrude into their play space, five- and six-year-olds are more tolerant and show early interest in cooperative activities. Early attempts at leadership may also emerge in four- and five-year-olds.

The relationship between motor performance and social development is very important for the preschool child. Efforts to seek and gain approval occur frequently for the young as they utilize various movement patterns. Because motor skills are highly visible, they can easily be reinforced by the observant parent. The relationship of success in motor skills followed by parental praise encourages the child to explore other skills. Of course, the absence of success in play and game skills will lead to avoidance of these activities by young children, underlining the importance of structuring skills to ensure positive experiences.

Later Childhood (7 to 12 Years)

Children ages 7 to 12 are provided many opportunities to utilize the movement skills that were developed during the early childhood years. As children enter school, their environment expands and the basic movement patterns are used continuously in various interactions with their peers. The combined effects of experience, age, and maturation improve dramatically the elementary-school-age child's motor performance. In this section some of these changes will be discussed.

Physical Growth

Changes in height and weight in the age period from 6 to 12 are relatively slow and constant in comparison with the early childhood and adolescent periods. During this time, therefore, children are provided an excellent opportunity to refine and expand the basic movement patterns that they have established during the early childhood period.

Differences in the pattern of growth rate for boys and girls may also be detected during the later childhood period. In general, gender differences in height and weight are not significant until after approximately age 10, when girls reach puberty and achieve a size advantage that is apparent until about age 14. The hip-shoulder ratio for boys and girls also changes during this time, with the shoulder being wider than the pelvis for boys and the pelvis being wider than the shoulder for girls. The leg length of boys and girls also increases in proportion to the size of the trunk. This is particularly true for boys, so that by late childhood boys generally have legs proportionally

Examples of Voluntary Movement Pattern Seven–Twelve years of age:

- Refinement of Movement Patterns
  - Jumping farther and higher
  - Running faster
- Throwing farther and more accurately
- Catching easier
- Mature striking movements
- Dribbling

longer than those of girls, which was not the case during infancy and early childhood.

Refinement of Movement Patterns

Development of the basic locomotor and manipulative patterns occurs primarily in early childhood. As previously discussed, children learn the process of how to perform essential skills at very early ages. Many changes in skill performance occur during the early years. For example, the process that six-year-old children use to throw a ball is vastly different and more efficient than the process exhibited by a three-year-old. Continued refinement of the skills learned in early childhood occurs between the ages of 6 and 12 years, the later childhood period. Improved performance is noted in this age group because of several factors, including maturity, practice, and changes in size. This last factor, size, is particularly important. Bigger and stronger children are capable of performing many movement patterns more efficiently and effectively than can younger children.

The increase in functional complexity, noted in 7 to 12-year-olds, is attributed primarily to two different, but related processes—differentiation and integration (Gallahue & Ozmun, 2005). Differentiation is the gradual progression of movement patterns demonstrated by infants to the more refined movement patterns of children. Integration refers to the coordinated interaction of muscle and sensory systems. The relationship of the two processes is illustrated by the efforts of a young child to catch a ball. Early efforts rely primarily on trapping the ball (figure 2.16) and progresses only when the more mature visually guided reaching and grasping behavior is evident. This differentiation in the use of the arms, hands, and fingers followed by integration of the eyes and hands is crucial to success with hand-eye coordination tasks and to normal development. The intent of this section is to discuss how the skills learned in early childhood are further developed and refined in later childhood. The data presented herein assume that cultural change in America with regard to female sports has contributed to change in

Figure 2.16 The initial stages of catching a ball are exhibited by this youngster.

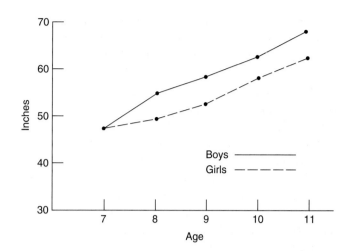

Figure 2.18 Standing long jump performance by age and sex. (Adapted from Cratty, Bryant J.: *Perceptual and Motor Development in Infants and Children*, 2nd ed. Englewood Cliffs, NJ, Prentice-Hall, Inc., 1979, p. 207; and Keogh, J. F.: *Motor Performance of Elementary School Children*, Monograph, University of California, Los Angeles, Physical Education Department, 1965.)

skill performance. Data on fundamental skills have been shown to be stable over time (e.g., Burton & Rogerson, 2003; Gabbard, 2004), with recent data by Hauberstricker (1997, in Gabbard, 2004) showing that females continue to make improvements from 14 to 18 years of age.

Jumping

The improvement children ages 7 to 12 make in both a vertical jump and a jump for distance is illustrated in figures 2.17 and 2.18. With respect to the vertical jump, boys and girls compare favorably until age seven, after which boys tend to

excel. Both sexes, however, improve dramatically in their vertical jump ability. A similar pattern is observed when analyzing boys' and girls' ability to perform a standing long jump. Until the age of seven both sexes perform equally. After this time both groups improve dramatically, with the boys achieving at a higher level.

Running

The speed at which young children can run a short distance has frequently been used as an indication of running efficiency. As indicated in figure 2.19, improvements in running speed occur as children grow older.

Figure 2.17 Vertical jump performance by age and sex. (Adapted from Cratty, Bryant J.: *Perceptual and Motor Development in Infants and Children*, 2nd ed. Englewood Cliffs, NJ, Prentice-Hall, Inc., 1979, p. 206; and Johnson, R. D.: "Measurements of Achievement in Fundamental Skills of Elementary School Children." *Research Quarterly*, 33:94–103, 1962.)

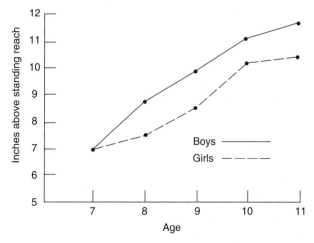

Figure 2.19 Running speed by age and sex. (Adapted from Espenchade, Anna S., and Eckert, Helen M.: *Motor Development*, 2nd ed. Columbus, OH, Charles E. Merrill Publishing Co., 1980; and Johnson, Warren R. (Ed.): *Science and Medicine of Exercise and Sports*, 1960.)

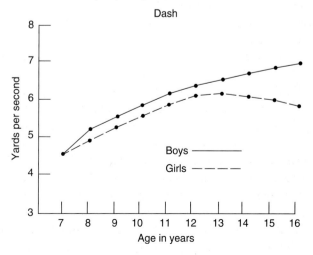

Throwing

As children emerge from the early childhood period, most can throw using a reasonably mature movement pattern. During the next few years, significant gains are made in the distance and accuracy with which children 7 to 12 years of age can throw a ball. Figure 2.20 illustrates that improvements in throwing distance occur in a linear fashion for both boys and girls, with boys achieving at a higher performance level than girls at each age. This gender difference may be attributed to the greater arm-shoulder strength of boys. The data in figure 2.19 shows similar trends across researchers.

The accuracy with which older children can throw also improves in a linear fashion.

Catching

Although few intensive studies have been conducted to analyze the developmental catching patterns of children ages 6 to 12 most recognize that with increasing age, children become more proficient in this skill. Catching is more difficult for children to master than throwing. Six-year-olds find catching a ball from a bounce easier than receiving a ball in flight. Similarly, larger balls are easier for the young to catch than are smaller balls (see figure 2.20). By age 12 however, most children can catch "on the fly" balls as small as a tennis ball with little difficulty.

Striking

Progress in the development of an effective striking pattern is indicated by the changes observed in patterns used at successive ages. These changes involve greater freedom or more definite use of body parts in the swing, the forward step, the hip and trunk rotation preceding the action of the arms in the swing, and the uncocking of the wrists during the swing. These changes begin to occur after six and one-half years, and it may be as long as two years before the child is capable of making mature striking movements.

Dribbling

Dribbling an object is a movement pattern that most children are exposed to and practice, yet it has not been studied extensively. Deach (1975), after studying children ages two to six, identified four stages of development. Stage 1 was a two-handed downward or diagonally forward overhand throw with no attempt to follow the ball. Stage 2 was an attempt to catch the ball after a single bounce. Stage 3 was an attempt to catch the ball after a single bounce, using one or more overhand swings with an outstretched arm. Stage 4 was a series of successive hits using a bent arm and palm/finger contact. In the final stage, the mature form is a rhythmic and a well coordinated series of pushes. Gallahue has identified the following elements as constituting the mature stage of dribbling (Gallahue, 1982; Gallahue & Ozmun, 2005):

- Feet placed in narrow stride position, with foot opposite dribbling hand forward
- Slight forward trunk lean
- Ball held waist high
- Ball pushed toward ground, with follow-through of arm, wrist, and fingers
- Controlled force of downward thrust
- Repeated contact and pushing action initiated from the fingertips
- Visual monitoring not necessary
- Controlled directional dribbling

The difficulty of the task of dribbling is compounded when the child moves while dribbling as contrasted to a stationary dribble. Dribbling while moving is a refined skill that should be introduced only after the child has successfully demonstrated the ability to perform a stationary dribble. This level of performance is normally not achieved prior to seven years of age.

Interest and Motor Activity

Children's interest in motor activities expands dramatically during the ages of 6 to 12. This is the period in which children move from participation in simple games and relays to lead-up activities for various sport experiences to membership in organized teams. Participation in school physical education classes as well as involvement in community-sponsored programs helps to nurture this interest in motor activity.

Figure 2.20   Mean throwing distance for boys and girls by age. Data from two longitudinal cohorts [1, 2] adapted from Keogh (1969) [K], Rippee *et al.* (1991) [R], and Nelson *et al.* (1986) [N].

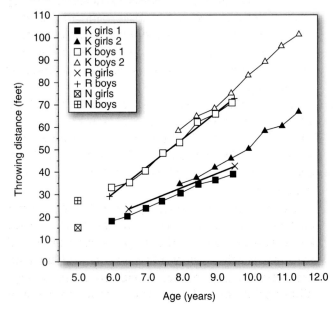

The primary educational emphasis during this critical time should be to expose children to a wide variety of activities and to create successful learning experiences. Curricular experiences that are limited to the popular fall, winter, and spring sports that are repeated year after year contribute little to the educational growth of children. Likewise, educational programs directed toward "playing the game" without first attempting to improve and refine the basic skills creates an environment that is loaded with failure. A concerted effort, therefore, must be made to expose children to developmentally sequenced motor activities so that all children, including those with disabilities, can grow and benefit. Without such a system, children's interest in motor activity will decline, and withdrawal will be likely, particularly for those who feel they are not proficient.

Social and Intellectual Changes

Social relationships and skills are widely extended during the 6 to 12 age period. Educators recognize that social growth, like physical growth, must be fostered through a developmental framework. At various stages the social needs of children change. Six-year-old children, for instance, prefer small group activities, whereas 12-year-olds seek identification with a group or club. Educational experiences should build upon these needs and be structured to foster social growth.

Individual differences in behavior patterns are observed during the ages of 7 to 12. It is difficult, therefore, to predict how the social behavior of a 9-year-old differs from that of an 11-year-old. For instance, although it is generally recognized that 11-year-olds enjoy team games, not all children of this age are socially mature enough to engage in team play. To force such children to participate in group games would be wrong and a violation of the principle of readiness. It should be noted that differences in behavior patterns are varied regardless of ability or disability. The development of social skills by children with disabilities may lag behind that of their nondisabled peers. However, this need not be the case if adequate and appropriate opportunities are provided for the social development of the students with disabilities.

One area of certainty is that children need and seek approval. The basic desire to feel important, wanted, and accepted is a primary need of children ages 6 to 12. Teachers must strive to ensure that each child is systematically recognized and valued as a unique individual.

Summary

An understanding of the patterns of development common to infants and children provides the physical educator with a means of assessing progress toward achieving the degree of development that is common for a given age period. This information can be very helpful as criteria to evaluate the degree to which a disabling condition is affecting normal growth and development. Development follows certain motor development and physical growth principles. There is an important distinction between voluntary and involuntary movement. The earliest movements that can be observed in the infant are reflexes. These actions are involuntary behaviors elicited by various types of external stimuli. An absent reflex or one that persists for too long may be an indication of neurological impairment. The precise process by which reflex actions are phased out and replaced by voluntary movements is not clearly understood. This is due, in part, to the differences found among individuals as well as to the lack of definitive timeliness dictating when reflexes will normally appear and disappear.

Postural control and locomotion are two movement problems that the infant must master. The ability to develop head control, sit without support, pull to a standing position, and perform selected locomotor acts such as rolling, crawling, and creeping is essential for later success in more refined movement patterns. Some of our limitations in determining with precision the initiation or absence of voluntary motor control may be attributed to an incomplete understanding of child development. Some have suggested that the reliance on a strict neuromaturational model with its motor control center approach to development may be too limiting in its view and appreciation for the environment and other factors important in the process of acquiring information. Much of the new view of development is being proposed by proponents of the dynamic systems theory.

In early childhood, ages two to six, children build and expand upon earlier development and establish the foundation for later refinement of locomotor and manipulative skills. This period, with its relatively uniform process of growth, allows for a great deal of movement exploration.

During later childhood, ages 7 to 12, the child is provided many opportunities to utilize the movement skills that were developed during the early childhood years. The combined effects of experience, age, and maturation dramatically improve the elementary-school-age child's performance. During this time frame children become more proficient in their locomotor and manipulative patterns, shifting to more refined movement patterns. Differences in the pattern of growth rate for boys and girls may also be detected during the later childhood period.

Paralleling the motor and physical development of infants and children is their emotional, social, and intellectual development. Change in the rate of development in these areas must be considered when evaluating the effects of a handicapping condition upon development.

Enhancing Activities

1. Observe a therapist or physician evaluate an infant for the presence or absence of selected reflexes.
2. Review a motor development test, such as the Denver II, to enhance one's understanding of the nature of the test and the type of test items used to evaluate motor development.
3. Observe children of different ages at a park or play space. Analyze the children's skills when running and throwing to compare for the different developmental patterns of children of various ages.
4. Select a specific manipulative pattern (e.g., catching) and test a child to assess the individual's performance level—initial, elementary, or mature.
5. Compare and contrast the movement patterns of a young child with a neurological impairment to that of a typically developing child of the same age. Develop a list of the similarities as well as the differences.

Selected Readings

Adolph, K. E. (1997). Learning in the development of infant locomotion. *Monographs of the Society for Research in Child Development, 62*(3, Se. No. 251).

Allen, M. C., & Capute, A. J. (1990). Tone and reflex development before term. *Journal of Pediatrics,* supplement, 393–398.

Authors. (1998). Baby. *World Book* (2nd ed.). Chicago: World Book.

Bayley, N. (1993). *Bayley Scales of Infant Development* (2nd ed.). San Antonio: Therapy Skill Builders.

Berkow, R. (1997). *The Merck manual of medical information* (Home ed.). New York: Pocket.

Berman, B. D. (1993). Difficult and challenging behaviors in young children: A neurodevelopmental perspective for assessment and intervention. *Infants & Young Children: An Interdisciplinary Journal of Special Care Practices, 6*(1), 26–34.

Brazelton, T. B., Als, A., Tronick, E., & Lester, B. M. (1979). Specific neonatal measures: The Brazelton Neonatal Behavior Assessment Scale. In J. Osofsky (Ed.), *The handbook of infant development.* New York: John Wiley and Sons, Inc.

Brazelton, T. B., & Nugent, J. K. (1995). *Neonatal Behavioral Assessment Scale* (3rd ed.). London: Cambridge University.

Bronfenbrenner, U., & Crouter, A. C. (1983). The evolution of environmental models in developmental research. In P. H. Mussen (Ed.), *Handbook in child psychology* (4th ed., pp. 357–414). New York: Wiley.

Burton, A. (1999). Hrdlicka (1931) revisited: Children who run on all fours. *Research Quarterly for Exercise and Sport, 70,* 84–90.

Burton, A. W., & Miller, D. E. (1998). *The assessment of movement skills.* Champaign, IL: Human Kinetics.

Burton, A. W., Greer, N, II, & Wiese-Bjornstal, D. M. (1992). Changes in overhand throwing patterns as a function of ball size. *Pediatric Exercise Science, 4,* 50–67.

Burton, A. W., Greer, N, II, & Wiese-Bjornstal, D. M. (1993). Variations in grasping and throwing patterns as a function of ball size. *Pediatric Exercise Science, 5,* 25–41.

Burton, A. W., & Rogerson, R. W. (2003). The development of throwing behavior. In G. Savelsbergh, K. Davids, J. van der Kamp, & S. Bennett (Eds.), *Development of movment coordination in children: Applications in the fields of egonomics, health sciences and sport.* (pp. 225–240). London: Routledge.

Carta J. J., et al. (1997). Developmental outcomes associated with "in utero" exposure to alcohol and other drugs. In M. Haack (Ed.), *Drug dependent mothers and their children: Issues in public policy and public health* (pp. 64–90). New York: Springer.

Cox, L., & Lubbers, T. (1999). *Make it take it!: Creating movement challenge kits for play at home or school.* Kearney, NE: Tekna.

Damiano, D. I. (1993). Reviewing muscle cocontraction: is it a developmental, pathological, or control issue? *Physical and Occupational Therapy in Pediatrics, 12,* 3–20.

Davis, W. E., & Burton, A. W. (1991). Ecological task analysis: Translating movement behavior theory into practice. *Adapted Physical Activity Quarterly, 8,* 154–177.

Deach, Dorothy F. (1975). Doctoral dissertation series; Publication 2390. Ann Arbor, MI: University Microfilms.

Dunn, J. M. (Ed.) (1991, August). PL 99–457, Challenges and opportunities for physical education. *Journal of Physical Education, Recreation, and Dance,* 33–48.

Eisenberg, A., Murkoff, H., & Hathaway, S. (1996). *What to expect the first year.* New York: Workman.

Eveleth, P. B., & Tanner, J. M. (1976). *Worldwide variation in human growth.* London: Cambridge University Press.

Frankenburg, W. K., & Dodds, J. B. (1991). *The Denver II developmental screening test.* Denver, CO: University of Colorado Medical Center.

Gabbard, C. P. (2004). *Lifelong motor development* (4th ed.). San Francisco, CA: Benjamin Cummings.

Gesell, A. (1928). *Infancy and human growth.* New York: MacMillan.

Gallahue, D. L., & Ozmun, J. C. (2005). *Understanding motor development: Infants, children, adolescents, and adults* (6th ed.). Dubuque: McGraw-Hill.

Gallahue, D.L & Ozmun, J. C. (2005) *Understanding motor development.* (6th Ed.). Dubuque: McGraw-Hill.

Haley, S. M., & Baryza, M. J. (1990). A hierarchy of motor outcome assessment: Self-initiated movements through adaptive motor function. *Infants and Young Children, 3*(2),1–14.

Haywood, K. M. & Getchell, N. (2009). *Life span motor development* (5th Ed.). Champaign IL: Human Kinetics.

Haywood, K. M., & Getchell, N. (2005). *Life span motor development* (4th ed.). Champaign, IL: Human Kinetics.

Keogh, J., & Sugden, D. (1985). *Movement skill development.* New York: MacMillan Publishing Co.

King, C. M., & Dunn, J. M. (1989). Classroom teachers' accuracy in observing students' motor performance. *Adapted Physical Activity Quarterly, 6*(1), 52–57.

Kunau, T. (2003). Computing infrastructure for life sciences: Confessions of an open source zealot. Conference presentation: Bioinformatic Technology: San Diego.

Lamb, M. E., Bornstein, M. H., & Teti, D. M. (2002). *Development in infancy: An introduction.* New Jersey: Erlbaum.

Leitschuh, C. A., & Dunn, J. M. (2001). Prediction of gross motor development quotient in young children prenatally exposed to cocaine/polydrugs. *Adapted Physical Activity Quarterly, 18,* 240–256.

Lester, B., & Tronick, E. Z. (1994). The effects of prenatal cocaine exposure and child outcome. *Infant Mental Health Journal, 15*(2), 107–120.

McCall, R. M., & Craft, D. H. (2000). *Moving with a purpose: Developing programs for preschoolers of all abilities.* Champaign, IL: Human Kinetics.

Miller, J. M., & Roid, G. H. (1994). *The Toddler and Infant Motor Evaluation.* San Antonio: Therapy Skill Builders.

Minnesota Department of Children, Families and Learning. (2004). *Active learning: A resource guide for designing and implementing developmentally appropriate movement experiences for young children ages 3 to 5.* [Manual]. Roseville, MN.

National Association for Sport and Physical Education. (2000). *Appropriate practices in movement programs for young children ages 3–5.* [Brochure]. Reston, VA.

National Association for Sport and Physical Education. (2002). *ACTIVE START: A statement of physical activity guidelines for children birth to five years.* [Brochure]. Reston, VA.

Neisworth, J. T., & Bagnato, S. J. (1996). *Assessment for early intervention: Emerging themes and practices.* In S. L. Odom & M. E. McLean (Eds.), *Early intervention/early childhood special education: Recommended practices* (pp. 23–57). Austin, TX: Pro-Ed.

NIDA pregnancy and drug use trends. Retrieved July 25, 2004, from http://www.drugabuse.gov/Infofax/pregnancytrends.html.

Norberg, S. (2001, July/Aug). Early signs of impaired motor development in infants and toddlers. *A Pediatric Perspective. Newsletter of Gillette Children's Specialty Healthcare, 10*(5), 1–3.

Pangrazzi, R. P. (2001). *Dynamic physical education* (13th ed.). Boston: Allyn and Bacon.

Piaget, J. (1952). *The orgins of intelligence in children.* New York: International Universities Press.

Piper, M. C., & Darrah, J. (1994). *Alberta Infant Motor Scale.* Orlando, FL: Saunders.

Saunders, S. W. (2002). *Active for life: Developmentally appropriate movement programs for young children.* National Association for the Education of Young Children, Washington, D.C. Champaign, IL: Human Kinetics.

Sherrill, C. (2004). *Adapted physical activity and sport: Cross-disciplinary and lifespan* (6th ed). Boston: McGraw-Hill.

Streissguth, A. P. (1997). *Fetal alcohol syndrome: A guide for families and communities.* Baltimore: Brookes.

Tanner, J. M. (1978). *Foetus into man.* Cambridge, MA: Harvard University Press.

Thelen, E., Kelso, J. A. S., & Fogel, A. (1987). Self-organizing systems and infant motor development. *Developmental Review, 7,* 39–65.

Thelen, E., & Smith, L. B. (1994). *A dynamic systems approach to the development of cognition and action.* Cambridge, MA: MIT Press.

United States Department of Health and Human Services (USDHHS), HHS Strategic Plan FY 2004–2009. Retrieved July 26, 2004 from www.aspe.hhs.gov.

Van Dyke, D. C., & Lin-Dyken, D. C. (1993). The new genetics, developmental disabilities, and early intervention. *Infants and Young Children, 5*(4), 8–19.

Wessel, J. A., & Zittel, L. L. (1995). *Smart Start: Preschool movement curriculum designed for all abilities.* Austin, TX: Pro-Ed.

Wessel, J. A., & Zittel, L. L. (1998). *I Can primary skills K-3.* Austin, TX: Pro-Ed.

Whitehall, J. (1988). *A dynamical systems approach to motor development: Applying new theory to practice.* Paper presented at the International Early Childhood Physical Education Conference, Washington, DC.

Wickstrom, R. L. (1983). *Fundamental motor patterns* (3rd ed.). Philadelphia: Lea and Febiger.

Wild, M. R. (1938). The behavior pattern of throwing and some observations concerning its course of development in children. *Research Quarterly, 9,* 20–24.

Motor Learning and Perception

CHAPTER OBJECTIVES

After studying this chapter, the reader should be able to:

1 Identify and describe the theories of learning.
2 Discuss the theories of learning and their application to motor learning.
3 Describe and discuss Thorndike's laws of effect, readiness, and exercise.
4 Explain the impact of Thorndike, Skinner, Tolman and Weiner.
5 Explain the laws of proximity, similarity, and closure and their relevance to the process of learning.
6 Identify and explain the various systems used to classify motor skills.
7 Recognize the commonly accepted motor skill tenets and their application to the teaching of students with disabilities.
8 Appreciate the value of recently developed motor learning theories and their potential application to individuals with disabilities.
9 Compare and contrast the views of the following perceptual-motor theorists: Kephart, Getman, Doman and Delacato, Barsch, Frostig, Ayres and Dunn.
10 Identify and describe the components of perception and their importance in the learning of various motor skills.
11 Explain how perception is developed.
12 Define the following terms and expressions: directionality, laterality, servomechanism, shaping, closed-loop, open-loop, figure-ground, body awareness, visual acuity.

Motor learning refers to the acquisition of skills involving muscular movement. The skills of movement with which physical educators have been traditionally concerned are gross motor in nature, *gross motor movements* being defined as those requiring vigorous action and large muscle-group contraction, for which a sizable amount of space is needed. This definition is not meant to imply that fine motor skills are not utilized in physical education activities; fine motor skills are nearly always involved, but usually as part of a larger body movement that is predominately gross motor. For example, the gross motor skill of throwing involves the fine motor movement of the fingers grasping the ball as part of the total movement.

Motor Learning Theories

Much of our understanding of how movement skills are learned is based on various theories of learning. While much useful information can be obtained by understanding the theories of learning, it must be emphasized that learning theories are based on verbal learning, and therefore these principles cannot always be directly applied to motor learning. Within this section, the theoretical approaches that seem to have had the most influence on our understanding of behavior in general, and motor skills in particular, will be discussed. The learning theories to be reviewed will be grouped under the heading of Behavior theories, Cognitive theories, and Human/Machine theories. Those who wish to study these theories in depth should refer to a psychology text on learning.

Behavior Theories

The earliest theory of learning, introduced around the turn of the 20th century, was *behaviorism*. This approach, which was based on the work of Edward Thorndike and J. B. Watson, is associated with the names of several well-known psychologists including Pavlov, Hull, and Skinner. The behaviorists are generally concerned with how two events that an individual perceives as occurring close together in time become associated. This approach is concerned with the individual's behavior (or response) and the events (or stimuli) that produced the behavior. For this reason, behaviorism is frequently referred to as the stimulus-response approach.

One of the earliest behaviorists, Pavlov, suggested that learning is the process of building conditioned reflexes through the substitution of one stimulus for another. His famous experiment in which a dog was conditioned to salivate at the sound of a bell provided early evidence of the ability to pair a conditioned stimulus (the bell) with an unconditioned stimulus (the food) to produce a particular response (salivation).

An early behaviorist who had a profound influence on education was Thorndike. He emphasized learning as a strengthening of the bond, or association, between a particular stimulus and response. Thorndike's research led to the development of several "laws" that are still recognized today. These include:

> the *Law of Readiness*, which emphasizes the idea of being prepared to learn (in the mood) and the importance of developmental readiness in children;
> the *Law of Effect*, which stresses that students will repeat responses that are satisfying, thus strengthening the relationship between the stimulus and the response;
> the *Law of Exercise*, which is divided into the *Law of Use* and the *Law of Disuse*. The effect of these laws stated in very straightforward terms is that skills will only be retained if they are used.

Perhaps the best known of all the behaviorists is B. F. Skinner, whose work led to the formulation of many principles related to the use of rewards and reinforcement in the shaping of behavior. Unlike Thorndike, who focused on the S-R bond (Stimulus-Response bond), Skinner stressed the importance of reinforcing the response itself and its probability of occurrence. A central component of Skinner's

theory is *shaping*, which involves the ⟨...⟩ desired behavior. The application of sl⟨...⟩ settings is commonly referred to as b⟨...⟩ This approach has been successfully ⟨...⟩ education programs for students with d⟨...⟩ this approach requires the teacher to ⟨...⟩

1. set goals to be achieved;
2. pretest to establish the current ability level;
3. set up the environment so as to remove irrelevant stimuli and center the learner's attention on the task;
4. shape a slow, step-like progression of intermediate goals leading toward the final goal; and
5. at all stages reinforce correct responses with appropriate rewards.

The influence of the behaviorists and their theories has had a profound impact on education, including the teaching of motor skills in physical activity settings. As will be emphasized in other chapters within this text, an understanding of behaviorism and its correct application is important in developing positive learning environments for students with disabilities.

Cognitive Theories

The cognitive theorists developed primarily as an alternative to the behaviorists. Whereas behaviorists were primarily concerned with the environment and its influence on behaviors, the cognitive theorists stressed the importance of an individual's interpretation of the environment. The supporters of the cognitive approach argued that learning is not a trained or paired response to a stimulus but involves cognition—the process of knowing—which involves both awareness and judgment. Both theories emphasize, however, that reinforcement, repetition, and perception are relevant to learning. As will be explained later, the difference between the behaviorists and the cognitive theorists is mainly one of emphasis.

Gestalt theory was one of the earliest and best known of the cognitive theories. The supporters of this approach, known as *Gestaltists,* were interested in problem solving, perception, and other processes that individuals use in order to develop appropriate behaviors in response to situations. They were concerned about how individuals abstract meaningful relationships from the environment and use this information to solve problems.

The Gestaltists, with their interest in perception and the organization of sensory data, developed several laws to explain the cognitive process. Three of the laws, proximity, similarity, and closure, are particularly relevant to the process of learning.

The *law of proximity* refers to the grouping of stimuli that are close together in time or space. **From a learning standpoint this suggests that instructional material should be organized into modules or groups.**

The *law of similarity* suggests that students find homogenous groups easier to identify than heterogenous groups. **The implication of this law is that teachers must organize materials so that they are logical and related.**

The *law of closure* emphasizes that some learners, if given part of the information, may be able to provide the rest of the response. **The value of this law is very apparent when working with students who have sensory or cognitive impairments. Emphasis must be placed on providing verbal and sensory cues that are appropriate and challenging to the individual.**

The relationship between the behaviorists and cognitive theorists was emphasized in the work of E. C. Tolman, published in 1934. Although a proponent of the cognitive approach, Tolman emphasized that initial learning is based on a mental trial-and-error process and therefore involves stimulus-response associations. He believed that beyond initial learning, the learner organizes the stimuli to form a cognitive map that provides cues for future repetitions. Tolman's views provide a valuable link between the theories of behaviorism and cognition. **The implications of this for teaching motor skills to those with disabilities suggests that for initial learning, particularly with low-functioning individuals, the use of a behavioral approach is appropriate, but when possible, students should be challenged to recognize and understand the principles employed in performing a motor skill.**

Human/Machine Theories

The technological advances made during and following World War II led to a wealth of new ideas and approaches for studying human behavior. The development of the computer, a primary example of the "machine age," helped to make this possible. Using the computer as a model for simulating how individuals receive and process information, the human/machine theorists combined elements of both the behaviorists and the cognitive theorists. Similar to the behaviorists, they were interested in observable behavior and like the cognitive theorists, they were interested in understanding how information was processed in the brain.

One of the first of the human/machine theories, *cybernetics*, was developed by N. Weiner in 1961. Cybernetics means self-guidance and control of one's own behavior. Proponents of this approach believe that learning is determined by the sensory effects of the movement that accompanies a response. Similar to a computer, an individual accepts stimuli (input) and responds to stimuli (output) and has an internal mechanism (brain) to control and store information.

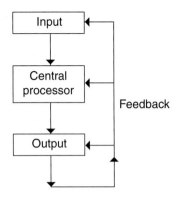

Figure 3.1 The servomechanistic model approach emphasizes the role of feedback for controlling ongoing activity. If the activity is terminated, feedback information can be stored in memory for future usages.

While the cybernetics approach accepts the computer model, emphasis is placed on the role of feedback in which some output is stored and some is fed back into the system. The cybernetics model may be described as a *servomechanism,* or closed-loop system. As illustrated in figure 3.1, in a servomechanism or closed-loop system, there is a direct link between output and input based on continual feedback.

Information theory, another example of a human/machine theory, is concerned with the amount of information an individual can process. The early work in information theory was based primarily on probability theory. Using this approach, analyses were undertaken to assess how much information was needed to solve selected problems. Simulations were developed using the computer as a model with its ability to be programmed to make yes–no responses.

The work in information theory has been expanded today to focus on how people receive information, attend to it, organize, process, and store information, and ultimately develop a plan of action. As suggested earlier, there is a great deal of interest in how much information can be handled; or stated in computer language, what is the channel capacity. **Information theory, therefore is concerned with very pertinent questions related to the teaching of motor skills: When is the system overloaded or underloaded? And what is the optimum amount and type of information for efficient and effective learning?** These are obviously questions of fundamental importance when teaching students with disabilities.

An information theory model is presented in figure 3.2. Similar to the cybernetics model, the information theory model stresses the importance of input, central processor (central nervous system), and output. The information theory model focuses on the capacity of the individual to process information, whereas the cybernetics model emphasizes the importance of feedback.

The last human/machine theory, *hierarchical control,* builds on the cybernetic and information theories by

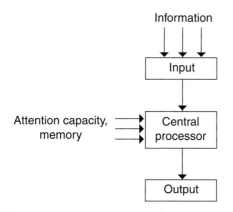

Figure 3.2 The information processing model approach calls to our attention the kinds of processes that are internally activated to organize information, leading to appropriate decisions and effective movements.

stressing the role of the central processes in controlling and directing movement. Humans, similar to computers, use programs (plans of action) to execute basic or routine patterns. These basic programs are deemed to be lower order and can be combined with other basic programs to produce more complex or higher-order programs. For the beginner, it will be necessary to become proficient with lower-order programs before combining those lower-order programs into more complex or higher-order programs. As skill increases, the process of selecting routines will improve. The relationship between lower-order and higher-order programs serves to explain the seemingly automatic responses observed in highly skilled performers. A model of hierarchical control is presented in figure 3.3. The process of distinguishing lower-order from higher-order programs can be facilitated by the use of task analysis, which will be described later in this chapter.

The theories of motor learning described in this section are all evident to a certain degree in physical education programs for students with disabilities. For some individuals with severe and profound disabilities, particularly those with mental retardation, the use of a behavioral approach is

Figure 3.3 The hierarchical control model approach describes central control properties with master, or executor, routines and subroutines. Behavioral control is expressed in a hierarchical fashion: as skill increases, the type and level of control changes.

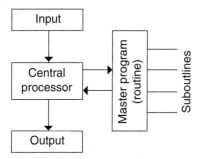

appropriate. Problem-solving methods and efforts to encourage creativity (cognitive approach) are frequently observed in physical education programs for individuals with various disabilities including individuals with sensory or orthopedic impairments. Recent efforts to explain human behavior through the use of computers have helped to explain and support some of the instructional approaches used with students with disabilities. For example, channel capacity discussed in relation to information theory provides helpful information when deciding how best to present information to a student with mental retardation. Likewise, the distinction between lower-order and higher-order programs stressed in the concept of hierarchial control emphasizes the need to master appropriate developmental activities before undertaking complex skills. Other examples of the relationship between the motor learning theories and teaching students with disabilities will be covered in the section Motor Skill Tenets, as well as included, where appropriate, throughout the text.

Classification of Motor Skills

In an effort to impose some order on the many different types of motor skills, several classification systems have emerged. Familiarity with the classification systems, or taxonomies, as they are sometimes called, is important for several reasons. First, they provide a means of bringing some order to the very diverse field of motor skills. Second, knowledge of the classification systems helps teachers to recognize the similarities as well as the differences in respective skills. This information is very important in developing appropriate motor learning experiences for students with disabilities. Using the following classification systems will allow the teacher to make informed decisions about the level of difficulty and complexity of various skills.

Movement Skills

Burton coined the term "movement skills" to identify a skill that is "a qualitative expression of movement performance, or a specific class of goal-directed movement patterns, such as running, throwing, hammering, driving, writing, or speaking" (Burton & Miller, 1998, p. 367). For Burton, "motor abilities" are individual traits or capacities that underlie the performance of a variety of movement skills. Hence, movement skills are observable, goal-directed movement patterns. Motor skills describe the internal process that is *inferred from* the movement performance. The taxonomy of movement skills Burton presented is seen in figure 3.4. Here six main levels are depicted:

1. **Foundations of movement skills:** These skills are important for all movement skills (e.g., balance and postural control, muscular strength and endurance,

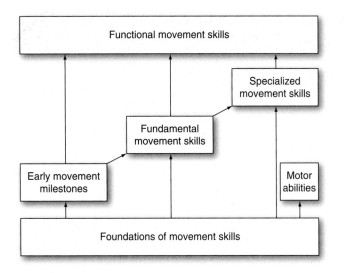

Figure 3.4 Burton taxonomy of movement skills.

neurological functioning, perception, skills such as cognition, motivation and affect).

2. **Motor abilities:** These include skills like agility, balance, and coordination. Burton found that many tests of movement competency are based on assessing motor abilities.

3. **Early movement milestones:** Early movement milestones are locomotor (e.g., roll over) and object control skills (e.g., object manipulation) performed before the onset of upright locomotion, bipedal locomotion, or both.

4. **Fundamental movement skills:** Walking is often the functional marker that distinguishes the transition into fundamental movement skills. The fundamental movement skills are, therefore, locomotor and object control skills performed in an upright or bipedal position *in all cultures of the world.* This includes skills like walk, run, jump, hop, throw, and catch.

5. **Specialized movement skills:** These skills are defined as those mature fundamental movement patterns for sport skill performance, as well as specific complex movement skills.

6. **Functional movement skills:** These are skills from early milestones, as well as fundamental or specialized skills, that are performed in naturally occurring environments of the individual (e.g., the difference between testing a person with a brain injury in a clinical setting for movement and later observing that person in a favorite activity of movement, such as walking through a garden of fragrant flowers).

Burton (Burton & Miller, 1998) believed that the utility of this taxonomy was its direct influence on the selection of a test instrument to measure an individual's movement performance and, hence, the results that the professional would obtain. If a young child with a disability who is ambulatory was tested for fundamental movement skills, then this would translate easily into appropriate curriculum in the physical education class. The skills tested are easily observed in elementary physical education classes. However, if the same child was tested for motor abilities, then the underlying skills contributing to movement skill performance are not easily translated into the day-to-day curriculum in physical education.

One month after Burton's untimely death in 2001, his further work on movement skills and motor abilities was published (Burton & Rogerson, 2001). This work revisited the differences between motor abilities and movement skills, with the notion that his earlier assumptions could be refuted and a General Motor Ability (GMA) could be useful in defining and assessing movement performance. Ulrich (2002) viewed this as an admirable ability: to discount earlier work in the name of advancing the science. The synthesis of Burton's GMA remains challenging, and scholars and students alike will need to further validate the truth of the term's application in the field of specialized physical education assessment.

More and more, the concept of "observable movement skill performance" is finding its way into best practice in assessment in specialized physical education, particularly with the emphasis on functional skill acquisition for students with disabilities. Thus, the Burton taxonomy provides a valuable source of categorization and, hence, assessment and intervention strategies for practitioners in specialized physical education.

Gross and Fine Motor Skills

As stated in the introduction to this chapter, physical educators have classically referred to motor skills as either gross or fine. Unfortunately, there is no standard criterion by which to identify a skill using these terms.

Discrete, Serial, and Continuous Skills

This classification describes a continuum on which some skills have a distinct beginning and end and some skills involve a continuous or repetitive series of movements. Discrete skills involve only a single exertion, such as shooting an arrow or throwing a baseball. A skill is serial in nature when the beginning and ending components can be identified, but events follow each other in sequence, such as a gymnastics routine on the parallel bars. Continuous skills refer to those tasks that are repetitive in nature, such as running, walking, and swimming.

Open and Closed Skills

In 1957, the British psychologist E. C. Poulton suggested that skills might be classified as either open or closed, depending upon the extent to which the performer must conform to a standard sequence of movement and the extent to which effective performance depends on environmental events. For example, diving is a closed skill because the required movement is consistent and the environment is fixed. However, tennis is an open skill. The game situation is constantly

TABLE 3.1   **Taxonomy Based Upon Environmental and Movement Requirements**

| | Nature of Movement Required by Task | | | |
| | Total Body Stability | | Total Body Transport | |
Nature of Environmental Control	No LT/M	LT/M	No LT/M	LT/M*
Closed (spatial control: stationary environment)	Sitting Standing	Typing Writing	Walking Running	Carrying or handling objects during locomotion Javelin throw
Open (temporal/spatial control: moving environment)	Standing on a moving train Log rolling Riding an escalator	Reading a news-paper on a moving train	Walking in a moving train Dancing with a partner	Running and catching a moving object Throwing on the run Dribbling in basketball

Source: from George H. Sage, *Motor learning and control, A neuropsychological approach.* Copyright (c) 1984 Wm. C. Brown Communications, Inc. Dubuque, IA.

*LT/M = Independent limb transport and manipulation, usually involving maintaining or changing the position of objects in space.

changing, and thus the individual playing tennis must respond within an unpredictable environment.

Variations on the open and closed classification system have been proposed by various individuals. B. N. Knapp in 1963 suggested the idea of a continuum from motor skills that are predominantly habitual to those that are predominantly perceptual. A. M. Gentile and her

colleagues in 1975 believed that the type of movement should also be considered. In their model, type of movement was subdivided into (a) total body stability or total body movement and (b) movement of the limbs for changing or maintaining the position of objects in space (table 3.1).

The work of Gentile and her associates has been clarified and expanded by others. In table 3.2, Magill (1993) provides

TABLE 3.2   **A 2 × 2 Diagram Representing the Four-Category Classification System**

| | | Response-to-Response Variability | |
		No Change	Change
Environmental Conditions	Stationary	Category 1 The object of the response remains stationary, and there is no change in response requirements from one response to the next.	Category 3 The object of the response remains stationary, and the response requirements change from one response to the next.
	In Motion	Category 2 The object of the response is in motion, and there is no change in the response requirements from one response to the next.	Category 4 The object of the response is in motion, and the response requirements change from one response to the next.

Source: Data from A. M. Gentile et al., "The Structure of Motor Tasks in Movement," 1975, 7:11–28 as appeared in Richard A. Magill, *Motor Learning Concepts and Applications,* 4th ed., Wm. C. Brown Communications, Inc., Dubuque, IA.

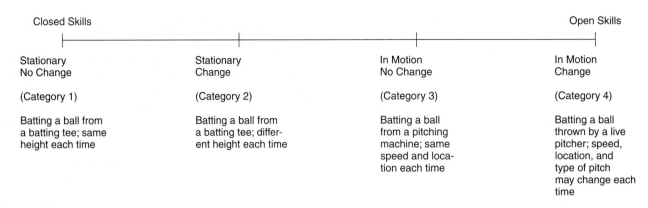

Figure 3.5   The four categories from the Gentile et al. (1975) system placed on a continuum having closed- and open-skill categories as its extremes. Four different types of ball-batting tasks are presented to show how the categories are different. (Source: from Richard A. Magill, *Motor Learning Concepts and Applications*, 4th ed., Wm. C. Brown Communications, Inc., Dubuque, IA.)

an excellent example of the four way classification system (response variability by environmental conditions) proposed by Gentile et al. Figure 3.5 extends the example in relationship to open and closed skills.

Theories of Movement Control

The nature of open and closed skills has generated a great deal of attention in helping to explain how individuals control movement. Adams (1971) proposed the first model which addressed this critical question. His approach, which today is perceived as somewhat incomplete, focused on closed-loop skills. Adams, while recognizing that his theory was limited, believed it was important to establish a framework useful for understanding movement control by focusing on simple skills.

Adams reasoned that every closed-loop system must have a reference mechanism that can be used to assess the status of a movement being made. In Adams' theory this is known as the perceptual trace. Essentially, the perceptual trace is responsible for comparing feedback about what the movement is currently like with what it should be like. If error is detected, a command is sent to stop the movement. The goal of practice is to make sure that the perceptual trace gets stronger, thus allowing the individual to advance to the motor stage of learning where the movement can be made automatically.

Although Adams' theory focused on a closed-loop approach to control, it is clear that imbedded within the theory is information related to an open-loop process. The Adams theory suggests that it is the open-loop, specifically the memory trace, that is responsible for initiating the movement in contrast to terminating the movement which is left to the closed-loop.

In 1975, Schmidt identified limitations in the Adams theory and proposed an alternative theory of motor control and learning which today is known as Schmidt's

schema theory (1982). According to this theory, the performer solves motor problems by responding to a motor schema, which is an abstraction of four sources of information:

1. the desired outcome of the movement;
2. the initial conditions, or physiological and postural readiness for the movement;
3. knowledge of past actual outcomes of similar movements; and
4. knowledge of past actual sensory consequences of similar movements.

Schmidt theorizes that the motor schema is developed as the student discovers the relationship among these sources of information. The motor schema can be characterized as a set of rules that generate instructions for producing movement.

Schmidt proposed two motor control components.

1. a generalized motor program that is the general memory representation of the action to be controlled. Stated simply, this program is responsible for controlling general actions, such as throwing, kicking, walking, and running.
2. a motor response schema that is responsible for the specific rules governing an action in a given situation. In practical terms, this suggests that with practice the learner abstracts different pieces of information from every action related to a motor skill. For example, with experience and practice, the learner acquires sufficient information to use the skill of kicking successfully in a variety of situations and conditions.

While the applied aspects of Schmidt's theory appear very promising, the research carried out with special populations has been limited and restricted primarily to individuals classified as mentally retarded (Del Rey & Stewart, 1989;

Poretta, 1982). Eidson and Stadulis (1991) suggest that while Schmidt's schema theory seems quite useful for motor skills that are closed, its applicability for tasks that have complex generalized demands must be viewed cautiously. The practical significance of this suggests that in teaching complex skills (i.e., skills with high environmental demand) the traditional approach of breaking the skill down and employing repetitive practice sessions may still be the best approach.

Dynamic Systems Theory

In recent years a new theory of motor control, dynamic systems theory, has been introduced as an alternative to the theories of Schmidt and Adams. The early proponents of dynamic systems theory as applied to special physical education included Bev and Dale Ulrich of the University of Michigan, Allen Burton from the University of Minnesota, and Martin Block from the University of Virginia.

Dynamic systems theory, as introduced in chapter 2, deemphasizes the influence of a central control center and emphasizes the role of information in the environment and the dynamic properties of the body and limbs. Perception and action are closely connected so that the execution of motor skills is dictated by the relationship between perceptual information and the motor system. This suggests, therefore, that unlike Adams and Schmidt, who recognized the importance of a command control center in the execution of motor skills, dynamic systems theorists argue that muscles and joints function as "collectives" so that an action can be carried out according to the dictates of the situation (Magill, 1993). The collectives, known as coordinative structures or action units, are developed through practice or experience, or may exist naturally. An example would be the young child who hits a ball from a batting tee. Given earlier practice, the youngster uses coordinative structures (joints and muscles), developed through earlier experience, to swing the bat, recognizing changes that might occur in the environment (e.g., height of ball, size of ball etc.). The command for this action, rather than coming from a central executive, is self-organized according to a coordinative structure. The muscles and joints used to swing the bat are constrained to work together with the understanding that changes in the environment may dictate further refinements in the skill. As Whitehall (1988) has emphasized, the dynamic systems theory contends that patterns are not prescribed but emerge from interaction among body, task, and environment with little central input. It is important to note that while dynamic systems theorists deemphasize the importance of the central command center, they do recognize that commands can come from the central center. However, they also articulate clearly that the commands can come from various sources within and external to the person.

The various theories reviewed here offer much promise for improving the motor and physical activity programs provided to infants, children, and youth with disabilities. Our understanding of mechanisms that control movement is expanding at a dramatic rate and while the work of Adams, Schmidt, and proponents of the dynamic systems theory might seem contradictory, collectively these efforts represent a significant breakthrough in our understanding of how individuals with disabilities acquire motor skills. Adams and Schmidt, for example, explain nicely the relationships inherent in a hierarchical system. A command is given and, following a very short period of time, action occurs. Feedback is provided as to the outcome of the action and, where necessary, corrections are made. The dynamic systems theorists, while recognizing the work of Adams and Schmidt, argue that there is more than one control center and specifically emphasize the importance of the joints and muscles and the environment in expanding the ability to perform motor skills.

The available literature concerning the application of these theories to individuals with disabilities is very limited. However, it is clear that the information presented holds much promise for improving our understanding of how individuals acquire information. The dynamic systems theory, in particular, speaks to some of the practical challenges encountered by many teachers of specialized physical education. For example, many teachers have recognized that our traditional views of motor learning (i.e., a linear acquisition of skills in a building block arrangement) do not seem to hold true for individuals with disabilities. Specifically, at times it appears that some children learn skills out of sequence, making greater gains in some areas and less than expected improvements in others. The approach and explanation to this problem varies. Some teachers emphasize, correctly so, the uniqueness of each student with a disability, and provide a rich and challenging curriculum. Others, however, seem to stall and spend more time on trying to "catch-up" those areas which seem to be lagging behind or conclude that the neuromaturational delay is too great and move to different skills. The dynamic systems theory offers the possibility that we need to be consistently conscious of the dynamic aspect of learning and the relationship between the central command center, other command centers located in the joints and muscles, and the environment. This theory helps to balance the relationship between the central nervous system and other important ecological variables in the learning environment. In summary, dynamic systems theory offers much promise as a foundation upon which to build exciting and relevant physical education programs for students with disabilities.

Motor Skill Tenets

The research and empirical evidence produced by the serious study of the phenomenon of movement has established certain tenets that are useful to the physical educator in teaching motor skills to students with disabilities. Those most relevant to the purpose of this book are reviewed in the following paragraphs.

- **The ability to learn a motor skill is influenced by growth and maturation.** A child normally can learn a specific motor activity when she or he has achieved the actual physical growth required to accomplish the movement. Motor readiness is affected not only by physical size but also by the level of maturation of the neuromuscular system. Maturation occurs as a result of experience and physiological changes that are produced naturally as age increases. Maturation is also related to the motivation to learn. It is important to understand the contribution that "readiness" and interest to learn a new skill has for a child with a disability. For some students, depending on the specific disability, this must be closely assessed.

   To determine the readiness of a child with a disability to learn, the teacher must be very sensitive to the child's reaction to the learning of motor movement. Pressuring the child to learn an activity when it is not possible for him or her to do so is detrimental to the child's well-being. On the other hand, it is necessary to encourage the child to explore his or her motor potential by trying to achieve various motor feats. This is sometimes referred to as increasing a student's repertoire in physical activity. Later, the student can decide if

this activity is one he wants to continue. However, initially the teacher must work out a procedure that will encourage but not pressure the child to explore the activity. Toward this end, it is useful to evaluate the motor achievements of the child with a disability by making a comparison of his or her motor development with that of nondisabled youngsters in the same age group (described in chapter 2) and by careful assessment of the child's mental, emotional, and physical limitations.

- **The best way to perform any given skill is dictated by mechanical and physiological principles of movement.** Application of the principles of movement ensures the most effective performance, regardless of anatomical and physiological differences in body structure. When a child's physical structure deviates markedly from normal, the most acceptable/typical means of performing a skill may not be possible. The child with a disability will need to be encouraged to explore so that he or she can find the best way to perform the skill in question, using the principles of movement as a guide. Burton offers a model for this exploration in his top-down approach to assessment (Burton & Miller, 1998). (See figure 3.6.) Here the student is given the goal (e.g., playing soccer) and the teacher observes how the student is able to perform the movement skills. For some students with a disability, the ability to perform a skill is very functional but may not necessarily be done in a "typical pattern." This atypical pattern should not preclude exclusion from the activity or require extensive intervention. Use of Burton's assessment sequence offers a systematic approach to the decisions faced by teachers who are interested in engaging students with

Motor Skill Tenets

The ability to learn a motor skill is influenced by growth and maturation.

The best way to perform any given skill is dictated by mechanical and physiological principles of movements.

A new skill is learned through reinforcement and repetition.

Practice alone does not lead to improved performance.

A child progresses in the learning of movement at a specific rate that is uniquely his own.

Emotion affects the process of learning motor skills.

The learning of motor skills is specific; that is, learning one skill does not necessarily improve performance in another.

A performer's learning ability is enhanced when she succeeds at a specific task.

A performer learns faster when practice sessions are separated by adequate periods of rest.

A motor skill that is overlearned will be retained for a longer period of time.

Gross motor skills and continuous tasks have been found to be retained longer and more effectively.

Students with disabilities learn motor skills in accordance with the same learning principles as students without disabilities; however, students with disabilities may take longer.

Although the learning of motor skills is a continuous process, stages have been identified to facilitate assessment.

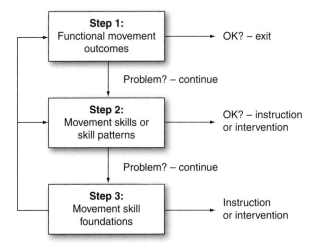

Figure 3.6 A three-step, top-down assessment sequence.

disabilities in the activities in a physical education curriculum.

- **A new skill is learned through reinforcement and repetition.** Reinforcement refers to any condition or event following a response that increases the probability that the response will be repeated. The instructor must determine the type of reinforcement that produces the best learning in any situation and then utilize that reinforcement. It should be noted that the child's knowledge that a certain effort by him or her produces a desired result is also a type of reinforcement, and the one that in the long run is probably the most effective. However, because many individuals with mental retardation are unable to understand the final consequence of an act, immediate goals must be stressed and reinforcement must be immediate and extrinsic; mastery of several parts of the whole is too abstract a concept for most of these children. For individuals with other types of disabilities, these concepts are critical. Many instructors feel compelled to vary the activities or fail to set a schedule for learning that builds upon success or the use of task analysis. It is here that younger children need more practice time (repetition) in a skill area. The teacher may get bored, but the student is enjoying the attainment of mastery. On the other end, it is important not to continue in a unit area for too long. If the student's behavior is one resulting from boredom, then it is important to move on to other skill areas. Some of this boredom has been observed when a remedial approach with older students is used. Instead, these older students will need modification and adaptation *for the skills they are interested in learning,* as opposed to repetition and failure given a defined skill.

Repetition of motor movement does tend to establish that movement as part of an individual's repertoire of movements. Therefore, repeated performance of the new skill should be encouraged by the teacher. To effect and establish improvement in the quality of the movement, however, the performer must be aware of what she or he is working toward and how to achieve it and, in general, must be motivated to improve. This motivation occurs when teachers know their students, the students' interests, and what motivates them. When a student appears unmotivated, then it is time to discuss this concern with parents or other teachers to develop ways to further engage the student in the class. There are times in the lives of all students when motivation is low for whatever reason.

- **Practice alone does not lead to improved performance.** If the teacher is not careful, errors may be practiced or boredom from mere repetition may occur. Practice sessions should be structured to develop the youngster's attention to relevant cues. The strategy of working with relevant cues is a potent one for individuals who may have sensory processing difficulties. In most cases, being sensitive to the modality the student uses most frequently for learning (e.g., vision, audition, kinesthesis) is also a potent teaching strategy. Here the instructor is teaching to the child's strength. In addition, the time devoted to practice should be of sufficient duration and quality to ensure the development of skill.

- **A child progresses in the learning of movement at a specific rate that is uniquely his or her own.** The teacher should determine as early as possible the learning pace of students and take that into consideration in setting goals for them. It must be kept in mind that individuals may learn different activities at different rates; for example, a child may rapidly learn to throw but have a more difficult time learning to kick a ball. For those with normal intelligence, the rate of motor learning shows very little relationship to intelligence as measured by an IQ test. However, there is a fairly high relationship between speed of learning and intelligence when the IQ falls below 70, particularly if it is lower than 60. In these cases, the rate of acquiring information is slower.

- **Emotion affects the process of learning motor skills.** It is incumbent upon the teacher to create an emotional atmosphere that is conducive to learning, taking into consideration that individuals may respond differently to the same situation. Confusion often exists concerning the effects of emotions on the learning of motor skills, arising from the fact that ability to perform physically is increased under stress in an emotional situation. For example, *during the time that a skill is being learned,* extreme emotion is actually detrimental to the learning process. The reaction of the body to a highly emotional situation that permits the successful exertion of great physical effort is one *that occurs after a skill has been learned.* The teacher must be alert to the characteristic emotional responses of each student in order to create the best possible climate for learning. Even though emotional responses to anxiety, fear, and humiliation may not be expressed overtly, these responses may be a strong deterrent to learning. Physical education class is the one academic area in which it is very obvious to the whole class that a student is either very successful or struggling with a skill performance. For the struggling student, this situation can be very embarrassing and can result in compensatory strategies to avoid certain activities. The student who goes against the rules of the class or a game, resulting in removal from part or all of the class, may be developing an inappropriate strategy to avoid embarrassment.

- **The learning of motor skills is specific; that is, the learning of one skill does not necessarily improve performance in another.** Transfer of the learning of one skill to the learning of another skill can occur but it is not automatic. The transfer occurs only under certain circumstances: (1) when two activities have identical elements and (2) when a principle learned in one situation can be generalized and applied in another situation. The ability to generalize a principle or a skill from one situation to another is particularly difficult for individuals with cognitive impairments. For these students and for others who struggle with the transference of skills, the teacher can help students make a transfer in learning by creating opportunities for the development of meaningful generalizations, providing practice in applying the generalizations in actual situations, pointing out the likenesses between activities in which transfer can occur, and providing a variety of different kinds of motor activities so that the possibility of transfer from one activity to another is increased.

- **A performer's learning ability is enhanced when he or she succeeds at a specific task.** "Nothing succeeds like success" is as true for motor skill performance as for any other endeavor. Hence, the teacher should choose activities for the student with disabilities that can be achieved with some degree of success (figure 3.7) and will provide the incentive for the student to progress to more advanced skill performance. If a student continually fails at a movement task, then motivation will decline.

Figure 3.7   Motor activities should be chosen that are challenging, fun, and allow for success.

Task Analysis

A complex task may be broken down into parts to encourage quick success in the learning of one or more segments before they are combined in the performance of the whole task. The student should be kept informed of his or her progress and be praised for any improvement, regardless of how small or unimpressive it is. In table 3.3, an example of a task analysis for the skill of throwing a ball underhand is presented. At each level from Phase I to Phase VI the skill becomes increasingly complex. For some students, beginning instruction at Phase VI may be appropriate; for others, instruction at an earlier phase or step may be necessary. Presenting a skill in this manner assists students in seeing that they can be successful even though they may not have mastered the entire task.

Physical education teachers are familiar with developmental progressions for teaching fundamental skills such as catch and kick. They are also familiar with teaching lead-up games/low-organized games that provide the initial learning for specific sports (e.g., Pangrazi, 2004). Task analysis can be used in either of these situations when a teacher observes that a student needs further analysis of the skill components so that the task can be performed.

The kind and amount of praise given must be in keeping with the child's maturation and level of ability. For a child who has much success, the praise may be minimal for small successes or may be reserved entirely for greater

TABLE 3.3 Example of a Task Analysis for the Underhand Throw

Terminal Objective: The student, standing, will perform an underhand throw swinging the arm backward and then forward while stepping forward simultaneously with the opposite foot and releasing the ball at the end of the swing in a manner that causes the ball to fly in the direction of the target.

Phase I The student, standing 5 feet from the target, will swing the arm backward and then forward, releasing the ball at the end of the swing in the direction of the target. The teacher will physically assist the student to bring his or her arm back and then forward.

Phase II The student, standing 5 feet from the target, will swing the arm backward and then forward, releasing the ball at the end of the swing in the direction of the target. The teacher will assist the student to bring his or her arm back.

Phase III The student, standing 5 feet from the target, will independently swing the arm backward and then forward, releasing the ball at the end of the swing in the direction of the target.

Phase IV The student, standing 5 feet from the target with one foot forward, one foot back, and knees bent, will swing the arm forward, releasing the ball at the end of the swing and in the direction of the target.

Phase V The student, standing 5 feet from the target and with knees bent, will swing the arm backward and forward, releasing the ball at the end of the swing and in the direction of the target while the teacher is pushing the student's opposite foot forward simultaneously with swing.

Phase VI The student, standing, will perform an underhand throw, swinging the arm backward and then forward while stepping forward simultaneously with the opposite foot and releasing the ball at the end of the swing in a manner that causes the ball to fly in the direction of the target.

The following steps apply to Phase VI.

Steps:

1. 7 feet
2. 15 feet

achievements. But a child whose improvement is slow and whose achievement is small needs to know that he or she has been successful when something has been done well, and he or she must be assured that others recognize and appreciate his or her accomplishment. The task-analysis process complements this need.

- **A performer learns faster when practice sessions are separated by adequate periods of rest.** Children learn faster when their interest is high. Long practice sessions tend to dull this interest. To prevent the detrimental effect of loss of interest, the teacher should keep instructional periods short and change activities frequently, stopping for periods of rest when interest begins to wane.

 Fatigue detracts from the learning process. Children with physical disabilities often tire more easily than their nondisabled peers and the teacher must be continuously alert to signs of fatigue during the teaching of a physical activity to those with physical disabilities. Fatigue is also a factor in learning for youngsters with mental retardation. If, as can often be the case, these children are in poor physical condition, they will tire

easily from physical exertion. In addition, they usually exhibit short attention spans. Therefore, the teacher will need to provide frequent periods of rest and to change the type of activity often to achieve peak learning potential.

- **A motor skill that is overlearned will be retained for a longer period of time.** Overlearning can be defined as the process of repeating a task until its performance is automatic, that is, without conscious effort being exerted to accomplish the task. When a motor skill is overlearned, the length of retention time is very high, sometimes lasting a lifetime. A good example is bicycling, a skill that is overlearned by youngsters through constant repetition during the years when bicycling is most popular. In their adult years, these people can, after many years of not riding, mount a bike and ride without any loss of skill.

 The point at which skill is overlearned varies with each individual. Children who are mentally retarded will require many more repetitions in performing a skill to reach the point of overlearning than will those who are not mentally retarded.

- **Gross motor skills and continuous tasks have been found to be retained longer and more effectively than other types of learning material.** In addition, for material that is serially learned, that which is learned first is retained best; the last learned is mastered second best; whereas the middle part is last to be retained. Retention of movement is greater when it has a natural relationship to other movements. The movements of skipping provide a good illustration. Although the hop is often taught to youngsters as a component of the total movement, the ability to perform the hop will be retained longer if it is related to and practiced with the other movements of the skip. Many physical skills have this kind of interrelationship of movements that form a definite rhythmic pattern of performance. Teaching the movements in their natural pattern ensures longer retention than teaching them in isolation. It should be noted that children with developmental disabilities, like those typically developing, cannot skip until they learn to hop; but the long-term retention of the skill of hop is benefited by using it in the skip.

- **Students with disabilities learn motor skills in accordance with the same motor learning principles as students without disabilities, but may take longer.** Because some students with a disability learn more slowly than do students without disabilites, they require more extensive and intensive motor skill instruction to compensate for their slower learning rates. This implies that educational gains for those with disabilities will be greatest when teachers work cooperatively to encourage practice time in the movement activity. At home, parents can be encouraged to reinforce those skills that have been learned at school. The students can engage in after-school programs (summers included) in the community where further socialization and practice time can occur. Good communication between home and school facilitates movement activities that the student is learning and enhances the student's opportunities to reinforce learning. Some parents also need information from the physical education teacher regarding community programs that are particularly suited for the student. For some parents, observing the physical education class can help them to understand the skill levels of their child for physical activity. Some parents underestimate and some overestimate their child's abilities, so observation can validate movement performance skills.

- **While the learning of motor skills is a continuous process, stages in the learning of motor skills have been identified.** P. M. Fitts and M. I. Posner in 1967 identified these to be the cognitive, associative, and autonomous phases.

1. The cognitive phase occurs early in learning as the student makes attempts at understanding the nature of the activity to be learned. The student has to understand the purpose of the motor skill and devise strategies for performing the skill. During this phase the student is also expected to respond to verbal information and to translate this into action. For many children, particularly those with a cognitive or learning problem, the ability to understand verbal information and translate the meaning of "adult" words can be a problem.

2. The associative phase requires the student to translate and put into action the information learned in the cognitive phase. Success at this stage requires the teacher to implement positive practice conditions to promote the learning of the activity.

3. The autonomous phase occurs when the skill, through practice and repetition, has been refined to the point that it is automatic. Because little conscious control over the movement is required, the performer is free to attend to other things simultaneously. This explains why a basketball player can dribble a ball while at the same time contemplating strategy that will lead to the scoring of a basket.

An understanding of the stages of learning helps to explain why some students with disabilities require special and individualized attention. Helping students to understand the skill (cognitive phase) and perform the skill (associative phase) will require additional instructional and practice time. Later in this book, the specialized skills teachers can use to assist students will be discussed.

A word of caution concerning the Motor Tenets discussed in this section seems appropriate. Unfortunately, little research in the area of motor learning has actually been conducted with populations that are disabled. Therefore, the instructional practices that are applied to students with disabilities are based on research conducted with nondisabled populations. While this is logical, because those with disabilities are more similar than dissimilar to the nondisabled, additional research in this area would serve to enhance our understanding of those motor learning principles that appear appropriate for both the populations with and without disabilities.

Perceptual-Motor Learning

In the 1960s, a number of men and women in the physical education profession directed their attention to an aspect of motor learning that had not been previously emphasized or thoroughly examined: the perceptual process that occurs while performing a motor skill. The interest was triggered by the earlier publication of the theories and experimental work in perceptual-motor learning by two men: Newell C. Kephart, a psychologist, and Gerald N. Getman, an optometrist. Kephart's book, *The Slow Learner in the Classroom,* appeared in 1960, and two years later Getman published *Improve Your Child's Intelligence.* In the decade after their publication, both books were widely read, and they had tremendous influence on the development of perceptual-motor programs in the physical education curriculum. The books were followed by works by such prominent perceptual-motor theorists and practitioners as Jean Ayres, Ray H. Barsch, and Marianne Frostig, and by some who are lesser known.

Although differences of opinion existed among these people about other aspects of perceptual-motor learning, they were in agreement that perception is the recognition and interpretation of stimuli received by the brain from the sense organs in the form of nerve impulses, and that a motor response to the interpretation is perceptual-motor. Today this definition is accepted universally.

For the teacher of individuals with disabilities, there are many reasons to be familiar with these early perceptual-motor theorists. First, they are individually often misunderstood by well-intended professionals, as well as parents. Thus, an advocacy arises to apply a theoretical perspective to a child's movement program. These approaches are often seen as "magic bullets" that will remediate the disability or certainly enhance the student's ability to learn motor and even academic skills. Finally, these theories resurface under different names. In the end, it is important to be familiar with research findings that advance the understanding of how sensory information is processed for individuals with and without disabilities, and how that information translates into a motor response. As the science of perception advances for people with specific disabilities, such as autism or learning disabilities, greater understanding will be gained in movement performance.

Early theorists also agreed that movement is an important key in the development of perception; that understanding the concept of left and right (laterality) is vital to the process of moving the eyes left to right in reading; and that improvement in eye-hand coordination is related to the perceptual concept involved in eye-hand coordination and is critical in learning to write. Kephart considered movement the basis of intellectual development. Others of this group believed that the learning involved in perceiving and interpreting perception in movement is automatically transferred to perceptual learning in academic activities, particularly reading and writing. A review of the beliefs espoused by major perceptual-motor theorists is presented in the following paragraphs.

Newell C. Kephart

One of the early perceptual-motor theorists, Newell Kephart proposed that the inadequate development of certain motor skills may tend to inhibit the development of later, more complex skills. Infants first learn, according to Kephart, through the medium of movement. As they explore and locate objects, higher levels of learning become possible through feeling and manipulating these unknown objects. This latter process of matching the perceptual system with the motor system was referred to by Kephart as the perceptual-motor match. In the modern mechanistic world, Kephart warned, many of the opportunities to explore the environment are reduced and thus children have fewer opportunities to develop perceptual-motor matches. For instance, children no longer play with kitchen items such as coffee pots because many of these items are now electric, expensive, and off-limits. Kephart believed that without opportunities to match perceptual and motor data, later difficulties with academic skills such as reading and writing would occur. Remediation for Kephart, therefore, meant that instead of working on reading skills for the youngster with a reading difficulty, efforts should be directed toward treating the basic skills, motor and visual training, upon which reading skills are built. It is this focus on teaching generalization rather than highly specific skills that made Kephart's approach different from those of earlier educators. Although the research results on the effectiveness of his program are contradictory, recent findings have not supported Kephart's generalization theory.

Gerald N. Getman

Getman's training as an optometrist led him to explore the relationship between intellectual development and visual development. For Getman, a child's growth, behavior, and cognitive development conform to a basic sequence of visually related development. Distinction is made by Getman between sight and vision. Sight is considered to be simply the basic biological response of the eye to light. Vision, by contrast, is the interpretation of what is seen. The importance Getman attaches to visual perception is repeatedly emphasized throughout his writings by statements such as "vision is intelligence."

Getman's support for motor activity is found in the six-stage training program he recommends. These stages include:

1. General Motor Patterns (basic movement skills such as creeping, crawling, and walking)
2. Special Movement Patterns (eye-hand coordination)
3. Eye Movement Patterns (matched movement for both eyes)
4. Visual Language Patterns (effective communication patterns)

5. Visualization Patterns (visual memory skills)
6. Visual Perceptual Organization (relationship of vision to other perceptual modalities)

Concern has been expressed regarding various aspects of Getman's work. The criticism generally focuses on two points: the strong emphasis placed by him on visual perception and the lack of scientific evidence to support his theory.

Doman and Delacato

One of the most controversial theories proposed concerning the development of perception and its relationship to the motor area was advanced in the late 1950s by Robert and Glen Doman and Carl Delacato. These three professionals, representing the fields of education, physical therapy, and physical medicine, believe that many perceptual, motor, and cognitive disabilities stem from inadequate neurological organization. According to them, neurological development follows the biogenetic postulate that ontogeny recapitulates phylogeny. This means that individual human development repeats the pattern of human evolutionary development. If individuals do not follow the sequential continuum of neurological development, Doman and Delacato hypothesized, they will exhibit problems of mobility and communication. The development of the brain, therefore, is of central concern to the Doman-Delacato team. They have traced the phylogenetic development of the brain from the lowest level of living vertebrae to humans. If injury to the brain occurs at any level of development, the child will show evidence of neurological dysfunction. According to the theory of neurological organization, never are all the cells of the brain damaged; those that remain intact can be trained to perform the functions of those that are damaged. Doman and Delacato, therefore, have proposed a treatment technique in which the brain is "patterned" through the active and passive manipulation of the arms, legs, and head. In short, they attempt to restructure the organization of the developing nervous system.

The premise of the Doman-Delacato theory, neurological organization, and their treatment effect have been heavily criticized by both the medical and the education field. Although their approach has received some favorable reviews by parents of brain-injured children, experimental studies have not supported their program.

Ray H. Barsch

Ray Barsch's support for perceptual-motor programs was expressed in his Theory of Movigenics. This theory relates learning to efficient movement patterns. As one moves more efficiently, the perceptual processes are enhanced, which Barsch theorizes contributes to intellectual development. His educational philosophy, therefore, relies heavily on a "physiologic" approach in contradistinction to the more traditional or psychiatric approach. This belief is expressed clearly in Barsch's Movigenic Curriculum, which emphasizes 12 dimensions of learning. Three of the dimensions, muscular strength, dynamic balance, and motor planning, highlight the importance Barsch places on movement. Like the approaches of authors previously discussed in this chapter, Barsch's approach is essentially nonlanguage, with the primary emphasis being on perceptual-motor learning. Unfortunately, few studies are available that either support or refute Barsch's work. It seems clear today, however, that a student with a language disorder will benefit from a program specifically designed to enhance language development, not motor development.

Marianne Frostig

Marianne Frostig, working with several of her associates, in 1964 proposed a visual perceptual training program. The intent of the program was to assist young children with visual perception problems, including those who are deaf, blind, mentally retarded, and have poor reading readiness skills. According to Frostig, visual perception is the ability to recognize and interpret visual stimuli by associating them with previous experiences. The Frostig program focuses on five perceptual skills:

1. figure-ground perception
2. perception of position in space
3. perception of spatial relationships
4. perceptual constancy
5. visual-motor coordination

As suggested by the title of the perceptual skill, movement plays an important part in the Frostig program. In a book written by Frostig and Maslow (1970), *Movement Education: Theory and Practice,* movement experiences are viewed as essential to serve as a foundation for later perceptual skills. Activities are proposed to develop visual-motor coordination, manipulation, body awareness, and the basic movement skills of coordination, agility, balance, flexibility, strength, speed, and endurance. Frostig and her associates do not identify with a particular developmental theory. Instead, they have remained eclectic, selecting elements from various educational viewpoints.

Jean Ayres

Jean Ayres, an occupational therapist, believed that perceptual and academic skills improve through participation in sensory-motor experiences. She supported this view by explaining that the development of higher brain cells is dependent on the function of lower brain cells. Ayres suggested, therefore, that students with learning difficulties will respond positively to sensory-motor treatment programs because kinesthetic, vestibular, and tactile stimulation affect the brain stem and enhance cortical function. The ultimate goal of the Ayres program is to improve sensory-motor integration, enabling the central nervous system to achieve a higher functioning state, improving both motor and academic skills.

In reviewing the work of Ayres, many have questioned the quality of the early research studies conducted to support her beliefs. In the early years, Ayres' research showed that academic learning and reading proficiency appear to function independently of sensory motor integration. In the past, physical educators have been cautioned about using sensory integration techniques. Typically these techniques are used by occupational therapists (TO). Dr Winnie Dunn's work is a solid resource for OTs and use of sensory integration techniques for children with disabilities. A description of her work follows.

Winnie Dunn

Winnie Dunn is an occupational therapist who is recognized for her professional work in understanding the impact of sensory processing on learning, behavior, and development. For Dunn, sensory processing is an essential component of child development and helps the child to learn, to feel safe and comfortable within his environment, and to form effective relationships with others. For some children, sensory processing difficulties can interfere with participation in daily life at school, at home, and in the community. Through her extensive research and written work, Dunn has produced the Sensory Profile assessments that observe and measure sensory processing and regulation behaviors in infants, toddlers, children, adolescents, and adults (Brown & Dunn, 2002; Dunn, 1997, 1999a, 1999b, 2002). Her Sensory Profile assessment tools are used extensively in the United States by occupational therapists, educators, psychologists, and physicians concerned about children who are struggling in their everyday life activities. Her research has shown that there is a relationship between children's sensory processing patterns and their performance in daily life activities.

Dunn does not make a distinction between learning strategies used in the classroom or those that could be applied to the gymnasium. More broadly, she is dedicated to students' success through knowledge about how students process sensory information and that application to academic tasks and life activities.

Commentary

Physical educators concerned with methods and techniques of teaching motor movements were quick to incorporate the perceptual-motor concepts established by Kephart and others into their practices and procedures. Programs of

perceptual-motor skills were rapidly established in schools, particularly at the elementary level, or were incorporated into the existing physical education curricula. It is understandable that many practitioners were drawn to the theories espoused by the early perceptual-motor advocates, because the importance placed on motor development greatly enhances the role of physical education—in fact, it makes the teaching of physical education activities basic to the learning of many fundamental academic skills.

Many of the concepts that served as the bases for these perceptual-motor programs are in serious question today. Because the concepts were largely unsubstantiated by objective research, some ran counter to conclusions from research evidence that were even then well-established. Others of these concepts have been refuted by recent research findings.

Research has established that the learning of motor skills is specific. This applies also to perceptual-motor movement, because perception is involved in all voluntary muscular movement except reflex action. There is very little evidence to indicate a direct relationship between learning specific perceptual-motor skills and learning to read and write.

Although researchers have found that many of the motor activities that were devised to improve perception in academic endeavors are not successful in this purpose, they are useful in developing the motor skills involved in the activities. Perception and interpretation of stimuli in the performance of the particular skills also may be improved. Although transfer of neither the motor skills nor the perceptual-motor responses to other activities occurs, the capacity of the child in both areas is improved and is thus likely to enhance his or her future performances.

There is little doubt that perception is of vital importance to volitional movement. Emphasis in teaching directed toward perception in movement is of value in improving faulty perception in movement.

Components of Perception

When the word "perception" is used, most people think of visual perception. This is somewhat understandable because vision is the dominant sense in most people. However, as indicated in figure 3.8, vision is not the only source of sensory input. Information can be received through the channels of sound (auditory), touch (tactile), smell (olfactory), taste (gustatory), awareness of body position (kinesthetic), as well as sight (visual). In complex motor activity, the senses are used in an integrated manner to allow for efficient movement. In the game of basketball, for instance, players use vision to shoot a basket, sound to hear the referees and their

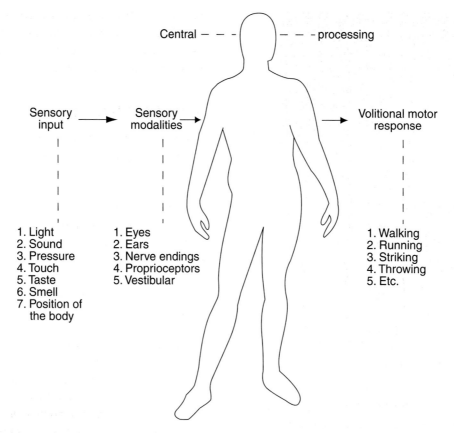

Central — — – — — – processing

Sensory input →   Sensory modalities   →   Volitional motor response

1. Light
2. Sound
3. Pressure
4. Touch
5. Taste
6. Smell
7. Position of
   the body

1. Eyes
2. Ears
3. Nerve endings
4. Proprioceptors
5. Vestibular

1. Walking
2. Running
3. Striking
4. Throwing
5. Etc.

Figure 3.8   Overview of perceptual-motor system.

teammates, touch to feel the ball, and kinesthetic sense to recognize their body position in relation to other players and the basket. As will be discussed in the chapters devoted to specific disabilities, students who do not have the use of some of the basic senses—for example, those who are deaf or blind—can participate successfully in various activities by relying on the other senses and, when necessary, through modifying the activity.

In the following section, the perceptual modalities and their component parts will be identified.

Visual Perception

Effective control of the visual system, or seeing what one wants, when one wants to see it, involves utilization of several skills that develop during childhood.

- **Visual acuity,** the ability to see objects clearly, improves until age 10 when maximum acuity is attained for most children.
- **Perceptual constancy,** the ability to determine if different objects are the same size, shape, and color, is also a necessary visual perceptual skill. Although infants appear to have some perceptual constancy skills, this trait follows a developmental course that extends through childhood.

- **Depth perception,** an important visual skill, is closely related to perceptual constancy. This skill involves perceiving three dimensions in proper perspective and having awareness of distance between objects or points. Scientists cannot agree whether depth perception is present in infants or is a developed skill.
- **Visual figure-ground** is a perceptual skill that involves distinguishing a figure from its background. Although it is generally recognized that form discriminations are among the first made by children, complete figure-ground mastery is slow to develop and normally continues to develop into adolescence.
- **Visual tracking** is the ability to perceive a moving object. Although infants as young as one month perceive and follow large objects, this trait continues to improve through the childhood years. As children become older and more experienced, the ability to track small objects moving at a rapid pace is remarkable.

Although the components of the visual perceptual system have been discussed separately, they work in an integrated fashion. For instance, successfully hitting a pitched ball requires that the ball can be seen clearly (visual acuity), followed as it leaves the pitcher's hand (visual tracking), and detected from among the many items in the background, such as the pitcher and fans (visual figure-ground). For

Figure 3.9 Catching a ball requires visual tracking skills and experience.

some students, the young and those with disabilities, the visual perceptual requirements of many skills may be too great, requiring that appropriate modifications be made. In the example given before, a simple modification would be to hit a stationary ball from a batting tee rather than a pitched ball, thus eliminating the visual process of tracking.

Auditory Perception

Auditory perception, similar to visual perception, consists of many identifiable subskills.

- **awareness,** the ability to indicate that there is sound or no sound;
- **discrimination,** the ability to discriminate between different tones and frequencies of sounds;
- **direction,** the ability to determine the direction from which sound is coming;
- **figure-ground,** the ability to distinguish a specific sound or sound pattern from other noises occurring at the same time.

Very few studies have analyzed the process of auditory development. It does appear clear, however, that infants are sensitive to sound from birth onward. Furthermore, infants appear to respond more favorably to low-pitched sounds rather than to high-pitched sounds.

Simple observation indicates that sound is an integral part of many of our games and physical education activities. Teammates' shouting, spectators' noise, and the teacher's whistle are only a few of the many sounds found within the gymnasium. If there are students who cannot perceive auditorily, as is true with students who are deaf and hearing-impaired, the teacher must rely on the other sensory systems to ensure positive learning experiences.

Kinesthetic Perception

Visual and auditory perception enables humans to receive, organize, integrate, and interpret a vast amount of never-ending stimuli. Such is also the case with kinesthetic perception. Instead of using an eye or an ear to receive information, the kinesthetic system utilizes proprioceptors located in tissues surrounding and adjacent to joints and in joint capsules. Whereas eyes and ears help people to remember a sight or sound, proprioceptors help us remember a movement or body position. This is a valuable system, one that is constantly used in the teaching and learning of many movement skills. Three skills that are closely related to kinesthetic perception—balance, body awareness, and laterality—will be discussed here.

1. **Balance,** the ability of the individual to position the body in response to the effects of gravity, is controlled in part by the *vestibular system.* This system, located in the inner ear, is a very important mechanism in helping individuals maintain balance in both a stationary and a static position, or when changing body positions. The latter type of balance is referred to as dynamic balance. Some individuals with hearing impairments have a defective vestibular system and they require a wide base of support to maintain balance when they walk.

2. **Body awareness** refers to an understanding of the position of the body in space and the relationship of body parts to each other and to external objects. Newborns are not capable of perceiving much about their environment. As children grow, they become aware of their capability of moving their extremities, head, and trunk. Later on, children learn labels and associate particular terms with various body parts. The labeling of body parts is one of the first body awareness characteristics a child develops. DeOreo and Williams (1980) indicate that at the age of five years, 55 percent of children accurately label their

Body Awareness Characteristics

- Labeling body parts
- Knowledge of what body parts can do
- Knowledge of how to move body parts efficiently

body parts. Linear improvements are found until age twelve, at which point there is 100 percent accuracy.

Two other important areas in the development of body awareness are knowledge of what the body parts can do and knowledge of how to make the body parts move efficiently. Knowledge of what the body parts can do refers to the child's ability to recognize the parts of a motor act and the body's potential for performing it. For example, children should be able to identify the correct body part when asked to respond to the following statements: I see with my . . . ; I talk with my . . . ; I snap my . . . , etc. The third area, knowledge of how to make the body parts move efficiently, refers to the ability to organize the body parts for a particular motor act and the actual performance of the act. For example, the child, when asked, should be able to: Touch the nose to the shoulder; touch the elbow to the knee; click the heels and arch the back.

3. An important aspect of the development of body awareness is the concept of **laterality.** This means simply that children develop an ability to distinguish between the two sides of the body. This trait is developed in children by the age of three to four. Although they may not be able to correctly apply the label "left" or "right," young children do understand that they have two feet, two hands, and two eyes and that these body parts are on two different sides of the body. Laterality is considered by many as the foundation for the development of other body awareness characteristics.

4. **Sensory dominance,** the preferential use of one eye, hand, and foot over the other, is closely related to the development of laterality. Individuals who develop a preference for the use of the eye, hand, and foot on the same side of the body are said to have pure dominance. Those who happen to have one of the preferred body parts on the opposite side of the body have mixed dominance. Children normally exhibit a hand preference by age four and foot preference by age five. Eye preference appears later, and in some instances, a pure preference for one eye over the other apparently never fully develops. Preferential use of the eye and hand on the same side of the body shows a definite developmental trend with age. The eye-hand preference of five- and six-year-olds has a trend toward being mixed, whereas the eye-hand preference of 9- to 11-year-olds has a trend toward pure preference.

5. **Directionality** is a kinesthetic sense that is also closely related to laterality. The ability to identify and relate objects and their positions to one another without the use of one's own body is referred to as directionality. More simply stated, directionality is evident when a child can indicate that an object in the room is to the right of a second object in the room without using his or her own body as a reference system. Children who have difficulty with directionality find it necessary to position their body between the two objects before they can indicate which is to the left or right of the other. Children take time to learn about their body in relationship to objects. Kindergarten and elementary PE programs often include obstacle courses to learn concepts such as "over," "under," "around," and so on.

Tactile, Gustatory, and Olfactory Perception

Tactile perception refers to the ability to interpret sensations by touching or feeling. This perception is used in learning many movement skills. Through experience, children quickly learn to distinguish between a hard and a soft ball, and between rough and smooth running surface textures. Tactile sensation is of paramount importance to certain students with disabilities, such as individuals without sight who frequently learn to perform various activities by feel. For example, a person who is visually impaired performing the basic skill of walking uses a cane to feel the sidewalk in contrast to other areas such as curbs and grass. Youngsters who are mentally retarded, too, learn many concepts such as smooth and rough by holding, feeling, and manipulating objects of various textures.

Very little is known about the development of taste and smell in children. Children do have a larger distribution of taste buds in their mouths than do adults, but it is not known whether children have a greater sensitivity to taste. With respect to smell, it is clear that young infants recognize pleasant from unpleasant odors, but precisely how this perceptual process develops is not clearly known. Movement skills generally do not require a highly refined taste or smell sensory input system.

Development of Perception

The Gestalt psychologists of the early 1900s felt that perception was not learned but was instead a factor of maturation. They reasoned that perception matured at a predetermined rate and experiences had little influence on the development. However, research accomplished since the early 1900s provides sufficient evidence to reject that theory. Today's evidence does support the concept that the process of perceiving can be improved through certain educational procedures. Perception does not necessarily improve automatically as the result of engaging in a given activity, however. Some children, through participation in an activity that involves the utilization of a specific sense, learn by themselves through trial and error to make an appropriate motor match with the sensory input. Others, because of learning disabilities, do not; they require specific assistance in interpreting sensory input and reacting to it with a suitable motor response.

Relying on dynamic systems theory, Block (1993) and Burton (1987) suggest that for some children, including those with various disabilities, deficits in movement performance might, in some cases, be related to a difficulty in perceiving what the environment affords them for action. This difficulty with a perception as it is related to an affordance suggests that children with disabilities may over- or underestimate their ability related to various tasks (e.g., distance that can be jumped) or they may misread the environment and use contextually inappropriate movements. For example, an object such as a ball might afford throwing, kicking, or bouncing, depending upon the person's expectation and environmental constraints. For the child with an affordance problem, the concern, of course, is that the child might be misjudged (i.e., viewed as not possessing the skill) when the problem may be related to an inability to properly read the environment. In some cases the individual may be confused by the environment and not perform at all or "read" the environment to call for an action different than that intended.

The human body perceives through different sense modalities. Each modality is different in function, providing a specific type of stimulation. The modalities that are usually involved in increasing the sensitivity and in improving the interpretation and reaction to the interpretation are sight, hearing, touch and pressure, and kinesthesis (the sensation of the location of body parts and of movement in muscles, tendons, and joints). Individuals use many modalities in a given movement experience. For some individuals, one modality is a dominant preference. The termed "multimodality" is often used to describe the teaching strategy used to accommodate the range and preference of modalities that a group of individuals would use to learn physical activity skills.

Children with learning disabilities cannot organize a sufficient amount of sensory information at one time to enable them to make an effective motor response. In addition, they may be deficient in one of the modalities of sensory input, for example, the auditory input. Therefore, the amount of sensory stimuli directed at a child with learning disabilities must be reduced to the level at which the child is able to absorb, and the teacher must be aware of which modalities are more easily accessed by that student. Children with learning disabilities who do not perform the task requested of them can be misjudged to be either oppositional in their behavior or lacking in intelligence. The real reason for nonengagement in the activity may be more directly related to sensory overload or a modality dominance. For these students, the task at hand may be made simpler by breaking it down into its components, thereby reducing the inputs of many different sensory stimuli at one time. This does not mean that various methods of providing sensory information should not be utilized. If the teacher finds that the student is not assimilating the information

from one source of sensory input/modality, other sources should be tried. For example, a child may not learn how to perform a skill by watching a demonstration (visual), but may get the idea when manual kinesthesis is used to lead the child through the required movements.

Although it is not established clearly how sensory interpretation and response to interpretation can be improved, it is generally conceded that practice in utilizing the senses and responding to the interpretation of the sense perceptions has value in effecting improvement of the process. The practice has to include cognition or conceptualization of the process of perception-interpretation; that is, there has to be an analysis of the deficient perception supplemented by analysis of the perception of the normally functioning senses to arrive at an interpretation that will produce the desired result. For example, children with problems of visual discrimination in size must use the normal perceptions from senses other than sight to evaluate the size of the object they are looking at. They then compare the result with the visual input they receive ordinarily and make the necessary adjustments to achieve agreement between the visual input and the input from the other senses. Much practice in simple repetitive exercises designed specifically for the deficiency is required to improve the interpretation of the stimuli.

Much the same procedure is utilized with children who have problems in reacting with appropriate motor movement to a sensation. For example, a child who cannot balance well on the balance beam must first analyze the sensations received just before losing balance. Then, through experimentation the child must discover the movements of the body that eliminate those sensations. Practice in consciously substituting these for the unsatisfactory movements will eventually result in an automatic response of the muscles to maintain balance when a fall is imminent. Examples of activities designed to enhance the perceptual process are found in table 3.4.

In utilization of motor activities to enhance the perceptual process, one must keep in mind that some of these movements require complex muscular coordination, as in throwing or kicking a ball, and others require intellectual recall, as in naming the body parts, and hence are relatively specific—not automatically transferred to the performance of other activities of coordination or intellectual recall. It is not known how general the perceptual processes are. For example, there is insufficient evidence to determine how readily the learned ability to determine the figure-ground relationship in one situation is transferred to another.

Because of the specificity of coordination and the possibility that perceptual processes also may be somewhat specific, a large number of experiences in sorting figure-ground relations and reacting in various situations are necessary to establish a general ability to distinguish a figure

TABLE 3.4	**Examples of Activities to Enhance the Perceptual Process**

Perceptual Area	Task
Visual	
Tracking	Watch a swinging, suspended ball.
Constancy	Reproduce on a chalkboard a shape that is provided by the teacher.
Depth perception	Throw a ball to the near basket rather than to the far basket.
Figure-ground	Kick a ball to a student standing in front of other children.
Auditory	
Direction	Point to the direction of a sound, e.g., a whistle.
Discrimination	Identify which bouncing ball sounds soft and which one sounds loud.
Figure-ground	Recognize the teacher's voice from among many voices in a crowded gymnasium.
Kinesthetic	
Body awareness	Touch and say the name of the body part located on a partner.
Laterality	Bend the body to the right (left) while in a standing position.
Directionality	Throw a ball from an off-center location to the right or left into a basket in the center of the room.

from its background. This would be true not only in the example given for a figure-ground recognition activity but also for all of the perceptual processes. The activities given in table 3.4 are only examples to provide information on the types of activities that may stimulate various perceptual processes.

Impairment of Perception

Research has not supplied the educator with all the answers concerning the nature of perception and its relationship to movement. It is postulated that the perceptual difficulties discussed previously may be caused by brain injuries or by malfunction of the portion of the nervous system that interprets perception.

It is possible that such injury or malfunction occurs in one phase of perception but that other phases may be unimpaired. Application of this concept can be very helpful when teaching students with various disabilities. For example, for individuals with visual and hearing impairments, the primary deficits will occur in sensory input. Individuals who have mental retardation will normally experience problems with interpreting input as well as processing of information. Impairment in the kinesthetic sense, as a result of muscular or nerve damage, will create unique challenges for those with orthopedic or neuromuscular disorders. Training the malfunctioning phase of perception or substituting another sensory organ for the one that is not functioning properly may help to overcome the motor problem that the perception problem creates.

However, in cases where no specific problem exists but where there is a nonspecific form of poor motor function, can the blame be placed upon any one perceptual area of malfunctioning? Probably not; it is reasonable to expect that the quality of motor ability fits a normal bell-shaped curve the same way it is supposed that intelligence does. If this is the case, it can be assumed that low general motor ability, or a large portion of it, is not caused by an organic lesion or malfunctioning of the nervous system but that the ability to learn motor movement is inherent within the neuromuscular system.

The Awkward Child

Children who demonstrate characteristics of nonspecific awkwardness do not necessarily respond positively to perceptual-motor activities designed for children with perceptual disabilities. Motor awkwardness appears to be general in nature; however, in close observation of awkward children it can usually be noted that the awkwardness occurs in some specific movements and not in others. The awkwardness may, for example, appear in the skills of jumping, hopping, and skipping but not in throwing and catching.

To effect remediation of motor awkwardness in the specific skills in which it occurs, the first step is to determine the reason for the awkwardness. To make such a determination in the case of awkwardness in running, for example, the teacher observes the child running and watches for such faults as

1. failure to coordinate the arm and leg movements,
2. failure to swing the leg straight forward in each stride, and
3. twisting of the trunk from side to side with each stride. (For description and techniques of such an evaluation, see chapter 6.)

After identification of the movement fault or faults that produce awkwardness in performing the skill, the child is taught how to overcome the problem and achieve a well-coordinated performance. Such instruction is much the same as that used to help any child break the habits of ineffective skill performance and achieve more efficient and graceful movement.

Unfortunately, although much has been written about awkwardness and related coordination problems, few serious efforts have been made to develop appropriate remediation programs (Burton, 1990). While it is outside the parameters of this chapter to provide a complete description of a remediation program, an example might prove helpful.

A useful framework for helping children with coordination problems has been proposed by Burton (1990). In his instructional hierarchy (figure 3.10), the child unable to coordinate the arms and legs while doing a jumping jack would be moved from level 3 to level 2 to work on between limb coordination. Suggested activities would include anything that required using the limbs together (e.g., two arms or two legs or the arm and leg on the same side). The movements should be done using the same (in-phase) or opposite (out-of-phase) movements. To make the skill easier, the movements should be executed first using as simple a position as possible (e.g., in a supine position). The relevant parameters (e.g., distance, time, and speed) should be varied to ensure success. However, if the child is unsuccessful at level 2, then he/she would be moved to level 1, between joints. At this level, possible activities might include anything that required use of only one arm or leg (e.g., throwing, striking). As success is achieved at level 1, the youngster would be advanced to level 2. It is important to emphasize that the tasks should be varied incorporating the appropriate parameters and aids (e.g., use of weights or cues [ribbon] on the arms or legs may be helpful). The goal is to

Figure 3.10 Knowledge of the instructional hierarchy helps teachers ensure student success. (Source: from "Applying Principles of Coordination in Adapted Physical Education" by Allen Burton. *Adapted Physical Activity Quarterly* (Vol. 7, No. 2), p. 136, © 1990 by Human Kinetics Publishers.)

Instructional Hierarchy for Working with Persons Who Have Movement Coordination Problems

Coordination level	Program focus	
3 Between limb pairs (total body)	Coordination	Control
2 Between limb (within limb pairs)	Coordination	Control
1 Between joints (within limb)	Coordination	Control

provide a program with clearly stated goals and instructional techniques that are reinforcing and creative.

Developmental Coordination Disorder

The American Psychiatric Association in its *Diagnostic and Statistical Manual of Mental Disorders* (DSM-IV, 1994) identified a movement syndrome classified as Developmental Coordination Disorder (DCD). The World Health Organization (2001) added an international consensus that some children who are clumsy or awkward may have this disorder. What remains problematic is how to screen, assess, or provide intervention for such children. The problems are not limited to gross motor skills but encompass other developmental skills. The revised DSM-IV-TR (2000) retains the description of the disorder. Research is being conducted to address the concerns of difficulties of motor coordination both in Europe and with colleagues in the United States (e.g., Polatajko, 1999; Sugden & Wright, 1998). The diagnostic criteria (DSM-IV, 1994) for DCD are:

A. Performance in daily activities that require motor coordination is substantially below that expected given the person's chronologic age and measured intelligence. This may be manifested by marked delays in achieving motor milestones (e.g., walk, crawl, sit), dropping things, "clumsiness," poor performance in sports, or poor handwriting.

B. The disturbance in Criterion A significantly interferes with academic achievement or activities of daily living.

C. The disturbance is not due to general medical condition (e.g., cerebral palsy, hemiplegia, muscular dystrophy) and does not meet the criteria for pervasive developmental disorder.

D. If mental retardation is present, then the motor difficulties are in excess of those usually associated with it.

Many clinicians believe that problems with coordination persist and contribute to difficulties in academic, behavioral, and psychosocial problems, as well as physical problems. Many educators also believe that children with DCD are not a homogenous group, but vary in the nature of their motor difficulties and their reactions to their difficulties. Physical educators with years of experience in the gymnasium often report children who struggle and appear awkward. Additional work on the diagnosis and interventions for these children is required. However, many physical educators have found that a definition of motor development as an adaptive change toward competence (Keogh & Oliver, 1968; Keogh, Sugden, Reynard, & Calkins, 1979) acknowledges that these children simply develop differently and therefore need different teaching strategies which could be implemented into the regular physical education lesson (Mally, 2002). Such children have difficulty with issues of timing and need extra practice; they do better when instruction is nonthreatening and noncompetitive and the activities are low-arousal and fun. In sum, when research evidence guiding modifications and adaptations is lacking, teachers can assume a best practice model of engaging each child as a unique person with strengths and weaknesses in movement, identify interests in movement, and develop positive experiences with movement activity for the child.

Summary

Within this chapter information has been presented concerning motor learning and perception and their importance to an understanding of how individuals acquire skills. Various theories of learning and movement control were reviewed with the recognition that aspects of each theory have some application in the teaching of motor skills to students with disabilities. There are also overlap and common elements among the various theories of learning.

Motor skill tenets were identified to assist the reader in recognizing some of the applied aspects of information that have been derived through a study of motor learning. Special attention was directed toward the importance of success, reinforcement, practice, and feedback in the teaching and retention of a motor skill. Information about how skills can be classified was included to emphasize the similarities and differences related to various skills. Knowledge in this area will lead to a better understanding of task complexity and the appropriateness or inappropriateness of introducing selected skills, depending upon the student's background and readiness.

Due to the continuing interest in perceptual motor programs, the theories of prominent individuals were reviewed. Although these theorists have aided in a significant way our understanding of the importance of motor activity in the lives of infants and children, including the child with a disability, there is insufficient research to support the various claims made by proponents of these programs.

The components of perception, including how perception is developed, were reviewed. Knowledge in this area serves to underline the importance of perception in the acquisition of knowledge, including motor skills. Although it is obvious that many have experienced the loss of one of the senses, innovative ways have been developed to help individuals to compensate successfully.

Finally, the chapter should serve to highlight that although information concerning motor learning and perception has been generated, little research is available that specifically applies to individuals with disabilities. Until such time as a more adequate research base exists, teachers will apply the known information cautiously, using experience and common sense as guides within the context of best practice in both physical education and specialized physical education.

Enhancing Activities

1. Decide whether the following motor skills should be classified as open or closed; gross or fine; continuous or discrete: archery, soccer, bowling, walking, and typing. Identify other skills and challenge your classmates to classify the skills.
2. Interview other professionals such as physical therapists, occupational therapists, reading specialists, and special educators to obtain their views regarding perceptual-motor programs.
3. Select a novel motor skill, such as tossing a tennis ball backward over the shoulder, and teach the skill to a child using the motor skill tenets listed in the chapter.
   For example, emphasize success, reinforcement, length of practice sessions, and retention of the skill.
4. For the following populations, identify perceptual and motor learning mechanisms that can be employed to help them compensate for their disabilities: visual impairment, orthopedic impairment, learning disability, and cerebral palsy.
5. Utilizing the theories of learning described earlier, explain how the process for teaching a motor skill might vary when employing a behavioral approach compared with a cognitive approach.

Selected Readings

Adams, J. A. (1971). A closed-loop theory of motor learning. *Journal of Motor Behavior, 3,* 111–149.

American Psychiatric Assoication (1994). Category 315.4 Developmental coordination disorder. *Diagnostic and statistical manual* (4th ed.). Washington, D.C.: APA.

American Psychiatric Association. (2000). Diagnostic and statistical manual of mental disorders (5th ed.). Washington, DC: Author.

Arnheim, D. D., & Sinclair, W. A. (1979). *The clumsy child* (2nd ed.). St. Louis: C. V. Mosby Co.

Block, M. E. (1993). Can children with mild mental retardation perceive affordances for action? *Adapted Physical Activity Quarterly, 10*(2), 137–145.

Brown, C., & Dunn, W. (2002). *The Adult Sensory Profile.* San Antonio: Psychological Corporation.

Burton, A. W. (1987). Confronting the interaction between perception and movement in adapted physical education. *Adapted Physical Activity Quarterly, 4,* 257–276.

Burton, A. W. (1990). Applying principles of coordination in adapted physical education, *Adapted Physical Activity Quarterly, 7,* 126–142.

Burton, A. W., & Rogerson, R. W. (2001). New perspectives on the assessment of movement skills and motor abilities. *Adapted Physical Activity Quarterly, 18,* 347–365.

Burton & Miller (1998). Movement Skill Assessment. Champaign, IL: Human Kinetics.

Delacato, C. H. (1963). *The diagnosis and treatment of speech and reading problems.* Springfield, IL: Charles C. Thomas.

Del Rey, P., & Stewart, D. (1989). Organizing input for mentally retarded subjects to enhance memory and transfer. *Adapted Physical Activity Quarterly, 6,* 247–254.

DeOreo, K., & Williams, H. (1980). Characteristics of kinesthetic perception. In C. B. Corbin (Ed.), *A textbook of motor development.* Dubuque, IA: Wm. C. Brown Publishers.

Dummer, G. M. (1985). Developmental differences in motor schema formation. In J. Humphrey & J. Clark (Eds.), *Current selected research in motor development* (chapter 11). Princeton, NJ: Princeton Books.

Dunn, W. (1997). The impact of sensory processing abilities on the daily lives of young children and families: A conceptual model. *Infants and Young Children, 9*(4), 23–35.

Dunn, W. (1999a). *The sensory profile.* San Antonio: Psychological Corporation.

Dunn, W. (1999b). *The sensory profile manual.* San Antonio: Psychological Corporation.

Dunn, W. (2002). *The infant toddler sensory profile.* San Antonio: Psychological Corporation.

Dunn, J. M., & Fredericks, H. D. (1985). Behavior management applied to mainstreaming in physical education. *Adapted Physical Activity Quarterly, 4,* 338–346.

Eidson, T. A., & Stadulis, R. E. (1991). Effects of variability of practice on the transfer and performance of open and closed motor skill. *Adapted Physical Activity Quarterly, 8,* 342–356.

Fitts, P. M., & Posner, M. I. (1967). *Human performance.* Belmont, CA: Brooks/Cole Publishing.

Frostig, M., & Maslow, P. (1970). *Movement education: Theory and practice.* Chicago: Follett Publishing Co.

Gabbard, C. P. (2004). *Lifelong motor development* (4th ed.). San Francisco, CA: Cummings.

Gallahue, D. L. (1982). *Understanding motor development in children.* New York: John Wiley and Sons, Inc.

Gentile, A. M., Higgins, J. R., Miller, E. A., & Rosen, B. M. (1975). *The structure of motor tasks.* Quebec City: Movement 7.

Kephart, N. C. (1971). *The slow learner in the classroom* (2nd ed.). Columbus, OH: Charles E. Merrill Publishing Co.

Kerr, R. (1982). *Psychomotor learning.* Philadelphia: Saunders College Publishing.

Magill, R. A. (1993). *Motor learning concepts and applications.* Dubuque, IA: Brown and Benchmark.

Mally, K. (2002). Developmental Coordination Disorder. Presentation, May 2002, University of Minnesota, Minneapolis.

Pangrazi, R. P. (2004). *Dynamic physical education for elementary school children* (14th ed.). San Francisco: Cummings.

Polatajko, H. J. (1999). Developmental coordination disorder (DCD): Alias the clumsy child syndrome. In K. Whitmore, H. Hart, & G. Willems (Eds.), *A neurodevelopmental approach to specific learning disorders* (pp. 119–133). London: MacKeith.

Poretta, D. L. (1982). Motor schema formation by EMR boys. *American Journal of Mental Deficiency, 87,* 164–172.

Poulton, E. C. (1957). On prediction in skilled movement. *Psychological Bulletin, 54.*

Project Beacon: Perceptual-motor activities handbook. (1977). Fairfax, VA: Fairfax County Public Schools.

Sage, G. H. (1984). *Motor learning and control.* Dubuque, IA: Wm. C. Brown Publishers.

Schmidt, R. A. (1975). A schema theory of discreet motor skill learning. *Psychological Review, 82,* 225–260.

Schmidt, R. A. (Ed.). (1982). *Motor control and learning.* Champaign, IL: Human Kinetics Publishers.

Schmidt, R. A., & Wrisberg, C. A. (2000). *Motor learning and performance* (2nd ed.). Champaign, IL: Human Kinetics.

Singer, R. N. (1982). *The learning of motor skills.* New York: Macmillan Publishing Co.

Skinner, B. F. (1938). *The behavior of organisms: An experimental analysis.* New York: Appleton-Century-Crofts.

Sugden, D. A., & Wright, H. C. (1998). *Motor coordination disorders in children.* Thousand Oaks, CA: Sage.

Tolman, E. C. (1934). Theories of learning. In F. A. Moss (Ed.), *Comparative psychology.* Englewood Cliffs, NJ: Prentice-Hall.

Ulrich, D. A. (2002). A model career worth developing. *Adapted Physical Activity Quarterly, 19,* 2–7.

Weiner, N. (1961). *Cybernetics.* New York: The M.I.T. Press and John Wiley and Sons, Inc.

Wertheimer, M. (1961). Psychomotor coordination of audio-visual space at birth. *Science, 134,* 1692–1693.

Whitehall, J. (1988). A dynamical systems approach to motor development: Applying new theory to practice. Paper presented at the International Early Childhood Physical Education Conference, Washington, DC.

Williams, H. G. (1983). *Perceptual and motor development.* Englewood Cliffs, NJ: Prentice-Hall, Inc.

Williams, H. G. (1986). Development of sensory-motor functioning in young children. In V. Seefeldt (Ed.), *Physical activity and well-being* (pp. 105–122). Reston, VA: American Alliance for Health, Physical Education, Recreation, and Dance.

World Health Organization. (2001). *International classification of functioning, disability and health.* Short Version. Geneva, Switzerland: WHO.

Zaichkowsky, L. D., Zaichkowsky, L. B., & Martinek, T. J. (1980). *Growth and development.* St. Louis: C. V. Mosby Co.

Understanding Individuals with Disabilities

CHAPTER OBJECTIVES

After studying this chapter, the reader should be able to:

1 Recognize the reality that each individual with a disability is unique and has a unique history of family and life experiences.
2 Appreciate the importance of others, namely parents, siblings, peers, and teachers, in helping the individual with a disability to adjust and be successful in the school setting.
3 Appreciate the importance of a positive professional–parent collaboration in delivering special education.
4 Identify various activities that teachers can use to help nondisabled students increase their sensitivity to their peers who have disabilities.
5 Compare and contrast the effects of a mild versus severe disability on the adjustment of the individual with the disability, as well as the adjustment of the person's family.
6 List and discuss various strategies employed by parents to accept and integrate a child with a disability into the family.
7 Identify and explain the response commonly experienced by parents upon learning that their child has a disability.
8 Analyze the impact of a child with a disability on the organizational structure of the family.

Success in working with individuals with disabilities is dependent upon understanding their special problems. It is significant that for many individuals with a disability, the most difficult problems are psychological in nature rather than physical. Ways have been found to reduce, if not actually eliminate, the physical pain of a disability. Many mechanical devices have been created and methods of rehabilitation developed to assist the person with a disability in achieving more normal use of the body. Medical treatment and the careful regulation of diet and activity enable many individuals disabled by functional diseases to lead normal lives in many respects. But regardless of how nearly normal body function and physical performance may be, the presence of the disability creates the potential for many psychological problems. Such problems have their origin in both the individual's reactions to the disabling condition and the responses of others to it.

Satisfactory resolution of these problems to achieve a desirable level of adjustment is often difficult and may constitute the major obstacle in the education of the person with a disability.

For teachers working with children and youth with disabilities, the understanding of the individual and the disability is imperative for the collaborative work required in the educational setting. The federal educational mandate, IDEA, '97, assumed a collaborative relationship between the school and parents of children with disabilities. The Beach Center on Disability (2004) has conducted research on the interpersonal relationships required of parents and professionals to provide positive collaborative work in the delivery of special education services (Blue-Banning et al., 2004; Nelson, Summers, & Turnbull, 2004; Summers et al., 2004; Wang et al., 2004). Their work shows that despite the decades of mandated services to individuals with disabilities and the spirit of the law to collaborate, the collaboration has been a difficult process for parents and professionals. This chapter will discuss the unique aspects of the individual with a disability within the context of the skills that the physical education teacher will need to be a positive advocate for such a student. Collaboration with families is imperative in this success.

To understand the person with a disability is to understand that each person is *unique,* with a unique biological make-up and history that includes the home environment, parenting, and life experiences (e.g., Bronfenbrenner & Crouter, 1983) (figure 4.1 *A* and *B*). For parents of a child with a disability, "respecting their child" means that professionals value their child as an individual rather than a disability label (Blue-Banning et al., 2004). As one parent reports, "If they perceive someone as being less than human then they are going to treat that someone as an object . . . I want [my son] to . . . feel like he belongs to the human race, like there's a place for him, like he fits in" (p. 197).

There is much in the child development literature regarding the interactive influence of nature and nurture (e.g., Rutter & Taylor, 2002). This means that a person's genetic factors and environment (family, parenting, home, school, etc.) interact and have a profound influence on how

Figure 4.1B Parents of children with disabilities want professionals to respect their child.

an individual matures. Consequently, it is an "it depends" answer when someone attempts to explain how an individual will develop (Bronfenbrenner & Crouter, 1983). Therefore, it is difficult to describe exactly which factors are shared by all people with disabilities. Although some research has described this, it should be taken as a general guide and must be filtered through the current thinking of the interaction of the uniqueness of the individual and his unique life.

Teachers participating in IEP meetings and in the ongoing communication with parents within an educational setting require information on how to communicate with families. The following chapter will discuss general information regarding adjustments followed by specific information on the current thinking on the collaborative family and professional partnership.

Factors Affecting Adjustment

Satisfactory solutions are achieved through the process of adjustment, a term used to describe the changes an individual undergoes in order to adapt to the environment. Adjustment begins at the moment of birth and is a continuous process throughout life. Certain innate factors, the result of inheritance, influence the kind of adjustment that is made in response to the stimuli of the environment. These factors are intelligence, physical appearance, temperament, and degree of disability.

Intelligence

By recognizing that child behavior is influenced by a number of factors, in general, the degree of native intelligence can

Figure 4.1A A child with a disability is a unique person with a unique family and developmental history.

influence the amount and quality of the direction and control of behavior. In many cases, a more intelligent child is potentially better able to direct and control her personal behavior, although it is recognized that certain life situations and experiences can overwhelm this. However, the greater ability to reason potentially enables the results of certain actions to be anticipated and acted upon accordingly. Because of the greater depth of understanding, a child with typical intellect has the capability to avoid many undesirable behaviors to achieve ends. Children with mental retardation are often able to learn socially acceptable behavior, but because of difficulties with the ability to generalize, they are unable to apply the learned behavior when they are in new and unexpected circumstances.

Physical Appearance

Physical appearance is an important factor in the development of behavior tendencies because of the responses of others to physical characteristics such as body build, facial features, and obvious deformities. We are aware that even such slight deviations as more-than-average height or weight can cause others to respond with a certain amount of teasing or even ridicule. Greater deviations from normal cause more intense responses, even to the extent of casting the one who deviates in an inferior social role. Child development research in school settings validates that children who are perceived as attractive are treated more positively by teachers and other adults than children who are not.

Temperament

Behavioral tendencies are also influenced by what is generally called temperament. There are many different theoretical approaches to temperament. The work of Rothbart and colleagues represents a good fit for the developing child, as emphasized in earlier chapters. Here the expression of the child's temperament is the result of the child's own unique genetic heritage, the environment in which the child is being raised, and the child's past and present experiences (e.g., Rothbart, 1989; Rothbart, Ahadi, & Hershey, 1994). Temperamental features like fearfulness or impulsivity contribute both to how the child expresses her emotions and how parent-child interactions occur.

Degree of Disability

Attention recently has been focused on the extent or degree of disability and its effect on adjustment. Although more research is needed in this area, some of the common assumptions of the past are now being seriously questioned. For instance, it was once widely accepted that the greater a person's disability, the more difficult it is for the individual to accept it or to achieve proper adjustment. Some have recently argued, however, that a person who is nearly "normal" in appearance and function may have a more difficult time adjusting than one who has a severe disability. Those who support this position postulate that an individual with a more severe disability recognizes that the disability is obvious to all and accepts his or her position, whereas the individual with a mild disability may try to hide or deny the disability. Future research will help to clarify this phenomenon. Until then it seems apparent that one should not assume that an individual that is mildly disabled will have fewer adjustment problems than those who are severely disabled.

Social-Environmental Influence

A continual interplay exists between the conditions arising from the individual with a disability and the conditions of the social environment—the attitudes and responses of others. Society tends to react in definite ways to any deviation from the norm. Sometimes the reaction is one of ridicule, curiosity, or maudlin sympathy; in the case of those close to the person with a disability, the reaction is often one of indulgence or overprotectiveness. The combined reactions of those in the social environment toward the one who deviates mentally or physically from the norm greatly influence that individual's adjustment. The responses of parents, peers, siblings, and teachers can significantly contribute toward a favorable social environment for the student with a disability.

Parent Reaction

Raising a child is recognized by most as a rewarding, but difficult and challenging task. As reported by Glass (1983), few couples are prepared for the realities of parenthood and the birth of a first child can be ". . . one of the most significant and stressful life events experienced by individuals." The birth of the first and subsequent children affects the marital relationship, economic status, and social status of a couple in very significant ways, some of which may be viewed by the couple as positive or negative. Whatever negative aspects may occur, they are usually overshadowed by the excitement of the baby and the infant's first responses such as the first smile and first sound.

In contrast, the experiences for parents of abnormal babies, particularly when the severity of the disability is apparent at birth, can be devastating. The birth of a child with a severely disabling condition places the parents in a very awkward position. While it is customary in our society to respond positively to the birth of an infant, society views the birth of an infant with a disability negatively. Awareness of society's perception adds stress to an already stressful situation for the parents and may interfere with the marital relationship. In addition the parents may be faced with extra hospital and medical costs and in some cases extensive and extended medical treatment and further bills. Given these stresses and the sudden time frame in which they occur, it is understandable that there are common reactions among parents to the initial impact of the birth of a child who is disabled. Among the most frequently identified responses are shock, denial, and grief.

When the infant's disability is apparent at birth, the initial parent reaction may be overwhelming. The stage of shock is likely to encompass feelings of anxiety, guilt, numbness, confusion, helplessness, anger, and despair. Unfortunately, it is at this time that many parents fail to receive the support they need or, in some cases, fail to comprehend the assistance that is available. Some parents avoid family and friends because of their own shame and uncertainty, as well as others' reactions.

The response of some parents to the birth of a child with a disability is to deny that a problem exists. These parents frequently suggest that the apparent delay is just that, and as the child develops, the deficits will be outgrown. For some, the denial process will involve obtaining additional professional opinions, hoping to find confusion and disagreement among the "experts." Although many parents overcome the denial stage, a conscientious effort must be made to minimize the length of this stage so that the child will receive the necessary treatment as soon as possible.

Parents of newborn children who are disabled experience grief for two reasons: first, there is grief associated with the loss of the expected normal child. Second, the parents need time to adjust to the child actually born to them. In this latter situation, some parents grieve because of their fear that their child will die. Grief can continue for some time after the baby is born.

Severe Disability

As children with disabilities grow and enter childhood and then adolescence, their parents continue to be faced with many adjustments. This is particularly so for parents of children with severe disabilities (see chapter 14). The realization for some that their child will not achieve sufficient independence to leave home will require an alteration in the normal family life cycle. The nature of the impact relates to expectations, family reorganization, prolonged and intensive care, provision of services, and fear of the future. It is for these reasons that some families go through adjustments at different times, yet retain the view that their child is a unique and special part of their family.

In a culture that is very conscious of chronological age, it is understandable that parents of children with severe disabilities are reminded at selected intervals of the child's life that their youngster is less than perfect. These include the expected milestones such as walking at age 14 months and riding a bike at age five as well as socially imposed norms such as driving a car at age 16 and eventually leaving home. Many parents indicate that they are at a loss to really know what to expect. For this reason many parents have found that observation of other children with the same disability as that of their child helps them to form reasonable expectations. Joining parent groups also provides an opportunity to share information about development in light of the child's disability.

The presence of a child with a range of disability levels, but particularly individuals with severe disabilities, also has an impact on the family and its organizational pattern. In our society parents normally formulate certain expectations for their children based on the order in which they are born. The parents' perception of the child changes as the youngster becomes older and assumes more responsibility within and outside the home. The organizational structure of the family with a child with a severe disability, however, is altered to accommodate the child's slower rate of development or very different rate of developmental patterns. In some families, the child with a severe disability is always perceived to be the youngest regardless of the child's age and order of birth.

Parents of children with severe disabilities recognize that many of the tasks associated with infancy, such as feeding, dressing, and diapers, are extended for a longer period of time or may remain indefinitely. The parenting responsibilities associated with infancy are never easy and may be overwhelming when there appears to be no end in sight. Age of the parents, too, becomes a factor as they reach middle age. The prolonged and intensive care needed by some children with severe disabilities requires additional time as well as physical and fiscal responsibility.

The nature of the disability will require the provision of services beyond those normally provided for nondisabled children. In addition to medical costs, children with severe disabilities will require the assistance of other specialists including physical and occupational therapists, speech and language specialists, vocational trainers, and counselors. Parents will need assistance in identifying the services needed and finding appropriate service providers. Obtaining the necessary medical assistance can also be a challenge. Many parents experience frustration when attempting to find medical specialists such as dentists, ophthalmologists, and audiologists who are comfortable in treating a child or adolescent with a severe disability.

Perhaps the major impact facing parents of a child with a severe disability is the fear of the future. This fear response is heightened as the child grows and the parents are faced with concerns about their own health and provisions for their son or daughter after their death. Alternative placements, including group homes and institutions, place additional stress on the parents and the major decisions that confront them. It is not surprising that parents of children with severe disabilities experience greater parent burnout and more isolation than other parents. Divorce rates for parents of children with severe disabilities have been reported to be twice that of the national average.

Mild Disability

Although research exists concerning parents of children with severe disabilities, little information is available concerning parents of children with mild disabilities. There is some evidence to suggest that the parent-child relationship for the child with a mild disability may be more disturbed than that of the youngster with a severe disability. The impact felt by the family may be attributed to several factors including identification, type of disability, cause of the disability, and treatment.

Unlike the child with a severe disability, the child with a mild disability may not be discovered until preschool, kindergarten, or early elementary school. This discovery may come as a surprise to parents or it may serve as an affirmation of their own concern about the child's development. Parent response, therefore, may range from anger to relief. One of the advantages of later identification is that the family has formed a close tie to the child and the child has been accepted as a member of the family without labels.

The type of disability is also an important factor in determining the impact of a child with a mild disability on parents. In general, society tends to be more accepting of visible disabilities such as physical and sensory impairments and less accepting of hidden disabilities such as learning and emotional impairments. The use of labels such as "mentally retarded" are normally difficult to accept and may generate various defense mechanisms. Children with learning disabilities create unique problems for the parents as they struggle to understand the nature of this disability and its implications.

Many parents are concerned with the cause of the disability. This can be a very frustrating search because for several of the major learning disorders, including learning disabilities, mental retardation, and emotional disturbances, the exact or precise cause is usually unknown. Some parents believe that they are the cause of their child's disability. They may go to extremes in their thinking regarding this, associating some event (dropping the child, for example) as the probable cause. Some may believe the cause is due to their own use and misuse of alcohol or stimulants. Parents of children with emotional disturbances may accept major responsibility because of the widespread belief that parents, at least in part, contribute

to the development of the child's emotional problems. Some parents have begun to speak out on this issue, arguing that there are few studies available to support this claim.

The impact of raising a child with a mild disability can be lessened for many parents if they know that treatment, including education, is available to assist their child. In this respect parent groups have become essential in assisting new parents to interpret professional recommendations, retrieve information, and secure needed services. The impact of raising a child with a mild disability can be minimized if quality services, including education, provided by caring professionals are available (Blue-Manning et al., 2004).

Family Dynamics

Given the previous text, it should not be surprising to note that families with children with special needs are more likely to be overprotective of the child with special needs; have an imbalance in the amount of support provided by primary caregivers; and have marital relationships that become subordinate to parental roles.

Although the challenges associated with raising a child with a disability are significant, many parents find genuine joy and satisfaction in raising their child. Some parents employ coping strategies to assist them in their relationship with their youngster. For example, some parents learn to accept their child with a disability by altering their expectations. Instead of continually comparing their youngster to selected developmental scales, they begin to accept and appreciate the individual progress made by their child. Parents also learn to cope by seeking solutions to the problems their children are encountering. The emphasis is not on fixing or correcting the child but instead focuses on a healthy concern that the youngster receive the best treatment and education possible. Some parents find it helpful to learn as much as they can about their child's disability and in a sense become an authority regarding the condition. In some instances the interest of the parent has led to formal education and a profession in a related area. Lindemann and Lindemann (1988) suggest that the key to raising a child with a disability is for each member of the family to maintain some personal identity, activities, and interests. If this is done, the final result will be a family in which the presence of the child with a disability, brother or sister, will enrich the lives of all.

There are, of course, some coping patterns that are more negative in their effects on the child. Some parents may choose to overprotect their children in an effort to insulate and isolate the youngster from situations that entail risk and possible failure. Withdrawal is a strategy some parents employ to avoid discussions about their children as well as situations in which the child's presence might lead to questions or comments from others including friends, family, and strangers.

Sibling Reaction

In recent years additional attention has focused on the reaction and needs of siblings of individuals with disabilition. Not surprisingly, the reaction of many siblings to their brother or sister is determined to a large extent by the reaction of their parents. Young children, in particular, usually follow the example set by their parents. During the teen years the need to be accepted and liked by others is very important. Teenagers strive to be part of the norm and to be accepted. Having a sibling with a disability is different and may lead to embarrassment if their friends make insensitive remarks. Some young people avoid confrontations by not bringing their friends home and by avoiding family outings to public places.

Guilt, too, is a reaction experienced by many siblings. This is normally associated with their negative feelings toward the sibling who is disabled. Some also experience guilt because they are not disabled.

Fear is also a reaction of many siblings of children with disabilities. Younger siblings may fear that they, too, will become disabled. Older siblings may fear that someday they will become the parent of a child with a disability or that they will be expected to care for their brother or sister after the death of the parents.

Resentment sometimes appears to be a reaction of siblings. This may be attributed to several factors, including neglect because of the excessive amount of time the parents seem to spend with the sibling who is disabled. Some siblings resent the amount of time that they are asked to contribute to the care of the child with a disability. Young people, too, may see their sibling with a disability as a drain on the financial resources of the family, which seems to interfere with the family's ability to buy selected items.

Although many siblings have spoken very positively about life with a brother or sister with a disability, studies are mixed on the effects of being raised with a sibling with a disability. One thing does appear clear: Siblings of children who are disabled need information. They need to know about the sibling's disability and how to explain the disability to their friends. Young children need basic answers to questions such as, How did this happen? Will it happen to me? They also need support, encouragement, and reinforcement for their accomplishments. Finally, siblings of children with a disability need to be recognized without continual reference to their sibling who is disabled. Sensitive teachers can be very helpful in assisting the sibling to make a positive adjustment.

Peer Reaction

In recent years, more students with disabilities are receiving their instructional program in the mainstream of education. When students are properly placed, individuals with and

Figure 4.2 Encouragement and positive reinforcement are essential in the development of skills.

without disabilities benefit from the opportunity to interact. Teachers have learned from experience that a favorable classroom environment requires that students become more sensitive to the needs of their fellow students. Even children with minor differences, such as those who are overweight or wear glasses, find it embarrassing to be called names, such as "fat" or "four-eyes." Obviously, to be labeled a "retard" or "deaf and dumb" can be devastating to a person attempting to secure a place in the educational mainstream. Such examples are not without support, as there is some evidence to suggest that students without disabilities have many misconceptions about their peers with disabilities.

The results of surveys provide clear direction for public schools and teachers. Acceptance of students with disabilities and the concept of integration are not enough. Schools must assist students without disabilities to improve their knowledge of disabling conditions and persons who have various diseases. To do otherwise may create a situation in which initial acceptance may lead to avoidance and rejection if understanding and expectations are not emphasized from the start. Direct contact is of critical importance in improving understanding between groups of people. In addition, planned educational experiences should be undertaken to assist students without disabilities to relate in a positive way to peers with disabilities. Later in this chapter specific suggestions to help the teacher accomplish this goal will be presented.

Teacher Reaction

A positive and accepting teacher attitude toward the student with a disability is essential for creating a favorable learning experience. The manner in which the teacher responds to the special student communicates much to the student and his/her peers. If the teacher appears apprehensive and fearful, it is likely that other students will follow this lead. Teachers, therefore, must analyze carefully their own attitudes toward those who are disabled. Some teachers have recognized that they, like many others, are afraid of the student with special needs. Other common responses include a tendency to underestimate the student's capabilities, to worry unnecessarily about liability, and to be sympathetic and overprotective. Teachers who recognize these feelings are in an excellent position to undertake special projects to improve their understanding. For instance, one can read about the etiology of the student's disability, observe other children with similar disabilities, talk with other teachers who have worked with the student, observe the student in various settings, develop a list of the student's *abilities,* and talk with the parents. Teachers may also find it necessary to enroll in graduate courses or inservice workshops to receive more formal training in the field of adapted physical education. Many of these courses provide opportunities for the teacher to work in a practicum setting with special students under the guidance of an experienced teacher. As teachers become more familiar with the needs of students with disabilities, they will learn the subtle but important distinction between empathy and sympathy; the student needs understanding but not sorrow. Teachers will also learn to become more sensitive; to view the student not as a disabled individual but as an individual who has a disability, with abilities that are far greater in number than his or her disabilities.

A number of investigators (Jansma & Schultz, 1982; Patrick, 1987; Rizzo, 1984; Rizzo & Vispoel, 1991, 1992; Rizzo & Wright, 1988; Rowe & Stutts, 1987; Stewart, 1988, 1990; Tripp, 1988) have analyzed various factors related to the attitude of physical educators toward teaching students with disabilities. Research findings suggest that the attitude of physical education teachers toward working with those students with disabilities can be improved if coursework and inservice experiences provide information about the nature of various disabilities. In addition, the attitude of teachers can be positively affected if teachers are provided supervised practicum experiences to work directly with students with disabilities. Innovative work by Rizzo and Vispoel (1991, 1992) highlights that the attitude of physical educators varies according to the type of disability. They have noted, for instance, that students with behavior disorders tend to be perceived less positively than individuals with learning disabilities or mental retardation (Rizzo & Vispoel, 1992). This suggests, therefore, that greater emphasis may need to be placed on selected skills (e.g., behavior management) to ensure that teachers feel adequately prepared and positive about providing services for all students.

Most important, teachers will come to appreciate the challenge of adapting games and activities so that the student

with a disability will benefit from and appreciate the many positive experiences inherent in the physical education class.

There must be continuous interplay among parents, peers, and teachers to create a favorable social environment for the student with a disability. Teachers and parents, in particular, must communicate to ensure that the special student adjusts favorably. Cooperative planning and frequent interaction help parents and teachers maximize the assistance available to the young person with a disability.

Family and Professional Partnerships

The recent emphasis on parent involvement in the education of children with disabilities was communicated clearly with the emphasis on the role of parents in both the Individualized Educational Plan (IEP) and the Individualized Family Service Plan (IFSP) IDEA '97. This emphasis has generated new enthusiasm for the partnership that should exist between home and school in the education of all children, particularly those students with special needs. Parents of children with disabilities have communicated, too, that they want to be partners, that they need assistance, and that they want their input to be taken seriously. For future physical educators, this means that additional opportunities to meet and work with parents of children with disabilities should be given top priority. Future educators must also provide information and be receptive. The expectations of teachers were nicely summarized by one parent who reported, ". . . Let us process our grief over the fact that our children are not perfect. Give us information about our children's disabilities. And give us cautious 'optimism.' Let us know the potential range of limitations their disabilities may present, but let us also know what these special children may also be able to do. Allow us faith and belief in the future. And you professionals, 'just be human'" (Royeen, 1992, pp. 66–67). According to the research, it is important that professionals fulfill not only the "letter of the law," but also the spirit (Blue-Banning et al., 2004).

A significant change in federal education law since the mandate of PL 94-142 in 1975 has been the changing role of the parents. Parents have always been identified as significant in the process of delivery of special education services, but the reality was that they were typically overwhelmed by the numbers of educational staff and, at times, by the information presented in IEP, and later in IFSP, meetings. Parents have commented for decades on this reality. For many, the cry has been "Listen to me, I am this child's parent!" Parents have tried to explain to professionals that they do indeed know their child. Too often, professionals have acted as if this were not the case.

According to IDEA '97 parents are involved in decision making and advocacy when they participate in the IEP development, give consent, have access to records, participate in hearings, and protect the confidentiality of student records. Under the special education law, parents serve as advocates for their child with a disability. Conducting extensive interviews with parents of children with disabilities to study Family Quality of Life (FQL) given this advocacy role, Wang and colleagues (2004) reported on parents' perceptions of their advocacy. One mother said, ". . . I feel that I am my son's greatest advocate. Because there is no one else that is going to speak up for my son but me." Another parent poignantly added, ". . . Who will listen for those who cannot hear? Who will have vision for those who cannot see? Who will speak for those who cannot speak? Who will stand up for those who cannot walk?"

Wang and colleagues studied 78 families of children with disabilities, 80 percent of whom had a child with moderate to severe disabilities, and found that improved partnerships between schools and parents were dependent on:

- viewing family members as equal partners in the decision-making process
- respecting family values and beliefs
- listening to families nonjudgmentally
- recognizing family expertise about its own child
- communicating a child's strengths
- using words that families can easily understand
- being friendly
- protecting family privacy
- avoiding conflict when family opinions differ

A total of 137 families and 53 professionals were interviewed in a qualitative research study aimed at developing guidelines for successful family and professional partnerships (Blue-Banning et al., 2004). A profound point emphasized in the report was the need for a "common sense of ordinary decency" in creating positive partnerships. The study identified six themes of collaborative partnerships as well as indicators for each theme. Each theme was valued by both the professionals and the families as leading toward positive collaboration. A summary with sample indicators follows:

1. **Communication:** The quality is positive and the quantity is understandable.
   a. Indicators: Being tactful, open; listening, coordinating information
2. **Commitment:** There is a shared sense of the importance of the child, the family, and the goals identified.
   a. Indicators: Demonstrating commitment, flexibility, accessibility; the child is not "a case"
3. **Equality:** Equality is pervasive and all members feel equally powerful in influencing outcomes.
   a. Indicators: Avoiding use of "clout"; validating others, fostering harmony
4. **Skills:** People are competent, fulfill their roles, and use recommended practice in their role.
   a. Indicators: Expect child to progress, consider whole family and whole child, be willing to learn
5. **Trust:** A shared sense of assurance about reliability and dependability of members.
   a. Indicators: Reliability, discretion, child is safe
6. **Respect:** Members exhibit esteem through their actions and communication.
   a. Indicators: Valuing the child, being nonjudgmental, being courteous, avoid being intrusive

These findings are important for physical education professionals to understand and to adapt to their work with families when providing special physical education services to students with disabilities. Physical educators have unique opportunities to be positive about physical activity and the value it has for the life of the student with a disability. The trained special physical educator has much to offer each student and family. Oftentimes special physical educators must be advocate for the student in the school physical education program, and must advocate with their colleagues in special education, administration, and in the community in which they live.

The Role of the Teacher

The environment of the individual with a disability does, as was suggested, play an important role in adjustment. Because any disabling condition reduces the social interaction between the person and his or her environment, the environment cannot make the same contribution that is possible with nondisabled people. Nevertheless, the help and understanding of those in the person's environment make a tremendous difference in the quality of the adjustment. No one develops a socially acceptable personality and becomes well adjusted entirely by personal efforts; individuals must have the help of family, friends, teachers, and classmates.

We are primarily concerned here with the role of teachers in promoting a positive environment for the wholesome personality development of the child with a disability. Any educational endeavor to help the child make a more satisfactory adjustment must include the promotion of better understanding among the children with whom the child with a disability comes in daily contact in the classroom and on the playground. These children constitute the greater portion of the child's social environment. If they can be given a fuller understanding of the role that society forces on the disabled, if they can acquire respect for a person with a disability as an individual rather than as a deviate, many of the difficulties imposed by the disability can be alleviated.

In developing a favorable climate in the classroom for the acceptance of students with disabilities, the teacher may discuss with the students the reasons for liking and disliking certain people. The importance that is sometimes attached to attractive physical appearance may be pointed out and contrasted with more meaningful personal attributes. The teacher might emphasize that performing to the best of one's ability is just as admirable and worthy of respect as being the most outstanding performer. Attention should be directed toward the concept that one does not have to excel in popular spectator sports such as football and basketball; success, according to one's ability, in an adapted game of beep baseball is of no less significance than success in the more popular games. Specific activities that teachers can undertake to help students increase their sensitivity to their peers are presented in the following paragraphs.

Invite People with Disabilities to Speak to Students

All too frequently there is a tendency to generate good ideas and to develop plans of action without first involving those people who are affected by the decisions. People with disabilities have much to offer in any discussion about the nature, severity, or effects of various impairments. Some people with disabilities feel very comfortable addressing groups and explaining such interesting information as the

Figure 4.3 Teachers have a responsibility to help students appreciate the ability of their peers with a disability.

process blind people use to prepare a meal or to walk down a sidewalk. As one would expect, not all people with disabilities enjoy addressing large or even small groups. For this reason and because of the candidness of students' questions, the selection of speakers should be done carefully. Most professional advisory groups, such as the National Disability Sport Association and the local ARC (Association for Retarded Citizens), have lists of speakers who are qualified to address student groups and are interested in doing so. "Disability awareness" is a prominent part of school activities, as well as teacher preparation programs in special physical education (for activities see Disability Awareness, in Lieberman and Houston-Wilson, 2002).

Interview People with Disabilities

The interview is an activity suitable for older, more mature students. The specific assignment is to locate a person with a disability and then to ask a series of questions relative to the effects of the individual's disability on performance of daily living activities. The questions should be general, with the primary goal being to encourage interaction of people with and without disabilities. Most students who undertake this exercise find varied responses by people with disabilities to the interview process—some are enthusiastic, some agree reluctantly, and some firmly reply no.

Obtain Films and Books That Provide Information about People with Disabilities

Today many excellent resources are available at reasonable cost. For example, the humorous film *What Do You Do When You See a Blind Person?* may be obtained free or for a nominal charge from the State Commission for the Blind. Likewise, a *School Alert Kit*, which presents an enlightened discussion of epilepsy, may be obtained free by contacting the local chapter of the Epilepsy League of America. A partial list of books, films, and agencies of and for those with disabilities is found in Appendix II on the CD.

Obtain Appliances, Assistive Devices, and Equipment That Assist Persons with Disabilities to Function in Society

Opportunities for young people to explore the function and operation of wheelchairs, for instance, can prove to be a very interesting experience. With the help of individual Braille alphabet cards, supplied by the American Foundation for the Blind, students can be given basic lessons in reading and writing Braille. Older children can use these cards to create and decipher jokes written in Braille. Young children can use their pencil erasers to form Braille impressions on sheets of aluminum foil and then try to decipher each other's messages. Similar valuable and enjoyable experiences can be created to illustrate the use of other devices such as hearing aids, canes, and walkers.

Simulate Disabling Conditions

Individuals of all ages are intrigued with opportunities to experience what it might be like to be disabled. Although such activities never fully simulate a disability, they do provide additional understanding and serve as the basis for some quality discussions. A few simulation exercises that have successfully been used include:

1. Permitting students to serve as guides for their blindfolded classmates. For a demonstration of the correct procedure for serving as the sighted guide the students should observe the film *What Do You Do When You See a Blind Person?*, which may be obtained from the State Commission for the Blind. Then, the students should attempt specific tasks while blindfolded, such as throwing a ball at a sound and identifying different objects by touch, and perform movement activities, such as hitting a ball and swinging a golf club. Finally, students should take turns assisting each other to perform the activities while simulating blindness.

2. Utilizing wheelchairs borrowed from hospitals and community agencies, permit students to have the experience of sitting in and operating a wheelchair. As with the simulation of visual impairments, encourage the participants to perform routine physical activities, such as shooting a basketball or serving a volleyball. Students should also be asked to use the washroom. Many young people find that this experience helps them become more appreciative of the skill and ease with which wheelchair users can move. Novice wheelchair users also quickly become aware of the frustrations that can be generated by the inaccessible architectural features found in many public buildings.

3. Students can also be asked to perform various tasks utilizing only one arm or leg. Assistive devices such as canes, walkers, and braces can be borrowed to allow opportunities to simulate disorders, such as amputations and cerebral palsy. Using a crutch instead of a foot to kick a ball provides the student with a different perspective concerning the ability of a peer. Swinging a bat with only one arm helps the nondisabled student appreciate the special skill and strength a student with an amputated arm must develop to participate in a game of softball. Examples such as these in which students participate in a game or sport while simulating the loss of an arm or leg contribute to an awareness of the unique talents that individuals with disabilities develop.

Space does not permit discussion of other simulated experiences that can be undertaken. Those identified, however, do serve as examples that can be expanded or changed to fit the needs of various student groups.

Essential to the entire process of simulation is the opportunity to hold discussions after the experiments. Questions that may be asked include, "How did it feel to be blindfolded?" "Was your guide helpful?" "Did people stare at you in your wheelchair?" "Were buildings difficult to enter?" Discussions about such questions are a must to help clarify young people's feelings and concerns. Not all of the answers are available, but the process should serve to make students more empathetic toward people with disabilities and should thus assist in the integration of children with disabilities into the mainstream of physical education. With empathy comes understanding and with understanding, the process of successful mainstreaming begins.

Reverse Mainstreaming

A process that is very helpful to many teachers who are preparing for the first time to introduce children with disabilities into a regular education class is to identify a small number of select nondisabled students to serve as aides in a special physical education class. This approach, which is frequently referred to as reverse or counter mainstreaming, has many advantages. It allows students with disabilities the opportunity to benefit from peer interaction in a setting with which they are familiar as well as providing them with an opportunity to enhance their skill level before integrating into the regular class. Nondisabled students benefit from this arrangement, as it affords them the experience of interacting in an environment that is different from that to which they are accustomed. This new sensitivity will assist them to better comprehend the feelings students with disabilities have as they enter the regular physical education class. Many teachers have found reverse mainstreaming helpful because it allows them to observe children with and without disabilities interact. Discussion sessions should be held with both groups of students to respond to questions and concerns they may have. These sessions generate information that will assist the teacher to lay the foundation for successful integration of students with disabilities into the physical education mainstream.

Reverse mainstreaming, with its emphasis on direct contact between children with and without disabilities, is an effective mechanism to facilitate attitudinal change. It should be stressed, however, that these experiences are most beneficial with young children who are less likely to have developed fixed attitudinal responses to those who deviate from the norm. Initial efforts should also be structured and directed toward exposing students to individuals with mild and moderate disabilities before moving to those who are severely mentally retarded and emotionally disturbed.

The activities that have been described will do much to eliminate the wall of isolation with which many youngsters with disabilities have had to contend. Integrating those with disabilities may at first require additional planning time. Dividends, however, will be evident as youth with and without disabilities grow in their awareness and appreciation of individual differences. Mainstreaming programs offer hope that more children will learn to recognize others' abilities rather than their disabilities.

In addition to helping others understand and accept people with disabilities, an educational program should be directed toward helping these youngsters develop skills and abilities to offset their shortcomings, and to find satisfactory substitutes for the desires they cannot fulfill and the activities they cannot perform. In these ways those with disabilities may overcome the fear, shame, and social inadequacies that cause them to seek refuge in escape, projection, and other unacceptable behavior. The special physical education program can make significant contributions to the total educational program by helping those with disabilities to develop better motor skills, improve body mechanics, increase physical fitness, and enhance body image. The special contributions of various kinds of physical education activities will be presented in the chapters dealing with the specific types of disabilities.

Summary

How an individual reacts to a disability has much to do with the person's long-term adjustment. Psychological problems, when they do occur, have their origin in both the individual's reaction to the disabling condition and the response of others to it. Each individual with a disability is unique with unique experiences of caregiving, homelife, and successes.

Many factors affect the individual's adjustment to a disability. These include the individual's intelligence, temperament, degree of disability, and physical appearance. Individuals with disabilities, similar to the nondisabled, use various mechanisms to adjust to their disability. These mechanisms, which include sublimation, compensation, identification, projection, escape, rationalization, and repression, are acceptable unless the individual resorts to these mechanisms too frequently and too intensely. Unfortunately some individuals with disabilities rely on these mechanisms more than they should.

The reactions of others have much to do with the ability of an individual with a disability to develop normally and lead a happy life. Key individuals in this respect include parents, siblings, peers, and teachers. Raising a child with a disability can be a very demanding task. For many parents integrating and accepting a child with a disability will take time. Some parents experience a grieving phase before they accept and make the necessary adjustments in their lives to fully integrate the child into the family unit.

Siblings and peers, too, play an important role in the life of an individual with a disability. A conscientious effort must be made to ensure that friends and siblings understand the child's disability, including areas of limitations and strengths. The goal is to improve their understanding and sensitivity toward the needs of those with a disability. Siblings and peers will normally follow the lead of other adults, primarily parents and teachers, as they improve their understanding and acceptance of a child with a disability.

Developing positive professional and family collaborative efforts is vital to the education of the student with a disability. Parents see themselves as advocates for their child in the school setting, and they ask that they be regarded as knowledgeable.

There are many techniques that teachers can employ to help young people become more empathetic and sensitive to the needs of their disabled peers. These include inviting people with disabilities to class, interviewing individuals with disabilities, and simulating disabling conditions. Some children will benefit, too, from the opportunity to work with students in special classes. This approach, frequently referred to as reverse mainstreaming, creates opportunities for nondisabled students to help and be helped as they learn and work with their disabled peers.

The underlying theme throughout this chapter is that when the physical educator works with the child with a disability he is also working closely with the student's family. The physical education program can be a supportive, positive experience for the student, as well as for the family's development of adjustment and appreciation of the unique person with a disability in their family.

Enhancing Activities

1. Review the information on developing positive collaborations with parents and service providers. Describe how this can be applied to the delivery of adapted physical education in a school.
2. Develop a list of various support organizations and groups within the community that offer services to individuals with disabilities and/or their families. Identify the services provided.
3. Interview students on the college campus to obtain their views of individuals with disabilities. Does their response vary as to the type of disability, such as visual impairment contrasted to orthopedic impairment? If you know them well ask how they would respond if they were to be the parent of a child with a disability.
4. Review the list of activities identified in the chapter to help students increase their sensitivity toward those with disabilities. Think of other suggestions that could be added to the list.

Selected Readings

Auxter, D., & Pyfer, J. (1985). *Adapted physical education and recreation.* St. Louis: Times Mirror/Mosby.

Bardach, J. L. (1979). Psychological adjustment of handicapped individuals and their families. *Awareness Papers.* Washington, DC: White House Conference on the Handicapped.

Beach Center on Disability. (2004). University of Kansas. (www. beachcenter.org).

Blue-Banning, M., Summers, J. A., Frankland, H. C., Nelson, L. G. L., & Beegle, G. (2004). Dimensions of family and professional partnerships: Constructive guidelines for collaboration. *Exceptional Children, 70*(2), 167–184.

Bolton, B. (1976). *Psychology of deafness for rehabilitation counselors.* Baltimore: University Park Press.

Bronfenbrenner, U., & Crouter, A. C. (1983). The evolution of environmental models in developmental research. In P. H. Mussen (Ed.), *Handbook in child psychology,* Vol. 1, (4th ed., pp. 357–414). New York: Wiley.

Cruickshank, W. M. (Ed.). (1980). *Psychology of exceptional children and youth* (4th ed.). Englewood Cliffs, NJ: Prentice-Hall, Inc.

Daniels-Mohring, D., & Lambie, R. (1993). Dysfunctional families of the student with special needs. *Focus on Exceptional Children, 25*(5), 65–67.

DeLoach, C., & Greer, B. G. (1981). *Adjustment to severe physical disability: A metamorphosis.* New York: McGraw-Hill Book Co.

Dunn, J. M., & Boarman, A. M. (1979). A need: Better understanding of people with special needs. *Campfire Leadership,* Winter 6–9.

Faerstein, L. M. (1981). Stress and coping in families of learning disabled children: A literature review. *Journal of Learning Disabilities, 14*(7), 420–423.

Featherstone, H. (1980). *A difference in the family.* New York: Penguin Books.

Garrison, K. G., & Magoon, R. A. (1972). *Psychology: An interpretation of psychology and educational practices.* Columbus, OH: Charles E. Merrill Publishing Co.

Gath, A. (1977). The impact of an abnormal child upon the parents. *American Journal of Psychiatry, 130,* 405–410.

Glass, J. (1983). Pre-birth attitudes and adjustment to parenthood: When 'preparing for the worst' helps. *Family Relations, 32*(3) 377–386.

Hardman, M. L., Drew, C. J., & Egan, M. W. (1984). *Human exceptionality.* Boston: Allyn and Bacon, Inc.

Jansma, P., & Schultz, B. (1982). Validation and use of a mainstreaming attitude inventory with physical educators. *American Corrective Therapy Journal, 36,* 150–158.

Kirtley, D. D. (1975). *The psychology of blindness.* Chicago: Nelson-Hall Publishers.

Kübler-Ross, E. (1970). *On death and dying.* New York: MacMillan.

Lieberman, L. J., & Houston-Wilson, C. (2002). *Strategies for INCLUSION.* Champaign, IL: Human Kinetics

Lindemann, J. D., & Lindemann, S. J. (1988). *Growing up proud: A parent's guide to the psychological care of children with disabilities.* New York: Warner Books Inc.

Lindgren, H. (1969). *Psychology of personal development.* New York: American Book Co.

Marion, R. L. (1981). *Educators, parents and exceptional children.* Rockville, MD: Aspen Systems Corp.

Miller, A. G., & Sullivan, J. V. (1982). *Teaching physical activities to impaired youth.* New York: John Wiley and Sons, Inc.

Nelson, L. G. L., Summers, J. A., & Turnbull, A. P. (2004). Boundaries in family-professional relationships: Implications for special education. *Remedial and Special Education, 25,* 165–253.

Patrick, G. (1987). Improving attitudes toward disabled persons. *Adapted Physical Activity Quarterly, 4,* 316–325.

Rizzo, T. L. (1984). Attitudes of physical educators toward teaching handicapped pupils. *Adapted Physical Activity Quarterly, 1,* 263–274.

Rizzo, T. L., & Wright, R. G. (1988). Selected attributes related to physical educators' attitudes toward teaching students with handicaps. *Mental Retardation, 26,* 307–309.

Rizzo, T. L., & Vispoel, W. P. (1991). Physical educators' attributes and attitudes toward teaching students with handicaps. *Adapted Physical Activity Quarterly, 8,* 4–11.

Rizzo, T. L., & Vispoel, W. P. (1992). Changing attitudes about teaching students with handicaps. *Adapted Physical Activity Quarterly, 9,* 54–63.

Roberts, R. N., Rule, S., & Innocenti, M. (1998). *Strengthening the family-professional partnership in services for young children.* Baltimore: Brookes.

Robinson, N. M., & Robinson, H. B. (1976). *The mentally retarded child.* New York: McGraw-Hill, Inc.

Ross, A. O. (1964). *The exceptional child in the family.* New York: Grune and Stratton.

Rothbart, M. K. (1989). Temperament and development. In G. Kohnstamm, J. Bates, & M. K. Rothbart (Eds.), *Temperament in childhood* (pp. 187–248). Chichester, England: Wiley.

Rothbart, M. K., Ahadi, S. A., & Hershey, K. I. (1994). Temperament and social behavior in childhood. *Merrill-Palmer Quarterly, 40*(1), 21–39.

Rowe, J., & Stutts, R. M. (1987). Effects of practica type, experience and gender on attitudes of undergraduate physical education majors toward disabled persons. *Adapted Physical Activity Quarterly, 4,* 268–277.

Royeen, C. B. (1992). A glimpse of the human experience: Parenting infants and toddlers who are disabled. *Infants and Young Children, 5*(2), 65–67.

Rutter, M., & Taylor, E. (Eds.). (2002). *Child and adolescent psychiatry.* Oxford, UK: Blackwell.

Schulz, J. B. (1982). A parent views parent participation. *Exceptional Education Quarterly, 3*(2), 17–24.

Seligman, M. (1979). *Strategies for helping parents of exceptional children.* New York: The Free Press.

Seligman, M. (1983). Siblings of handicapped persons. In M. Seligman (Ed.), *The family with a handicapped child.* New York: Grune and Stratton.

Sherrick, C. E., Swets, J. A., & Elliott, L. L. (1974). *Psychology and the handicapped child.* Washington, DC: U.S. Dept. of Health, Education, and Welfare.

Shontz, F. C. (1980). Theories about the adjustment to having a disability. In W. M. Cruickshank (Ed.), *Psychology of exceptional children and youth* (4th ed.). Englewood Cliffs, NJ: Prentice-Hall, Inc.

Stewart, C. G. (1988). Modification of student attitudes toward disabled peers. *Adapted Physical Activity Quarterly, 5,* 44–48.

Stewart, C. G. (1990). Effects of practica type in preservice adapted physical education curriculum on attitudes toward disabled populations. *Journal of Teaching in Physical Education, 10,* 76–83.

Summers, J. A., Hoffman, L., Marquis, J., Turnbull, A. P., Poston, D., & Nelson, L. G. L. (2004). Measuring the quality of family-professional partnerships in special education services. *Exceptional Children, 72,* 65–82.

Tew, B. J., Payne, H., & Lawrence, K. M. (1974). Must a family with a handicapped child be a handicapped family? *Developmental Medicine and Child Neurology, 16,* 95–98.

Tripp, A. (1988). Comparison of attitudes of regular and adapted physical educators toward disabled individuals. *Perceptual and Motor Skills, 66,* 425–426.

Turnbull, A. P., & Brotherson, J. J. (1984). *Assisting parents in future planning.* Papers presented at the CEC 62nd Annual Conference, Washington, DC.

Wang, M., Mannan, H., Poston, D., Turnbull, A. P., & Summers, J. A. 2004. Parent's perceptions of advocacy activities and their impact on family quality of life. *Research and Practice for Persons with Severe Disabilities, 29*(2), 144–155.

Zuk, G. H. (1962). The cultural dilemma and spiritual crisis of the family with a handicapped child. *Exceptional Children, 28*(8), 405–408.

Managing the Learning Environment

The chapters in this section are concerned with the practical aspects of providing a good physical education program for students with disabilities. Ideas are suggested for effective planning and operation of the program and for instructional and evaluative procedures that foster motor learning.

OBJECTIVES

The section is designed to help the reader to:
- Organize and provide special physical education services that emphasize desirable instructional and placement practices consistent with federal regulations.
- Utilize effective and contemporary instructional methods in the delivery of appropriate physical education services to students with disabilities.
- Analyze screening instruments and evaluation tools to determine their appropriateness for use with special populations.
- Recognize the various assistive devices used by individuals with disabilities and the effect these devices may have on the instructional program.

CHAPTER 5

Teaching Special Physical Education

CHAPTER OBJECTIVES

After studying this chapter, the reader should be able to:

1 Recognize and appreciate the attributes and professional qualifications of teachers of special physical education.
2 Identify and describe the components of the Individualized Education Program (IEP) and the Individualized Family Service Plan (IFSP).
3 List the persons participating in the IEP/IFSP meeting and the rationale for their inclusion.
4 Discuss the importance of the IEP/IFSP and its relationship to quality education for students with disabilities.
5 Recognize the similarities and differences between the IEP and IFSP.
6 Identify, analyze, and apply selected principles of movement toward the education of students with disabilities.
7 Recognize the value of task analysis, as well as ecological task analysis, as an educational approach in teaching physical education to students with disabilities.
8 Describe the various approaches that can be employed to prevent and alleviate inappropriate behavior.
9 Recognize various medications used by students with disabilities will have effects on motor performance.
10 Compare and contrast various teaching methods and their application to students with disabilities.

No doubt the recent reauthorization of the Individuals with Disabilities Education Act of 1997 (IDEA '97), now referred to as the Individuals with Disabilities Education Improvement Act of 2004 (IDEA, 2004), will impact the delivery of special physical education. A review of IDEA 2004 from the Council for Exceptional Children (CEC) indicates that physical education remains a part of special education. Therefore, the spirit of the law is that if children and youth with disabilities need special modifications, adaptations, and placement considerations for success in physical education, then they should have access to them. It is important to retain the spirit of the law in this transition from the last reauthorization to the current one. For it is in this spirit that physical educators and special education teams can provide services to families who want the best education for their child with special needs. Since 1975 when the authors first began working in special education, special physical educators have been advocates for those with special needs. Federal laws such as IDEA develop through litigation, which means that the law's full interpretation is, at some level, defined by the lawsuits that followed. Many parents and professionals have advocated for important provisions in the law. Now we enter a new era in carrying forth the mandates as well as the spirit of education for individuals with disabilities.

It is the function of the teacher to provide a positive learning environment. As a consequence, certain changes occur in the student. In physical education the most obvious changes will undoubtedly be the improvement of motor skills and a higher level of physical fitness. This will be evident not only in the success with which the students participate in games and physical education activities but also in general movement pattern improvement. Another desirable change that will occur, but that is likely to be less obvious to an untrained observer, is the student's increased understanding and appreciation of his or her personal abilities and attributes. This manifests itself in an improved attitude toward self and toward others. For many individuals with disabilities, success in physical activity can be the first step toward better adjustment and the development of more wholesome personality traits. In order to provide the kind of learning situation that makes these desired results possible, the teacher needs both knowledge and training as well as certain special qualities of character and personality. Because of the specific challenges that a physical or mental disability creates for an individual, a teacher of students with disabilities must possess certain attributes and knowledge. Due to the increased inclusive philosophy of school districts, there is a growing use of the consultative model in the delivery of physical education services to children and youth with disabilities.

It is precisely this last point that has caused a great deal of frustration in today's public schools. Like teachers in other fields, general physical education teachers often feel inadequate when faced with the prospect of teaching students with disabilities. Although this is an understandable response, it is one that is perhaps too readily accepted. Students with disabilities, as was stressed in chapter 4, are more similar to than different from those without disabilities. Therefore, many of the basic techniques that all teachers of physical education use can be applied successfully in teaching the special population. The purpose of this chapter is to review and reinforce some of the educational concepts that apply to all students and to highlight, where necessary, additional or new skills that teachers will find helpful in working with individuals with disabilities, particularly those students who have severe disabilities.

stabilizing influence, must represent to the students the ultimate in successful adjustment. A teacher who is unable to resolve personal psychological problems is not likely to be able to assist students in solving their problems. Behavior on the part of a teacher that is particularly immature may even contribute to the maladjustment of students, rather than help them make satisfactory adjustments to their disability.

Patience and a sense of humor are indispensable qualities in any good teacher. Those who work with students with disabilities need to be endowed with a generous portion of each, for progress often proceeds very, very slowly. When the results of long hours of work do manifest themselves, however, they are extremely rewarding to the student and to the teacher. Equally important is the quality of sensitivity. This entails a recognition of the individual with a disability as a person, one who has special needs but not necessarily one who is special. People with disabilities appreciate efforts to help them learn but they also wish to be independent, self-sufficient, and, to the greatest extent possible, "normal." The special physical education teacher needs to be sensitive to this desire and respond to it by providing a quality program without fanfare or unnecessary focusing of attention on the student with a disability.

Creativity is yet another desirable quality in the teacher of those who deviate from the norm, for it may be necessary for the instructor to improvise equipment as well as techniques for performing skills. When facilities and equipment for the teaching of adapted activities are limited, the imaginative teacher adjusts and modifies the available facilities and equipment to fit the requirements of the program. The creative teacher meets the challenge of an unusual handicapping condition by devising suitable adaptations of the activities to meet the needs of the particular individual. Moreover, the teacher who is imaginative and creative is far better able to encourage and promote creativity in those whom he or she teaches. Creativity can be so easily stifled

Attributes of the Teacher of Special Physical Education

Perhaps the single most important attribute the teacher of students with disabilities can possess is emotional maturity. Emotional maturity is the ability to solve problems and adjust to the circumstances without undue emotional involvement. The teacher of the disabled must be a

Teacher Attributes

- Emotional maturity
- Stabilizing influence
- Patience
- Sense of humor
- Sensitivity
- Creativity
- Organized
- Positive attitude

in physical education because of the tendency to enforce conformity in order to impress patterns in skill performance upon children.

Organizational ability is essential in the good physical education teacher. Regardless of the method of teaching used, carefully planned class procedures and well-organized class activities are time and energy savers. They make achievement of the desired goal easier and more certain. Class instruction left entirely, or even partially, to chance results in wasted time and motion, in poor learning, and in poor teaching.

A positive attitude toward students with disabilities is an indispensable teacher attribute. The teacher must be sensitive and empathetic but not overly solicitous. Students who are disabled deserve equal treatment and modifications, where appropriate, in instruction, activity, and equipment. Most students and their parents do not seek or expect special treatment beyond that which is necessary to create an equitable learning experience.

Unfortunately this is apparently not well understood by many teachers of physical education. Recent studies suggest that the attitude of physical education teachers toward those with disabilities is not positive. Some researchers have suggested that this may be due to insufficient coursework and field experience focusing on the needs of students with disabilities. Rizzo (1984) found that physical education teachers were more positive in their attitude toward teaching those with mental retardation than physical disabilities. He also suggested that the attitude of physical education teachers was less positive as the grade level advanced, with high school teachers less favorable in their attitudes toward teaching students with disabilities than elementary or intermediate teachers. Through additional studies, Rizzo and Vispoel (1991) have also found that physical education teachers have more favorable attitudes toward teaching students with learning disabilities in mainstreamed physical education classes in contrast to students with behavior disorders or mental retardation. A particularly encouraging finding of Rizzo's work is that a teacher's perception of competence has much to do with the teacher's attitude toward teaching individuals with disabilities. This suggests, therefore, that the attitude of teachers toward students with disabilities can be improved if provided coursework and structured practicum experiences.

It is hoped that coursework; the media; printed material, including this text; and the significant achievements of individuals with disabilities will help future generations of physical educators to recognize, appreciate, and accept the challenges and rewards associated with teaching students with disabilities. Most educators who have taught those with disabilities recognize that the energy expended is returned many times over.

Professional Qualifications of the Teacher of Special Physical Education

Regarding the qualifications a teacher needs in order to instruct adapted activities, it should be said that the background subject areas are essentially the same as those for physical education. A thorough knowledge of sport and game skills is very important, as is a sound understanding of the nature of the human body and its response to exercise. Training in methods of teaching and the psychology of learning, including motor learning, is very necessary.

In addition to knowledge pertaining to physical education generally, the teacher should acquire some specific information about the causes, nature, and psychological implications of the various disabilities. It is necessary to understand the effects of exercise upon these conditions and how sports and games may be utilized to improve the social and emotional as well as the physical well-being of individuals with disabilities. The teacher must also have a basic knowledge of emergency treatment of minor injuries and, most particularly, the practices that are applicable to certain disabilities, such as the emergency care to be administered to an individual experiencing a seizure or insulin shock.

In recent years, some states have developed standards and certification procedures for teachers of adapted physical education. Although there is not universal agreement among state education officials, administrators, and professionals about the number of hours and courses that should be required for a certificate, there is a growing interest in identifying the competencies that these professionals should possess.

It is clear that simply selecting more experienced teachers to serve as the teachers of students with disabilities will not guarantee success. Vogler, Vander, Mars, Cusimano, and Darst (1992) report that there is no reason to believe that mainstreamed students will benefit more in physical education from experienced as contrasted to novice teachers. Their work suggests that teachers need specific expertise or experience to be successful in providing appropriate physical education programs for students with disabilities. For this and many other reasons, the Physical Activity Council of the American Alliance for Health, Physical Education, Recreation, and Dance (AAHPERD) developed guidelines identifying the competencies that representatives of this organization believe are important. The competencies identified are, for the most part, limited to those with direct relationship to teaching students with disabilities in regular physical education classes or those that would serve as the basic foundation for the more specialized competencies of the adapted physical education specialist. A modified list of competencies identified by AAHPERD for both the generalist and the specialist is presented in table 5.1.

Dempsey (1987) surveyed selected higher-education professors and specialists in adapted physical education to rate the competencies as to their importance. The study was designed to validate the competencies and to compare the observations of knowledgeable university professors to those of public school specialists in adapted physical education. Both groups were in agreement that the competencies were appropriate. In addition, the two groups were comparable in their overall ratings of each of the competency statements. While differences were noted, there was general consensus with both groups that the competencies were appropriate for the training of specialists in adapted physical education.

TABLE 5.1 Competencies for the Generalist in Physical Education and the Specialist in Special Physical Education*

Competency	Generalist	Specialist
1.0 Biological Foundations		
1.1 Kinesiology	Demonstrate understanding of functional anatomy and its relationship to individuals with or without disabilities.	Demonstrate proficiency in evaluating and analyzing motor performance in terms of motor dysfunction and in applying biomechanical principles that affect motor functioning to posture and to neurological, muscular, and other specific health needs.
1.2 Physiology of Exercise	Demonstrate ability to design and conduct physical education programs that adhere to sound physiological principles.	Demonstrate ability to design and conduct physical education programs for individuals with disabilities that adhere to sound physiological principles.
1.3 Physiology and Motor Functioning	Demonstrate understanding of anatomical and physiological deviation and the effects such deviations have on motor performance.	Demonstrate the ability to apply an understanding of physiological motor characteristics for individuals with physical, mental, sensory, neurological, and other specific health needs to programs designed to improve the motor performances of these individuals with disabilities.
2.0 Sociological Foundations		
2.1 Sport, Dance, Play	Demonstrate understanding of the ethnic, social, and cultural aspects of sport, dance, and play and the importance of these in the lives of all, including the disabled.	Demonstrate the ability to analyze the significance of sport, dance, and play in the lives of individuals with disabilities.
2.2 Cooperative/Competitive Activities	Demonstrate understanding of the potential of cooperative/competitive activities for human interaction and social behavior and knowledge of organizations that conduct appropriate activities for the disabled.	Demonstrate ability to apply understanding of the potential for human interaction and social behavior occurring in cooperative/competitive activities for individuals with disabilities; cooperate with organizations that conduct adapted sport, dance, and play programs for individuals with disabilities.

*Adapted from a statement prepared by the American Alliance for Health, Physical Education, Recreation, and Dance, 1980.   *Continued.*

TABLE 5.1   Competencies for the Generalist in Physical Education and the Specialist in Special Physical Education (*continued*)

Competency	Generalist	Specialist
2.3 Social Development	Demonstrate understanding of social learnings involved in experiencing human movement and its effects on perception, motivation, and personality for individuals with and without disabilities.	Demonstrate ability to apply understanding of the potential that sport, dance, and play provide for social interactions among individuals with and without disabilities.
3.0 Psychological Foundations		
3.1 Human Growth and Development	Demonstrate understanding of human growth and development, including how deviation in normal growth and development can result in disabilities and atypical motor development.	Demonstrate ability to apply understanding of deviations in human growth and development and atypical motor development to assist individuals with physical, mental, sensory, neurological, and other specific health needs.
3.2 Motor Learning	Demonstrate proficiency in applying principles of motor learning to teaching and learning motor skills.	Demonstrate ability to apply principles of motor learning, including motivation techniques, to the teaching and learning of motor skills by individuals with disabilities.
3.3 Self-Concept and Personality Development	Demonstrate ability to help students with and without disabilities develop positive self-concepts and overcome attitudinal barriers that can affect interpersonal relationships and development of positive self-concepts.	Demonstrate ability to apply skills and techniques in the teaching of physical and motor skills to assist individuals with disabilities to overcome attitudinal barriers that can affect interpersonal relationships and development of positive self-concepts.
3.4 Management of Behavior	Demonstrate an understanding of principles of motivation as they affect human behavior and promote motor performance and apply various methods for developing appropriate student behavior.	Demonstrate ability to apply appropriate techniques for managing behavior, including techniques of motivation to enhance acceptable behavior and promote motor performance.
4.0 Historical and Philosophical Foundations		
4.1 Historical Development	Demonstrate understanding of the historical development of physical education, including the role and significance of professional organizations in the development of professional standards and ethics.	Demonstrate understanding of the historical development of adapted physical education, including the role and significance of professional and voluntary organizations in the development of professional standards and ethics related to adapted physical education.
4.2 Philosophical Development	Demonstrate understanding of the philosophies of physical education, current issues, and emerging trends in physical education and identify ways that individuals realize and express their individualities and uniquenesses through physical education, sport, dance, and play.	Demonstrate understanding of the philosophies of adapted physical education, current issues, and trends in adapted physical education and identify ways individuals with disabilities realize and express their individualities and uniquenesses through physical education, sport, dance, and play programs.

Continued.

TABLE 5.1   Competencies for the Generalist in Physical Education and the Specialist in Special Physical Education (*continued*)

Competency	Generalist	Specialist
5.0 Assessment and Evaluation		
5.1 Program Goals and Objectives	Demonstrate understanding of goals and objectives of physical education, including programs and activities for individuals with disabilities.	Demonstrate ability to develop instructional objectives that lead to fulfillment of physical education goals in psychomotor, affective, and cognitive domains by individuals with disabilities.
5.2 Screening and Assessment	Demonstrate ability to select, construct, and administer various assessment instruments for measuring physical and motor performance.	Demonstrate proficiency in using appropriate instruments to assess and interpret the motor performances of students with disabilities.
5.3 Evaluation	Demonstrate proficiency in using appropriate evaluative procedures to determine student progress.	Demonstrate proficiency in applying appropriate instruments and evaluative procedures to determine student progress in adapted physical education.
6.0 Curriculum Planning, Organization, and Implementation		
6.1 Program Planning	Demonstrate ability to plan instructional programs that emphasize physical and motor fitness development.	Demonstrate ability to plan individual physical education programs that are adapted to individual student needs based on goals and objectives established by an interdisciplinary team.
6.2 Individual Instruction	Demonstrate ability to apply strategies for individualized instruction in regular physical education settings based on student's current level of performance.	Demonstrate ability to implement appropriate physical education programs for individuals with disabilities based on each student's current level of performance using appropriate strategies, including task-analysis techniques.
6.3 Program Implementation	Demonstrate understanding of role and significance of physical educators as members of interdisciplinary teams.	Demonstrate ability to function effectively as a member of an interdisciplinary team using appropriate techniques for facilitating interdisciplinary communication among all persons working with individuals who are disabled.
6.4 Safety Considerations	Demonstrate knowledge of specific safety considerations for individuals with disabilities as they participate in physical education, sport, dance, and play activities.	Demonstrate understanding of scientific bases for specifically contraindicated exercises and activities, including transfer techniques for individuals with disabilities.
6.5 Health Considerations	Demonstrate knowledge of special health considerations when individuals with disabilities participate in physical education, sport, dance, and play activities.	Demonstrate understanding of the effects of medication, fatigue, illness, posture, and nutrition on the mental, physical, and motor performances of individuals with disabilities.

Suphawibul (1990), in a study similar to that of Dempsey's, using a sophisticated culturally sensitive translation of the competencies, found that Thai physical educators, both university adapted physical educators and practicing teachers, agreed that the AAHPERD competencies were appropriate for Thailand.

A review of table 5.1 indicates that the primary difference between the competency level of the general physical education teacher (generalist) and that of the special physical educator (specialist) is one of degree. Obviously both groups are expected to be knowledgeable with respect to the physical education needs of individuals with disabilities and receptive to providing needed services. It is recognized, however, that the generalist is not as knowledgeable about disabilities nor as experienced in working with those with disabilities. There also is a difference in the role of the generalist and specialist. Whereas the regular physical educator should be competent to teach those with mild and moderate disabilities, the special physical educator has primary responsibility for structuring and ensuring that those with severe disabilities receive appropriate instruction in physical education. In addition, the special physical educator frequently is asked to provide indirect service to the student with disabilities by serving as a consultant to other physical education teachers. In this latter role, the special physical educator frequently serves as a member of the school system's special education staff, performing many services such as assessing the motor and physical fitness levels of students with disabilities, assisting with the writing of the Individualized Education Program (IEP), recommending placement options, providing teaching suggestions to physical educators, recruiting and training volunteers, and informing other teachers about the motor and physical fitness needs of the disabled.

The precise role of the special physical educator is dependent upon many factors, including the size of the school system, the number and type of special students, and the extent to which the regular physical educators are available and prepared to provide programs for students with special needs. A schematic of the role relationship responsibility between the general and special physical educator is presented in figure 5.1. Placement of the Xs in figure 5.1 denotes who has primary responsibility for the specific function. An X placed somewhere between the general physical educator and special physical educator emphasizes that many responsibilities are shared, with one party assuming a greater degree of responsibility. The functions and responsibilities of both professional groups are important in providing appropriate physical education services to the special student.

Figure 5.1   Schematic of the shared responsibilities of special and general physical educators of students with disabilities.

Degree of Responsibility for Various Special Physical Education Functions		
FUNCTIONS	**General Physical Educator**	**Special Physical Educator**
Screen	X	
Assess		X
Write IEPs/IFSPs	X	
Recommend Placement	X	
Recruit Volunteers	X	
Train Volunteers		X
Serve on Multidisciplinary Team	X	
Inservice Teachers		X
Implement Program / Mildly Handicapped	X	
Implement Program / Moderately Handicapped	X	
Implement Program / Severely Handicapped		X
Consult with Teachers		X

The most ambitious effort to date to identify the skills needed by professionals to be qualified to deliver special physical education services is the National Standards Project directed by Luke E. Kelly. This project, funded by the Office of Special Education and Rehabilitative Service, is designed to identify the content that specialists in adapted physical education should possess to teach students with disabilities. The work thus far has led to the identification of a knowledge base which is grouped into fifteen content areas or standards (Kelly, 1995). The standards include:

Human Development
Motor Behavior
Exercise Science
Measurement and Evaluation
History and Philosophy
Unique Attributes of Learners
Curriculum Theory and Development
Assessment
Instructional Design and Planning
Teaching
Consultation and Staff Development
Program Evaluation
Continuing Education
Ethics
Communication

The ultimate goal of the National Standards Project is to create a valid examination that can be taken by professionals to demonstrate they possess the knowledge to be effective as practitioners. Given the wide support for the project from both university personnel and physical education teachers, it is probable that the National Standards Project will enhance the overall quality of services provided to individuals with disabilities.

Developing Individualized Education Programs (IEPs)

One of the significant features of IDEA '97 and IDEA 2004 is the requirement that an Individualized Education Program (IEP) be developed for each student with disabilities. Some people refer to this as the "plan" for the student, hence, the Individualized Education Plan (also known as IEP). There are two main parts of the IEP requirement, as described in federal law and the regulations that accompany this law:

1. the IEP meeting(s), at which parents and school personnel jointly make decisions about a child's educational program, and

2. the IEP document itself, which is a written record of the decisions reached at the meetings.

The original federal educational law, The Education of All Handicapped Children Act of 1975 (PL 94-142), has been reauthorized over the years. Regarding physical education, the reauthorizations have never lost the reality that physical education is an academic area under special education. Therefore, reference is sometimes made to PL 94-142 when discussing the law and its requirements. It is considered "the law" after which reauthorizations have occurred.

Purposes of the IEP

The IEP process is designed to accommodate a number of important functions. Some of these, as identified by the federal government, are indicated in the following paragraphs (Federal Register: Part XII, January 14, 1981, p. 5460).

The IEP meeting serves as a communication vehicle between parents and school personnel, thus allowing them as equal participants to jointly decide the student's educational needs and to identify the necessary special education and related services. The IEP meeting also helps to resolve potential differences between parents and school officials concerning the educational programs as well as anticipated outcomes.

A practical purpose of the IEP is to identify in writing the resources necessary to enable the student to benefit from the educational program that has been developed. Furthermore, the IEP is a management tool that is used to ensure that each student with a disability is provided special education and related services appropriate to the student's special learning needs.

The IEP also may be used as a compliance or monitoring device. Local school personnel as well as State Department of Education officials can review individual IEPs to determine whether a student is receiving the educational program agreed to by the parents and the school. An evaluation of the student's progress toward meeting the stated educational goals and objectives is also possible by periodically examining the IEP.

IEP Team Members

Although the exact composition of the IEP team will vary from one school system to the next, IDEA '97 specified that certain participants must be included in all IEP discussions. School officials have been responsible for ensuring that the following participants are present at the IEP meeting. IDEA 2004 regulations have changed some of the following. Implementation of the regulations should be referred to by school district.

1. **A representative of the public agency, other than the child's teacher, who is qualified to provide, or supervise**

the provision of, special education. Various individuals, including building principals, counselors, and special education administrators, normally are selected to fulfill this role. The key factor is that the person selected must be thoroughly familiar with the local school's special education program, and federal and state law.

2. **The child's teacher.** Obviously, the person selected to fill this role is the teacher who has the most contact with the student. IDEA '97 specified that the child's regular education teacher must be present. Therefore, those present can be the regular classroom teacher, a special educator, or a specialist such as a speech therapist or physical educator. Of primary importance is that the person selected to fill this role cannot also serve as the school's representative to the team, as identified in point 1.

3. **One or both of the child's parents.** As discussed earlier, one of the basic premises of IDEA '97 and IDEA 2004 is that parent input into the IEP plan is considered extremely important. For this reason, school systems should take whatever steps are necessary to ensure that parents are involved in the IEP deliberations. This means scheduling the meeting at a time convenient for parents as well as informing parents of their right to disagree with the recommended Individualized Education Program.

    Some parents also may require the assistance of an interpreter if they are deaf or their native language is one other than English. Regardless of the provisions made to solicit parent input, a small percentage of parents will elect not to become involved in the IEP process. In these cases, the IEP meeting may still be held but school officials should be prepared to document, if asked, their attempts to solicit parent input. In some cases the State Department of Education will appoint surrogate parents for students living in state institutions whose parents are deceased, unknown, or express no interest in their child's welfare.

4. **The child, where appropriate.** Students with disabilities, like their nondisabled peers, frequently have helpful comments to make about the educational experiences that are to be provided for them. It is for this reason IDEA '97 emphasized the importance of student input. The final decision as to whether the student will participate as a member of the IEP team rests with the parents, except in cases where the student is of majority age. IDEA 2004 continues this focus.

5. **Other individuals, at the discretion of the parents or agency.** This last category for membership on the IEP team simply indicates that both the local school and the parents have the right to invite others to participate as members of the IEP team. For the school this means that on occasion it may be desirable to have additional school personnel involved in the IEP deliberations. Likewise, parents may feel the need to be accompanied by a relative or friend who is more knowledgeable about education and its relationship to their student. In some instances, parents have also felt it necessary to be accompanied by legal representation. The important point is that both the parents and the school may invite others to participate without asking the other party's permission.

The members identified previously are charged with the responsibility of developing an appropriate educational program for each special student. To accomplish this task requires that the team meet at least annually and more frequently if necessary. **Because physical education is an integral part of special education, the IEP team must also decide on the type of physical education program for the student.** This is a critical decision that, if not handled properly, can result in inappropriate physical education services for the special education student. Some of the potential difficulty arises because of the composition of the team and the absence of a person knowledgeable about the area of physical education. Some school systems have resolved this problem by inviting a representative of physical education to serve on the IEP team, particularly for the student with more severe disabilities. Other school systems, desiring to keep the official IEP team small, have used pre-IEP meetings to obtain the input of specialists such as physical educators. Either system seems to work well. **The important point is that the IEP team makes critical decisions that affect the quality of physical education services that are eventually implemented.**

Content of the IEP

The IEP document is an important source of information that specifies the special education programs and services to be provided the student. Many districts have electronic IEPs. Each IEP must include the following information:

1. A statement of the child's educational performance;
2. A statement of annual goals. IDEA 2004 only requires statements of the goals. In the past the IEP had to indicate short-term instructional objectives but IDEA 2004 does not require this. Currently school districts will chose whether or not to have objectives;
3. A statement of the specific special education and related services to be provided to the child and the extent to which the child will be able to participate in general educational programs;
4. The projected dates for initiation of services and the anticipated duration of the services;
5. Appropriate objective criteria and evaluation procedures and schedules for determining, on at least an annual basis, whether the short-term instructional objectives are being achieved; and
6. A statement of the needed transition services for students beginning *no later* than age sixteen and annually

thereafter (and when determined appropriate for the individual, beginning at age fourteen or younger), including, when appropriate, a statement of the interagency responsibilities or linkages (or both) before the student leaves the school setting.

The reauthorization of IDEA as IDEA 2004 is a response to the need to reduce paperwork generated by the IEP. Therefore, the new law emphasizes that IEPs will be generated and managed using technology. In many school districts, the use of computer software programs to generate and monitor IEPs is already being implemented. In the future, there will be a stronger emphasis on this management technique.

Physical Education and the IEP

A careful analysis of the following elements is critical to the development of a meaningful IEP. Information on physical education must be included in the student's IEP. In the following paragraphs, information on physical education and its relationship to the content of the IEP are discussed.

Present Level of Educational Performance (PLEP)

"Present level of educational performance," as the title implies, simply means those physical education skills the student presently possesses. To ascertain this information requires that an appropriate evaluation with resulting assessment be conducted to determine the student's physical and motor fitness levels. Without this information the school representatives will be at a disadvantage at the IEP meeting when called upon to make recommendations concerning the student's special physical education needs.

Detailed information concerning evaluation and the resulting assessment recommendations is outlined in chapter 6. To summarize, physical educators must be aware of federal mandates on evaluation as well as the state's laws regarding eligibility criteria. Assessment information about the special student's motor ability may be derived from a variety of sources, including standardized and nonstandardized testing (formal and informal measures). Some of these are as follows:

School Records

What physical education skills has the student previously been taught? How did the student do? Were any behavior problems observed? Did the student attend class on time? Were dressing and undressing before and after class a positive or problem area? Information such as this, which should be easily obtained from school records, is very helpful to the IEP team.

Norm-Referenced Tests

Comparing the performance of a student to the performances of a group of similar individuals is referred to as a norm-referenced comparison. Norm-referenced tests can help the teacher to determine the student's present level of performance, but they do little to identify an acceptable criterion level of performance.

Criterion-Referenced Tests

This type of test helps the IEP team to determine how a student's performance compares to a defined standard. Normally, the utilization of this approach requires the availability of a curriculum that is sequenced and in which tasks such as throwing a ball are broken down into smaller steps. An excellent example of this approach is the *I CAN* program, a set of physical education curricular materials that promote the concept of systematic teaching based on a criterion-referenced assessment procedure.

The use of both norm-referenced and criterion-referenced tests is discussed more fully in chapter 6.

Observations

Physical educators may find it necessary from time to time to use a readily available assessment tool, and their own powers of observation, to document the need for special physical education services. Not all youngsters can be effectively evaluated by norm- or even criterion-referenced assessment procedures. Students with cerebral palsy, orthopedic impairments, and multiple disabilities are examples of the types of special populations that may require teachers to rely primarily on their observational skills to assess performance levels. Teachers who may be apprehensive about their ability to observe accurately can videotape examples of the student's movement skills to share with others at the IEP meeting. Such a procedure frequently provides valuable information to assist the rest of the team to focus on the individual's physical education needs.

The assessment process is the seed from which the Individualized Education Program develops. Without accurate and adequate information, conclusions may be drawn that will result in inappropriate goals and objectives as well as inappropriate program placement. Additional information on evaluation procedures will be presented in chapter 6.

Goals and Objectives

Under IDEA 2004 the goals will become the guideposts for determining whether the student with a disability is benefiting from the educational program developed by the IEP team. Goals provide direction and serve as a means to communicate to the child and members of the team that a particular area such as cardiorespiratory endurance needs work. States determine the manner in which the goals and, in the past, objectives are written. The following are examples of physical education goals, although some states may require different content:

Joe will improve his overhand throw from immature to mature.

Mary will improve her physical fitness performance on the 600-yard walk-run test.

Matthew will learn to skip.

A more experienced physical educator can see overall areas where a student with a disability needs goals in physical education, and can write goal statements to that effect. In other cases, experience and personal preference, or district guidelines, influence goal statements that are greater in number and seem to be written as general objectives. Obviously, computerized goal statements will ease the burden of creating these goals. Although a child with a disability is unique, despite a common category of disability, sometimes the overall goal/need for that child can be generalized and implemented. For example, as is described in chapter 17, individuals with disabilities often have lower fitness levels than their nondisabled peers. The Brockport Physical Fitness Test (BPFT) has a computer-generated list of goals and objectives categorized by disability area.

In the past, for each of these goals, objectives were developed that define more precisely the behaviors that will be taught to the student. Essentially, each objective should specify the behavior, the conditions under which the behavior is to be performed, and the level of criteria accepted as appropriate. Using the first goal, objectives for teaching Joe the overhand throw, stated in behavioral terms, might include:

1. Using a tennis ball, Joe will throw the ball overhand and hit a four-foot by four-foot target ten feet away eight out of ten times;
2. Using a tennis ball, Joe will throw the ball overhand and hit a four-foot by four-foot target twenty feet away eight out of ten times;
3. Using a tennis ball, Joe will throw the ball overhand and hit a two-foot by two-foot target ten feet away eight out of ten times;
4. Using a tennis ball, Joe will throw the ball overhand and hit a two-foot by two-foot target twenty-five feet away eight out of ten times.

Depending on the particular student, the objectives might vary in a number of ways such as in the size of target or distance to target, as well as in the accuracy expected. For some students, the objective might focus simply on the throwing pattern.

In the past, one need only develop a sufficient number of objectives for each goal to indicate to other members of the team the process and level of behavior deemed appropriate. For each objective, a projected date for reaching the specified criterion must be provided. It remains to be seen how the use of objectives will be lerpreted by states and school districts under IDEA 2004. Nonetheless, objectives

are a systematic method for determining how the student can reach a specified goal.

Special Education and Related Services

Under IDEA 2004 physical education is identified as a special education service. The primary concern in this section is, therefore, devoted to the type of physical education program to be provided. Specifically, the question of whether the student with a disability requires special physical education must be discussed. If the student's present level of educational performance, including motor, cognitive, and affective, is acceptable, the student is placed in the general physical education program and expected to learn at a rate equivalent to that of other nondisabled peers. Sometimes the placement of students is such that they can benefit from both a general and specialized physical education setting. Requests for special assistance do not eliminate the possibility of placing the student in the general physical education class. Some individuals, for example, may simply need the assistance of an aide or volunteer. Of course, students with more severe disabilities may require help that can best be met in a special physical education experience. If so, services of this nature must be provided.

Physical educators will need to utilize the services of other related professionals to best fulfill the physical education needs of some students. Related services include, but are not limited to, the following:

speech therapy
physical therapy
occupational therapy
work experience
medical service
social services
transportation
recreation

Obviously, physical educators and the students they teach would benefit from the assistance of many of the professionals identified here. For instance, many individuals with Down syndrome experience congenital cardiovascular system problems; engaging such children in active movement skills without the consultation and advice of a physician would be inappropriate.

Educators should be cautioned to remember, however, that related services are *related* and should not be used to supplant physical education programs. Physical therapy, for instance, is a valuable and necessary service for many students with disabilities. However, justifying physical therapy as a replacement for a physical education program places too much emphasis on the commonality of the shared word "physical" and does a disservice to professionals in physical therapy and physical education, as well as to the student who can benefit from both programs.

Time Line for Service

The following is written from IDEA '97 with the understanding that IDEA 2004 will be interpreted further regarding student goals. Under IDEA '97, each IEP is normally written to cover a time period of up to twelve months. For each goal and objective, a time line is established that provides a general estimate of when the student should achieve a particular goal. It is generally recognized that predicting when a "milestone" is to be reached is very difficult. Some students, for instance, reach the objectives much sooner than expected, whereas others achieve few, if any, of the stated objectives. When the teacher sees unusual deviations from the projected time line, it is best to request that the school personnel call for an IEP meeting to identify, with parent consultation, new goals and objectives or more realistic time lines for those previously developed.

Evaluation Procedures

The Individualized Education Program (IEP) must include a plan that specifies the procedure to be used to evaluate the student's progress. This review must be done at least annually. Many school systems have responded to this requirement by indicating the extent to which the student has achieved the goals and objectives specified in the IEP. It should be emphasized, however, that the IEP is not a performance contract that imposes liability on a teacher or public agency if a student does not meet the IEP objectives. According to the Rules and Regulations for Public Law 94-142, a stipulation that has continued with the reauthorization as IDEA 2004 is that, "While the agency must provide special education and related services in accordance with each handicapped child's IEP, the Act does not require that the agency, the teacher, or other persons be held accountable if the child does not achieve the growth projected in the written statement" (1981).

Transition Services

Over the years, the concept of transition services was added into the law when amended since PL 94-142. Transition services address the needs of students moving from early intervention programs into preschool programs, as well as those students moving out of the school program and into the community. Specifically, IDEA '97 provided a definition of transition services and added transition services to students' IEPs, and in the case of early intervention, to the IFSP. Specifically, the term "transition services" means a coordinated set of activities for a student, which promotes movement

from one program area to another. For older students, the transition from school to postschool activities includes postsecondary education, vocational training, integrated employment, continuing and adult education, adult services, independent living, or community participation. The goal, of course, is to ensure that students and other community resources are fully integrated to the extent that students with disabilities can move easily from the school setting to other environments, including those used for various recreational pursuits. Physical educators, thus, are expected to be cognizant of procedures for ensuring that skills and activities learned in the school setting can be generalized easily and successfully into other settings (e.g., community fitness centers, roller skating rinks, swimming pools, etc.).

IDEA also made it clear that cooperating and participating agencies are responsible for providing services identified within the IEP. Specifically, the law states that where a participating agency, other than the educational agency, fails to provide agreed upon services, the educational agency shall reconvene the IEP team to identify alternative strategies to meet the transition objectives. This, of course, places the school in a unique position to not only work cooperatively with participating agencies, but also to monitor the quality of their services. Transition services remain in IDEA 2004.

Individualized Family Service Plan

Closely related to the IEP is the Individualized Family Service Plan (IFSP) mandated by the Education of the Handicapped Act Amendments of 1986. The law has been amended to include both infants and toddlers, as well as preschool children. One of the critical aspects of IDEA has been the IFSP for infants and toddlers. The major components of the IFSP include:

1. A statement of the child's present levels of development (cognitive, motor, speech/language, psychosocial, and self-help);
2. A statement of the family's strengths and needs relating to enhancing the child's development;
3. A statement of major outcomes expected to be achieved for the child and family;
4. The criteria, procedures, and timelines for determining progress;
5. The specific early intervention services necessary to meet the unique needs of the child and family including the method, frequency, and intensity of service; and
6. The projected dates for the initiation of services and expected duration.

Differences Between IEP and IFSP

1. IFSP is family centered.
2. IFSP is designed for smooth transition for infants to school at age three.

While it is clear that there are many similarities between the IEP and IFSP, there are also some differences. First, the IFSP is family-centered with as much commitment and emphasis placed on the family as the individual child. As Deal, Dunst, and Trivett (1989) stated, "Major emphasis is placed on both enabling and empowering families. Enabling families means creating opportunities for family members to become more competent and self-sustaining with respect to their abilities to mobilize their social networks, to get needs met and attain desired goals. . . . Empowering families means carrying out interventions in a manner in which family members acquire a sense of control over their own development course as a result of their effort to meet needs" (p. 33). Second, the IFSP is designed to make certain that for the infant (age zero to two) that there is a transition plan to ensure a smooth integration into the school at age three. Additional information about the motor development and activity needs of infants and toddlers will be presented in chapter 15.

Consultation in Physical Education/Physical Activity

In some school districts, physical educators who work with students with disabilities act primarily as consultants. Many physical educators are not trained in consultation. Figure 5.2

Figure 5.2 Stages of the consultation process. (*Sources:* Bergan, 1977, 1995; Bergan & Kratochwill, 1990; Caplan, 1970; Caplan & Caplan, 1999 in Buysee & Wesley, 2005.)

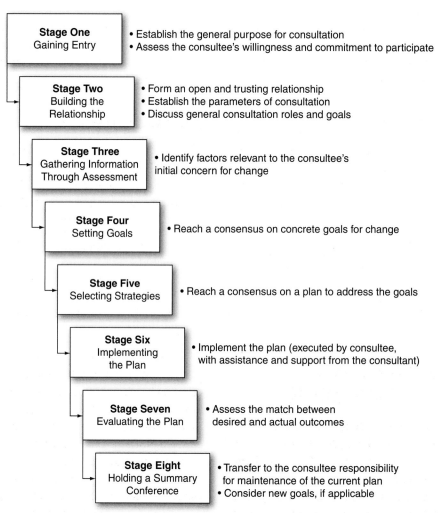

Stage One
Gaining Entry
• Establish the general purpose for consultation
• Assess the consultee's willingness and commitment to participate

Stage Two
Building the Relationship
• Form an open and trusting relationship
• Establish the parameters of consultation
• Discuss general consultation roles and goals

Stage Three
Gathering Information Through Assessment
• Identify factors relevant to the consultee's initial concern for change

Stage Four
Setting Goals
• Reach a consensus on concrete goals for change

Stage Five
Selecting Strategies
• Reach a consensus on a plan to address the goals

Stage Six
Implementing the Plan
• Implement the plan (executed by consultee, with assistance and support from the consultant)

Stage Seven
Evaluating the Plan
• Assess the match between desired and actual outcomes

Stage Eight
Holding a Summary Conference
• Transfer to the consultee responsibility for maintenance of the current plan
• Consider new goals, if applicable

outlines the process for consultation (Buysee & Wesley, 2005). This model can be adapted for different stages in the delivery of special physical education. The consultee here could be a school district, a special education teacher, an aide, a parent, or a general physical educator; in summary, it is anyone who may seek the expertise of a physical education teacher in order to deliver special education services for a student.

Systematic Approaches to Teaching

In recent years, there has been much greater emphasis placed on the systematic analysis of instruction. Much of this is attributed to growing recognition that selected process variables such as the amount of time spent in the academic or instructional environment and the number of opportunities to respond or perform is very important to the success of the learner. Many believe that a measure of the amount of learning time (frequently referred to as academic learning time, ALT) suggests that increases in on-task time leads to educational gain. For students with disabilities, it is clear that the efficient use of instructional time is critical. DePaepe (1985), for instance, found that with the assistance of peer tutors the ALT time in physical education was greatly enhanced. Houston-Wilson et al., (1997) and Webster (1987), too, suggested that peer tutors were effective in increasing the amount of ALT in physical education.

Other investigators have suggested that the frequency with which students have an opportunity to respond (OTR) in physical education may be as important as the amount of on-task instructional time. Houston-Wilson et al., (1997), for instance, found that trained peer tutors were very effective in helping students with developmental disabilities increase their OTR in physical education.

Both ALT-PE and OTR-PE offer excellent methods for assessing important process variables (instructional time and frequency of response) which are vital to achieving desired learning objectives for students with disabilities.

Analyzing and Applying Principles of Movement

In teaching motor skills to those with disabilities, the teacher must understand and develop the ability to analyze the movements made by the student and to apply the mechanical principles of movement to achieve the most effective performance possible for the particular student. Analysis of movement consists of determining which essential parts of the body are involved in a given movement and how these parts relate to each other in the performance of the movement. Knowledge of anatomy and kinesiology is, of course, extremely useful in making an accurate analysis.

Every individual differs from every other anatomically, physiologically and neurologically; therefore, the best way to perform a movement varies, to some extent, for each person. Consequently, the best way for each student to perform a particular skill can be most effectively determined by analyzing his or her movements in order to understand how he or she moves and then, by applying the principles of movement, to discover the most efficient and effective way to utilize the movements in the performance of the skill. This approach recognizes that an individual's movement performance is the product of his uniqueness as a human being, as well as the environment in which the performance takes place and the parameters that are placed on the task. Therefore, individuals with disabilities may have their own unique way of performing a specific movement pattern or skill; this performance may be their optimal way.

Laws of Motion

All movements, including human movements, are regulated by the laws of motion. In human movements, the chief elements are those related to maintaining stability and equilibrium.

Principles of Stability

Achieving stability is important in all action as well as in all stationary positions. The successful performance of such activities as standing, sitting, running, jumping, and bouncing requires some degree of stability. In maintaining stability, the body is governed by certain principles:

1. When the center of gravity is lowered, greater stability is achieved.
2. The larger or wider the base of the support, the greater the stability.
3. When the center of gravity is over the base, stability is greater.

When the body is lowered, as in bending the knees, the center of gravity is lowered, thereby providing more stability. In activities in which force must be received, such as catching a fast ball, greater stability can be created by lowering the body, thereby making it more capable of receiving the force without losing balance. Balance is more easily maintained in a sitting position than standing; hence, one who is on crutches may increase stability by sitting to play some types of games, such as bowling or shuttle badminton, rather than trying to balance with crutches in the erect position.

A larger base allows a greater range of body movement before the center of gravity moves beyond the base to cause the loss of balance. This is particularly evident in walking a narrow beam; maintaining balance in this kind of activity is difficult because the base of support is relatively small. In movement that requires a stable base, spreading the feet creates a larger base. A case in point is when a person balances with a cane; the triangle made by the feet and the cane affords more support as the size of the triangle is increased.

It should be noted that a wide base does not always create the most efficient position. If the stance is so wide that the legs are at an extreme angle to the ground, muscular efficiency is decreased so that, actually, any advantage created for maintaining balance by a wide base is nullified by the decrease in the muscular efficiency of the legs used in maintaining balance.

When the center of gravity is near the center of the base, greater stability is created. Many directions for performing skills include a suggestion to distribute the weight evenly in order to give better balance to the body. Such distribution brings the center of gravity to the center of the base. If the participant must make a quick move or start in a specific direction, he or she leans the body in that direction so that the balance is easily disturbed by the shifting of weight. In starting a race, the body is leaned forward and the center of gravity falls near the front of the base. In running rapidly, the center of gravity falls in front of the base so that, in a sense, the body falls forward and the legs "run up under the body." When slowing from a fast pace, the body is straightened so that the center of gravity is brought back near the center of the base.

Principles of Moving the Body

The movement of the human body or any part of it is governed by these laws of motion:

1. An object at rest will remain at rest, or if in motion will remain in motion at the same speed in a straight line unless acted upon by a force.
2. When a body is acted upon by a force, its resulting change of speed is directly proportional to the force and inversely proportional to the mass.
3. For every action, there is an equal and opposite reaction.

The tendency of the body to remain either stationary or in motion is known as inertia. The more the object weighs, the more force is required to overcome its inertia. Also, the faster the movement of the object, the greater the difficulty in overcoming its inertia. In initiating movement, the inertia is overcome by use of force. Once an object is moving, less force is required to keep it moving. In propelling a wheelchair, for example, less energy is required to push it after it is moving than to bring it into motion. The same is true of the body. An individual attempting to move from a sitting position to a standing position will find it much easier to complete the movement entirely than to stop halfway and then continue rising.

If unequal forces are applied to two objects of equal mass, the object to which the greater force is applied will move at a greater speed. If equal forces are applied to two masses of different sizes, the larger mass will move at a slower rate. For example, if two girls are batting balls and one of the girls consistently hits the ball with more force, her ball will travel much farther; however, if the girls are hitting with equal force but one has a heavier ball, the heavier ball will travel a shorter distance than the lighter ball.

The equal and opposite reaction is perhaps most easily illustrated by the swimmer pushing backward against the water—the water moves backward as the swimmer moves forward. This reaction is not so obvious when the performer pushes against a large solid object, such as a wall or the ground, because of the large size of the object in relation to the performer who is exerting force against it; movement of the large object is insignificant in relation to the movement of the performer and, therefore, is not noticed.

When the body is not supported by a surface but is in the air, the equal and opposite reaction occurs within the body itself. For example, when one jumps from a diving board with the arm extended to the side, and then swings that arm to the front of the body, the entire body will turn in the direction opposite to that in which the arm is moving. The speed of the turn is increased if the extended arm is bent as it is brought to the front. The rotary motion of turning is accelerated by shortening the radius of the body when the arm is brought close to the body. Conversely, the rotary motion is decreased when the radius of the moving body is increased. Application of this principle is, as should now be apparent, very important in diving and tumbling activities.

Still another factor that must be considered when absorbing force is the relationship of the force to the size of the area that bears the brunt of the impact. Force concentrated on a small area of body surface is likely to cause more serious injury than the same amount of force spread over a larger area. For this reason, injury is more likely in a fall in which the weight is taken on one foot than when the weight is distributed equally on both feet.

In catching an object, both factors (absorbing the force over a longer time and spreading the force over a larger area while receiving it) are important for the safety and success of the performer. Consequently, to catch a ball that has been thrown hard, the elbows are bent to help absorb the force; to catch large balls, the body is leaned backward as the ball is caught. A baseball glove helps to disperse the impact of the ball over a large area of the hand as well as to lengthen the time it takes the ball to slow down. The padding acts as a cushion that reduces the force over a longer period of time.

Disability and Force

In many instances, individuals with disabilities, especially orthopedic and neurological impairments, will not be able to perform the movements described in the principles of absorbing force. In these cases, it is necessary to first determine if participation in the movements is contraindicated. If not, an analysis of those movements that can be performed should be made in order to determine what movements may be substituted for the lost movements. For example, a person who lacks the ability to bend the knees to lower the body closer to the ground while falling may use the arms to help absorb the force of the fall. The arms are slightly bent to take the force of the fall, and the body is lowered quickly to the ground to increase the distance over which kinetic energy is lost.

Principles of Imparting Force to an Object

Many of the activities in physical education require the projection of a ball or an object into the air. In throwing a ball there are three main concerns:

1. the speed of the throw,
2. the distance, and
3. the direction in which the ball will travel.

The speed and the distance that the ball is thrown are dependent upon the speed at which the hand was traveling at the moment of release. The speed that the hand can acquire

Figure 5.3   When mobility is impaired, principles of imparting force to an object must be modified.

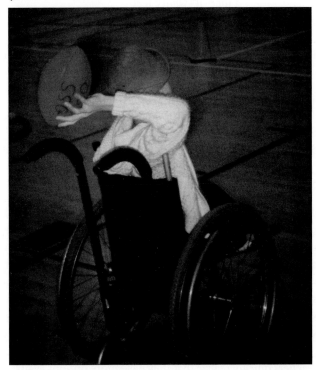

depends upon the distance it travels before the ball is released. Therefore, it is advantageous to make the backswing of the throwing movement as long as possible by rotating the body, shifting the weight, and taking a step. The use of these movements to create distance is effective only if they are synchronized, so that each one is added to the preceding movement to take advantage of the momentum already created.

The distance that the ball will travel depends not only on the force exerted in the throwing but also on the angle at which it is released (figure 5.3). As soon as the ball leaves the hand, gravity has a tendency to pull it downward. The pull of gravity becomes more noticeable as the ball is slowed by the resistance of the air. A greater distance can be obtained if the ball is thrown upward as well as forward because the ball will stay in the air longer and, hence, travel farther. The throwing angle that gains the most distance is approximately forty-five degrees.

The follow-through is an important part of the throw. Stopping the movement immediately after the release of the ball tends to produce a short, jerky movement throughout the total throw and affects the direction and distance of the throw. Furthermore, stopping the throw abruptly may cause injury to the arm because the muscles that must contract for the throw may be damaged by the tremendous force exerted in the opposite direction.

The direction in which the ball travels depends upon the direction in which the force was applied at the moment of release. In most throwing, the hand describes an arc in the throwing process; when the ball is released, it goes off at a tangent to the arc described by the hand. The release of the ball must be timed so that the tangent is in the desired direction. It is easier to release the ball at the correct time when the hands are moved in a flatter arc at the time of the release. A ball that is too large to hold in the fingers and must be held in the palm is more difficult to release at the right time than one held in the fingers. Keeping the palm of the hand directly behind the ball as it moves in the desired direction will keep the ball moving in that direction.

The direction of flight may be influenced by winds as well as by any spin that is placed on the ball when it is released. A spin to the right causes the ball to curve to the right; a spin to the left causes it to curve to the left.

When an implement such as a bat or a racket is used to apply force to an object, the implement becomes an extension of the arm. The arm in throwing or batting is a lever; with the addition of an implement, the resistance arm of the lever becomes longer. Hence, greater momentum can be created. When a bat is swung in an arc, the end of the bat is moving much faster than the hands that are holding it. Consequently, when the ball rebounds, it does so at a much faster rate than if the bat were only moving at the speed of the hands.

The direction the ball travels is even more difficult to control when using an implement than when throwing. The angle of the ball as it leaves the striking surface is determined by the angle at which it hits the surface. The ball will bounce from the object at an angle opposite to that at which it struck; so, in batting a ball the bat must strike the ball at an angle opposite the direction of the intended flight of the ball. To cause the ball to rebound in the same direction that it came from, it must strike the implement at right angles.

Teaching Principles of Movement—Suggestions for Specialized PE

There is no agreement among teachers on the value of teaching the principles of movement to participants before they engage in performance of skills. Research studies have not helped to clarify the issue. **Some studies have indicated that students perform better when they are taught the mechanical principles before attempting performance; other studies have shown that students perform better without having been exposed to such knowledge.** Whether participants profit from instruction in principles of movement appears to be dependent upon how the information is presented. The following suggestions are offered as ways in which maximum benefit may be gained from the teaching of the principles to students before their participation in motor activities:

1. Select the principles to be taught in relation to the ability of the students to understand them.
2. Simplify the presentation, when necessary, to fit the situation and the ability of the students to comprehend.
3. Avoid belaboring the obvious—do not offer explanations when the concept is already well understood by the participants.
4. Avoid lengthy sessions of discussion.
5. Integrate the teaching of principles with the teaching of a skill or movement.

In the authors' work with students with orthopedic disabilities, the students have shown themselves to be more capable of *experimenting intelligently* to find the best kind of movement to fit their needs and abilities if they have some understanding of movement principles. Consequently, it is recommended that the principles be taught to students with disabilities with close adherence to the previous suggestions.

Task Analysis

Because learning motor skills is more challenging for students with disabilities, it is essential that activities be taught in a systematic way, starting with easier and then moving to more difficult components of an activity (figure 5.4). To accomplish this goal, many teachers use a process referred to as task analysis, a technique in which the components of an activity are identified and then ordered according to their level of difficulty. Each component is then broken down into smaller instructional units so that students will be taught at a level where they can achieve initial success before moving to more advanced levels. For example, the skill of roller skating is a complex motor activity comprised of many essential components. To successfully roller skate, students must be able to stand, walk, glide, stop, and turn on skates. After the components are identified, they should be ordered from least to most difficult. Using the roller skating example, standing on skates obviously would be taught prior to turning on skates. The next step, breaking the components into smaller instructional phases, is the heart of the task analysis process. For instance, the component of walking on skates might be taught as follows:

Selected Component: Walk on Skates

PHASE I: Walk on carpet squares attached to feet for ten feet

PHASE II: Walk on wood blocks attached to feet for ten feet

PHASE III: Walk on one skate, with a block under the other foot, for ten feet

PHASE IV: Walk on two skates on a shag rug for a distance of ten feet

PHASE V: Walk on two skates on a shag rug for a distance of twenty feet

PHASE VI: Walk on two skates on an indoor carpet for a distance of twenty feet

PHASE VII: Walk on two skates on a gymnasium floor for a distance of twenty feet

The following steps apply to Phases IV-VII:

Step 1: With teacher assistance

Step 2: With assistance of an object such as a chair, rope, walker, and so on

Step 3: Without assistance

There are several important features of the task analysis process that must be emphasized. First, this procedure permits both the teacher and the student to see progress. For some students, the activity of roller skating will be extremely frustrating unless the activity is broken down into some smaller meaningful steps. For both student and teacher, many successful experiences will be shared as the student masters various tasks, then components, and finally the entire activity.

A second positive aspect of task-analyzing skills is that teachers quickly realize that they have more options available

Figure 5.4 The analysis of movement principles must be individually applied to individuals with disabilities.

to them than they might have initially recognized. Breaking any component of an activity into smaller instructional packages will help the teacher to stretch his or her imagination to try new and creative methods of helping students learn. For instance, in the roller skating example, the use of carpet of varying textures is an idea generated by a teacher who was convinced that there had to be a way to increase friction and thus reduce the free roll of the skates. Other teaching ideas might include using old skates with rusted, immovable wheels or having students walk on skates surrounded by a tall box for support.

The task-analysis process also lends itself as a valuable tool for helping to evaluate the students' accomplishments. Figure 5.5 illustrates the relationship between the students' accomplishments and the amount of time required at each phase. In this example, the phase must be performed correctly for two consecutive days before moving to the next phase. Some teachers might prefer that the student have three or four consecutive days with an X before moving to the next phase. These are decisions that the teacher makes for each individual student based on a variety of factors.

Figure 5.5 also identifies another positive feature of task analysis: Breaking skills down and charting student progress helps teachers make sound educational decisions. For instance, in figure 5.5, it appears that the student is having difficulty learning Phase IV, Step 2. What this suggests to the teacher is that the distance between Steps 1 and 2 of Phase IV is too great for this student. Therefore, it will be necessary to branch this specific task. For example, Phase IV, Step 1 requires that the student walk on two skates on a shag rug

for a distance of ten feet with teacher assistance. Although the student is able to successfully complete this task, the next phase and step are apparently too difficult. In analyzing Phase IV, Step 2, the only difference in this task from the preceding one is that the student must do the task with the assistance of an object instead of a teacher. In inserting a branch into this program, several options could be employed. For instance, the teacher might want to monitor the amount of assistance, slowly fading from two-hand assistance to one-hand assistance prior to going to Phase IV, Step 2. In this example, the use of various amounts of teacher assistance would be identified as branches and added to the student's Task Analysis Evaluation Sheet. This example suggests that even though an activity can be broken into components and in turn into tasks, not all students learn tasks or the components in the same order. Therefore, although a task-analyzed physical education curriculum is helpful, no sequenced curriculum will ever be developed that can be applied universally to all students. The task-analysis approach is essential, however, as an aid to assist teachers in becoming sensitive to individual students' learning needs by creating positive and successful educational experiences.

Ecological Task Analysis (ETA)

While task analysis continues to be a very effective instructional approach, particularly for individuals with severe disabilities (Dunn, Morehouse, & Fredericks, 1986), Davis and Burton (1991) caution that this approach is not without limitations. They argue that traditional approaches to task analysis have focused too much on the task and not enough on the performer or the environment in which the task is to be performed. Building on the work of others, namely Gibson (1979) and Newell (1986), Burton and Davis offer a new approach to task analysis known as Ecological Task Analysis. The ecological approach to task analysis, depicted in figure 5.6, focuses on the environment, the performer, as well as the task that is to be learned. Burton and Davis argue that the primary difference between the ecological and regular approach to task analysis is that the "wholeness" of the skill to be learned is not divided into small parts such that the meaning of the skill is lost. Proponents of this approach, therefore, would argue that task sequences may vary considerably depending on the performer and environmental constraints. An application of the ecological approach would therefore lead the teacher to practice the "goal" of the task; e.g., locomotion using related movement skills such as rolling, creeping, and so on in various settings or environments. **The "correctness" of the response is based on the performer's perception of the task, the environment, and his or her personal attributes.** In this respect, the ecological approach does not rely on the anatomical approach commonly used in many traditional approaches to task analysis.

TASK ANALYSIS EVALUATION SHEET

Component   __WALK ON SKATES__

Student's Name _____

Starting Date   _____

Ending Date   _____

Date

PHASES	3/11	3/12	3/13	3/14	3/15	3/16	3/17	3/18	3/19	3/20	3/21	3/22	3/23	3/24	3/25	COMMENTS
I	0	X	X													
II			X	0	X	X										
III							0	X	X							
IV (1)										X	X					
IV (2)												0	0	0		
IV (3)																
V (1)																
V (2)																
V (3)																
VI (1)																
VI (2)																
VI (3)																
VII (1)																
VII (2)																
VII (3)																

Figure 5.5   Example of a task analysis evaluation sheet for monitoring student progress.

Figure 5.6   Ecological Task Analysis helps to understand the relationship among the environment, skill, and performer in analyzing the movement performance of an individual.

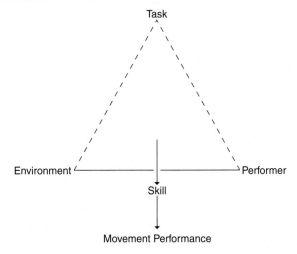

Task

Environment ← — — — — — → Performer

Skill

Movement Performance

While the ecological task analysis approach appears to be consistent with what proponents of task analysis have long proposed, the ecological approach emphasizes correctly the need to focus on the learner and not the task and to emphasize the teaching and learning of skills in various environments. Ecological task analysis also holds much promise for directing future research efforts because of its sound theoretical premise and relationship to new research in motor development, including dynamic systems theory discussed earlier in chapter 3.

Motivating the Student with a Disability

Motivation cannot be thought of as a direct cause of all behavior. It is simply a concept that is used to explain why human behavior occurs. Wloodkowski (1977) states that most psychologists and educators use the word motivation "to describe those processes that can

    A. arouse and instigate behavior,

    B. give direction or purpose to behavior,

    C. continue to allow behavior to persist, and

    D. lead to choosing or performing a particular behavior."

Various theoretical concepts exist as the basis for ways to motivate behavior. Theorists of the different concepts have their own body of research to support and their own vernacular to express the ideas and methods particular to their theories about motivation. However, the theories do overlap, so that it is possible to utilize methods advocated by different theories in combination to produce the best results in motivating the learner. Also, certain concepts of various theoretical bases appear to be more effective in motivating some individuals than do others.

The last point can best be illustrated by the theories of humanism and behaviorism, the two theories most commonly utilized by educators. Basic to the humanistic approach is the idea that a reasoning process must be evoked in the learners so that they arrive at decisions that are best for themselves as individuals and for the society in which they live, and then act upon the decisions accordingly. Intrinsic rewards rather than extrinsic ones are used to motivate and reinforce learning. The behavioristic approach emphasizes extrinsic rewards and relies primarily on manipulation of the external environment to produce the desired behavior. There is more concern for the outcome, rather than the means by which the outcome is achieved, than is the case with humanism.

Experience with learners of various levels of intelligence confirms that development of a reasoning process that enables a person to make a decision with respect to the most desirable behavior is dependent upon the capacity to reason and possess an adequate degree of emotional stability. Hence, motivational methods of humanism have not proved to be as effective with those who are mentally retarded and emotionally disturbed as the methods of the behaviorists have.

Researchers have found the use of extrinsic rewards to be very effective in producing desired behavior in those with mental and emotional disabilities. However, the preponderance of research indicates that although extrinsic rewards can be quite effective in altering behavior temporarily in a controlled setting, such rewards are less influential in effecting changes of a permanent nature outside the nonreinforcing environment. Individuals who are capable of reasoning at an adequate level appear to develop a more lasting positive behavior pattern when they achieve an understanding of the values of conduct and develop

appropriate levels of self-esteem, aspiration, and achievement. This statement is not to be construed to mean these attainments should not be sought with those with behavior disorders and severe mental retardation; rather, the intent is to indicate that the use of intrinsic rewards is not always as effective with these individuals as it is with their nondisabled counterparts. (The technique of using these procedures will be discussed in chapter 14, as well as later in this chapter.)

Self-Esteem and Level of Aspiration

There is evidence to indicate that persons strive to behave in a manner that is consistent with how they look at themselves. Some individuals develop concepts about themselves that lead them to look for ways to be successful, whereas the concepts of others appear to cause them to actually avoid success. Seligman (1975) contends that the relationship between negative student self-esteem and motivation is a "learned helplessness." Children learn to try not to succeed because they believe they are unable to do anything right, so why make the attempt?

Closely associated with self-esteem is level of aspiration. Those who have low self-esteem generally set relatively low goals if they set goals at all. Without appropriate goals individuals do not perform effectively and learning is hampered.

Children with the ability to understand should be appraised of the relationship of self-esteem and level of aspiration to achievement. They should be helped to realistically judge their abilities and assisted in setting their goals high enough to produce the best efforts and optimum results.

Need for Achievement

Investigators of motivation have found that the need for achievement is an important factor in motivation. Alschuler (1973) and Wloodkowski (1977) have found that individuals with high achievement motivation tend to exhibit certain characteristics:

1. interest in excellence for its own sake rather than the reward it brings,
2. preference for assuming personal responsibilities for the outcomes of their efforts,
3. setting of goals after considering the probabilities of success of a variety of alternatives,
4. greater concern with the medium- to long-range future than persons with low achievement and motivation.

To promote a need for achievement in students who lack it, teachers should encourage the development of these characteristics.

Excellence for Its Own Sake

The teacher can contribute to an attitude of striving for excellence and to an appreciation of accomplishment rather than concentrating on the extrinsic reward success will bring. Emphasis should be placed upon the instability of the extrinsic reward as compared to sound accomplishments that will lead to further success. Extrinsic rewards to encourage achievement should only be used in those classes and with those individuals who are incapable of understanding the limitations of these rewards and so need them as motivation to achieve a desired result. In many cases competition with others has value in promoting the striving for excellence. When the emphasis is only upon beating someone else regardless of the quality of performance, however, competition actually becomes detrimental to establishing the concept of excellence for its own sake.

Taking Personal Responsibility for the Outcome

When possible, the student should be helped to make sense out of experiences by attempting to conceptualize what happened and why it happened. Analyzing the experience and its results will help develop an understanding of what could have been done differently and how the results could have been changed. The student must be made to understand, if possible, that one's actions produce results and one must be responsible for the results. However, knowing the cause of the results will enable the student, in most cases, to take more appropriate action to gain better results.

Setting Goals

All children, regardless of age or mental capacity, set goals. Some of these goals may be very simple and short term. As soon as children are capable of doing so, they should begin to set long-term goals. Teachers can offer assistance in this by helping children to understand the reasons they really wish to achieve a goal and the effort required to reach the goal. Children also need help in analyzing their abilities in order to determine the possible level of achievement.

The setting of instructional objectives by the teacher can help motivate as well as give the student insight into the process of setting goals. It is argued by some that behavioral objectives are more effective than instructional objectives in motivating learning because the learners are able to anticipate the results of their actions. Regardless of the type, well-thought-out objectives, explained by the teacher to the students, will help them with their own goal setting, as well as motivate them to achieve the goals the teacher has set.

Preventing Behavior Problems

Students with disabilities, similar to those without disabilities, present behavior problems from time to time. These can range from minor problems, such as fidgeting in class and becoming unnecessarily upset over losing, to more serious problems such as aggressive or disruptive behavior. The goal of all teachers is to minimize behavior problems by creating a positive teaching and learning environment. Ackerman and Dummer (1982) have suggested the following strategies to help teachers reinforce desirable behaviors and to prevent behavior problems.

Structuring the Physical Environment

Before children enter an instructional environment they should know what they are expected to do, where they should go, and what to do when they get there. The room should be organized with activity areas and equipment clearly marked. Activity stations, for instance, can be lettered or numbered to help students who have difficulty following directions.

Modeling

Teachers must serve as effective models for their students. All students, including those with disabilities, look to the teacher as a standard for proper conduct. Teachers, therefore, must be particularly careful in their comments about other students and the manner in which they provide feedback or correction. A favorable response by a teacher to an overweight student, who although lacking in skill tries hard, can serve as an effective catalyst for acceptance of the student by others. Teachers also can serve as effective models by dressing appropriately for the activity, participating in the activity, and allowing students to challenge ideas without becoming defensive or negative.

Reinforcing Desirable Behavior

The sensitive teacher of students with disabilities seeks every possible opportunity to provide positive reinforcement. Using techniques such as verbal praise and public recognition increases the likelihood that appropriate behaviors will be exhibited again in future class sessions. The use of positive reinforcement can be infectious. In classes where this approach is consistently used, students will reciprocate by reinforcing the teacher and other students, as appropriate.

Regulated Permission

There are times when it is desirable to permit exceptions or deviations in the normal class routine for a student who is having difficulty. For example, a student who finds it exceptionally difficult to stand in line before returning to the classroom could be assigned the responsibility of gathering and returning equipment to the proper area. This same concept pertains to the student who comes to the gymnasium angry about something that happened earlier in the day. There are times when the teacher can avoid major confrontations by altering the student's program to allow time to regain composure. The use of this strategy will require that the teacher speak with the student about the exception and the circumstances that led to the exception. Care must be exercised to avoid a situation in which the student expects exceptions as a matter of routine.

Developing, Stating, and Enforcing Consequences

Students need to know that there are rules, standards of behavior, and consequences for inappropriate behavior. The rules must be clear and reasonable and the consequences appropriate to the infraction. Most importantly, the teacher needs to help the student understand that the consequence is related to a rule violation and not designed to suggest that the teacher dislikes the student. The message must be, "I dislike what you did," rather than, "I dislike you." The teacher must find an appropriate time (when the student is not upset) to state and review rules and standards of behavior. It is of little value to discuss rules and behavior when a student (or a teacher) is upset. Instead, clear understandings with consequences communicated ahead of time maximize student learning and facilitate a much smoother behavioral management within class time.

Student and Teacher Contracts

There are times when it is desirable for the teacher and student to develop a contract as part of a conference in which a problem is acknowledged, expected behaviors are identified, and rewards and consequences are specified. This approach has been effectively used with students with behavior disorders. Effective contracts require student input to ensure that the expected behavior and consequences are clear and obtainable. Contracts have been used to motivate students to reduce weight, for example, or to reduce inappropriate behavior such as objectionable language and negative comments about another student.

Dealing with Atypical Behavior

There are times when the intensity, frequency, and duration of a student's behavior may be so severe that it is clearly atypical. For example, individuals who persist in being abusive to themselves or others normally require assistance beyond that designed to prevent behavior problems.

One of the primary concerns facing today's teacher is how to deal with inappropriate student behavior. This is particularly true for teachers who work with disruptive, aggressive, and self-destructive individuals. It is very difficult to teach motor skills to students who are constantly abusing themselves or their peers.

Although various strategies may be used in dealing with atypical behavior, the approach offered here is based largely on the theory and techniques of behaviorism, which has been shown to be the most effective way to deal with extremely antisocial behavior by individuals who are mentally retarded and emotionally disturbed. Suggestions for reducing antisocial behavior reflect primarily behavioral techniques, although the author does borrow from other theoretical concepts when appropriate. The technical vocabulary used in this section is chiefly that of the behaviorists (Dunn & Fredericks, 1985; Dunn & French, 1982). The primary focus will be on helping teachers apply their knowledge of learning theory to students with behavior problems.

Laying the Foundation

Prior to initiating any effort to help a student overcome a behavior problem, it is essential that the teacher talk first with the school administration to determine if other teachers have noted similar concerns and what, if anything, has been done to remediate the problem. Efforts should also be made to contact the student's parents. For students previously identified as having a disability, it may be necessary to request an IEP meeting. Meeting with the parents provides an excellent opportunity to explain to them the nature of the problem from the teacher's perspective and to ask if the

Dealing with Atypical Behavior

1. Lay the foundation
2. Identify inappropriate behavior
3. Establish a baseline
4. Develop a plan of action

parents have noted similar problems. Conversing with parents also helps the teacher and school officials clarify whether the parents are aware of any specific reason that may account for the abnormal behavior.

Every effort should also be made to enlist the support of fellow teachers and special personnel such as counselors and school psychologists. Their knowledge and wealth of experience will contribute much to the success of any efforts to help the student with a behavior problem. When a plan of action is developed for dealing with the student's behavior, the cooperation of parents, school officials, and colleagues is necessary to ensure that a conscientious effort is undertaken to respond to the student's behavior problems in a consistent manner.

Identifying Inappropriate Behavior

A concise description of what the teacher believes to be inappropriate behavior must be supplied. The importance of this process cannot be overemphasized because it is the foundation of the other steps to dealing with atypical behavior. To emphasize this point, let us assume that a basketball coach explains to one of the players that the youngster's lay-up shot is poor. Upon hearing this remark, the player asks, "Coach, what do you mean by poor? What am I doing wrong?" Faced with this question, the experienced coach will explain in descriptive terms the weakness of the player's shot, such as wrong foot take-off, wrong hand, improper eye placement, and so on. The same sort of specific description of inappropriate behavior is also required of teachers.

Teachers sometimes make broad sweeping statements about students and their behavior, such as, "Tom is bad." To deal with this behavior, however, the teacher will have to clearly identify the behavior—hitting other children and throwing objects, for example—that has led to the conclusion that Tom is bad. Teachers should strive to state the questionable behavior in descriptive terms that can be observed and measured by others. Inappropriate behavior can be measured only if the criterion of inappropriateness is clearly stated. Once teachers have made this initial step, they are in a position to systematically deal with the identified behavior and to evaluate the results of their attempts.

Establishing a Baseline

Once a specific behavior has been identified, it becomes necessary to measure the frequency of the behavior's occurrence. The recording of the behavior's frequency prior to initiating a plan for remediation helps to establish a baseline that can be referred to later as continuous and final measures are taken. It is through this procedure that the effects of the behavior program can be evaluated.

Techniques for Dealing with Inappropriate Behavior

- Positive reinforcement
- Modeling
- Extinction
- Time-out
- Interference
- Proximity control
- Humor

Although there is some controversy regarding the most accurate means of charting behavior, it is generally concluded that the most practical method for teachers is to simply count the occurrence of a behavior per unit of time. For the sake of convenience, the suggested procedure calls for the teacher to mark on a conveniently located card the number of times the inappropriate behavior appears.

Before the teacher establishes a baseline, the behavior should be observed each day at various times and under different circumstances for at least a week. At the end of this period, the tabulations per day are added and averaged, thus resulting in a behavior baseline value.

Developing a Plan of Action

The exact process that a teacher uses to decrease the frequency of an undesirable behavior depends on many factors. The uniqueness of the individual and the specific behavior to be remediated are simply two of the important variables that must be incorporated into a plan of action. Of course, the more severe the behavior problem, the greater the need for a well-developed strategy. In developing a specific plan, teachers are encouraged to use the assistance of specialists within their school system, such as school psychologists and behavior-management consultants, to help them with this important task. Indicated here are some general concepts to help teachers improve their understanding of how to deal with inappropriate behavior. For sake of clarity, the following techniques will be described and discussed separately; however, frequently these techniques are utilized together in various combinations.

Positive Reinforcement

Positive reinforcement is defined as any pleasant event that follows a behavior and strengthens the future frequency of that behavior. This technique is generally recognized as the most powerful tool for increasing selected behaviors. Children and adults, with and without disabilities, all respond favorably to positive reinforcement; people continue to do those activities for which reinforcement is provided. The key to this system, then, is the identification of appropriate reinforcers. It must be emphasized at this point that an event that follows a response is not a reinforcer unless it increases the frequency of a specified response. Educators are often tempted to identify certain items, such as ice cream, candy, trinkets, and so forth, as reinforcers. This is an unwise procedure, however, because students are not all the same and they therefore obviously do not all value similar items.

The basic or primary reinforcers used with children with disabilities include the categories of consumables (ice cream, candy, food treats); manipulatables (toys, trinkets, hobby items); visual and auditory stimuli (films, records, and animations); and social stimuli (verbal praise and attention). Although some students, specifically the seriously emotionally disturbed, require basic reinforcers, the goal of the positive reinforcement procedure is to help students learn to respond to natural forms of social praise. Many teachers have found it useful to implement a positive reinforcement procedure that employs a token system (Bennett, Eisenman, French, Henderson, & Shultz 1989). A token is a tangible item having no value of its own that is given for acceptable behavior to be exchanged at a later time for an item of value. The use of a token system has many advantages. It permits students to exchange tokens for items that personally appeal to them at a time mutually convenient for both teacher and student. Physical education teachers have found the token system a practical and manageable system. In figure 5.7 a schematic of a reinforcement hierarchy is presented. Although the ultimate goal is to have students respond to an intrinsic reward, this is not always possible.

Once the positive reinforcement system has been identified it is necessary next to decide on a reinforcement schedule. When the teacher is initially attempting to establish a behavior—to increase the student's compliance, for example—it is generally best to reinforce the student every time

the desired response is made. This is called a continuous reinforcement schedule. Gradually, the teacher may introduce a fixed ratio schedule where a reinforcer is provided every three times the student demonstrates compliant behavior. Later, as the behavior is established, the continued permanency of the behavior is ensured by introducing a variable ratio schedule. Therefore, the behavior may be reinforced on the average of one out of every three, four, five or more times it appears. Changing reinforcement schedules, however, must be done carefully. Generally, it is best to consult with other school specialists before initiating a reinforcement schedule change.

Modeling

Frequently, children demonstrate inappropriate behavior because they do not know or have forgotten the proper way to behave. In an attempt to increase the student's repertoire of desirable behaviors, the behavior of others can often be utilized as examples of the types of behavior that should be exhibited. This system, whereby appropriate behavior is demonstrated for the student, is referred to as modeling.

The utilization of models is not a new concept for physical educators. For example, the teaching of most sport skills is greatly enhanced if either the teacher or a student leader can effectively demonstrate (model) the skill being taught.

Modeling has been successfully employed with special students. It is a particularly effective technique to use in a mainstreamed physical education class. For example, the teacher who is working on having children attend for longer periods of time to specific motor skill tasks can reward a student who is practicing by saying, "John, I like the way you are working hard." The strategy, of course, is to always speak loudly and enthusiastically while standing close to the student who needs to work harder. In some cases, it may also be necessary to be more direct by saying, "Mary, have you watched how hard John is working?" The message to the student is that if you work hard, the teacher will provide some strong positive verbal reinforcement. It is essential, therefore, that the teacher immediately reward the students who

Figure 5.7 Hierarchy of the reinforcement system.

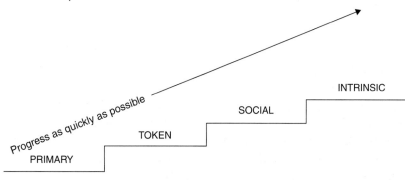

suddenly decide that they, too, would like some attention from the teacher. Various situations will arise when the student with a disability also can serve as the model, thus helping others to recognize that effort, and not perfection, is the name of the game.

The conduct of teachers, too, can often serve as a model for youngsters. Therefore, teachers should conduct themselves in a manner consistent with the behavior expected of their students. To do otherwise would be hypocritical.

Extinction

If a behavior has been learned under conditions of positive reinforcement, it follows logically that the particular behavior can be unlearned by withdrawing the reinforcer. This technique of gradually decreasing a previously reinforced behavior by withholding the reinforcer is known as extinction. Take, for example, the young child who insisted upon wandering around the gymnasium while the other children engaged in activities directed by the teacher. The teacher's natural reaction, upon seeing this student's purposeful attempt not to be part of the group, was to go to the student and lead him back to the group. This sequence of behavior, the child leaving and the teacher retrieving him, happened several times over a two-day period before it occurred to the teacher that by always retrieving the student, he was in effect positively reinforcing the youngster's behavior. The teacher also noted that although the gymnasium doors were open, the child never attempted to leave. Therefore, the teacher elected to focus his direct attention on the children who were participating and to ignore the child who was aimlessly walking around the gym. To the teacher's delight, by reinforcing the children who were in the right spot at the right time and by watching the nonjoiner for safety purposes only, the wandering student soon became more and more interested in the group experiences. The strategy of ignoring the child and then reinforcing him when he did participate was a successful technique for extinguishing an undesirable behavior.

Although the previous example concisely describes the extinction technique, rarely does this procedure work as effectively or as efficiently as indicated in the example. Sometimes the teacher utilizing this technique has difficulty extinguishing a behavior problem for two reasons:

1. Identification of all the reinforcers that are maintaining a behavior is difficult, and
2. even if the reinforcers can be identified, it is virtually impossible to control all of them.

For instance, many people other than teachers, such as classmates, siblings, parents, and neighbors, reinforce student behavior; obviously, to manage the actions of all of these individuals would be a difficult task.

Physical educators who utilize extinction for the first time should be aware of additional concerns. First, when the extinction plan is initiated, the immediate reaction of many students will be to increase their level of undesirable activity. So by not attending to a child's use of abusive language, for instance, the youngster's cursing may at first become louder and more frequent. Second, the length of time required to completely diminish a behavior by the use of extinction alone may weaken the will of even the most patient teacher. Third, it is recommended that this procedure not be employed with certain behaviors exhibited by students who are emotionally disturbed, particularly self-destructive behaviors. Finally, although there is some research that would indicate that extinction alone may be used to reduce undesirable behavior, most authorities agree that extinction should be combined with other techniques, specifically positive reinforcement, to be most economical and efficient in producing changes in behavior.

Time-Out

The behavior of some students, particularly those with severe behavior disorders, can be disturbing and harmful to themselves as well as to others. When confronted with behavior problems that can be dangerous, teachers often rely upon a technique called time-out. Basically, this procedure involves removing the student quietly and gently from the room to a designated time-out area. During this transfer from the classroom, the teacher should make every effort not to positively reinforce the student's behavior by chastisement. The purpose of time-out is to remove the student from a setting that appears to possess positively reinforcing elements. Time-out also provides the student with an opportunity to recover composure in a quiet, private area. As soon as the undesirable behavior stops, the student should be permitted to return to class. Time-outs are also successfully used to manage behavior *when the student knows when to give himself a time-out*. Therefore, meetings can be held with the student to identify the problem(s) and have the student determine a consequence. This technique has been used with young children as well as older students. With young children, the discussion should be kept in simple terms and focus on the positive. For example, "Michael, I really like the way you have lots of excitement for our physical education class. I think you love playing the games. What do you think we should do if you have so much excitement that you cannot follow the rule in class about saying positive words to people?" If the student has difficulty, assist him with the use of choices. Some students are surprised that they are being allowed to have a say in the consequences for their behavior. Therefore, the teacher may say, "Do you want to give me a sign that you will step out for a little while? Or, do you want me to give you a special sign?"

Many classrooms for students with severe behavior problems contain a specially designated time-out area. Generally, the time-out area is plain and free from distractions. Physical educators, because of their utilization of both indoor and outdoor facilities, may find it necessary to design their own time-out areas in each facility. Before employing a time-out procedure it is essential that the teacher review with school administrators and parents precisely the conditions under which the system will be employed.

Beyond the formal techniques of positive reinforcement, modeling, extinction, and time-out, there are some informal approaches teachers can use to deal with undesirable behavior. Ackerman and Dummer (1982) have identified several of these, three of which will be briefly described: signal interference, proximity control, and humor.

Teachers employ a variety of signals that communicate to students approval or disapproval for selected behaviors. Some of the nonverbal techniques that can be employed include: eye contact, hand gestures, snapping fingers, frowning, or various body postures. These signals, if employed before the behavior gets out of control, can be very effective in stopping or minimizing the intensity of the inappropriate behavior.

A very old but effective strategy to use when a teacher senses that a student's behavior is beginning to deteriorate is for the teacher to move close to the child. This action, when done in a noncombative way, serves to remind the student of the behavioral expectations for the class. The close presence of the teacher may assist the student in regaining self-control and/or ceasing the undesirable behavior.

Most teachers are aware that humor can be very effective in defusing a tense situation. A funny comment by the teacher creates the opportunity for the student to gain self-control and time for the teacher to think before removing the student or using some other behavioral strategy. Of course, care must be exercised to avoid ridicule or sarcasm. The humor must be in good taste and appropriate to the situation.

Medication and the Student with a Disability

Medications used by some students to assist with learning given problematic behavior(s) are considered *part of* a comprehensive approach to behavior management. The student, as well as the adults working with the student, are still required to take responsibility to learn and shape behavior into skills that are considered more adaptive for the individual. For example, children who have been severely abused may be angry and defensive. For some, this maladaptive

behavior has protected them from further abuse, whereas in other instances, it has only made it worse. A full and coordinated program to help the child deal with anger and to develop appropriate social skills is important. Medication is often a part of the student's overall program to regain a healthy life and be ready to learn in school.

The use of prescribed medication as an aid in the management of learning, behavior, and convulsive disorders is known as drug therapy. This treatment approach is used with students of various disabilities, including those with learning disabilities, mental retardation, behavior disorders, epilepsy, and cerebral palsy. Students are sometimes provided medication to manage such behaviors as short attention span, tendency to be distracted, restlessness, and tantrums. Although exact figures are unavailable, it is clear that a large number of students are on medication for various disorders, including hyperactivity, behavior problems, and epilepsy.

Although the decision as to the type of medication and dosage is a medical decision, educators are interested in drugs and the role of the school in drug treatment. Teachers recognize, for example, that if a particular drug treatment is successful, the probability that a student will benefit from educational programs is greatly enhanced. If, however, a particular medication does not seem to have an effect on the student's behavior, then this information needs to be shared with the student's physician. Fortunately, an increasing number of physicians are becoming aware of the remarkable sensitivity teachers have concerning drug treatment programs. Sleator and Sprague (1978) believe that drug treatment programs will not be effective unless physicians routinely obtain input from teachers about the student's performance. Some educators and physicians have developed a close relationship in which information about drug treatment programs and their effects are exchanged. Kennedy, Terdal, and Fusetti (1993) note that blood studies, laboratory studies, and neurological teams are not as helpful in evaluating the effectiveness of medications as behavior ratings by parents, caregivers, and teachers.

Physical education teachers must also recognize that some drugs have side effects that may improve or impair the student's motor performance. Discussion about a student's educational progress in physical education, therefore, may be misleading unless information concerning the individual's medication is available. Awareness of this information may also explain any sudden or unusual change in behavior. Drug treatment is an important variable that must be combined with other information to help teachers make wise educational decisions.

Category of Drugs

Various terms are used to describe drugs. Drugs may be referred to by their generic names or their trade names. For example, Dilantin, a trade name for a drug used as an anticonvulsant in grand mal epilepsy, is known by its generic name as phenytoin sodium. The generic name is normally used in medical literature and by scientists throughout the world. The trade name, however, is a registered trademark that may vary from country to country.

Two major categories are used to identify the drugs frequently used in treating childhood disorders. These are psychotropic and anticonvulsant, or antiepileptic, drugs (Gadow, 1979). Drugs that are prescribed primarily for their effects on mood, behavior, and cognitive processes are known as psychotropic drugs. As the name implies, anticonvulsant drugs are used in the treatment of convulsive disorders.

Psychotropic drugs have commonly been divided into six categories: stimulants, major tranquilizers, minor tranquilizers, antidepressants, hypnotics, and sedatives. Drug use with children and youth is currently under the scrutiny of parents, physicians, and educators. Educators should work with the family and medical personnel when students are taking prescribed medications. The names of drugs change, with some distinction being made between a drug that is still under patent protection and those drugs that do not have patents and have been "copied" by other drug companies. The copied drug is sometimes referred to as "generic" or "formulary." Additionally, health plans restrict the use of certain types of more expensive drugs in favor of the generic. Even pharmacists are confused regarding health insurance plans and allowable drugs. It is best to work directly with families and medical personnel on understanding the name of their child's drug and the condition for which it has been prescribed. The drugs mentioned here are for reference only; this list is not comprehensive.

Medication Side Effects

Although drug treatment has been widely accepted as an effective treatment approach for various childhood disorders, it is important that teachers be aware of possible side effects that may occur as the result of a particular drug. For example, Ritalin has been shown to be effective in improving hyperactive children's motor performance (Lere, Lere, & Artner, 1977), cognitive levels (Sprague & Sleator, 1975), behavior (Gadow, 1977), and school achievement (Gittelman-Klein et al., 1976). Other drugs are also used by physicans to work with hyperactivity.

It is also clear that with some drugs detrimental side effects may occur in some children. These may be temporary or long-term problems. Using Ritalin again as an example, the most common side effects observed during the early stages of treatment with this drug are insomnia and loss of appetite. Other side effects that may be observed include headaches, nausea, moodiness, and irritability. These side effects may disappear as children develop a tolerance for Ritalin. In some instances a change in the amount or type of medication may also be necessary.

The use of Ritalin also has been shown to be associated with health concerns. These include the possibility of an increase in blood pressure and heart rate (Ballard, Boileau, Sleator, Majjey, & Sprague, 1976), as well as a decrease in height and growth rates (French & Jansma, 1981). Insufficient data are available, however, to conclude that these findings apply to all users of Ritalin. Further studies are needed to evaluate the effects of several variables, such as dosage levels, length of treatment, and individual differences. Some have noted, for instance, that the retarded weight and height growth observed in some Ritalin users is temporary and when the treatment is ended, normal growth rates will be achieved (Roche, Lipman, Overall, & Hung, 1979).

Knowledge of which medication students are taking is helpful in developing physical education programs. Teachers who are aware of this information can communicate with parents and physicians concerning any unusual behavior that may be observed. Teachers might also be less likely to err in assessing the student's motor performance. Assessment information taken during a change in drug treatment, for instance, could alter the student's motor performance and mask the individual's true capability. Major tranquilizers, for example, are frequently used to treat children with mental retardation who are hyperactive, aggressive, or self-abusive. Unfortunately, major tranquilizers such as Haldol and Mellaril also affect the extrapyramidal tract, which coordinates motor activities—especially walking, posture, muscle tone, and patterns of movement. This problem can be corrected by attempting to alter the recommended dosage. The physical education teacher will obviously be at a major disadvantage in determining the student's present and potential motor ability until the adverse reaction is treated.

Awareness of the side effects of drugs is also essential in preparing a physical education experience that is safe for the student. The side effects of some medications may cause problems such as drowsiness, balance dysfunction, and lack of muscle coordination. These problems not only interfere with the student's performance but also can lead to unsafe activity experiences for the students. Asking a student who is experiencing a drug-related problem with balance to perform gymnastic stunts involving height is an unsafe practice.

Teaching Methods

Teaching is an art. A method of teaching is a general procedure used by the teacher to help the student understand and apply the information that is being presented. In physical education, the methods most commonly used are the direct

Teaching Techniques

- Verbalization
- Visualization
  - Demonstration
  - Videos
  - Photos, posters, diagrams
  - Written materials
- Kinesthesis
  - Exploratory
  - Manual
  - Reverse manual
- Direct or Traditional Method
- Problem-Solving or Indirect Method
- Synthesis of Methods

or traditional method, the indirect or problem-solving method, and a synthesis of both. The direct method has been most frequently utilized by teachers in the past. The problem-solving method has come into use fairly recently and is rapidly gaining popularity. A synthesis of the two is not generally recognized as a method, although it is widely practiced; for this reason and for others that will be discussed later, it is included as one of the methods of teaching physical education.

Techniques of teaching may be defined as special ways the teacher handles instructional problems efficiently and deals effectively with the varied responses of different children. Teaching techniques used by physical education teachers are of three general types: verbalization, visualization, and kinesthesis. *Any of the techniques may be used with any method of teaching.* Before examining how they are used with a specific teaching method, the various techniques will be described to provide the background necessary for understanding the use of the terms in the later discussion.

Techniques of Teaching

Verbalization

Verbalization refers to the use of the spoken word in the process of teaching. Describing a skill or explaining the strategy of a play vocally is an example of the use of the technique. The oral presentation of a motor problem to be solved is included in this category. Oral reports and class discussions are other examples of utilizing verbalization in classroom teaching, although their use is more limited in the teaching of physical education than in other types of classes. Some concepts are best communicated to students

by means of verbalizing them: their presentation cannot be clearly made in any other way. For example, in the demonstration of a skill, verbalization is frequently employed to clarify a concept that could not be clearly identified without the use of a descriptive oral explanation. This technique also has obvious advantages for certain populations, such as those with visual impairments. See figure 5.8 for an example of using a verbal instruction technique. The instructor is at eye level with the student and has his attention as the instructions are provided.

Visualization

Visualization is a technique that employs the visual attention of the students. Included under this general heading are demonstrations, filmstrips, videotapes, posters and pictures, diagrams, and the printed word.

Demonstration is a most effective tool, particularly when used with the traditional method of teaching. In a good demonstration, the skill is executed in correct form one or more times, depending upon its complexity. The students then attempt to execute the skill by duplicating the movements they have observed. The teacher may need to simulate the disability of the student being taught in order to give a meaningful demonstration. Even if it proves impossible for the teacher to duplicate exactly the adjustment that must be made by the student, the demonstration will still

Figure 5.8   This instructor has good eye contact with his student as well as the student's attention. This increases the ability of the student to benefit from verbal instructions.

be useful to the student with a disability, because it will help to identify the objective of the movement. Doing this will provide the insight the student needs to know how to best achieve similar results for himself or herself through experimentation.

"Technically enhanced visualization" resoures such as videos, DVDs, CDs, and Internet resources such as YouTube, are effective for showing the proper techniques of performing skills. Many of these have a certain limitation for use in the special class, however, because they show how the skills are performed by individuals who do not have the disabilities that these students must circumvent in their performances. But if the teacher is prepared to describe possible adaptations of the skills for the students watching the video, a very effective teaching situation can be developed. Alert students with active minds and imaginations also may be assigned to watch the videos and plan possible adaptation of the skills. These can then be discussed with the teacher and tried out under his or her supervision, or they can be set up as problems to be solved by the student. Teachers should be alert for examples that show exercise and activity as performed by individuals with disabling conditions.

Still pictures, posters, and diagrams may be used effectively to illustrate correct skill techniques. Pictures of performers executing the skills are less desirable than ones in which an adapted technique is illustrated, but they are nevertheless extremely useful. Diagrams of plays on the blackboard are used to good advantage in teaching students with disabilities who may be less familiar with the strategy of games than are other students who have participated in sports more widely. As discussed in chapter 12, students with autism are successfully taught the skill and the schedule for physical education using visual aids, particularly in the form of pictures.

The use of *the printed word* is a technique that has been largely overlooked as an effective teaching tool in physical education. Textbooks, pamphlets, and other written materials can be particularly advantageous in the special class in a dual program situation. Depending upon their reading level, students with disabilities who know little about a particular activity may be assigned to read about it before work in that activity begins so they will be familiar with the terminology and the general performance of the activity.

There are many textbooks available, some designed especially for a comprehensive activity course in physical education and others devoted entirely to the skills and strategy of a particular sport or recreational activity. Most of these are suitable for use by high school students. They are directed chiefly toward the nondisabled, but the student with a disability may still utilize much of the instruction. For example, in teaching weight-lifting to a student who suffers a chronic dislocation of the shoulder, the instructor might direct the student to read about all of the lifts except those that bring the arms higher than the shoulders—the only lifts the student could not perform.

Textbooks designed for activity classes usually offer a brief history of the game and stress the care of equipment and the playing courtesies, all of which are essential if the student is to attain the fullest possible understanding and appreciation of the activity. Although effective and well-organized teachers can manage to bring this additional information to their classes, their jobs are made considerably easier by the use of a textbook. Moreover, by assigning the students to acquire this information from books, a little more time is gained for working in the physical activity with individual students.

Worksheets are helpful to students who are working by themselves. An example of the kind of worksheet that may be used is given in figure 5.9. A photocopied form such as this will aid students in determining the cause of their skill faults, and also will show their progress.

Kinesthesis

The use of kinesthesis refers to the involvement of muscular activity in the teaching-learning situation. There are different ways of using kinesthesis as a teaching technique, although it must be taken into consideration that this type of learning has different phases. Identifying the phase of teaching using kinesthesis is important for a teacher of physical education.

When students attempt to perform a skill and must make an adjustment in stance or grip because it doesn't feel right, they are making use of kinesthesis. Of course, in the case of beginners, students will not know how the correct form feels. In fact the correct form may feel more awkward than the incorrect. This is often the case in assuming the grip of a golf club or in making an overhand throw. It is only after students begin to associate the desired result with the correct form that they will begin to "feel right" about their performance.

In a sense, the adjustment that students make when their muscular movements have not achieved satisfactory results is a phase of kinesthesis. Adjusting the serve in table tennis after the ball has fallen short of the net is a learning related to kinesthesis. Of course, the eyes tell the player that the serve was no good, but the adjustment in the muscular movement made to perform the skill more accurately is kinesthetic in nature.

Attempts to correct errors in order to achieve a more satisfactory performance are referred to as **exploratory kinesthesis.** Such exploration is an integral phase of the learning of any new activity and is particularly to be fostered among students who are disabled.

Still another phase of teaching that employs kinesthesis is that of actually leading the student's hand, arm, or part of

	Practice Guide	
Techniques	Common Errors	My Errors
Grip	Gripping too high on the handle	
Strokes in General	Standing too close to the bird while stroking Failure to use the wrist in the stroke Failure to place the shot away from the opponent Telegraphing shots or using strokes in a specific pattern	
Overhead Stroke	Allowing the bird to drop too low before stroking	
Forehand Stroke	Failure to hit the bird up when it has dropped lower than the net	
Backhand Stroke	Failure to abduct the wrist in the backswing and snap the wrist forward as the swing comes forward	
Serve	Failure to watch the bird while serving Failure to use the wrist in stroking Repeatedly serving to the same spot Moving the feet during the serve Holding the bird too close to the body; this causes the bird to go into the net Setting up the bird for the opponent which may be caused by holding the bird away from the body or by not using enough or too much wrist in the stroke	
Net Shots	Hitting net shots too high	
Drives	Hitting up on the bird	
Court Positions	Failure to return to the proper position after stroking the bird Encroaching on partner's court area Backing up for deep shots instead of pivoting and running back	

Figure 5.9 Practice guide for badminton.

the body involved in the activity through the performance of the skill. This technique is called **manual kinesthesis** (figure 5.10). It is extremely helpful to students who have failed to grasp the fundamentals through exploration, visualization, or verbalization. With students who have sensory deviations, as in the case of blindness, the technique is invaluable. It would be practically impossible, for example, to teach a boy who is blind to catch or throw a ball unless his hands were led through the movements by his instructor. Some students, particularly those who are blind, find a process known as **reverse manual kinesthesis** effective. In this technique, the student holds on to the instructor as the instructor executes the task. For example, the teacher permits the student to get the feel of a golf swing by having the student stand behind the instructor and hold on to the instructor's hands. Students who are blind learn much by feeling the movements involved in successful execution of a task.

Techniques of Teaching: Use of Cues/Prompts

The techniques of teaching referred to as verbalization, visualization, and kinesthesis have been incorporated into a well-recognized use of cues or prompts when working with individuals with disabilities in physical activity. Cues and prompts are used in a hierarchy to enable students to learn skills and develop knowledge in movement performance. It is understood that because of an individual's disability, a particular teaching technique is more appropriate than

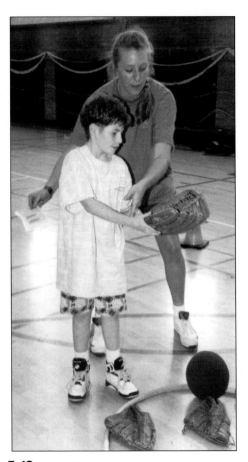

Figure 5.10 Manual kinesthesis is helpful to a student unable to grasp the fundamentals of performing a skill.

others, and that technique can be used at different times in the learning process. The hierarchy is as follows:

- using the technique of verbalization, the cue/prompt at the highest level is *verbal*
- using the technique of visualization, the cue/prompt at the next lowest level is *visual*
- using the technique of kinesthesis, the cue/prompt at the lowest level is *physical*

In addition, individuals have a preferred method of learning: some prefer auditory, some visual, and some moving or kinesthetic. Many physical educators readily admit that they learn through moving; whereas music teachers are often auditory (verbal), as well as kinesthetic learners (if they play an instrument rather than being a vocalist).

For a teacher, the easiest method of instruction may be to verbally explain a skill or tell the students the rules of the game. But for some students who have auditory processing difficulties or for whom auditory is not their preferred mode of learning, these instructions are confusing and they become lost. Successful physical education teachers use a multimodality approach: auditory, visual, and physical. This ensures that the students will have their mode of learning addressed.

The prompt hierarchy is useful when teaching skills. A student with a disability such as mental retardation may learn a skill by seeing a demonstration of the skill (visual) and then listening to *key words* used (verbal) as they are being physically assisted through the movement (kinesthetic).

In the case of some disabilities, the teacher is instructed to teach to the student's strength; that is, some children prefer a certain learning technique. When teaching the skill, the use of a prompt hierarchy helps the student engage in the successful performance of the skill. It is appropriate to fade the prompts so that, if possible, the student comes to a point where she only needs a verbal cue to know to perform the skill or participate in the game. For some students, the fading may take a long time or may not be realistic: some cues will need to remain in place (e.g., a yellow cone to help the student with directionality of the line-up). The reality is that all students benefit from multimodality teaching as well as from the use of prompt hierarchies. Even as adults, when we learn a new movement skill (e.g., golf), the prompt hierarchy is appropriate.

Direct or Traditional Method

Basically, in the direct method the teacher selects the activity or skill to be learned and instructs the participants by describing the skill or by using one of the visual techniques to show how the skill is performed. The participants then attempt the skill, and the teacher assists each student in making the adjustments in movement necessary to perform the skill according to the prescribed standards.

The procedure is often described as consisting of the three Ds: Demonstration, Diagnosis, and Direction. The three Ds are discussed in the following paragraphs as they apply to the teaching of the students with disabilities.

Various techniques of demonstration have already been described. To present to students with disabilities the best method of performing a skill will require considerable insight and imagination on the part of the instructor. Teachers must try to put themselves in the place of the awkward child who has difficulty learning to skip or the student who is blind who desires to become a wrestler. At times it may be helpful for the teacher to attempt the skill simulating the disability; for example, attempting the side stroke in swimming without using one of the legs so as to demonstrate more clearly for the student who has lost a leg. Not all disabilities can be simulated successfully: loss of both arms, for instance, seriously affects the balance of the body, and in the attempt to perform a skill without the use of arms, the instructor will not be confronted with the same problem of balance as the armless student. Consequently, the teacher's demonstration will be limited in its value to the student except to the extent that it gives insight into the movement. The demonstration must, therefore, be supplemented with analysis of the student's movements as the skill is attempted.

We have just spoken of the need for diagnosis of the skill performance in the case of a student for whom a demonstration is not entirely satisfactory. Diagnosis goes beyond this, however; it is an integral factor in teaching skill improvement. Every good physical educator becomes an expert in diagnosing or analyzing learning difficulties and in giving clear, explicit directions to students to enable them to acquire a new pattern of movement.

It is not enough for the teacher to show a learner how to do the skill and to diagnose the student's learning difficulties; the instructor must also direct the student in overcoming his or her difficulties. Direction is extremely important in the teaching of students with disabilities, for these students want intensely to succeed in performing the skill, and the more quickly any learning difficulties can be overcome the sooner the skill can be mastered.

The techniques that are utilized by the teacher are dependent upon the circumstances and the objectives that are sought. Beginning teachers must choose their techniques on the basis of what they know about the needs of students with disabilities and on their prediction of the success a particular technique will have in accomplishing the changes they hope will be effected in the students. In addition, they may utilize the suggestions for performing sports skills in chapter 16 as a springboard for exploration and experimentation to determine the best teaching techniques for each individual student.

Problem-Solving or Indirect Method

In the problem-solving method, the teacher presents a motor task in the form of a problem to be solved by the students in the class. Basically, the problems are offered as a guide to the students to help them discover the movements their bodies are capable of and how they may control these movements to accomplish a specific goal. The method is very effective in teaching sports skills, particularly to those who have orthopedic and neurologic disabilities, because it necessitates experimentation with movement to determine the best way to perform the skill within the limitations imposed by the disability.

The nature of the problem to be solved by the students is determined by their level of maturation, past experiences, and the medical limitations established by the physician. It is very important that both the teacher and the student understand the kinds of activities and specific movements that are contraindicated by a student's disability so that he or she will not attempt anything that may be harmful during exploration of various movements in the attempt to solve the problem.

To use the problem-solving method effectively, the teacher must decide not only the general area of motor learning to be examined but also the kind of problem that will evoke most effectively the exploration of the selected area. Problems in motor movement may take two forms:

1. *A Single Problem.* The single problem consists of a simple motor task to be solved by the individual student. For example, the boy on crutches could be given the problem: Can you balance your body with the use of only one crutch? All problems should be organized and stated in such a way that, when they are resolved, the student will have gained a fuller understanding of how the body can be controlled in movement and the extent and kinds of movement the body is capable of performing.
2. *Sequence of Subproblems Leading to the Answer of a Major Problem.* This approach has been described as *guided discovery* or *independent discovery,* depending upon the role the teacher plays.

In guided discovery, the teacher presents the major problem to the participants and then guides them toward a solution by posing subproblems that, when solved, will provide answers that lead to the resolution of the major problem. An example that illustrates the procedure follows:

Major problem (For students who have the use of only one arm): How can a golf ball be stroked most effectively by using one arm to hold the club?

Subproblems:

1. How should the grip be taken on the club to get the firmest hold?
2. Where on the club should the grip be taken to achieve the best leverage and the best control?
3. Which movement produces the most power in hitting the ball, a forward or a backward movement?*
4. Is it now necessary to adjust the grip to execute the stroke with optimum power and control?

Effectively conducted guided discovery should lead to independent discovery. Independent discovery, as the name implies, is a form of problem-solving that requires the student to work independently in the search for the solution to the motor problem. The major problem is divided into subproblems by the student, who develops them so they will lead to the solution of the major problem. The student then experiments with each subproblem until he or she has worked out a satisfactory solution to each one. The solutions are then combined to provide the answer to the major problem.

In many situations involving a student with a disability, independent discovery will need to be a cooperative endeavor

---

*The teacher should be aware that when using the right arm to stroke the ball with a backward movement, a left-handed club is used; when making a forward stroke a right-handed club is used.

between the student and the teacher. For example, solving the problem of how a student with an amputated hand can swim the crawl stroke will require the student to try various positions and movements. The teacher will observe and, applying knowledge of mechanical analysis, suggest additional variations with which the student may experiment. Following this pattern of cooperative effort between student and teacher, a solution will eventually be discovered.

In some disability areas, the problem-solving approach may be very difficult for the student to utilize. For example, with students who do not generalize well or for whom concrete and predictable activity is preferred, this method of teaching may be difficult. From an instruction standpoint, the teacher should explore whether this method matches a student's need and the student is actually learning, or whether the technique is only causing the student frustration.

Synthesis of Methods

In actual practice, many physical education teachers combine the problem-solving and traditional methods of teaching. The author believes such a synthesis is a highly effective way of teaching youngsters with disabilities. It unites the best of each method and permits flexibility so that the teacher can choose the method best suited to a specific situation and to personal talents and abilities.

A synthesis of the two methods is likely to be more effective in helping students to achieve the objectives of the program than the exclusive use of either method may be. It allows students to be creative and experimental and impresses upon them the possibilities of movement their bodies can achieve. It will encourage them to think reflectively and to apply the process of logical reasoning in solving the problem. But if, at any time, the teacher should sense a lack of security among the students with the problem-solving method, or confusion arising from failure to solve the motor task, the instructor can shift to the more direct approach. When time is a factor in developing a phase of the program, certain aspects of the motor problem being considered can be taught with the traditional techniques, since they generally require less time. Review of formally learned skills and evaluation of performance may also generally be more efficiently handled by traditional methods.

Summary

Physical education teachers of students with disabilities utilize many of the same attributes helpful in teaching any student: namely patience, creativity, a sense of humor, and an appreciation for individual differences. These attributes, combined with the unique professional qualifications identified by professional organizations, equip today's physical educator with the necessary skills and knowledge to provide effective instruction for students with disabilities. Successful teachers know that they must have a thorough understanding of federal and state legislation pertaining to the disabled. This information will be valuable in ensuring that Individualized Education Programs (IEPs) include instruction in physical education with appropriate goals and objectives. The Individualized Family Service Plan (IFSP) addresses the motor needs of infants and toddlers. Physical education teachers should also have an appreciation of the least restrictive environment and the importance of creating opportunities for students with and without disabilities to interact.

One of the specialized skills the teacher of special physical education should possess is the ability to analyze and apply the principles of movement to students with disabilities. A strategy that can be very helpful in this respect is task analysis, a process by which the components of an activity are identified and then ordered according to their level of difficulty. Ecological task analysis is also recommended. Teachers should also know how to motivate students and create positive learning environments. An understanding of the process to use when inappropriate behavior occurs is also essential. Knowledge of various medications and their effects on students will help in establishing meaningful assessment data and establishing appropriate baselines.

Teachers of special physical education should be familiar with direct and indirect teaching methods and the appropriateness of these when combined with the techniques of verbalization, visualization, and kinesthesis. As the appreciation for these and other skills helpful in teaching increases, the teacher's sensitivity toward the needs of the student with a disability will deepen. There also will be a growing awareness that good teaching is good teaching and that students with disabilities, like students without disabilities, respond to a concerned and knowledgeable teacher.

Enhancing Activities

1. Develop a task analysis for a selected activity and utilize the analysis with a student who has a disability. Then develop an ecological task analysis.
2. Contact a local school district and ask permission to observe an IEP meeting. Obtain the IEP forms used by the district and develop an IEP for a selected student.
3. Interview physical education teachers to obtain their views and perspectives on teaching students with disabilities. Do they tend to be generally positive or negative in their attitude toward the disabled?
4. Obtain a copy of the *Physicians' Desk Reference* and review.
5. Review the competencies identified in table 5.1 to determine how many of these you now possess.
6. Observe a physical education class and tally how many positive versus negative comments are made by the teacher and the students in the class. Focus on any student that appears to be exhibiting inappropriate behavior. Analyze the situation to see what changes you might recommend in the teaching environment.

Selected Readings

Ackerman, V., & Dummer, G. (1982). *Behavior management in physical education: A handbook for teachers.* Maryland State Department of Education and Towson State University. (*Note: These two organizations published the manuscript.)

Alschuler, A. (1973). *Developing achievement motivation in adolescents.* Englewood Cliffs, NJ: Educational Technology Publications.

Baker, C. E., Jr. (1988). *Physicians' desk reference* (42nd ed.). Oradell, NJ: Medical Economics Company, Litton Division.

Ballard, J. E., Boileau, R. A., Sleator, E. K., Majjey, B. A., & Sprague, R. L. (1976). Cardiovascular responses of hyperactive children to methylphenidate. *Journal of the American Medical Association, 236,* 2870–2874.

Bennett, F., Eisenman, P., French, R., Henderson, H., & Shultz, B. (1989). The effect of a token economy on the exercise behavior of individuals with Down Syndrome. *Adapted Physical Activity Quarterly, 6,* 230–246.

Buysee, V., & Wesley, P. W. (2005). *Consultation in early childhood settings.* Baltimore, MD: Paul Brookes.

Davis, W., & Burton, A. (1991). Ecological Task Analysis: Translating movement behavior theory into practice. *Adapted Physical Activity Quarterly, 8,* 154–157.

Deal, A., Dunst, C., & Trivett, C. (1989). A flexible and functional approach to developing individualized family support plans. *Infants and Young Children: An Interdisciplinary Journal of Special Care Practices, 1*(4), 32–43.

Dempsey, S. (1987). *A comparison of college/university professors and specialists in adapted physical education in their perception of the importance of a specified set of professional competencies.* (Doctoral dissertation.)

DePaepe, J. L. (1985). The influence of three least restrictive environments on the content motor ALT and performance of moderately mentally retarded students. *Journal of Teaching in Physical Education, 3,* 34–41.

Department of Education. (1981, January 19). Part XII, assistance to states for education of handicapped children; interpretation of the Individualized Education Program (IEP). *Federal Register.* Washington, DC: Author.

Department of Health, Education, and Welfare, Office of Education. (1977, August 23). Education of handicapped children, Article II, implementation of Part B of the Education of the Handicapped Act. *Federal Register.* Washington, DC: Author.

Dunn, J. M. (1979). *Adaptive physical education: A resource guide for teachers, administrators, and parents.* Salem, OR: State of Oregon, Mental Health Division.

Dunn, J. M. (1991). P. L. 99–457: Challenges and Opportunities for Physical Education. *Journal of Physical Education, Recreation, and Dance, 47,* 33–34.

Dunn, J. M., & Fredericks, H. D. B. (1985). The utilization of behavior management in mainstreaming in physical education. *Adapted Physical Activity Quarterly, 4*(2), 338–346.

Dunn, J. M., & French, R. (1982). Operant conditioning: A tool for special educators in the 1980s. *Exceptional Education Quarterly, 3*(1), 42–53.

Dunn, J. M., Morehouse, J. W., & Fredericks, H. D. (1986). *Physical education for the severely handicapped.* Austin, TX: Pro-Ed Publishers.

Fait, H. F. (1976). *Experiences in movement: Physical education for the elementary school child* (3rd ed.). Philadelphia: W. B. Saunders Co.

French, R., & Jansma, P. (1981). Medication, learning disabilities, and physical education. *American Corrective Therapy Journal, 35,* 26–30.

Gadow, K. D. (1977, April). *Psychotropic and anticonvulsant drug usage in early childhood special education programs III. A preliminary report: Parent interviews about drug treatment.* Paper presented at the Annual Meeting of The Council for Exceptional Children, Atlanta, GA. (ERIC Document Reproduction Service No. ED 139 182.)

Gadow, K. D. (1979). *Children on medication: A primer for school personnel.* Reston, VA: The Council for Exceptional Children.

Geddes, D. (1981). *Psychomotor individualized educational programs.* Boston: Allyn and Bacon, Inc.

Gibson, J. J. (1979). An ecological approach to visual perception. Boston: Houghton Mifflin.

Gittelman-Klein, R., Katz, S., Klein, D. F., Abikoff, H., Gloisten, A. C., & Kates, W. (1976). Relative efficacy of methylphenidate and behavior modification in hyperkinetic children: An interim report. *Journal of Abnormal Child Psychology, 4,* 361–379.

Houston-Wilson, C., Dunn, J. M., van der Mars, H., & McCubbin, J. A. (1997). The effect of peer tutors on motor performance in integrated physical education classes. *Adapted Physical Activity Quarterly, 14*(4), 298–313.

Kelly, L. E. (1995). *Adapted physical education national standards.* Champaign, IL: Human Kinetics Publishers.

Kennedy, P., Terdal, L., & Fusetti, L. (1993). *The hyperactive child book.* New York: St. Martin's Press, p. 276.

Lere, R. J., Lere, P. M., & Artner, J. (1977). The effects of methylphenidate on the handwriting of children with minimal brain dysfunction. *Journal of Pediatrics, 91,* 127–132.

Londeree, B., & Johnson, L. E. (1976). *Motor fitness test for the moderately mentally retarded.* Washington, DC: AAHPERD.

Newell, K. M. (1986). Constraints on the development of coordination. In M. G. Wade & H. T. A. Whiting (Eds.), *Motor development in children: Aspects of coordination and control* (pp. 341–360). Dordrecht: Martinus Nijhoff.

Rizzo, T. (1984). Attitudes of physical educators toward teaching handicapped pupils. *Adapted Physical Activity Quarterly, 1*(4), 267–274.

Rizzo, T. L., & Vispoel, W. P. (1991). Physical educators' attributes and attitudes toward teaching students with handicaps. *Adapted Physical Activity Quarterly, 8*(1), 4–11.

Roche, A. F., Lipman, R. S., Overall, J. E., & Hung, W. (1979). The effects of stimulant medication on the growth of hyperkinetic children. *Pediatrics, 63*(6), 847–850.

Seligman, M. (1975). *Helplessness.* San Francisco: Freeman Press.

Sherrill, C. (1993). *Adapted physical education and recreation* (4th ed.). Dubuque, IA: Wm. C. Brown Publishers.

Sleator, E. K., & Sprague, R. L. (1978). Pediatric pharmacotherapy. In W. G. Clark & J. del Guidice (Eds.), *Principles of psychopharmacology* (2nd ed.). New York: Academic Press.

Sprague, R. L., & Sleator, E. K. (1975). What is the proper dose of stimulant drugs in children? *International Journal of Mental Health, 4,* 75–104.

Suphawibul, M. (1990). *Competencies for adapted physical educators in Thailand.* Unpublished dissertation. Oregon State University.

Turnbull, A. P., Strickland, B., & Brantley, J. C. (1978). *Developing and implementing IEPs.* Columbus, OH: Charles E. Merrill Publishing Co.

Vogler, E. W., van der Mars, H., Cusimano, B., & Darst, P. (1992). Experience, expertise, and teaching effectiveness with mainstreamed and nondisabled children in physical education. *Adapted Physical Activity Quarterly, 9*(4), 316–329.

Webster, G. E. (1987). Influence of peer tutors upon academic learning time—physical education of mentally handicapped students. *Journal of Teaching in Physical Education, 1,* 393–403.

Wessel, J. (1976). *I CAN program.* Northbrook, IL: Hubbard Scientific Company.

Winnick, J., & Hurwitz, J. (Eds.). (1979). *The preparation of regular physical educators for mainstreaming.* Brockport, NY: SUNY Press.

Wloodkowski, R. W. (1977). *Motivation.* Washington, DC: National Education Association.

Evaluation

CHAPTER OBJECTIVES

After studying this chapter, the reader should be able to:

1 Appreciate the need to evaluate the motor performance of students with disabilities and the benefits ranging from student screening to communication between home and school.
2 Comprehend the federal requirements of federal and state law related to the evaluation of students with disabilities, including assessment of the motor domain.
3 Identify the general and specific types of motor performance tests.
4 Explain the similarities and differences among the following types of tests and provide an example of each: developmental scales; motor skill tests; perceptual-motor tests; motor ability tests; and physical fitness tests.
5 Explain the differences and similarities between norm-referenced and criterion-referenced tests and the appropriate use of each.
6 Locate and retrieve sources of information about various tests that can be used to assess the motor and physical fitness performance of students with disabilities.
7 Define and apply various terms such as "validity," "reliability," "standard error of measure," and "standard score," which are used in describing and analyzing tests of physical fitness and motor performance.
8 Identify and discuss the process and elements to be used in selecting motor and physical fitness tests to employ with students with disabilities.
9 Analyze tests to ensure that the statistical properties of a test are such that the test is appropriate for use with students with disabilities.
10 Identify and discuss issues pertinent to the evaluation of the motor and physical fitness performance of students with disabilities.

Implicit in the term "special physical education" is the mandate to provide students with a physical education experience that is of greatest benefit to them as individuals. Good decisions concerning how to provide the best possible physical education program to students are based on sound evaluation of their individual needs and abilities. Periodically, evaluation must also be made to determine the amount of improvement that has occurred and to discover the kinds of activities and kinds of procedures and techniques in teaching that are proving most effective.

Standardized and nonstandardized tests are used to evaluate motor performance in physical education. However, because fundamentals of developing, administering, and interpreting such tests are established in courses of measurement and evaluation required of physical education majors, written test development will not be discussed and only such information as is germane to evaluating movement skills of those with disabilities will be presented in this chapter.

The terms "assessment" and "evaluation" are often used interchangeably in special education. For our purposes, assessment is the assigning of numbers to a movement performance, and evaluation is the resulting judgment(s) made by the professional based on the assessment data (Burton & Miller, 1998). It is critical in the use of standardized, nonstandardized, and observational assessment to realize the importance of the physical educator's expertise in interpreting the data for the special education team, the student, and the family. This chapter will illustrate the factors to be considered for making professional judgments regarding student movement skill performance for special education eligibility, placement, and the ongoing evaluation of student's progress in learning.

IDEA '97, and the reauthorization, IDEA 2004, requires that a student must first be evaluated to determine her ability to perform successfully in the general education curriculum. When it is determined that the student is unable to participate successfully in the curriculum for her grade, then consideration for special physical education services is initiated to determine if the student meets eligibility requirements. Each state determines its own eligibility requirements given the federal mandate to provide a free, appropriate, public education (FAPE) for all students. **For physical educators, consideration is given to the extent that the student can participate in the general physical education curriculum, the modifications and adaptations that are needed for success, and the physical education placement implied by the student's needs.** For example, is the student able to participate in the aquatics unit but not in the football unit? Is the student able to participate in any of the general education curriculum or does she need a specialized adapted physical activity program?

As described in chapter 3, the terms "movement skills" and "motor abilities" (Burton & Miller, 1998) will be used to guide the assessment of students and the resulting evaluation results. Movement skills are the observable skills, whereas motor abilities are felt to be inferred in the movement performance. The focus on observable movement skills is appropriate given the current focus in special education on evaluating functional skills that students need in order to be successful in their educational life (Kleinert & Kearns, 2001) and, in this case, for the physical education class (e.g., Lieberman & Houston-Wilson, 2002). Observable movement skills are applied to skills performed in infancy and toddlerhood, on through preschool, early elementary, elementary, middle, and high school (see chapter 3, figure 3.4).

Need for Evaluation

There are many reasons why students with disabilities benefit from a physical education program that includes a strong evaluation component. One of the obvious reasons is that evaluation helps teachers, parents, and students recognize progress and in turn permits an effective exchange of communication between the school and home. Teachers also can use the results of student progress to analyze their own effectiveness as well as their methods of instruction and the curricular materials that they have utilized. The value of evaluation is so numerous and varied in special education

Purposes of Evaluation Program

- Screening
- Establish eligibility for special physical education service
- Develop individualized physical education programs
- Analyze educational progress
- Review curricular effectiveness
- Communication between home and school

that students must be evaluated in a variety of educational areas, including movement performance. In the following paragraphs some of the benefits derived from evaluation will be examined.

Screening

One of the primary aspects of an evaluation program is screening for students who are suspected of having developmental delays in movement skill or who are in need of assistance, within the parameters of special education services, to be successful within their physical education class. Through this process, individuals who have specific needs can be identified. Currently, when screening is formally conducted, written permission of the parent or legal guardian is expected. Screening tests differ from a comprehensive test of movement performance, in that screening tools identify selected skills considered important for development in a specific domain(s). Such tests help "red flag" children who are not developing within a range considered typical for their age. For example, the Denver Developmental Screening Tool (Denver II) (Frankenburg & Dobbs, 1992) screens across early childhood skills: gross motor, language, fine motor-adaptive, and personal-social. The test is developed for use with ages beginning at the first month of life through age six years. If delay is identified, then additional tests that are more comprehensive and in-depth can be administered to confirm or refute the findings of the screening test. It is then up to the special education team to decide if the student can be considered eligible to receive services. To be effective, the screening procedure must be efficient, time-effective, and highly reliable.

Informal screening also occurs when adults observe that a student is not performing, in movement skills or with developmentally appropriate games and sports, at the same level as his peers. Sometimes this is referred to as the "concern and reflection stage" in the referral process (Colarusso & O'Rourke, 2003). Here, in informal ways, observations are made by parents in the home and community, physicians in their offices, special educators at recess time, and general physical education teachers in the gymnasium. Sometimes, in consultation with adapted physical educators, observations can be systematic and repeated in a similar setting across a similar time. If there is an unofficial consensus that a problem may exist, or if deep parental concern is voiced, then formal screening assessments can be initiated leading to more comprehensive assessments for special education eligibility if necessary.

Establish Eligibility for Special Physical Education Service

A second purpose of an evaluation program is to establish which students are eligible for special physical education services. Students identified as potential candidates through the screening process are referred for further evaluation to confirm the results of the screening. Additional tests are conducted to determine whether the student qualifies for special education services. Further testing also helps to pinpoint the student's specific strengths and weaknesses and particular educational needs. It is at this stage that the question of whether the student's movement skill performance warrants special physical education services is answered. Moreover, it is necessary and consistent with the intent of IDEA 2004 to assess the student's motor and fitness skills so that an objective decision can be made about the student's physical education needs.

In some states, prereferral interventions must take place before a comprehensive evaluation is initiated to determine eligibility for special education services. Teachers and a team of support staff must identify interventions and implement them to determine whether success can be attained in the general education class if accommodations and modifications are made (Colarusso & O'Rourke, 2003). This prereferral and resulting level of intervention has reduced the number of inappropriate referrals for special education.

Develop Individualized Physical Education Programs

The additional evaluative information generated when determining the student's eligibility for special physical education services is the cornerstone in developing Individualized Education Programs. This aspect of the evaluation program assists in translating the assessment results into a meaningful program. Annual instructional goals that reflect the student's strengths and weaknesses can be developed to serve as the foundation upon which a physical education program, specific to the needs of the students, can be built.

Analyze Educational Progress

A periodic review of the annual goals and objectives coupled with further evaluation provides a mechanism whereby the effectiveness of the physical education experience can be determined. This aspect of the evaluation program is essential. Information obtained through this process informs the teacher, parents, and student about the extent to which educational progress has occurred. Areas where significant gains were made as well as areas where the instructional gains were minimal can also be identified. Teachers, therefore, can begin to systematically analyze their instructional process. A lack of student progress may lead a teacher to conclude that a specific instructional methodology is not appropriate for a given student. Questions can also be raised about the educational material utilized or the environment in which the experience was provided.

Review Curricular Effectiveness

Evaluation of student progress has many curricular ramifications. For instance, the lack of improvement in a student's physical fitness program may be due to the insufficient time allocated for the program. Likewise, some students may not progress because the curricular sequences are too difficult, requiring that skills be further task-analyzed and broken down into smaller steps. Evaluation results can also help to analyze the effectiveness of educational experiences in alternative placements. A review of the progress of a student who has recently been integrated into a general physical education class can only be effectively conducted if sufficient evaluative data are available.

Communication between Home and School

Communication with students and their parents is greatly enhanced if there is a well-developed evaluation plan available within the IEP. The evaluation plan is not to be confused with the evaluation conducted to establish eligibility for special education services. Herein, evaluation plans refer to the means by which the IEP goals for the student are monitored. Teachers, naturally, feel more comfortable talking about a student's achievement if some objective data are available to support their position. Parents and students also more readily accept input if they feel teachers are attempting to be objective rather than subjective in their remarks. An evaluation plan helps the communication process because parents recognize and appreciate efforts to determine progress in their children's performance. Educational accountability requires that there be an evaluation plan to show student progress from year to year.

Evaluation is a valuable process whereby teachers, students, parents, and administrators can systematically analyze the effects of instruction. To maximize the benefits of education for each special student requires that certain variables, such as the amount of instruction time, placement setting, nature of the activity, and number of aides or volunteers, be monitored closely. Evaluative data are essential, therefore, to help school personnel and parents recognize that changes in these or other variables may have an effect on the student's progress.

Evaluation and Legal Requirements

The Education for All Handicapped Children Act of 1975 (PL 94-142) emphasized the importance of the evaluation process in the delivery of educational services to students with disabilities. The law established a framework in which evaluation became the cornerstone to the type of program provided and a reference point for educational outcomes. As discussed in earlier chapters, PL 94-142 has been amended several times. The most recent reauthorization is Individuals with Disabilities Education Improvement Act of 2004 (IDEA 2004). Through the reauthorizations since 1975, the essential provisions of this federal educational law have changed. Now, physical education is not an academic area under special education. It is important that all educators, including teachers of physical education, have a clear and comprehensive understanding of federal law for students with disabilities and the provisions related to evaluation.

In the following paragraphs, information will be provided to assist the teacher in understanding the requirements that must be adhered to in the process of assessing the special education student. Table 6.1 provides an example of the safeguards of federal law against assessment abuse.

Identification

Every state is required to develop a plan for identifying, locating, and evaluating all students with disabilities within the state. Most State Departments of Education work in cooperation with local education agencies to implement a plan for identifying school-age students in order to deliver services to individuals with disabling conditions. Identifying students with suspected problems also applies to the area of physical education, where students should be routinely and systematically observed for delay and the inability to succeed in physical education without assistance. Teachers have a right and responsibility to refer those students whose motor and physical fitness levels deviate significantly.

Prereferral

The referral plan employed by most school systems involves a variety of procedures. Standardized tests are used, as well as other informal techniques, such as teacher checklists and systematic observation of student performance. School records may also be consulted as a source of information. As mentioned previously, some states are requiring a prereferral where, in the case of physical education, teachers put in place at least two interventions for students who deviate from their peers in motor and fitness skills. If these interventions fail, then a referral for eligibility for special physical education is made. This process involves the teacher and the parents.

Due Process

Federal law ensures that children with disabilities and their parents are guaranteed procedural safeguards. This protection, commonly known as due process, means that parents and their children will be informed of their rights, with the provision that they may challenge educational decisions that they feel are unfair. Informing the parents of their rights is an important process that must be administered in an organized and systematic manner. For this reason, most local education agencies assign this responsibility to an administrator, normally the director of special education. What will follow, therefore, is a summary of some of the important due process considerations.

Permission Prior to Evaluation

A written notice must be given to the parents indicating that their child has been referred and that the school requests permission to conduct an evaluation for the purpose of determining whether the child requires special education services. Parents must give written permission before the evaluation can be conducted. The letter sent to the parents seeking permission to evaluate must include a reason for the evaluation and a list and description of the tests to be used. A copy of the parents' rights must also be included. Figure 6.1 on page 122 is an example of a form that includes the necessary information.

The school is responsible for documenting that permission to test was obtained. Furthermore, all communication with the parents must be clearly presented and, if necessary, in the native language of the parents.

Results of the Evaluation

The results of all tests conducted with the student must be interpreted in a meeting with the parents. Persons who are knowledgeable about the tests administered must be available to respond to any questions the parents may have about the test process or the obtained results. Finally, the parents must be told whether their child has a condition that qualifies under IDEA 2004 (see table 6.2 on page 123) and, if so, what special education and related services will be provided. Younger children ages three through nine are discussed in chapter 15.

TABLE 6.1   Safeguards of Federal Legislation Against Assessment Abuses

Past Abuses	Safeguards
Students evaluated for special education without notice to parents or parental consent	Prior written notice must be given to parents before evaluation; parents must give consent before evaluation [121a.504]*
Culturally biased tests used in evaluation	Tests must be selected and administered so that they are not racially or culturally discriminatory [121a.530]
Non-English-speaking students assessed in English	Tests must be provided and administered in the child's native language or other mode of communication, if feasible [121a.532]
Tests administered by untrained or poorly trained personnel	Trained professionals must administer tests according to the test instructions [121a.532]
Poor-quality assessment instruments used for evaluation	Tests must have been validated for the specific purpose for which they are used [121a.532]
Tests used that penalized individuals with disabilities	Tests must be selected so that they do not discriminate against the individual on the basis of disability (unless their purpose is the identification of the disabling condition) [121a.532]
Placement in services based solely on IQ scores	No one procedure may be used as the sole criterion for determination of the educational program [121a.532]; tests selected for use in evaluation must include not merely those that yield a single general IQ score [121a.532]
Placement decisions made without a complete evaluation of the individual	Individuals must be assessed in all areas related to the suspected disability (e.g., health, vision, hearing, social and emotional status, general intelligence, academic performance, communicative status, motor ability) [121a.532]; information from a variety of sources (aptitude and achievement tests, teacher recommendations, physical condition, social and cultural background, adaptive behavior) must be documented and carefully considered [121a.533]

*The numbers in brackets refer to a section of the *Code of Federal Regulations;* 45 CFR 121a contains regulations promulgated under the Education of the Handicapped Act (PL 91-320), as amended by the Education of All Handicapped Children Act (PL 94-142) and the Individuals with Disabilities Education Act (PL 101-476).

Outside Evaluation

If the parent wishes, an independent evaluation of the student can be conducted to confirm or refute the findings of the local school. The parents must pay for the independent evaluation unless the results obtained differ from the information previously provided by the school system, in which case the cost is borne by the school district.

Hearings

If the parents and the school system cannot agree on the evaluation findings, efforts to mediate the differences should be undertaken. This process normally requires that both sides review their positions and continue to talk and negotiate in an effort to resolve the differences. When mediation fails, an impartial hearing officer is appointed to hear

---

PRIOR NOTICE AND CONSENT FOR EVALUATION

Dear _____ :　　　　　　　　　　　Date _____

We would like to inform you that your child, _____ , is being referred for individual testing which will help us in his/her educational planning. Following is a description of any records, reports, or previously administered tests which were used as a basis for recommending this evaluation: _____

_____

The following options for dealing with the above concerns were considered and rejected for the reasons specified: _____

_____

The evaluation procedures and / or test will include the areas checked below:

☐ ACADEMIC ACHIEVEMENT
Assessment of basic skill development measuring current achievement in reading, mathematics, spelling, and other areas as appropriate.

☐ BEHAVIOR AND/OR PERSONALITY
Assessment of current emotional/social development, adaptive behavior, or personality.

☐ COMMUNICATION DEVELOPMENT
Assessment of current communication skills including the ability to use speech and/or language clearly and appropriately.

☐ HEARING
Assessment including air and bone conduction, pure-tone audiometry, and discrimination tests as appropriate.

☐ INTELLECTUAL DEVELOPMENT
Assessment of general intelligence measuring current verbal and/or nonverbal intellectual functioning.

☐ PHYSICAL
Assessment of coordination of body movements in small and large muscle activities.

☐ OTHER _____
(Specify areas)

Following is a description of any other factors which are relevant to the proposed testing: _____

_____

An explanation of your rights regarding the identification, evaluation, and placement of your child according to State Administrative Rules is on the reverse side of this form.

Since State Law requires that the district receive written consent before proceeding with testing, please sign this permission form and return it as soon as possible. If you have any questions, please feel free to contact me.

_____　_____　_____
Name/Title　　　　　　　　　　　Telephone　　　　　　　　　　Date

I understand and agree to the above described individual testing or other evaluation. I also understand that the granting of consent is voluntary and may be revoked at any time. I have received a copy of my rights.

Permission is *given* to conduct the evaluation as described _____ _____
　　　　　　　　　　　　　　　　　　　　　　　　Parent/Guardian　　　Date

Permission is *denied* to conduct the evaluation as described _____ _____
　　　　　　　　　　　　　　　　　　　　　　　　Parent/Guardian　　　Date

PLEASE RETAIN GOLDENROD PARENT COPY FOR YOUR RECORDS
Please return other copies to: _____　　_____
　　　　　　　　　　　　　　　Name/Title　　　　　　　　　　　　　Location

Figure 6.1 Parental consent for evaluation form.

both parties, review the available information, and render a decision.

Confidentiality of Records

Only parents of the special education student and authorized school personnel are permitted to review the student's records. This confidentiality clause includes all available evaluation information. Other persons who request to review the file may do so only after the parents have given written permission. The names, dates, and purposes for which the file was reviewed by persons other than the parents or authorized school personnel must also be maintained.

When the school system determines that certain information is no longer pertinent or helpful, the material may be destroyed if the parents are notified and they agree with the decision.

TABLE 6.2	Federal Law Categories of Disabilities

Autism	Emotional disturbance
Hearing impairment including deafness	Mental retardation
Other health impairment	Orthopedic impairment
Speech or language impairment	Specific learning disability
Visual impairment including blindness	Traumatic brain injury

Adapted from the Federal Law definition of disability, IDEA 2004, 34 C.F.R., Section 602.3.

Standards for Evaluation

The legal requirements of the federal law not only help to ensure that an evaluation process will be utilized but also help to establish standards that must be adhered to in the evaluation process. This is a marked departure from some of the past practices in which the label of handicap was primarily related to the student's intelligence quotient without concern for the performance capabilities of the student in other areas. Specific provisions of IDEA '97 related to standards for test selection, administration, and test examiner are presented here. IDEA 2004 regulations may differ slightly.

Test Selection

The instruments used to gather evaluative data must be valid tools designed to reflect the student's aptitude or achievement level, or whatever other factors the test purports to measure, rather than reflecting the student's impaired sensory, manual, or speaking skills. **It is essential that more than one test procedure be utilized to determine the student's educational status.** This means that more than one test instrument is necessary and that formal as well as informal evaluation techniques are desirable. Total reliance on norm-referenced tests alone, for example, will not provide meaningful motor fitness test scores for students with severe and/or multiple disabilities. More detail on the implementation of test selection is described later in this chapter.

A major shift has taken place in evaluation of a student for special education (and upheld in IDEA 2004) in that there must first be documentation that the student cannot succeed in the general education class without modification and adaptations or, in some cases, a segregated physical education class. Thus, the evaluation process must include documentation that this criterion for eligibility has been met.

Test Administration

Many students with disabilities have communication problems. For this reason, it is important that tests be administered in such a way that they measure the students'

ability rather than their communication skills. Adaptations in test protocol may be necessary, therefore, for students who have visual and hearing impairments. Students whose native language is other than English will also require special attention to be certain that tests do not discriminate because of a language barrier. The important concern is that the test measure the students' motor abilities and performance levels rather than measure their communication and language skills. When the standardized test protocol has been adapted, this must be included in the report and care must be taken with interpretation of test results. In some cases where the adaptations have changed the test, norms are *not* reported, but rather test results describe what the student **was able to do** given the test. For example, if the student with visual impairment needs extra physical assistance in the Test of Gross Motor Development (Ulrich, 2000), such assistance should be noted and the findings reported.

Test Examiners

IDEA 2004 emphasizes the importance of a multidisciplinary team approach to assessment. Incorporating the expertise of several professionals increases the probability that an accurate evaluation relevant to the student's educational needs will be made. Professionals involved in the assessment process must be trained and qualified to administer tests and interpret test results. Whereas federal law emphasizes the importance of qualified test administrators, it does not specify, for instance, the qualifications necessary to administer tests of motor ability. These decisions must be made by local school systems. Assigning this responsibility to special physical educators is logical because of their expertise, as well as their ability to relate test results to the educational programming available in the physical education setting.

Approach to Testing

According to Burton (Burton & Miller, 1998), the approach to testing a student is either bottom-up or top-down. Bottom-up is considered the classical developmental approach where a hierarchy of movement skills are identified beginning at the younger ages progressing to the later years of high school. A graphic display of the hierarchy of curriculum is presented in figure 6.2. Assumed within this hierarchy is that there are developmental movement skills accompanying the progression that the student makes from early school years to the later years. Using the bottom-up approach, the student is not allowed to progress on to the next level/activity until competency has been reached in the lower skill areas. It is felt that lower-skill accomplishment later contributes to more complicated skill accomplishment. Therefore, the instructional strategy is to move the student along a developmental progression that is felt to be both normative and curriculum-based.

The top-down approach recognizes that functional ability in a skill or game area may be reachable by the student without all the assumed prerequisite skills. This is particularly apropos for students with disabilities who may never be able to perform all the lower-level skills. For example, a child with spastic cerebral palsy who has increased tone in the muscles of the arms may never demonstrate the criterion of "throw" as described on the Test of Gross Motor Development (Ulrich, 2000). The spasticity may impede performance, but this child can throw a ball. It is functional.

Another advantage of using a top-down approach is the recognition that children with disabilities may not perform the typical developmental sequences expected even at the younger ages. For example, some children with cerebral palsy never crawl; but some will sit up, shuffle forward on their bottom (scoot), and then stand up and walk (Largo, Molinan, Weber, Comedale-Pinto, & Duc, 1985). Thus, the top-down approach is useful with younger children. Figure 6.3 outlines the approach to both assessing from a top-down approach and also for instruction. Note in this figure that the goal is identified and then the student is given choices in the movement skill. This can include setting out a number of different types of balls if the skill is throwing or kicking for soccer. The instructor tests the movement task and observes how the student is able to perform the task. Then a series of steps are taken by the instructor to ascertain whether manipulating some of the variables makes any difference in the performance. It is felt that for evaluation purposes, the process could stop here. The remaining steps move into instruction.

This top-down approach is consistent with an ecological task analysis approach to teaching skills (Davis & Burton, 1991) where the unique characteristics of the individual, the task, and the environment in which the task is being performed become important considerations in predicting and understanding the individual's movement performance. See figure 6.4 on page 126 for an example of an ecological task analysis checklist that could be utilized in an instructional setting.

The top-down approach is also consistent with some of the informal evaluation approaches outlined later in this chapter.

Figure 6.2 Physical education hierarchy of curriculum model from Kelly (1989). Adapted from the *Journal of Physical Education, Recreation & Dance*, volume 60, issue 9, 1989, pages 29–32. JOPERD is a publication of the American Alliance for Health, Physical Education, Recreation and Dance, 1900 Association Drive, Reston, VA 22091.

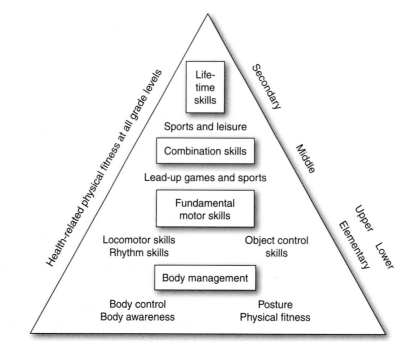

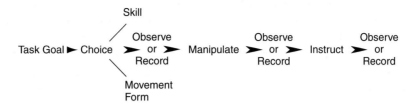

Steps:

1. Select and present the task goal—one of the functional movement categories. Structure the environment and provide verbal and other cues to the student that allow for an understanding of the task goal.

2. Provide choices—have the student practice the task, allowing him/her to choose the skill and the movement form. Observe and/or record the skill choice and movement form in qualitative measures and the performance outcome in quantitative or qualitative measures.

3. Identify the relevant task dimensions and performer variables. Manipulate one or two task dimensions to find the optimal performance level. Observe and/or record the skill choice, movement form, and performance outcomes in qualitative and/or quantitative measures, and compare results with previous measures.

4. Provide direct instruction in skill selection and movement form. Manipulate task variable to challenge the student. Observe and/or record the skill choice, movement form, and performance outcomes in qualitative and/or quantitative measures, and compare results with previous measures.

Figure 6.3 Ecological task analysis model for assessment and instruction of movement tasks. This is also known as top-down approach. (Source: from Davis, W. E., & Burton, A. W. (1991). Translating movement behavior theory into practice. *Adapted Physical Activity Quarterly, 8*(2), 167.)

Test Selection for Qualifying Students for Special Physical Education The federal educational law under IDEA 2004 has identified disability categories (see table 6.2). For a student to receive special education, he must first have a disability (ages three to six are exceptions to this, see chapter 15). Then, the student must be tested to determine if he meets state eligibility requirements for service provision. **To have a disability does not mean that the student receives services in all areas addressed under special education.** Each state has the discretion to determine eligibility criteria. Figure 6.5 on page 127 is an example of criteria for the state of Minnesota. Area 1 lists the disability areas using state terminology. Under Area 2, the criteria for eligibility has two main subsections: the first is based on the use of a normed test where the student can be identified as being below 1.5 standard deviations (SD) below the mean for their age; and the second uses numerous other methods of documenting the need for adapted physical education. The use of these alternative methods requires that two tools be chosen. These alternative methods are as follows:

1. Motor and skill checklists
2. Informal tests
3. Criterion-referenced measures
4. Deficits in achievement related to the defined curriculum
5. Medical history and reports
6. Parent and staff interviews
7. Systematic observations
8. Social, emotional, and behavioral assessments

This chapter provides descriptions of both types of evaluation tools: those that have standardization procedures and are norm-referenced, and those without such procedures. It is the "without" that has come to the forefront for special educators for a number of reasons. One is that it is difficult to find evaluation tools that are normed for the populations that special education serves. Second, focus of special education service is to target skill development that is functional for the student. Many of the tools identified in the informal methods (those without standardization procedures) potentially allow the special educator the opportunity to assess within the physical education curriculum and, hence, the functional skills the student needs.

These informal tests require the application of the physical education teacher's professional judgment in documenting skill development as well as helping to design appropriate IEP goals in the motor performance and making placement decisions with the IEP team. For example, a systematic observation of a student in a general physical education class can clearly document the inability of the student to be successful compared with her peers. Combine this with a checklist of what the student can do in a grade-level curriculum in physical education, and there is not only good evidence that the student needs assistance, but also a direct link into the curriculum interventions. See figure 6.6 on page 128 for an example of curriculum-based assessment.

Ecological Task Analysis Checklist			Movement skills or patterns					
				Throw with 1 hand overhand				
					Throw w/1 hand underhand			
						Throw with 2 hands		
							Roll with 1 hand	
								Roll with 2 hands
Task	Factor	Factor						Outcome
Propel ball	from 5'	tennis ball		X				10/10
to player on	from 5'	softball		X				10/10
first base,	from 5'	8" playground ball			X			10/10
8/10 times	from 10'	tennis ball		X				7/10
	from 10'	softball		X				5/10
	from 10'	8" playground ball					X	7/10
	from 15'	tennis ball	X					5/10
	from 15'	softball				X		2/10
	from 15'	8" playground ball					X	4/10
	from 20'	tennis ball	X					2/10
	from 20'	softball				X		1/10
	from 20'	8" playground ball					X	3/10

Figure 6.4 Sample score sheet for collecting data in Step 2 (see figure 6.3). Adapted from *Movement Skill Assessment* by Allen Burton, Human Kinetics.

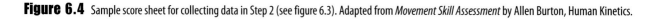

Motor Performance Tests

Testing is performed within specialized physical education to evaluate the student for eligibility of services, ongoing progress monitoring, and instructional purposes. The following test types can be used to work with students with special needs.

General Types

Several procedures may be used to assess the motor performance of students with disabilities. In the following section, some of the more commonly used procedures are presented. As will be discussed, each of the assessment procedures is

MP/S Developmental Adapted Physical Education (D/APE) Criteria Checklist
MINNEAPOLIS
PUBLIC SCHOOLS

☐ Initial
☐ Reevaluation

Learner's Name _____ DOB _____ Grade _____

School _____ Date of Evaluation Team Meeting _____

In order for a learner to be eligible for Developmental Adapted Physical Education: Special Education, the criteria in Areas 1 and 2 must be met.

Area 1

Yes No
☐ ☐ The learner meets the criteria for one of the disability categories.(Check below)

☐ autism spectrum disorders ☐ mental impairment
☐ deaf/blindness ☐ physical impairment
☐ EBD ☐ other health impairment
☐ SLD ☐ visual impairment
☐ hearing impairment ☐ DD (ages 3 to 6–11)
☐ severe multiple impairment ☐ traumatic brain injury

AND

Area 2

Yes No
☐ ☐ The team determines the learner is in need of specially designed physical education instruction because:

Yes No
☐ ☐ The learner's performance on an appropriately selected, technically adequate, norm-referenced psychomotor or physical fitness instrument is 1.5 SD or more below the mean.The instrument was individually administered by an appropriately licensed teacher.

or

☐ ☐ The learner's development or achievement and independence in school, home, and community settings is inadequate to allow success in the regular physical education program as supported by written documentation from 2 or more of the following: motor and skill checklist; informal tests; criterion-referenced measures; deficits in achievement related to the defined curriculum; medical history or reports; parent and staff interviews; systematic observations; and social, emotional, and behavioral assessments. Indicate the two or more sources below:

_____

_____

Figure 6.5 Eligibility requirements for state of Minnesota.

valuable in a comprehensive approach to evaluating the motor characteristics of the students with special needs.

Norm-Referenced Tests

In the past, most physical education tests were called norm-referenced tests. This type of evaluation procedure consists of developing a test and then administering it to a randomly selected group of individuals which become the normative sample. The test results from this normative sample become the criteria against which subsequent test takers can compare individual performances. The norm is the average performance of the normative sample group. The comparisons help the teacher to identify students who are in need of special physical education assistance.

In the examiner's manual, which accompanies norm-referenced tests, information about the test's validity, reliability,

Jump

1. Demonstrate jumping using good form which includes: _____
   a. knees and hips are flexed and arms swing backwards.
   b. swing both arms forward and upward as knees and ankles extend.
   c. land lightly on 2 feet, bending knees and ankles to cushion shock of landing.
2. Jump forward 18 inches using good form. _____

Hop

3. Demonstrate hopping using good form which includes: _____
   a. spring lightly upward, taking off with ankle extension and landing lightly on ball of the foot.
   b. knees and arms are relaxed.
4. Hop 2 times on right foot, transfer, 2 times on left foot. _____

Skip

5. Demonstrate skipping using good form which includes: _____
   a. the skip is a step hop, the step with a long count and the hop on a short count.
   b. spring from toes and land on ball of the foot.
6. Demonstrate skipping in good form at a slow and fast speed. _____

Slide

7. Demonstrate sliding using good form which includes: _____
   a. a long step is taken to the side on one foot, bringing the other to the first.
   b. spring lightly from toe and land on ball of the foot.
8. Demonstrate sliding at a slow/fast speed and left/right using good form. _____

Bounce

9. Demonstrate bouncing a ball with one hand using good form which includes: _____
   a. wrist flexed, fingers relaxed and spread.
   b. directing ball with slightly cupped hand and fingers spread.

Kick

10. Use a toe kick to propel a ball to a partner 20 feet away. _____

Rope Jump

11. Jump rope using good form which includes: _____
    a. keeping hands below waist level while turning rope.
    b. jumping over rope lightly and close to ground.
    c. continuously turning rope over head on each jump.

Body Awareness

12. Correctly identify right and left sides of body and correctly move the body upon command: forward, backward, sideways, right, left, up, and down. _____
13. Demonstrate walking forward and turns on low balance beam. _____
14. Clap to an even and uneven rhythmic beat. _____

TOTAL [X] =   _____
Percent [(X/14) ×100] =   _____

Figure 6.6 A curriculum-based assessment with items derived from the Minneapolis Public Schools physical education curriculum for second graders (Minneapolis Public Schools, 1991).

and objectivity is presented. The directions for administering, scoring, and interpreting the tests also are provided so that the test procedure is standardized. Also found in the test manual are tables and graphs that express the normative data as standard scores, such as age equivalents or percentages, and so on, thus permitting comparisons with others of similar age.

Physical education teachers who administer the tests must follow the standardization procedures in order for the test to be valid. This then allows the teacher to use the norms in the manual to interpret the movement performance of the student being tested. If the teacher does not follow the standardization procedures of the test, then the test is not considered a valid representation of the student's skill. If, on the other hand, the performance of the student is reported as a unique score for the person (e.g., percentage of what that student could perform of the skill), then the test is not a norm-referenced test, but rather serves more as a checklist. To report the data as obtained in a checklist is considered

Motor Performance Tests

- Norm-referenced
- Criterion-referenced
- Task analysis
- Observation
- Self-evaluation
- Interviews

informal testing and is still a valid means of testing a student. The informal testing is a part of nonstandardized testing and is a valid way to determine what the student is capable of performing.

Criterion-Referenced Tests

Another type of referenced assessment is the criterion-referenced tests, which are well suited to evaluation in physical education. In the criterion-referenced test, a criterion or level of mastery of certain information or skills is established for each item of the test or for the test as a whole. See figure 6.7 for an example given for the skill of hop. The score achieved by the test taker describes how well the criterion was met. Some criterion-referenced tests have a standardized procedure and have been used with a normative sample to develop the norms. Therefore, they are also norm-referenced and will be noted as such in the manual for the test.

Task Analysis

This assessment procedure is closely related to the criterion-referenced process. With task analysis, the components of a specific task are identified and then arranged from least complex to most complex. Students are evaluated to determine whether they can master the final, most difficult step of the task. The last step may be thought of as the criterion, and in this respect the task analysis evaluation approach is identical to the criterion-referenced procedure. If, however, the student cannot master the final step, the assessment continues to determine the parts of the task that the student can perform. Assessment using a task-analyzed approach provides a great deal of useful information for later instruction. See figure 6.8 for an example of a task analysis for striking a Nerf® ball off the batting tee. This example includes a task analysis of the performance objectives.

Recent analysis of the value of task-analytic evaluation procedures has been challenged and strengthened by the work of Davis and Burton (1991). They have argued correctly that teachers need to be very careful about developing a sequence of a specific skill (e.g., catching) and then assuming that all learners will master the skill following precisely the order of subtasks as defined. The traditional task-analytic approach, which normally uses either an anatomical or developmental perspective, if used rigidly, places too much emphasis on the sequence of the skill and fails to adequately consider individual variation found within groups of learners. Davis and Burton recommend that the traditional approach to task analysis be modified to recognize that the

Figure 6.7 Criterion-referenced skill of hop from Test of Gross Motor Development (TGMD-2) Ulrich, 2000.

Section VI. Subtest Performance Record

Preferred Hand: Right ☐ Left ☐ Not Established ☐
Preferred Foot: Right ☐ Left ☐ Not Established ☐

Locomotor Subtest

Skill	Materials	Directions	Performance Criteria	Trial 1	Trial 2	Score
Hop	A minimum of 15 feet of clear space	Tell the child to hop three times on his or her preferred foot (established before testing) and then three times on the other foot. Repeat a second trial.	1. Nonsupport leg swings forward in pendular fashion to produce force			
			2. Foot of nonsupport leg remains behind body			
			3. Arms flexed and swing forward to produce force			
			4. Takes off and lands three consecutive times on preferred foot			
			5. Takes off and lands three consecutive times on nonpreferred foot			
					Skill Score	

Task Analysis

Desired or target behavior: The child will demonstrate a mature two-hand striking pattern by hitting a foam ball with a wiffle-ball bat successfully off a batting tee 9 out of 10 times. (Other types of balls and striking implements may be substituted for the bat and ball in accordance with the individual's skill level).

Steps (Task analysis of the desired or target behavior)

1. Demonstrates familiarity with the equipment that will be used to perform the striking pattern.
2. Both hands are held correctly on the bat, with the dominant hand on top.
3. Visually attends to the object (ball) that will be used to perform the striking pattern. (Use brightly colored balls.)
4. Is in proper position in relation to the batting tee. (If necessary, a physical cue such as foot steps taped on the floor can be used.)
5. Brings the bat 2 inches back from the batting tee and strikes the foam ball in a horizontal plane.
6. Brings the bat 1 foot back from the batting tee and strikes the ball in a horizontal plane.
7. Brings the bat back to shoulder height with both elbows flexed and strikes the object in a horizontal plane.
8. Develops proper contact and follow-through upon contacting the ball.

Once the process of the task is mastered the instructor can have the individual increase the striking velocity. (However, do not increase the swinging velocity at the expense of sacrificing control of the striking pattern.)

If an individual is displaying difficulty moving from one step to the next, then the task analysis may need to be altered or broken down to smaller steps. Dunn, Morehouse, and Fredericks (1986) define this procedure as branching. For example, the child accomplishes the following:

1. Brings the implement back to shoulder height with both elbows flexed and strikes the object in a horizontal plane
2. Properly grips the bat and brings it back to shoulder height with both elbows flexed
3. Stands with feet shoulder-width apart and knees comfortably flexed
4. Turns body slightly to the side
5. Turns the head and eyes toward the object on the batting tee
6. Positions weight on the back foot
7. Begins the horizontal swing with a lateral step forward on the front foot
8. Begins to extend the arms forward toward the object on the tee
9. Rotates the hips in the direction of the object
10. Shifts weight to the front foot upon contacting the object

Figure 6.8 Task analysis of strike.

capability of the performer varies due to individual and environmental constraints. For example, the approach used by a student with cerebral palsy to catch a ball will be different than a student without a neurologic impairment. Likewise, environmental constraints (e.g., the size of the ball and elements such as wind) should be considered in assessing the performance of any student. In using task-analytic procedures, it is important also to make sure that the parts (subtasks) of the skill are similar to the "whole" task so that the desired goal "catch a ball" is clear. Some of the new thoughts and arguments regarding task-analytic assessment approaches have helped to reinforce the need to always be attentive to individual differences land focus on what students *can* do as well as areas needing further work. As noted

in figure 6.4, the relationship between assessment and instruction using an ecological task-analytic approach should be dynamic and interactive.

Lieberman and Houston-Wilson (2002) have focused on physical education unit adaptations; an example of soccer modifications and adaptations are presented in figure 6.9. A circle is used to indicate if the skill has been introduced by the instructor. A check is used to identify which of the modifications would be appropriate for the given student. This form of modifying and adapting the activity is based in ecological task analysis. Also described are assessment through rubrics (see figure 6.10 on page 132). Rubrics are similar to a task-analytic approach to teaching, as well as checklists and teacher rating scales. Instead of using the term "branching" common

Potential Modifications and Adaptations

Equipment	Rules	Environment	Instruction
__ Auditory balls	— Ground pass	__ Bright boundaries	✓○ Peer tutor entire unit
__ Bright balls	__ Timed dribble	__ Carpet squares	__ Physical assistance
__ Tactile balls	__ Undefended	__ Shooting line	__ Hand signals
__ Bell balls	__ Time limitations	__ Tactile lines	__ Verbal cues
✓⊘ Nerf balls	__ Boundary limitations	__ Auditory lines	__ Close proximity
stuck under	__ Free shooting	✓ Cones	__ Signs
wheelchair	__ Throw-ins	__ Ropes	__ Brailing
10/21	__ Walk with ball	__ Clap behind goal	__ Bright clothing
__ Bells on net	__ Run with ball	__ Limit mobility	__ Discovery learning
__ Buzzer on net	✓○ Cooperation vs.	✓○ Smooth surface	✓○ Task analyze
__ Radio	competition 10/28	entire unit	10/23-11/2
__ Fan	__ Peer place ball	✓⊘ Can be goalie 10/30	used rubrics
__ Wheelchair	__ Free kicks	*bored	__ Slow down
✓○ Front bumper 10/21	__ Stay in assigned area	__ Music	__ Demonstrate
__ Smaller goal	✓○ Hands used for protection	__ Watch film	__ Feedback
__ Assigned area	10/28	__ Modify field size	__ Indirect
✓○ Ball size larger	✓○ Pass to everyone	__ Cones in front of net	__ Direct
10/23	__ 5 passes	✓○ Stations 10/21-25	✓○ Task style
__ Soft ball	__ Space as a defender	__ Decrease distractions	__ Problem solving
__ Wider goals	__ No heading		__ Lane soccer
__ Bright goals	__ 5 dribbles		✓○ Smaller groups
__ Flags	__ Do defense for 5 sec.		10/28-11-2
✓○ Pinnies 10/28	__ Pass before goal		cooperative games
__ Cones	__ Shooting zone/score		__ Small sided games
__ Whistle	__ Minimum 3 passes		
__ Bigger nets			
__ Shin guards			
__ Flip cards			
__ Ball on string			

Figure 6.9 Unit adaptations for soccer. A check = modification works well; a circle = indicates instructor has tried the variable; a circle with a line through it indicates instructor tried variable but it did not work and date is added to the right.

to task analysis, the phrase "rubric analysis" is used when there is a need to further break down the skill for the student. Rubrics are felt to be easily translated into curriculum content for the student and can be reported in the IEP meeting.

Observation

All evaluation techniques involve observation. What is meant by the use of the term here, however, is technology and non-technology oriented observation to capture the student's performance. Videotapes are used today as aids in recording motor performance. This process permits the evaluator to enlist the aid of other professionals to analyze the student's skill level. Some individuals, such as those with cerebral palsy and various orthopedic impairments, who are difficult to assess with traditional instruments, can be effectively evaluated through the use of a visual recording of their effort. Further recording of their performance at periodic intervals provides an effective means of evaluating skill improvement over time. Parents, too, find a visual recording of their youngster's motor skills a helpful process in assisting them to recognize the importance of physical education and its contribution to total development. As a

tool in the assessment process, observations are best done with emphasis on a systematic approach where observations are made across repeated classroom/gymnasium settings. In this manner, physical education teachers can provide more validity to their observations of repeated examples of movement performance for parents and members of the IEP team or motor team.

Non–technology-oriented observations include systematic evaluations of how the student is performing in her class, be it the general physical education program or otherwise. The teacher can observe for a specific amount of time, note the time, and then describe what skill is being performed by the class and how the student is performing. In this case, the observer must first make nonjudgmental descriptive statements. For example, "the class was running laps around the gymnasium. All of the students ran for five minutes. Lynn ran for two minutes and stopped and rested." At the end of the observation time (e.g., after class), the teacher can formulate an evaluation of the student's performance. In the case cited, the teacher may observe that Lynn has lower cardiovascular endurance than his peers. A sample format is provided in figure 6.11 on page 133.

Soccer

Task	Sport games: soccer, dribbling
Task description	Student can dribble using both inside and outside of the foot against a defender
Scale components	Type and velocity of performance, radius of direction change, with or without defenders
Rubric level & Color	**Rubric descriptors**
1-white	Attempts to dribble with dominant and nondominant foot
2-yellow	Dribbles with inside of each foot, through 10 cones set 7 feet apart, up and back, without losing the ball
3-orange	Dribbles fast with outside of each foot, through 10 cones set 7 feet apart, up and back, without losing the ball
4-green	Dribbles fast with inside and outside of each foot, through 10 cones set 5 feet apart, up and back without losing the ball
5-blue	Student can dribble against a defender with inside and outside of the foot for 30 yards
6-brown	Student can dribble against a defender, through 10 cones set 5 feet apart, up the field, without losing the ball
7-black	Student can dribble against 2 defenders, for 30 seconds, within a 20-yard radius, using the inside and outside dribble, without losing the ball
Task	**Sport games: soccer, passing**
Task description	Student can perform an exact pass using the inside and outside of the foot to a standing and moving partner
Scale components	Type and number of performances, from stationary pass to passing while in motion
Rubric level & Color	**Rubric descriptors**
1-white	Attempts to pass with dominant and nondominant foot
2-yellow	Student can pass with inside of the foot to a partner standing 10 feet away, using each foot, 10 times
3-orange	Student can pass with outside of the foot to a partner standing 10 feet away, using each foot, 10 times
4-green	Student can pass with inside and outside of the foot to a partner standing 20 feet away, using each foot, 10 times
5-blue	Student can pass using only the inside of the foot to a partner, moving up and down the field, without losing control
6-brown	Student can pass using only the outside of the foot to a partner, moving up and down the field, without losing control
7-black	Student can pass to a partner 20 yards up the field, leading the receiver on the run, within 5 feet of the foot, 8 times out of 10

Figure 6.10 Rubric for soccer.

As noted in chapter 5, two processes which lend themselves nicely to evaluation of individual performance include academic learning time (ALT) and opportunity-to-respond (OTR). Both of these variables have been shown to be related to student performance (Houston-Wilson, 1993). Using opportunity to respond as an example, Houston-Wilson found that the use of trained peer tutors was effective in assisting students with developmental disabilities learn discrete motor skills. This point is illustrated by analyzing the performance of one of the students in the Houston-Wilson study. As noted in figure 6.12 on page 134, a definite improvement in performance with the use of a trained peer tutor was observed. Graphic presentations such as these provide meaningful information for parents and surrogates and assist them to recognize the capability and talent of their students.

Observation Form
Physical Education

Student Name: _Lynn Walker_ _____ Date Observed:_____

Observer Name: _____ Title: _____

Description of class: 25 students are participating in a general education program with 1 physical education teacher

Time	Class Activity	Target Student's Performance
9:00	Warm up to music -Walk around gym 3X *Most students walked 3X around gym.* -Jog around gym 3X *Most students walked 3X around gym.*	*Lynn walked around 1X.* *Lynn ran .5 of gym and rested on bench.*
9:20	Stations for throw to target -5 stations -Different skill levels *All students engaged in stations.*	*Lynn participated in stations and was at the lowest level skill station (throwing bean bags into a hoop on the ground from a distance of 5 feet). He did not want to leave this station.*
etc.		
etc.		
etc.		

Comments: *Lynn appeared to enjoy the physical education class (smiling and watching the teacher) but his skill level was well below his peers for the cardiovascular activity and the throwing skill.*

Recommendations: *Lynn is functioning below his age peers today in his cardiovascular activity and performance in fundamental skill of throw and it is recommended that he . . . .*

Figure 6.11 A sample of a systematic observation form with partial data. This can be repeated to gather a representative sample of the student's performance in a physical education class.

King and Dunn (1991) report that with proper training, teachers can be used effectively to observe and report the performance of students who are performing at a high or low level. Visual recording of the student's performance, including a thoughtful analysis provided by the teacher, in combination with other sources of valid test data, provides a powerful and helpful communication device between the school and home.

Self-Evaluation

Self-evaluation is an important skill and every student should be encouraged to develop the ability to evaluate his or her own progress toward achieving the objectives of the program. Self-evaluation of the kind involved in problem-solving can, and should, be more widely used by teachers of students with special needs regardless of the method of teaching used. To institute self-evaluation in a more traditional program, the teacher must be certain that the objectives are clearly recognized by the students; involving them in setting up the objectives is an especially good way of accomplishing this.

Once the objectives have been identified, the student is then provided with a checklist on which selected objectives

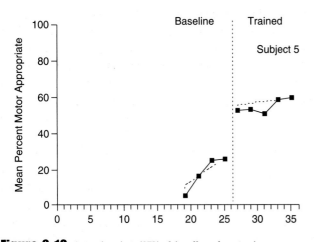

Figure 6.12 A visual analysis (OTR) of the effect of a trained peer tutor on the motor performance of a student with a developmental disability. (Adapted from Houston-Wilson, C. (1993). The effect of untrained and trained peer tutors on the motor performance of students with developmental disabilities in integrated physical education classes. Ph. D. dissertation, Oregon State University, Corvailis, OR.)

are listed for the student to accomplish in a given unit of time. The decision as to whether the objective has been met is made by the student based on the criterion identified for each objective. Although various rating scales can be used, a popular system is to have the student place a plus sign by those objectives that are completed and a check by those requiring more teacher assistance. A zero suggests that more practice is required. Self-evaluation techniques are not as structured as other assessment procedures, but they supply valuable information that can be used for individual programming.

Interviews

An increasingly popular assessment tool is the use of interviews to obtain information about a student's motor performance capabilities and interests. This technique can be used with many people, but it has been restricted primarily to use with parents and students. In each situation, the questions used should be individually developed for the specific student.

Parents can be asked questions related to the individual's developmental history. Information about motor tasks their child accomplished at specific ages can be very useful. This information is helpful in planning for those with congenital disabilities as well as for those individuals who have developed a disabling condition. As the student progresses in the education system, particularly at the transition period of the IEP beginning at age 14 (required under IDEA 2004), interviews with the parents are helpful in taking into account the family values and desired physical activity for their child. In addition, the student may be interviewed. In

this manner, there is time to formulate plans for teaching the necessary skills as well as working with the reality of engaging in those activities outside of the school physical education program.

Students should be interviewed to obtain their perceptions of their physical fitness levels and motor performance capabilities. Students' views as to the value of physical education and their activity preferences provide information that can make the difference between eliciting either a positive or a negative response to the physical education experience. The input of students at the Individualized Education Program (IEP) meeting can be a valuable addition to the team and, when possible, should be encouraged. An interview with the student prior to the meeting helps the student to focus his or her thoughts for more effective input. Currently, students who are old enough and capable can and do participate in their own IEP.

Specific Types

Currently, a number of assessment tools used for years in adapted physical education have been re-normed and revised. Others have fallen out of favor with the shift toward more authentic assessment and goals directed toward more functional skill development for students with disabilities. Although it is beyond the scope of this text to discuss each of the tests, examples of some of the tests will be presented in this section. The tests identified will follow the Burton Taxonomy of Movement Skills (Burton & Miller, 1998); see figure 3.4. The skills are organized as follows: early movement milestones, fundamental movement skills, specialized movement skills, and motor abilities. Tests are designed and constructed to perform specific purposes and functions. In this section, various types of tests that have been used to measure different aspects of motor performance will be reviewed. The selection of tests used herein is not comprehensive.

Types of Motor Performance Tests

- Curriculum-based
- Fundamental movement skills
- Specialized movement skills
- Motor ability
- Motor skill
- Movement performance behavioral objective-type
- Customized
- Perceptual-motor
- Physical fitness

Early Movement Milestones—Fundamental Movement Skills

Educators for many years have been interested in a basic question: At what age do children exhibit certain motor characteristics? The work of Shirley (1931), Bayley (1935), and Gesell (1925) generally is recognized for its significant contribution in establishing developmental progressions that are useful in evaluating a child's acquisition of a specific skill compared to the average chronological age at which other children acquire the skill. In recent years, the revised Denver Developmental Scale, the Denver II (Frankenburg & Dobbs, 1992), has become a popular instrument to use in screening young children for evidence of developmental delays. A review of the scale, which appears in figure 6.13, identifies items that are used to evaluate children from zero to six years of age in fine motor, gross motor, social, and language skills. Although helpful information can be obtained with the use of developmental scales, the results must be interpreted carefully because of the difficulty of obtaining accurate test information with young children as well as the diverse and unique growth pattern exhibited by some children. For example, infants prenatally exposed to drugs have been assessed using the Motor Assessment of Infants (MAI) (Chandler, Andrews, & Swanson, 1980) which was found to be more sensitive in identifying infants at risk for motor problems.

Early movement milestones are identified as those locomotor and object control skills performed before the child is upright and bipedal in locomotion. This skill area is assumed to be the time before the infant becomes a toddler. Many physical educators specializing in working with young children do not work directly with infants, yet they do work with preschoolers who have movement skill delays. They also work with pediatric occupational and physical therapists who play a large role in the assessments of infants who qualify for early intervention programs and services. Once the child is upright in locomotion, the child moves into the fundamental movement skills classification with their locomotor and object control skills (e.g., run, jump, skip, throw, kick).

Physical educators working with preschool children who are typically developing and those who have disabilities work with a combination of standardized and nonstandardized assessment tools. In addition to the Denver II, another example of assessment tools that therapists and educators use is the Peabody Developmental Motor Scales, 2nd edition (PDMS-2) (Folio & Fewell, 2000), to determine a Gross Motor Quotient that includes testing reflexes, stationary ability, locomotion, and object manipulation. The Peabody II is used with children from infancy to six years of age.

Curriculum-Based Assessments

The work of Diane Bricker, Jane Squires, and colleagues has produced a number of assessment tools for use in early intervention programs, such as the Assessment, Evaluation, and Programming System for Infants and Children from Birth to Three Years and Three to Six Years, 2nd edition (AEPS) (Bricker, 2000). Gross motor skill is a component of the system, and activities of assessment link directly into the curriculum. Squires (1999) has also developed the Ages and Stages Questionnaire for children birth to five years of age. Gross motor skill is a component of the scales. Physical educators may also find the social-emotional scales of the Ages and Stages Questionnaire (ASQ-3) helpful (Squires, Bricker, & Twombly, 2002). The Hawaii Early Intervention Profile (Furuno et al., 1988) is also a reference for assessment linked into curriculum activities. These assessments have validity and reliability reported in their manuals, although there are no reported norms.

The I Can Primary Skills K–3 (Wessel & Zittle, 1998) and Smart Start: Preschool Movement Curriculum (Wessel & Zittle, 1995) provide valuable assessment information and link directly into physical education curriculum.

Fundamental Movement Skills

The Test of Gross Motor Development (TGMD, TGMD-2) developed by Ulrich (1985b, 2000) is an excellent example of a well-developed movement skill test. The purpose of the TGMD is to identify children ages three to ten years who lag significantly behind their peers in the execution of gross motor skill patterns. Two subtests, locomotion and object control, assess different aspects of gross motor development. In the TGMD first developed by Ulrich in 1985, the gross motor patterns of the run, gallop, hop, leap, horizontal jump, skip, and slide comprise the test items in the locomotion subtest. Included in the object control subtest are the motor patterns of the two-hand strike, stationary bounce, catch, kick, and overhand throw. The results of the test provide criteria and norm-referenced assessment data. The test is easy to administer, and the equipment, directions, and performance criteria for each skill are clearly identified. Some sample items from the TGMD are found in table 6.3. According to Ulrich (2000), the TGMD is commonly used today both nationally and internationally to assess the motor performance of typically developing children and those with disabilities. The TGMD-2 (2000) has norms for the object control skills listed by gender because a gender difference persists in these skills at the early ages. The norms are now listed in six-month increments for both locomotor and object control skills. This current breakdown considers the difference in performance between a younger four-year-old and an older four-year-old child, (Ulrich, 1986, 2000).

In assessing the skills of younger school-age children when fundamental skills are emphasized in the physical education curriculum, attention to choosing tests that are process or product oriented is important. Product tests focus

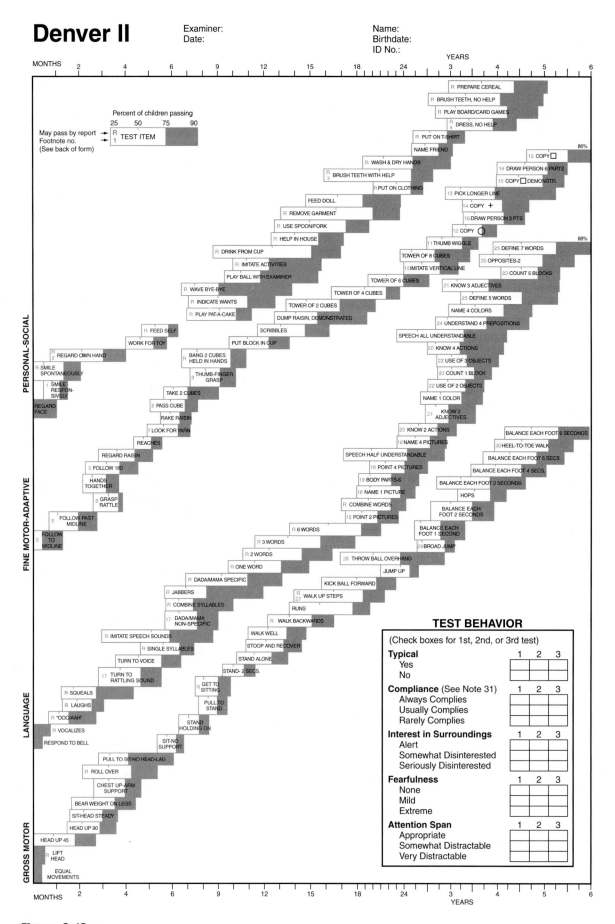

Figure 6.13 Denver Developmental Screening Test.

1. Try to get child to smile by smiling, talking, or waving to him. Do not touch him.
2. When child is playing with toy, pull it away from him. Pass if he resists.
3. Child does not have to be able to tie shoes or button in the back.
4. Move yarn slowly in an arc from one side to the other, about 6″ above child's face. Pass if eyes follow 90° to midline. (Pass midline; 180°)
5. Pass if child grasps rattle when it is touched to the backs or tips of fingers.
6. Pass if child continues to look where yarn disappeared or tries to see where it went. Yarn should be dropped quickly from sight from tester's hand without arm movement.
7. Pass if child picks up raisin with any part of thumb and a finger.
8. Pass if child picks up raisin with the ends of thumb and index finger using an over hand approach.

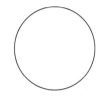

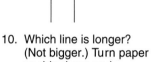

9. Pass any enclosed form. Fail continuous round motions.

10. Which line is longer? (Not bigger.) Turn paper upside down and repeat.(3/3 or 5/6)

11. Pass any crossing lines.

12. Have child copy first. If failed, demonstrate.

When giving items 9, 11, and 12, do not name the forms. Do not demonstrate 9 and 11.

13. When scoring, each pair (2 arms, 2 legs, etc.) counts as one part.
14. Point to picture and have child name it. (No credit is given for sounds only.)

15. Tell child to: Give block to Mommie; put block on table; put block on floor. Pass 2 of 3. (Do not help child by pointing, moving head or eyes.)
16. Ask child: What do you do when you are cold? . . . hungry? . . . tired? Pass 2 of 3.
17. Tell child to: Put block on table; under table; in front of chair, behind chair.
18. Ask child: If fire is hot, ice is ?; Mother is a woman, Dad is a ?; a horse is big, a mouse is ?. Pass 2 of 3.
19. Ask child: What is a ball? . . . lake? . . . desk? . . . house? . . . banana? . . . curtain? . . . ceiling? . . . hedge? . . . pavement? Pass if defined in terms of use, shape, what it is made of or general category (such as banana is fruit, not just yellow). Pass 6 c
20. Ask child: What is a spoon made of? . . . a shoe made of? . . . a door made of? (No other objects may be substituted.) Pass 3 c
21. When placed on stomach, child lifts chest off table with support of forearms and/or hands.
22. When child is on back, grasp his hands and pull him to sitting. Pass if head does not hang back.
23. Child may use wall or rail only, not person. May not crawl.
24. Child must throw ball overhand 3 feet to within arm's reach of tester.
25. Child must perform standing broad jump over width of test sheet. (8-1/2 inches)
26. Tell child to walk forward, ⚭⚭⚭⚭⟶ heel within 1 inch of toe. Tester may demonstrate. Child must walk 4 consecutive steps, 2 out of 3 trials.
27. Bounce ball to child who should stand 3 feet away from tester. Child must catch ball with hands, not arms, 2 out of 3 trials.
28. Tell child to walk backward, ⟵⚭⚭⚭⚭ toe within 1 inch of heel. Tester may demonstrate. Child must walk 4 consecutive steps, 2 out of 3 trials.

DATE AND BEHAVIORAL OBSERVATIONS (how child feels at time of test, relation to tester, attention span, verbal behavior, self-confidence, etc.)

Figure 6.13 *Continued*

Section VI. Subtest Performance Record

Preferred Hand: Right □   Left □   Not Established □
Preferred Foot: Right □   Left □   Not Established □

Locomotor Subtest

Skill	Materials	Directions	Performance Criteria	Trial 1	Trial 2	Score
1. Run	60 feet of clear space, and two cones	Place two cones 50 feet apart. Make sure there is at least 8 to 10 feet of space beyond the second cone for a safe stopping distance. Tell the child to run as fast as he or she can from one cone to the other when you say "Go." Repeat a second trial.	1. Arms move in opposition to legs, elbows bent			
			2. Brief period where both feet are off the ground			
			3. Narrow foot placement landing on heel or toe (i.e., not flat footed)			
			4. Nonsupport leg bent approximately 90 degrees (i.e., close to buttocks)			
			Skill Score			
2. Gallop	25 feet of clear space, and tape or two cones	Mark off a distance of 25 feet with two cones or tape. Tell the child to gallop from one cone to the other. Repeat a second trial by galloping back to the original cone.	1. Arms bent and lifted to waist level at takeoff			
			2. A step forward with the lead foot followed by a step with the trailing foot to a position adjacent to or behind the lead foot			
			3. Brief period when both feet are off the floor			
			4. Maintains a rhythmic pattern for four consecutive gallops			
			Skill Score			
3. Hop	A minimum of 15 feet of clear space	Tell the child to hop three times on his or her preferred foot (established before testing) and then three times on the other foot. Repeat a second trial.	1. Nonsupport leg swings forward in pendular fashion to produce force			
			2. Foot of nonsupport leg remains behind body			
			3. Arms flexed and swing forward to produce force			
			4. Takes off and lands three consecutive times on preferred foot			
			5. Takes off and lands three consecutive times on nonpreferred foot			
			Skill Score			
4. Leap	A minimum of 20 feet of clear space, a beanbag, and tape	Place a beanbag on the floor. Attach a piece of tape on the floor so it is parallel to and 10 feet away from the beanbag. Have the child stand on the tape and run up and leap over the beanbag. Repeat a second trial.	1. Take off on one foot and land on the opposite foot			
			2. A period where both feet are off the ground longer than running			
			3. Forward reach with the arm opposite the lead foot			
			Skill Score			

on the amount of a certain skill that a student can perform (e.g., throw for a distance, number of throws correct). Process tests are looking at the quality of the movement, such as form in a throw. Tests that take into account both process and product are the I CAN series by Janet Wessel (1976). Here skills are organized from criterion-referenced checklists plus levels of assistance. The I CAN series, though issued many years ago, remains a valuable resource for teachers.

For students who are severely involved, the MOVE curriculum (Mobility Opportunities Via Education) (Bidabe & Lolar, 1990) has produced the Top-Down Motor Milestone Test. This test is useful in understanding the basic skills of sit, stand, and walk as they relate to being a physically active individual engaging in functional activity.

Specialized Movement Skills

According to Burton and Miller (1998), specialized movement skills are those fundamental movement skills used in combinations to accomplish specific tasks such as shooting a free throw or spiking a volleyball. For Burton, they are recognized as also having a basis in the early movement skills. Practically speaking, they are skills most physical educators understand as part of the curriculum as students get older. Examples of these tests are sometimes the self-make checklists constructed by the physical education teacher and are based on years of observation and experience. Others are tests developed by professional organizations, such as the AAHPERD Basketball Test (1984), or are constructed by experts in a given sport area (e.g., golf, gymnastics, tennis serve). The Brockport Aquatics Checklist (Houston-Wilson in Lieberman & Houston-Wilson, 2002) is another current example of assessment of specialized skills.

Motor Ability Tests

Burton and Miller (1998) considered motor ability tests to be in a separate category. Tests of motor ability are designed to provide information about a student's motor capabilities in comparison to individuals of similar age and gender. This type of test is based on the assumption that there are underlying abilities that determine a student's motor performance. In addition it is assumed that these abilities can be identified and measured by specific motor tasks. Motor ability tests are usually standardized with normative scores provided. Werder and Kalakian (1985) have identified the following as reasons for administering motor ability tests:

1. To determine general motor deficiency
2. To determine motor deficiencies in specific subtest areas
3. To provide empirical data to meet criteria for placement into a special physical education program
4. To determine relative areas of strengths and weaknesses in motor ability

The Bruininks-Oseretsky Test of Motor Proficiency (BOTMP) was a popular test of motor ability used extensively in the first decades of federally mandated special education beginning in 1975 with PL 94-142. The test is designed to assess eight factors:

1. running speed during a shuttle run;
2. selected types of balance;
3. bilateral coordination movements;
4. strength and endurance of selected muscle groups;
5. different types of upper-limb coordination, including visual tracking;
6. specific types of visual-motor control;
7. upper-limb speed and dexterity in various movements; and
8. response speed.

The complete test battery provides three estimates of motor ability: a gross motor composite score, a fine motor composite score, and a general index of motor proficiency. A shorter version of the test can be used in screening when a brief overview of motor ability is desired. The complete battery, which consists of forty-six separate items, requires approximately sixty minutes to administer, whereas the fourteen-item short form can be completed in about twenty minutes.

Although motor ability tests such as the Bruininks-Oseretsky are helpful in identifying students with motor deficiencies, their use in a pre-and-post design as a means of measuring individual student growth and progress over a period of time is limited. Burton and Miller (1998) reported numerous psychometric difficulties with the test. In general, the shift to more functional-based assessment for individuals with disabilities has made the Bruininks-Oseretsky difficult for physical educators to use. The test is in favor with some occupational therapists for the attention given to fine motor skills and hand-eye coordination; however, this test is not used widely in physical education. Pre-and-post measures, using a general motor ability test, ignore the research literature available on transfer of learning. Changes in the student's score will not occur unless by chance, or **unless there is practice of the items of the test** or of items of sufficient similarity to permit a generalization to be made about one skill that can then be transferred to the performance of a test item. Also the data from BOTMP is not easily transferred into curriculum.

Many professionals who obtained pre- and post-measures with motor ability tests frequently become concerned because they do not find any student improvement. This does not mean, however, that the students did not improve in specific skills, but rather that general tests are frequently unable to detect the individual progress in overall motor ability. This difficulty could be resolved by providing a program that emphasizes the various items found on the motor ability test. For the most part, however, teaching the test items would result in a sterile physical education program and would provide little gain in improving overall movement skill development. One solution to this dilemma is to supplement motor ability tests with information derived from tests of movement skills. As will be explained in the next section, these tests focus on specific skills and utilize a criterion-referenced format.

General Considerations in Motor Testing

Because of the IEP process and the interdisciplinary nature of working with children with disabilities, physical educators must be able to communicate their reasons for selecting a specific tool(s) for the assessment of a student's movement skills performance, how the IEP can be constructed from the data provided in the motor domain, and how objectives will be developed that help monitor the student's progress toward specific annual goals. The following explanations are given to assist educators in these situations.

Motor Skill Tests

Parents, students, and teachers are all interested in the basic question of whether there is change in the student's motor performance. This implies, therefore, that a system should be implemented in which the student's progress is monitored at regular intervals to detect improvement in performance. Measures are taken on skills that are important and basic in the life function and play of children. These essential skills, as discussed earlier, are referred to as basic skills.

Behavioral Objective-Type Tests

An effective measuring device for evaluating basic motor skills is the behavioral objective. This type of behavioral objective is a statement describing the skills to be learned in terms that make possible an easy determination of whether or not the skill has been accomplished. For example, a behavioral objective for a specific type of balance might be: "Walk the total length of a balance beam that is six feet long, four inches wide, and two inches high." The statement clearly establishes the instructional objective, and the teacher knows the objective is met when the student is able to perform the skill described. The evaluation in the behavioral objective is explicitly a test of a specific skill; in this instance, it is a measure of a type of balance. The results of the test provide information only about a specific kind of balance skill: walking on a balance beam. No information is provided about the ability to balance on the hands, or head, or to perform other activities requiring a specific kind of balance. Information is also specific to a particular student

and is, therefore, criterion-referenced. The *ABC program,* developed by Janet Wessel, is an excellent example of an instructional system for students with special needs that incorporates a behavioral objective-type of evaluation system. The OSU Data Based Gymnasium (Dunn & Moorehouse, 1986), a program using a similar format, has been successfully employed with students with severe disabilities.

Customized Motor Skill Tests

Utilizing the concept of behavioral objectives, tests can be developed to evaluate the quality of performance in motor skills of every kind. For example, a test can be made to determine how efficiently and effectively a student can make an overhand throw. The test would need to give consideration to the components of the throw: for example, "the arm was brought back behind the shoulder, a step was made with the opposite foot as the throw was made, the elbow was preceded by the upper arm, the wrist was snapped when the ball was released," and so forth. Such a test provides information about the effectiveness of the specific movements of the throw. It does not provide much information about total coordination of the arm muscles in any other motor skill that is not similar to overhand throwing. Tests of this kind can be used to tell a good deal about the motor ability of a student, however, especially if the skills to be tested are basic skills frequently used in the student's everyday life. Skills such as walking, running, throwing, catching, striking, and kicking can be labeled as basic skills for most children because of their frequency of use in play and in everyday activities.

In designing a test to evaluate the components of a skill such as the overhand throw, it is necessary to task-analyze the movements required to perform effectively. The analysis is based upon the principles of movement—for example, the use of various parts of the body to apply force over a long period of time. To be able to teach and evaluate movement, one has to know how the movement is most effectively performed. Also, consideration must be given to the physical capacity of the individuals being tested. The overhand throw test, for example, must be modified for those under the age of six. Most children younger than six lack the maturity required to perform this skill in the most efficient way. The test would require further modification if it were to be used with students with orthopedic disabilities.

To make adaptations, an assessment must first be made of the child's limitations and potentialities. For example, if the individual is partially paraplegic, consideration must be given to the potential for movement in the arms. It may be found that flexion and extension of the fingers are possible but only flexion remains in the lower arms (i.e., the biceps are functional but not the triceps). Throwing a ball in the usual way is impossible because of the inability to extend the arm; however, a throw over the shoulder is possible.

Analysis of the movements involved in throwing a ball over the shoulder produces these components in the performance of the best possible over-the-shoulder throw:

1. good grasp of the object,
2. hyperextended wrist at the start,
3. sharp contraction of the biceps,
4. sharp flexion of the wrist, and
5. release of the ball at the proper time so that it is propelled in a straight line.

Perceptual-Motor Tests

The best known of the perceptual-motor tests is the Purdue Perceptual-Motor Survey (PPMS). This test, designed to be administered to children ages six to ten, measures perceptual-motor abilities in five areas. The areas and the behaviors assessed in each area include the following:

1. Balance and posture: walking a balance beam and jumping
2. Body image and differentiation: identification of body parts, imitation of movement, obstacle course, Kraus-Weber, and "angels in the snow"
3. Perceptual-motor match: drawing a circle, drawing two circles simultaneously, drawing a lateral line, and drawing two straight vertical lines simultaneously
4. Ocular control: movement of eyes following a flashlight, and convergence on objects
5. Form perception: copying seven geometric forms

Roach and Kephart (1969), the test developers, emphasize that the test was not designed to diagnose but rather to allow the clinician to observe perceptual-motor behavior in a series of behavioral performances. The scoring procedures for the test battery are subjective and qualitative. An example of the test form is provided in figure 6.14. Given the nature of the scoring system, primarily a checklist, and the limited information regarding the validity of the PPMS, the instrument should be used cautiously and as a supplement to other assessment data.

Many of the perceptual-motor ability tests were developed by special educators, whereas the older motor performance tests were developed by people with training in physical education. The two groups frequently use different constructs and different groupings of skills in developing their tests. Vocabularies differ, as does the use of terms. Special educators often use a single term to encompass several components that have traditionally been identified by two or more terms by physical educators. For example, "bilateral integration," a term popularized by special educators to describe a smooth working together of the right and left sides of the body, includes the traditional physical education concepts of agility and specific kinds of coordination.

Unfortunately, the tests developed by special educators often have ignored the research performed by those in physical education that provides evidence of the specificity of motor skills; hence, special educators have made greater claims for the validity of their tests as measurements of perceptual-motor ability than evidence would warrant. The perceptual-motor tests are valuable educational tools, but they do not provide the overall measurement of motor ability that is often claimed. Rather, they offer information concerning the ability to perform a specific motor skill.

Physical Fitness Tests

Tests of physical fitness are designed to assess the health-related aspects of a student's performance. The five areas most fitness tests attempt to assess are muscular strength, muscular endurance, cardiovascular endurance, flexibility, and body composition. Although many tests of physical fitness are available, few tests have been specifically developed for individuals with impairments. Exceptions to this statement include Brockport Physical Fitness: A Health-Related Test for Youth with Physical Disabilities and Mental Disabilities (Winnick & Short, 1999). This is designed for youth ages 10 to 17 years to test their fitness skills. The Brockport has criterion-referenced fitness standards and computer applications to assist the physical educator in designing intervention programs for the individual. Other tests include the AAHPERD Special Fitness Test for the Moderately Mentally Retarded, the AAHPERD Youth Fitness Test for the Mildly Mentally Retarded, and Buell's Test for blind and partially sighted.

Unfortunately, some physical educators have taken the position that any valid test of physical fitness can be used to assess the fitness level of students with disabilities. For example, the AAHPERD Health-Related Fitness Test has been used to test the fitness level of many special students. This test has not been validated for use with any special population. Caution must be exercised in utilizing any test that has not been validated for use with specific populations. Traditional tests of cardiovascular endurance, in particular, have not been used successfully with individuals with selected disabilities. Pizarro (1990) and Baumgartner and Horvat (1991) indicated that field tests that assess endurance must be interpreted carefully when used with individuals with mental retardation. Fernhall and Tymeson (1988) noted, however, that the one and one half mile could be used successfully with adults who are mildly mentally retarded. Rintala, Dunn, McCubbin, and Quinn (1992) found that the Rockport Walking Test could be used successfully as a measure of predicted cardiorespiratory fitness with adult

Perceptual-Motor Survey

Name _Jim Smith_   Address _447 N. Elm_

Date of Birth _9/7/98_   Sex _M_   Grade _5th_

Date of Exam _10/10/08_   Examiner _TJ_   School _Hansen_

		Score 1	2	3	4
Balance and Posture	Walking board: Forward			X	
	Backward		X		
	Sidewise	X			
	Jumping			X	
Body Image and Differentiation	Identification of body parts				X
	Imitation of movement			X	
	Obstacle course		X		
	Kraus-Weber				X
	Angels-in-the-snow		X		
Perceptual-Motor Match	Chalkboard Circle		X		
	Double circle	X			
	Lateral line		X		
	Vertical line			X	
	Rhythmic writing Rhythm	X			
	Reproduction		X		
	Orientation	X			
Ocular Control	Ocular pursuits Both eyes		X		
	Right eye	X			
	Left eye	X			
	Convergence		X		
Form Perception	Visual achievement forms Form	X			
	Organization			X	

Figure 6.14 Purdue Perceptual-Motor Survey record form.

moderately mentally retarded men. Rintala et al. questioned the use of running tests with this population of individuals with mental retardation, explaining that the running cadence and pace is a problem. Although less is known about the validity and reliability of other health-related fitness tests for populations with disabilities, Pizarro (1990) found that the modified sit-up test, sit and reach, and skinfold measure used in AAHPERD's Health-Related Fitness Test, with modifications, were reliable for individuals with mild and moderate levels of mental retardation. In an effort to address this problem as well as provide norms for individuals with sensory and orthopedical disabilities, Winnick and Short (1985) developed a fitness test for individuals with orthopedic and sensory disabilities that incorporates, with

modifications, many of the items found in the Health-Related Fitness Test. A summary of this test follows.

Project Unique is a test of physical fitness that was designed for use with children and youth ages ten to seventeen. The test is the outgrowth of an extensive field study in which 3,914 youngsters from twenty-three states and the District of Columbia were assessed. Youngsters and individuals with visual, auditory, and orthopedic impairments as well as those without disabilities were included in the study. The test items for all populations, with modifications where appropriate, are identified in table 6.4. Norms are provided that can be used to compare a student's performance with other youngsters with similar disabilities as well as individuals without disabilities of similar age and gender. Project

TABLE 6.4   An Outline of Project UNIQUE Physical Fitness Test Items According to Major Participant Groups

Test Items	Normal, Auditory Impaired, Visually Impaired[a]	Cerebral Palsy[a]	Paraplegic Wheelchair Spinal Neuromuscular[a]	Congenital Anomaly/Amputee[a]
Body Composition Skinfolds	X	X	X	X
Muscular Strength and Endurance				
Grip Strength (Strength)	X[b]	X[c,f]	X[g,h]	X[b,j]
50-Yard/Meter Dash (Power-Speed)	X	X[d]	X[d]	X
Sit-Ups (Power-Strength)	X	—	—	X[i]
Softball Throw for Distance (Power-Strength)	—	X[e]	sub.[g,h]	sub.[i]
Flexibility				
Sit and Reach	X	X	—	X
Cardiorespiratory Endurance				
Long Distance Run	X	X	X	X

[a]Items may require modification or elimination for selected group subclassifications (see test administration section).
[b]The broad jump may be substituted for grip strength tests as a measure of strength for these groups.
[c]Grip strengths measure power-strength for males with cerebral palsy.
[d]The dash measures power-endurance for individuals in this group.
[e]The softball throw is recommended for females only as a measure of power-strength.
[f]The arm hang may be substituted for grip tests for males.
[g]The arm hang or softball throw for distance may be substituted for grip strength measures (strength factor) for males.
[h]The softball throw for distance may be substituted for grip strength measures (strength factor) for female participants.
[i]The softball throw for distance may be substituted for sit-ups (as a power-strength factor) in cases where the sit-up would be considered inappropriate.
[j]Males may substitute the arm hang for grip tests (strength factor).
Source: Winnick, J., & Short, F. (1985). Physical fitness testing of the disabled (p. 7). Champaign, IL: Human Kinetics Publishers.

Unique is an excellent example of a physical fitness test based on current information with practical and valuable application to special populations.

Issues in Evaluation

Physical educators are confronted with several issues in their efforts to select the best procedure for evaluating the motor performance levels of students with disabilities. In the following paragraphs, some of the more critical issues will be discussed to assist the teacher in understanding some of the important factors that must be considered in selecting appropriate tests.

Motor Fitness versus Physical Fitness

Federal education law that mandates services to those students who qualify for special physical education defines physical education as including "motor fitness and physical fitness." Many of the tests developed in the past to evaluate students in physical education have combined tests of motor fitness and physical fitness into a single test battery. Analyzing student performance with this type of test is difficult and frustrating because of the uncertainty about whether the students' performance should be attributed to their motor fitness or physical fitness levels. The issue is not whether one should assess the students' motor fitness levels in contrast to their physical fitness levels, but rather that the distinction between motor fitness and physical fitness is recognized. Physical fitness is related to the concept of health and includes the five generally accepted areas of physical fitness: cardiorespiratory endurance, flexibility, muscular strength, muscular endurance, and body composition. Motor fitness, however, is related to the students' motor skill performance (e.g., fundamental motor skills) and includes those factors believed important (e.g., reaction time, balance, coordination, and agility) in the development of various motor tasks.

Norm-Referenced versus Criterion-Referenced

Specialists in the education of children with disabilities struggle with the issue of whether it is best to evaluate the student with norm-referenced or criterion-referenced instruments. In reality, this is a minor point that can be clarified easily once the use of each test is understood. Norm-referenced tests are helpful in screening for motor problems, in comparing students, in program evaluation, and in the placement of students. Criterion-referenced tests are valuable as aids in assessing student progress and for making day-to-day instructional decisions about individual students. As such, criterion-referenced tests lead directly into the physical education curriculum. As Davis explains it, "A major advantage of the criterion-reference test is that it accommodates an individualized approach to testing and programming more than the norm-referenced approach" (Davis, 1984). Some criterion-referenced tests also may be utilized as a screening test. This is true, for example, with the TGMD discussed previously. Because the criterion is the most effective movement for performing the basic skills, students who cannot accomplish one or more of the criteria with maximum efficiency in accordance with their capabilities are immediately identified as needing work to improve the skills in which they are deficient. Inability to effectively execute a large number of basic skills given the student's age is indicative of the need for special help.

Generality versus Specificity in Evaluation

Whether a general motor ability test can be used to evaluate students is a question that has generated a great deal of discussion. Some feel that tests that measure constructs such as motor ability and intelligence are limited in their usefulness and may provide misleading information. Even tests that measure components within the domain of motor ability, such as balance, are perceived by some as being too general. For example, the ability to do a handstand does not provide an indication of the ability to balance the body while standing on one foot with the eyes closed. To assume that an evaluation of either skill measures the other is incorrect, as is the assumption that a measurement of either evaluates total balancing skill.

Those who accept the concept that motor evaluation is specific argue that assessments should be made of the specific motor skills that are the foundation of general motor ability. These foundation skills are those often referred to as the basic skills: the skills that are used most frequently and are most important in the daily life functions and play of children. The specific skills that constitute the basic areas will vary in different environments and also may be quite different from one student to the next. For example, in a society devoid of dancing and games that utilize skipping and galloping, the skills of skipping and galloping would not be basic for children. Walking and running are not basic skills for a student who uses a wheelchair. For such a child, the skill of propelling would be a basic skill; for others it

would not be. Obviously, for students with disabilities, tests of basic skills provide a meaningful indicator of their progress toward individually designed goals. General tests of motor ability, although valuable as screening tools, must be used with caution when serving as precise indicators of the motor performance of students with disabilities.

Process versus Product

Process and product evaluation both have been widely used with students. Those who favor the process system argue that the most important aspect of student performance relates to the mechanics or the process of how the skill is executed. For example, in the skill of throwing a ball, students would be evaluated on their ability to grasp the ball, step with the correct foot, look at the target, use an overhand motion, rotate the body, and follow through. Evaluators using the product approach focus on the results of the throw. Therefore, the primary measures would be how far the ball was thrown and with what degree of accuracy.

Both process and product evaluation are important and should be used for specific purposes. The process system is helpful in working with novice performers and for incorporating evaluation into the process of teaching, particularly when used with a task-analyzed curriculum or for employing the ecological task analysis approach recommended by Davis and Burton (1991). Product evaluation is helpful in obtaining an overview of the student's ability to perform specific motor tasks and for comparing students.

Selecting Tests to Evaluate Motor Behavior

Due to the large number of tests available that purport to measure motor performance or some aspect of this construct, it is essential that educators evaluate the various instruments carefully. Presented in this section is a discussion of the test qualities that should be considered prior to selecting instruments to evaluate motor performance.

Purpose of the Test

A fundamental question that must be asked when surveying the various motor tests is, What is the purpose of the test? For example, is the instrument designed as a screening tool or is the intent of the test to evaluate changes in motor performance? Is it a test of motor fitness, physical fitness, or both? These and many other questions related to the test's purpose should be analyzed.

The important concept is that a test should be used only for the purpose for which it was developed. Using a test of

> ### Test Qualities to Consider
> - Purpose of test
> - Standardization and normative scores
> - Statistical properties
> - Administrative factors

> ### Statistical Properties
> - Test validity
>   - Content validity
>   - Criterion-related validity
>   - Construct validity
>   - Effects on validity
> - Test reliability
> - Objectivity
> - Scoring
> - Ecological validity
> - Independent test reviews

general motor ability as an instrument for assessing student change in motor performance is not acceptable. Likewise, using most criterion-referenced tests of basic motor skills as the sole instrument for comparing the performance of various students also has limitations.

Standardization and Normative Scores

Standardization refers to the process of administering a test in a systematic and consistent way to a large sample of individuals. The test developer must demonstrate that the standardization group is representative. This means that the group should have the same proportion of demographic variables as the national population or as the subpopulation with whom the instrument is to be used. Project Unique is an example of a physical fitness test that used a systematic sampling procedure to ensure that selected disability populations were adequately represented by geographic regions. Other important factors that must be considered in assessing a test's standardization sample is the currency of the sample—whether the sample represents a recent census report and sample size. Generally speaking, the larger the sample size, the more likely it is to be representative of the specific population.

Normative scores, based on the group used to standardize the test, are usually reported as standard scores, percentile ranks, and age or grade norms. These scores are used to describe the distance of a student's test score from the mean in terms of standard deviations. Examples of standard scores are T scores and z scores. T scores have a mean of fifty and a standard deviation of ten, whereas the mean for the z score is zero with a standard deviation of one (figure 6.15). Stanine scores also are frequently used as standard scores. Stanine scores have a mean of five and a standard deviation of two. Percentiles are also frequently used in physical education to report student scores. A percentile tells the percentage of a norm group that falls at or below a specific score. Age and grade norms are derived by computing the average raw scores made by students of a given age or particular grade level. Many tests provide several normative scores, allowing the teacher to decide which scores would be appropriate for different occasions. For example, student

scores on the Test of Gross Motor Development (Ulrich, 2000) may be reported as standard scores and percentiles. Age equivalents may be available, but these are no longer in favor with parents and physical educators. The families tire of hearing how far the child lags behind typical development. As the child matures, too often the gap becomes larger and larger. Physical educators find that reporting strengths and weaker areas is more in line with the intent of the federal law and special education: It allows the creation of IEPs based on realistic goals and objectives for the student. Parents may be interested in percentiles, whereas school administrators may focus closely on the standard scores to verify qualification for services.

Statistical Properties

Test developers must provide statistical information to help prospective users determine if the test is designed in conformity with accepted educational measurement procedures. Some important statistical properties include the test's validity, reliability, and objectivity. These and the procedures used to score the test will be reviewed in the following paragraphs.

Test Validity

A test is considered valid when it measures what it purports to measure. Although this is a clear statement and a reasonable expectation, it is, unfortunately, not always easy to establish validity. Procedures used to establish validity of motor tests include content validity, criterion-related validity, and construct validity.

Content Validity This term refers to a process whereby the content of a particular body of information is defined and a test constructed to measure the extent to which students have acquired the necessary information. For example, a test

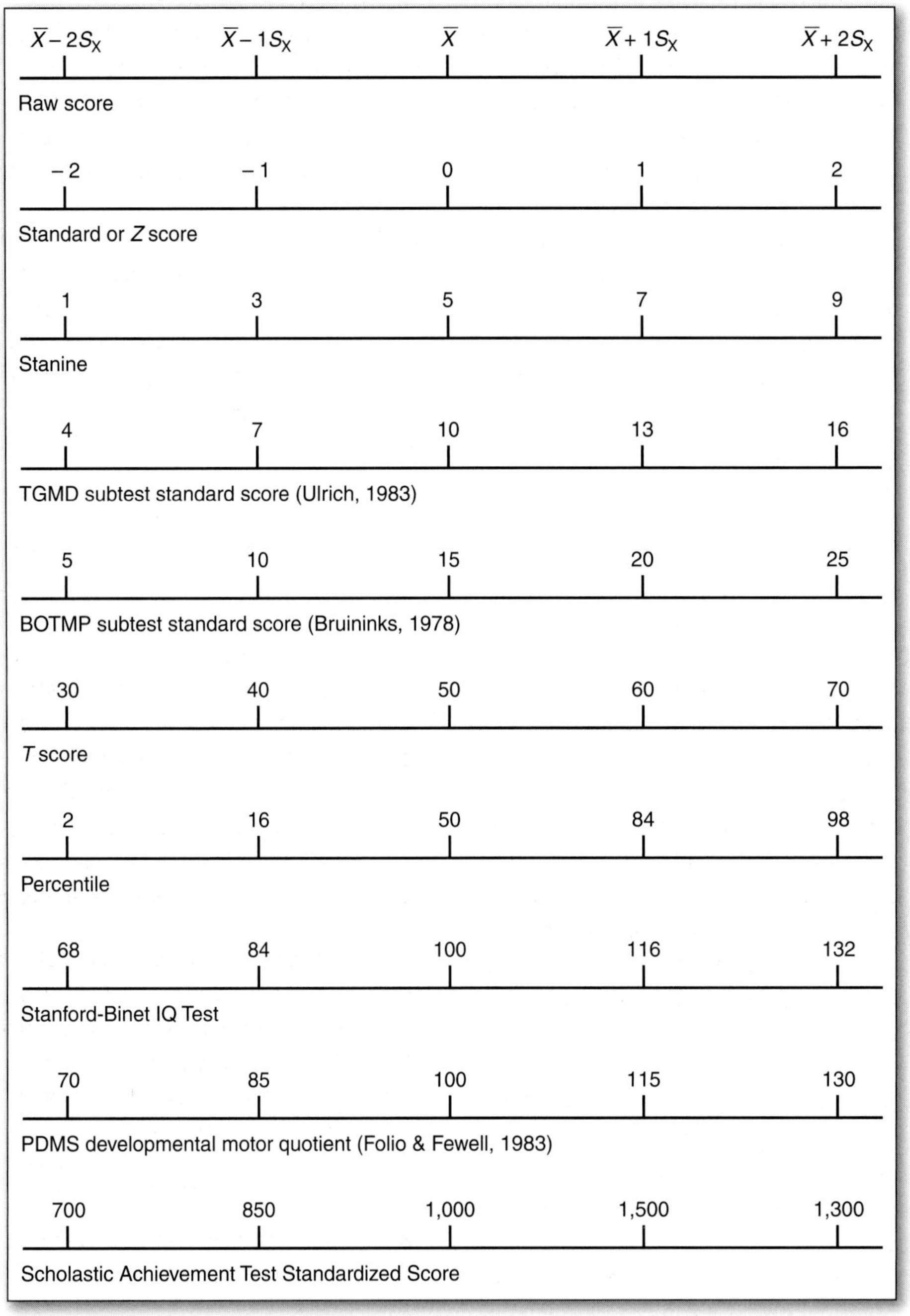

	$\bar{X} - 2S_X$	$\bar{X} - 1S_X$	$\bar{X}$	$\bar{X} + 1S_X$	$\bar{X} + 2S_X$
Raw score					
Standard or *Z* score	−2	−1	0	1	2
Stanine	1	3	5	7	9
TGMD subtest standard score (Ulrich, 1983)	4	7	10	13	16
BOTMP subtest standard score (Bruininks, 1978)	5	10	15	20	25
T score	30	40	50	60	70
Percentile	2	16	50	84	98
Stanford-Binet IQ Test	68	84	100	116	132
PDMS developmental motor quotient (Folio & Fewell, 1983)	70	85	100	115	130
Scholastic Achievement Test Standardized Score	700	850	1,000	1,500	1,300

Figure 6.15 A comparison of various types of score transformations.

could be developed to measure a special student's ability to perform the tasks involved in a game such as kickball. The content, or the skills in kickball, would first be identified, and then certain aspects of the various skills would be selected for purposes of testing the individual. The test is valid if it measures those aspects of the skill that are most important. Logic is an important process in establishing content validity. This means that statements must be provided by the test developer that demonstrate that the test items selected are representative of the larger area from which they were developed and that a logical procedure was used to select the appropriate items.

Criterion-Related Validity This type of validity refers to the extent to which a test is related to an external criterion. For example, some tests of cardiorespiratory endurance, such as Cooper's Twelve Minute Run Test (1970), are validated by comparing the individual's running performance over a specified distance to the amount of oxygen that an individual can utilize while running on a treadmill. If individuals who consistently perform well on the criterion (i.e., they have a large oxygen intake capacity) run the specified distance quicker than those who have a small oxygen capacity, one may argue that the test has criterion-related validity. For example, Rintala et al. (1992) validated the Rockport Walking Test as a measure of cardiorespiratory fitness by comparing the performance of men with mental retardation as to their peak maximal oxygen uptake using a treadmill and standardized laboratory procedures.

Other examples of criteria against which a new test can be compared include teacher evaluations, parent expectations, performance on other tests, and success in school.

Construct Validity Unlike content or criterion-related validity, construct validity is used when the quality to be measured is difficult to define. Items such as intelligence and motor ability are examples of constructs that investigators have historically attempted to define and measure. The process used in construct validity involves defining the construct and then comparing the test performances of individuals who represent extremes on the particular construct. A test of intelligence, for instance, could compare test scores of individuals with different levels of intelligence, including the mentally retarded. Rarick and McQuillan's (1977) effort to identify the factor structure of motor abilities of individuals with moderate mental retardation is an excellent example of construct validity.

Effects on Validity It is important to recognize that tests are valid only under certain conditions and for specific populations. A test designed to be individually administered, for example, loses its validity when the conditions are altered by administering the test to the entire class. Likewise, a test that has validity when used with students without disabilities may not remain valid when given to students with special needs, because this is not the population for which the test is intended. In essence, then, a test that is valid when given under the conditions intended for testing students *without* disabilities may not be appropriate for testing those *with* disabilities. This is an important consideration that must be weighed carefully in the selection of tests to be administered to any special population.

Test Reliability A test is reliable if it consistently measures those variables it is designed to measure. Reliability is frequently determined for physical and motor fitness tests by comparing the scores of students from trial to trial or day to day. If students perform in a similar manner on the same test each time it is given under like conditions, the test is considered to be a reliable measure.

An important factor in establishing test reliability is the development of specific instructions for how the test should be administered. Special adaptations for students with disabilities should also be specified. Frequently, it is necessary to establish reliability for tests that have been modified for use with students with disabilities. With some special populations, particularly the mentally retarded, the variability evident in the students' responses is so great that special efforts will be necessary to obtain an acceptable level of reliability.

An attempt must also be made to ensure that the conditions under which the test is given are similar to the conditions intended for administration of the test. Changing the procedures for administering the test or conducting the test in a different type of environment may alter its results. Also, students may not perform in a consistent manner because of such factors as the effects of fatigue or warm-up or the degree of motivation, thereby affecting the outcome of the test. An excellent discussion of the implications of testing the motor performance of special populations is reported by Stewart, Dummer, and Haubenstricker (1990). Although their discussion is specific to the deaf, the general concepts presented, including the dangers of administering and interpreting test results from invalid tests, are applicable to many individuals and populations with disabilities.

Standard Error of Measurement One of the primary reasons for determining a reliability coefficient is to use it in estimating the test's standard error of measurement (SEM). The SEM is actually the standard deviation of the error distribution around a true score and may be computed using the following formula:

$$\text{SEM} = \sqrt{1-r}$$

where 1 is a constant and r represents the reliability coefficient. Manuals for standardized tests will report the SEM for that test.

The SEM expresses classical test theory and is a very practical tool for helping students to obtain specialized physical education services. Classical test theory assumes that, from a measurement perspective, error always exists in the movement performance observed. This means that an error may have been created by the examiner, the examinee, or because of the environment. For example, the examiner may not have been expert in administering the test, the student could have been having a "bad day," and the environment may have been too noisy for testing.

Classical test theory is expressed in the following equation: Observed score = True score + Error. To account for this error, the SEM can be calculated to give a range of where the student's true score would probably fall. Therefore, the SEM establishes the limits that anyone can place on a particular test score. For example, a female student achieves a standard score of 79 for her Gross Motor Quotient (GMQ) on the Test of Gross Motor Development-2. According to the test manual, the SEM is 5 for a child who is six years of age. This means that 1 SEM = 5. Based on a Confidence Interval of 68%, we can say that her true score 68 percent of the time would be somewhere between 74 and 84. This is calculated by adding 1 SEM (5) to her standardized score, and subtracting 1 SEM from her standardized score: 79 + 5 = 84 and 79 − 5 = 74.

The practical application of this is found if we look closer to see if this girl qualifies for special physical education. States have discretion in determining eligibility for special education services if they have a categorical disability identified under the federal educational law. In Minnesota, a child meets eligibility for adapted physical education if she is one and one half SD from the mean using a standardized psychomotor instrument. Looking at the normal curve, the seventh percentile is at one and one half SD below the mean. The manual for the TGMD-2 indicates that this girl's original GMQ score of 79 would put her in the eighth percentile. Technically, she would not qualify for services, yet this student is clearly a very low-skilled student. If the physical educator looks in the manual to find the SEM and then calculates the simple math (+ and − the SEM off her GMQ), then her range can be reported. She then qualifies for the services she most likely needs.

Objectivity

A special form of reliability is objectivity. This measure relates to how well different test examiners can give the same test to the same individuals and obtain similar results. Objectivity is a factor that must be considered in test selection. Tests that require special training to administer and score will obviously not be objective unless all individuals who give the test have developed the appropriate test examiner skills.

Scoring

The procedure used to score tests is a variable that should be studied when reviewing different tests. Some tests generate only a raw score reflecting the student's actual performance; other instruments allow for scores to be converted for comparative purposes. Norm-referenced tests, for instance, will frequently report scores as standard percentiles, which permits comparisons between students. Some tests identify specific criteria that must be met on individual tasks and then each test item is scored on a pass-fail scale. The percentage achieved on a specific criterion is yet another scoring system incorporated into some tests. The test reviewer must decide whether the scores to be obtained provide the type of information desired.

Ecological Validity

Several authorities have suggested that tests used to assess the performance of individuals with disabilities should be ecologically valid (Davis & Burton, 1991; Zittel, 1994). This suggests that the test should be sensitive to the child's comfort level and be administered in an enviroment familiar to the individual. This is especially true for preschool children with special needs and individuals with moderate to severe levels of mental retardation. Administering a test in a familiar environment by an examiner known to the student helps to ensure that the test results more accurately represent the individual's true ability. A good example of an ecologically valid instrument is the I Can Pre-Primary Motor and Play Skills (Wessel, 1980). With this test battery, the test is administered by a caregiver in a familiar setting, using material known to the child.

Independent Test Reviews

The process of selecting a test and assessing its quality has been made easier by the availability of selected references. *The Buros Mental Measurement Yearbook*, for example, provides concise reviews of many tests including some commonly employed with students with special needs. The reviews are conducted by knowledgeable individuals who are asked to provide an objective and independent review of various properties associated with the tests. Reviews of tests also may be found in selected professional journals. *The Adapted Physical Activity Quarterly* frequently publishes reviews or papers that critique selected tests. An excellent example is the paper authored by Zittel (1994) in which she analyzed nine gross motor assessment instruments frequently used with preschool children.

Sources such as these are extremely useful in helping professionals to make informed decisions about the quality and usefulness of a test. This information adds credibility to the test ultimately selected for use with special populations. Burton and Miller (1998) have closely reviewed over 45 test instruments with a description of the test and stated uses, ages, validity, reliability, standardization, equipment, and time, as well as publisher and the book/journal citation.

Brown and Bryant (1984) have developed a consumer's guide for professionals to assist them in the process of selecting tests. A sample of the guide is found in figure 6.16. The guide summarizes in a formal way, using a checklist format, many of the test properties that have been discussed in this chapter.

Reviewer _____

A Consumer's Guide to Tests in Print

Test Name (Date of Publication): _____
Test Author(s): _____
Publisher, City, State: _____
_____

Test Score Being Reviewed: _____
Content Area: _____
_____

Administration:
1. Administration:
   ☐ Group or individual
   ☐ Individual only
   ☐ Group only

2. Administration requires terms of:
   ☐ 14 minutes or less
   ☐ 15–29 minutes
   ☐ 30–59 minutes
   ☐ 60 minutes or longer
      ☐ Other: _____

3. Administration is:
   ☐ Timed
   ☐ Untimed
   ☐ Both timed and untimed

Age/Grades for Intended Use:
   ☐ Preschool (0 through 5 years or through kindergarten)
   ☐ Primary (6 through 8 years or grades 1–3)
   ☐ Elementary (9 through 11 years or grades 4–6)
   ☐ Junior High (12 through 14 years or grades 7–9)
   ☐ Senior High (15 through 18 years or grades 10–12)
   ☐ Adult (19 years or greater)

Examiner Characteristics:
   ☐ The test is administered easily after reading the manual.
   ☐ Administration requires special training beyond familiarity with the manual.
   ☐ Administration is restricted to certified examiners, examiners with specific licenses,
      or examiners who have completed supervised practice with the instrument.

Format Characteristics:
Format requires the subject to:
1. Input:
   ☐ Listen
   ☐ Read print
   ☐ Look at stimuli (pictures, objects)
   ☐ Understand sign language
   ☐ Read braille
      ☐ Other: _____
         ☐ Draw
         ☐ Write print
         ☐ Write braille
         ☐ Use sign language
         ☐ Other: _____

Scoring:
1. Scoring is:
   ☐ Computer only
   ☐ Manual only
   ☐ Both computer and manual

2. Scores are interpreted in:
   ☐ Age equivalents
   ☐ Grade equivalents
   ☐ Percentile ranks
   ☐ Standard scores

2. Output:
   ☐ Speak, minor (yes/no, one word responses)
   ☐ Speak, major (phrases, sentences required)
   ☐ Manipulate objects
   ☐ Mark answer sheet
   ☐ Point

Figure 6.16   Reviewer's evaluation form. (Adapted from Brown, L., & Bryant, B. R., "A Consumer's Guide to Tests in Print" in *Remedial and Special Education, 5*(1), 57.)

Administrative Factors

The ease with which a test may be given is an important consideration in determining its usefulness in the school setting. Significant factors relate to the amount of time required for administration as well as the facilities and equipment needed.

Time

Tests of motor fitness vary considerably in the amount of time required to administer them. Some require only a few minutes, whereas others involve several test sessions over a two-day period. If a test is long but provides needed information,

Section II: Standardization and Normative Scores

A. Normative Scores
☐ No normative scores are reported or only age/grade equivalent scores are available.
☐ Percentile ranks are reported.
☐ Standard scores are reported.

B. Size of the Standardization Group
☐ The size of the standardization group is not specified or does not meet the criteria below.
☐ The standardization group contains 75–90 subjects in most chronological age intervals or academic grade levels for which a normative table is presented; in addition, there are 750–999 subjects in the total group.
☐ The standardization group contains 100 or more subjects in each chronological age interval or academic grade level for which a normative table is presented; in addition, there are 1,000 or more subjects in the total group.

C. Demographic Characteristics of the Standardization Group
☐ The characteristics of the standardization group are not specified or are not representative of the appropriate population.
☐ The characteristics of the standardization group correspond approximately to the census data for a specified region or population on at least three of the following: sex, domicile (urban/suburban/rural), socioeconomic status, geographic region, and race/ethnicity.
☐ The characteristics of the standardization group correspond approximately to national census data on at least three of the following: gender, domicile (urban/suburban/rural), socioeconimic status, geographic region, and race/ethnicity.

D. Recency of Test Standardization
Standardization was completed in:
☐ 1968 or before.
☐ 1969–1978.
☐ 1979 or after.
If no standardization date is given, use the test publication date.

Section III: Reliability

A. Internal Consistency Reliability
Internal consistency reliability is:
☐ not reported or is below 0.80 at most ages.
☐ between 0.80 and 0.89 at most ages.
☐ 0.90 or above at most ages.

B. Stability Reliability
Stability reliability is:
☐ not reported or is below 0.80 at most ages.
☐ between 0.80 and 0.89 at most ages.
☐ 0.90 or above at most ages.

Section IV: Validity

Validity is:
☐ not reported: or validity studies are not acceptable in design or significance of results.

Figure 6.16 Reviewer's evaluation form. (Adapted from Brown, L., & Bryant, B. R., "A Consumer's Guide to Tests in Print" in *Remedial and Special Education, 5*(1), 57.)

then it should be used. Motor tests designed primarily as screening instruments to identify students who may need further evaluation must be constructed so that they are time efficient, thus increasing the probability of their widespread use.

Caution must be exercised when attempting to shorten the necessary testing time by evaluating a group of students together. The performance of some students is dramatically affected when peers are permitted to observe their motor skill evaluation.

Facilities and Equipment

The examiner's manual that accompanies most tests provides information about space requirements and necessary equipment. Fortunately, most motor skill tests are developed to be used in school settings, and thus, the test developers recognize the space and equipment limitations with which some school systems must deal. There are, however, a few tests that, if used, involve the purchase of specialized equipment. Although the costs may be justified because of the type of information provided by a specific test, the budgetary impact of the purchase should be considered prior to incorporating this test into the physical education evaluation program.

The materials and equipment in some test kits may be reproduced with the permission of the publisher. Making duplicate copies of test material is a practical way to reduce costs while making the tests readily available throughout a school or school system.

Test Examiner

Each test should be reviewed carefully to determine the level of training required for potential users of the test. Despite the fact that many of the motor performance tests can be routinely administered and evaluated by personnel with preparation as physical educators, some do require additional expertise. This is particularly true of some of the tests designed to measure certain elements of perceptual-motor skills.

Special qualifications are also necessary to administer tests to some students with disabilities. For instance, personnel who test students with hearing disabilities will need sufficient signing skills to communicate effectively so that the results will not be invalid. Likewise, examiners of individuals who are mentally retarded should have sufficient training to ensure that a given test is assessing the student's motor rather than cognitive level.

The quality of information obtained through the evaluation process is closely related to the skills of the examiner. Every effort must be made to utilize personnel who have a thorough background in physical education and who are knowledgeable about appropriate motor tests and their use with special populations.

Although it is beyond the scope of this book to discuss all of the motor tests that have been used with students with disabilities, for more information refer to Burton and Miller (1998), who reviewed more than 45 tests of movement skill (pp. 333–353). The physical educator can use this resource to identify tests that match a student's assessment needs and can also find important psychometric properties to use in reports within special education.

Summary

Quality physical education programs require that, periodically, appropriate measures be taken to assess the effectiveness of the educational experience. Given this information, sound decisions can be made regarding modifications, if any, that should be made in the program. Recognizing the value of evaluation, the framers of the Individuals with Disabilities Education Act mandated that comprehensive assessments, including measures of the student's motor performance, be an integral part of the services provided for children with disabilities. Federal statute requires that screenings be conducted to ensure that all students requiring assistance are identified. No child can be identified as disabled unless a thorough, non-biased assessment is conducted. Besides screening and determining eligibility for special education services, evaluation is also helpful in formulating goals and objectives for the Individualized Education Program and for reviewing student progress toward meeting the IEP goals.

Evaluations of the motor fitness and physical fitness of students with disabilities should be comprehensive and should include, where possible, both criterion- and norm-referenced measures. Normative data provides meaningful information concerning the youngster's performance compared to similar students. Because of the diverse nature and needs of students with disabilities, it is not always possible or desirable to use a norm-referenced test. In these instances, criterion-referenced measures that compare the child's performance to predetermined criteria are very helpful.

Various types of tests can be used to evaluate motor performance. These include developmental scales, and tests designed to measure motor ability, motor skills, perceptual-motor skills, and physical fitness. Within the chapter, a number of the popular tests used in special physical education programs are identified and described. In selecting a test it is important to identify tests that adhere to high standards of test construction. The purpose of the test and its statistical properties, validity, and reliability should be analyzed carefully.

Although there are some excellent tests that can be used in the special physical education program, teachers must be careful to use tests only for the purposes for which they were originally intended. This includes, too, special care to ensure that tests are ecologically valid and responsive to performer and environmental constraints. Professionals must also be cognizant of the various issues in evaluation, and must be conversant with the latest findings regarding the administration and interpretation of test results. Most importantly, teachers must recognize that good evaluation enhances the instructional process and helps in making wise educational decisions. Without an effective evaluation program, communication with parents and other professionals will be limited and issues of accountability and quality of service will surface. Evaluation takes time, but the effort is essential for determining student progress and for assessing the overall effectiveness of the special physical education program. A good evaluation system is the cornerstone of a quality special physical education program.

Enhancing Activities

1. Administer one of the tests identified in this chapter to a child with a disability.
2. Interview a parent and a teacher to obtain their views regarding evaluation of a child for physical education class. Try to solicit their views on other issues related to evaluation and the IEP process for physical education.
3. Using the guide for evaluating tests found in figure 6.4, select one of the tests identified in this chapter and conduct a review of the test and its various properties.
4. Provide examples of test procedures that appear to be ecologically sensitive to variations in the student's movement performance.
5. Create a form for a systematic observation of a student in a physical education class. Evaluate whether the form was helpful in providing information to a physical education teacher about the student's placement in a general physical education class.

Selected Readings

American Alliance for Health, Physical Education, Recreation, and Dance (AAHPERD). (1976). *Testing for impaired, disabled, and handicapped individuals.* Washington, DC: Author.

Arnheim, D. D., & Sinclair, W. A. (1979). Basic motor ability test. In *The clumsy child.* St. Louis: C. V. Mosby Co.

Ayres, J. (1980). *Southern California Test of Sensory Integration.* Los Angeles: Western Psychological Services.

Baumgartner, T., & Horvat, M. (1991). Reliability of field based cardiovascular fitness running tests for individuals with mental retardation. *Adapted Physical Activity Quarterly, 8,* 107–114.

Bayley, N. (1935). The development of motor abilities during the first three years. *Monographs of the Society for Research in Child Development, 1*(1), 1–26.

Bayley, N. (1969). *Bayley scales of infant development.* The Psychological Corporation. New York: Harcourt, Brace, Jovanovich, Inc.

Bidabe, L., & Lolar, J. M. (1990). *Mobility opportunities via education.* Bakersfield, CA: Office of Kern County Superintendent of Schools.

Bowman, R. A., & Dunn, J. M. (1982). Effect of peer presence on psychomotor measures with educable mentally retarded children. *Exceptional Children, 48*(5), 449–451.

Bricker, D. (2000). *Assessment, evaluation, and programming system for birth to three years and three to six years* (2nd ed.). Baltimore: Brookes.

Brigance, A. H. (1978). *Brigance diagnostic inventory of early development.* North Billerica, MA: Curriculum Associates, Inc.

Brown, L., & Bryant, B. R. (1984). A consumer's guide to tests in print: The rating system. *Remedial and Special Education, 5*(1), 55–61.

Bruininks, R. H., Bruininks, B. D., (2005). Bruininks-Oseretsky test of motor proficiency, 2nd Ed. Circle Pines, MN: AGS Publishing.

Buros, O. K. (1985). *Mental measurement yearbook* (9th ed.). Highland Park, NJ: Gryphon Press.

Burton, A. E., & Miller, D. E. (1998). *Movement Skill Assessment.* Champaign, IL: Human Kinetics.

Chandler, L. S., Andrews, M. S., & Swanson, M. W. (1980). *Movement assessment of infants: A manual.* Rolling Bay, WA: Movement Assessment of Infants.

Colarusso, R., & O'Rourke, C. (2003). *Special education for all teachers.* Dubuque, IA: Kendall/Hunt.

Cooper, K. H. (1970). *The new aerobics.* New York: M. Evans and Company, Inc.

Cratty, B. J. (1969). Cratty six-category gross motor test. In B. J. Cratty (Ed.), *Motor activity and the education of retardates.* Philadelphia: Lea and Febiger.

Cratty, B. J. (1971). Body-image screening test for blind children. In B. J. Cratty (Ed.), *Movement and spatial awareness in blind children and youth.* Springfield, IL: Charles C. Thomas.

Criterion-referenced physical fitness standards for adolescents with disabilities (1994). *Palaestra, 10,* p. 55.

Davis, W. E. (1984). Motor ability assessment of populations with handicapping conditions: Challenging basic assumptions. *Adapted Physical Activity Quarterly, 1,* 125–140.

Davis, W., & Burton, A. (1991). Ecological task analysis: Translating movement theory behavior into practice. *Adapted Physical Activity Quarterly, 8,* 154–177.

Department of Health, Education and Welfare, Office of Education. (1977, August 23). Education of handicapped children, part II, implementation of part B of the Education of the Handicapped Act. *Federal Register.* Washington, DC: Author.

Dunn, J. M., Morehouse, J. W., & Fredericks, H. D. (1986). *Physical education for the severely handicapped.* Austin, TX: Pro-Ed Publishers.

Fait, H. (1982). Evaluation of motor skills of the handicapped: Theory and practice. *Practical Pointers.* Washington, DC: American Alliance for Health, Physical Education, Recreation, and Dance, 5(8).

Fernhall, B., & Tymeson, G. (1988). Validation of cardiovascular fitness field tests for adults with mental retardation. *Adapted Physical Activity Quarterly, 5,* 49–55.

Folio, M. R., & Fewell, R. R. (2000). *Peabody Developmental Motor Scales* (2nd ed.). Austin, TX: Pro-Ed.

Frankenburg, W. K., & Dodds, J. B. (1991). *The Denver II developmental screening test.* Denver, CO: University of Colorado Medical Center.

Frankenburg, W. K., & Dobbs, J. B. (1992). *Denver II training manual* (2nd ed.). Denver: Denver Developmental Materials.

Furuno, S., O'Reilly, K. A., Hosaka, C. M., Inatsuka, T. T., Zeislof-Falbey, B., & Allman, T. (1988). Hawaii early learning profile. Palo A lot, CA: VORT.

Gesell, A. (1925). *The mental growth of the preschool child: A psychological outline of normal development from birth to the sixth year, including a system of developmental diagnosis.* New York: Macmillan.

Godfrey, B. B., & Kephart, N. C. (1969). Godfrey-Kephart movement pattern checklist—Short form. *Movement Patterns and Motor Education.* New York: Appleton-Century-Crofts.

Hammill, D., Brown, L., & Bryant, B. R. (1986). *A consumer's guide to tests in print.* Austin, TX: Pro-Ed Publishers.

Houston-Wilson, C. (1993). The effect of untrained and trained peer tutors on the Opportunity to Respond (OTR) of students with developmental disabilities in integrated physical education classes. (Unpublished dissertation). Oregon State University.

Hughes, J. (1979). *Hughes basic gross motor assessment.* Denver, CO: Office of Special Education, Denver Public Schools.

King, C. M., & Dunn, J. M. (1991). Classroom teachers' accuracy in observing students' motor performance. *Adapted Physical Activity Quarterly, 6,* 52–57.

Kleinert, H. L., & Kearns, J. K. (2001). *Alternate assessment: Measuring outcomes and supports for students with disabilities.* Baltimore: Brookes.

Largo, R. H., Molinari, L., Weber, L., Comedale-Pinto, L., & Duc, G. (1985). Early development of locomotion: Significance of prematurity, cerebral palsy and sex. *Developmental medicine and child neurology, 27.* In A. Burton & D. Miller, *Movement Skill Assessment.* Champaign, IL: Human Kinetics.

Lieberman, L. J., & Houston-Wilson, C. (2002). *Strategies for INCLUSION: A handbook for physical educators.* Champaign, IL: Human Kinetics.

Londeree, B., & Johnson, L. E. (1976). *Motor fitness test for the moderately mentally retarded.* Reston, VA: AAHPERD.

Loovis, E. M., & Ersing, W. F. (1979). Ohio State University SIGMA. In *Assessing and programming gross motor development for children.* Cleveland Heights, OH: Ohio Motor Assessment Associates.

McLoughlin, J. A., & Lewis, R. B. (1986). *Assessing special students* (2nd ed.). Columbus, OH: Charles E. Merrill Publishing Co.

Ness, R. (1974). *The standardization of the basic movement performance profile for profoundly retarded institutionalized residents.* (Unpublished dissertation). North Texas State University, Denton, TX.

Oregon Department of Education. (1981). *Adapted physical education in Oregon schools.* Salem, OR: Author.

Orpet, R. E., & Heustis, T. L. (1971). *Move-grow-learn movement skills survey.* Chicago: Follet Publishing Co.

Peabody Developmental Motor Scales. (1974). IMRID Behavioral Science Monograph No. 25, George Peabody College, Nashville, TN.

Piper, M. C., & Darrah, J. (1994). *Motor assessment of the developing infant.* Philidelphia: Saunders.

Pizarro, D. C. (1990). Reliability of the health related fitness test for mainstreamed educable and trainable mentally handicapped adolescents. *Adapted Physical Activity Quarterly, 7,* 240–248.

The Psychological Corporation. (1978). *McCarthy screening test.* New York: Harcourt, Brace, Jovanovich, Inc.

Rarick, G. L., & McQuillan, J. P. (1977). Motor proficiency assessment. In *The factor structure of motor abilities of trainable mentally retarded children: Implications for curriculum development.* Berkeley, CA: Department of Physical Education, University of California, Berkeley.

Rintala, P., Dunn, J., McCubbin, J., & Quinn, C. (1992). Validity of a cardiorespiratory fitness test for men with mental retardation. *Medicine and Science in Sports and Exercise, 24*(8), 941–945.

Roach, C., & Kephart, N. C. (1969). *The Purdue perceptual motor survey tests.* Los Angeles: Western Psychological Series.

Seaman, J. (Ed.). (1988). Testing the handicapped: A challenge by law. *Journal of Physical Education, Recreation and Dance, 59* (1).

Shirley, M. (1931). The first two years, a study of twenty-five babies. Minneapolis: University of Minnesota.

Squires, J. (1999). *Ages and Stages Questionnaire.* Baltimore MD: Brookes.

Squires, J., Bricker, D., Twombly, E. (2002). *Ages and stages questionnaire: social emotional.* Baltimore, MD: Paul H. Brookes Publishing Company.

Stewart, D., Dummer, G., & Haubenstricker, J. (1990). Review of administration procedures used to assess the motor skills of deaf children and youth. *Adapted Physical Activity Quarterly, 7,* 231–239.

Trembath, J. (1977). *The Milani-Comparetti motor development screening test.* Omaha, NE: Meyer Children's Rehabilitation Institute, University of Nebraska Medical Center.

Ulrich, D. A. (1985a, August). *Current assessment practices in adapted physical education: Implications for future training and research activities.* Paper presented at the annual meeting of the National Consortium on Physical Education and Recreation for the Handicapped, New Carollton, MD.

Ulrich, D. A. (1985b). *Test of gross motor development.* Austin, TX: Pro-Ed.

Ulrich, D. A. (2000). *Test of gross motor development-2.* Austin, TX: Pro-Ed.

Vodola, T. (1976). *Project ACTIVE maxi-model: Nine training manuals.* Oakhurst, NJ: Project ACTIVE.

Werder, J. K., & Kalakian, L. H. (1985). *Assessment in adapted physical education.* Minneapolis, MN: Burgess Publishing Co.

Wessel, J. (1980). *I Can pre-primary motor and play skills.* East Lansing, MI: Field Service Unit in Physical Education and Recreation for the Handicapped.

Wessel, J. A. (1976). *I CAN.* Northbrook, IL: Hubbard Publishing Company.

Wessel, J. A., & Zittle, L. L., (1995). *Smart start.* Austin, TX: Pro-Ed

Wessel, J. A., & Zittle, L. L. (1998). *I Can primary skills K-3.* Austin, TX: Pro-Ed.

Winnick, J. P. (1979). *Early movement experiences and development: Habilitation and remediation.* Philadelphia: W. B. Saunders, Co.

Winnick, J. P., & Short, F. X. (1985). *Physical fitness testing of the disabled: Project Unique.* Champaign, IL: Human Kinetics Publishers.

Winnick, J., & Short, F. (1999). The Brockport physical fitness test manual. Champaign, IL: Human Kinetics Publishers.

Zittel, L. (1994). Gross motor assessment of preschool children with special needs: Instrument selection considerations. *Adapted Physical Activity Quarterly, 11,* 245–260.

Conditions Resulting in Enervated and Impaired Movement

Discussed in this section are disorders that occur so commonly in school-age children that physical educators are very likely to find students with these conditions in their classes. The chapters on the various kinds of disorders briefly describe the etiology and pathology, discuss special considerations in planning the program, and suggest kinds of activities that may be offered.

OBJECTIVES

This section is designed to help the reader to:
- Recognize the cause and characteristics of the disabling conditions found in the school setting.
- Appreciate students with disabilities as unique individuals with specific needs that are different in some ways but similar in other ways to those of their nondisabled peers.
- Individualize instruction in the physical education program consistent with the developmental needs of students with various disabling conditions.
- Recognize the breadth and depth of special physical education services that range from instruction in regular programs to special classes and include programs for those with mild as well as severe disabilities.

Orthopedic Disabilities

CHAPTER OBJECTIVES

After studying this chapter, the reader should be able to:

1 Recognize the various types of orthopedic disabilities and their implications for planning appropriate physical education activities and programs.
2 Understand the common characteristics of orthopedic impairments that are caused by injury, are congenital, or are the result of bone growth diseases.
3 Understand the relationship of the spinal cord segments to the spinal vertebrae and the use of the level of impairment to the spinal cord segments as descriptive of function.
4 Appreciate and be sensitive to the various techniques used to assist those with bowel- and bladder-control problems and the implications of these related to physical education.
5 Understand the important role physical activity has in helping individuals with orthopedic impairments to develop physically fit and active lifestyles. This role includes a strong physical education program that is developmentally appropriate and includes sports activity.
6 Develop appropriate program and activity modifications for individuals with various orthopedic impairments.
7 Recognize some of the unique physiological and biomechanical characteristics of those with orthopedic impairments and the implications of these in developing conditioning programs for optimal training levels.

"Orthopedic" is derived from the Greek words meaning "to straighten the child," and in modern usage is applied both to a specific type of disability and to the branch of medicine concerned with its prevention and treatment. An orthopedic disability is one that does not allow the individual to properly perform the motor and locomotor functions of the body and limbs. Such disabilities affect the functions of the bones, joints, and tendons.

The public attitude toward individuals with orthopedic disabilities has changed immensely since the Middle Ages, when the only hope one had of acceptance within the society was to become a court jester. Today the individual with an orthopedic disability has opportunities for treatment, rehabilitation, gainful employment, and social acceptance far beyond the dreams of even the most imaginative court jester. Although much remains to be done, especially in equalizing social and employment opportunities, those

with orthopedic disabilities have, over the years, generally suffered less from a lack of public understanding of their needs and problems than have most other populations with disabilities.

Care for children with orthopedic disorders was extremely limited until the nineteenth century, when the work of several prominent orthopedic surgeons in England, continental Europe, and the United States began to direct attention to the prevention and remedial treatment for crippling conditions. Concern about the plight of children with orthopedic disabilities remained almost entirely medical until the closing years of the century, when the increasing number of such children aroused interest in adequate educational provisions for them. Special schools for "crippled" children were established, as were special classes within the public schools. Currently, students with orthopedic disabilities are mainstreamed, when appropriate, into the regular classes of the public schools, including classes in physical education. A number of hospital programs for children with orthopedic disorders exist throughout the country, and these provide educational instruction as well as medical and therapeutic treatment. However, advanced treatment techniques and the desire to return children to their homes as quickly as possible have greatly reduced the actual time the children spend in the hospital. The result is that more students receive their education in the public schools than in the hospitals.

Because of the lack of uniformity in defining the conditions of crippling and orthopedic disabilities, statistics of incidence are neither very meaningful nor very accurate. The number can be doubled or cut in half by the inclusion or exclusion of individuals with certain conditions. It is consequently not possible to determine how many cases of youngsters with orthopedic impairments exist currently or how many of these may be expected to be found in the regular school, the special school, or the hospital.

The orthopedic conditions presented in this chapter are those found among school-age students. The discussion is divided into three sections: disorders that immobilize lower limbs, disorders that limit ambulation, and disorders that affect other body movements. This organization allows specific orthopedic disabilities that cause similar movement problems to be brought together under one heading, permitting emphasis to be placed on the movement potential of students with similar limitations rather than on the disabilities and restrictions imposed by each type of orthopedic disability. Before discussing the specific orthopedic conditions, needs and adjustments as well as program planning will be presented.

Teaching Those with Orthopedic Disabilities

When normally active human beings find their usual movements restricted by disease or accident, they face the necessity of changing many of the patterns of their daily living. The degree to which they are able to make these changes determines to a large extent how satisfactory their adjustment will be. The age and the suddenness with which the incapacitating disability strikes appear to have considerable effect upon the adjustment that individuals make. Very intense emotional reactions usually follow, for example, a sudden loss of limb by amputation, but these usually subside as the individuals discover they are still capable of many of the activities of their former life. Students with disabilities are likely to make a satisfactory adjustment as they acquire compensatory motor skills. Youngsters with a limb missing

from birth or early infancy may have a deep-seated but less easily detected emotional disturbance as the result of the continual frustration they experience in attempting to do the things that other children do. On the other hand, they may have made an entirely adequate adjustment as the result of having acquired such satisfactory compensatory skills that they and those with whom they associate do not think of them as different. If students have not made this kind of adjustment, they need help in overcoming their fears and frustrations so that better adjustment will be possible.

The incapacitation produced by an infectious disease like spondylitis is usually much less sudden than that resulting from amputation. Nevertheless, a strong emotional reaction is usually evidenced during the early stages of the disease, which increases as the disease progresses and the movement limitations become more evident. It is likely to continue even after the disease has been terminated if the limitation to normal locomotion remains. The most common emotional reactions are withdrawal, hostility, and aggressiveness.

The age of the child presents certain other problems in adjusting to the disability. Children and adolescents are particularly susceptible to the reactions others have to the cosmetic appearance of their disabilities. They may worry unduly about how they look and become overly sensitive to the responses others have to their appearance. The anxieties thus aroused are not easily relieved.

Orthopedic disorders occurring early in life frequently limit the child's opportunities for play and other social contacts and greatly restrict the development of satisfactory social growth. Courage, resourcefulness, and initiative fostered in the vigorous exchanges of childhood play activities are commonly deficient in children with physical disabilities who are deprived of opportunities to engage in play.

These desirable characteristics are also frequently lacking in adults with orthopedic disabilities, stemming from their inability to participate in the normal patterns of living. In addition, many of them have inferiority feelings or have excessive anxieties usually related to their inability to support themselves economically. On the whole, a change of any kind is more difficult as age advances, owing to the force of daily habits. Consequently, unless the adult is given a good deal of help, satisfactory adjustment is very difficult.

The lack of active play in the lives of these youngsters and adults has detrimental physiological, as well as psychological, results. General body fitness is lacking. Coordination is poor. There is increased susceptibility to injury and hypokinetic diseases.

To achieve satisfactory adjustment, individuals with orthopedic disabilities must compensate for their lack of success in physical performance or they must seek satisfying substitutions. Some people compensate by achieving superiority in intellectual endeavors; in the development of

Figure 7.1 This boy needs only upper body strength to enjoy the physical activity of kayaking. (NCPAD.) This photo is reproduced from the National Center on Physical Activity and Disability at www.ncpad.org. It may be freely distributed in its entirety as long as it includes this notice but cannot be edited, modified, or otherwise altered without the express written permission of NCPAD. Contact NCPAD at 1-800-900-8086 for additional details.

musical, artistic, or literary talents; or in the creativity of crafts. Some measure of compensation can be achieved by nearly everyone, but compensation is not enough—satisfactory substitutions for the loss of motor skills must also be found.

Physical activity can make one of its most significant contributions to the welfare of those who have disabilities by enabling them to enjoy the pleasures of active participation in activities and sports through the teaching of substitute motor skills. This is, of course, only part of the role of physical education for those with orthopedic disabilities. Play provides the incentive for the improvement in motor skills, and as locomotion increases, morale receives a needed lift. When more complex game skills are achieved or former skills are reacquired, the youngster's self-esteem reestablishes itself and he or she looks forward with greater confidence and reassurance to achieving satisfactory substitutions for lost skills (see figure 7.1).

As participation becomes more active, physical fitness is increased and body mechanics are improved. The individuals become more skilled in the use of previously unused portions of the body and in the use of the assistive device, if one is required. Because they can play better and longer, owing to the improved conditioning and better playing skills, they enjoy themselves more and others enjoy playing with them. In such an atmosphere of social acceptance, the first steps may be taken toward a more satisfactory adjustment.

Planning the Physical Activity Program

In some cases, during the early stages of treatment, it is necessary to confine youngsters with orthopedic impairments to a hospital setting. Although these stays are usually short, it is imperative that an educational program, including physical education services, be provided for these students. The physical education program in this situation should be concerned with those big-muscle activities used for leisure-time play and the promotion of body conditioning, rather than with the correction of the handicap for the purpose of increased motor function. This latter and important aspect of the child's program must be left to the discretion of the related services personnel, primarily the physical and occupational therapists. Consequently, the physical education program should be carefully planned in consultation with the medical authorities so that muscles will not be used incorrectly, thus negating the therapeutic treatment.

The Hospital or Special Program

During the hospital stay or active treatment stage, the physical education teacher must consider the medical problems that are related to specific types of disabilities. Weakened muscles must not be strained by overwork; the muscles of the set antagonistic to the weaker ones must be protected from overdevelopment, which would produce muscular imbalance; an injured joint in the spinal column must be protected from all movement. In most cases of crippling diseases, after the disease is arrested and muscular reeducation is nearly complete, the physical education activities need to be limited only by the structural limitations of the student.

One of the important objectives of the physical education program for children in special schools and hospitals is to provide play opportunities that encourage them to try the motor skills that they are acquiring or relearning under the care of the physical therapist. Consequently, the program must be carefully planned to provide good progression of skills and experiences. When the very simple skills are satisfactorily mastered, more complex ones can be introduced, and finally very complex skills can be taught. The variety of skills required by the games should be as wide as possible.

The students should be prepared for the great amount of practice that may be necessary to accomplish a skill. If they understand this, they will not become discouraged when they compare their present rate of skill acquisition with their rate before their disabilities. Words of encouragement and praise should be spoken often by the instructor. Students with mental retardation or emotional disturbance in special programs will need extra encouragement in overcoming the limitations in movement imposed by their orthopedic disability. They must be helped in setting realistic goals for themselves and in accepting the fact that improvement in motor skill, however small, is very worthwhile.

The General School

A student returning to school after hospitalization with an orthopedic disability may display no apparent aftereffect; others may exhibit a mild or even severe movement disorder. Although there may be no visible debility, the physical education teacher should not automatically include the student full time in the regular physical education curriculum. Possible muscular weakness or lack of endurance may not be observable. The teacher should not attempt to include the student in the activities until he or she has received medical recommendations as to the amount of activity in which the student should engage and the kinds of activities that will prove most beneficial, as well as those that should be monitored carefully. With this knowledge the teacher will be able to plan the kind of program that will help students increase their general level of fitness and motor efficiency so that they will be better able to meet the physical demands of daily life.

The returning student who has a moderate or severe disability may need considerable help in achieving maximum physical efficiency. Upon receipt of the medical report, the teacher should work out a carefully planned, graduated program of exercises and activities to meet the special needs of the student. It is advisable to secure medical approval of the planned program. Students who have considerable residual paralysis or a limb amputation are also likely to need a great deal of help in making a satisfactory adjustment to their disability. Because of their possible concern about their appearance and their inabilities to perform motor skills, they may experience more anxieties about physical education class than about other phases of their school life. The teacher can help alleviate their fears by assisting them to find a solution that is satisfying to them concerning dressing and showering in the presence of others, and by preparing them to meet the challenges of their restrictions with good humor rather than with fear of embarrassment or ridicule. These concerns should be addressed in the Individualized Education Program (IEP) meeting, at which time parental input can be obtained.

Many students who have had their orthopedic disability for much of their lives achieve a high level of motor efficiency by the time they enroll in physical education. Special instruction for them may need only to be directed toward refinement of movement patterns and the introduction of new skills. Other youngsters, however, require the same kinds of physical education programming considerations as those with recently acquired orthopedic disabilities.

The activities of the special program for those with orthopedic disabilities will be determined by the nature and extent of the impairment and the general debility (see figure 7.2). The early phases of the program for the returning student will be largely exercises and games to increase physical fitness and improve posture and body awareness. As the physical condition and motor performance improve, modified games,

Figure 7.2 Age-appropriate physical activity is enjoyed in the community through the physical education class, or as the result of instruction/practice during the class. (NCPAD.) This photo is reproduced from the National Center on Physical Activity and Disability at www.ncpad.org. It may be freely distributed in its entirety as long as it includes this notice but cannot be edited, modified, or otherwise altered without the express written permission of NCPAD. Contact NCPAD at 1-800-900-8086 for additional details.

dances, and team sports can be introduced into the adapted program. Specific suggestions are made following the discussion of the orthopedically disabling conditions in each of the three sections of this chapter. When the situation warrants it and to the maximum extent possible, the student with a disability should be included in the activities of the regular class.

Disorders That Immobilize Lower Limbs

Many types of orthopedic disorders can cause such severe paralysis of the lower limbs that the use of a wheelchair or similar device is required to achieve locomotion. The two types of such disorders the physical educator most frequently encounters are traumatic spinal cord injuries and spina bifida. The two conditions are similar in that they both produce lesions in the spinal cord and result in subsequent paralysis of the lower limbs.

The following terms are used to label the spine:

C, cervical,
T, thoracic,
L, lumbar,
S, sacral,
the tailbone is referred to as coccyceal.

The spine consists of a spinal cord surrounded by bony structures called vertebrae. The spinal cord is segmented and spinal nerves exit the spinal cord at each segment. These

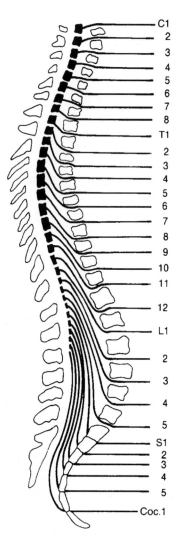

Figure 7.3 Nerves emerging from different levels of the column.

nerves carry movement messages from the brain as well as signals to the brain. The spinal segments and nerves are numbered (C1, C2, C3, . . . T1, T2, T3, . . . L1, L2, L3, . . . S1, S2, S3, etc.) and the vertebrae are similarly numbered (C1, C2, C3, etc.). The relationship of the spinal cord segments and nerves to the surrounding protective vertebrae is seen in figure 7.3. As can be seen, the spinal cord segment is not always colocated at the similarly numbered vertebra (the spinal cord is shorter than the vertebral column). **Spinal injuries are described in terms of spinal cord levels, not vertebral levels.** For example, the neurologic injury resulting from a significant fracture of the T12 vertebra is not necessarily limited to the T12 spinal segment and nerves. The injury may involve lumbar and sacral neurologic levels. Therefore, when reporting on a spinal injury, it is important to specify the injured spinal cord segment and spinal nerve roots, as well as the vertebral injury. The physical educator will be most interested in how this injury affects functional use of muscles and the resulting ability to perform movements in a physical activity program.

The physical educator is a member of the team of education personnel that works with the medical information available regarding the level of injury and resulting paralysis. At some point, the orthopedic surgeon or physiatrist will have made an evaluation about movement paralysis. As the individual's condition is evaluated by physical and occupational therapists, additional information is gained regarding functional levels of movement. **In addition, the physical educator must observe the individual in the physical education classes in order to make professional judgments about the level of functioning given the curriculum, the particular interests of the individual, and the goals and interests of the student's family members.**

The understanding of how a spinal cord injury affects movement performance is complex. From a medical standpoint, the following is taken into account: the areas of injury in the spine, whether the nerve roots have been damaged, and whether the cord is intact. There can be other sources of an injury that impact motor performance; for example, if the head was concussed resulting in cognitive impairment, or the eyes were damaged resulting in impaired vision. In addition, the physical educator must be aware of any problems affecting bowel and bladder function. Some individuals with spinal cord injuries need assistance with elimination. The physical educator must inquire with the student or the family on the type of device the student uses, and the use and care of this device for physical activity. Because their condition requires them to remain seated, or lying on the back, for long periods of time, persons with spinal cord injuries commonly develop decubitus ulcers (bed sores) on the back and buttocks. The major cause of such ulcers is pressure of the body weight on these areas. Pads can be placed to relieve the pressure and to help prevent the ulcers from developing.

Fitness Levels and Activity Considerations

The fitness level of individuals in wheelchairs is generally low (Davis, 1993; Shepard, 1990). This is often attributed, in part, to the unnecessary activity restrictions placed on individuals with spinal cord injuries. According to the National Center on Physical Activity and Disability (NCPAD) (2004), exercise programs can be geared to improving the fitness level of the individual, as well as functional independence. The activities to include in the program vary according to the level of functional skills of the individual. As individuals begin their exercise program, NCPAD encourages them to work closely with a physician who specializes in spinal cord injury. It is assumed that with young children in school programs of physical education, the medical specialist's information will be critical in helping the physical educator understand what to engage the student in within the physical education curriculum, when modifications are needed, and when an activity area needs to be substituted for another activity. For example, if a student cannot engage in a volleyball unit because of quadriplegia, then another activity such as a swim unit might be more appropriate. (More information on adaptations for aquatic programs is found in chapter 16.)

To engage in an exercise program, NCPAD recommends choosing a facility that is staffed with knowledgeable personnel. This is appropriate for younger children and also for older school-age students and with adults. For younger children, this is probably the school's physical education program. For adults, community recreation facilities are important resources. NCPAD recommends exercising three to four times per week using both an at home program and a facility program.

NCPAD recommends interval training to improve cardiovascular fitness where work and rest is built into the program. (Again, the activities of the exercise program depend on the level of functional ability.) For those with access to equipment, rowing machines and treadmills adapted for wheelchairs are used. Muscle strength training and endurance exercises are also recommended by NCPAD. Here the individual increases the intensities of the weight to gain strength and varies the muscle groups trained in order to avoid overuse injuries. Working at 70 to 75 percent of the maximal life, the individual performs 10 to 12 repetitions for two to three sets. NCPAD states that lifting through the full range of movement is important even if physical assistance is necessary. Muscle endurance is measured by the number of times the individual can lift moderate weights. For the person who uses a wheelchair, this endurance is critical for health and mobility. Two pieces of equipment are used in multi-station weight machines: the "Equalizer" and the "Uppertone Gym." Equipment that is easily transportable includes elastic tubing, free weights, and weights attached with velcro to the wrists and ankles.

Flexibility is maintained by range-of-motion exercises and helps to protect the individual from pain or injury. It also enhances the integrity of the joint. The physical educator should know which exercises the individual is using (based on the work of the individual's physical therapist or medical doctor) so the educator can encourage the individual to stay loyal to her program. It is important that the physical educator focus on the activities of physical education and avoid setting a one-to-one exercise program only. The individual with a spinal cord injury needs access to the general education curriculum to the extent possible, as well as to the facilitation of participation in community physical activity in recreation programs and to specialized athletic competition, if the individual is interested. Today, more competitive programs are available for individuals with spinal cord injuries; for example, downhill ski programs. Yet, if the individual is not interested in competition, then a less competitive approach to engaging in activity outside of the school setting can be facilitated. NCPAD promotes incorporating sports and recreation program involvement into the life of an individual with a spinal cord injury for physical as well as psychological well-being. Athletes who compete in sports are classified by functional ability to create equity in the competition. The classification systems, or functional profiles, differ for different sports. Information on classification is found in chapter 18. There are currently many more competitive athletic programs for adults with spinal cord injuries, such as basketball, tennis, swimming, downhill skiing, and floor hockey. NCPAD lists resources by state (www.ncpad.org) and local city and county recreation departments should be contacted.

Precautions with exercise and individuals with spinal cord injuries include being sensitive to the reality that the interruption in communication between the body and the brain may affect the inability of the individual to adjust to changes in blood pressure and heart rate during exercise (figure 7.4). Careful observation of the student is recommended, as well as assisting the student in recognizing the need to pace himself in a physical activity.

Skin integrity is challenged when the sensations of pain are disrupted by a spinal cord injury. Therefore, skin breakdown can occur in areas subjected to prolonged pressure (e.g., hips, heels, tailbone).

Hypotension, or lowered blood pressure, can cause dizziness or lightheadedness during exercise in the individual with a spinal cord injury; this is referred to as orthostatic hypotension. NCPAD recommends that the individual stay hydrated, change positions slowly and, if necessary, wear compression stockings to encourage more normal circulation of the blood throughout the body.

Some individuals with a spinal cord injury also have respiratory involvement, which makes them at risk for infections, congestion, and either shortness of breath or rapid breathing. The physical educator can obtain information on these and other conditions from the medical personnel, physical therapist, or speech therapist, and thus become knowledgeable about how to facilitate appropriate exercise exertion without causing the individual distress, as well as what actions to take if the individual is in distress.

Spina Bifida

Students with spina bifida have an impairment resulting from development that took place before birth. Spina bifida is a deviation in the normal development of the fetus where the arch of the vertebrae does not close around the spinal cord. This can occur at different locations on the spinal cord and can vary in severity. The lumbar area of the spinal cord is the most often affected, but incomplete development can occur at other levels of the spine.

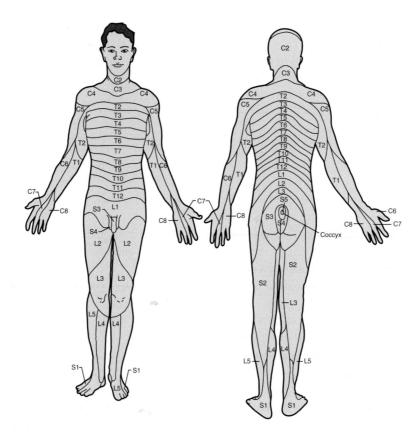

Figure 7.4 Cutaneous distribution of spinal nerves. (Source: Barr, M. L., & Kieman, J. A. (1988). *The human nervous system: A medical viewpoint* (5th ed.). Hagerstown, MD: Harper & Row.)

The exact cause or causes of this neural tube development failure have not been identified. The occurrence risk for spina bifida and related anomalies in siblings and offspring of those with spina bifida is slightly higher than the expected occurrence in the general population; also, the incidence is higher among the Welsh and Irish.

Classification

Spina Bifida Oculta The term "oculta" means hidden, and individuals with spina bifida oculta may have no visible signs of the anomaly in their spinal cord. Here the spinal arch is not closed, but the spinal cord retains its normal position and is not damaged (see figure 7.5 *A*). Symptoms of this impairment may not occur until later in life, when the vertebra may slip and cause the individual pain.

Myelomeningocele Myelomeningocele occurs when the spinal cord is damaged. Here the cord or the membranes that cover the cord protrude through the open vertebra arch (see figure 7.5 *B*). This open arch is called the myelomeningocele. In this condition, muscle weakness is associated with the areas where the spinal cord nerves innervate the muscles; for example, there can be loss of bladder or bowel function, or atrophy in the calf and thigh muscles.

For individuals with more severe forms of spina bifida, a neurologist examines the infant. Other medical specialists may also be involved: neurosurgeon, pediatric orthopedic

Figure 7.5 Two types of spina bifida. *(A)* Spina bifida occulta and *(B)* myelomeningocele. (Source: Williamson, G. G. (1987). *Children with Spina Bifida: Early Intervention and Preschool Programming* (p. 2). Baltimore, MD.: Paul H. Brookes Publishing Co.)

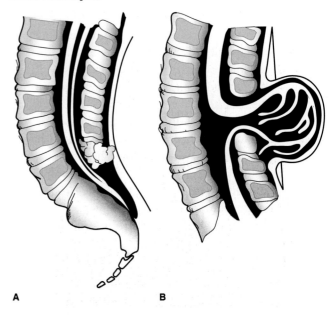

A   B

surgeon, and urologist. As the child grows, frequent monitoring by a medical team is recommended. Because of the nerve damage, there is often lack of sensation, and the skin must be protected from ulcers. Individuals with myelomeningocele, like all those with paralysis, are very susceptible to skin ulcerations (sores) because of the loss of sensation in the skin. Obesity may also become a problem, and the incidence of congenital heart disease seems to be higher in children with spina bifida.

Many students with spina bifida are latex sensitive and must avoid this substance in the classroom and gymnasium. This sensitivity can have very serious effects for some individuals, resulting in anaphylactic shock. For educators, communication with the family is imperative. It is also helpful to check with the Spina Bifida Association of America (www.sbaa.org) to find out which items are to be avoided.

Individuals with myelomeningocele are at high risk for developing hydrocephalus owing to increased spinal fluid that accumulates in the brain. The head is often disproportionally larger than expected for their body size. Shunts implanted in the head help to relieve the accumulation of the fluid by draining it off into the stomach. In individuals with spina bifida, the torso is longer compared to the legs. Sometimes the children have braces on their legs because of weaker muscles. In some cases, the students use wheelchairs or a combination of a wheelchair and crutches (see figure 7.6).

Some individuals with spina bifida have cognitive deficits, but many have normal intelligence. Sherrill (2004) observes that the limited mobility in infancy can contribute to delays in motor development. Scoliosis, lordosis, kyphosis, or a combination of these may be present at birth or may appear later as a result of rapid growth accompanied by the absence of a complete vertebral column.

Social challenges are faced by children with spina bifida. Some of this is caused by their use of assistive devices for mobility (crutches, canes, wheelchairs), larger head size, and the need for external collection devices for bladder control. In early life, these children can experience numerous and lengthy hospitalizations, which can affect the typical development of age-appropriate social skills. In addition, as is often the case in other disability areas, parents can be overprotective of their child.

Treatment

Prior to the 1950s, myelomeningocele infants were left untreated and the vast majority died within a few months. Today improved surgical techniques and drug treatments can lead to prolonged life in many patients. Unfortunately, however, paralysis and other serious problems present at birth are not reversible and treatment is not completely ameliorative. Extensive and continuous medical treatment of a child with a poor prognosis places heavy emotional, social, and economic burdens on the family. Complete evaluation is made and a decision for treatment is reached based on economic, social, familial, and medical factors.

The tube and shunt valve do not require special care and normally the child with a shunt is not overly restricted from activity (figure 7.7). The only movement that is usually to be avoided is prolonged hanging upside down (this position may interfere with the flow of fluid and disrupt the valvular function of the shunt) and sports such as soccer, where the head might be hit.

Periodically the shunt may have to be replaced due to the growth of the child, obstruction in the tube, or malfunction of the valve. Teachers and parents need to be aware of warning signs that may indicate possible problems with the

Figure 7.6 This young woman uses both crutches and a wheelchair for ambulation.

Figure 7.7 *(A)* Ventriculoatrial shunt. *(B)* Ventriculoperitoneal shunt.

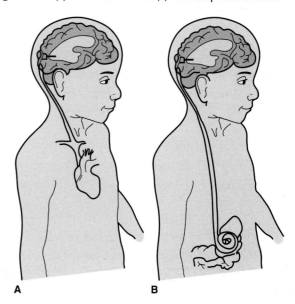

A   B

shunt. The warning signs that follow should be brought to the attention of the child's physician:

1. Increase in head size
2. Behavioral changes such as extreme irritability or fussiness
3. Increase in sleepiness
4. Seizures
5. Diminished reaction to the environment, or lethargy
6. Forceful vomiting
7. Swelling or redness of the skin in the area of the shunt
8. Headaches
9. "Setting sun" eyes (iris only partially visible due to a downward gaze) (Williamson, 1987, pp. 83–84)

There are two important urological considerations. One is the prevention of infection and renal dysfunction and the other is the prevention of socially unacceptable incontinence. Controversy exists as to which of the several treatment methods available is best. As yet, none seems to be satisfactory in all cases. Treatment varies with the individual and depends on urinary tract involvement, the sex and age of the person, and the preference of the family and physician.

Successful micturition may be brought about by manual pressure on the lower abdomen (Credé maneuver) for some persons or by a catheter from the bladder for others. The use of the catheter, known as catheterization, requires inserting a catheter (a tube) through the urethra into the bladder for the withdrawal of urine at set intervals. For young children, catheterization must be done by a teacher or aide, but later students learn to perform this procedure without assistance (figure 7.8).

Figure 7.8 Catheterization, a means of withdrawing urine from the bladder, is used by persons with spina bifida, spinal cord injuries, and other conditions that cause urinary incontinence. The catheter is lubricated and then inserted about six inches into the penis or about three inches into the female opening. Parents can generally instruct teachers as to the correct procedure.

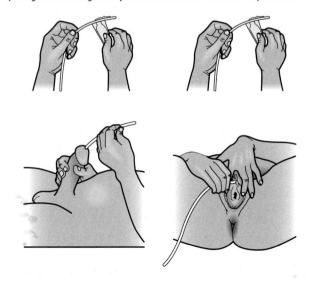

For boys, a urinal bag with penile attachment may be used. When progressive upper urinary tract damage is evident, surgical diversion is recommended. The most common is the ileal loop. In this diversion the ureters are brought into a loop of the bowel, which is opened to the outside through the abdominal wall, thus eliminating the bladder as a collection bag. Antibiotic drugs are used to combat infections.

Bowel management through diet, medication, and the use of suppositories and enemas when necessary is relatively successful. Further treatment is generally not necessary.

Treatment for infants with spina bifida has improved dramatically over the decades. Those who survive may still face paralysis, continued threats of infection, and genitourinary problems. Concurrent with improved treatment practices are new methods of screening and detection of spina bifida during the fetal period that provide the possibility of prevention through early identification.

Physical Activities

The following activity suggestions are focused on engaging the student with spina bifida in a physical education program that is age appropriate, develops his social skills, and allows him to have fun in physical activity while learning valuable lessons about the role that fitness plays throughout his life. Because of the advances in medical management of these children, their lives are longer and can be fulfilling. Physical education has a special role to play in the lives of these students; one that separates the students from many of the therapeutic modalities of their lives. Each student with spina bifida has a unique personality and history. The physical educator can take advantage of the student's interests and can expand that knowledge in the physical education program. In the end, individuals with spina bifida will gain in successfully managing their own physical health.

Younger students

The kinds of motor activities in which a student in a wheelchair can engage depend upon the specific nature of the disability. For those with spinal injuries, including spina bifida, the activity choices depend on the severity and level of the lesion. The physical educator will need to assess the movement potential of each student, utilizing knowledge of the level of injury, the resulting paralysis, and actual observation of the student. Careful attention when observing the ways in which the student manipulates his or her body to perform daily routines will provide possible clues as to the potential for movement. Teachers will notice, for instance, that children with spina bifida frequently have visual-motor problems requiring special assistance when teaching games that involve balls and objects that are thrown or struck.

Persons with paraplegia, after recovery from the initial injury, can perform most physical education activities from the wheelchair. For younger children, catching and throwing games are easily devised; target games using bean bags are also readily developed. Bouncing balls off walls is another activity possible for the child in a chair. Even a game of modified handball is possible; the child bats the ball so that it returns to him or her or to a partner, who in turn bats it to the wall. A ball suspended from the ceiling with a heavy cord makes an excellent piece of equipment for teaching catching and throwing skills to the child who needs a wheelchair (figure 7.9). In addition, the suspended ball can be used for various activities, such as throwing at a target drawn on a board or at empty milk cartons or plastic bottles standing on a table (Webster, Levy, Bryant, & Prusakowski, 2001).

The child in a wheelchair can also take part in parachute play. There is no reason why he or she cannot engage in all of the common activities of parachute play, including exchanging places with another player while the parachute is in the air, by substituting locomotion of the chair for walking and running. The same substitution is possible in most basic skill games.

Older students

Older students can be offered many of the activities included in the general education program, with only such modifications as are necessitated by the need to remain in the chair. Again, the Burton top-down assessment approach described in chapters 5 and 6 is recommended. Given the curriculum, the

Figure 7.9 After each hit, the suspended ball returns to the student in the wheelchair, eliminating problems of retrieval.

physical educator can observe the individual in the activity and decide what, if any, modifications are needed to successfully engage in the activity. The way in which the skills are performed usually requires some adaptations; specific suggestions for these are made in the chapters on various activities, and Lieberman and Houston-Wilson (2002) have provided a good framework for making adaptations for many activities. Here, options for modifications of game regulations and equipment can be identified. For example, the playing area for games and sports is usually reduced in size, playing equipment is lighter, and frequently the handles of rackets and mallets are extended to increase the range of the reach. In team games, the area that each player must cover is reduced, the assignment of duties is made on the basis of the players' abilities, or two people with different abilities share an assignment. For rhythm and dance activities, the size of the formations is increased to accommodate the wheelchair in the maneuvers.

Fitness Activities

The National Center on Physical Activity and Disability (NCPAD, 2004) stresses the importance for individuals with spina bifida to engage in fitness activities. NCPAD sees practical importance in fitness activity for individuals with spina bifida to control weight and prevent deconditioning. For young children, physical fitness activities are those engaged in when they are playing games and playing in a neighborhood open space such as a park or playground. Later, they will become more fit with regular activity such as sports or recreational physical fitness. Specific activities in the physical education program for fitness for older students with spina bifida should be age appropriate. A description of this follows.

Swimming is an especially good activity for total physical conditioning. Students with bowel- and bladder-control problems can use waterproof pants to eliminate potential embarrassment while in the water. For individuals with paraplegia, special attention should be given to providing exercises to achieve and maintain physical fitness. Especially important for the person with paraplegia are activities that strengthen the arms and shoulder girdle, because optimal strength in these muscles will make propelling the wheelchair and transferring to and from it easier and less exhausting (Coutts, McKenzie, Loock, Beauchamp, & Armstrong, 1993; Glaser, 1989). Emphasis should also be given to activities that encourage a full range of motion in the spastic muscles to aid in the prevention of contracture (Jeffrey, 1986).

For individuals with paraplegia, weight training can be used to develop muscular strength. NCPAD (2004) recommends strength training using free weights, weight machines such as Nautilus, a medicine ball, wall pulley, and Therabands. Wheelchair push-ups can be performed every 10 to

60 minutes each day and held for 30 to 60 seconds. The elbows must be bent slightly on the extension. NCPAD recommends strength training three days per week and exercises should be varied to avoid overuse of the muscles.

NCPAD also draws on the recommendations of the American College of Sports Medicine (ACSM) regarding cardiovascular training for individuals with spina bifida: 20 to 60 minutes of continuous aerobic exercise, or multiple sessions of 10 minutes in duration, three to five times per week. The maximum heart rate (MHR) for individuals with spina bifida may be much lower than normal. Measure of perceived exertion will be moderate to strong. This means that although the MHR may be lower, individuals with spina bifida will perceive their effort appropriately.

NCPAD also encourages people with spina bifida to monitor their urinary cycle and empty their bladder before exercise. Thermoregulation difficulties make it imperative that individuals with spina bifida wear appropriate exercise clothing for the weather and drink fluids as necessary. Those with spina bifida need to check the skin for pressure sores when engaged in wheelchair sports and regularly perform pushups to alleviate pressure from sitting. People should be trained to assist individuals with spina bifida for transfers from the wheelchair to accessible exercise machines. Stretching spastic muscle groups is recommended to avoid increasing an excessive spastic condition.

Persons with quadriplegia can also engage in conditioning with weights if certain adaptations are made. In total quadriplegia, a head harness attached to wall pulleys is supplied. For those with partial quadriplegia who have some arm movement, special weight resistance exercises are possible.

Several organizations promote competition on local, national, and international levels for persons with paraplegia and quadriplegia. Through the school physical education teacher, students as young athletes can be encouraged to compete in local events. As the student's interest develops for competition, other community-based programs that lead to local and national competition can be explored. Events include archery, bowling, basketball, table tennis, swimming, weightlifting, shooting, and tennis. Classification systems based on the levels of injury have been developed so that no player or team will have an unfair advantage over another. More information on this can be found in chapter 18.

Disorders That Limit Ambulation

Many orthopedic disorders affect ambulation, the ability to walk. This section includes a discussion of the disabilities that make walking difficult. However, these disabilities may,

in severe cases or cases of multiple disabilities, require the person to use a wheelchair. If so, modifications can be made to accomodate a slower speed of ambulation or alternate means of locomotion.

Congenital Hip Dislocation

Congenital dislocation of the hip refers to a partially or completely displaced femoral head (in relation to the acetabulum of the hip) that is present at birth. Defective development of the acetabulum, termed dysplasia of the hip, accompanies the condition. In time, with continued dislocation, the acetabulum changes in shape, becoming triangular or oval rather than flat, and may become filled with fibrous tissue.

Congenital hip dislocation occurs more commonly among girls than boys. It is more often unilateral than bilateral, and the left hip is affected more often than the right. It is the fourth most common congenital defect. Prolonged malpositioning of the hip joint produces a chronic weakness of the leg and hip muscles. If the condition is left untreated, ambulation becomes difficult; however, if adequate medical treatment, consisting of bracing and surgery, is received early in life, the prognosis for normal locomotion is very good. No modifications may be needed.

Foot Deformities

Foot deformities are seen when the foot is positioned atypically. This condition is often congenital but it can also be acquired when other conditions, such as spastic paralysis, are present. Various medical terms are used for these foot deformities. The term "equinus" (latin for horse) is used in orthopedic medicine; horses walk on their toenails, and thus the term is often used to refer to the abnormal foot position for walking. Foot deformities include appearances of the heel lower than the toes, the toes and sole of foot turned out, the toes and foot turned in, and combinations of the lower heels and toes/sole turned in or out.

The most common foot deformity seen in physical education and in early childhood education programs is "toe walking," wherein the child puts more weight on the toes than on the heels. According to experts (Speciality Services, 2004), toe walking is commonly seen in toddlers, who eventually assume a normal gait. Toe walkers who are older may have a neurologic etiology for the atypical foot position. Toe walking has levels of severity that are measured by the height of the heel from the ground. It is recommended that the physical education teacher follow the family and orthopedic surgeon's management of the foot placement. Surgery is typically a last resort and there are numerous variables to take into account based on the suspected cause of the abnormal foot position.

Another common foot deformity is "club foot." Here the child turns the foot inward and walks on the outside edge of the foot. The club foot is often smaller than the normally developed foot of the child and, for some children, both feet are affected. The calf muscles can be smaller and, for some children, there is a shortening of certain tendons. Treatment at birth is coordinated by an orthopedic surgeon and the type of intervention is based on the severity of the deformity. When the foot is in better alignment, functional ability is good and is not affected by the persistence of smaller feet and calf muscles.

In all the different foot deformities, the physical educator is best advised to consult with the family, follow the orthopedic surgeon's management plan, and complete any accompanying physical therapy interventions. From this point, the modifications and adaptations, if they are needed for physical education, would be individualized while the student engages in age-appropriate physical activity.

Disorders of Growth of the Bone

Typically, it is the orthopedic surgeon who identifies why and where the bone is not growing. Bone growth disorders are described by location: at the epiphysis, physis, metaphysis, and the bone diaphysis (see figure 7.10). Bones typically grow at the ends, not in the middle. When children are growing bone, there may be structural problems that occur at specific sites on the bone. This can cause pain and difficulties during participation in physical activity.

Osgood-Schlatter Disease

Osgood-Schlatter disease is a common cause of knee pain in teenagers who are still growing. Pain can come from the swelling below the knee joint on a prominence on the leg bone (tibia). Inflammation of the patellar tendon that stretches over the knee cap and attaches to the top of the shin bone also may occur (see figure 7.11). The pain comes from the growth plate in the bone in the area of the tibial

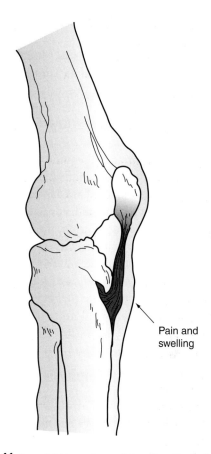

Figure 7.11 Osgood-Schlatter disease. Pain and swelling in the area of the insertion of the tendon into the tibia is the common complaint of those affected with this condition.

tuberosity. Typically bones grow at the ends rather than the middle. Pain occurs when the bone is growing and the cartilage near these points is not as strong as the bone.

This disease was once more common among young boys, ages ten to fifteen, than among girls. Because of the increased activity levels of girls, an increasing number of females are now experiencing discomfort from Osgood-Schlatter disease. Most authorities believe that this disease is the result of trauma that may produce major changes in the area as a result of one isolated event or the accumulation of several smaller injuries to the knee.

The disease responds well to treatment. Usually vigorous use of the knee is contraindicated for a period of six to nine months. During this time the student is restricted/limited in activities that involve running, jumping, climbing, and bicycling.

This disease varies in levels of severity; therefore, pain management should be coordinated with medical personnel. Returning to sports is dependent on the individual's pain tolerance. According to physicians, ". . . An athlete will not be 'damaging' their knee by playing with some pain" (Specialty Services, 2004). The best treatment is still to rest from the activity.

Figure 7.10 Location of bone growth disorders.

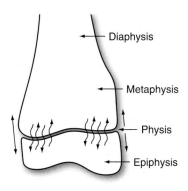

Kyphosis

Kyphosis is a disturbance of the normal vertebral growth in the cervical and upper thoracic region. The epiphysis or cartilage of one or more vertebra may be inflamed, resulting in fragmentation of the vertebra(e). The etiology is generally unknown and the disease appears to have an active phase in which activity is contraindicated.

The amount of pain and discomfort associated with kyphosis varies from individual to individual. Some complain of no pain and insist that they be allowed to participate in any activity of their choosing. If the student's activity level is not restricted, particularly forward flexion, the kyphotic slump may increase. Consultation with parents is recommended.

Treatment varies depending on the severity of the kyphosis. Sometimes surgery is indicated and, in other cases, exercises and pain medications are all that is required. Children with kyphosis typically lead normal lives (Specialty Services, 2004).

Slipped Femoral Capital Epiphysis

Slipped Femoral Capital Epiphysis (SFCE) occurs in adolescents when the growth plate is weakened in the femoral head that fits into the cup of the pelvic bones. Then a slip occurs at this place in the hip. This weakening of the growth plate can be caused by different endocrine disorders as well as by obesity or trauma. Treatment is surgical. Depending on the level of treatment of the SFCE, the physical educator will need to coordinate modifications and adaptations with input from the student, family, and medical personnel.

Leg Amputation

Prognosis is good with amputation of the lower limbs. Good prosthetic solutions to lower extremeties has positively influenced patient outcomes. Amputation, the loss of all or part of a limb, may be due to several factors. Among these are congenital conditions in which the infant is born with all or part of a limb missing. Other reasons for amputation are tumor, trauma, and disease. Amputation may be performed to arrest a malignant condition. Traumatic amputation may occur as the result of accident, or the damage may be so extensive as to require surgical removal of the limb. The diseases responsible for most amputations are those, like diabetes and arteriosclerosis, that cause circulatory problems. Such problems occur more often in the legs than in other parts of the body. The terms that are used to identify amputations are presented in figure 7.12. This information is valuable in helping the teacher to interpret medical information and in its educational relevance to the affected student.

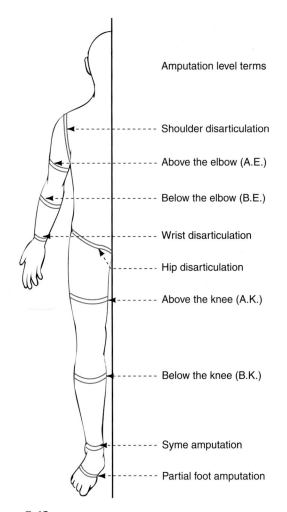

Amputation level terms

— — — — Shoulder disarticulation

— — — — Above the elbow (A.E.)

— — — — Below the elbow (B.E.)

— — — — Wrist disarticulation

— — — — Hip disarticulation

— — — — Above the knee (A.K.)

— — — — Below the knee (B.K.)

— — — — Syme amputation

— — — — Partial foot amputation

Figure 7.12 Terms used for amputation levels.

The person with a leg amputation can be readily fitted with a prosthesis. The problems of ambulation will vary with the specific level of amputation. Those with below-knee amputations can readily learn the use of the prosthesis in locomotion. Many young individuals with an amputation learn to use their prostheses so well that walking effectiveness is altered very little.

Those with amputations above the knee but below the hip may have difficulty in developing a proper walking gait because the gait pattern is drastically changed due to the loss of the knee joint. Steps are shortened to prevent a movement that would tend to flex the artificial knee as it is swung forward. The individual must lean forward at the hips and, when the foot strikes the ground, the hip must be extended to prevent bending of the knee. As the weight passes over the artificial leg, the thigh is flexed and the artificial limb flexes at the knee, owing to the weight of the lower part. The hip is then extended to bring the body weight over the artificial foot as it is planted on the ground.

A common fault in walking for the person with above-the-knee amputation is the abduction or rolling gait. As weight is borne on the good leg, the opposite side of the body is raised, elevating the hip and causing the prosthesis to swing out from the body as well as forward.

Amputation of both lower extremities obviously adds serious problems. However, the basic technique in walking is approximately the same. The chief difference is the need to manipulate two artificial limbs rather than one.

Physical Activities

A student with an orthopedic disorder affecting ambulation may or may not use an assistive device to aid locomotion. If the assistive device is a cane or crutches, few problems arise to hinder participation in physical education. Many of the activities suitable for students in wheelchairs are also appropriate for these children. The chief difference is that those with canes or crutches need to learn to balance themselves in such a manner as to free one hand for use. The kind of crutches as well as the manner of use will vary from one situation to the next. In most cases it is easier to use the arms in activities if crutches with cuffs are used. The balance can be maintained by one crutch while the other arm is free. The crutch does not fall to the ground because it is anchored to the forearm. Activities such as volleyball, throwing a ball, and striking with one hand can all be readily accomplished.

All students whose ambulation is impaired are at a disadvantage when speed of locomotion is required. Such activities should be adapted so that the distance the player has to travel is limited. For example, in badminton the regulations can be changed so that the objective becomes to hit the bird back to the opponent with a disability rather than to place it where he or she cannot return it. In addition, the court of the player with a disability can be reduced in size to compensate for his or her movement limitation. Decreasing the speed needed to move from one place to another also allows more efficient participation by these students. Using a balloon for a ball in a game of toss is an example of a way in which the requirement for fast movement can be modified, since a balloon, when thrown, moves at a slower rate through the air than does a ball.

Activities for young children can be adapted from some of the basic skill games described in chapter 15. For example, children who have difficulty moving can participate in games such as softball, circle ball, wonder ball, or target toss from a sitting position in a chair (see figure 7.13). Children with some degree of functional leg movement can play softball, bowling, driving pig to market, partner toss, and similar games in which leg agility is not essential. These children can also participate in singing games like Here We Go Over the Mountain, and Way Down Yonder in the Paw-Paw Patch by substituting walking for skipping.

The student with a leg prosthesis has a problem in maintaining balance. The individual with a unilateral

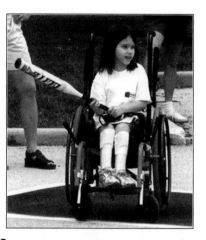

Figure 7.13 Children who have difficulty moving can still participate in games such as softball. This photo is reproduced from the National Center on Physical Activity and Disability at www.ncpad.org. It may be freely distributed in its entirety as long as it includes this notice but cannot be edited, modified, or otherwise altered without the express written permission of NCPAD. Contact NCPAD at 1-800-900-8086 for additional details.

amputation should practice maintaining his or her balance on the prosthetic limb so as to be able to use the sound foot for other purposes in game situations, for example, kicking a football or trapping in soccer. Balance on stairs is easier to maintain if the sound limb leads when ascending and if the prosthesis leads when descending.

Certain devices placed near the person with a leg amputation can help the individual with balance (e.g., table), or the person can sit in a straight back chair.

In most cases, individuals with single-leg prostheses can develop balance and other locomotion skills so that they are able to participate in all physical education activities. Many become active in athletic competition such as football or baseball, both as amateurs and as professionals. These athletes usually train in the same manner as others. Strengthening exercises are done while wearing the prosthesis, thus strengthening the muscles that control the device.

The prosthesis is not worn in the water, and a missing leg will cause a change in the center of gravity in swimming. Consequently, the swimmer experiences difficulty in maintaining a prone or back position because the body tends to turn in the water toward the heavier side (away from the missing limb). Proper stroking can eliminate the problem (see chapter 16).

Students with an orthopedic disability enjoy movement in the water that is not possible out of the water. Although not encouraged to stand erect in the water, they can do so without much risk because the buoyancy of the water reduces the pressure of body weight on the head of the femur. For others, the water buoyancy makes control of the body easier by minimizing the effects of weak muscles and the lack of balance and stability that hinders or restricts movement out of

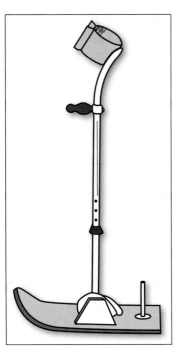

Figure 7.14 Outrigger ski.

the water. Assistive devices that must always be worn otherwise can usually be removed for swimming.

Many individuals with unilateral leg amputations have been very successful in skiing. Those with below-the-knee amputations can usually wear regular skis with their prostheses. Skiers who have a single above-the-knee amputation employ a three-track ski technique, in which one regular ski and two handheld outriggers are used. The outrigger consists of a Löfstrand crutch attached by a hinge to a short ski (figure 7.14). The outrigger is constructed to allow only limited movement at the hinge. A movable spike is inserted at the rear of the ski. The spike is lifted when skiing downhill and can be lowered to sink into the snow when skiing over flat terrain or moving uphill.

Disorders That Affect Other Body Movement

The first two sections of this chapter have been directed toward orthopedic disabilities that prevent or impede ambulation. This section will discuss other orthopedic disorders that affect body movement but do not necessarily impose limitations on locomotion to any great extent; included are scoliosis, torticollis, spondyloses, and arm amputation. Under certain conditions, some of these disabilities indirectly affect walking gait because the resultant deformity causes problems in body balance that, in turn, disturbs the normal gait.

Scoliosis

When a body with a normal spinal column is viewed from the back, the right and left sides of the body are symmetrical, both shoulders and both hips are at the same level, and the spinal column is straight. Most individuals will show a very slight deviation in the spinal column. A slight deviation is usually not noticeable during casual observation and, if it does not become progressively worse, is of no consequence. However, a lateral curvature that is obvious must be considered an abnormal condition.

The lateral curvature of the spine is accompanied by a twisting of the vertebrae and takes its name, *scoliosis,* from the Greek word *skolios,* meaning twisting or bending. The lateral curve may be to the right, left, or a combination of both. If it is to the right or left, it is called a C curve. An S curve is one in which the lower part curves in the opposite direction. In the latter condition, one of the curves is usually the primary curve while the other is a secondary curve developed to compensate for the first in restoring equilibrium to the trunk as a whole. An uncorrected C curve will eventually encourage the development of an S curve.

The C curve takes its name from the direction of convexity of the curve. A left C curve is to the individual's left and causes the right shoulder to be lowered and right hip to be raised (figure 7.15 A). The reverse is true of the right C curve. A condition of convexity of the curve, present at birth, is usually a left C curve. A curve that develops after birth is usually to the right.

In most S curves the primary curve is to the left, in the upper portion of the spine. The right shoulder will be held lower than the left, while the left hip will be raised higher than the right (figure 7.15 B).

Figure 7.15 Diagrammatic illustration of the slant of shoulders and hips in scoliosis. *(A)* C curve to left. *(B)* S curve to left.

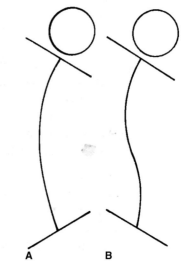

A   B

Scoliosis may be functional or structural in nature. If the curve tends to disappear when a hanging or prone position is assumed, it is probably functional. The causes of scoliosis are varied. A shortened leg, disease, injury, congenital conditions, and faulty postural habits, often due to hearing and vision problems, are the most frequent causes. Seldom does scoliosis in its early stages cause pain or noticeable fatigue. However, in the later stages the muscular pull necessitated by the abnormal condition of the spine may cause back fatigue and frequent pains. It is, moreover, a definite cosmetic concern.

Scoliosis is a common problem affecting 10 percent of the school-aged population, with 2½ percent requiring some form of medical attention. Students should be periodically checked for evidence of scoliosis until growth is complete. Some questions used to screen are listed in figure 7.16. Questions 9 and 10 require that the student assume the Adam's position with the legs straight, hips flexed, and arms hanging freely in line with the toes. This position enables the teacher to look down the student's back to check for symmetrical muscle development. Diagnosis of scoliosis is made by a physician.

Treatment

Treatment for scoliosis depends on the amount of curvature of the spine and the age of the individual. In young children, if the curve is moderate (less than 25 degrees), then they are followed by a pediatric orthopedic surgeon until the skeleton has reached maturity. When children are still growing, and have a greater curvature of the spine (greater than 25 degrees), they can wear braces to keep the curve from becoming more severe; the brace is worn under the clothes.

Surgery has two phases. First, stainless steel rods are placed at the point of greatest curvature. Later, bone grafts can be added to fuse the spine into the correct position obtained by the rods. Students can return to activity when energy permits and 6 months after the corrective surgery; there are no permanent activity restrictions (Specialty Services, 2004).

Figure 7.16 Simple test for early detection of scoliosis.

	Yes	No	
1.	____	____	Is one shoulder higher than the other?
2.	____	____	Is one scapula (shoulder blade) more prominent than the other?
3.	____	____	Does one hip seem higher or more prominent than the other?
4.	____	____	Is there a greater distance between the arm and the body on one side than on the other, when the arms are hanging down loosely at the sides?
5.	____	____	Does the child have a "swayback" (lordosis)?
6.	____	____	Does the child have "round shoulders" or "humpback" (kyphosis)?
7.	____	____	Is there a larger "crease" at one side of the waist than at the other side?
8.	____	____	Does the child seem to "list" or lean to one side?
9.	____	____	Is there a hump in the rib area?
10.	____	____	Is there a hump in the lumbar region (near the waist)?

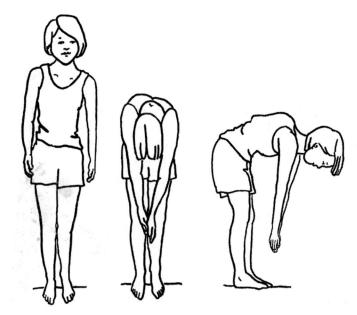

Torticollis

In this disorder the neck is persistently held at a tilt, with the chin pointing in the opposite direction. This is caused by a contracted sternocleidomastoid muscle. This disorder may be congenital or hysterical, or it may be caused by pressure on the nerves, by muscle spasm, or by inflammation of the glands in the neck. Treatment is symptomatic; that is, it differs depending on the symptoms.

Spondylolisthesis

Spondylolisthesis is a structural defect in the vertebrae which leads to a forward slippage of one vertebra over another. As a result, motion in bending forward is restricted and often painful. The pain may be aggravated by lordosis (swayback). Treatment consists of maintaining proper posture. In more advanced cases, surgery is usually performed to stabilize the joint.

Arm Amputation

Arm amputation may occur at various levels (see figure 7.12). Causes of upper limb amputations are the same as those discussed earlier in this chapter under the heading *Leg Amputation*. The prosthesis of the individual with an arm amputation does not substitute as well as the prosthesis of the person with a leg amputation. It is almost impossible to develop a mechanical device that substitutes for the human hand and fingers in both function and appearance. Nevertheless, it is possible to achieve considerable dexterity with the utility arm and split hook in performing manual tasks, including racquet and paddle games in physical education.

Physical Activities

Physical education activities for those with orthopedic disorders that affect other body movements must be selected to meet the students' special needs and limitations, with consideration for their interests and movement potential and in consultation with the medical doctor and the physical and occupational therapists working with individuals in the schools.

Students with torticollis and scoliosis are usually not greatly restricted in movement. Those with torticollis are able to perform all activities except those that place an undue stress upon neck muscles. Some, because of spasms in the neck muscles or limited movement in the neck, cannot participate in the forward roll, the headstand, or similar activities.

Scoliosis does not interfere with the normal performance of motor activities unless there is extreme deformity.

Locomotion may be affected to some degree, as may movements of the body that require extreme flexibility, such as tumbling. Activities that place undue stress on the spinal column, such as football, may be contraindicated.

Weight-lifting programs for those with scoliosis can be initiated with the approval of the orthopedic physician. All exercise that affects the muscles on only one side of the spinal column should not be attempted without approval by the physician. Most symmetrical exercises can be participated in without adding further to the imbalance of the body. Chin-ups, passive hanging from a bar, and pushing or pulling equally with both hands are examples of suitable exercises.

Activities for those who have spondylolisthesis should be suspended until the inflammation is brought under control. If there is no permanent damage to the spinal column, the student can resume normal activity. If damage does occur, the activities selected must not cause undue twisting or stress and strain on the spinal column.

The congenital arm amputee or student who has had a single arm since early life usually has made sufficient motor adaptation by the time he or she reaches school and will require little assistance in making adaptations in motor skill performance. Students with a recent amputation, in contrast, will need to relearn some skills before they are able to participate in most activities. Also, they must adjust to their disability. Many individuals, after losing a limb, become self-conscious and tend to withdraw from activity. The physical education teacher can be of great assistance to such students by encouraging them to try the suggested modifications of the activities. When they find that they can perform many skills that they thought they could never engage in again, they are very likely to begin to accept their loss and adjust more successfully.

Those who have lost a single arm, if it is not the dominant arm, can play most basic skill games and participate in more advanced physical education activities without significant modifications, except in the technique of catching. If the dominant hand is lost, the student can learn to use the other hand. Performing the skill with this hand will at first seem awkward, but practice will overcome this. The development of arm dexterity should be initiated with simple throwing activities such as throwing bean bags or darts at a target. Devices can be specially built by an orthotist to fit into the arm prosthesis for the purpose of holding sports equipment such as gloves. Students having difficulty in learning to catch with one hand may wish to have such a device made. How to catch a ball with a glove and one arm is described in chapter 28 on the CD, in the section on softball.

Most racquet games are not affected by single-arm amputation. In the case of the double-arm amputee with sufficient stump, a paddle or racquet can be attached to the stump to enable play of many racquet games (chapter 27 on the CD). Swimming, as mentioned previously, is a good activity for single or double amputees and others with orthopedic disorders affecting body movement.

Of course, students who have use of their feet can participate in activities that chiefly require foot action, such as soccer, goal kicking, and various running events.

It is possible for the student with double-arm amputation to play volleyball by using parts of the body to play the ball; the head and knee are the most effective for this.

Soccer handball, a game developed at the University of Connecticut for those with limited use of their arms, can be played by participants who have upper-limb involvement in both arms. It is played in a handball court with a soccer ball. The ball is kicked against the wall. The serve, to be good, must be kicked against the front wall and must return behind the service line. The ball is allowed to bounce once. It may hit any wall or combination of walls and remain in play. The ball may be played with any part of the body.

Thermal Injuries

Two million people sustain burn injuries each year; 100,000 seriously enough to require hospitalization. The exact number of children who are affected by a serious or life-threatening thermal injury each year is difficult to estimate but is not insignificant. The effect of a thermal injury can be devastating, including the loss of an extremity, disfigurement, and severe contractures.

Burns may be caused by several things including fires, chemicals, and scalding from extremely hot water. Recent efforts to treat burns and other thermal injuries have been so successful that today many individuals survive what were life-ending injuries a few years ago. This means that educators, including physical educators, must be sensitive to this disability population and specific instructional needs they may require.

Rehabilitation for the burn victim begins the first day after the accident. One of the primary goals of treatment is to maintain joint motion and to avoid, where possible, contractures.

Deformities caused by contractures can be prevented or minimized by proper positioning of the patient both in bed and in a chair, appropriate splinting and bracing, performing selected exercises, and participating in a general conditioning program.

Active, passive, and resistive exercises of both the burned and unburned area should be performed frequently. The purpose of the exercise program is to:

1. Prevent or minimize functional and cosmetic deformities.
2. Prevent deconditioning.
3. Prevent complications of prolonged bed rest and immobilization.
4. Enhance the individuals's self-worth and confidence by preserving the ability to perform activities of daily living.

These programs, while normally developed by the physical therapist, can be implemented by the physical educator in consultation with the medical team. In addition, rehabilitation specialists recommend that burn victims participate in a program of fitness and conditioning activities as soon as possible. This is done to ensure that the individual maintains an appropriate level of fitness and to emphasize a positive outlook toward an active life.

The child with a thermal injury should be encouraged to return to school as soon as possible. The physical education program for the youngster should be similar to that of any other youngster, with modifications as necessary. Because the child may be wearing a splint or brace, the physical educator may need to assist the child in removing, cleaning, and reapplying the device. Some children may wear a jobst, an elastic support made to fit a particular area of the body. The jobst applies pressure to the burned area to help minimize the amount of scarring.

Physical education teachers will need to be sensitive to the burn-injured child's reaction to the sun and to chlorine in swimming pools. Normally, activities in the pool and in sunlight are not contraindicated. However, consultation with the youngster's physician may be appropriate.

Summary

Significant strides have been made in the past twenty-five years in the treatment and rehabilitation of individuals with orthopedic impairments. Injuries that only a few years ago would have resulted in certain death are now treatable. This has created opportunities and challenges for medical personnel, including therapists, to develop effective treatment programs. Contrary to past practice, effective treatment requires that all aspects of the individual's life be considered, including school for children and adolescents. In addition, greater attention is now paid to the quality of the individual's life, including his or her level of fitness. Recent studies have indicated, for example, that the fitness levels of individuals in wheelchairs are lower than expected but that training programs can be effective in increasing important variables such as oxygen consumption.

The implications, therefore, for physical educators are clear. Programs should be developed that contribute to functional health and fitness. The medium through which this may be accomplished includes all of the activities commonly engaged in by individuals without disabilities. Modifications can be made, where necessary, to accommodate the individual with orthopedic impairment in regular physical education classes. Separate classes may be scheduled as appropriate to accommodate any special activity needs that may exist.

The athletic accomplishments of some athletes with orthopedic impairments have helped to dispel the myth that those with spinal cord injuries and other bone and joint disorders are incapable of high performance levels. Those with orthopedic impairments, similar to those who are nondisabled, enjoy and benefit from participation in physical activity. While the activity may initially be therapeutic in nature (e.g., increasing the range of motion for a severely burned individual), the ultimate goal is to contribute to and enhance the quality of life.

Enhancing Activities

1. Attend an athletic event such as a track and field meet for athletes with spinal cord injury and note the various techniques used by individuals with different levels of spinal cord injury.
2. Visit the orthopedic section of the local hospital and, given permission, observe the treatment and rehabilitation programs conducted by various professionals such as the occupational and physical therapist.
3. Compare and contrast the resting and exercise heart rate of an individual with orthopedic impairment

(e.g., one with a spinal cord injury) to that of a person with no disabilities. Discuss the findings with your professor and/or an exercise physiologist.
4. Develop a short survey of selected questions related to physical education and activity programs and ask students with and without orthopedic impairments to respond. Questions such as, "How often do you exercise?" "Where do you exercise?" and "Why do you/do you not exercise?" will generate some interesting observations.

Selected Readings

Adams, R. C., & McCubbin, J. A. (1991). *Games, sports, and exercises for the physically disabled* (4th ed.). Philadelphia: Lea and Febiger.

Anderson, E. M., & Spain, B. (1977). *The child with spina bifida.* London: Methuen and Co., Ltd.

Bartshaw, M. L., & Perret, Y. M. (1986). *Children with handicaps: A medical primer* (2nd ed.). Baltimore: Paul H. Brookes Pub. Co.

Bigge, J., & O'Donnell, P. A. (1976). *Teaching individuals with physical and multiple disabilities.* Columbus, OH: Charles E. Merrill Publishing Co.

Bleck, E. E., & Nagel, D. A. (1982). *Physically handicapped children: A medical atlas for teachers* (2nd ed.). New York: Grune and Stratton.

Brewer, E. J., Jr. (1970). *Juvenile rheumatoid arthritis.* Philadelphia: W. B. Saunders Co.

Conditions (2009). Johns Hopkins University, Department of Orthopaedic Surgery. Retrieved at www.hopkinsortho.org/orthopedicsurgery/toewalking.html April 23, 2009.

Coutts, K., McKenzie, D., Loock, C., Beauchamp, R., & Armstrong, R. (1993). Upper body exercise capacity in youth with spina bifida. *Adapted Physical Activity Quarterly, 10,* 22–28.

Cratty, B. J. (1976). *Developmental games for physically handicapped children.* Palo Alto, CA: Peek Publications.

Cratty, B. J. (1989). *Adapted physical education for handicapped children and youth* (2nd ed.). Denver: Love Publishing Co.

Davis, G. M. (1993). Exercise capacity of individuals with paraplegia. *Medicine and Science in Sports and Exercise, 25*(4), 423–432.

Davis, G., & Glaser, R. (1990). Cardiorespiratory fitness following spinal cord injury. In L. Ada & C. Canning (Eds.), *Key issues in neurological physiotherapy* (pp. 155–196). London: Butterworth and Heinemann.

Dibner, S., & Dibner, A. (1973). *Integration or segregation for the physically handicapped child.* Springfield, IL: Charles C. Thomas.

Freeman, J. M. (Ed.). (1974). *Practical management to meningomyelocele.* Baltimore: University Park Press.

Garwood, G. S. (1979). *Educating young handicapped children: A developmental approach.* Germantown, MD: Aspen Systems Corporation.

Glaser, R. M. (1989). Arm exercise training for wheelchair users. *Medicine and Science in Sports and Exercise, 21,* 5149–5157.

Holmes, L. B., Driscoll, S. G., & Alkins, L. (1976). Etiologic heterogeneity of neural-tube defects. *New England Journal of Medicine, 29,* 365.

Jeffrey, D. L. (1986). The hazards of reduced mobility for the persons with a spinal cord injury. *Journal of Rehabilitation, 52,* 59–62.

Lieberman, L. J., & Houston-Wilson, C. (2002). *Strategies for INCLUSION.* Champaign, IL: Human Kinetics Publishers.

Lockette, K. F., & Keyes, A. M. (1994). *Conditioning with physical disabilities.* Champaign, IL: Human Kinetics Publishers.

Michael, J. W. (1989). New developments in prosthetic feet for sports and recreation. *Palaestra, 5*(2), 21–22; 32–35.

Nash, C. L., Jr. (1980). Current concepts review scoliosis bracing. *The Journal of Bone and Joint Surgery, 62A,* 848–852.

National Center on Physical Activity and Disability (NCPAD). (2004). *Spina bifida—Physical activity guidelines factsheet.* Retreived at www.ncpad.org April 23, 2009.

Nicosia, J. E., & Petro, J. A. (1983). *Manual of burn care.* New York: Raven Press.

Sawisch, L. (1990). Strategic positioning in the disabled sports community: A perspective from the new kids on the block. *Palaestra, 6*(5), 52–54.

Schaller, J., & Wedgewood, R. J. (1972). Juvenile rheumatoid arthritis, a review. *Pediatrics, 50*(9), 40–53.

Scoliosis. (1979). New York: The Scoliosis Association, Inc.

Shepard, R. J. (1990). *Fitness in special populations.* Champaign, IL: Human Kinetics Publishers.

Sherrill, C. (2004). *Adapted physical activity, recreation and sport* (6th ed.). Dubuque, IA: McGraw-Hill.

Taylor, H., Haskell, S. H., & Barret, E. K. (1977). *The education of motor and neurologically handicapped children.* New York: John Wiley and Sons, Inc.

Tecklin, J. S. (1989). *Pediatric physical therapy.* Philadelphia: J. B. Lippincott.

Webster, J. B., Levy, C. E., Bryant, P. R., & Prusakowski, P. E. (2001). Sports and recreation for persons with limb deficiency. *Archives of Physical Medicine and Rehabilitation, 82*(3), S38–44.

Williamson, G. G. (Ed.). (1987). *Children with spina bifida.* Baltimore: Paul H. Brookes Publishing Co.

Cerebral Palsy

CHAPTER OBJECTIVES

After studying this chapter, the reader should be able to:

1 Recognize the various types of cerebral palsy and their characteristics.
2 Understand the importance of the primary reflexes and the role that they play in controlling and/or inhibiting the movement of the individual with cerebral palsy.
3 Identify various treatments for cerebral palsy, including physical therapy and orthopedic surgery.
4 Appreciate the importance and limitations of physical therapy in the treatment of cerebral palsy.
5 List and discuss the secondary disabilities, such as epilepsy and mental retardation, that sometimes accompany cerebral palsy.
6 Recognize and discuss important objectives and features in developing a physical activity program for individuals with cerebral palsy.
7 Analyze activities and their appropriateness for the student with cerebral palsy.
8 Appreciate the importance of the psychosocial aspect of physical activity to the overall development of the student with cerebral palsy.
9 Understand the physical and motor characteristics of cerebral palsy and the importance of physical activity, body-image activities, breathing exercises, and physical fitness to the development of the student with cerebral palsy.

Based on what we know today about the causes and prevalence of cerebral palsy, it would be safe to say that this condition has probably affected people for many centuries. However, until relatively recently, cerebral palsy has received little significant attention from those in medicine, education, or the social services. The great strides of medical science over the past century have been largely responsible for stimulating attention to and concern about those with cerebral palsy.

W. J. Little, an English orthopedic surgeon, is credited with being the first physician to document and analyze the condition of cerebral palsy. His published reports on sixty-three children, describing the manifestations of their condition, appeared in the early 1860s, and the disorder became known as Little's disease. The term was changed to spastic paralysis in the 1930s and finally to cerebral palsy in the 1940s.

In spite of improved medical treatment, those with cerebral palsy face many difficulties. Lack of public understanding of the condition hinders opportunities for personal development. Because of the distortion of speech and facial expressions, the disorder may cause many misconceptions and stigmas to become attached to the individual with cerebral palsy, producing social isolation. Other physical manifestations of the various cerebral palsy conditions may make movement difficult, giving rise to problems in performing motor skills including the activities of daily living.

Through the efforts of advocacy groups, the educational, occupational, and social opportunities for persons with cerebral palsy are continually improving. The extent to which individuals with cerebral palsy can avail themselves of these new opportunities will depend, in part, on the amount of independence they can attain in their motor behavior. It is in the achievement of this objective that the physical educator's expertise is needed.

The Nature and Causes of Cerebral Palsy

Cerebral palsy is a condition resulting from brain damage that is manifested by various types of neuromuscular disabilities. These disabilities are characterized by the dysfunction of voluntary motor control. The lesion causing the brain damage is found in the upper motor neurons of the cerebrum and brain stem, thus affecting the functions of the central nervous system.

To date, cerebral palsy is incurable. However, the condition is amenable to therapy and training, and the motor functions of those with this impairment can be improved. In addition, cerebral palsy is nonprogressive, also referred to as a "static injury to the central nervous system" (Sanger, Delgado, Gaebler-Spira, Hallett, & Mink, 2003); that is, the extent of the lesion will not increase, so the condition will not worsen or result in death. However, some of the characteristics of the disorder are ever changing. For example, muscle tone can change over the course of time. Cerebral palsy impacts the development of the central nervous system. The degree of this interference is related to the extent of the lesion. Generally, the earlier the occurrence of cerebral palsy, the more extensive will be the interference. Thus, because approximately 90% of all those affected contract cerebral palsy early, either at birth or during the prenatal period, many of those with cerebral palsy have multiple disabilities.

According to the United States Cerebral Palsy Athletic Association (USCPAA) (2005), congenital cerebral palsy is a brain injury incurred in utero and accounts for 70% of children who have cerebral palsy. During the birth process, brain injury can result, and this accounts for 20% of cases of cerebral palsy. The exact cause of this brain injury remains unknown, although lack of oxygen at birth is known to cause brain damage that can result in cerebral palsy. In the United States, 10% of children with cerebral palsy acquired it in the first few months or in the early years of life. Children with "acquired cerebral palsy" have experienced either a brain infection (e.g., meningitis, viral encephalitis) or a head injury such as occurs from child abuse, a motor vehicle accident, or a fall.

The incidence of cerebral palsy in the United States is estimated at about one million people (Healthcommunities, 2004). In 2001 the number of diagnoses of cerebral palsy was 8,000 infants and 1,200 to 1,500 preschool children (USCPAA, 2009). Cerebral palsy does not appear to be related in any way to socioeconomic structures; however, it is more prevalent among Caucasians, the firstborn, and males. Of those affected, about 10% will be so severely disabled that they will require intensive care for the rest of their lives. The remaining 90% can be found in various educational settings, ranging from regular public school classes to special education classes.

Types of Cerebral Palsy Conditions

In medical settings, the term "dystonia" is often used to describe a movement disorder where the muscle contraction is abnormal and considered involuntary. According to Sanger and colleagues (2003), "Dystonia is an involuntary alteration in the pattern of muscle activation during voluntary movement or maintenance of posture" (p. 92). Dystonia is now often used to describe cerebral palsy in general. There are four current classifications of cerebral palsy (Centers for Disease Control and Prevention, 2004):

1. spastic
2. athetoid
3. ataxic
4. mixed

Some experts disagree about the different types of cerebral palsy because they are based on the movement pattern observed. In reality, individuals rarely have one type of cerebral palsy. What is observed is often the dominant type. In addition, modern surgeries can change the movement patterns. For example, a selective dorsal rhisotomy reduces the spasticity associated with spastic type cerebral palsy. Spasticity is no longer the main problem; rather, a dysfunctional muscle tone is present with involuntary muscle movements. This can look like a sudden body turn, or a sudden movement into a flexed position. Therefore, physical education instructors should know the manifestations of the type of cerebral palsy, and the ramifications of any surgical procedures the student has undergone. In addition, physical educators working with individuals with cerebral palsy in physical activity programs need to consider themselves as part of a multidisciplinary team with colleagues such as those in occupational therapy, physical therapy, and speech therapy, as well as the special educator. (In some states, special education teachers seek particular endorsements with their teaching license for working with students with orthopedic impairments.) Physical educators can better understand the movement capabilities of the individual with cerebral palsy when they are up-to-date with the student's current physical capabilities. For students with cerebral palsy, changes in the assistance they need varies over their lifetime. Therefore, the level of assistance from allied professions such as occupational therapy and physical therapy also varies. Referred to as "episodic," therapists understand that these students have life-long conditions where the need for interventions is required at some times more than others (MDE, 2002). It is considered the best practice when therapeutic interventions are provided to make the individual's life more satisfying, not change the disease or disorder itself (Dunn, 2000). This is also the basis of modification and adaptations for physical activity enjoyment and success for individuals with cerebral palsy.

Muscle tone is extensively described for individuals with cerebral palsy, and it is important for physical educators to understand these conditions and the ramifications for movement activities in physical education programs. Important terms associated with muscle tone are hypertonic and hypotonic. It is also important to understand the *location on the body* where the affected muscles are hypertonic or hypotonic. These terms will be presented in the discussion that follows.

Spastic Cerebral Palsy

People with spastic cerebral palsy have increased muscle tone, referred to as hypertonia, wherein the muscles are stiff and their movements can be awkward. The individual can have hypertonia when the muscle involvement is located in both legs more so than in the arms (spastic diplegia); on one side of the body (spastic hemiplegia); involving the whole body (face, trunk, legs, arms) (spastic quadriplegia); or involving all four limbs (tetraplegia). The term "plegia" and the accompanying descriptor with cerebral palsy is not to be confused with paralysis used to describe nerve damage resulting from spinal cord injuries (such as the late actor Christopher Reeves, whose quadriplegia was the result of an accident which severed his spinal cord in the cervical area). According to Sanger (WE MOVE, 2004), some clinicians prefer the term "paresis" rather than "plegia."

Spasticity in cerebral palsy results from a lesion in the motor cortex. The motor cortex is the area in the central nervous system composed of motor neurons grouped together to form tracts. These tracts originate in the upper central portion of the cerebrum and proceed downward through the brain into the spinal column. It is in this area that voluntary motor actions originate.

Spasticity is the most prevalent type of cerebral palsy. It is characterized by a persistent and increased hypertensity of muscle tone. This spasticity is considered "velocity dependent," meaning that when the muscles of a limb experience a passive movement from someone else (such as when a teacher tries to move an arm or leg), the muscle resistance will increase depending on how fast the other person is moving the limb. Individuals with spastic cerebral palsy are sometimes required to have someone move their limb through a stretching exercise to avoid contractures of the affected limb. If the teacher grasps the limb and moves it too quickly, the muscles in the limb will have a strong resistance. Again, this can happen when someone takes hold of the spastic arm or leg and tries to move it, as in a *therapy session*, to increase the range of motion (ROM), which helps prevent contractures. If a spastic limb is moved slowly, there is less likelihood of resistance. On the other hand, spasticity does not interfere with attempts by the individual with voluntary movements. Sanger (2004), an expert from Stanford University, does not consider the difficulties with voluntary movements truly related to the spasticity, but rather by symptoms associated with spasticity, such as weakness, dystonia, or ataxia. Although these attributions to the cause of the difficulties continue to be explored by experts in science, the physical educator observes problems with voluntary movement in a person with spastic cerebral palsy. Physical educators may observe that movement is usually restricted, jerky, and uncertain, with inconsistent control. On any given occasion, a movement may be very slow and deliberate or very explosive. In addition, the individual with spasticity tends to respond to the slightest stimulation, whether visual, verbal, or tactile, with a muscular reaction. Oddly enough, it is the spasticity that can help children maintain a position like stand: The muscles are rigid and thus help support the child against gravity. However, spasticity can lead to rigid fixed joints, which is why children with cerebral palsy receive therapies for range of motion and are referred to physical education programs for movement activities appropriate for their age group.

Another common characteristic of the individual with spasticity is a hyperactive stretch reflex. The stretch reflex, which is monosynaptic (passing through a single nerve junction), serves as a protective agent for the skeletal muscles. When a muscle is stretched too quickly, the reflex causes the antagonist muscles to contract to prevent the stretching muscle from being injured by a violent overstretch. This reflex is elicited by muscle spindles located throughout the skeletal muscles. The proper stimulation of these spindles is controlled by various motor centers in the brain.

When the normal neurologic controls of a healthy muscle are greatly reduced, the stretch reflex is disturbed both in

Characteristics of Spastic Cerebral Palsy

- Persistent and increased hypertensity of muscle tone
- Velocity dependent
- Movement is usually restricted, jerky, and uncertain, with inconsistent control
- Responds to the slightest stimulation
- Hyperactive stretch reflex

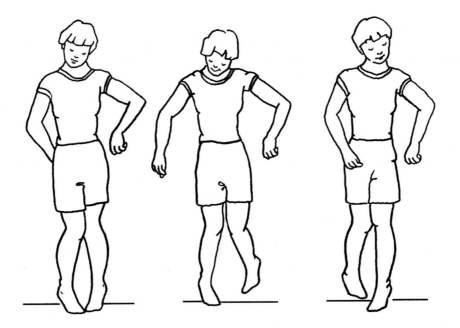

Figure 8.1 Typical scissors gait of individual with cerebral palsy.

timing and in strength. Any sudden stretch will result in a strong contraction. A frequent result of the hyperactive stretch reflex is a sudden contraction followed by repeated jerks. This reaction is known as clonus.

Spasticity tends to affect the flexor muscle groups; thus, the maintenance of proper posture becomes very difficult. In addition, the individual with spasticity may have pathological reflex problems that also affect movement ability. If the lower limbs are spastic, they may be rotated inward and flexed at the hip joint, and the knees may be flexed and adducted, while the heels are lifted from the ground. These characteristics force a crossing of the legs through the midline during the walking gait, producing a scissors-type movement called the scissors gait (figure 8.1). When the upper limbs are involved, the person may have pronated forearms with flexion at the elbows, wrists, and fingers (figure 8.2). Mental impairment is more frequently associated with spasticity than with any other type of cerebral palsy.

Figure 8.2 A walking pattern of an individual with spastic hemiplegia.

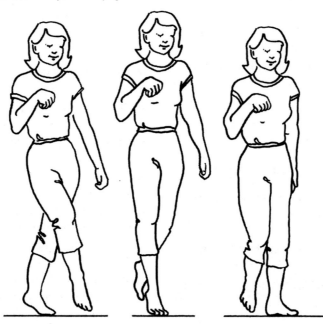

Athetoid Cerebral Palsy

People with athetoid cerebral palsy have difficulty with smooth, coordinated movements and maintaining their body posture. The movements in their face, arms, and trunk appear purposeless. Low muscle tone, referred to as hypotonia, is characteristic of athetoid cerebral palsy.

Athetosis is caused by a lesion in the area of the basal ganglia called the globus pallidus. This area is composed of large masses of neurons located deep within the center of the cerebrum. It is this part of the brain that controls purposeful movement. Because the damage to the brain occurs outside of the pyramidal tract, the athetoid type of cerebral palsy is sometimes referred to as extrapyramidal. Today it is understood that "most children with CP have both pyramidal and extrapyramidal signs . . . (which) are present simultaneously" (Sanger et al., 2003, p. 90).

About 10% of children with cerebral palsy have athetoid cerebral palsy. At times the movements are slow and rhythmical, whereas on other occasions they are jerky and fast. In addition, the individuals with athetoid cerebral palsy are hampered by a problem known as overflow. This is manifested by extraneous movements that accompany voluntary motion. The combination of overflow and involuntary movement produces a situation in which the body position is constantly in a stage of change.

The muscles of the head and upper limbs are commonly affected. Frequently seen movements of the upper limbs include constant flexion and extension of the fingers, wrists, and elbows, plus the drawing of the arms backward while palms are held downward. Lack of head control is a major problem. In many cases the head is continually drawn back and the face turned to one side. Accompanying this are facial contortions in which the mouth is frequently open; this pro-duces drooling and makes eating and speaking very difficult. Other individuals may be affected by inward rotation of their feet.

The amount of athetoid-type movements is reduced when the person is relaxed and calm and increased when the person is nervous and tense. Athoid cerebral palsy is not commonly characterized by mental retardation.

Ataxic Cerebral Palsy

People with ataxic cerebral palsy exhibit a lack of coordination when engaged in voluntary movements. Their speech is not varied in tone, and odd pauses between phrases and syllables occur. The major manifestations of ataxia are a reduced sense of balance, which results in frequent falls, and a reduced sense of kinesthesis, which produces uncoordinated movements. Examples of ataxic problems are inconsistent foot placement in locomotion, overshooting when reaching for objects, and a general loss of manual dexterity. The person with ataxia usually exhibits a very awkward gait.

Ataxic cerebral palsy is the result of a lesion in the cerebellum, the area located below the cerebrum and posterior to the brain stem. The cerebellum acts as the feedback mechanism of the brain and organizes the information to coordinate muscular functions. Although this is the third-most common type of cerebral palsy, ataxia accounts for less than 10% of the cases. The condition is usually acquired rather than congenital.

Mixed Type

In some individuals it is apparent that more than one type of cerebral palsy is evident. In these cases the term "mixed type" is used. The term is applied as a classification term when more than one type is prevalent and no single type predominates. Those with the most frequent combination of types of cerebral palsy exhibit both tenseness of movement associated with the spastic type and lack of control associated with the athetoid type. Obviously, the student with the mixed type of cerebral palsy experiences significant problems with motor control. Studies now suggest that the frequency of mixed type is much higher than previously thought.

Characteristics of Athetoid Cerebral Palsy

- Difficulty with smooth, coordinated movements
- Difficulty maintaining body posture
- Movements in face, arms, and trunk appear purposeless
- Low muscle tone
- Extraneous movements accompany voluntary motion
- Constant flexion and extension of the fingers, wrists, and elbows
- Drawing of arms backward while palms are held downward
- Lack of head control
- Facial contortion

Characteristics of Ataxic Cerebral Palsy

- Reduced sense of balance
- Reduced sense of kinesthesis
- Very awkward gait
- Lack of coordination
- Speech is not varied in tone

As science continues to develop a clearer understanding of the neurology of cerebral palsy, there will be a better understanding of classifications. Currently there is no pure form of cerebral palsy, but rather the diagnosis is made when a type predominates the movement pattern(s) as observed by the clinicians (see Sanger et al., 2003, for detailed information from the Task Force on Childhood Motor Disorders, which represented over 35 institutions).

A guide to understanding the motor performance of mixed type cerebral palsy is that a young child can have hypertonic limbs with a hypotonic trunk. As the child gets older, the tight muscles can become tighter, which means their tone is becoming more inflexible. A muscle held in one position is weak. If a tight, inflexible muscle is stretched without strengthening it, then the situation worsens. Strengthening must occur in the core muscles of the trunk as well as the limbs. Strengthening tight muscles once was avoided. Now it is understood that these muscles can and should be strengthened. Weightlifting and calisthenics are now acceptable forms of physical activity for individuals with cerebral palsy. First, the muscles must be warmed up with locomotor activity and then stretched before strengthening programs can be undertaken.

Major Reflex Problems

Many of the movement problems of persons with cerebral palsy are reflexive in nature. These movements depend solely upon the proper stimulus and cannot be controlled. All individuals are born with certain reflex patterns which are the foundations upon which motor behavior is developed (discussed in chapter 2). These reflexes are present within the first few months of life and then are suppressed by higher brain centers as the infant develops control of its movements. In many persons with cerebral palsy, several reflex patterns persist for a longer-than-normal period and, in effect, retard motor development. Winnick and Short (1985) explain the importance of this information: **"If reflexes, when elicited, are uneven in strength, too weak or too strong, or inappropriate at a particular age, neurological dysfunction may be suspected.** Various reflexive behaviors are quite predictable and are expected to appear at particular ages and to be inhibited, disappear, or be replaced by higher order reflexes at later ages. Failure of certain reflexes to disappear, be inhibited, or be replaced may inhibit the development of voluntary movement" (1985, p. 50). Whenever reflexes continue to be exhibited, and thus not extinguished within a typical time frame in early childhood (see chapter 2), there is concern that the development is abnormal. In an individual with cerebral palsy, there are involuntary reflexes that are retained and not extinguished, and therefore have an effect on the child's posture and movement.

A reflex often seen is the asymmetric tonic neck reflex (ATNR) described in chapter 2. This reflex can be elicited given the right stimulation. For example, if a person with cerebral palsy is surprised by a ball thrown at him, or is removed suddenly from his wheelchair, or is anxious, then a teacher may observe the individual in an ATNR position. Figure 2.3B depicts an infant in this position, but an older child, youth, or adult with cerebral palsy can also exhibit this involuntary reflex.

The presence of this reflex inhibits the child's ability to control the arm and interferes with early efforts to crawl and sit without support. Later in life, it can also interfere with an ease of performing fundamental skills of object manipulation. **Careful observation of the individual will inform the teacher of the times when the student is more prone to the reflexive response. If it does occur, it will sustain itself for awhile and then should subside.**

As described in chapter 2, the tonic reflex is initiated when the head is moved. Flexion of the head causes extension in the legs, whereas extension of the head is accompanied by flexion of the legs. In some instances the reflex is not strong and changes in muscle tone may occur without any changes in the position of the limbs. The presence of the tonic reflex creates major challenges in the infant's ability to sit independently. Movement of the head causes postural responses that are difficult to control (Batshaw & Perret, 1986). Again, a teacher can see this reflex exhibited when attempting to help a student into or out of a wheelchair. Instead of having a flexed leg, the legs will shoot out, or the head will arch back. Care should be taken to work closely with the physical therapist to know how to position students with cerebral palsy so as not to elicit this reflex.

When lifting and carrying very young children with cerebral palsy, care should be taken not to "send the child into extension." For example, in children with normal tone, parents often pick them up by the trunk and place them facing the parent's shoulder or trunk. With a child with cerebral palsy, it is often best to pick him or her up at the trunk facing away from the adult and place an arm under the back of the knees, giving pressure to bend the knees of the child. This "breaks up the tone in the legs," thus avoiding the child's extension. Then the child can be carried facing outward in a sort of sitting position, with the back of the trunk held against the chest of the adult.

Also, when assisting older children in transfers into and out of wheelchairs for physical activity, the proper techniques should be followed so as to not elicit a reflexive action. Again, the physical therapist is a valuable resource for understanding how to implement and successfully carry out these activities.

With the positive support reflex, the infant extends the legs when the balls of the feet come in contact with a surface

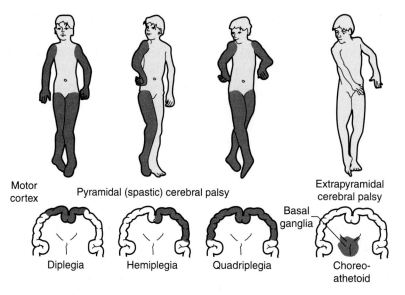

Figure 8.3 Different regions of the brain are affected in various forms of cerebral palsy.

(figures 2.8*A* and *B*). For the child with cerebral palsy, the extension of the legs leads to a rigid position of the legs accompanied by adduction and internal rotation of the hips. The child cannot "get out" of this position. The legs are in extension and rigid. Unfortunately this response interferes with, rather than helps with, walking and standing because the child is unable to voluntarily get out of the position.

Topographical Classification

Cerebral palsy affects different parts of the body. To describe the portion involved, the topographical classification utilized for paralysis of the body due to any cause may be applied, although the individual with cerebral palsy is not paralyzed, but rather the limbs are "involved." (As mentioned before, some physicians and therapists describe the individual as having a "paresis" in the affected limbs.) The classification is as follows:

1. Monoplegia: only one limb is involved.
2. Paraplegia: only the legs are involved.
3. Diplegia: primarily, legs are involved; arms are slightly affected.
4. Hemiplegia: limbs on one side of the body are involved.
5. Triplegia: three limbs are involved, usually the legs and one arm.
6. Quadriplegia: all four limbs are involved.

Quadriplegia is more frequently found in athetoid cerebral palsy; the other types occur more often in the spastic cerebral palsy condition. Spastic hemiplegia is the most common involvement. Figure 8.2 shows a walking pattern of an individual with spastic hemiplegia. Here the right side of the body has higher tone. Note the flexed arm and the high tone

in the right leg with the heel not touching the ground on the phase where the foot is placed on the ground. The individual is not paralyzed, but the limbs on one side of the body have greater tone/spasticity. In figure 8.1 a "scissors gait" is depicted that, in addition to being a walking pattern, also shows the involvement at some level of the legs and arms. This gait can be seen within different topologies of spastic cerebral palsy. In figure 8.3, the topographical classification system and its relationship to the area of the brain affected is presented. It should be noted that there is some disagreement about the appropriateness of the medical label extrapyramidal cerebral palsy (Sanger et al., 2003). Again, continued research into the cause of the types of cerebral palsy will likely reveal increased insight in the future.

Treatment

With an understanding of the functional ability of the individual with cerebral palsy, the physical educator can teach motor skills, sports, and games for the individual to utilize in play, leisure, and health-related physical activities. Some understanding of the medical care in the treatment of cerebral palsy is important to physical educators. Such knowledge enables them to plan an appropriate program of physical activity engagement for the individual with cerebral palsy.

Medical Treatment

Medical treatment of individuals with cerebral palsy has changed dramatically over the last decade. Physicians have become more aggressive in their treatment of cerebral palsy, although some of the procedures are considered less invasive than in the past. Now, orthopedic surgeons brace the hands, wrists, and lower limbs.

There are two major objectives in the use of braces:

1. to keep spastic muscles stretched to prevent contractures and structural deviations, and
2. to hold a hand or leg in a functional position.

A person wearing a brace should in most instances keep the brace on during physical education (swimming not included). The physical educator must be clear on what the precautions with bracing are, and should receive this information from the physician or the physical therapist working with the student. It has been noted by therapists that if the bracing is not functional for the student, then the student often loses that brace; the more helpful it is to the student, the more the student will not go without the support. Surgery is performed on individuals with cerebral palsy to improve the performance of a movement pattern. The information on surgical procedures can be obtained from the family and the medical doctor, particularly if the surgery is recent. Otherwise, the physical educator will need to be observant of how the student moves and what ways best involve the student in the curriculum of the physical education class.

Physical Therapy

The physical educator must work with the physical therapist when students with cerebral palsy are in the physical education class. Referred to as the "motor team" by some school districts, professionals in these disciplines can share knowledge that is essential for the success of their students. First and foremost, physical therapy is not a substitute for physical education for individuals with cerebral palsy. Physical therapy is provided under IDEA 2004 to support the education of the student with a disability: ". . . services as are required to assist a child with a disability to benefit from special education." An academic area under special education is physical education. The student's IEP team, under consultation with the physical therapist, makes a determination regarding the support needed for successful participation in education by the student with a disability. Therefore, physical therapy activities can be used to support the provision of special physical education.

The focus in the delivery of service in physical therapy and occupational therapy in the educational system is on

1. client-centered services, and
2. functional-based interventions that relate to the activities that the students need in order to be successful in the home, school, and community (MDE, 2002).

Therapists are keenly aware that focusing on the unique needs of the student with cerebral palsy acknowledges that the similar diagnosis does not infer a similarity in individuals with the disability. Rather, to assist an individual to be successful educationally, the student has to be the center of the focus: unique needs and interests must be accounted for in the interventions. Second, as has been stated, functional interventions are the focus. Parents and advocacy groups serving individuals with disabilities insist on this focus.

Another critical factor is that delivering therapy services is episodic in that there are times when more support is required than at other times in the academic life of the student: The need for and level of therapy can come and go over the course of time. Students have life-long conditions that they will need to learn to manage to achieve goals that are important to them (MDE, 2002). That being said, there are times when physical therapies are inappropriate to be implemented in the school setting. One marker for inappropriateness is when the intensity of therapy is so great that it interferes with the student's learning and is not related to an educational need.

Without question, physical therapy is a primary source of movement education for the individual with cerebral palsy. There are many different theories and methods employed, but in a generic sense they can be divided into those methods developed to treat spasticity and those developed to treat athetosis. Today, many physical therapists do not adhere to a pure system, but use procedures from various methods in order to accomplish their objectives. Physical educators working with students who have cerebral palsy should become familiar with current procedures. Much of the current thinking says to provide services in the education system that help students understand how they can care for themselves and how they can develop compensatory strategies for movement activities. Compensatory strategies mean that the individual learns the ways that his body can best perform an activity. For physical education, this may mean learning how to swim given the disability. Swimming is a highly recommended physical activity for individuals with cerebral palsy. However, given the differences in tone (hypotonic or hypertonic as the cerebral palsy is exhibited) that make the typical stroke patterns less appropriate, individuals learn swimming skills based on their capabilities.

Bleck and Nagel (1982) caution that therapy should not be viewed as a magical method for overcoming a permanent motor disorder. They add that "Passive 'hands-on' therapy in cerebral palsy has not been effective and has been given up in favor of active programs that emphasize functions, fun, games, and sports for the school aged child" (p. 81). In this light, they recommend that the expertise of therapists be used in developing and modifying motor programs. The hands-on approach has been successful with children younger than age three years. After that, a more functional approach is more successful in helping individuals with cerebral palsy be physically active. According to experts in physical therapy (e.g., Bleck, 1987; Fetters & Kluzik, 1996), controversy exists about the approach to treatment using different therapeutic modalities. Neurodevelopmental therapy as originally presented by Bobath (1971), compared with an infant stimulation approach, was explored in a classic study (Palmer et al., 1988) with trends in the data favoring infant stimulation. **Studies like the latter and others appear to support the recommendation of Rimmer (NCPAD, 2004) that a more ecological approach to working with individuals with cerebral palsy is required.** It is understood that different approaches have been considered and employed for individuals with cerebral palsy, but physical educators working with students with cerebral palsy need to understand the approach *currently* being used with their particular student's therapists.

Strength Development Through Physical Activity

Individuals with cerebral palsy must have sufficient strength and endurance to perform the functional skills of daily living as well as participate in recreational sport activities (Fernandez, Pitetti, & Betzen, 1990). As described under *Mixed Types* in this chapter, most of the concepts used in strength-development programs for the nondisabled can be applied to programs for individuals with cerebral palsy. There are some unique characteristics of cerebral palsy that require careful attention. Some guidelines are suggested in the following list:

1. **Strive for muscle balance.** Because many individuals with cerebral palsy have overdeveloped flexors in relation to extensors, normally the program for the student with cerebral palsy should be developed to strengthen the muscle extensors. The goal is to achieve as much balance as possible between muscle groups.

2. **Emphasize range of motion.** Programs designed to improve muscle strength and endurance will be successful if efforts to improve the range of motion in a particular joint are also emphasized. This means that stretching activities should be included in the strength-development program.

3. **The type of resistance utilized may affect development.** A resistance training program, when properly applied, can improve the strength of the extensor muscle while helping to normalize the tone in the opposing muscle group through reciprocal inhibition. In general, isokinetic exercises that hold constant the speed and resistance applied to the muscle are preferred over isotonic exercises. However, isotonic exercises in which the muscle is moved through a range of motion at a variable speed and resistance (the use of barbells, for example) have been found as effective as isokinetic exercises in subjects with non-handicapping conditions (Sanders, 1980). Equipment used in isotonic training is also more readily available than that used in isokinetic programs. McCubbin and Horvat (1990) provide guidelines for resistance exercise training for persons with cerebral palsy.

4. **Progression is important.** In initiating a strength-development program, it is important that the program be individualized. This means that the amount of weight and type of exercises selected should be appropriate to the youngster. It is also essential that light weights be selected initially and that the focus be on executing the exercises slowly and correctly. Adequate time must be allowed before and after the strength program to allow for stretching exercises. The length and intensity of the program should also be modified for the individual with cerebral palsy. The amount of energy expended by some students with cerebral palsy in performing an exercise contrasted to that of the nondisabled is much greater (Rose, Gamble, Medeires, Burges, & Haskell, 1990).

5. **The position of the individual is important.** Because of the difficulties some individuals with cerebral palsy have counteracting the forces of gravity, it may be advisable for the individual to perform the weight exercises in a seated or supine position. The role of the uninhibited reflexes and their effect on movement must be considered in selecting the best position.

6. **Explain the movement pattern.** As the youngster engages in different weight-training exercises, explain what is happening to the muscles and joints and the sensations the individual should be experiencing. Many individuals with cerebral palsy have a difficult time dif-

Guidelines for Adapting Strength Training Programs for Individuals with Cerebral Palsy:

1. Strive for muscle balance
2. Emphasize range of motion
3. The type of resistance used may affect development
4. Progression is important
5. The position of the person is important
6. Explain the movement pattern
7. Recognize unique needs

ferentiating a normal from an abnormal movement sensation.

7. **Recognize unique needs.** For some students with cerebral palsy, participation in an active weight-resistance training program is the current rule rather than the exception. Focus should be on functional activities for strength that focus on age-appropriate strengthening activities in line with what the student *can do* rather than cannot do. For a younger child, this will be games and play. As the student gains in age and interests, sports can be added if they are in line with the student's functional capacity. The use of co-contraction exercises is effective in enhancing the functional levels of strength for a youngster with more severe disabilities. Again, the physical therapist can be consulted on these activities so that the physical educator can work them into the individual's physical education program (Campbell, 1995).

Analysis of functional ability can be done by the physical therapist using assessment tools such as the Pediatric Evaluation of Disability Inventory (PEDI) (Haley, Coster, Ludlow, Haltiwanger, & Andrelles, 1992) and the Gross Motor Function Measure (GMFM) (Boyce et al., 1991). Physical educators can also use the Top-Down Motor Milestone Test (TDMMT) (Bidabe & Lollar, 1990) which is part of the MOVE curriculum (Movement Opportunities Via Education). With younger children, measures taken from the assessment tools of the Peabody Developmental Motor Scales–2 (PDMS–2) (Folio & Fewell, 2000) and the Brigance Diagnostic Inventory of Early Development (BDI) (Brigance, 1991) are helpful in determining what movement skills the student is capable of performing.

According to the National Center on Physical Activity and Disability (NCPAD, 2004), there is increasing evidence that strength programs help individuals with cerebral palsy (e.g., Damiano & Abel, 1998; Kramer & MacPhail, 1994). It was not until recently that the myth about engaging individuals with cerebral palsy in strength training was dismissed. Prior to this, strengthening muscles in individuals with cerebral palsy was contraindicated. Now, however, the possibility is being explored that strengthening muscles would improve quality of life in those with cerebral palsy.

An excellent example of a progressive-resistance training program for an individual with spastic cerebral palsy has been reported by Horvat (1987). The program used both free weights and weight machines to perform a variety of exercises. Initial weights were set at 30% of body weight to allow the subject to complete at least ten repetitions of each exercise. Prior to each session, fifteen minutes were devoted to stretching various muscle groups. As a result of the eight-week training program, improvement was found in strength, endurance, and range of motion on both sides of the body.

The program demonstrated that a common-sense approach to training in which stretching, low amounts of weight, and a high number of repetitions are combined can produce desirable outcomes.

Exercises and activities to increase flexibility should be an essential aspect of the physical fitness program for individuals with cerebral palsy. As previously described, these youngsters experience contractures, which limit their range of motion. The lack of flexibility affects overall physical performance.

The goal of the stretching program is to teach appropriate flexibility exercises and to encourage individuals to incorporate the program into their daily activities. Self-monitored programs will help to ensure that these needed but time-consuming exercises are performed daily but not to the detriment of other important aspects of the physical education program.

The type of stretching that is recommended for individuals with cerebral palsy is static rather than ballistic stretching. In static stretching the movements are slow and deliberate with the muscles stretched to the point of discomfort but ordinarily not to exceed 10 percent overstretch.

Teaching Those with Cerebral Palsy

Basically, cerebral palsy cannot be extinguished, but therapies and education can work to develop compensatory strategies for physical education activities. A few considerations will facilitate the development and implementation of these strategies. First, in addition to motor dysfunction, many individuals with cerebral palsy have concomitant problems. These problems or disturbances often are associated with the common group of syndromes related to brain damage. In addition, the problems that students with cerebral palsy exhibit in areas such as behavior are also influenced by that which is typical for any individual: personality, interests, life circumstances, environmental offerings, parenting, and socioeconomic status. In addition to the motor dysfunction, included are the associated problems of intellectual functioning, sensory loss, speech and/or language disorders, and disturbances of communication or behavior. Although the reported percentage of individuals with cerebral palsy with secondary disabilities varies, the figures do support the view that the student with cerebral palsy is frequently a student with multiple disabilities.

Currently, the term "secondary conditions," or "other health problems," is used to describe the reality that individuals with cerebral palsy often have other concomitant conditions (Wilber, Mirra, Klein Walker, & Allen, 2002). In the past, the term "secondary disabilities" was favored.

However, according to NCPAD guidelines regarding exercise and cerebral palsy, these secondary conditions are important to consider when facilitating involvement in exercise programs; for example, controlling the problems of pain associated with musculoskeletal deformities causing hip pain that contributes to participation in physical activity (Turk, Geremski, Rosenbaum, & Weber 1997).

Mental Retardation

The incidence of mental retardation in the cerebral palsy population has been estimated to be as high as 76 percent. The highest incidence of retardation appears in the spasticity and rigidity conditions. Because of the problems in accurately measuring the IQ of these individuals, estimates of the incidence of mental retardation are not totally reliable; however, the academic performance of many is below the level of their peers. However, it is important to remember that some individuals with cerebral palsy have intelligence with the normal range.

Perceptual Deficits

Perceptual deficits are another problem of the individual with cerebral palsy. Some of these deficits are a result of delayed development due to an inadequate foundation of motor functions; others are probably neurological. Many of the perceptual problems are in the visual and tactile modalities. A majority of individuals with cerebral palsy have sensory deficiencies, with a major portion of these being visual problems.

Social-Emotional

In spite of the movement and learning problems individuals with cerebral palsy must cope with, probably their greatest adjustment needs have to do with their emotional well-being. Because of their motor inadequacies, communication problems, and, in some cases, differences in appearance, they often experience social rejection or excessive sympathy. The acceptance that all persons seek is often denied them. Some may also deal with the rejection and shame from their parents and relatives. Without a proper atmosphere of acceptance, these individuals have a very difficult time developing a good self-concept and consequent feelings of adequacy and contentment. Instead, tremendous frustration, which may be coupled with excessive fears, is a common occurrence.

A number of professionals in the field believe that some of the emotional problems observed in individuals with cerebral palsy are a result of specific brain damage. This opinion is substantiated to some extent by the observation of several pronounced behaviors with certain types of cerebral palsy. For example, those with spastic cerebral palsy often exhibit withdrawal traits and are not usually overresponsive to affection. However, regardless of the influence of structural damage on their emotional stability, it can reasonably be assumed that most of their emotional problems are environmentally related.

Other

Seizures (which may be due to epilepsy) and learning disabilities also occur. In addition, nearly all of these individuals have speech defects caused by their inability to control the muscles of speech. Their problems in communicating are a great barrier to social and academic adjustments. The need for speech therapy by this population must not be minimized.

Planning the Physical Activity Program

Planning the physical activity program and involvement in physical education and community recreation has overarching goals. One is to keep the program focused on functional activity goals for the student. The physical educator must ask: What skills, knowledge, and movement experiences does this student need in order to succeed in the physical education program, at home, and in his or her community recreation programs? What are the physical activity interests of this student, and in what physical activities is the family interested in seeing the student participate? The second goal of the program is to cooperate with and coordinate with the physical therapist, if there is one involved in the student's educational program.

Repetition of functional activities is important. Therefore, functional mobility goals can be incorporated into the physical education program (e.g., Block, 2000) and vice versa, the goals in physical education can be incorporated into the student's leisure life in the community and in related classroom assignments; for example, writing about a sport interest or hero. In the actual physical education activity, repeating the functional activity helps students both learn the skill and retain it. This acknowledges the team approach in delivering special education, but also recognizes that intellectual deficits or learning disabilities contribute to devising strategies that encourage learning. Repetition across the educational day within various settings can help many students with cerebral palsy learn the skills identified in their IEP.

Another goal is to modify the activity, not the student. As noted previously, cerebral palsy cannot be cured. An individual will not have less cerebral palsy as a result of a good physical activity program. Instead, that individual will be more physically fit, have a broader understanding of activity interests, and will have had enjoyable movement experiences with classmates and friends.

Finally, regarding physical activity, strength training is an important goal for the student with cerebral palsy. Strength training is useful because it helps activity performance in physical education, as well as performance of the activities of daily living (ADL). Developing the skills needed in the performance of ADL is the domain of the occupational therapist (OT). Again, physical educators can work with the OT personnel to encourage not only ADLs but also planning interventions for skills in object control (e.g., reach, grasp, release) and in developing strategies for games and sports where grasp is required. For example, a number of adaptations have been made for students with low grip-strength who want to play a game of broom ball, floor hockey, or even golf. Also, OT goals can be worked on within the physical education program; for example, if there is a need to develop some skill in manual manipulation, activities such as placing objects in a container, rearranging blocks, and striking with rackets can be offered if developmentally appropriate.

The program for students with cerebral palsy is also governed by two other objectives: (1) to enhance physical development and muscular control, and (2) to assist psychosocial development. Development in these areas can be accomplished not only by encouraging social interaction but also by promoting acquisition of sport and leisure activity skills that can add enjoyment to life and provide an avenue for further social endeavors. Through the IEP team's assessments, which include those of the physical therapist and the adapted physical educator, an appropriate plan can be devised for the student with cerebral palsy.

Program Goals

1. Focus on functional activities
2. Cooperate and coordinate with the physical therapist
3. Repeat functional activities
4. Modify the activity, not the student
5. Perform strength training
6. Enhance physical development and muscular control
7. Assist psychosocial development

Evaluation

A thorough evaluation of the facilities and equipment must also be made as part of the comprehensive planning of the program. Ramps to help the student reach elevated teaching stations should be provided. Lockers should be assigned that will not require the student to maneuver a narrow aisle. Certain areas of the shower facilities must be equipped with benches and hand supports under the shower heads to make safe showering available. In addition, the equipment should be investigated to determine its appropriateness. When possible, special equipment should be purchased. Many times, special equipment can be constructed by the teacher or other school personnel. This is an excellent alternative when budgets are restricted. As with all other programs, the scope of the program that can be offered is, to a large extent, dependent upon the facilities and equipment available. Thus, adequate attention to these factors will greatly enhance the program.

Two additional items that must be considered in planning the program are scheduling and placement. Whenever possible, these students should be integrated with their peers. For a small minority this may not be realistic and, therefore, placement in a special class may be necessary.

Special classes should be scheduled in facilities that can be utilized adequately by the students. **Consideration should also be given to the extra time needed by the students to prepare for class, to change afterward, and to move to and from the facilities.**

It is important to ensure that the program is challenging and offers a genuine learning experience. Individuals with cerebral palsy can learn, and it is the responsibility of the physical education teacher to recognize their motor potentials and to develop these abilities through physical education.

Assessment for Physical Activity

When assessing individuals with cerebral palsy for the physical education program, it is important to choose tools that will provide a valid representation of what the student *can do*. In the past, the focus on choosing tools that had norms administered with standard protocols forced many specialists to use tools that had never been normed on individuals with cerebral palsy. For example, the Bruininks-Oseretsky Test of Motor Proficiency (BOTMP) (Bruininks, 2005) is used extensively by occupational therapists by focusing on subsections of the test related to fine motor tasks. This tool has recently been renormed. It had fallen out of favor with physical educators when assessing for eligibility for special physical education (Burton & Miller, 1998). One of the main drawbacks of the BOTMP is that the items tested are not easily translated into the intervention strategies for use in the curriculum of physical education. This is particularly apparent when attempting to use the BOTMP for students with cerebral palsy. The student ends up failing many of the items owing to the cerebral palsy (e.g., lack of ability to move quickly, exhibit good balance, or to be precise with skills like throwing).

The Test of Gross Motor Development-2 (TGMD-2) (Ulrich, 2000), which is used broadly in adapted physical education, can also be problematic for a student with cerebral palsy. For example, the student may use a wheelchair for locomotion; thus, the locomotor subsection of the TGMD-2 is not appropriate because the student cannot perform the skills, and consequently an overall gross motor quotient (GMQ) for the student cannot be obtained. In these cases, the TGMD-2 can still be a valuable tool for assessment, but the criterion-referenced test becomes more of a checklist and is reported as such. Often, physical educators want to use the TGMD-2 with a child who is delayed in motor skills and therefore beyond the ages for which the test was validated (three to ten years of age). The reality is that the test can be used, but not the norms. Instead, the educator reports the information as a checklist; however, caution is needed here. Often students with cerebral palsy will never be able to perform all the criteria within the range of typical development of a skill (e.g., throw), so the checklist approach does not work. Instead, the Burton top-down approach to assessing participation in an activity is more appropriate (Burton & Miller, 1998) as described in chapters 5 and 6. The underlying theme in using the top-down approach for an individual with cerebral palsy is that the individual may have a very functional way of participating in an activity. This movement performance may not contain all the components of typical developmental patterns, but is very functional.

Aside from depending on physical and occupational therapy testing to identify the functional motor support needed in the education of the student, the physical educator must contribute to the IEP team's understanding of the services the student needs. **Valid assessment for qualifying for special physical education can be determined by nonstandardized testing.** The physical educator must use professional judgment in presenting valid information for use by the team to make appropriate placement decisions for physical education. Thus, nonstandardized testing is often recommended. As described in chapter 5, this approach includes the following tools: curriculum-based assessment, systematic observation of the student's performance in relationship to the norm in the general physical education class, interviews with the student's parents, and checklists for specific skills in motor and physical fitness. In Minnesota, the physical educator needs to provide evidence of two of these approaches and make recommendations as to the extent the student can be involved in the general physical

education curriculum, or needs other placements and supports. Understanding which modifications and adaptations are appropriate can be guided by a review of the equipment, rules, environment, and instruction techniques (Lieberman & Houston-Wilson, 2002). (See figure 8.4.)

As the student moves through the educational system, the notion of developing transition plans in physical education is required. Beginning at age 14, the transition plans become part of the student's IEP. For the physical educator, the question is: What life-long activities will this student be able to participate in after graduation from high school? It is here that assessment of leisure interests is important. This can be done through a questionnaire given to the student, a family member, or both. Some physical educators have developed their own questionnaires based on the locale of the school and the particular resources of the geographic area; for example, downhill skiing may be more accessible in Utah than in Hawaii.

The reality is that the norm-referenced measure of psychomotor performance for physical education does not serve the needs of many students with cerebral palsy. And as the student moves into the upper grades, there is a need to address lifetime leisure and physical fitness activities as opposed to the fundamental movement skills or motor abilities of the student. In the early days of PL 94-142, the resources were scarce for assessment. Over the years, the spirit of the law has adjusted assessment guidelines. The reality is that professional judgment is needed to assess the individual for eligibility and for ongoing development of IEP and movement goals. This nonstandardized assessment is discussed in chapter 6.

The young child with cerebral palsy needs to be involved in the general physical education program with peers to the extent possible. The child needs age-appropriate games and activities as well as learning experiences in the fundamental movement skills. These will serve the child well as she moves into the upper grades in physical education. Some students will be impressed with competitive athletics; others may not. But for both groups of students, physical education in the schools can be the place where they learn what they can do in physical activity, how to socialize and play with their peers, and how to make physical activity a part of their life.

Physical Activities

As is true in program planning for all individuals with disabilities, the Individualized Education Program (IEP) meeting is the key to the quantity and quality of educational and related services. Maximum benefits for the student with cerebral palsy will be realized through the concerted efforts of educators and different therapists working cooperatively to respond to the individual's educational, social, psychological, and physical needs.

Tag Games

Equipment	Rules	Environment	Instruction
— Poly spots	— Have spots on floor	— Constant movement	— Make student calm self
— Soft, long objects	— Must use soft object	__ Bright boundaries	before starting
— Time-out chair	— Same locomotor activity	__ Rough boundaries	__ Peer tutoring
— Pinnies	— Use first names	__ Check understanding	__ "It" students do different
— Scarves	— Everybody is "it"	__ Big smile to class	skill
— Sponge balls	— Steal teammates' scarves	__ Ice arena	__ Direct
— Cones	— If tagged, 5 push-ups	__ Mats	__ Indirect
— Whistle	— Gender rule	__ Flat surface	__ Small group
— Carpet squares	— Touch rule	__ Mirrors	__ Physical assistance
— Scooters	— Bumpers up	__ Remove leg rest	__ Feedback
— Radio	— Airplane space	__ Large area	__ Positive role model
— Hula hoops	— Partner tag	__ Boundaries	__ Demonstration
— Pillow polo stick	— Animal walk	__ Circles	__ Verbal cues
— Bean bags	— 10-second rule	__ Lines	__ Brailing assistance
— Hard scarves	— Start/stop signal	__ Music	__ Nonverbal cues
— Different size balls	— Activity book	__ Smaller lines	__ Quality movement
— Bright color objects	— After tag do a skill	__ Smaller distance	__ Stress cooperation
— Tagging objects	— More than 1 person	__ Flags	__ Instruction feedback
— Wands	— Practice moving safely	__ Safety zone	__ Proximity
— Nerf balls	— Use soft stick to tag	__ Goals	__ Verbal cues
— Tape	— Clap 4 times then run	__ Groups for tag	__ Peer runners
— Wiffle balls	— Partner is "it"	__ Uncluttered	__ Command style
	— Walk, no running	__ No confusing sounds	__ No time factor
	— Tag on body parts	__ Good lighting	__ Task analyze
	— Blindfold partner	__ Level surface	__ Speak naturally
	— Change locomotion	__ Large movement	__ Braille tags
	— Run on balls of feet	__ Movement friendly	__ Preorient child
	— Tag softly	__ Outside on grass	__ Utilize all senses
	— Don't throw at face	__ Cooperative	__ Guided discovery
	— Freeze when tagged		
	— Follow the leader		

Figure 8.4 Considerations for modification and adaptation in low-organized and tag games.

Figure 8.5 Students with movement disorders can participate successfully in physical education and sport activities.

Because programming for students with cerebral palsy is individualized, the activities selected should be determined by the type and severity of the disability, the amount of muscular training that has occurred, and the interest level of the student. Thus, the physical educator looks at what the student *can do* and builds the program from there (figure 8.5). Facts that are important to ascertain are:

1. What body parts are affected by cerebral palsy?
2. What reflex problems are present?
3. What is the person's personality and emotional skill?
4. What medication is being used and what are the effects of the drugs?
5. Are there any perceptual motor deficits?
6. Are there learning disabilities?
7. What is the verbal ability of the student?
8. What recreation experiences has the student had?

Spastic Cerebral Palsy

The type of cerebral palsy will determine the adaptations that are needed. **Keeping in mind that most cerebral palsy cases are now considered a mixed type, it is important to**

be aware of some of the following facts. When working with individuals with primarily spastic cerebral palsy, activities requiring great agility and fast-moving actions should be avoided. The student will fail in these when compared with their peers. (The authors once watched a child with cerebral palsy do a line-race across a field on a summer day. The child was a significant distance from all the others in his class. It was very obvious that he had a form of cerebral palsy. The director of the program had him do the activity repeatedly, and the student was repeatedly last!) For some students, the environment should be structured to minimize external stimuli. Loud noises and sudden movements will cause the person to become tense and go into an extension; such a student has an abnormal reflex response. Movements that elicit the unwanted responses must be avoided. Movements that are continuously repeated are easier for those with spasticity. Also, some primitive reflexes may be elicited during activities; for example, an ATNR. If so, present the activity toward the side that the person is facing.

Athetoid Cerebral Palsy

When instructing those with athetoid cerebral palsy, the emphasis must be on creating a relaxed atmosphere where the student can remain calm because body tension and excitement tend to increase the athetoid symptoms. Frequent rest periods can be planned. For some students, an important aid in the performance of motor skills is an apparatus that can be utilized to create distal stabilization, which is the stabilization of an opposite limb during the performance of a movement. This procedure tends to reduce involuntary movements. Basically the student with primarily an athetoid cerebral palsy will have problems with overflow and involuntary motion. The level of cognitive impairment will also affect performance and understanding of movement skills and activities.

Ataxic Cerebral Palsy

For those individuals with ataxia cerebral palsy, adjustments must be made for severe balance and coordination problems; for example,

1. conducting balance activities on the floor instead of on a balance beam,
2. using very soft balls to reduce the possibility of injuries in catching, and
3. creating wider spaces between objects in the agility run.

Persons with ataxic cerebral palsy do not perform well in skills requiring balance and kinesthesis; they are able to move the body successfully but have difficulty responding to objects, as in the instances of picking up or catching or kicking objects in a game situation. Because of their poor kinesthesis, they often move too far or not far enough in executing the required movement. Success will be more likely if the skill can be performed in a stationary position. Kicking the ball while running will be very difficult for those who are ataxic, but if they can stop and then make the kick the chances of performing the skill successfully are immeasurably better.

Carry-over leisure activities are an important aspect of the program. Community activities that the individual can engage in should be taught. Examples of activities that have been successfully taught to these students include bowling, table tennis, horseshoes, and swimming.

Swimming is an excellent activity. The buoyancy of the water allows students with cerebral palsy to have a freedom of movement that they cannot have out of water. The water also provides a superb environment for the student to practice walking. Special techniques for the teaching of swimming skills to students with cerebral palsy are presented in chapter 16.

It is also recommended by some authorities that muscular relaxation training be given to these students. There is considerable disagreement, however, as to the effects of such training. More research is still needed to determine its appropriate use. Chapter 29 on the CD explains the techniques of such training.

Thanks to the United States Cerebral Palsy Athletic Association (www.ndsaonline.org), opportunities now exist for individuals with cerebral palsy to participate in organized sports programs. UCP's purpose is to promote competitive sport programs and recreational opportunities for persons disabled by cerebral palsy and similar disorders. Local, state, national, and international meets are held to allow athletes with cerebral palsy to demonstrate their skills in various dual and team sports. An eight-category classification system is used to ensure that individuals compete fairly and equitably with athletes who have a similar type of cerebral palsy, degree of involvement, and mode of ambulation. Additional information on the advocacy association for individuals with cerebral palsy will be presented in chapter 18.

In addition to these general suggestions, there are some specific activities that should be incorporated into the physical education program of a student with cerebral palsy. These include experiences designed to enhance body image, breathing capacity, and physical fitness.

Body Image

Children with cerebral palsy frequently lack a complete understanding or awareness of the movement capability and location of their body parts. Activities, therefore, should be designed to help the student overcome this difficulty. For young children, this will require simple games designed to help the students name and identify body parts. As they progress, more attention can focus on helping them become aware of the body's position in basic movements such as rolling over or throwing a ball. It is very important to help students focus on their movement patterns by questioning them as they participate in various games. For example, questions such as, "Which hand are you using?" and "Which way are you moving?" help the student become more aware of the body's capability and its relationship to space and other objects. For some students, the teacher may find it necessary to provide nonverbal cues, such as touching the student's arm while emphasizing, "*This* is your right arm."

Physical Fitness Activity Levels

The level of physical fitness for many individuals with cerebral palsy is such that special efforts should be undertaken to help students improve their performance in this important area (Rintala, Lyytinen, & Dunn, 1990). Cardiovascular endurance, in particular, is a physical fitness component about which there is a growing body of literature to support the contention that individuals with cerebral palsy can improve the efficiency of their heart and lungs, thereby increasing their stamina. To do this, however, requires that a systematic program be developed in which students are provided opportunities to stress their cardiorespiratory system. Individuals in wheelchairs, those who walk with the aid of an assistive device, and those who walk unaided but with an unusual gait can all undertake activities that stress the cardiorespiratory system gradually over time. The basic premise of the program is that the student is asked to move greater and greater distances, with a gradual reduction in the amount of time taken for a given distance. Monitoring the individual's pulse rate can be used as an informative way to help the student appreciate the benefits of a systematic cardiorespiratory fitness program (see chapter 17).

Facilitating physical fitness in individuals with cerebral palsy is known to be hampered by the lack of access to transportation, the cost of activity involvement and, for some, the medical concerns and complications. Nonetheless, NCPAD emphasizes that physical fitness testing is important for children with cerebral palsy, and that adults with cerebral palsy, who are competitive athletes, benefit from their high level of physical fitness. Certainly these adults have found that cerebral palsy does not negate seeking and maintaining good physical fitness. Many of the studies concerning cerebral palsy and fitness involve small numbers of participants, which limits the ability to generalize. However, cerebral palsy is a condition that is known for its wide diversity in affecting movement performance. Hence, physical educators can take each individual as a unique person with

unique abilities for movement activities. The models of assessment and program development discussed in earlier chapters will be of assistance in framing a program for and with the individual with cerebral palsy.

Wheelchairs

For the student who uses a wheelchair for ambulation, it is very important that the individual be removed from the chair periodically during the day to prevent excessive contractures. The physical education period provides an excellent opportunity for the student to learn and explore new movement skills while on a mat. It is essential, however, that the teacher employ correct lifting and handling techniques with children with cerebral palsy. For example, when the student is on a mat and the teacher wants to place the individual back into the wheelchair, it is best to first roll the child on his or her side and bend the head and shoulders forward, thus facilitating the bending of the hips. Physical therapists can provide additional information to help the teacher learn other valuable lifting and handling techniques.

Selecting Alternative Experiences

The motor characteristics of the student with cerebral palsy require that the teacher not only adapt activities but select alternative experiences when necessary. For example, if the class is working on the skill of ball throwing, various adaptations of the skill can be utilized, like using a ball of different weight or size, or changing the size and distance of the target. Any adaptation of an activity must be done carefully, recognizing the unique needs of the student with cerebral palsy. For instance, using a lightweight ball to help a child learn how to kick a ball is considered an acceptable teaching technique. However, this approach for the individual with hemiplegic cerebral palsy may not be appropriate. As illustrated in figure 8.6, the use of a light, small ball with this

Figure 8.6 Children who are hemiplegic benefit from opportunities to kick large heavier balls. Heavier balls add resistance, whereas lighter balls encourage a backward lean that increases stiffness in the leg and in the bending of the arm. (Adapted from Finnie, Nancie: *Handling the Young Cerebral Palsied Child at Home*, New York, E. P. Dutton and Co., Inc., 1975, p. 267.)

TABLE 8.1 An Example of a Traditional, Adapted, and Alternative Objective

Goal: Participation in games involving throwing

Skill: Throwing

Objective (traditional): Given a softball, the child will assume a stride position and employ the overhand method to throw a given distance of 20 feet with 80% success.

Objective (adapted): Given a Nerf ball, the child will throw a distance of 20 feet with 80% success. The child will be stabilized at the hips by an assistant.

Objective (alternative): Given a wheelchair with foot pedals, the child will balance an 8-inch ball on the lap and, placing one hand, fisted or open, between the legs and under the ball, lift the ball up, and at the same time push it forward. The ball must travel 10 feet in the air with 80% success.

Courtesy of Joan Kelly, Adapted Physical Education Specialist, Eugene, Oregon, Public Schools.

child increases extension in the leg and flexion of the arm with a backward body lean as the kick is performed. Using a heavier, larger ball, however, forces the student to keep the leg flexed and body weight over the ball. This improves overall body balance and position, thus increasing the probability of success.

For some, however, adaptations of the skill may not be helpful. In these cases an alternative experience may be necessary. A skill becomes an alternative activity when the skill is modified to such an extent that the traditional skill may not be easily recognized, or the child is unable to assume the physical posture required by the traditional skill. An example of a traditional, adapted, and alternative objective is presented in table 8.1. For some students with cerebral palsy, successful physical education experiences require a teacher who can adapt and, when necessary, design alternative experiences.

There is much that is not known or understood about the motor characteristics of cerebral palsy. For example, there is some uncertainty about the amount of time these individuals require to process information prior to the execution of a motor task. Parks, Rose, and Dunn (1989), in a study of adolescents with mild spastic hemiplegia, found that the premotor component of a fractionated reaction time task with these students was longer than that of their nondisabled counterparts. These findings suggest that teachers will need to allow for additional processing time when instructing students with spastic cerebral palsy, including those who do not have a cognitive deficit. Sensitivity to this need will help to create a favorable and positive learning environment. Future research will help to confirm some of these findings and to shed new light on methods of teaching those with cerebral palsy.

Summary

Cerebral palsy is a condition resulting from brain damage that may be incurred before or during birth or at any time in later life. There are various types of cerebral palsy; the spastic and athetoid conditions are the most prevalent. Cerebral palsy affects different parts of the body, with the topographical classification of hemiplegia being the most common.

The major problem confronting the individual with cerebral palsy is learning to move the body as efficiently and effectively as possible. Treatment for cerebral palsy includes physical therapy, medication, and to a lesser extent biofeedback. While treatment for cerebral palsy can be helpful, no cure for this disorder exists. The goal of the treatment program is to minimize the effect of selected reflexes while helping the individual acquire functional skills that can be used in daily life.

In addition to the obvious neuromuscular problems, many individuals with cerebral palsy have secondary disorders. Concomitant problems may include mental retardation, speech and language disorders, sensory disabilities, and epilepsy. While not all individuals possess all or even some of these secondary disorders, many do. This suggests that the population with cerebral palsy is significant and varied. Treatment programs today, therefore, emphasize a multidisciplinary approach in the delivery of medical treatment and educational programs.

Physical education is an important and essential service for individuals with cerebral palsy. Modern treatment of cerebral palsy emphasizes the importance of helping the individual function effectively in the activities of daily life. This requires, among other things, that the person be healthy and physically fit. Physical educators can be effective in helping young students with cerebral palsy develop appropriate levels of cardiorespiratory fitness, muscular strength and endurance, and flexibility.

Furthermore, efforts must be directed toward teaching motor skills essential to successful participation in sports, games, and play activities. There is a growing awareness that the individual with cerebral palsy can perform physical feats that only a few years ago were thought to be impossible. Organizations such as USCPAA (the United States Cerebral Palsy Athletic Association) have been helpful in dispelling myths about cerebral palsy while promoting a realistic and positive image of individuals with this disorder.

Enhancing Activities

1. Attend an athletic event sponsored by the United States Cerebral Palsy Athletic Association. Observe the various athletes and the differences in movement capability and performance by classification.
2. Interview an adult with cerebral palsy. Through discussion, obtain the individual's perception of the disability and the effectiveness of various treatment techniques.
3. Develop a physical fitness program for an adolescent with cerebral palsy. If possible, implement the program under the guidance of your professor.
4. Confer with a physical therapist to obtain his or her view of cerebral palsy and the effectiveness of various treatment techniques.
5. Write a paper defending the importance of physical education as an essential aspect of the education of the child with cerebral palsy.

Selected Readings

Batshaw, M. L., & Perret, Y. M. (1986). *Children with handicaps: A medical primer* (2nd ed.). Baltimore: Paul H. Brookes Publishing Co.

Bertoti, D. B. (1988). Effect of therapeutic horseback riding on posture in children with cerebral palsy. *Physical Therapy, 68,* 1505–1512.

Best, G. A. (1978). *Individuals with physical disabilities.* St. Louis: C. V. Mosby Co.

Bidabe, L., & Lollar, J. M. (1990). *Mobility opportunities via education.* Bakersfield, CA: Office of Kern County Superintendent of Schools.

Bigge, J. L., & O'Donnell, P. A. (1976). *Teaching individuals with physical and multiple disabilities.* Columbus, OH: Charles E. Merrill Publishing Co.

Blackman, J. A. (1984). *Medical aspects of developmental disabilities in children birth to three.* Rockville, MD: Aspen Systems Corporation.

Bleck, E. E. (1979). *Orthopedic management of cerebral palsy.* Philadelphia: W. B. Saunders Co.

Bleck, E. (1987). Goals, treatment, and management. In *Orthopedic management in cerebral palsy* (2nd ed.). Cambridge University Press.

Bleck, E. E., & Nagel, D. A. (1982). *Physically handicapped children: A medical atlas for teachers* (2nd ed.). New York: Grune and Stratton.

Block, M. E. (2000). *Including students with disabilities in general physical education* (2nd ed.). Baltimore: Brookes.

Bobath, B. (1971). Motor development, its effect on general development, and application to the treatment of cerebral palsy. *Physiotherapy, 57,* 526–532.

Boyce, W. F., Gowland, C., Hardy, S., Rosenbaum, P. L., Lane, M., Plews. N., Goldsmith, C., & Russell, D. J. (1991). Development of a quality-of-movement measure for children with cerebral palsy. *Physical Therapy, 71,* 820–832.

Brigance, A. H. (1991). *Revised Brigance Diagnostic Inventory of Early Development.* North Billerica, MA: Curriculum Associates.

Brown, A. (1975). Review: Physical fitness and cerebral palsy. *Child: Care, health, and development, 1,* 143–152.

Bruininks, R. H., Bruininks, B. D., (2005). Bruininks-Oseretsky test of motor proficiency, 2nd Ed. Circle Pines, MN: AGS Publishing.

Burton, A. W., & Miller, D. E. (1998). *Movement skill assessment.* Champaign, IL: Human Kinetics.

Campbell, S. K. (1995). The child's development of functional movement. In S. K. Campbel (Ed.), *Physical therapy for children* (pp. 3–37). Philadelphia: Saunders.

Centers for Disease Control and Prevention (CDC). (2004). What is cerebral palsy? Retrieved July 2004 from www.cdc.Gov/ncbddd/dd/ddcp.htm

Cotton, E., & Parnwell, M. (1967). From Hungary: The Peto method. *Special Education, 56*(4), 7–11.

Cruickshank, W. (1976). *Cerebral palsy: A developmental disability* (3rd ed.). Syracuse, NY: Syracuse University Press.

Damiano, D. L., & Abel, M. F. (1998). Functional outcomes of strength training in spastic cerebral palsy. *Archives of Physical Medicine and Rehabilitation. 79*(2), 119–125.

Denhoff, E. (1976). Medical aspects. In W. M. Cruickshank (Ed.), *Cerebral palsy: A developmental disability.* Syracuse, NY: Syracuse University Press.

Dunn, W. (2000). *Best practice in occupational therapy.* Thorofare, NJ: SLACK.

Edgington, D. (1976). *The physically handicapped child in your classroom.* Springfield, IL: Charles C. Thomas.

Eichstaedt, C. B., & Kalakian, L. H. (1987). *Developmental/ adapted physical education* (2nd ed.). New York: Macmillan Publishing Co.

Fernandez, J. E., Pitetti, K. H., & Betzen, M. T. (1990). Physiological capacities of individuals with cerebral palsy. *Human Factors, 32,* 457–466.

Fetters, L., & Kluzik, J. (1996). The effects of neurodevelopmental treatment versus practice on reaching of children with cerebral palsy. *Physical Therapy, 76,* 346–358.

Finnie, N. (1975). *Handling the young cerebral palsied child at home.* New York: E. P. Dutton.

Folio, M. R., & Fewell, R. R. (2000). *Peabody developmental motor scales* (2nd ed.). Austin, TX: Pro-Ed.

Frost, H. (1972). *Orthopedic surgery in spasticity.* Springfield, IL: Charles C. Thomas.

Haley, S. M., Coster, W. J., Ludlow, L. H., Haltiwanger, J., & Andrellos, P. (1992). *Pediatric evaluation of disability inventory.* Boston: New England Medical Center Hosptials.

Harris, F. (1971). Inapproprioception: A possible sensory basis for athetoid movements. *Physical Therapy, 51*(7), 761–770.

Harris, S. R. (1990). Therapeutic exercises for children with neurodevelopmental disabilities. In J. V. Basmajian, & S. Wolf, (Eds.), *Therapeutic exercise* (5th ed., 163–176). Baltimore: Williams and Wilkins.

Healthcommunities. (2004). *Cerebral palsy.* Retrieved July 2004 from www.neurologychannel.com

Heward, W. L., & Orlansky, M. D. (1988). *Exceptional children* (3rd ed.). Columbus, OH: Charles E. Merrill Publishing Co.

Holland, L. J., & Steadward, R. D. (1990). Effects of resistance and flexibility training on strength, spasticity/muscle tone, and range of motion of elite athletes with cerebral palsy. *Palaestra, 6*(4), 27–31.

Horvat, M. (1987). Effects of a progressive resistance training program on an individual with spastic cerebral palsy. *American Corrective Therapy Journal, 41*(1), 7–11.

Jones, J. A. (1988). *Training guide to cerebral palsy sports* (3rd ed.). Champaign, IL: Human Kinetics Publishers.

Kramer, J., & MacPhail, H. (1994). Relationships among measures of walking efficiency, gross motor ability, and isokinetic strength in adolescents with cerebral palsy. *Pediatric Physical Therapy, 10,* 3–8.

Kurtz, L. A. (1992). Cerebral palsy. In M. Batshaw & Y. Perret (Eds.), *Children with medical disabilities: A medical primer* (3rd ed., pp. 441–469). Baltimore: Paul H. Brookes Publishing Co.

Levitt, S. (1985). *Treatment of cerebral palsy and motor delay* (2nd ed.). Boston: Blackwell Scientific Publications.

Lieberman & Houston-Wilson (2002). *Strategies for INCLUSION: A handbook for physical educators.* Champain, IL: Human Kinetics.

Lugo, A. A., Sherrill, C., & Pizarro, A. L. (1992). Use of a sport socialization inventory with cerebral palsied youth. *Perceptual and Motor Skills, 74,* 203–208.

McCubbin, J. A., & Horvat, M. (1990). Guidelines for resistance exercise training for persons with cerebral palsy. *Palaestra, 6*(2), 29–21; 47.

Minnesota Department of Education (MDE). (2002). *Occupational and physical therapy in educational settings. A manual for Minnesota practioners.* Minneapolis. Author.

Mullins, J. B. (1979). *A teacher's guide to management of physically handicapped students.* Springfield, IL: Charles C. Thomas.

National Center on Physical Activity and Disability (NCPAD). (2004). *A brief history of therapy in the treatment of cerebral palsy.* Retrieved July 2004 from www.ncpad.ord/ disability/fact_sheet.php?sheet=119&section=954

Palmer, F., Shapiro, B., Wachtel, R., Allen, M., Hiller, J., Harryman, S., Mosher, B., Meinert, C., & Capute, A. (1988). The effects of physical therapy on cerebral palsy. *New England Journal of Medicine, 318,* 803–808.

Paneth, N., & Kiely, J. (1984). The frequency of cerebral palsy: A review of population studies in industrialized nations since 1950. *Clinics in Developmental Medicine, 87,* 46–56.

Parks, S., Rose, D. J., & Dunn, J. M. (1989). A comparison of fractionated reaction time between cerebral palsied and non-handicapped youth. *Adapted Physical Activity Quarterly, 7,* 379–388.

Pitetti, K. H., Fernandez, J. E., & Lanciault, M. (1991). Feasibility of an exercise program for adults with cerebral palsy: A pilot study. *Adapted Physical Activity Quarterly, 8,* 333–341.

Rintala, P., Lyytinen, H, & Dunn, J. M. (1990). Influence of a physical activity program on children with cerebral palsy: A single subject design. *Pediatric Exercise Science, 2,* 46–56.

Rood, M. (1954). Neurophysiological reactions as a basis for physical therapy. *Physical Therapy Review, 34*(9), 444–449.

Rose, J., Gamble, J. G., Medeiros, J., Burgos, A., & Haskell, W. L. (1990). Energy expenditure index of walking for normal children and for children with cerebral palsy. *Developmental Medicine and Child Neurology, 32,* 333–340.

Rothman, J. G. (1978). Effects of respiratory exercises on the vital capacity and forced expiratory volume in children with cerebral palsy. *Physical Therapy*, *58*(4), 421–425.

Sanders, M. (1980). A comparison of two methods of training on the development of muscular strength and endurance. *Journal of Orthopedic Sports Physical Therapy*, *1*(4), 210–213.

Sanger, T. D., Delgado, M. R., Gaebler-Spira, D., Hallett, M., & Mink, J. (2003). Classification and definition of disorders causing hypertonia in childhood. *Pediatrics*, *111*(1), e89–e97.

Sherrill, C. (1993). *Adapted physical activity, recreation and sport* (4th ed.). Dubuque, IA: Wm. C. Brown Publishers.

Sugden, D. A., & Keogh, J. (1990). *Problems in movement skill development*. Columbia, SC: University of South Carolina Press.

Turk, M. A., Geremski, C. A., Rosenbaum, P. F., & Weber R. J. (1997). The health status of women with cerebral palsy. *Archives of Physical Medicine and Rehabilitation, 78*(12), 10–17.

Ulrich, D. A. (2000). Test of Gross Motor Development-2. Austin, TX: Pro-Ed.

USCPAA. (2005). Retrieved June, 2005 from www.ndsaonline .org

WE MOVE. (2004). Spasticity. Retrieved July 2004 from www.mdvu.org with section authorship by Terence Sanger, MD, PhD.

Wilber, N., Mitra, M., Klein Walker, D., & Allen, D. (2002). Disability as a public health issue: Findings and reflections from the Massachusetts survey of secondary conditions. *The Milbank Quarterly*, *80*(2), 393–421.

Winnick, J. P., & Short, F. X. (1985). *Physical fitness testing of the disabled*. Champaign, IL: Human Kinetics Publishers.

Winnick, J. P., & Short, F. X. (1991). A comparison of the physical fitness of non retarded and mildly retarded adolescents with cerebral palsy. *Adapted Physical Activity Quarterly*, *8*, 43–56.

Young, R. R., & Delwaid, P. J. (1981). Drug therapy and spasticity. *New England Journal of Medicine*, *304*(1), 28–33.

Sensory Impairments

CHAPTER OBJECTIVES

After studying this chapter, the reader should be able to:

1 Appreciate the historical and changing perspective of the importance of physical activity and its contribution to the well-being of students with sensory impairments.
2 Recognize the various communication techniques utilized to help those with auditory and visual impairments benefit from educational programs and activities.
3 Analyze various games and activities commonly played by children and suggest modifications in these experiences to accommodate the special needs of those with sensory impairments.
4 Identify and describe the common causes of sensory impairment and the degree of sensory loss associated with each.
5 Identify adaptations made to games such as soccer, volleyball, tennis, and horseshoes for individuals with sensory impairment.
6 Explain the classifications systems used to describe the magnitude of the visual or hearing loss.
7 Identify the special equipment and instructional techniques used to teach physical education to those with visual and/or hearing impairments.
8 Describe the following terms used to describe programs and services for the visually and hearing impaired: congenital, adventitious, legal blindness, myopia, hyperopia, nystagmus, astigmatism, strabismus, Braille, mobility orientation, beep baseball, goal ball, hearing impaired, blind, deaf, decibel, hertz, ASL, finger spelling, speech reading, and deaf-blind.
9 Identify and describe general guidelines that can be employed to develop appropriate programs for students with sensory impairments.
10 Identify the different sports and recreation associations available for individuals who are sensory impaired.

The term "sensory impairment" describes a condition in which one or more of the senses are diminished in their effectiveness to respond to stimuli. Such a condition may be present from birth or may develop at any time during life as the result of injury or disease. The lack of sensory response to stimulation may be total or partial. Difficulties for the person involved are created by any sensory impairment regardless of the time of incurrence or the degree of severity.

The discussion in this chapter will be limited to visual and hearing impairments and to a combination of the two, referred to as dual sensory impairment. Visual impairment is a generic term that includes a range of visual acuity (Bloomquist, 2003a).

Much of the information presented concerning the causes, special needs, and adjustment problems of persons with either of the disabilities also applies to those with dual impairment and can serve as a foundation for a fuller understanding of the presentation of the dual sensory disability.

Visual Impairments

Physical education for those with visual impairments has a long and interesting history. In the 1830s three schools for blind children were founded in the United States, providing the first educational opportunities for such children. One of these schools, Perkins Institute in Boston, had as its director a medical doctor who was an enthusiastic advocate of the benefits of physical exercise. He organized a program of vigorous physical activity that included playing outdoors, swimming in the ocean, and working on gymnastic apparatus. His program was far in advance of the physical education in the public schools of his day.

Gradually other schools for the visually impaired were established. Some of these made provisions for physical training classes in which gymnastics constituted the chief activity. Military training, which received emphasis in the public schools following the Civil War, displaced gymnastic training in schools for the visually impaired. The consequence was that marching and military exercise or formal gymnastics have served as the core of physical education for students with visual impairments in many schools until very recent times. In other schools, the play movement that swept the country in the early part of this century encouraged administrators to begin athletic programs in wrestling and track and field. Intramural teams in these sports became prevalent, and soon varsity teams entered into interschool competition.

Today physical education programs at the special schools offer a balanced variety of activities, including intramural and interscholastic sports. Dr. Charles Buell, a physical educator who is blind and former Athletic Director at the California School for the Blind, was instrumental in formulating many of the ideas used in physical education classes for the visually impaired throughout the United States. Many students with visual impairments who in former years would have been enrolled in special schools now attend public schools where they participate in regular physical education or special physical education as their needs require.

The Nature of Visual Impairments

Approximately one child out of every four or five has some significant deviation from the accepted norm of good vision. A large majority of these have such slight deviations that they are not extremely detrimental to the child or are remediable either medically or by wearing prescribed lenses. For these children no special educational provisions need be made. However, about one out of every fifteen hundred has such severe deviations from normal vision that he or she cannot read books printed in regular type and so require materials printed in large type or Braille.

Visual acuity, the ability to clearly distinguish forms or discriminate details, is commonly measured by the use of a chart having several lines of progressively smaller letters or symbols. The person being tested reads the chart from a specific distance. Visual acuity, as determined by the number of lines the individual is able to read, is expressed in a numerical ratio. For example, a ratio of 20/200 indicates that the person being tested had to stand twenty feet from the chart (the first number in the ratio) in order to see what someone with normal vision can see from two hundred feet (the second number).

The degree to which students are impaired is determined largely by how greatly their vision deviates from normal. **Those with visual acuity of 20/200 or less with glasses are considered legally blind, but most of those so classified have some useful sight.** They may be able to perceive light, form, or movement and are, consequently, considered to be partially sighted (table 9.1). The partially sighted have traditionally been enrolled in schools for the blind along with the totally blind because their visual impairments require special educational methods and equipment. However, the enrollment of partially seeing students in regular school systems, with some special arrangements made for their needs, is now common practice. Sometimes their

TABLE 9.1   Degrees of Visual Acuity

Legal Blindness.   Visual acuity of 20/200 or less or a field of vision less than 20°. Students so designated are eligible to receive special assistance from state and federal sources.

Travel Vision.   Visual acuity from 5/200 to 10/200 inclusive. Enough sight is present to allow moving or walking without extreme difficulty.

Motion Perception.   Visual acuity from 3/200 to 5/200 inclusive. Movement can be seen but usually not the still object.

Light Perception.   Visual acuity less than 3/200. A bright light can be distinguished at a distance of three feet or less but movement cannot.

Total or Complete Blindness.   Inability to see light.

Tunnel Vision.   A field of vision of 20° or less. The field of vision is so drastically narrowed that the person sees as though looking through a tube.

instruction is provided in special classes with a teacher trained in methods of instructing the partially sighted and with equipment designed especially for their needs. In other situations they are accommodated in the general classroom.

The age at which individuals lose sight has as much bearing on their educational needs as the degree to which their vision is affected. Blindness at birth may be more challenging than blindness that occurs later in life, because it prevents the individual from establishing visual concepts of any kind.

Causes of Visual Impairments

The primary function of the eye is to receive visual input and to transmit this information to the brain via the optic nerve. This is a complicated procedure in which the eye collects light reflected from objects in the visual field and focuses these objects on the retina. The visual information is then transmitted from the retina to the optic nerve. In a normal eye, refraction occurs when a ray of light is deflected from its course as it passes through various surfaces of the eye (figure 9.1).

First, light focuses on the cornea; then it passes through a watery liquid known as the aqueous humor. Next, light passes through the pupil, a circular hole in the center of the eye that contracts or expands according to the amount of light reaching the eye. The light then enters the lens, which is curved to reflect the light more before it enters a jelly-like fluid known as the vitreous humor. A clear image finally reaches the retina and is transmitted to the brain via the optic nerve.

The ability to see normally is a very complex process involving various intricate parts of the eye. It is understandable, therefore, that problems can develop that interfere with normal sight. Although there are many causes of visual impairments, only those that more commonly occur will be presented here.

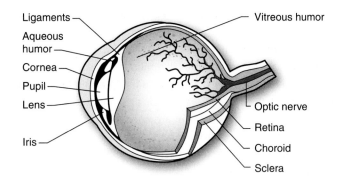

Figure 9.1 Diagram of the human eye.

Visual impairments may be due to congenital problems or to difficulties that occur later in the student's development. Those who are born with visual disorders are referred to as *congenitally blind*; those who develop problems later are referred to as *adventitiously blind*. Causes of visual impairments may be classified as refractive errors, eye muscle disorders, or diseases and genetic defects.

Refractive Errors

Refractive errors occur when the visual image is blurred due to improper focus of the light rays. **Myopia** (nearsighted), **hyperopia** (farsighted), and **astigmatism** (blurred vision both near and far) are three common refractive errors. Fortunately, refractive problems can be corrected for most individuals through the use of prescription glasses or contact lenses.

Muscle Imbalance

Some students experience visual problems because the eyes do not work together. Although each eye's retina sees a separate visual image, normally the brain coordinates the eyes so that one visual image is perceived. For some, however, the

Figure 9.2 (*A*) Cataract: A clouding of the lens which causes a general loss of detail in what a person sees. The field of vision is unaffected, but glaring light conditions, distortion, and double images can prove annoying. (*B*) Macular degeneration: The most common eye disease, macular degeneration causes loss of vision in the central field, making it difficult to read or do close work.

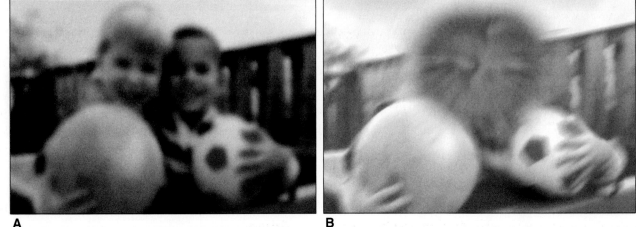

A   B

muscles that surround each eye are not synchronized, resulting in vision that is distorted. Normally this condition is characterized by **nystagmus**, rapid side to side or up and down movement of the eye; **strabismus**, misaligned vision in which the eyes either cross or turn out; or **amblyopia**, domination by one eye due to the inability of the two eyes to focus clearly on an object.

Genetic Disorders and Diseases of the Eye

According to Bloomquist (2003a), causes of a visual impairment due to birth defects include cataracts (see figure 9.2 *A* and *B*) and optic nerve disease. In the past, young children experienced retinopathy caused by excessive oxygen in incubators, but now that is uncommon in individuals younger than 18 years of age. Elderly individuals may experience visual impairments caused by such diseases as diabetes, macular degeneration, glaucoma, and cataracts.

Teaching Those with Vision Impairment

Children with impaired vision have the same needs for physical activity as other children, but their lack of normal vision does in numerous instances restrict their play activities to such an extent that they are noticeably retarded in their physical development. Fear of injury instilled in them by protective parents reduces their natural interest in big-muscle movements such as running, climbing, and jumping, which are an inherent part of most children's play and contributes to their muscular growth and the development of coordination. As a result, physical vitality and resistance to certain diseases are low and excess weight is often a problem. Posture may be poor both because of the lack of strength in the postural muscles and because of the lack of visual examples of good posture to emulate.

Because the urges of children who are blind to move and play are frustrated, they often develop certain mannerisms known as **blindisms**. These are physical movements through which, it is thought, the child who is blind seeks to fulfill the need for muscular movement without moving about through space. **Rocking back and forth, twitching of the head, and jerking of the limbs are characteristic blindisms.** It is desirable to overcome these mannerisms, because they set children with visual impairments apart from their seeing peers. Moreover, in working to eliminate the blindisms a greater sense of security in moving about in space will be developed. Teaching children who are blind to pursue physical and recreational pursuits will give them alternative activities during idle time other than blindisms or self-stimulation.

Those who are visually impaired may have personality problems as well as physical incapacities. Because of their fears of activity, those who are visually impaired tend to pursue solitary and sedentary occupations. This limits their social contacts, which may in turn feed a feeling of inferiority. Frustrations experienced in attempting normal activity or normal social relations contribute to maladjustment. Fantasies and daydreaming are common among the visually impaired who have made unsatisfactory adjustments to their circumstances.

The age at which individuals lose their sight has considerable effect upon their social adjustment. Children who have been without sight since birth have more difficulty in social adjustment than those who had achieved some degree of social maturity before losing their sight. However, the latter may experience anxieties and fears about their future, resulting in extreme cases of despondency and depression.

The age at which the impairment occurs likewise influences the movement patterns. These are also governed by the degree to which the person can see. Those who have gained assurance from previous experiences or from their ability to see slightly will move about with less awkwardness and with more confidence than others whose fears are heightened by lack of such assurance.

To compensate for their lack of sight, individuals who are visually impaired tend to develop their other senses to a higher degree than sighted people. Some believe the visually impaired have a "sixth sense" because they have developed such an awareness of their environment that they appear to perceive things that their sighted associates cannot. There is no evidence to support the concept that those with visual impairments have an unnatural or mystical gift that enables them to perform activities that would seem possible only for the seeing. The adroitness with which a person without sight walks down the crowded sidewalk avoiding other walkers and obstacles, negotiates the curb, and crosses with the light seems almost superhuman to the fully visioned, who cannot conceive of doing this themselves without the use of eyes. Behind the skill of the walker who is visually impaired is a highly developed kinesthetic sense, the ability to listen closely to auditory clues, and extensive experience in the interpretation of the various stimuli to the other senses. The person's "sixth sense" is actually the acute development of the other senses.

Planning the Physical Activity Program

Planning an activity program for the individual with a visual impairment is vital to the success the individual has with being physically active, exercising, engaging in games and, for some, being involved in competitive athletics. Exercise for individuals with a visual impairment produces the same positive psychological benefits as it does for those without such an impairment (Bloomquist, 2003a), including:

- more opportunities to improve socialization skills;
- practice and improvement in balance skills, which may be low;

- improvement in self-image, confidence, and spatial orientation;
- improvement in cardiovascular fitness; and
- decrease in obesity. (p. 325)

According to Lieberman and Coward (1996), the benefits of physical activity are similar for both visually impaired and sighted individuals. These authors believe that games help students refine their movement skills and engage in physical activities that produce health benefits. These specialists in physical activity for individuals with visual impairments recommend the following:

- Locate age-appropriate games that meet the needs of all students in a class;
- Make only the needed modifications;
- Implement and monitor the game: provide positive feedback, adjust the game if necessary, or make a mental note to adjust in the future;
- Re-examine the game for appropriateness: Was the game enjoyable and did it allow the students to practice needed skills or develop new ones?

Integration in Physical Activities

Several effective teaching procedures may be utilized to integrate a student with a visual impairment into the general physical education class. Before these procedures can be used, of course, the teacher must ascertain the degree to which the student can perceive and how well he or she has developed compensatory skills. Of fundamental importance is for the teacher to ascertain how well the student can see. For example, the teacher should question the student as to his/her visual abilities (e.g., can the student see light, shadows, outline of faces, and colors such as white versus red). With this knowledge about the student, the teacher can make simple modifications in the activities to accommodate the youngster in the games of the class.

An example should suggest many more similar possibilities to the physical education teacher. Assume that a student with partial vision is to be integrated into a softball unit with sighted students. The teacher, in consultation with the student, must devise a system to help the individual learn the fundamentals of softball. As presented in chapter 5, the teacher would first identify the tasks involved in the game of softball and then systematically explore ways the various tasks could be modified. The game of softball, for instance, requires students to hit, run bases, pitch, field, catch, and throw. Modifications for the task of hitting might include having the student hit using a batting tee; hit with a larger bat; use a larger, brightly colored ball; swing at a pitched ball with the verbal assistance of the teacher or a classmate; or use an audible ball. Each of these modifications must be

---

TABLE 9.2 Sample Modifications for the Game of Softball

Task	Modification
Hitting the ball	Use a larger, bigger bat
	Use a larger, brightly colored ball
	Use a batting tee
	Use an audible ball
	Swing at a pitched ball with the verbal assistance of the teacher
Running the bases	Follow a guide rope
	Use the natural contrast of worn base path to grass field
	Shorten the distance between bases
	Run with a partner
	Run to sound provided by audible device or teammate's coaching
Fielding a ball	Use the buddy system for assistance
	Modify rule so that if player who is visually impaired picks the ball up before runner reaches base, the runner is out
	Modify the rule to allow for an out when ball is thrown to the closest player or base
	Use an audible ball

studied carefully by the teacher with a view to identifying the one most closely approximating the original task that can be performed successfully by the student. Use of a substitute batter should be made only if none of the other options were successful. Modifications for other softball skills are given in table 9.2 and offer an example of the way in which games can be adapted for participation by players with visual impairments.

The ultimate aim is to have the students without disabilities recognize the student who is visually impaired as an asset rather than a liability for the team. Utilization of modifications like those suggested before promotes the development of such recognition. However, the teacher sets the tone for how the student with visual impairments is received. If the teacher is overly protective and solicitous of the student in the class, such will be the general attitude displayed by the class. Acceptance of the students for who they are, with an appreciation of the talents and abilities they display, will be

the response of the class if this is the attitude demonstrated by the instructor.

Peer tutoring is an effective method of instruction in a general physical education class for individuals with visual impairment (e.g., Lieberman & Houston-Wilson, 2002). Training the peer tutor to assist the individual with visual impairment is critical to the success of this instructional method for learning movement skills, games, and sports. These authors offer "kid terms" to explain visual impairment that can be used to assist in training peer tutors and also with inclusion in the general physical education classes (see table 9.3). Older students with vision have reported a reciprocal benefit from participating in leisure activities such as cross-country running or training for competitions with the individual with visual impairments.

The discussion that follows identifies several factors that physical educators must consider in teaching movement experiences to students who are visually impaired. The

TABLE 9.3 Disabilities in Kid Terms: for Use with Peer Tutoring

Blind or Visually Impaired
- Children who are blind or visually impaired have difficulty seeing.
- They have this disability because of a birth accident, an accident after birth, or a sickness.
- Some kids can see a little bit and walk around by themselves; some kids can see a little bit but need some help getting around; and some kids cannot see anything and need help in getting around.
- With practice and a cane or a seeing-eye dog, kids may be able to walk around school and their neighborhood by themselves.
- These kids will eat by themselves and use the clock system. You can tell them their milk is at 12:00, which means their milk is at the very top of their plate, and their fork is at 9:00, which means their fork is just to the left of their plate.
- They can dress themselves, and they know which clothes are which color by brailling the color on the tag of the shirt.
- They find out what is happening in their environment, who is around them, and where they are going by having people tell them.
- Do not be afraid to use the words "see" or "look" in a sentence. They will use these words and you can too.

Inclusion Ideas
- You can guide your classmates by allowing them to grab your elbow and walk one step behind you. This will allow them to let go if they want to.
- You can assist them in getting their food in the lunch line, and you can tell them where their food is on their plates.
- You can describe their environment to them, such as who is in the room, what the weather is like, and what equipment is around the gym.
- You can answer their questions and make sure they are included in conversations.
- Do not ever leave a room without telling them you are leaving. They may want to talk to you and not know you are gone, and this is embarrassing.
- You can make sure they are included in games and activities in your neighborhood or on the playground by adapting the equipment, the playing area, or the rules

information applies to students taught in the regular program as well as students enrolled in special classes or special schools for the blind.

Play Areas

The play area, indoors and out, should be a large, uncluttered space. As a safety precaution the play area should be free of nonessential equipment and unnecessary obstructions. For outdoor playing fields, hedges and shade trees are considered desirable boundaries rather than walls or fences, which present a certain element of danger for all students, including those who are visually impaired. Boundaries for games can be indicated by varying the composition of the court as, for example, having the in-bounds area composed of asphalt or an all-weather surface and the out-of-bounds area of sand or grass. Players will then be able to tell by foot sensitivity when they have stepped out of bounds. Newspaper tightly secured to mark the out-of-bounds area on a floor or field is an inexpensive method to achieve this effect.

Boundaries in the indoor playing area should be painted in white for the benefit of those students able to distinguish white. The gymnasium should be well lighted to present the best possible seeing conditions for those who are able to perceive light. A contrast in playing surfaces in the gymnasium can be achieved with wood and concrete or the composition surface, which is becoming increasingly popular. Rope taped to the floor is also a cheap and safe way to distinguish boundaries.

Students who are blind should have a thorough verbal introduction to an unfamiliar playing area before they are allowed to play. They should know the size and shape of the area and the nature of the boundaries before they engage in activity in the area. To orient the students, the teacher should walk with them around the area, including the locker room facility, describing the essential details and, when appropriate, having the student feel an area or object. Specific areas—such as entrances, exits, and other permanent fixtures—should be identified for the student. These permanent fixtures, commonly referred to by individuals who are blind as **anchor points**, serve as valuable reference points for orientation. In the play area, a few simple games or contests might be played to help the students gain familiarity with the playing area before engaging in strenuous play.

To guide children with visual impairments in running activities and to give them greater security, guide ropes and rings that are grasped in the hands may be suspended from wires strung across the gymnasium well above the heads of the participants. For outside running events, guide ropes can be placed along the path of the runners to guide them. The runners will need some type of warning at the finish line; this may be a knot tied at the end of the rope, or some sort of auditory signal such as a whistle may be sounded.

Special Equipment

Playground equipment for younger children may be the same type found on any playground, including swings, jungle gyms, and teeter-totters; however, greater care must be exercised in locating them by the child with a visual impairment to avoid possible injury. Swings should be constructed with no more than two swings on the stand; a third swing in the center is difficult to reach without danger when the other two swings are occupied. The use of guard rails or ground markers is a necessary safety precaution to prevent youngsters from bumping into equipment or being hit by flying swings.

It is recommended that balls to be used by students who are blind be larger in size and softer than regulation balls and that they be yellow or white to make them more easily seen by those with some vision. Bells, rattles, or buzzers inside the balls help to indicate their location to players who are blind.

A portable aluminum rail is a useful aid to the blind in bowling. The rail may be used on bowling alleys or on the gymnasium floor when plastic bowling sets are being used. Stationary bicycles, common equipment in physiology of exercise laboratories, are excellent for use by the blind in physical conditioning. Information concerning the purchase of the previously mentioned special equipment can be obtained through the American Foundation for the Blind (www.aft.org).

Only such playing equipment as is actually in use should be permitted in the playing area to ensure maximum safety. Children who are blind can memorize the location of the permanent fixtures but cannot avoid superfluous equipment that has been left in their way. The youngsters also can memorize the place in the storage closets where each item of equipment is kept. They are then capable of securing the needed items and returning them at the end of the play period.

Communication Aids

Instruction in physical education, similar to other curricular areas, requires that students read assigned material, take tests, and complete class reports. For the student who is blind, this usually requires some special considerations when disseminating written material. For some, such as those who can read printed material with the aid of a magnifier, the modifications will be minor. Others may need printed material that is enlarged with the use of fonts found in many computer software programs. In figure 9.3, the large print is illustrated. The American Printing House for the Blind (www.aph.org) publishes books with enlarged print.

For students unable to read printed letters that are one-quarter inch high, reliance on the Braille system is an alternative means of written communication. Braille is a tactile

Large-print books for the visually impaired use type

of the size shown in this sample. Fewer characters fit on each line; so the width of the line increases as does the length of the page in large-print books.

Figure 9.3 Sample of large print type size.

alphabet system developed in the nineteenth century by Louis Braille, a blind Frenchman. The Braille alphabet is a code system, not a language, consisting of raised dots arranged in various positions within a six-dot cell. Letters, numbers, mathematic symbols, and abbreviated words are represented in the Braille system by various configurations of raised dots (figure 9.4). Braille may be written by the use of a Braille writer, a device similar to a typewriter, or a slate and stylus to produce the raised dots. Portable electronic Braille notetakers are also available, as well as desktop computer-driven Braille embossers.

In many schools, resource teachers for the visually impaired are common. Cooperative planning with these professionals will assist the physical education teacher in selecting the best system for preparing written material. These experts also can help transfer assignments and tests into Braille or enlarged type. Some material may also be recorded, enabling the student to complete reading assignments and tests by listening to tapes.

Instructional Approach—Teaching

The introduction of new skills requires a kinesthetic approach. The teacher and perhaps a few of the students who have learned the skill may demonstrate it while those without sight examine with their hands the parts of the body involved. (An inspection of people and objects with the hands is called "brailling" in the vernacular of the blind.) In teaching the golf swing, for example, the student can stand behind the instructor with arms around the instructor and with hands on the instructor's hands. At times it may be helpful for the teacher to place the student's hands, feet, and other parts of the body into the desired positions. Lengthy verbal explanations should be avoided. However, clear and concise descriptions that accompany the kinesthetic approach may be used with great effectiveness. In planning the teaching of a skill, sighted instructors may gain greater insight into the problems that the skill will present to their students who are visually impaired if they close their eyes while performing the skill.

Teaching Games and Group Activities

A whistle is an essential piece of equipment for the instructor of students who are visually impaired, and it may be blown to identify for the students the teacher's location, to signal for attention, or for other purposes. A meaningful set of signals may be worked out with the students. Because of the noise found in most gymnasiums, a megaphone is useful to teachers in making their voices heard to the players. The visually impaired player will need to be given a great many details of the progress of the game that players with normal vision would observe naturally. For example, if a kickball game is in progress, the player will need to be told which players are on which bases, who will kick next, the placement of players on the field, and when an out or a score

Figure 9.4 The braille system for representing numbers and letters. (Courtesy of American Foundation for the Blind, Inc.)

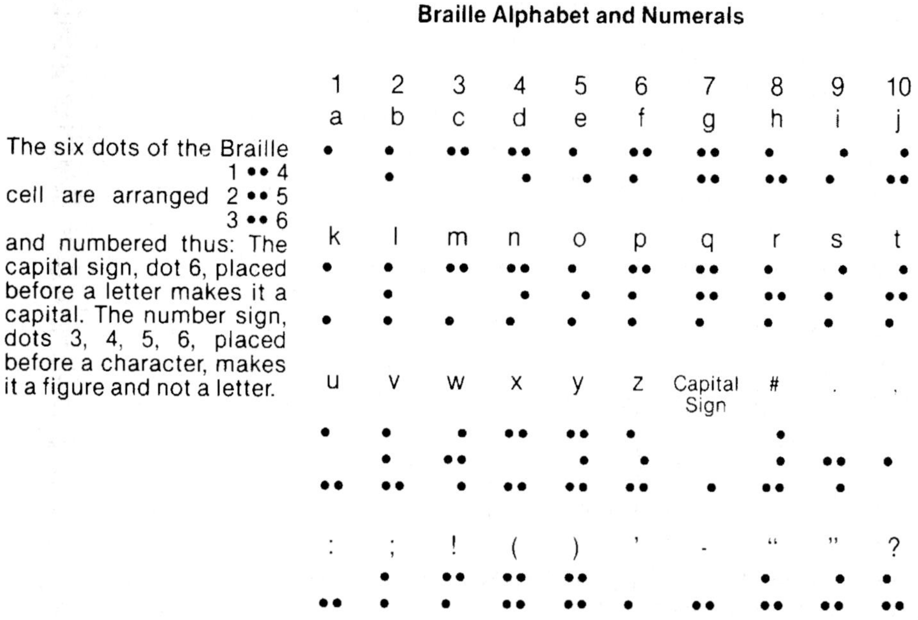

Braille Alphabet and Numerals

The six dots of the Braille cell are arranged 1 •• 4, 2 •• 5, 3 •• 6 and numbered thus: The capital sign, dot 6, placed before a letter makes it a capital. The number sign, dots 3, 4, 5, 6, placed before a character, makes it a figure and not a letter.

is made. Here again, the teacher can select the most useful information to give to the player.

Nearly all the varieties of activities offered to sighted students in the physical education curriculum can be presented to youngsters who are blind. Some require more adaptation than others, but children who are blind enjoy and need participation in the same games, sports, and physical activities as other children. In addition, the activities can help them overcome some of the problems, physical and emotional, that are the direct result of the visual impairments. Students with visual impairments should participate with their sighted peers. If special instructional assistance is needed, it should be in addition to general instruction in physical education.

Mobility and Orientation—Critical Considerations for Teaching the Child

The ability of a student with visual impairments to move about independently is one of the primary goals of his or her total educational development. Orientation refers to the ability of nonsighted students to use their remaining senses to relate their body position to other objects. Mobility refers to the ability to move from one point to a second point. Obviously, both skills are important if the student who is visually impaired is to be independent.

Although the specific techniques used in mobility training are provided by professionals with specialized preparation, physical educators can reinforce many of these concepts in games and play experiences. For instance, asking students to locate a sound (a radio or metronome, for example) in the gymnasium provides not only a useful experience but also one that reinforces the basic concept of direction taking. Blindfolding students who are sighted and having them engage in similar experiences offers them an opportunity to appreciate the mobility skills some students who are blind develop. Relay races with sighted, blindfolded students, and nonsighted children, also can be conducted with the use of a sound device at the end of each line or by using the aid of teammates' voices. For older students, more advanced games can be developed in which the sighted and the nonsighted students are asked to follow first a constant sound and then later an intermittent sound. Measures can then be taken to compare how far the sighted students veer from the path compared to their classmates who are visually impaired. Such comparisons may help sighted students understand how adept many students with visual impairments are in moving efficiently toward a sound or signal.

Teachers also can help reinforce the student's skill in walking with a sighted guide. This technique requires that the nonsighted individual grasp a sighted person's arm just above the elbow. With the hand on the guide's arm, the student who is blind then walks about one-half step behind the guide. The person who is visually impaired must learn to follow the guide and to "read" movement or changes in the guide's body position. The guide must learn to provide verbal cues such as "step up," "step down," "turn to the right," and so on, when leading a person who is blind. Other students in the class should be shown the proper way to walk with their visually impaired classmates. This will not only provide the nonsighted individual an opportunity to practice trailing with a number of different guides, but also will develop a skill that sighted students can employ to assist others with visual impairments outside the school.

Guidelines for Free Play Activity

Although children should be encouraged to use the playground equipment on their own during the leisure hours, they should be given explicit instruction in the use of the play equipment for their own safety and for that of others. All children should be taught the skills involved in the use of the apparatus and the safety measures that must be observed. This is especially true of children with visual impairments.

The teacher may find some hesitancy on the part of some children who are blind to play on the equipment. This is most likely to be true of those who have led extremely sheltered lives. The teacher must begin with the children at their level of motor skill development and their level of self-confidence and strengthen both by encouraging participation at the tempo they will accept. In very young children and very timid ones, it may be necessary to inspire a desire for carefree play on the equipment.

Chair seats on swings and teeter-totters require less balancing skill and promote confidence and security. In introducing these pieces of equipment, the teacher should tell the children something about how they look and how they are used while the children explore them with their hands. Each child may be assisted in sitting on the equipment and trying it with the help of the teacher. A reassuring grasp on the shoulders or arm promotes confidence during the first attempts. When a certain amount of confidence has been developed, mounting and dismounting and safety precautions can be taught to the children.

The safe and enjoyable use of the slide requires careful instruction by the teacher. The children must be taught to wait their turn at the bottom of the ladder and not to climb the steps until the one who is having a turn signals by clapping the hands that he or she is going down the slide. Upon reaching the bottom of the slide, the child must inform the one who is waiting at the top that the slide is clear.

To encourage reluctant children the teacher may first have to help them sit on the slide near the end and hold them as they slide down. This may be done several times at increasing heights. Children should be shown how they may slow down the speed of the slide by forcing their feet against the sides.

Jungle gyms and parallel ladders can be dangerous if improperly used by either sighted or nonsighted children. Children often have sufficient confidence to get on the bars but do not have sufficient skills and strength to perform with safety. A low single bar can be utilized to develop sufficient arm and hand strength and to develop skill in hanging or swinging the body through space. Or a child may be started out very low on the jungle gym where the danger of falling would be minimal. On the parallel ladders, a thick board may be placed between the rungs of the two upright ladders of a very high ladder. This lessens the distance of the drop. The board can also be used as a bouncing board to spring up and down on, which is an excellent exercise in itself.

Special Safety Considerations for glasses and the eyes

The student who wears glasses for corrected vision may present a safety problem in vigorous sports participation. If the glasses cannot be removed during play, the student should either wear the special type of rugged glasses made to withstand rough treatment or wear glass guards. Many glasses today are plastic and designed to be shatter proof. While these improvements are excellent, they do not necessarily lessen the need for protective eyeware. It may be necessary to give the glasses protection and support in some instances by placing adhesive tape over the stems of the glasses at the temples.

Another problem with which the teacher must be concerned is a condition of **retinal detachment**. Individuals with partial sight who suffer from progressive myopia sometimes have this condition, in which there is partial detachment of the retina from the choroid. It will be necessary to safeguard such individuals from situations that might produce a blow to the head, as such a jar may cause further detachment that can result in total blindness. Contact sports and diving are contraindicated for them. However, persons with corrected myopia can participate in contact sports with safety. The physical education teacher should be informed of any contraindications by contacting the student's parents, or eliciting this information in an interview with parents.

Physical Activities for Primary Grades

In the primary grades, physical education activities and games are often utilized as tools in the learning of reading, number concepts, and other areas of study. There are many methods of doing this, and each primary school teacher has worked out numerous ways that might be employed in teaching children who are blind. Many activities suggest themselves, and the suggestions made in subsequent paragraphs are given only as a foundation from which other ideas will spring.

For teaching number concepts, the turns taken in certain activities may be counted, such as the number of times a ball is bounced or the steps taken on a balance beam. In developing reading readiness the background of meaningful experience is expanded, and toward this end numerous physical activities may be utilized. Exploration of the surrounding areas, following paths and sidewalks, going up and down hills, and climbing trees are a few possibilities.

Many of the singing games and mimetic games of the primary grade level need no adaptation for those who are blind. A game such as London Bridge does not need any modification. Other games may need only slight modifications to offset the disadvantage of being unable to see the other players. In the game Red Light and Green Light, which is recommended for children who are blind because it encourages them to run freely and swiftly, the teacher should name those who are moving on the call of "red light," because the children who are blind will not be able to tell which runners should be brought back.

Because persons who are blind need to develop greater spatial awareness, activities in physical education should promote learning to move the body through space and to relate the body's location to other people or objects that share the space. Motor exploration activities are an excellent vehicle for such learning. In motor exploration, students are not trying to find the most effective way to make a movement; rather they are experimenting with a number of different ways of moving to discover the one that is most efficient for and most satisfying to them. In the process they learn a great deal about moving the body through space. Suggested motor activities for exploration of space are as follows:

Movement While Stationary

The objective in these activities is to learn how the body can be moved without locomotion.

1. Starting with the arms at the sides, move them up and down. (If the arms are bare, the wind currents created by the movements can be felt on the arms.)
2. Move any part of the body except the arms but do not move from the original space.
3. Lift up one leg and then try to lift up the other. (Because this is impossible to do, it teaches the concept of motor limitations.)

Exploring Locomotion

Elementary skills of locomotion are rolling, crawling, walking, running, jumping, and variations of these. Exploration of these skills helps children to learn the variety of ways the body can be moved from place to place. In teaching locomotor skills to children who are blind, it is important to clearly identify for the student a stationary point where all movement skills begin and end. This will help students to feel secure and confident as they engage in various movement activities.

1. Move from one place to another, not allowing the feet to touch the floor.
2. Move about the play area, trying to create an impression of being tall, small, wide, flat, round, and so on.

Communication through Movement

In this phase of exploratory movement, children learn the ways in which the body may be used to communicate emotions and ideas.

1. Move like, and make noises like, a dog. (Previous to this activity, children will need an opportunity for brailling a dog, listening to it bark, and developing an idea of how it moves.)
2. Move in a manner to show fear, anger, happiness, and so on. This also helps the children learn to display emotion.
3. Move to depict a gentle rain, a hot sunny day, and a snowstorm. Important concepts about weather can also be taught through this activity.

Manipulation of Objects

Having discovered movements that can be made with the body, the child is ready to explore the use of the body in the manipulation of objects. The ball is the most common object of manipulation in physical education and so it will be used in the sample activities.

1. Make the ball move, using the hand, foot, head, shoulders, and so on.
2. Move the ball so that it makes different sounds.
3. Throw a ball (suspended from the ceiling by a cord) at different speeds.

Relaxation

Muscular relaxation is another activity that lends itself to exploration. Learning to relax is not always easy, and participation in the exploratory activities helps to develop an understanding of the process. Suggestions for such activities are made in the discussion of relaxation in chapter 29 on the CD.

Spatial Awareness

Excellent activities for teaching spatial awareness also can be presented by the direct or traditional method. Possibilities include the following:

1. Walk in a straight line. (Children who are blind have a tendency to veer to the side of their dominant hand or weave back and forth.)
2. Follow sounds; for example, a drum beat, a voice, footsteps.

3. Slide a hand along a rope that encloses a small area while walking around it; retrace the steps without touching the rope.
4. While walking, turn on command to make a ninety-degree turn, a forty-five-degree turn, and so on.
5. Follow a cord stretched between two points. At the farther point, release the hold on the cord and return to the starting point.

Physical Activities for Older Children

There are many games suitable for elementary and high school students that need no modification. Many dual competitive games such as arm wrestling or leg wrestling can be presented without modification. In tag games and other games in which the players need to make their location known to the one who is "It," the players may make vocal sounds. When sighted players are participating in the game, these students may join hands with a nonsighted player and play as a couple. Certain games with balls such as dodge ball and wall ball are easily modified by slight rule changes that prevent seeing players from having undue advantage and provide for the calling out by players so that opponents who are blind can locate them by the sound of their voice.

Some games lend themselves more easily than others to adaptation for playing by students who are blind or have limited vision. As a guide for the selection of those games that can be readily used without much modification, Buell (1974) suggests these eight characteristics:

1. Blindfolding one or two players
2. Sounds whereby the sightless know what is happening
3. Different duties for students who are blind and partially seeing
4. Running to a goal easily found by those who are totally blind
5. Limited playing area such as gymnasium or tennis court
6. Direct contact as in wrestling
7. Line or chain formations
8. The possibility of players pairing up in couples

Because individuals who are blind rely so much on sound to receive their impressions, they are particularly receptive to the rhythm not only of music but also of the human activities that surround them. The knowledge thus gained of rhythm patterns is a valuable asset in learning to dance. All types of dance may be taught to those who are blind: musical games, folk dances, modern dance, and social dancing. All types of dance can be taught at almost any age level as soon as children have learned to move freely, with confidence and skill, through space.

Although the needs of those with visual impairments are similar to that of the sighted, special attention must be directed toward the physical fitness of these students. Winnick and Short (1985) reported that the fitness level of students who are visually impaired was inferior to that of their nonimpaired peers. The reason for this is generally attributed to the restricted activity level of the visually impaired. Because of their visual limitations these children do not experience some of the natural movement and play associated with an active childhood. Special efforts, therefore, must be directed toward ensuring that those who are visually impaired participate in programs that encourage the development of physical fitness. Without such a program, the lack of physical activity will lead to further losses of stamina, strength, and flexibility. Weitzman (1985) advocates that walking programs, if done with sufficient intensity, are very effective in helping those who are visually impaired improve their cardiorespiratory levels of fitness. Equally important is the observation that for some students who are visually impaired the "high" associated with being physically active leads to an improved self-concept. Rowing, cycling, dance aerobics, and cross-country skiing are all activities high in endurance that students who are visually impaired, with modifications, can engage in successfully. Programs should be structured with goals so that change in performance can be documented and reinforced.

Bloomquist (2003a) recommends that when a teacher is testing individuals for exercise, he or she should use manual and visual orientation of all testing equipment and facilities, and keep the facility clear of clutter. She explains that there is greater difficulty in mobility when the visual impairment is due to loss of field of vision than when the individual has loss of acuity. Nonetheless, her recommendations for activities include individual sports such as swimming, weight training, dance, track and field, golf, and aerobics. Goal ball competition, a game played with all individuals blindfolded and a ball that makes a sound, is also recommended.

Sports

Students who are blind participate in many team and individual sports. The type and the modification depend upon the extent of the student's visual impairment. Some students who are visually impaired, for instance, have sufficient residual vision that they can participate in various sports with their sighted peers. For those with more serious visual impairments, however, the modifications are more extensive and require careful planning on the part of the teacher.

Popular team sports include basketball, football, and volleyball. Students who are partially sighted adapt well to **basketball**; those who are legally blind will require major modifications of this activity. For instance, the player without sight will find shooting baskets and playing such games

as Around-the-World and Twenty-One enjoyable. Students with severe visual impairments may find participating in the game as their team's free-throw shooter a fulfilling activity and one that allows them to be a part of a team experience.

Football is a popular sport in which many visually impaired students can successfully participate. Those with limited vision can play on the line as a center or guard. Rule modifications are simple, including having the player who is carrying the ball shout to identify his or her position. Some partially sighted players have become so proficient at football that they have participated on regular high school teams.

Volleyball, particularly the lead-up game of newcomb, is an enjoyable activity that many partially sighted students can play. In this game, the ball is played on the first bounce or may be caught and thrown rather than hit while in the air. Students also may be allowed to move toward the net, feel the top of the net, and throw the volleyball over the net. Time limits can be imposed on how long the ball may be held and the number of consecutive throws limited.

There are many individual sports that students who are visually impaired have found enjoyable. Some of these include **track and field, bowling, golf, wrestling, gymnastics, and swimming**.

Track and field is such a popular sport among the blind that many of the residential schools sponsor interscholastic teams. The competitive events usually included are the 50- and 100-yard dashes, the mile and two-mile run, the standing high jump and long jump, the triple jump, and the throwing events.

In **training for running events in track,** the participant who is totally blind can run with a partially seeing partner by using the partner's footsteps as a guide or by running at his or her side, lightly and intermittently brushing the partner's arm. Overhead wires with drop cords that slide along the wire that runners can grasp in their hands will aid them in keeping a steady course. Guide wires about hip high along one side of the track, which students can slide their hands along as they run, are good for the training period. Later, as confidence and skills develop, another wire is placed on the other side so that runners run between—and are guided by—them without placing their hands on the wires. This permits greater speed in running. If the runners swerve off the course, the wires brush against them and remind them to adjust their position. A less elaborate but effective system for assisting the visually impaired runner is to use a rope instead of the guidewire. In this system large knots are tied toward the ends of the rope to warn the runner that the end of the rope is near. To avoid rope burns, a relay baton can be placed over the rope and held by the runner while running. In running events, teammates or coaches are stationed at the end of the run to serve as callers. Their task is to call the runner's name, thus providing a constant cue to guide the runner. Some investigators have reported that use of sighted guides and guide wires are less restrictive and generate faster times than using a caller.

Bowling and golf are very popular individual sports for students who are blind or visually impaired. Bowlers who are blind orient themselves by feeling the sides of the alley or by using the guide rail if it is available. With golf, the only adaptation is the necessity of playing with a sighted person who locates the ball and provides verbal feedback. Swimming offers an unusually fine activity for the person who is visually impaired. The nature of the confined environment combined with the availability of lane markers makes this activity one that many students who are blind have participated in with little modification. An audible locator such as a buzzer or battery-operated radio may be placed at the ends of the pool lane to assist swimmers who are visually impaired with their turns. Many swimmers who are visually impaired count the number of strokes per lap and use this as a guide for marking the end of the pool and for making turns. Diving may also be successfully undertaken by individuals who are blind. The only modification necessary here is helping the person who is blind locate the end of the board. Most prefer to hold onto the diving board rail and then crawl on hands and knees to the end of the board.

Wrestling is the sport in which students with visual impairments have most distinguished themselves. Athletes who are blind have successfully competed against sighted opponents at the high school level, university level, and the Olympics. The only rule modification that is necessary is that wrestlers who are blind begin the match in a standing position with a hand-touch start and initial contact must be from the front.

Unfortunately, students who are visually impaired have only recently been introduced to **winter sports**. Skiing is rapidly becoming a very popular sport among the blind. This activity requires that the person ski with a partner. Some ski instructors prefer to ski in front of the blind skier, leading them down the slope, whereas others prefer to ski behind, providing the visually impaired skier with verbal directions. Likewise, many students who are blind are finding ice skating enjoyable. Orientation to the skating surface and boundaries is the only necessary modification.

Two sports—**goal ball and beep baseball**—have been specifically developed for participation by individuals who are visually impaired. In goal ball, three players compose a team. The objective of the game is to roll a large ball with a bell in it across the opponent's goal while the other team tries to stop it. The defensive team may stop the ball from a sitting, lying, or standing position. Each player must wear a helmet, mouth piece, elbow pads, and blindfold. The team that scores the most total goals in two five-minute halves

wins the match. Because all players wear blindfolds, this is an excellent activity to encourage interaction between sighted and nonsighted players.

Beep baseball, which was introduced in 1975, is governed by the National Beep Baseball Association (www.nbba .org). Similar to baseball, this game is played on a regulation size diamond. Each team has five players who are blind plus a sighted catcher and pitcher. All equipment information can be obtained through the website for The National Beep Baseball Association. The ball is a regulation sixteen-inch softball with an audible device inside. Only two bases are used, first and third. Each base is a thirty-six-inch tall plastic cone with a speaker in the top. The sighted players serve as the pitcher and catcher for their own team and as spotters when their team is in the field. The role of the spotters is to help their nonsighted peers locate the ball. Each batter is allowed seven pitches with fouls counting as strikes except on the last strike. When a fair ball is hit, one of the two bases is activated by the umpire and emits a buzzing sound. The batter must run to the buzzing base. The concept of running to either first or third as randomly determined by the umpire is designed to equate the reaction time of batter and fielder. If the batter reaches the base before being tagged, a run is scored. The team who scores the most runs in six innings with three outs per inning wins the game.

Deaf and Hard-of-Hearing

Auditory losses of varying degrees of severity constitute as a group one of the most common disabilities affecting children and adults. Statistics show that approximately 9 percent of the American population experience some hearing loss (The National Center for Health Statistics, 1994). These hearing losses range from slight deviation from normal hearing to total loss of sound perception. Less than 10 percent of the children and youth enrolled in schools for the deaf are totally devoid of hearing.

Too often in the past a hearing loss has been considered to be a "handicapping" condition in much the same way as the loss of sight and to affect the individual in much the same way—socially and psychologically. Such thinking was to be expected in view of the fact that both conditions arise from a complete or partial loss of one of the senses. However, this tendency to regard a visual and hearing loss as similar has retarded a true consideration of the implications of a hearing loss. Helen Keller reflected on her own life and declared that deafness was a far greater hardship than blindness. She observed that blindness cuts people off from things, deafness cuts people off from people (Dolnick, 1993). Despite this dire perception of hearing loss as a condition that isolates people, deaf individuals argue that deafness is not a disability.

They offer that deaf people constitute a subculture and that they comprise a linguistic minority. The deaf argue that treatment and educational programs should not focus on "fixing" them but rather they should be recognized and accepted as unique and culturally different. While this view of the deaf person as an ethnic minority is not universally accepted, the movement has led to some rethinking of educational and treatment programs for the deaf and hard-of-hearing. This includes important questions of where, what, and how to teach this population. Strident supporters of the deaf culture movement suggest, too, that deaf individuals are best reared and educated in settings with members of their own culture. Given that 90 percent of deaf children are born to hearing parents, this creates some challenging concerns for parents and educators in developing and delivering the desired educational programs and activities. The goal is not only to assist the deaf and hard-of-hearing in learning but to recognize their unique sociocultural perspective.

The Nature and Causes of Hearing Loss

Individuals with hearing loss may be referred to as deaf or hard-of-hearing depending on the degree of loss and, to some extent, on the communication ability of the individual. The term "deaf" may be used to encompass all forms of hearing loss as is common among groups such as the American Athletic Association for the Deaf (AAAD). Within educational settings, primarily for funding or school purposes, it is common to make a distinction between the terms "deaf" and "hard-of-hearing."

In working with students with hearing impairment, the terms "deaf individual," or "deaf student," is not considered in violation of the person-first language within the delivery of services to individuals with disabilities. For the most part, in disability advocacy, this regard is the exception. Individuals who are deaf often prefer the reference "deaf person." This is part of their identity and they do not consider themselves disabled. Issues of inclusion in schools has challenged the notion that it is the least restrictive environment in which to learn for people who are deaf. Debate by Butterfield (1991) and Decker (1993) addresses these issues.

In 1975, the Executives of American Schools for the Deaf defined the terms "deaf," "hard-of-hearing," and "hearing impaired" (Larson & Miller, 1978) as follows:

Deaf—a person who is unable, with or without a hearing aid, to process speech through the ears alone.

Hard-of-hearing—a person who has a condition which makes it difficult to understand speech, with or without hearing aids. Individuals who are hard-of-hearing, therefore, have hearing that is deficient but functional. Deaf persons, on the other hand, have nonfunctional hearing.

Hearing impaired—a generic term used by some individuals to identify those with hearing impairments, including those who are deaf or hard-of-hearing. The deaf community rejects the term "impaired," arguing that: (1) they are not impaired, and (2) the term "impaired" suggests that they are deficient and in need of medical treatment.

Modern educational methods for students with hearing loss make the maximum use of the residual hearing that they possess. Consequently, it is important that educators teach students who are hard-of-hearing more nearly like hearing students than like students who are deaf.

Hearing loss may also be described in terms of its age of onset. Hearing impairments may be either congenital, present at birth, or adventitious, occurring later in life. The child who is deaf from birth will not be able to learn to speak spontaneously. The needs of this youngster are very different from those of a child who acquires a hearing loss after the age of seven, when speech and language are well developed. Frequently, the terms "prelingual" and "postlingual" are used to distinguish the impact of a hearing loss on the ability of the student to speak. Those with a postlingual hearing loss normally, with special assistance, retain the ability to speak.

Like the eye, the ear is a complex organ, capable of discriminating the intensity and frequency of various sounds. Sound is first received by the outer ear and transmitted to the middle ear before it finally reaches the inner ear, where it is transferred to the brain via the auditory nerve. As illustrated in figure 9.5, the function of the outer ear is to collect sound waves and transmit them via the auditory canal to the middle ear. In the middle ear, the sound passes from the tympanic membrane to the ossicular chain, where the vibrations created by the motion of the stapes, incus, and malleus move the sound from the outer to the inner ear. The inner ear is divided into two sections, the vestibule and the cochlea. The latter part, the cochlea, is the critical element in hearing. As the stapes bone moves, the oval window moves, transmitting the sound from the middle ear to the fluid-filled cochlea. Inside the cochlea are thousands of tiny hair cells that are set in motion. Movement of the hair cells in turn causes electrical impulses to be sent to the brain.

Also located in the inner ear are three small loops called the semicircular canals. Although the semicircular canals do not contribute to the hearing process, they are extremely important in helping individuals maintain balance.

Hearing disabilities are usually structural in origin, and damage to any part of the ear, outer, middle, or inner, can result in a hearing loss. The three types of hearing loss are classified as conductive, sensorineural, or mixed.

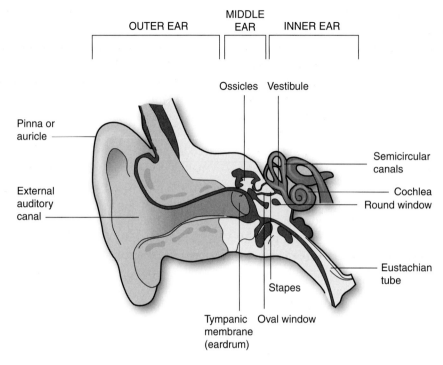

Figure 9.5 Diagram of the human ear.

Conductive Hearing Loss

This disorder is caused by a physical obstruction to the conduction of the sound waves to the inner ear and the deafness is never total. This is due to causes such as impacted wax, which can be readily removed by a physician, or an infection, which can be treated medically with relatively good chances for arresting or improving it, particularly in its early stages. A hearing aid is very useful in improving a hearing loss due to conduction difficulties. The other cause of conductive hearing loss is otitis media (infection of the middle ear) due to colds, sinus infections, allergies, or blocked Eustachian tubes (Bloomquist, 2003b).

Communication Techniques For Deaf Persons

- Oral method
- Total communication approach
- Speech reading
- American sign language
- Finger spelling
- Cued speech
- Bilingual/bicultural system
- Hearing aid
- Cochlear device

Sensorineural Hearing Loss

Sensorineural hearing loss is usually a more serious condition and less likely to be improved by medical treatment. It is caused by damage to the cells or nerve fibers that receive and transmit the sound stimuli. The loss of hearing may range from mild to total disability. Some degree of sensorineural deafness is common among the aging. A certain amount of high-tone nerve deafness appears to be part of the natural process of aging in many people, just as many of the elderly suffer hardening of the arteries and deterioration of eyesight. This condition is in fact so prevalent that the most common cause of nerve deafness is attributed to aging.

In children and young adults the most frequent cause of sensorineural deafness is congenital, the nerve having been injured or destroyed before or during birth. However, research into the causes of deafness in children has shown that a number of cases heretofore classified as hereditary were actually associated with certain contagious diseases that the mother contracted during the early months of pregnancy. Rubella, mumps, and influenza all have been indicated as causes of deafness in infants whose mothers were afflicted during early pregnancy.

Cases of sensorineural deafness that have a noncongenital origin are classified as acquired deafness. Among the common causes are brain infections such as meningitis, brain fever, and sleeping sickness and communicable diseases such as scarlet fever, measles, influenza, and others.

At one time it was considered that hearing aids were of little value to those with sensorineural hearing loss, but with the improvement of the quality of hearing aids, it has become possible to successfully fit more and more persons with this type of hearing loss. Many cochlear implants have been performed successfully, allowing deaf people to hear.

Prolonged loud sounds of any spectra can produce a temporary threshold shift (auditory fatigue); recovery usually takes place within a day. The more intense the sound, the shorter the exposure time necessary before a temporary fatigue takes place. Continual exposure eventually produces a permanent hearing loss. As a general rule, the ears should not be exposed to sounds over 130 decibels (units of loudness) longer than momentarily. There is some evidence to suggest that prolonged listening to amplified music is causing hearing losses in young men and women, especially among the musicians themselves. In these cases, the hearing loss occurs in the higher frequency ranges. The combined sounds of the environment, such as street noises in a city, often reach levels of intensity that may cause hearing loss.

Mixed Loss

When both conductive loss and sensorineural loss are present, the result is classified as a mixed loss. Individuals who experience this disorder may have what is referred to as a significant air conduction/bone conduction gap. If the conductive aspect of the hearing loss is stabilized, the probability of receiving assistance through the use of a hearing aid is good. The individual then functions similarly to those who experience only a conductive loss.

Measurement and Classification of Hearing Loss

An audiologist is a professional who specializes in assessing hearing loss. With the use of an instrument known as an audiometer, the audiologist measures hearing acuity, the sharpness or clarity with which sound is received. The audiologist uses the audiometer to present tones that vary in intensity (loudness) and frequencies (pitch). The results of the hearing examination are recorded on a graph called an audiogram (figure 9.6).

Two units of measurement are noted on the audiogram. A decibel (dB) refers to loudness of sound. A loud shout at a distance of one foot is measured at 110 decibels, whereas ordinary conversation is about 60 decibels.

Degrees of hearing loss are classified differently by various authorities, but the classification most frequently used in educational circles divides the losses into five categories. These include:

- **Slight (27 to 40 dB)**—may have difficulty hearing faint or distant speech. Although some students with slight hearing loss will require speech reading instruction as well as speech correction, normally these individuals

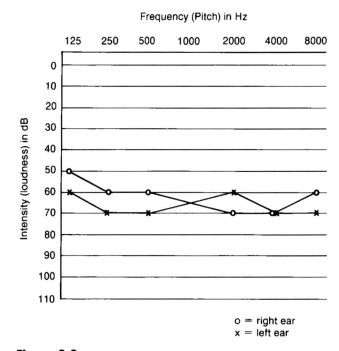

Figure 9.6 Example of an audiogram.

will not have difficulty in school and will experience no disadvantages in the physical education class.

- **Mild (41 to 55 dB)**—can understand conversational speech at a distance of three to five feet. Obviously, these individuals are unable to follow much of the conversation and instruction in the physical education class without special assistance. Several forms of help—including hearing aids, speech reading, and favorable seating or roving privileges—can be utilized to improve communication with students who have a moderate hearing loss. (The use of the latter in physical education is discussed later in this chapter.)

- **Marked (56 to 70 dB)**—conversation must be loud to be understood. Students with this degree of loss have difficulty following group discussion. It is also likely that these individuals have a limited vocabulary and speech is affected. The aids identified for students with mild hearing loss also benefit those with this greater degree of hearing loss.

- **Severe (71 to 90 dB)**—means that the individual may not hear loud voices one foot from the ear. The student with a severe hearing loss may be able to discriminate vowels but not all consonants. Like the student with a marked loss, this individual has difficulty with speech and needs the assistance of aids and special instructional techniques in those subjects that require a high level of language skills.

- **Profound (91 + dB)**—cannot rely on hearing as their primary channel for communication. Although these individuals may have some residual hearing and, therefore, hear loud noises, they are more aware of vibrations than of tonal patterns. It is probable that children with a profound hearing loss will need the assistance of an interpreter. Most of these students, however, are capable of participating in the regular physical education class if they have not been deprived of these experiences earlier in their development.

Teaching and Communicating

The most obvious adjustment that the deaf person must make is the loss of the normal means of communication. A new way of receiving messages must be found if the disability is acquired after speech has been learned. If the loss of hearing is congenital or acquired before speech has been learned, a means of conveying as well as receiving communications must be learned. Deaf persons who could not speak were once taught signing as the sole means of communication, but deaf children are now being taught to speak by the technique of properly utilizing the mouth and vocal cords in the production of sounds. They also receive speech reading and usually signing instruction.

Considerable controversy exists among those who work with the deaf as to the extent to which deaf people should be taught to communicate by speech, speech reading, and signing. One faction contends that signing should not be taught at all and that the educational efforts should be directed entirely toward learning to speech read and to speak because such communication skills are closer to normalcy. This approach is known as the **oral method.**

Opponents say that signing, speech reading, and speech should all be taught to give the deaf child the widest possible communication skills. Their approach is referred to as the **total communication approach** and is frequently referred to as a philosophy rather than an educational method. The emphasis with total communication is placed on maximizing the student's ability to communicate using the best of both systems.

Educators should recognize, however, that students who speech read do not read every word, but rather they follow conversation by observing the speaker's lips, mouth, and facial expressions for clues to determine the essence of what has been said. Obviously, this is a difficult skill and one that requires considerable effort, practice, and training to master. In tests using simple sentences, deaf people recognize perhaps three or four words in every ten (Dolnick, 1993). Not all students with hearing impairments speech read.

For those students who are taught to communicate manually, the **American Sign Language (ASL)** system is frequently used. With this approach, hand gestures and body positions are used to represent words and concepts. For many words, the gesture is closely related to the action being described. Physical education teachers, therefore, may find that some communication with ASL is possible even without formal training. For example, the sign for throw is the arm motion of overhand throwing. Figure 9.7 presents other signs frequently used in the physical education setting.

A second form of manual communication is **finger spelling,** in which there is a distinct hand position for each letter in the alphabet (see figure 9.8 on page 215). In this system each word is spelled letter by letter. Total reliance on finger spelling as the sole means of communication is not feasible because of the amount of time required to spell each word. This system, therefore, is frequently combined with other methods. Finger spelling is particularly helpful for spelling words and proper names for which no sign exists. Deaf-blind persons also can make use of finger spelling by feeling the user's hand to decipher the letters.

Cued speech (Cornett, 1982), a supplement to speech reading and a substitute for signing, is a communication approach used by some individuals who are deaf. It consists of eight signs or shapes of the hand and four hand positions that signify all the vowels and consonants in the English language (other positions apply to other languages). These hand shapes and positions are used by a speaker to enable the deaf person to know which specific vowel or consonant sound is being made by the speaker in cases where the difference between the vowels or consonants cannot be distinguished by watching the lips and mouth of the speaker, because of the great similarity in the way the sounds are formed. For example, the words "bat," "mat," and "pat" are similar enough to appear to the speech reader to be the same; cued speech eliminates the confusion by informing the speech reader which of the consonants is being used.

Some argue that all of the communication systems for deaf individuals, including total communication, have serious limitations and thus the search continues for alternative approaches. A new approach, known as the bilingual/ bicultural system, has generated considerable controversy. In this approach, deaf students are first taught ASL and then eventually build on that knowledge to learn English as a second language. Critics of this approach fear that too much time will be devoted to ASL and not enough to the fundamentals of learning to write and read English. Hearing parents of deaf children fear, too, that the bilingual/bicultural movement will be too oriented toward a deaf culture and, therefore, potentially isolating the child from them and other hearing children and adults.

Hearing Aids

Students who are hard-of-hearing often have residual hearing, and, therefore, many find a hearing aid an invaluable assistance in achieving total development. The purpose of the hearing aid is to amplify sound. Contrary to the generally

Athletics

Ball

Start

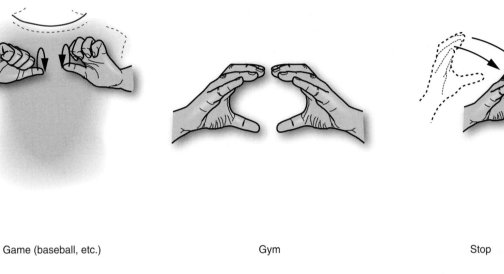

Game (baseball, etc.)

Gym

Stop

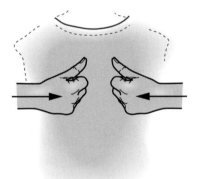
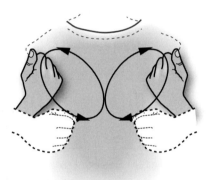
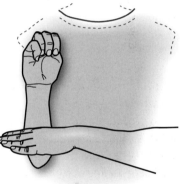

Referee

Team

Whistle

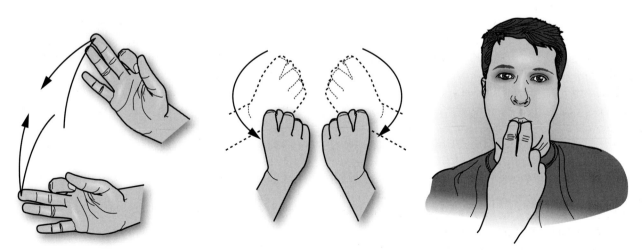

Figure 9.7 Example of signs commonly used in physical education instruction. These can be easily learned and used in class by teachers.

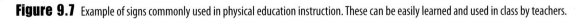

Finish

Bounce

Dive

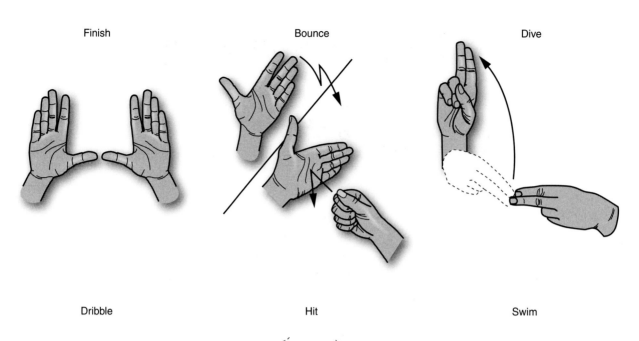

Dribble

Hit

Swim

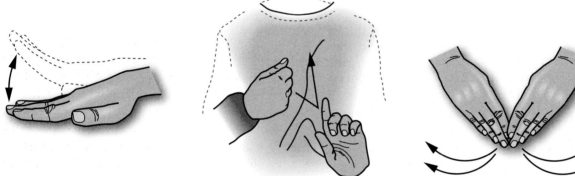

Good job

Tag

Throw

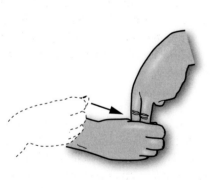

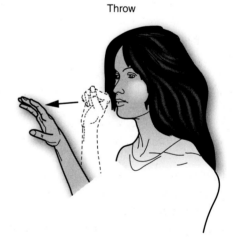

Figure 9.7 *Continued*

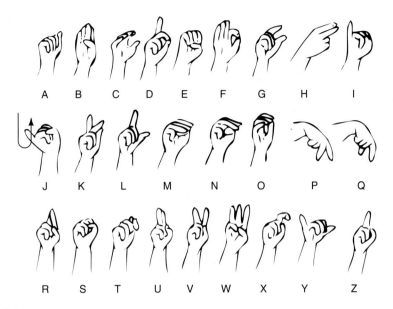

Figure 9.8 Finger spelling alphabet.

held concept, hearing aids do not make speech and sound clearer; those who hear distorted sounds will still experience distortion with a hearing aid. The value of hearing aids lies in enabling children with severe hearing impairments to learn to recognize the sound of their own name or in assisting those with a moderate loss to hear their own speech.

Although there are many different types of hearing aids, they are usually worn in one of three places: behind the ear, on the chest, or in eyeglasses. Each aid is composed of three primary components: an amplifier, a microphone, and a receiver. The microphone collects the sound; it is then amplified and transmitted to the ear. Students should be encouraged to wear their hearing aids throughout the day. It is important that they learn how to use the aid to help them interpret conversation. This cannot be done with proficiency if the student refuses to wear the aid or turns it off periodically. In the physical education setting the hearing aid should be worn as much as possible. Given the noise level in the gymnasium, and the inability of the hearing aid to selectively filter certain sounds, some students may choose to remove the hearing aid on occasion. Students also will need to remove the hearing aid for selected activities, such as swimming and team sports that involve body contact. The physical education teacher should be cognizant of when the student is or is not wearing the hearing aid and adjust the process for communicating accordingly.

The hearing aid should be periodically checked to ensure that it is properly functioning. Two common problems are batteries that are low and an ear mold that needs to be cleaned. Occasionally, the cord that connects the microphone to the receiver will be broken or defective. The hearing-impaired specialist or resource teacher can quickly teach the physical education teacher to detect and fix many of the minor problems associated with hearing aids, so that children need not be put at a disadvantage due to an easily remedied problem.

Individuals with profound bilateral deafness may benefit from implantation of a cochlear device. The cochlear implant consists of an external speech processor and implanted electrodes. A small wire runs from the receiver via the implant to the cochlea. Sounds are picked up by a microphone worn near the ear and transmitted through a wire to the speech processor, which converts the sound into an electrical signal sent to the cochlear implant. In selected patients the implant has produced excellent results. The cochlear implant enhances speech reading, recognition of sound, and allows for the discrimination of some words (Silverstein, Wolfson, & Rosenberg, 1992). Some deaf advocates argue that the cochlear implant is an invasion of the ear and a denial of deafness and its associated culture (Dolnick, 1993).

Adjustment

In addition to their loss of the usual conversational method of communication with others, those with severe deafness experience other losses that cause difficult problems of adjustment. The personal and social development of deaf children and youth is frequently reported as unusual. Keane, Tannenbaum, & Krapf (1992) cite several studies indicating that the deaf, as a group, manifest higher degrees of impulsivity, egocentricity, and rigidity than the population at large. Teachers and parents (Strika, 1989), too, report that deaf children appear to have more social and emotional problems than hearing children of the same age.

There are several factors that might help to explain the reported high frequency of social and emotional adjustment problems of deaf children and youth. These include:

- level of parental acceptance;
- availability of appropriate role models;
- reduction in level of communication and interaction; and
- limited school and extracurricular activities.

Solutions to help eradicate some of the reported social and emotional problems include: parent education and counselling programs; greater involvement of deaf individuals in programs for young deaf children; increased fluency in sign language on the part of parents, teachers, and other adults important in the life of a deaf child; and expanded and enriched educational and social opportunities (Fischgrund, 1994).

The early childhood literature recognizes that play is critical to the development of a healthy personality and physical education teachers are in a unique role to foster the social and emotional development of deaf and hard-of-hearing children and youth. First and foremost is the need to create an educational environment in which the deaf feel that they are part of and welcome in the physical education setting. Second, it is essential to develop success experiences so that deaf and hard-of-hearing students feel that they are progressing and enjoying the opportunity to participate in and learn various concepts related to movement. Third is the need to expand the ability of the teacher to communicate so that the student recognizes that his or her form of communication is accepted and valued. Additional tips for teaching students who are deaf and hard-of-hearing will be found later in the chapter.

Without the orientation of the auditory background and the symbols and warnings that are customarily provided by sound perception, the deaf are prone to frustrations and anxieties. This is particularly true in cases in which hearing is lost in adolescence or adulthood. The longer a person has had full powers of hearing, the more difficult is the adjustment to a severe hearing loss. The loss of background sounds contributes also to inaccuracy in the recognition of space and motion, and, as a consequence, the movements of the deaf are often vague and distorted.

Motor Performance of Deaf and Hard-of-Hearing Persons

Studies have been conducted since the 1930s to examine the motor performance of the deaf and hard-of-hearing. These investigations have focused primarily on measures of balance, fine and gross motor skills, and motor ability. Efforts have also been made to compare the performance level of the deaf and hard-of-hearing to those without a hearing loss. For the most part, the studies that have been conducted are not definitive because of the failure to control for factors such as cause of the hearing loss and level of hearing loss. A comprehensive review of studies which have been conducted to examine the motor performance of students with hearing losses has been reported by Goodman and Hopper (1992). The following generalizations, however, may be made about the motor performance of the deaf and hard-of-hearing:

1. Some deaf students may have balance problems, depending upon the cause of the hearing loss. If the cause results in an inner-ear problem, it is also probable that the vestibular system, particularly the semicircular canal, where the sense receptors for balance are found, will also be affected.

2. The extent of the hearing loss may have an influence on motor performance. Some deaf students, therefore, may be less proficient in some motor skills than those who are hard of hearing. This difference, however, may be due to previous experience with game and movement skills rather than to the extent of hearing loss. The deaf students' greater difficulty in receptive and expressive communication skills may also contribute to these differences.

3. Compared to hearing students, some deaf and hard-of-hearing individuals appear to perform at a lower level on many motor tasks.

4. In general, the deaf and hard-of-hearing were found to be more similar in motor performance, with the exception of balance. Where differences were noted, much of the variance may be due to: (1) the extent of previous opportunities to participate in physical education activities and (2) inadequate communication in assessing the motor performance of deaf students (Pontecelli & Dunn, 1988).

Generally, these findings suggest that although much remains unknown about the motor performance of the deaf and hard-of-hearing, involving these students in physical education programs is highly desirable. Successful experiences will require teachers who are empathetic and willing to develop sufficient communication skills to assist the deaf student to benefit from the instruction offered. For students whose motor skills or communication skills, or both, are seriously limited, special physical education classes may be necessary. Most deaf and hard-of-hearing students, however, can successfully participate in regular physical education classes with minimal modifications.

The setting in which deaf and hard-of-hearing students are to be educated has generated considerable attention. Some have argued that the least restrictive environment for this population is a special class or special school placement. Butterfield (1991) summarizes this position eloquently by stating that the regular class placement lacks (a) cultural foundations unique to deaf individuals and essential for their optimal development and (b) appropriate support services vital for the education of such students. Decker (1993) believes that deaf students have more to gain than to lose by receiving their education with hearing peers.

Both Butterfield and Decker acknowledge that deaf students will not be successful in integrated settings unless there are adequate support services. In this respect, the Individuals with Disabilities Education Act (IDEA) emphasizes that deaf students should be provided interpreters, if this level of assistance is needed. The interpreter plays an essential role in helping the deaf student benefit from instruction. It is important to emphasize that the interpreter should be with the deaf student for all class periods, including instruction in physical education. The idea or suggestion that the active nature of the physical education class will not need the services of an interpreter should be challenged.

Planning the Physical Activity Program

It is estimated that approximately 4 to 5 percent of the school population actually experiences some hearing loss. Most children with hearing loss are enrolled in the regular schools, and generally speaking, such children are successfully included in the general physical education class. Winnick and Short (1985) reported, for instance, that individuals with auditory loss compared very favorably to the hearing students on selected tests of physical fitness. However, if the child's hearing loss has prevented normal participation in play activities to the extent that marked physical needs or personality problems are evident, the teacher should consider the case more carefully to determine if the child could profit more from participation in the special class. Children who have experienced recent hearing loss and are still in a period of adjustment may well profit from individualized instruction in a special physical education program, as may those with subnormal strength and coordination.

Students who need special help might benefit best by participation in both the general physical education and special physical education classes. This approach will allow the students to benefit from additional instructional time and provide opportunities to work on selected skills. Deaf students, too, will enjoy the advantage of having class time with other deaf students. This should help to increase opportunities for socialization with other deaf students and increase the probability of participating in sport programs sponsored by the American Athletic Association for the Deaf (Stewart, McCarthy, & Robinson, 1988).

Hearing Aids

Many students who are hard-of-hearing wear hearing aids that may be removed during physical education classes for some types of activities. Without this assistance to the individual's auditory perception, the student will again be disadvantaged in the amount of verbal direction he or she can comprehend. The teacher must anticipate this and be prepared to help the student make the necessary adjustment.

For calling roll or giving preliminary instruction to the class before the activity begins, the teacher should place the student with a hearing loss where the student will be in the best position to watch the instructor's face. During actual play, when the need to comment arises, the teacher may move close to those students who cannot hear well before speaking. Or the students may be granted "roving" privileges so that they may move about freely to a position at which they are better able to hear the speaker.

Modeling Desired Behavior

Other students in the class are usually very cooperative in helping those who cannot hear to make the right responses in game situations once they recognize that the student has a hearing loss. As long as the hearing students are unaware that deaf students respond the way they do because of a hearing loss and not because of personal peculiarities, they sometimes ignore or ridicule those with a hearing loss. Consequently, the physical education instructor must set the pattern for the class. **The teacher's kindness and patience in directing and explaining the class activities to the student with a hearing loss will be imitated by the others.** Soon the teacher will find that when such a student has muffed a play by being out of position, a teammate will quietly step over to indicate what was wrong.

Students with a hearing loss may demonstrate a lack of cooperation in class activities and undesirable behavior in competitive play. Such tendencies are related largely to their failure to have understood the directions or rules of the game. In the lower grades where the play is less dependent upon vocal directions and rulings, the deaf child is usually a considerably more successful participant than in later years when games become more dependent upon the comprehension of spoken words. Clear explanations directed at the student and careful demonstrations of the skill to be performed should do much to alleviate the misunderstandings that prompted the undesirable behavior. It is the teacher's responsibility to make sure that students understand what is expected, including how to play selected games and sports.

Verbal and Visual Aids for Teaching

Students with hearing losses need to be taught more factual information about a game than hearing children whose ears as well as their eyes have given them insight into the activity. The vocabulary of the game as well as the rules and playing strategy must be conveyed with greater care and exactness than is necessary for the student who can hear. Well-described and illustrated written materials may be used to good advantage for this purpose with students who read.

Visual aids have greater significance as a teaching technique in the instruction of the hard-of-hearing and deaf than in perhaps any other situation. Their use can substitute for considerable amounts of verbal instruction. Videotapes and slides can be used to good advantage, although slides will frequently require more explanation than videos. However, the required explanation can be shown on the screen in written form if the students are old enough to be good readers. The videotapes chosen should show performances of the skills in such a way that they are largely self-explanatory. Frequently, reruns of the demonstration will help to make it more clear to those who are trying to learn the correct techniques from the picture. Captioning on television has been well received by the deaf community and provides another important system that can be used to enhance instruction.

Movement Symbols A visual system for assisting the deaf and hard-of-hearing to participate successfully in physical education classes has been proposed by Schmidt and Dunn (1980). In their approach, movement symbols have been developed to help the student who is deaf or hard-of-hearing associate various movement responses with standard symbols. For example, in figure 9.9, the symbols for body awareness and space awareness are presented. A student learns, therefore, that a straight line centered on a nine- by twelve-inch card means stretch. Individual cards can also be combined to write movement sentences. For example, in figure 9.10, the movement sentence requires that the student do a stretch, curl, twist, and stretch without stopping. The movement cards can also be used with various apparatus such as the balance beam, or the cards may be placed around the room to permit the student to work independently at various stations.

Creativity is encouraged through the use of the movement symbols. Students quickly learn, for instance, that there are many ways to stretch. With a traditional approach in which the teacher relies primarily on demonstration, some deaf students associate the image of the teacher standing on tip-toes with arms raised above the head with the correct way to stretch. The movement symbol system helps the student to understand that the word "stretch" may be associated with many different movement patterns. Hearing students will find the movement symbol system fun and helpful as will other disability populations. The symbols may be made out of felt to accommodate the needs of students who are visually impaired to receive tactile information.

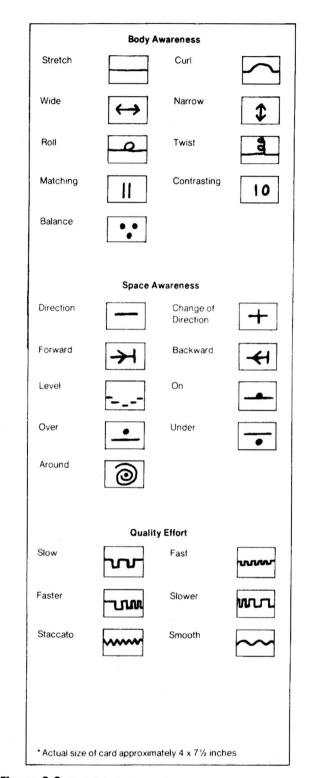

Figure 9.9 Symbols for fundamental movement.

Teaching Guidelines

Teaching guidelines that teachers of physical education should consider in providing appropriate physical education experiences for the deaf and hard-of-hearing include:

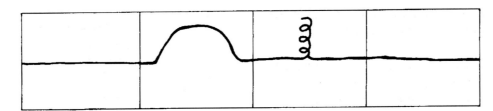

Figure 9.10 "Do a stretch, curl, twist, stretch movement sequence without stopping."

1. Good eye contact must be maintained. This means that the teacher will need to be in a position that enables the student to see the instructor's face. With young children, it may be necessary for the teacher to kneel or sit down on the floor when talking with them.

2. The teacher must speak clearly but avoid talking slowly or overemphasizing words. When it is apparent that the student did not understand the teacher's directions, repeat the instructions but use different words and phrases.

3. Sport terms are frequently difficult for the young deaf student to follow. For example, the meaning of the word "touchdown" is to "touch" "down." This word, however, takes on a very different meaning in the game of football. Instructors must make a special effort to explain sport jargon to the student with a hearing loss.

4. An overhead projector is a necessary visual aid in physical education classes that include students with hearing loss. This aid allows the instructor to speak facing the class while drawing diagrams and putting key words on the overhead. The teacher's ability to maintain eye contact while speaking and making notes helps both those with and those without a hearing loss to follow directions.

5. When outside, teachers should avoid standing in the shadow of buildings or trees or stationing themselves so that students must face the sun during group instruction. Shadows that descend over the face of the instructor interfere with the deaf student's ability to speech read or follow instructions. Having the student facing into the bright sun creates the same difficulty.

6. Some students with hearing loss find long verbal instructions very fatiguing. This is attributed to the intense listening effort that some have to maintain to follow the class discussion. Teachers, therefore, should recognize this special need and provide for frequent rest periods as well as employ alternative methods of providing information to the deaf.

7. When teaching the profoundly deaf student, it is important that the teacher ask frequent questions to ascertain whether the student is following the specific lesson. It is also important that only one question be asked at a time to avoid confusion.

8. Other students must be reminded that they should look at the deaf student when asking or answering a question. The teacher may need to repeat the student's statement so that it is clear to the deaf student as well as others in the class.

9. If possible, a hearing student should be assigned to serve as a peer aide for the student with a hearing loss. The aide's responsibilities include taking notes for communication purposes, helping in the orientation to new activities, and providing visual signals when required during play in team games. Weekly or monthly rotation of the peer aide is recommended to avoid overdependence. Caution must be exercised, too, to ensure that the aide provides assistance only when it is necessary. Lieberman (1995) found that deaf and hearing students benefitted when paired as peers in integrated physical education classes.

Physical Activities

There are few restrictions on the activities that may be offered to students with hearing loss in the regular or special physical education class in the usual school or in the physical education program of the special school. The limitations imposed on these students are of a social rather than physical nature. To help these students in their adjustment to their hearing loss and in their relationship with others takes precedence in planning the program to meet their greatest need.

Students who have sustained damage to the semicircular canal of the ear may have poor balance and experience dizziness. Certain limitations in activities are necessary for the safety of these students: Activities that require climbing on high equipment or demand acute balancing are usually prohibited.

Games and Sports

All the individual and team sports may be learned by individuals deaf and hard-of-hearing. Many special schools field basketball, baseball, and football teams that compete successfully against teams of hearing players. Deaf students enjoy competitive play and play to win, but more important than the winning or losing are the social contacts provided by the game and the acceptance of their worth by opponents with good hearing.

There are, of course, some hazards to the safety of the deaf and hard-of-hearing in competitive play because they are unable to hear signals and other warning sounds. As a precautionary measure, certain visual signals such as the waving of colored flags should be arranged. The instructor should be sure that each participant understands the meaning of each signal before play begins. If the opponents are also nonhearing, the signals should be agreed upon and understood by both teams. If the opponents can hear, they should be alerted to the need for the visual signals and for their cooperation in preventing accidents to hard-of-hearing players.

Fencing, archery, bowling, tennis, golf, and badminton are other sports with demonstrated appeal for students in both deaf schools and regular schools. Activities such as archery and bowling that can be participated in without others have great value as leisure-time activities for those who cannot hear, for whom some avenues of recreation are closed due to their hearing loss. Because listening to records, radio, concerts, and similar recreational pursuits that require normal hearing are lost to them, many deaf and hard-of-hearing people do not have adequate recreational outlets and their leisure hours are boring and depressing as a consequence. They should be taught some individual sports that they can participate in during leisure time; however, these should not be emphasized to the detriment of team play, which encourages the give and take of social intercourse so extremely vital to these students.

Bloomquist (2003b) recommends the removal of hearing aids before contact sports, gymnastics, self-defense, and aquatics programs. With the aquatics program participation, earplugs should be used if the student has tympanic tubes. Students with cochlear implants should avoid mats, plastic ball pits, or plastic equipment to prevent electrostatic discharge. Train individuals with hearing loss to be visually aware of nearby moving vehicles during activities such as cross-country running, cycling, and jogging. In case of an emergency in the school facility, use strobe fire alarms.

Swimming

Water play and swimming are enjoyed by individuals deaf and hard-of-hearing as much as by other active people. Although some may experience balancing difficulties in the water, nearly all progress similar to other children in learning the swimming skills. A modified stroke that permits the head to remain above water will be necessary for those who must not get water in the ears or who become disoriented when their heads are submerged.

Rhythmic Activities and Dance

Students of all ages with hearing loss take pleasure in rhythmic movement, even though their hearing of the rhythm in music is totally or partially restricted. For successful performance in musical games and dancing, the students must be taught the pattern of movement, with emphasis upon the length of time each phase of the movement is held before it is changed. To students with hearing this is evident in listening to the musical accompaniment, but for those who cannot hear adequately the teacher must accentuate the rhythm with hand movements so that the students can perceive visually what they cannot perceive by hearing. Some students will, of course, hear some of the music, and even those who do not hear melody experience musical vibrations. For this reason a percussion instrument is helpful in establishing rhythms.

Students should be taught simple tap or folk dances first. The basic steps may be presented in demonstration with the back to the students so they will not become confused as to which foot is being used, as is often the case when the teacher faces the class. Dances and musical games that are performed in circles or squares and involve complex formations are best taught in a straight-line formation and in short parts that are later put together in the required formation.

Motor Exploration

Motor exploration and the use of problems in motor movement to be solved through experimentation help those deaf and hard-of-hearing to lose their fears and inhibitions about moving freely in space. Because students proceed at their own pace and their own level of competence in motor movement, they are relieved of the pressures that they usually experience in more formal activities. With each small gain of confidence in their ability to move the body and to control it will come an increased willingness to expand movement experience. Eventually, the student's fears and inhibitions will diminish entirely.

Physical Fitness

Those who are deaf and hard-of-hearing may be underdeveloped physically, owing to their withdrawal from vigorous play activities; they may also be poorly coordinated and purposeless in their movements because of their lack of sound orientation. The physical education program at all levels should include a variety of activities for well-rounded physical development as well as specific exercises that develop cardiorespiratory endurance, flexibility, and muscular tone.

Balance

Although their value is questioned by some, balancing stunts and activities should be included for those students who have difficulty maintaining good balance because of damage to the semicircular canal. Such dysfunction is irreversible, but the kinesthetic sense can be developed and the eyes trained through practice to aid in maintaining body balance in compensation for the loss of semicircular canal control. Young children will enjoy such stunts as walking a line and performing the stork stand (standing on one foot). For older children, work on the pogo stick or on a low balance beam is effective in improving balance. Training in all sport activities encourages the development of better balance in those who lack it. The goal of any balance training that may be required should be to supplement and not supplant the regular instruction in physical education. Students who are deaf need opportunities to be included in activities along with hearing students; programs that pull students out of the mainstream should be discouraged and kept to an absolute minimum.

Dual Sensory Impairment

Individuals with dual sensory impairment experience the loss of both sight and hearing. The United States Office of Special Education defines the deaf-blind child as one "who has both auditory and visual impairments, the combination of which causes severe communication and other developmental and educational problems so that he cannot be properly educated in special education programs for the hearing impaired child or the visually impaired." The degree of loss of visual and auditory acuity that cannot be accommodated in special educational programs varies from situation to situation. However, a student with a visual ratio of less than 20/200 or a field of vision of twenty degrees or less who has a hearing loss of twenty-five decibels or more is usually unable to be educated in such programs and so is considered deaf-blind.

Concern for the education of the deaf-blind person has been relatively slow in developing despite the well-publicized success in teaching Helen Keller to read and communicate. Prior to the 1950s, education of the deaf-blind was confined to a very small and select group; most other such children were given little more than custodial care. During the 1950s interest in and efforts to provide for the educational needs of the deaf-blind gradually gained momentum. The endeavors were given impetus by the sudden increase in the number of children born with dual sensory impairments during the 1963 to 1965 rubella epidemic. In the wake of this disaster, many schools for the blind expanded their curricula to include programs directed toward the education of deaf-blind children. In 1968, ten original centers were established, each serving from one to seven states, to provide educational services for the deaf-blind. Research continues to assess needs of individuals with dual sensory impairment and recommendations for programs for the deaf-blind give considerable attention to physical recreation.

The Nature and Causes of Dual Sensory Impairment

The most common causes of dual sensory impairment are congenital defects. Other causes are linked to accidents and infectious diseases such as meningitis (inflammation of the membrane covering the brain and spinal column). In recent years, Usher's syndrome has become the leading cause of deaf-blindness. Usher's syndrome is a genetic condition resulting in deafness and is accompanied by a progressive blindness known as retinitis pigmentosa. Unfortunately, children who are deaf-blind as the result of rubella often have other disabilities as well. Among these are other physical disorders and mental and emotional problems.

Teaching Those Who Are Deaf-Blind

The child who is deaf-blind has challenges similar to those of blind children and those of deaf children. However, the effects of dual sensory deprivation are multiplicative rather than additive. The effects of both blindness and deafness are much more serious than the effects of either deafness or blindness alone, for where these disabilities occur separately, the healthy sense organs can be trained to compensate for the deficient one.

One of the great problems for the person who is deaf-blind is that very little foundation exists for the development of communication skills. The deaf individual is able to see communications between people, and the blind person is able to hear them, but the deaf-blind person has only limited resources for even knowing that people do communicate.

There is, of course, a great need to develop a means of communication for the deaf-blind individuals. Residual hearing, residual sight, or both can be the basis for communication if the child retains either or both. If there is no residual sight or hearing, communication will depend upon body contact using touch signs, signing in the hands, or both of these. In the former, the person who is teaching works with the student to establish certain interpretations of specific touches made on the body. Signing in the hands refers to the use of a manual alphabet in which words are signed or spelled out on the hand of the receiver. Many deaf-blind persons also learn to talk by use of the vibration technique, in which the hands are placed on the face and mouth of the talker to feel the vibrations created by the voice, the movements of the mouth, the control of the breath, and to some extent the placement of the tongue.

Like the individuals who are blind or deaf, the child who is deaf-blind needs to develop the unimpaired senses as well as learn to utilize fully any residual sight or hearing. Students who are deaf-blind must rely heavily on their tactile, kinesthetic, vestibular (inner ear balance), and olfactory sensations as

Figure 9.11 Activities designed to help students who are deaf-blind achieve an understanding of their body and its location in space are important.

stimuli for movement. The educational environment should provide opportunities for experiences that encourage such use.

Without the ability to communicate, children who neither see nor hear are isolated from the world around them. In their isolation they experience little of the social interaction required to develop a sense of well-being and to fulfill the basic need of belonging. Consequently, such children urgently need assistance in learning to relate to others, especially to their peers (figure 9.11).

Awareness of Body and Movement

The formation of a positive self-concept is important to normal social development. Knowledge of one's physical self, the body image, is necessary for the development of a concept of the self. Because they have great difficulty in learning to move about in their world, deaf-blind children have limited opportunities to develop an awareness of their body and to integrate their observations with other information to form a concept of themselves as persons. One of their most essential needs, therefore, is to have greatly expanded opportunities to utilize their bodies in movement.

Movement-related activities should be encouraged from birth with the goal of associating cues (visual, auditory, tactile) with various forms of movement. Van Dijk (1966) developed a system of teaching communication through movement. In this system, which consists of several stages, the teacher uses close body contact with the student to imitate various movements. As the student progresses, the amount of body closeness between teacher and student can be reduced. Throughout the instructional program, the goal is to introduce language by associating movement with cues that can be understood by the student.

Experiences that create tactile and social awareness and control of the body in gross and fine motor movements need to be provided. The total movement experience for deaf-blind children must be varied enough to help them understand their potential in movement and to provide the means to realize this potential.

Planning the Physical Activity Program

The physical education activities that can be presented to students who are deaf-blind depend upon their age and also upon the degree of deafness and blindness and the extent to which movement has been learned. **Movements that are taught should be presented in such a manner that they contribute to the communication skills of the person.** To accomplish this the physical education teacher must learn body signs for general communication from the teacher who works with the student so that the same signs can be used in physical education. Other signs will need to be developed to convey certain concepts of movement peculiar to physical education. The signs developed for this purpose should be used consistently, and additional signs should be introduced only when the previously learned signs are inadequate in instructing the child in a new motor movement.

One system that has been successfully employed with students who are deaf-blind mentally retarded is to rely on kinesthetic cues to communicate. For instance, in teaching a young deaf-blind student to reach for a ball, the teacher, with the student in a seated position, would tap the student's elbows as a signal to reach for the ball. If the student fails to reach, as requested, the instructor would then take the deaf-blind student's hands and physically assist the child to retrieve the ball. Additional feedback would be provided by moving the student's head up and down to indicate yes or side to side to indicate no.

The teacher must also develop a daily routine so that the deaf-blind student will know what to expect each day. The lesson should begin with the teacher identifying himself or herself to the child. A watch or ring that is normally worn every day is useful for this purpose; the child can feel it and know which person this teacher is. Following the introduction, a review of previously taught movements is desirable. The same order should be used in each review. After practice of the previously taught movements, a new movement can be introduced and the child allowed to experiment and practice it. The lesson may end with a familiar activity or game that the child particularly enjoys. Although the idea of sameness might appear boring or limiting to some teachers and students, it is essential that the program for deaf-blind students follow a consistent routine.

Physical Activities

Sample activities and teaching suggestions are given in the subsequent paragraphs. Each should be given a specific body sign. The teacher should give the sign each time before an activity starts, so that the student can become aware that this sign refers to the activity that follows. The activities are listed in order of difficulty of performance for most children. However, because of past experience or interest, some children may perform the most difficult skills more easily than the skills preceding them. The order also reflects the increased communication skill that will be developed as the activities progress.

Angels in the Snow

Place the child in a prone position on the floor. Touch arms, legs, and head one at a time, helping the child to move the parts touched.

Walking

Help the child to a standing position. Lead child gently forward by the hands until a step is taken. (A helper may be needed to push against the legs.)

Rocking in a Chair

Seat the child in the chair. Help child to rock, indicating the need to shift weight.

Rocking on Back

Lay the child on his or her back. Raise the child's legs to a pike position (knees to chest). Clasp your hands around the child's knees. Lift head and rock body gently back and forth. Help child shift weight to rock alone.

Rocking on Stomach

Place the child on his or her stomach. Raise legs and indicate they are to be held erect. Elevate head and shoulders and indicate that they are to be held up. Help the child to shift weight to rock the body.

Crawling

Help the child assume the position for crawling. Move limbs in the proper order to move forward in a crawl. (A helper is generally needed.)

Kneeling

Help the child take a position on knees with buttocks resting on the back of the legs. Lift buttocks off the legs to raise the trunk to the upright position.

Finger Play

Move the fingers of the child into various positions; for example, cross one finger over another, touch the thumb to each finger on the same hand, squeeze and release soft objects.

Rolling Down

Place the child on an incline mat and move the body so that it rolls forward and down the incline. Help child shift weight so that body rolls without assistance.

Rolling on the Level

Help the child to take a prone position. Move one leg over the other. Cross the arm on the same side over the body. Push the child over onto the stomach. Move the leg that was moved when the child was on the back over the other leg; pull the same arm across the back until the body turns onto the back.

Pushing and Pulling

Put the child's hands on the object to be pushed or pulled (for pulling, the fingers are placed around the object). Push or pull the arms until the object moves.

Rolling over a Medicine Ball

Place the ball on the mat. Position the child to lie on the stomach across the ball. Push on body to start the ball moving forward. Tuck the child's head so that the back of the head will land on the mat as the ball moves forward. Lift the hips and push them over the ball, lowering the hips to the mat.

Running

Pull the child along by the hand at a slow run. As the child gains confidence, run together, each holding opposite ends of a short length of rope.

Running Unaided

The child holds the guide rope while running (see discussion of this technique in the section on suggested activities for the blind).

Rebounding

Help the child to balance on an inner tube or a jouncing board. Lift at the waist or under the shoulders. Move the legs from flexion to extension in coordination with the lift and return. (A helper will be needed.)

Jumping

Put the child in a standing position and indicate that knees are to be flexed. Lift up and down, simultaneously helping the legs to flex or extend as in rebounding. (A helper will be needed.)

Tossing

Place the child's fingers in a grip around an object to be thrown (a bean bag is the simplest to handle). Lead the arm through tossing movements with one hand; with the other hand pull the object from the grasp. When the object is released without aid, move arm through the toss more vigorously to achieve forward movement of the object.

Striking

Set a large ball on a batting tee. Place a bat in the child's hands with the proper grip. Move the bat to within a few inches of the ball. Move the arms through the batting motion to strike the ball. As skill improves, move the bat farther from the ball. When introducing new equipment, such as the ball and bat, it is essential that the student be provided an opportunity to orient to the equipment by feeling and touching it.

Catching

Place the child's hands in the proper position for catching. Drop a ball onto the hands and immediately bring the arms up to entrap the ball between the arms and chest.

Moving to Drum Beat

Place a large drum near enough to the child to enable the vibrations to be felt. Beat the drum with one hand and move parts of the child's body in time to the beat.

Children with more advanced communication and motor skills will be able to participate in more complex activities than those just described. Possibilities are pullups, scooter-board riding, hula hoop play, bean-bag tossing at various targets, rebound tumbling on the trampoline, bouncing a ball, catching and rolling a ball, goal kicking, and moving through an obstacle course.

Older students will be able to participate with assistance in many activities, among them bowling, golf, shuffleboard, archery, weight training, track and field events, rhythms, dance, wrestling, and swimming. Adaptations of these are described in the chapters in which the activities are discussed.

Summary

Information in this chapter focused on sensory impairment, specifically those individuals with visual impairments or hearing loss or a combination of the two. Although the loss of sight or hearing is a major impairment, the focus of this chapter was to highlight that most individuals with sensory impairments function at a very high level and that they enjoy the same activities as individuals who are not disabled. Information about hearing loss and visual impairments were discussed separately.

Visual disabilities range from common eye disorders such as myopia (nearsightedness) to diseases such as trachoma which cause loss of sight. The causes of visual impairments may be classified as refractive errors, muscle imbalance, or genetic disorders and diseases of the eye. The degree of visual acuity is expressed in a numerical ratio such as 20/200, where the first number indicates that the person being tested had to be twenty feet from the chart in order to see what someone with normal vision can see at 200 feet from the chart. Legal blindness is defined as visual acuity of 20/200 or less or a field of vision less than twenty degrees.

In developing physical education programs for those with visual impairments, emphasis must be placed on developing an effective form of communication. Depending on the student's prior experience with activity and the nature of the visual impairment (for example, congenital versus adventitious), the exact approach will vary. Many, however, have found a physical assistance approach in which the student is guided through the movement to be very effective. Some have also found the technique of allowing those with visual impairments to touch the teacher while the skill is being performed effective in helping the student to get the feel of the skill. Communication aides—for example, Braille and special equipment—also can be used to assist the student who is visually impaired. The type of physical education activities used for those with visual impairments are basically the same as those used with the sighted. Some activities such as beep baseball and goal ball are unique sport forms for those with visual impairments. Modifications in activities will need to be made to accommodate the child with a serious visual impairment. Special effort must be made to encourage these youngsters to explore their environment and to participate in creative movement experiences.

Individuals with auditory loss, similar to those with visual impairments, vary considerably in their motor and physical fitness performance levels. Those students whose hearing loss is mild participate successfully with hearing children in play activities. Individuals with profound hearing losses require special modifications in the instructional environment for communication. Hearing losses may be classified according to the type of loss—conductive, sensorineural, or mixed, a combination of the two. Major importance is also placed on whether the hearing loss was congenital or after birth. Those individuals born deaf experience major problems in developing speech. Another factor that must be considered prior to developing physical education programs is to assess the degree of hearing loss, measured in decibels, as well as the hertz or pitch at which sound may be heard. Finally, the method of communication that the person is utilizing must be known. This can range from manual language including gesture (known as ASL) to finger spelling or speech reading. Many deaf and hard-of-hearing individuals use a combination of these methods.

Motor and physical fitness programs for the deaf and hard-of-hearing are very similar to those for the student who hears. The same activities, games, and sports are taught with modification in instruction as appropriate. Similar to the visually impaired, special effort should be made to encourage the student with a hearing loss to engage in creative movement. These experiences add considerably to the student's background and avoid the all too common reliance on demonstration as the only teaching technique. Throughout the chapter, guidelines for creating successful and favorable learning experiences were emphasized.

Information was also presented concerning the special needs of the deaf-blind population. Although the challenges of this population are similar to those with hearing or visual losses, the negative effects of dual sensory deprivation are multiplicative rather than additive. A major problem is the limited foundation that exists for establishing a communication system with this population. Physical assistance and kinesthetic cues have been successfully used in the physical education class. Efforts of this nature, while slow, have produced positive gains in both the physical and motor fitness levels of deaf-blind students.

Fortunately today there is an acceptance and understanding that individuals with sensory impairments enjoy and benefit from participation in physical and motor fitness activities. With proper instruction and adaptations as appropriate, their students can successfully and safely participate with their hearing and sighted peers in a variety of games and sports.

Enhancing Activities

1. While blindfolded, and with the assistance of a sighted partner, participate in a number of activities including walking on campus, visiting the student union, participating in a class, and going to a movie and exercise class. Keep notes on your reaction to performing these activities without sight. What was the reaction of your guide and others to your performance?

2. While blindfolded, participate in a game of goal ball with some players who are visually impaired.

3. Practice communication skills with a deaf student by using some simple signs or finger spelling. While wearing earplugs, watch others speak and try to follow their conversation.

4. Select a favorite skill or sport and modify the activity for a student who is visually or hearing impaired. Try the modifications with an appropriate student and make additional changes as necessary.

5. Visit a local school to observe the educational program employed with a deaf-blind student. Observe the various techniques used to communicate with the student.

6. Interview a deaf educator, a parent of a deaf child, and a deaf person to obtain their views on the various communication systems used with the hearing impaired. Do they agree or disagree on the value of ASL compared to speech reading? Do they agree that deaf students should be mainstreamed?

7. Using the system developed by Schmidt and Dunn, develop some movement sentences to use with deaf and hard-of-hearing students. This same approach can be used with the visually impaired if felt is placed on the cards that contain the symbols.

8. Attend a beep baseball game and/or a goal ball match. Identify similarities and differences in these activities compared to sport experiences for the nondisabled.

Selected Readings

Best, G. A. (1978). *Individuals with physical disabilities: An introduction for educators.* St. Louis: C. V. Mosby Co.

Birch, J. (1975). *Hearing impaired children in the mainstream.* Reston, VA: The Council for Exceptional Children.

Bloomquist, L. E. C. (2003a). Visual impairment. In J. L. Durstine & G. E. Moore (Eds.), *ACMS's exercise management for persons with chronic diseases and disabilities* (2nd ed., pp. 325–328). Champaign, IL: Human Kinetics.

Bloomquist, L. E. C. (2003b). Deaf and hard-of-hearing. In J. L. Durstine & G. E. Moore (Eds.), *ACMS's exercise management for persons with chronic diseases and disabilities* (2nd ed., pp. 320–324). Champaign, IL: Human Kinetics.

Buell, C. E. (1974). *Physical education and recreation for the visually handicapped.* Washington, DC: American Alliance for Health, Physical Education, and Recreation.

Butterfield, S. (1991). Physical education and sport for the deaf: Rethinking the least restrictive environment. *Adapted Physical Activity Quarterly, 8*, 95–102.

Collins, M. T., & Zambone, A. M. (1994). Deaf-blind children and youth, Education of. *International Encyclopedia of Education*, 1398–1402.

Corbett, E. E., Jr. (Ed.). (1975). *The future of rubella—deaf/blind children proceedings.* Dover, DE: Department of Public Instruction.

Corliss, E. (1978). *Facts about hearing and hearing aids.* Washington, DC: U.S. Department of Commerce, National Bureau of Standards.

Cornett, R. O. (1982). Center for Studies on Language and Communication, Washington DC: Gallaudett College. Personal communication.

Danyluk, A. W., & Paton, D. (1991). Diagnosis and management of glaucoma. *Clinical Symposia,* 43–44.

Decker, J. (1993). Least restrictive environment programming for individuals with hearing impairments: A response to Butterfield. *Adapted Physical Activity Quarterly, 10*, 1–7.

Dolnick, E. (1993). Deafness as culture. *The Atlantic Monthly,* September, 37–53.

Fischgrund, J. (1994). Deaf and hearing impaired youth, Education of. *International Encyclopedia of Education*, 1398–1402.

Goodman, J., & Hopper, C. (1992). Hearing impaired children and youth: A review of psychomotor behavior. *Adapted Physical Activity Quarterly, 9*, 214–236.

Heward, W. L., & Orlansky, M. D. (1988). *Exceptional children* (3rd ed.). Columbus, OH: Charles E. Merrill Publishing Co.

Keane, K., Tannenbaum, A., & Krapf, G. (1992). Cognitive competence: Reality and potential in the deaf. In H. C. Haywood & D. Tzuriel (Eds.), *Interactive assessment.* Berlin, Germany: Springer and Verlag.

Kratz, L. E. (1973). *Movement without sight.* Palo Alto, CA: Peek Publications.

Larson, A. D., & Miller, J. B. (1978). The hearing impaired. In E. L. Meyen (Ed.), *Exceptional children and youth: An introduction* (p. 431). Denver: Love Publishing Co.

Lieberman, L. J. (1995). The effect of trained hearing peer tutors on the physical activity levels of deaf students in integrated elementary school physical education classes. (Unpublished doctoral dissertation). Corvallis, OR: Oregon State University.

Lieberman, L. J. (2000). Peer-tutors' effects on activity levels of deaf student in inclusive elementary physical education. *Adapted Physical Activity Quarterly, 17*, 20–39.

Lieberman, L. J., & Coward, J. F. (1996). *Games for people with sensory impairments.* Champaign, IL: Human Kinetics.

Lieberman, L. J., & Houston-Wilson, C. (2002). *Inclusion.* Champaign, IL: Human Kinetics.

Mandell, C. J., & Fiscus, E. (1981). *Understanding exceptional people.* St. Paul, MN: West Publishing Company.

McGuffin, K., French, R., & Maestro, J. (1990). Comparison of three techniques for sprinting by visually impaired athletes. *Clinical Kinesiology, 44*(4), 97–100.

Meyen, E. L. (Ed.). (1978). *Exceptional children and youth.* Denver, CO: Love Publishing Company.

National Center for Health Statistics (1994). National Health Interview Data, Series 10, Number 188. Washington, DC: U.S. Department of Health and Human Services.

Nesbitt, J., & Howard, G. (1975). *Proceedings of the National Institute on Recreation for Deaf-Blind Children, Youth, and Adults.* Iowa City, IA: University of Iowa Press.

Pontecelli, J., & Dunn, J. M. (1988). The effect of two different communication modes on motor performance test scores of hearing impaired children. The national convention of the American Alliance for Health, Physical Education, Recreation and Dance. Poster Presentation.

Rosenthal, R. (1978). *The hearing loss handbook.* New York: Schocken Books.

Ryan, K. (1979). *Adapting physical education and recreation for the visually handicapped student.* New York: American Foundation for the Blind.

Schmidt, S., & Dunn, J. M. (1980). Physical education for the hearing impaired: A system of movement symbols. *Teaching Exceptional Children*, Spring, 99–102.

Silverstein, H., Wolfson, R. J., & Rosenberg, S. (1992). Diagnosis and management of hearing loss. *Clinical Symposia, 44*(3), 32.

Stewart, D. A., McCarthy, D., & Robinson, J. (1988). Participation in deaf sport: Characteristics of deaf sport directors. *Adapted Physical Activity Quarterly, 5*(3), 233–244.

Strika, C. (1989). Empathy and its enhancement in hearing impaired children. (Unpublished Dissertation). Syracuse, NY: Syracuse University.

Vander Kolk, C. J. (1981). *Assessment and planning with the visually impaired.* Baltimore: University Park Press.

Van Dijk, J. (1966). The first steps of the deaf-blind child towards language. *International Journal for the Education of the Blind, 15*(4), 112–114.

Weitzman, D. M. (1985). An aerobic walking program to promote physical fitness in older, blind adults. *Journal of Visual Impairment and Blindness, 79*(3), 97–99.

Wilson, G. B., Ross, M., & Calvert, D. R. (1974). An experimental study of the semantics of deafness. *The Volta Review, 76*, 408–414.

Winnick, J., & Short, F. X. (1985). *Project Unique.* Champaign, IL: Human Kinetics Publishers.

Nutrition for Healthy Children

Holly Willis, PhD, RD, LD
Carol Leitschuh, PhD

CHAPTER 10

CHAPTER OBJECTIVES

After studying this chapter, the reader should be able to:

1. List and discuss various tools that can be used for nutritional planning.
2. Identify the dietary goals for the United States.
3. Describe some of the common nutritional problems including those that are pertinent to students with severe disabling conditions.
4. Discuss various weight control strategies including the value of behavior modification in altering dietary habits.
5. Explain the important and critical relationship between diet and exercise in the prevention and treatment of obesity.
6. Apply selected criteria and guidelines to assess the potential effectiveness of selected weight control programs for children.
7. Recognize the inherent danger in some of the common eating disorders including anorexia nervosa and bulimia.
8. Recognize some of the unique dietary and exercise needs of selected disability populations.
9. Identify the components of a well-designed exercise program for the student who is obese.

Nutrition for Healthy Children

Nutrition is a positive, empowering aspect of health and lifestyle, because **good nutrition is the cornerstone to good health**. What children eat directly influences how they grow, perform, and feel. Nutrition practices have changed a great deal over the last 50 years. Currently, Americans live in a food-obsessed world, a "global nation" where cross-cultural practices may vary, yet healthy balanced meals remain important for all children and families.

Research suggests that eating habits established early in life tend to persist into adulthood. This means that practical nutrition education and good nutrition role models are essential for all children. However, in preparation for being physical educators and/or teachers, few have had *extensive* coursework in nutrition. Also, most schools do not have nutritionists on faculty to act as ready resources in understanding children's nutritional needs. Therefore, this chapter is co-authored by a registered and licensed dietitian. It contains valuable information about young children's growth and nutritional needs. These guiding principles are contained within this chapter:

- Children's nutritional intake and needs differ from those of adults.
- Nutrition requirements for children with special needs *may* or *may not* differ from children without special needs.
- Children of all body weights should be treated with respect and not singled out because their weight is higher or lower than other children.
- Discussions about nutrition should be empowering and should be framed to boost a child's self-esteem and self-image.

Success in physical activity has a strong positive force on a child's development of self-worth, social skills, and overall joy. This chapter provides a discussion about how to encourage children to choose healthy foods and how to achieve and maintain a healthy, active lifestyle.

This chapter includes useful information from an expansive group of experts and expert reports, including:

- *Healthy People 2010* presented by the National Institutes of Health http://www.healthypeople.gov/Document/HTML/Volume2/19Nutrition.htm
- MyPyramid from the United States Department of Agriculture http://mypyramid.gov/ and http://mypyramid.gov/kids/index.html
- Dietary Reference Intakes (DRIs) as established by the Institute of Medicine http://www.iom.edu/Object.File/Master/21/372/0.pdf
- National Center for Health Statistics and Centers for Disease Control and Prevention http://www.cdc.gov/nchs/about.htm

These references, and their obvious future revisions, should be used by physical educators and researchers as they come to understand appropriate ways to regard children's nutritional needs for growth and a healthy lifestyle. This chapter points out when a clinical expert is required to assess a child's nutrition. It is important that physical educators do not intervene with families and their children when a clinical specialist is needed. Fun, age, and developmentally appropriate physical activity gives life to all children at all levels of maturation, socialization, and psychological well-being. Pairing this belief with good nutrition is a combination for improved health.

Basic Nutrition: Dietary Guidelines for Americans

In the United States, the Dietary Guidelines for Americans (DGAs) serve as the basis for all national nutrition and physical activity recommendations. The DGAs are written to include general nutrition and activity messages for people of all ages, but are *not* specific to people with special health care needs. However, the types of healthy foods described by MyPyramid are often the basis for all healthy nutrition plans. These guidelines are updated every five years. The most recent version of the DGAs includes the MyPyramid Food Guide (which replaced the old "Food Guide Pyramid"). MyPyramid emphasizes a few key messages that are important for most people, regardless of age or ability. Examples of specific foods are described in the following section: Tips for Making a Child's Plate Healthy.

- Eat a variety of nutrient-dense foods
- Eat colorful fruits and vegetables
- Eat whole grains instead of refined grains whenever possible

- Eat low-fat foods (especially low-fat dairy products)
- Be physically active (see chapter on physical fitness and children)

MyPyramid is largely web-based and contains many ways to personalize information or recommendations. For example, the home page (www.mypyramid.gov) offers each user the opportunity to enter in an age, gender, and activity level. General information is tailored to fit these specifications. There is also a link to "Inside the Pyramid," which describes specific food groups and portion sizes. MyPyramid has an abundant assortment of resources and tools for health and physical educators, health care professionals, and parents.

Figure 10.1 is an example of the MyPyramid for Preschoolers, which is a close-up look at the MyPyramid for children two to five years of age.

Physical educators should not feel responsible for making specific recommendations when it comes to nutrition. The best messages they can send are to encourage all children and adults to consume good quality foods and balanced meals that include fruits, vegetables, whole grains, lean proteins, and low-fat dairy products. As appropriate, educators modeling good eating habits and talking about how they enjoy nutritious foods is also important.

Tips for Making a Child's Plate Healthy

(Adapted from Team Nutrition, an initiative of the United States Department of Agriculture Food and Nutrition Service)

1. Choose whole-grain foods, like whole-wheat bread, oatmeal, brown rice, and low-fat popcorn instead of refined products like white bread or white rice.
2. Vary the veggies. Go dark green and orange with vegetables—try spinach, broccoli, carrots, and sweet potatoes. The darker the color the better!
3. Focus on fruits. Eat them at meals, and at snack time, too! Choose fresh, frozen, canned, or dried, but go easy on the fruit juice.
4. Eat calcium-rich foods. To build strong bones, try low-fat and fat-free milk and other low-fat milk products several times a day. (Full-fat dairy products may be more appropriate for certain children. Ask your child's health care team.)
5. Go lean with protein. Eat lean or low-fat meat, chicken, or turkey. Or, try more dry beans and peas. Add chick peas, nuts, or seeds to a salad; pinto beans to a burrito; or kidney beans to soup.
6. Change the oil. Everyone needs oil, but some kinds are better than others. Aim for more fish, nuts, and liquid oils such as olive oil, corn, soybean, or canola.

MyPyramid for Preschoolers

Use MyPyramid to help your preschooler eat well, be active, and be healthy.

MyPyramid for Preschoolers is for children 2 to 5 years of age. Click on the blue button to get a customized MyPyramid Plan for your preschooler.

MyPyramid Plan

Explore ways to help your preschooler:

● **Grow up healthy.** Complete a growth chart especially for your child to find out more about normal development.

● **Develop healthy eating habits.** Raise a healthy eater by setting a good example and practicing positive habits.

● **Try new foods.** Help for picky eaters.

● **Play actively every day.** Add physical activity into your preschooler's day.

● **Follow food safety rules.**

You are the most important influence on your child. You can do many things to help your children develop healthy eating habits for life.

Figure 10.1 MyPyramid for children ages two to five helps children learn how to eat healthy.

7. Don't sugarcoat! Choose foods and beverages without sugar or sweeteners as a main ingredient. Added sugars contribute calories with few, if any, nutrients.

Food Allergies

It is estimated that as many as 8% of all children have true food allergies; these allergies may be even more prevalent in children with special needs. The following list includes some of the most popular food allergies (Kuehn, 2008).

- Milk
- Soy
- Eggs
- Wheat
- Peanuts (or other nuts)
- Fish (and shellfish)

True food allergies can cause severe reactions, including anaphylaxis. The health care team finds it important to consider the potential for food allergies when recommending or discussing healthy eating habits for children. Therefore,

parents should inform the IEP team of their child's food allergies.

Dietary Reference Intakes (DRIs): An FYI

The Dietary Reference Intakes (DRIs) are more specific than the DGAs. The DRIs are the general nutrient intake standards for healthy children and adults. They have been established for carbohydrate, protein, fat, fiber, and all vitamin and mineral intakes. The DRIs encompass the Recommended Dietary Allowances (RDA), Adequate Intakes (AI), Tolerable Upper Intake Levels (UL), and the Estimated Average Requirements (EAR). DRIs are broken down by age and have been established for toddlers and preschoolers; children ages 4-8, 9-13, 14-18 and adults 19-70. Specific intake levels can be found on the Institute of Medicine website at www.iom.edu or at http://www.iom.edu/Object.File/Master/21/372/0.pdf

The DRIs are not customized for children with special health care needs; however, they are often the basis for all children's healthy eating plans. Preschoolers and school-age children with special health needs are often at risk for the same nutrition-related problems as other children. Regardless of the child, attempts should be made to meet appropriate growth and developmental goals. Goals for specific nutrient intake (for children with or without special needs) are best handled on a case-by-case basis by a trained health care team, which includes a Registered Dietitian (RD) and Medical Doctor (MD). The health care team assesses all children for:

- Current and expected growth and development patterns
- Conditions that increase or decrease calorie needs
- Conditions that alter digestion or physiology of swallowing (i.e., severe cerebral palsy may make feeding and swallowing difficult)
- Food allergies, sensitivities, intolerances
- Access and resources to appropriate foods

In most cases, regardless of a child's ability, the health care team will still promote and encourage healthy, nutrient-dense foods (such as those described previously in Tips for Making a Child's Plate Healthy, or on mypyramid.gov). They will discourage using food as a reward in either the home or school setting. They will also consistently monitor the child for growth that is appropriate to the child's condition and age.

Some children will indeed have special needs when it comes to their nutrition requirements. As stated before, these needs should *not* be determined by the physical educator or the IEP team. However, reports from a registered dietician or medical doctor will be helpful when establishing actions that should take place during the school day (i.e., feeding tube use, or meals every two hours).

Feeding Problems

Children with special needs often display many of the same problems with eating/feeding as children without special needs. Natural feeding problems include many different scenarios, including:

- Short attention span at the meal table
- Poor coordination with utensils
- Food jags (child only willing to eat one or two specific foods for a period of time)
- Strong preference for liquids over solids, or foods with a specific texture
- Difficulty chewing or swallowing

It can be difficult to determine when eating/feeding behaviors are a "problem" or just part of a child's natural growth and development. Preschoolers are naturally curious and often enjoy the first stages of autonomy and independence; because of this, they are often disinterested in routine mealtime practices. It is important to recognize that feeding problems are common for all children between the ages of about two to five, but are something that can exist for lengthy or indefinite periods of time in children with special needs. For example, children with attention deficit hyperactivity disorder or autism may have no interest in meal time and may not respond to feeling hungry. Likewise, children with cerebral palsy may have life-long problems with chewing and swallowing. In situations like these, parents, teachers, and the IEP team need to work on individualized strategies (with the health care team's information) to accommodate the child's needs.

Most children will have temporary food patterns and preferences; this is okay for a while, with the focus that balance will occur in time. It is normal for children to eat limited foods at certain times in development. In general, children need to try new foods 8-10 times before they really like them. Parents and care providers should continually encourage variety and balance for nutritional intake, but should be wary of creating an issue around "good" or "bad" foods. Children can smell an agenda, and may become resistant to balance and variety if the issue is forced or made mandatory.

When it comes to kids, consuming a greater variety of food often equates to better dietary quality (this is because each type of food provides a different nutrient profile). Food variety can mean many different things. For example, variety could mean offering a sample of fresh, frozen, dried, or canned fruits and vegetables. Variety in food delivery might mean offering a mix of foods that can be eaten with fingers, with chopsticks, or as a picnic on the floor. Color variety is a wonderful way to support a varied nutrient intake; help children aim for eating every color of the rainbow at each meal. Food variety can be encouraged by preparing foods into different or unusual shapes—think pineapple cut with a star-shaped cookie cutter or zucchini pureed into tomato soup. With a little creativity, the possibilities are endless and so is the fun!

Vitamins and Minerals: A Quick Word for Educators

In general, most children who eat balanced meals do not require vitamin or mineral supplements. Parents who are concerned about their child's need for a supplement should consult with their child's health care team. Excessive amounts, or unbalanced proportions, of vitamins and minerals can be harmful. (This is why it is important to treat children's supplements like any other medication—*especially the ones that look like candy.*)

Vitamins are either water or fat soluble. The water-soluble vitamins include many B vitamins and vitamin C; the four fat-soluble vitamins are A, D, E and K. The list of minerals is extensive, but common minerals include calcium, potassium, and sodium. Each of these vitamins and minerals plays an important role in the regulation of metabolism, growth, and overall health. Vitamin and mineral deficiencies can occur over time if a child or adult does not eat a healthy, balanced diet that includes a variety of vegetables, fruits, whole grains, and plant or animal proteins.

Growth

It has been estimated that 15% of children may have special needs. Of this group, 40 to 60% of these children are at risk for at least some nutritional problems. The growth of children with special health care needs often differs from children without special health care needs because of reasons unrelated to nutrition. These reasons may depend on medications, severity of condition, impaired motor skills, or many other variables. For example, trisomy 21, Prader-Willi syndrome, and spina bifida are three conditions that commonly predispose children to become overweight. The reasons for this may include hypotonia, lower metabolic rates, lack of ambulation and mobility, or greater chances for excessive food intake. In contrast, cystic fibrosis, HIV, and cerebral palsy may predispose children to becoming underweight. The reasons for this may include increased work of breathing, higher metabolic rates, or feeding difficulties.

In either situation—overweight or underweight—children should be encouraged to choose and eat healthy foods that include whole grains, fruits, vegetables, and healthy fats. They should also be encouraged to participate in age- and condition-appropriate activities. Just because a child has special needs does not mean he/she cannot enjoy many of the same things that children without special needs enjoy! (United States Department of Health and Human Services, 2009).

Specialty growth charts have been developed for a number of conditions, including:

* Down syndrome (Trisomy 13, 18, 21)
* Achondroplasia
* Fragile X syndrome
* Prader-Willi syndrome
* Rubinstein-Taybi syndrome
* Sickle cell disease
* Turner syndrome
* Williams syndrome
* Cornelia deLange syndrome
* Marfan syndrome
* Spastic quadriplegia

However, it is important to recognize that specialty growth charts have limitations, since they are often developed from small sample sizes that lack racial and ethnic diversity. Though useful, specialty growth charts should be used in conjunction with other assessment tools.

Growth charts are available from the Center on Disease Control and Prevention (CDC). Visit http://www.cdc.gov/nchs/about/major/nhanes/growthcharts/charts/charts.htm. Specially growth charts are gender specific and are divided into the following categories:

* Weight for ages 2 to 20 years
* Stature for ages 2 to 20 years
* Weight for stature percentiles
* Body Mass Index (BMI) for age

If the physical educator is tracking any of these variables, the goal is to establish the start point and track over time to see individual growth across time. Each child is unique, but a stable trend across time is generally considered healthy. The key is to have growth remain steady each year. By nature, some kids will always fall in the lower or upper percentiles—this is normal. They should just be monitored for consistent growth.

Delayed Growth and Body Weight for Children with Special Needs

Improper nutrition frequently results in delayed growth in children both with and without disabilities. Diagnosing the cause of delayed growth in children with disabilities is more complex because of the lack of information on the effects of condition-related growth rate. Studies on children with mental retardation have indicated that such factors as dietary intake, appetite, activity level, medication, parental stature, overall health, and economic status may be important factors in the potential size and growth of the child. Addressing growth patterns for children with special needs or conditions is difficult, and should be discussed with the child's health care team.

Appreciate All Shapes and Sizes

It is normal for children to gain weight at different rates and at different times during their childhood. One of the best things that a teacher can do is to encourage children to celebrate their individual strengths and abilities. It is important to teach students that their most important qualities are not physical. (Healthy yes, but not just by standards of physical appearance. Remember, a slender person is not always a healthy person.)

Emphasis should never be placed on body type, weight, or size. Body shapes and sizes vary for many reasons. At the same time, a child's weight will fluctuate with growth spurts and patterns. The combination of these two factors makes it unreasonable to compare one child's size or shape to another. Similarly, it is harmful for parents, professionals, and teens to make body comparisons with the media, fashion industry, or film idols. Children (actually people of all ages) are much more beautiful when diversity is appreciated for qualities that are deeper than physical appearance. It is beneficial to address the human body's beauty in all its individual uniqueness.

In all situations, judgment should never be passed on a child's shape or size. Remember the "people first" approach, and make efforts to treat all students with the same courtesy, respect, and tact.

Body Mass Index for Children

Body Mass Index (BMI) is the most commonly used way to estimate body fat. It is simply calculated by dividing weight in kilograms by height in meters^2. For example:

Sarah is twelve years old, she weighs eighty pounds (thirty-seven kg) and is four feet eight inches (1.42m) tall.

Her BMI is $37 \div 1.42^2 = 18.3$. This is the 50th percentile for her age.

Nutrition professionals rarely use skinfold or caliper measurements. A BMI greater than the 85th percentile, but below the 95th percentile, means the child is at risk for being overweight. BMI less than the 5th percentile means the child is underweight. A BMI more than the 95th percentile means the child is overweight.

However, **weight loss is only indicated in children over seven years of age with a BMI greater than the 95th percentile for age.** When weight loss is indicated, it is done under close medical/clinical supervision. This means that the physical educator should *not* direct the weight loss. Rather, the physical educator should spend time creating healthy environments, providing positive role models, and offering all students the opportunities to make good lifestyle decisions.

BMI is generally *lowest* in children who are four to six years old. The BMI then increases from these ages into adulthood. For children, it is best to have a "BMI for age" in the normal range, not a specific BMI number as advised for adults. Children usually lay down fat first, then grow out, and then grow up! **In general, unless a child (up to age 18) has a BMI *more* than the 95th percentile for age, we encourage the child to maintain weight and not lose weight.** Children should be encouraged to maintain weight by making good, healthy choices about food and physical activity. When good choices are made and become habit, the hope is that weight will change gradually as they move into adulthood.

Overweight Children

Childhood obesity is on the rise in America. In the past three decades, the number of children who are overweight has more than doubled among two- to five-year-olds, and more than tripled among 6 to 11 year-olds. According to data published in 2006, nearly 19% of children age 6 to 11 were classified as overweight, and approximately 37% of children in this age range were considered at risk for overweight.

It cannot be overemphasized that a child's growth in height and weight will not always be proportional. It is reasonable to expect that all children will have periods when they grow out in weight, before they grow up in height. As a physical educator, it is important to monitor a child's growth over time and to consistently encourage healthy habits, before becoming concerned that a child is "too heavy" or "too thin."

Physical appearance is influenced by genetics, as well as the degree to which the child likes, has access to, and participates in physical activity. These factors are important to consider. It is natural for children to vary in appearance across ages and stages of development. However, at each developmental level, physical activity should be part of normal daily life. All children, overweight or not, can benefit from developing healthy eating and physical activity habits. Be active and eat well are goals for all stages of growth and development. Children need support from adults to learn and maintain these habits. Educators should set good examples with their own habits and provide an environment that empowers their students to make good decisions. For example, talking about eating fruit for a snack and encouraging students to choose fruit is something simple that can be done in the midst of students' activity time. Giving children the tools and the knowledge to make healthy lifestyle decisions will often take them further than even the most carefully planned program.

An enormous amount of effort and resources have focused on improving children's health and body weight. Nutrition and exercise is paramount for parents and professionals concerned about the health and body weight of children. **Physical educators have the greatest control and sphere of influence over the child's access and attitude toward age-appropriate/condition-appropriate physical activity.**

The greatest hurdle to overcome is often a child's low self-esteem and low motivation to participate where failure can be obvious: no other academic area is so visible for failure as the gymnasium or playground. Physical education classes offer a time for all children to move and to learn about physical activity skills and interests. Based on accepted practice with children who need specialized attention in physical education settings, the following is recommended:

1. Get to know the child's interests outside of physical activity. This provides a way for the teacher to talk with the child about his or her interests not related to weight or motor skill. This establishes rapport with the child and gives the teacher a fuller picture of who this child really is.

2. Recognize and correct the bias against body weight that may exist in the physical education staff, educational assistants, or other teachers. Check negative attitudes at the door and provide discussion time with staff members to encourage a compassion that allows each child to gradually gain physical activity skills and knowledge.

3. Adapt activities for an overweight child as needed, and include other children in the adaptation. Oftentimes other children in a physical activity class will also be interested in the alternative activity. Making adaptations for intensity and duration of the activity may actually increase the number of children who willingly participate.

4. Focus on the positive and the "personal best" of each child. (See examples in the chapter for children with emotional problems.) Allow for only positive comments from one child to another, and explain that each person in the class has a personal best that is his/her unique time/distance/skill. Positives can come in the form of "Hey, great green t-shirt today!" Everyone enjoys positive feedback.

5. Observe closely for overexertion and pace the child.

6. Continue to expose the child to a variety of activities. However, be sensitive to the differences in an individual sport (i.e., bowling or physical activity stations) versus a team sport (i.e., basketball or a simple game of tag) where physical fitness is a key component to success. For older children, a dual sport such as ping-pong is appropriate. (See chapters 26 and 27 on the CD for other suggestions.)

7. Stay away from a traditional fitness focus in the child's physical education program. If possible, it is recommended not to take the child out of classes to work on fitness goals. This may defeat the purpose of the intervention, since the child has little choice in the matter and the 1:1 focus can appear to be on the child's weight or inability to move well in class. Rather, adjust class activities accordingly and build from where the child is successful.

8. The IEP for each child should address modifications and adaptations to curriculum activity that will allow for successful participation.

9. Find ways to reward the student that are a natural part of the class for every student. This would require the physical educator to know which of his/her favorite teaching strategies would potentially work for the target child.

Eating Behaviors

Eating Behaviors in Teens

Nutrition needs increase substantially during adolescence. Needs are ultimately based on biologic/sexual/pubertal maturity and not actual age. Adolescents typically gain nearly 50% of their adult body weight during a relatively short period of time (about ages 11 to 18). It is important to remember that weight and height do not always change proportionally.

Overall calorie needs will increase for all teenagers, but are ultimately determined by activity level, metabolism, and requirements to support growth. Changes in calorie needs are highly individual and will vary depending on the person, his/her condition, and projected growth. (Note the specialty growth charts discussed in the beginning of the chapter can be referenced.)

The basis for healthy eating during the teenage years is similar to all other stages of life. Emphasis should be placed on high-quality foods, such as fruits, vegetables, whole grains, lean proteins, and low-fat dairy products. Most teenagers do not eat adequate fruits or vegetables, and often fall short of the recommendations for calcium. Environments that encourage nutrient-dense foods, especially fruits and vegetables, are important and beneficial.

Adolescent eating behavior is highly influenced by the individual's self-esteem, parents, authoritative role models, and the media. It is important to highlight and discuss positive role models and positive health practices with teens. Family meals should be encouraged, and nutrition messages given to teens should focus on areas important in their life; for example, how food impacts appearance, grades, sports performance, having energy for social activities, and even appropriate stress relief. Teenagers often respond better to messages that emphasize the present-tense benefits of eating well, such as having good skin and hair, strong bodies, or being smart and energetic. Long-term health messages, such as a reduced rate of cancer or heart disease in the future, are not effective for the adolescent population.

All messages to adolescents should promote self-esteem and a healthy body image. Adolescents with and without disabilities all want to be socially accepted. Good nutrition paired with fun age-appropriate successful physical activity experiences should be stressed and provided. The physical educator can reinforce these concepts while teaching.

Eating Disorders

Research suggests that 13% of girls and 7% of boys have some form of disordered eating behaviors. A large percent of teens report they have tried dieting. This is a problem for normal growth and development. Research also suggests that teens who try dieting are more likely to become overweight as adults.

Some students may exhibit the signs or symptoms of an eating disorder, like anorexia or bulimia. The best way to handle this situation is to approach the students and/or their family discretely. Be prepared to refer to a professional for help. Disordered eating of any kind is serious and beyond the scope of a physical educator's expertise. Signs and symptoms of common eating disorders include, but are not limited to, routinely skipping meals, making excuses for not eating, eating only a few certain "safe" foods, adopting rigid meal plans, wearing baggy or layered clothing, complaining about being fat, exercising compulsively, constant dieting, self-induced vomiting, unhealthy focus on body shape and weight, or having a distorted or negative body image.

An expert report suggests the following for helping to prevent eating disorders (Loth, 2009).

- Decrease emphasis on weight and body shape
- Provide a supportive food environment
- Model healthy eating habits and physical activity patterns
- Help children build self-esteem beyond looks and physical appearance
- Encourage appropriate expression of feelings and use of coping mechanisms
- As a professional, increase your understanding of eating disorder signs and symptoms
- Seek support in dealing appropriately as an adult with your own struggles about weight and shape

Trendy Diet Plans

When it comes to both children and adults, there is controversy about the health benefits of current popular diets. The American Heart Association (2009) (www.americanheart.org) recommends adopting healthy life-long eating habits and warns against any quick fix. There is no "superfood" that when eaten in combination with other foods will be "fat burning" or will produce radical weight reduction over the long term. This is especially true for children. All individuals should focus on eating moderate amounts of food from all food groups and not large amounts of "special foods." The AHA also reminds students that eating should, and can, be both enjoyable and fun.

Being a Role Model for Students

Physical educators can help children make good decisions in the following ways:

- Model good physical activity and eating patterns. Adults, like children, should exercise 60 minutes a day (see CDC guidelines in chapter 17), eat a variety of foods, and engage in consuming regular, balanced meals.
- Keep healthy foods available and convenient.

- Don't promote foods as "bad" or "off limits."
- Use praise, attention, time, and activities as rewards for behavior/performance—not food!
- Involve children in healthy meal and food decisions.
- Avoid food rules or coercions like: "No dessert until the plate is clean." This signifies that the food on the plate is bad and that dessert is good.
- Always consider the language you use when you talk about *your own* body weight or shape.

Model Nutrition Programs and Resources

- **Team Nutrition** is a program designed by the United States Department of Agriculture (U.S. Department of Agriculture). This program recognizes that schools are an important setting for healthy nutrition and physical activity strategies. It is designed to help improve children's life-long eating and physical activity habits, and is consistent with the principles of the Dietary Guidelines for Americans and the Food Guide Pyramid.

  For example, *Changing the Scene—Improving the School Nutrition Environment* is one of the Team Nutrition toolkits that is available to all schools. This toolkit addresses the whole school environment—including commitment to nutrition and physical activity, pleasant eating experiences, quality school meals, and other healthy food options. The kit is available to help local people and educators take action to improve the school's nutrition environment. It includes a variety of resources that can be used to address school environment issues that influence students' eating and physical activity practices.

  Figure 10.2 shows the heading from the webpage for Team Nutrition. Select the About Team Nutrition link for more information on the program and how to get your school involved.

- **Children in Balance** is an initiative developed by the New Balance Foundation and Tufts University. Their goal is to reverse and prevent childhood obesity by empowering community leaders and schools to build environments that promote healthy eating and increase physical activity in children. The initiative is responsible for conducting rigorous scientific research, and subsequently disseminating evidence-based interventions and "best practices" that foster positive changes in children's health. The website contains an extensive resource list for teachers, schools, and parents. http://www.childreninbalance.org/

Figure 10.2 Team Nutrition is designed to help schools improve life-long eating habits.

- **Fruits & Veggies—More Matters**™, a health initiative that replaced the 5-A-Day program, was designed to inspire and support both children and families to eat more fruits and vegetables. The Fruits & Veggies—More Matters™ website highlights the combination of great taste, nutrition, abundant variety, and various forms of many fruits and vegetables. This program's website also has resources specific for teachers and classrooms. http://www .fruitsandveggiesmorematters.org/
- **National Super Kids** was established in 1991 as a partnership between the National Cancer Institute and the Produce for Better Health Foundation. The Super Kids program includes resources for teachers and classrooms that encourage healthy eating—especially when it comes to fruits and vegetables. The website includes ways to get students excited about eating fruits and vegetables, as well as lesson plans and activities that are appropriate for children of all ages. The Teacher's Toolkit has a variety of information that could be incorporated into various classroom settings. http://www.dolesuperkids.com/ and http://www.dole5aday.com/html/Teachers.html

The *Healthy People 2010* Goals: More Aid for Supporting Childhood Nutrition

The CDC publishes recommendations for the nation's health. The *Healthy People 2010* Goals contain five general goals that involve children. http://www.healthypeople.gov/ Document/HTML/Volume2/19Nutrition.htm

These goals are listed as an aid to understanding what children in America need to be healthy. The goals are based on an extensive assessment of data collected since the formation of the last *Healthy People 2000* Goals. These goals will not make sense for all American children and their families, but they do stand as a general recommendation for the nation. For example, Goal #1 states that for the United States to be healthy, children and adolescents as a whole need to increase their *daily* physical activity. If any of the goals seem pertinent to helping a child be healthier in regards to nutrition or physical activity, then these guidelines are a support.

Goal #1: Increase daily physical activity among children and adolescents.

- The CDC recommendations in this text, chapter 17, are appropriate guidelines for children and adolescents.

Goal #2: Reduce the amount of time kids spend watching television, video games, and the Internet.

Goal #3: Decrease the consumption of energy-dense, high-sugar/high-fat foods like soda, ice cream, junk food, and fast food.

- The focus is for individuals two years and older to consume less than 10% of calories from saturated fat, and less than 30% of calories from total fat. In addition, this goal intends to increase the number of children (age 6 to 19 years) whose intake of meals and snacks at school contributes to good overall dietary quality.

Goal #4: Increase the consumption of nutritious foods like fruits, vegetables, whole grains, and skim milk.

- Increase the proportion of persons age two years and older who consume at least two daily servings of fruit.
- Increase the proportion of persons age two years and older who consume at least three daily servings of vegetables, with at least one-third being dark green or orange vegetables.
- Increase the proportion of persons age two years and older who consume at least six daily servings of grain products, with at least three being whole grains. Increase the proportion of persons age two years and older who meet dietary recommendations for calcium (500 mg for children age one to three years, 800 mg for children age 4–8, and 1300 mg for adolescents age 9–18).
- Increase the proportion of children and adolescents age 6 to 19 years whose intake of meals and snacks at school contributes to good overall dietary quality.

Goal #5: Create social, monetary, and policy-driven incentives that reinforce long-term environmental and behavioral change.

Enhancing Activities

Refer to any number of the resources cited in this chapter that are Web-based. Many of these sites have activities that can be used as enhancing activities for students. These are activities that are research-based as well as best practice-based.

1. Perform an in-depth review of a Web-based resource contained in the chapter and identify a program that could be implemented. Identify an age-related focus.
2. Within a selected site, identify practical resources that could be used with young children.
3. Continue the focus on an in-depth review of a site and identify a useful list of activities for adolescent ages to teach healthy nutrition.
4. Create a statement about nutrition and physical activity based on the any one of the resources provided in the chapter. Add some examples of activities. Present this page to the following physical education teachers: elementary, middle, and high school. Ask for their professional reactions to your paper. Take notes on the reaction and summarize the area where the teachers appear to agree or disagree with your presented material.
5. Obtain views about obesity in childhood from individuals studying in physical education or recreation or another selected related health discipline.

Selected Readings

American Heart Association (2009). (www.americanheart.org) retrieved April 24, 2009

Brown, J. E. (2008). *Nutrition through the life cycle* (3rd ed.). Belmont, CA: Thomson Wadsworth.

Economos, C. D., Hyatt, R. R., Goldberg, J. P., Must, A., Naumova, E. N., Collins, J. J., et al. (2007). A community intervention reduces BMI *z*-score in children: Shape Up Somerville first year results. *Obesity (Silver Spring), 15*(5), 1325–1336.

Flegal, K. M., Tabak, C. J., & Ogden, C. L. (2006). Overweight in children: Definitions and interpretation. *Health Education Research, 21*(6), 755–760.

Kuehn, B. M. (2008). Food allergies becoming more common. *Journal of American Medical Association, 300*(20), 2358.

Loth K. A., Neumark-Sztainer D., & Croll J. K. (2009). Informing family approaches to eating disorder prevention: Perspectives of those who have been there. *International Journal of Eating Disorders. 42*, 146–152.

Nicklas, T. A., & Hayes, D. (2008). American Diabetic Association. Position of the American Dietetic Association: Nutrition guidance for healthy children ages 2 to 11 years. *Journal of the American Dietetic Association, 108*(6), 1038–1044, 1046–1047.

Ogden, C. L., Carroll, M. D., Curtin, L. R., McDowell, M. A., Tabak, C. J., & Flegal, K. M. (2006). Prevalence of overweight and obesity in the United States, 1999–2004. *Journal of American Medical Association, 295*(13), 1549–1555.

United States Department of Agriculture, Team Nutrition (2008). (www.fns.usda.gov/tn) retrieved December 8, 2008.

United States Department of Health and Human Services (2008). Health Resources and Services Administration, Maternal and Child Health Bureau. Retrieved December 8, 2008, from http://www.mchb.hrsa.gov

Contributor:

Holly Willis MS, RD, LD is recognized for her enormous contribution in co-authoring this chapter. There is no chapter like "Nutrition for Healthy Children" in any textbook on physical activity for children with disabilities. Dr. Willis is a registered dietitian and a licensed nutritionist. Her knowledge about the growth and development of young children, with and without disabilities, comes from her extensive clinical training, teaching, and personal experience. We believe this information has been needed for many years in our discipline of adapted physical activity and are proud to present it in this newest edition of our text.

Mental Retardation

CHAPTER OBJECTIVES

After studying this chapter, the reader should be able to:

1 Recognize and understand the nature of mental retardation, its causes, classification systems, and prevalence.
2 Identify the learning, social, and emotional characteristics of individuals with mental retardation, appreciating the similarities and differences associated with this disorder.
3 Plan and implement a physical education program that is sensitive to and consistent with the needs of people who are mentally retarded.
4 Appreciate the diversity of talent and ability among individuals with mental retardation.
5 Comprehend the importance of utilizing a systematic instructional process when teaching physical education to those with mental retardation.
6 Explain the unique physical and motor characteristics of individuals with Down syndrome, including obesity, atlantoaxial instability, and congenital heart defects.
7 State the definition of mental retardation and the criteria for identifying someone as mentally retarded.
8 Evaluate the needs of students with mental retardation and identify selected motor learning concepts that can be applied to this population.
9 Explain why it is essential that there be close coordination between the school-based physical education program and services offered by other agencies such as the community park and recreation departments and sport organizations such as Special Olympics.
10 Defend the statement that most youngsters with mental retardation should receive their physical education program with their age peers.

According to the National Center on Physical Activity and Disability (NCPAD, 2004), participation in regular structured physical activity contributes to the health and self-esteem of children with developmental disabilities, even though it is documented that these children often have fitness levels lower than their nondisabled peers. It is well-documented that physical activity can make a major contribution in the lives of children and adults with and without mental retardation (Bar-Or, 1983; McCubbin, Frey, & Lavay, 1992; Savage et al., 1986; Seefeldt & Vogel, 1987). This includes participation in sports, recreation, and physical activities that lead to physical, psychological, and social development. Historically, individuals with mental retardation were left on their own for physical activity or, worse,

excluded from it altogether (Eichstaedt & Lavay, 1992). (Figure 11.1)

In 1970, Rarick and colleagues reported only 25 % of students who were "educably mentally retarded" received more than an hour of physical education each week while 45 percent received no physical education. Since this time there have been many legislative, vocational, academic, and favorable attitudinal gains toward individuals with mental retardation. Today, opportunities for individuals with mental retardation to learn with their nondisabled peers, participate in structured recreational programs, hold jobs, and even marry are commonplace. Unfortunately, societies have not always accepted individuals with mental retardation.

Figure 11.1 Child anticipating physical activity in gym program.

Throughout history, individuals with mental retardation were persecuted, enslaved, and frequently punished until death. It wasn't until the end of the eighteenth century that the work of Itard began what is today special education. More recently, the end of World War II saw individuals with mental retardation given the opportunity to participate in physical education. Finally, in 1965 physical education for students with mental retardation became a special interest to the profession. At this time the American Association of Health, Physical Education and Recreation (AAHPER[1]), in cooperation with the Joseph P. Kennedy, Jr., Foundation, established the Project on Recreation and Fitness for the Mentally Retarded to provide assistance and encouragement to schools and community agencies in the development of programs of recreation and fitness activities for those with mental retardation. The Special Olympics program, sponsored by the Joseph P. Kennedy, Jr., Foundation, also has contributed significantly to increased awareness of educators and the public to the value of physical activity for individuals with mental retardation.

Early researchers such as Cratty (1969), Fait and Kupferer (1959), and Rarick and his colleagues (1970) investigated the impact that participation in physical activities played on the lives of individuals with mental retardation. Since this time, considerable advances have been made in our understanding of the importance of training and participation in

physical activities for this population. Today, individuals with mental retardation participate in Little League Baseball; run in the Boston, Portland, and other famous marathons; and participate in their own World Games (formerly Special Olympics International Games) in which more athletes and countries participate than in the "regular" Olympics. Recognition that persons with mental retardation can learn is attributed to a large extent to the work of Jean Itard, a French physician. In 1799, Itard undertook a five-year program to educate an animal-like boy of twelve who was found in the forest of Aveyron, France. Although Itard considered his program a failure, others familiar with the boy observed definite improvement in the youngster's behavior. The ideas of Itard were introduced to the United States by one of his pupils, Edouard Seguin, who became superintendent of a Pennsylvania institution for the mentally retarded. During the 1800s many of the progressive ideas proposed by Seguin, such as emphasis on the whole child, individualized teaching, and good rapport between teacher and child, were incorporated into the programs of other publicly supported institutions, which were growing rapidly in number.[2]

Defining Mental Retardation

No one definition of mental retardation has been constructed that will satisfy all the professional disciplines (medical, psychological, educational, social, and legal) concerned with this population. Throughout the world, the term "mental retardation" has many different meanings and definitions. Even within the United States terms such as "idiot," "imbecile," "moron," "feeble minded," and "subnormal" were once commonly acceptable. More recently, terms such as "a student with intellectual disabilities" or "a person who is mentally challenged" (e.g., Colarusso & O'Rourke, 2003), as well as "individuals with cognitive impairment," have been used. The federal educational law IDEA 2004 continues to use the term "mental retardation." A "person first" language uses the phrase "individuals with mental retardation" to describe this group.

Like society's changing acceptance of individuals with mental retardation, revisions have been made to the definition. Originally produced by the American Association on Mental Deficiency (AAMD), the definition of mental

[1]Now the American Alliance for Health, Physical Education, Recreation, and Dance (AAHPERD)

[2]The authors note there are numerous terms accepted across the United States, Europe, and other countries to refer to individuals who have mental retardation. It is also noted that across the United States, state laws use various terms to refer to this same disability area (For example, Minnesota uses Developmental Cognitive Delay (DCD)). Since the current federal education law, IDEA 2004, continues to use the term mental retardation, we are remaining with that term in our chapter. We recognize there is freedom to add any and all terms used in a local for this disability area.

retardation has undergone many changes. For example, since the 1950s the definition was revised in 1959, 1972, 1983, 1992, and most recently in 2002. The most widely employed contemporary definition of mental retardation is that established by the American Association on Intellectual and Developmental Disabilities, (AAIDD), formerly the American Association on Mental Retardation (AAMR, 2002), formerly AAMD:

> Mental retardation is a disability characterized by significant limitations both in intellectual functioning and in adaptive behavior as expressed in conceptual, social, and practical adaptive skills. The disability originates before age 18.
>
> Five Assumptions essential to the application of the definition are:
>
> 1. Limitations in present functioning must be considered within the context of community environments typical of the individual's age peers and culture.
> 2. Valid assessment considers cultural and linguistic diversity as well as differences in communication, sensory, motor, and behavioral factors.
> 3. Within an individual, limitations often coexist with strengths.
> 4. An important purpose of describing limitations is to develop a profile of needed supports.
> 5. Within appropriate personalized supports over a sustained period, the life functioning of the person with mental retardation will improve.

A careful analysis of the definition clarifies some of the important considerations that must be met before classifying students as mentally retarded. Various terms used in the statement are defined as follows:

Limitations in intellectual functioning and adaptive behavior These include limitations in functional, social, and cognitive capabilities, and practical skills that people use to function day to day.

Significant limitation in intellectual functioning Intellectual functioning is determined by one or more of the standardized tests developed for that purpose. Two of the most frequently used tests include the Stanford-Binet and the Wechsler, the results of which yield an intelligence quotient (IQ). The mean IQ score for the population on both tests is 100 points with a standard deviation of approximately 15 points. Performance on a standardized intelligence test of greater than two standard deviations below the mean is required before a score can be considered significantly sub-average. According to the definition, therefore, persons with mental retardation possess an intelligence quotient (IQ) of less than 68 if using the Stanford-Binet or less than 69 on the Wechsler test. Due to the arbitrary nature of

these numbers, scores less than 70 also qualify under this definition.

AAMR (2002) defines criterion for mental retardation as an intelligence quotient (IQ) score that is understood in light of the standard error of measurement (SEM; see chapter 5) given for the test. The AAMR reports that if the SEM of most IQ tests is five, then the ceiling for mental retardation can go up to as much as a score of 75. This score is two standard deviations (SDs) below the mean.

In addition to an IQ score, a diagnosis of mental retardation is also made by identifying a significant limitation in adaptive behavior present before the age of 18. Adaptive behavior can be tested using standardized tests. Again the behavior must be at least two SDs below the mean in one of three types of adaptive behavior: conceptual, social, or practical; or an overall score for all three types of adaptive behavior. See figure 11.2 for the theoretical distribution of IQ scores and mental retardation.

Before the age of eighteen—Due to the ambiguity of the term "developmental period," as described in the earlier definition, this most recent definition clarifies this period by specifically identifying mental retardation beginning before the age of 18 years.

Adaptive skill areas—Adaptive skills are defined as the ability to meet the standards of social responsibility for a particular age group based on the level of support required in any adaptive skill. Levels of support include:

1. continuous,
2. substantial,
3. minimal, or
4. no support necessary.

Because these expectations vary for different age groups, the defects in adaptive behavior vary according to age as well. During infancy and early childhood significant delays in the maturation areas of communication, self-help skills, and sensory-motor activities are potential indicators of mental retardation. During childhood and early adolescence, primary focus is centered on the ability to learn the basic academic skills. The ability to make a living and to handle oneself and one's affairs with the prudence ordinarily expected of an adult in our society is the important determinant of the presence of mental retardation. According to AAMR, examples of adaptive behavior skills in three categories (reduced from AAMR's original 10 categories) are:

- Conceptual Skills
  - Receptive and expressive language
  - Reading and writing
  - Money concepts
  - Self-direction

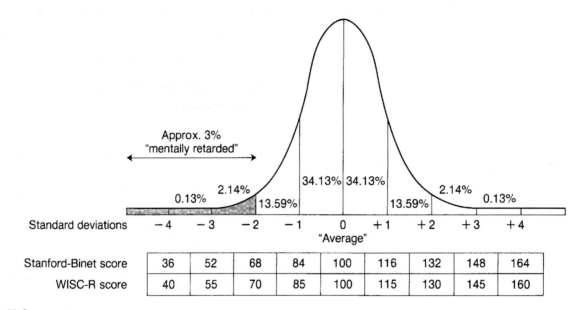

Figure 11.2   Theoretical normal distribution of intelligence.

- Social Skills
  - Interpersonal
  - Responsibility
  - Self-esteem
  - Gullibility
  - Naïveté
  - Following rules
  - Obeying laws
  - Avoiding victimization
- Practical Skills
  - Activities of daily living: eating, dressing, mobility, toileting
  - Instrumental activities of daily living: meal preparation, taking medications, using the telephone, managing money, using transportation, housekeeping activities
  - Occupational skills (working)
  - Maintaining a safe environment

The federal education law IDEA 2004 currently retains the definition of retardation as follows:

Mental retardation means significantly sub-average general intellectual functioning existing concurrently with deficits in adaptive behavior and manifested during the developmental period that adversely affects a child's educational performance. (34 C.F.R, 300.7, IDEA '97)

Schools focus on the degree of mental retardation (mild, moderate, severe, profound), whereas AAMR focuses on the amount of support needed (intermittent, limited, extensive, and pervasive) by the individual with mental

retardation to function in society (Colarusso & O'Rourke, 2003).

Due to the dynamic concept of mental retardation, a person may meet the criteria at one point in life but not at some other time or in different environments. As explained by Grossman (1973), "A person may change status as a result of changes or alterations in his intellectual functioning, changes in his adaptive behaviors, changes in the expectations of the society, or for other known or unknown reasons." As a result, IQ is no longer the determinant of the severity of mental retardation; rather, it is determined environmentally. For example, an individual might experience significant deficits in academic abilities throughout childhood but can successfully accomplish vocational skills which find that individual functioning "normally" during adulthood.

Classification of individuals with mental retardation is made with tests that measure intelligence and adaptive skill areas. The American Association on Mental Retardation has classified mental retardation as: (1) mild, or (2) severe. This is a departure from previous definitions in that IQ scores are now not used to determine *classification*. Previously, mental retardation was defined as:

1. mild, 52–69;
2. moderate, 36–51;
3. severe, 20–35; and
4. profound, below 19.

Standardized tests of adaptive behavior such as the Vineland Social Maturity Scale and the American Association on Mental Deficiency Adaptive Behavior Scales are frequently employed to determine extent of impairment in adaptive skills. Although the relationship is not perfect, persons who score low on the intelligence tests often score low on the adaptive skill scales and vice versa.

Severe Classification

Individuals with severe mental retardation are almost always identified at birth or shortly thereafter. The nature of their condition is usually attributed to a central nervous system defect with associated disabling conditions. The severeness of their mental retardation is such that training will focus on the self-care and functional life skills of toileting, dressing, eating, and drinking. Assistance in helping these individuals develop language and communication skills is typically provided. An individual with severe retardation may require complete supervision and care throughout life. Recent developments in instructional technology and vocational education have provided substantial improvements in self-sufficiency for this population.

The range of movement to be found in those who are totally dependent varies from random, meaningless movements to the intricate and controlled movements required by such skills as walking, running, catching, throwing, and climbing. The kinds of movements of which they are capable depend upon mental ability, absence or presence of physical disabilities, general level of physical fitness, and past experiences in physical education. With the downsizing of traditional state hospitals and institutions, many individuals with severe mental retardation are relocated into community-based residences and group homes that allow a greater level of independence than previously thought possible.

Mild Classification

Students with mild mental retardation have difficulty learning at a rate equal to that of their peers but are capable of learning basic academic skills. They can acquire from second- to sixth-grade achievement in reading, writing, and arithmetic by the age of sixteen. Their development is approximately one-half to three-fourths as fast as the average child; consequently, their academic progress is also at one-half to three-fourths the rate of the average child. Although their communication skills may be limited, they can adequately develop skills for most situations. Most students can learn to get along with others and can acquire enough skills to support themselves economically in adulthood. Many achieve a level of self-sufficiency such that they are not recognized as having mental retardation once they leave the school setting. Frequently they hold jobs, obtain a driver's license, and live independently with no supervision. The majority of these individuals are able

to participate in the same motor activities as their nondisabled peers.

The Extent of Mental Retardation

It is difficult to formulate a precise estimate on the prevalence of individuals with mental retardation. In 2001 the University of Minnesota Research and Training Center on Community Living conducted an extensive survey about disability in the United States. The Center reported that the prevalence of mental retardation in uninstitutionalized individuals was 7.8 per thousand, 11.3 per thousand for developmental disabilities, and 14.9 per thousand for combined mental retardation and/or developmental disabilities (Lawson, Coyle, & Ashton-Schaeffer, 2001). The normal distribution of intelligence (figure 11.2) shows a value that approximates the incidence of mental retardation in the United States. However, basing prevalence estimates on IQ scores alone neglects the most important criterion for mental retardation—deficits in adaptive skills.

IDEA 2004 allows early intervention programs to identify a significant number of at-risk children who may have been previously overlooked or not properly diagnosed. The mortality rate in this group is known to be high but is difficult to document. Frequently, a baby with mental retardation may not show significant signs for months or even years after birth. Usually, however, when parents of children with mental retardation look back, they can recognize that signs were present from infancy.

At the turn of the 20th century, the life expectancy of individuals with mental retardation was approximately nine years (Thase, 1982). Today, the life expectancy of individuals with mild retardation is probably about the same as that of other people. It is difficult to document since many individuals with mental retardation achieve a satisfactory degree of adaptive behavior and attain economic and social independence, and no longer are recognized as having mental retardation. For this reason they are often not identified and counted when community surveys are made, although most of them remain potentially vulnerable to adverse social or economic pressures. For individuals with severe mental retardation, life expectancy is substantially less, although they have been known to live to age seventy to eighty.

With the establishment of advanced medical technologies it is likely that the life expectancy of individuals with mental retardation will continue to increase. Statistics on survivorship among persons with Down syndrome, for example, indicate a much greater life expectancy for this group today than twenty or thirty years ago. As a result, the number of adults who may require help because of varying degrees of mental retardation probably is no more than 1 million to 1.25 million. Many of these persons are receiving disability or general welfare assistance or are dependent on relatives and friends. Thus, as a cause of lifetime disability and as a medical, social, and educational problem of unique extent and complexity, mental retardation today presents an outstanding challenge to science and society in the United States and throughout the world.

The Causes of Mental Retardation

Mental retardation can be caused by any condition that hinders or interferes with development before birth (prenatal), during birth (natal), or in the early childhood years (postnatal). While well over 300 causes have been identified, educators should note that teaching strategies are based on the characteristics of the student and not the cause (etiology) of mental retardation. Although we will discuss the etiology here, it is not the basis for teaching strategy. (This approach is consistent with other areas in special education).

Grossman (1973) identified ten separate etiological classifications of mental retardation, including:

Infection and Intoxication This grouping includes maternal and child infectious diseases and intoxication. Specific causes include: sexually transmitted diseases (syphilis); rubella (German measles); infections after birth (encephalitis) or anytime before or during birth (meningitis); intoxications due to alcohol (fetal alcohol syndrome), tobacco, or other drugs (cocaine). Less frequent is plumbism (lead-based poisoning) which had been the most common source of intoxication among children.

Trauma or Physical Agent Physical trauma or injury to the brain may occur prenatally, perinatally, or postnatally. This includes exposure to X rays, anoxia (lack of oxygen) during birth, or trauma to the skull due to accidents and/or child abuse causing excessive swelling, hematomas, or thrombosis.

Metabolism or Nutrition Disorders directly due to metabolic, nutritional, endocrine, or growth dysfunction should be classified under this category. More specifically, lipid storage (fatty acid) disorders such as Tay-Sachs; mineral (hypercalcemia), endocrine (thyroid dysfunctions), and carbohydrate disorders (idiopathic hypoglycemia); protein disorders such as phenylketonuria (PKU); and nutritional deficiencies (malnutrition, calorie deprivation) are found in this category.

Gross Brain Disease (Postnatal) This category includes new growths that develop and a large number of hereditary disorders in which the cause is unknown or uncertain. Examples include von Recklinghausen's

disease (a nervous disorder), multiple tumors of the skin and peripheral nerves, and tumors in the central nervous system and other organs.

Unknown Prenatal Influence This division is intended only for conditions for which no definite cause can be established but that existed at, or prior to, birth. Macrocephaly (accumulation of fluid within the cranium causing enlargement of the head), and microcephaly (insufficient skull growth) are two of the primary examples found within this category.

Chromosomal Abnormality Syndromes associated with chromosomal errors are included in this category. These disorders may be in the number or structure of chromosomes, or in both. Examples include Down syndrome, Fragile X, Prader-Willi, and Turner.

Gestational Disorders There is a high incidence of defects related to atypical gestation. Prematurity, low birth weight, and postmaturity are the primary subdivisions within this category.

Following Psychiatric Disorder Cases of retardation occurring after serious mental illness when there is no evidence of cerebral disorder due to disease fall in this category.

Environmental Influences This category is for cases in which retardation is caused by a sensory disability or by adverse environmental conditions (e.g., cultural deprivation or mistreatment) when there is no cerebral disorder due to disease. Examples include sensory disabilities such as blindness and deafness and situations such as maternal deprivation.

Other Conditions Included in this classification are cases in which there is no evidence of a physical cause or structural defect, no history of subnormal functioning in parents and siblings, and no evidence of an associated psychosocial factor.

As time goes on, more people are found to have specific diagnosable causes of their mental retardation that fit neatly into the first eight categories just discussed. Nevertheless, even today, in the majority of cases, no clear diagnosis of cause can be made, and in most of these there is no demonstrable pathology of the nervous system. Therefore, most cases of mental retardation are attributed to environmental influences and other conditions. Undoubtedly among those with mental retardation there are many people whose development has been adversely affected by nonspecific influences, such as inadequate diet, inadequate prenatal and perinatal care, and lack of adequate stimulation toward growth and development through learning opportunities. Mental development, like physical development, is promoted by the right kinds of activity and stimulation and is retarded when these are lacking. Indeed, mental and physical development tend to interact. In the developmental process, the years of early childhood when the nervous system is maturing and language is developing are certainly very critical.

Brain Damage and Mental Retardation

The term "brain damage" has not been adequately defined and is used differently by different people. Destruction of brain tissue or interference with brain development in the infant or young child frequently produces mental retardation as well as cerebral palsy, convulsive seizures, hyperactivity, and perceptual problems. Such damage accounts for a substantial percentage of severe mental retardation. Although it may be definitely shown in some cases of mild mental retardation, the extent of its contribution is not known and expert opinion is divided. Several factors may be at work in the same individual. For example, the premature infant is more vulnerable to brain damage, prematurity is more common among mothers who receive inadequate prenatal care, and inadequate prenatal care in turn is more common in the disadvantaged groups in our society; these same children are more apt to have inadequate postnatal opportunities for growth and development and to be subject to psychological and cultural deprivation.

The extent of psychomotor, perceptual, and sensory handicaps among those with mental retardation points to common causation in many cases. Most individuals with severe mental retardation have pronounced motor handicaps or impairment of hearing, vision, or speech, or a combination of several of these. Although the majority of those with mild retardation would not be readily identified as physically disabled, their general level of motor coordination is below average. There are people with limited intelligence who are gifted athletes.

Prevention of Mental Retardation

Progress is being made in the prevention of mental retardation, but it is proceeding, as might be expected, through a succession of small advances across the broad front rather than by any spectacular breakthrough. Each of the many contributing causes must be analyzed individually, with specific preventive measures devised when the cause has been found. Steps can be taken before conception, at birth, and during childhood.

Before conception, the education of parents has perhaps had the greatest impact on the prevention of mental retardation and other disabilities. This includes the passage of federal and state laws and nationwide advertising efforts which require warning labels on medications, tobacco and alcohol products, and the implementation of mandatory

seat belt laws. In addition, progress is being made in identifying the characteristics of mothers most likely to give birth prematurely, so that this indirect cause of mental retardation may be reduced. Recent advances in science have helped physicians to identify certain genetic factors strongly associated with mental retardation. These breakthroughs have led to genetic counseling, which provides information to prospective parents about the possibility that they may give birth to a child with a disability. Other tests such as amniocentesis detect the presence of selected genetic disorders, including Down syndrome, prior to birth.

Early intervention within the United States began with President Johnson's policies on funding programs which would promote intellectual and physical development in children of lower socioeconomic backgrounds. The program began as a cost-cutting effort to minimize future costs of caring for individuals with and without disabilities. The idea being that, if a child can be provided with a positive developmental trajectory, this will allow the child opportunities to be successful earlier and hopefully over the lifespan. As a result of these policies, legal mandates have since been introduced which help identify children at risk or developmentally delayed. Begun under PL 99-457, the Handicapped Infants and Toddlers Act of 1986, the law's attention to younger children has become an integral part of special education services (see chapter 15).

When working with very young children, the implementation of federal special education law follows a noncategorical approach and includes children who show delays in one or more of the following: cognitive development, physical development, psychosocial development, speech and language, and self-help skills. The focus of this legislation is to identify children at risk and to ensure they are provided educational opportunities they might not otherwise receive. This law also focuses on empowering families to get involved with the establishment of the Individual Family Service Plan (IFSP) and mandates educational programs for children ages three to five. Financial incentives are also provided to encourage services for the child and family as early as the first day of life. This law ensures that every effort is made to identify and provide needed services as early as possible. The law may have far-reaching implications for minimizing some of the deficits associated with mental retardation. Progress is being made against some of the more serious forms by such techniques as corrective surgery for malformations of the skull and the diversion of excess fluid in the brain through various shunting techniques. Infants who have inadequate blood sugar in the first few critical days after birth are now more readily identified and given corrective treatment. Damage resulting from Rh factor incompatibility can be prevented by treatment of the mother after the birth of her first child (the firstborn is not vulnerable to damage). Quick treatment in cases of lead poisoning or, better yet, action to prevent children from eating paint containing lead can undoubtedly prevent some cases. Further preventative measures include the removal of environmental contaminants, immunization of children for all preventable diseases, using bicycle helmets, seat belts, and car seats.

All of these steps have been effective in eliminating only a relatively small fraction of mental retardation. Increased attention to relevant basic and applied research and to the prompt application of new discoveries is essential in carrying forward this initial progress. Unfortunately, even with these advances, there are disturbing trends which still need to be addressed. In 1993 the Centers for Disease Control report showed that the number of babies born with fetal alcohol syndrome (FAS) tripled between 1979 and 1992. Reported cases leapt from 1 per 10,000 births in 1979 to nearly 4 per 10,000 in 1992 (Facts on File, 1993) and FAS is known to contribute to health problems, including mental retardation. Fetal alcohol syndrome (FAS) can result when a woman abuses alcohol (beer, wine, mixed drinks) during pregnancy. Some of the babies born to these women have the full spectrum of symptoms of FAS, and some do not. According to Dr. Ann Streissguth (1997), who directs the University of Washington's Fetal Alcohol and Drug Unit, the diagnosis of FAS is made when three criteria are met:

1. Growth deficiency in height, weight, or both, prenatally or postnatally.
2. A specific pattern of minor anomalies that include characteristic facial features including eye slits (short palpebral fissures), short upturned nose, a smooth or a long philtrum (the ridges running between the nose and lips), and a thin upper lip.
3. Central nervous system (CNS) damage, including small size of the brain (microcephly), tremors, hyperactivity, fine or gross motor problems, attentional deficits, learning disabilities, intellectual or cognitive impairments, or seizures. Mental retardation and developmental delays also qualify as CNS criteria but, like the other single items listed, they are not necessary for a diagnosis.

The diagnosis of FAS also requires "a presumed" history of maternal alcohol exposure. This means that an attempt is made to determine that the mother was abusing alcohol during pregnancy. This determination is often difficult because information is gathered retrospectively (months, or sometimes years, after the birth of the baby), or from an adoptive parent, or even from an adult with FAS. The diagnosis is more readily made with comprehensive information about the excessive or substantial regular intake of alcohol or heavy episodic drinking.

These individuals with FAS have varying degrees of mental retardation (Baer, Sampson, Barr, Connor, &

Streissguth, 2003; Streissguth, 1997). Some children are given the diagnosis of fetal alcohol effect (FAE) because they do not meet the full criteria for FAS. In addition, professionals currently refer to Fetal Alcohol Spectrum Disorders (FASD). This is not a diagnostic term, but an umbrella term to describe a range of effects of a child who is prenatally exposed to alcohol. According to the National Organization on Fetal Alcohol Syndrome (NOFAS, 2004), FASD covers terms for individuals with prenatal alcohol exposure:

- Fetal alcohol syndrome (FAS)
- Alcohol-related neurodevelopmental disorder (ARND)—those with cognitive and functional impairments
- Alcohol-related birth defects (ARBD)—physical features linked with FAS
- Fetal alcohol effect (FAE)

(See Streissguth, 1997, which remains a solid resource for families and communities regarding FAS.)

Teaching Those with Mental Retardation

Students with mental retardation exhibit certain common characteristics. However, like their nondisabled counterparts, they vary greatly in the extent to which they demonstrate specific characteristic behaviors. This appears to be the result of the idiosyncratic characteristics of this population. Students with mental retardation may exhibit unique problems which, in the educational setting, make progress challenging. For example, secondary health problems and sensory or physical impairments may influence educational outcome. Educators must learn to recognize these common behavioral patterns while also remembering to search for the individual qualities that are unique to each human being.

Students with mental retardation have the same basic needs, including recreational, vocational, educational, social, and others, as do their nondisabled peers. In addition, frequently these students need additional services beyond those normally provided to students with mental retardation. While educational outcomes may be different, the goal should be to promote activities which are safe, functional, and age appropriate for the student.

Learning Characteristics

Essentially, the learning characteristics of students with mental retardation are similar to those of their nonretarded peers in that they follow the same developmental sequence.

Primary differences are noted in the total amount of information gained and in the rate at which this material is learned. Other learning characteristics of individuals with mental retardation include a short attention span, difficulty in dealing with abstracts, and a limited ability to generalize information. It is widely recognized that individuals with mental retardation have attention deficiencies (Bergen & Mosley, 1994).

Since traditional educational programs have required students to sustain continuous attention for relatively long periods of time, teachers need to be sensitive to the unique needs and abilities of students with these learning traits. Research would suggest that attention training can significantly improve the performance of students with mental retardation but may not be transferrable (Del Rey & Stewart, 1989).

While teaching students with mental retardation, it remains imperative that information be presented in a way that is easily understood. Merrill (1990) reports it takes longer for individuals with mental retardation to encode and process information than their normal peers. Educationally, this requires providing students with the opportunity to rehearse and frequently repeat the same activities. Burger and colleagues (1980) suggest that when individuals with mental retardation are afforded opportunities to rehearse specific strategies, they are able to significantly improve performance.

Perhaps as challenging for the student with mental retardation is to generalize the information he or she learns and transfer those skills. This includes the inability to solve problems in different situations and effectively employ problem-solving strategies. Therefore, educators must use instructional strategies so that students with mental retardation not only attend to relevant stimuli, but are given the opportunity to rehearse and practice those skills in a variety of settings. Students who distract easily and/or have short attention spans may need additional visual cues and modeling as much as possible. Instruction should be designed which affords students opportunities to be successful.

Although the inability to transfer learned material, academic or social, from one situation to another is a major learning difficulty for students, the primary learning deficiency may be the failure of persons with mental retardation to effectively employ problem-solving strategies. Educators, therefore, must use procedures to present information in such a fashion that youngsters attend to relevant stimuli.

Applied behavior analysis is the instructional approach that has produced the most consistent educational improvements in students with mental retardation. Gains with this approach are attributed to its emphasis on the direct and continuous measurement of selected behaviors that have been systematically task-analyzed.

Social and Emotional Characteristics

The failure of students with mental retardation to keep intellectual pace with other students contributes to personality maladjustment and the development of undesirable behavior patterns. Much of the normal individual's social maturity and satisfactory adjustment is acquired in play situations throughout the formative years. This is not so with children with mental retardation, who frequently find themselves rejected by their nonretarded peers, or who, because of their low mentality, have no interest in group play. As a result, these students often feel inferior and then tend to devalue their skills and talents, resulting in further withdrawal and regression in ability. Understandably, these individuals are frustrated and develop an attitude of "I can't," which means "I have tried, I have failed, and I do not want to try again." Researchers have reported that individuals with mental retardation have significantly lower levels of self-esteem than their normal peers (Chiu, 1990). Historically, a greater emphasis has been placed on the cognitive, and not the social or emotional, functioning of children with mental retardation (Koop, Baker, & Brown, 1992).

Relatively few studies have investigated the effects of participation in physical activities on self-concept (Riggen & Ulrich, 1993). Anecdotally, teachers, coaches, and parents have long praised the numerous benefits of sports participation for children with mental retardation, including changes in self-esteem. Rarick (1971), and later Bell, Kozav, and Martin (1979), not only examined self-concept, but the influence of Special Olympic participation on physical fitness, social interaction, and community awareness. Both studies found significant improvements for athletes who participated in these events. More recently, Wright and Cowden (1986) and Gibbons and Bushakra (1989) found significant gains in feelings of self-concept and self-worth, respectively, with participation in Special Olympics training.

Conversely, some individuals with mental retardation, placed in circumstances in which more is expected of them than they can deliver, exhibit expressions of fear and aggression. Aggressiveness on the part of the child with mental retardation may be an attempt to cover weaknesses, to demonstrate worth, to attract attention, or to relieve tensions. Rebellious acts and other undesirable behavior are similarly motivated. On occasions those who have mental retardation may use their disability as a protective shield or in an outright bid for sympathy to compensate for their lack of social acceptance.

Physical and Motor Learning Characteristics

Comparative studies of children with mental retardation have shown they consistently score lower than other children on measures of strength, endurance, agility, balance, running speed, flexibility, and reaction time. Generally, the motor performance of youngsters with mental retardation tends to be two to four years behind their non-mentally retarded peers. These differences have been attributed to developmental lags and variability in performance (Moss, & Hogg, 1981; Porretta, 1985). Dobbins and his associates (1976; 1981) caution, however, that the motor performance of many boys with mental retardation compares favorably with their nondisabled peers when allowances are made for differences in body size. Some differences may be attributed to failure to understand the movement skill task rather than the inability to execute the skill. Newell (1985) believes that the motor deficiency in populations with mental retardation lies not in the coordination of the action but in its control. This line of reasoning suggests that the problem may be due to a deficiency in the biodynamic system—force, mass, and stiffness of muscles and joints.

Those with Down syndrome possess some unique physical characteristics worthy of a separate discussion. These individuals are often inappropriately referred to as mongoloids because of the resemblance of their facial features to those of the Mongol race. Although these similarities have been exaggerated, children with Down syndrome do tend to have a flat nose with eyes that appear to slant upward. Other visible characteristics include reduced head and ear size, a small mouth with abnormal teeth, and a protruding tongue. Small, square hands, and hair that is usually sparse, fine, and straight are

TABLE 11.1   Characteristics of the Child with Down Syndrome

Characteristics	Movement Implications
Lag in physical growth. (Growth ceases at an earlier than normal age and generally results in shorter height and smaller overall stature.) Lag is evident in motor development.	The child may need to participate in activities geared for younger age groups.
The circulatory system is less well developed. Arteries are often narrow and thinner than normal, and less vascular proliferation is evidenced. Many children (especially boys) exhibit congenital heart disorders, with heart murmurs and septum defects being the most common.	Although there is a need for the development of endurance, youngsters will have difficulty in endurance activities. It is necessary for all children to have a medical exam and for the instructor to develop a program with medical consultation.
Poor respiration and susceptibility to respiratory infections. (Underdeveloped jaw causes mouth to be too small for normal-sized tongue, inducing mouth breathing.)	Poor respiration may impede participation in endurance activities.
Perceptual handicaps.	Children may be clumsy and awkward. Activities to develop perceptual abilities should be emphasized.
Poor balance.	Since balance is important in most physical and motor activities, lack of balance will affect performance ability. Children need balance training.
Enjoyment of music and rhythmic activities.	The instructor should include rhythmic activities in the program to provide successful and enjoyable experiences and should use music as an aid in teaching.
Obesity.	General overall participation in activities that enhance weight reduction are recommended.
Flabbiness. (Hypotonicity, particularly associated with newborn infants.)	The instructor should provide opportunity for movement experiences at early ages and activities to increase strength at later ages.
Protruding abdomen, lack of muscle and ligament support around the joints, and pronated ankles.	Activities to enhance body alignment, increase muscle and ligament support around the joints, and abdominal exercises are recommended.
Ability to mimic.	Instructor should demonstrate activities and ask children to imitate them.

Source: from Winnick, J. P. (1979). *Early movement experiences and development: Habilitation and remediation* (p. 229). Philadelphia: W. B. Saunders Co.

other noticeable characteristics. Impairments in speech are quite common among this population. Physical educators should be particularly cognizant that these individuals are usually short and stocky with a tendency toward obesity. In the area of physical fitness, the Down syndrome population performs at a lower level than that of other individuals with mental retardation (Connolly & Michael, 1986). These differences may be due to their generally short stature and hypertonia, lack of muscle tone (Share & French, 1982), or inability to respond cardiovascularly (Piteti, Climstein, Campbell, Barrett, & Jackson, 1992). However, these individuals do well and improve through physiological training programs (Dyer, 1994). In addition, those with Down syndrome have a tendency to gain weight in their early teens after they have reached their maximum height (Glaze, 1985). Winnick (1979) has listed major physical and motor characteristics of Down syndrome children and the movement implications associated with these characteristics (table 11.1). Upper respiratory infection, heart defects, and poor muscle tone are also very prevalent among individuals with Down syndrome. A medical history is essential in developing physical education programs for this population.

Individuals with Down syndrome may suffer from a condition known as atlantoaxial instability, a malalignment of the first two cervical vertebrae. This condition exists in approximately 17 percent of all Down syndrome individuals. Because individuals with this disorder do not indicate any symptoms, X rays of the vertebral column are necessary. If the condition exists, but is not detected, forceful forward or backward bending of the neck, which is common in some sports such as gymnastics, may dislocate the axis, causing damage to the spinal cord (figure 11.3). School officials should follow the lead of Special Olympics (1983) and require all students with Down syndrome to have medical clearance before they can

be allowed to participate without restrictions in physical education and sports programs. In the absence of medical clearance, Down syndrome students should be restricted from participating in gymnastics, diving and butterfly stroke in swimming, high jump, pentathlon, and any warm-up exercise placing pressure on the head and neck muscles. This restriction should be temporary until the necessary clearance is obtained. If the diagnosis confirms atlantoaxial instability, the individual should be permanently restricted from these activities. In these situations other activities can be selected that are enjoyable and pose minimal risk to the student.

Recognition of these characteristics points to the need of students with mental retardation for successful experiences in group play. Although youngsters who have mental retardation cannot generally acquire the high degree of skill of nonretarded players, they can acquire sufficient skills to participate in enough different muscular activities to increase their physical fitness and improve their body mechanics. In addition to the physical benefits, play provides many opportunities for social development and emotional growth. Adherence to the rules of the game and to the sportsman's code of fair play provides incentive for self-discipline and self-control. Respect for one's own abilities and limitations and those of others is stimulated in the cooperation and sharing necessitated by the game situation. Many desirable learnings are claimed for sports in the training of nondisabled youngsters. However much these have been exaggerated for other children, they are essentially acceptable for those with mental retardation, whose other opportunities for learning to work and play with others are considerably restricted.

Students with severe and progressed mental retardation are in great need of personal attention in physical education; because of their physical and social limitations, they do not respond well in group play. They even experience difficulty in relating to just one person. Serving these children effectively requires a very low teacher-pupil ratio, usually one to one.

Planning the Physical Activity Program

Directing the play of the student requires careful organization on the part of the instructor. The ultimate goal is a physical activity program in which students can enjoy the experience while improving their movement proficiency. Additional planning considerations must focus on creating a program that can be conducted in an appropriate environment with suitable activities presented in a manner so that students can succeed.

In planning any program, particularly one funded by federal, state, and local taxes as many such programs are, it is essential that a clear statement of the rationale of the

Figure 11.3 Atlantoaxial instability. Dislocation of the atlas may injure the spinal cord.

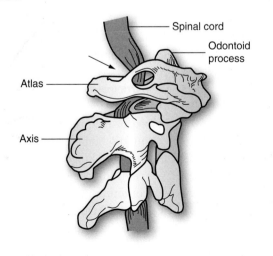

- Spinal cord
- Odontoid process
- Atlas
- Axis

program be developed. The essential question to be answered in the statement is, "Why this program with these activities for this group of students?" This question is legitimate, and it deserves a straightforward answer that can be understood by participants, their parents, school officials, and the public.

Those who support physical education for students with mental retardation often justify this support by stating that movement experiences improve intelligence, enhance self-concept, improve motor ability, and develop physical fitness. Although research evidence is extremely limited, support, to some extent, may be given to each of these. It would seem logical to suggest that physical education may be one of the few disciplines that contributes to all three learning domains: psychomotor, cognitive, and affective.

Nevertheless, it must be emphasized that the unique contribution physical education provides to those with mental retardation is in the area of motor development (figure 11.4). It has been established clearly that these youngsters are deficient in motor ability and in physical fitness (Faison-Hodge & Porretta, 2004; Pitetti & Fernhall, 2004). Furthermore, data supports conclusively the argument that improvements can be made in these areas if appropriate programs are provided (Eberhard & Eterradossi, 1990; Horgan, 1983).

Figure 11.4   Physical activity for individuals with disabilities helps improve fitness levels and enhances quality of life.

As students experience success in physical education, they often improve in self-concept and in general emotional development. Emphasis on motor skill development also provides opportunities to reinforce the youngsters' understanding of certain important concepts, such as shape, size, and color. It is important that the physical education teacher be aware of the activities that children are doing in the classroom. A coordinated curriculum involving special education personnel is necessary for the most efficient presentation of material to those with mental retardation.

Emphasis on motor skill instruction is a must in programs for students with mental retardation. Tasks such as reaching and grasping, which normally develop with maturation, will need to be taught to many of these youngsters. The value of psychomotor skills and their relationship to affective and cognitive learning will be apparent to all who work with students who are severely retarded. For these reasons, school officials and parents of the children will actively seek assistance from motor development specialists. Unfortunately, in the past too many professionals teaching those students have not had a sufficient background in motor skill development.

Class Placement

In recent years, classroom placement—and more specifically, issues of inclusion, mainstreaming, integration, least restrictive environment, and segregation—have come to the forefront within educational systems in the United States and Europe (Downs & Williams, 1994). Public Law 94-142, The Education for All Handicapped Children Act of 1975 and its successors, including IDEA 2004, emphasize that students with disabilities, including those with mental retardation, should be educated in the least restrictive environment. Although educators are in general agreement with this concept, means to implement this requirement have generated a great deal of controversy. Specifically, some feel that youngsters with mental retardation should be taught in separate special classes and others feel that these children should receive instruction in the general educational setting, the mainstream of education. In the field of physical education there are few studies available to support either position. It is apparent, though, that youngsters with mental retardation are capable of successfully participating in regular physical education classes. The topic of inclusion has become an emotional and controversial topic for many educators, parents, and students with and without disabilities. Block and Krebs (1992) have challenged previous thinking relating to placements in the least restrictive environment in special physical education. They focus on a continuum of support in school settings. Craft (1994) suggests that "inclusion can be successful when all children are not required to follow the same curriculum" (p. 23), and Block and Vogler (1994) report that "students with disabilities can receive an appropriate, individualized education within the general class setting" (p. 43). While this continuum provides numerous placement opportunities, it fails to include full-time special physical educators in the general or residential facility. Furthermore, they suggest that general physical education is the only environment which allows students enough flexibility to provide opportunities for interactions with a group of peers while still providing individual instruction.

While special physical education is not the LRE for all children with mental retardation, it is a necessary part of many students' IEPs. Often times, general physical educators are ill-prepared to adequately address the needs of students with mental retardation. This may be due to a lack of training, inadequate facilities and equipment, or perhaps personal misbelief or fear.

Others, including Block and Krebs (1992), feel that placement decisions into special physical education are frequently made on categorical labels rather than on systematic decision making. While labeling has drawn criticism from many parents, teachers, and administrators, labels are frequently necessary to receive adequate support services from federal, state, or local educational offices. In a study by Rarick and his associates (1981), data have been obtained to suggest that youngsters with mental retardation can benefit from placement in the general physical education class. Children with severe mental retardation will require classes that are specifically designed to meet their unique movement needs. It must not be assumed, however, that all youngsters fit these general guidelines. Occasionally, low functioning children with mental retardation have the competency to participate in some or all of the general physical education activities. Similarly, not all students with mental retardation will find success in the general class program. Therefore, placements must be individualized to respond to the unique needs of each student.

Placement flexibility is extremely desirable in movement programs for students with mental retardation. Some students may be placed in special classes; others may be placed with general classes for a small portion of every period. Some students may have sufficient skill to completely integrate for an entire physical education period. Placement consideration must be based on a careful evaluation of motor skill and physical fitness performance coupled with other factors such as the child's social maturity level, the level of support and modifications needed, and curricular considerations. Remember, too, that no placement decision is final, and periodic reviews should be made at least semiannually.

Teaching Environment

Educators often assume that physical education activities must be taught in a gymnasium. For many children, particularly those with mental retardation, this is an incorrect assumption; conducting classes within such a large space may actually interfere with their skill development. These youngsters are easily distracted and the presence of permanent or temporary equipment usually found in the gymnasium will compete with the teacher's ability to hold the attention of the students. **It is recommended, therefore, that instruction be confined to a small area when introducing a new skill. A distraction-free corner of the classroom will often be suitable for this purpose.** As the participants become proficient in the skill, opportunities should be provided to utilize the new skills within the larger environment of the playground or gymnasium.

Physical education teachers should strive to maintain a class size conducive to learning. The ratio of teacher to student will vary according to the motor skill level of the youngster and the ability of the teacher. Children with severe mental retardation will often require a one-to-one student-teacher ratio. For higher-functioning students, the class size may reach as high as one teacher to ten or twelve youngsters. As a general guide, it is strongly suggested that the physical education teacher not be asked to teach more youngsters with mental retardation per class than is the classroom teacher. Early indications suggest that using trained peer tutors can provide an invaluable resource to the classroom teacher and provide beneficial experiences for students with and without mental retardation (Houston-Wilson, 1993).

Student Interest and Motivation

In organizing any activity designed to assist students, it is essential to consider the interest level of the participants. Many students with mental retardation will come to the physical education class with high initial interest because the change to another type of class activity is interesting in itself. Moreover, if previous physical education periods have been fun, interest is high in anticipation of more fun. If natural initial interest does not exist among the students, as is often true when new skills are introduced, it can be aroused in various ways. Students with mild mental retardation can be introduced to a new game with simple, colorful pictures. Through cooperation with the classroom teacher, a short story related to the activity to be presented may be told. Or, if a song or music is to accompany this activity, it may be introduced in an interesting way before the actual activity is presented. Although considerable student interest may be generated, it is usually not sustained because the interest span of these students is relatively short. A change to an alternate activity, designed to achieve the same purpose as the initial activity, is indicated when interest lags.

Children with severe mental retardation do not always respond well to the use of pictures or stories as a means of motivation for desirable behavior. Generally, these children require individual attention and continuous stimulation and encouragement by the teacher, aide, or trained volunteer.

The technique of behavior modification has been a most successful method for reaching these children.

Equipment

To maintain the interest of the students, a wide variety of play equipment is desirable (figure 11.5). **Using a dynamic systems approach, one should ask:**

1. Does the equipment take into account the ability and/or size of the student?
2. Will the equipment stimulate interest and imagination?
3. Is the equipment safe?
4. Does the equipment stimulate social, locomotor, and manipulative activities?
5. Can the novelty of the equipment be easily manipulated? and
6. Does the equipment provide feedback on how well the movement was made?

There should be enough physical education equipment for each specific activity, so that no child need sit around idly waiting for a turn. An insufficient amount of equipment interferes with learning by reducing the maximum number of practice trials available to the student. Opportunities to explore with different items designed to achieve the same purpose, such as teaching students to throw using objects of various shapes, sizes, and substances, should be used to renew stimulation and interest.

In addition to the conventional equipment and supplies found in good physical education programs, many ordinary items can be adapted to offer variety and stimulate interest. Old tires, logs of various sizes, barrels, large pipes, boards and planks, saw horses, wooden and paper boxes, balloons, steps, and parachutes are some examples. An innovative teacher will discover many other items that can be used effectively in the program.

Teaching Methods and Techniques

Prior to the onset of the actual lesson, the instructor should ask themself several important questions:

1. What is the purpose of the activity?
2. Is the activity age appropriate?
3. Is the activity safe for individuals and/or groups?
4. How will the activity benefit students?
5. Is the teacher adequately prepared to teach the activity?
6. Is the activity meaningful (functional) and fun?

The problem-solving method has limitations in teaching motor skills to students with mental retardation because of their need for **structure** and **direction**; nevertheless, exploration can be rewarding for some students with cognitive dysfunction.

To increase the possibility that problem-solving will be successful as a method of teaching students with mental retardation, the following suggestions are offered:

1. Select problems that have a simple solution.
2. Keep the problems few in number and related to the same area of motor skill.
3. Explain and demonstrate how moving one part of the body while in motion can change the nature of the movement. For example, in solving the problem "Can you hop like a rabbit?" demonstrate a hop on two legs

Figure 11.5   Play equipment can be used to stimulate interest.

Teaching Techniques

- Demonstration
- Verbal cues and prompts
- Consistency
- Provide success-oriented experiences
- Encourage participation
- Offer praise
- Consistent discipline
- New and complex activities at the beginning of class

and then show how, by lifting one leg in hopping, or by raising the hands to the head to simulate bunny ears, the nature of the movement can be changed.

4. Repeat the same problem frequently, encouraging some small change in movement.

Modifying instruction to meet the individual's needs is a starting point toward successful learning. Throughout a student's education, parents should be an integral part of the planning and teaching team. While teaching individuals with mental retardation it is important to:

1. Use concrete materials that are interesting, age appropriate, and relevant to the student.
2. Present information and instructions in small sequential steps and review each step frequently.
3. Provide prompt and immediate feedback.
4. Stress and provide opportunities for success.
5. Teach tasks or skills that students will use frequently and can apply the tasks or skills to settings outside the school.
6. Break down activity and instruction into small steps or segments (task analysis).

The **direct method** is generally very successful for helping students with mental retardation learn motor skills. Of the various techniques utilized in the method, demonstration appears to be the most effective for teaching students with mild mental retardation. These students are great mimics, and much can be accomplished by encouraging them to imitate the demonstrated skill. The demonstration must be adapted to the intellectual abilities of the students. It is usually less successful when the students attempt the activity at the time it is being demonstrated. In some cases, it may be desirable to use physical assistance at the time the demonstration is being made; this may require manually moving the child's body parts through the desired movements. To avoid confusion, the instructor and child should face in the same direction when a new skill is to be demonstrated. This technique, known as mirroring, does not require the youngster to reverse the visual image. Similarly, when giving physical assistance, the teacher should stand behind the student, reaching around him or her, if necessary.

Physical assistance is effective in many situations, such as when teaching a child to ride a tricycle. Here the child may not be able to perceive the nature of the action required to pedal the tricycle until the teacher moves his or her feet alternately through proper movements. Physical assistance may be successfully used for teaching motor movement to the low-functioning student. When working with students of this level it is important that the teacher move the parts of the body in the same way each time to avoid confusion. The hold taken on the child should be firm and reassuring to promote confidence in attempting the movement.

Verbal cues and prompts can be utilized when teaching students with mental retardation in much the same way as with nondisabled youth. However, over-reliance on the use of verbalization with students who are severely retarded, many of whom have communication disorders, has definite limitations. It is possible to teach these students to understand and respond to a limited number of words related to the skills they are learning. Examples of such words are "sit," "grasp," and "step over." Only one or two words should be taught during a given period. The word that is being taught should be repeated over and over as the action it describes is being demonstrated by the teacher or being performed by the student. The word should be used alone rather than in a sentence. This does not preclude speaking in sentences. Rather, it is highly desirable that such communication take place because hearing sentences is important to the potential language development of the students.

Care must be exercised not to provide students with mental retardation more information than they can process during a given period of time. It is not uncommon to observe a response delay of several seconds in students with mental retardation, similar to that observed in very young children. During this interval of inaction, it is important that the teacher not become impatient and provide additional visual or verbal cues. This extra instruction interferes with information still in the processing system, thereby confusing the student.

Efforts must be made to assist students in recalling and retaining information. Consistency in the instructional environment—using similar cues or requests—is helpful in establishing efficient and effective gains in physical education. Likewise, in the teaching of any task it is essential for the teacher's directions to be as specific as possible. The instructor's failure to provide good visual, verbal, or manual cues often results in students not performing the task because of their inability to understand what is expected of them. For example, many students with mental retardation have difficulty learning the hand and foot placement required in the sprint start. Hand and foot prints cut out of cardboard or other material and placed on the floor can be invaluable aids in teaching this skill, especially if the prints are actual tracings of the student's own hands and feet. The use of various colored lines painted on the floor can help in-class organization by providing the teacher and students with several specific common points of reference. One can well appreciate the confusion that can arise from an inexperienced teacher's nonspecific command of "over there."

Instructional efforts should be directed toward providing success-oriented experiences for the participants. Recognition of this principle is especially critical for teachers of students with special needs, since so many of these individuals have failed in tasks for which they were ill-prepared. To overcome this difficulty, instructors of these students should recognize the importance of breaking skills down into minute components and listing them in a hierarchical sequence (task analysis). For each component, behavioral statements with criterion levels may then be developed so that teacher and student will know when to advance to the next step. An analysis of skill in this manner provides a means for the student to recognize success. The teacher, too, will become more cognizant that small but important improvements are being achieved.

Participation in play activities by everyone should be actively encouraged by the teacher. There should, of course, be no resort to pressure tactics. Students need and seek approval, and they can be led to cooperate and participate if they know that this is what the teacher wants and gives approval for. **Teacher participation, when possible, in the play and fitness activities of these students is also encouraged.** Students react favorably when they see that what is asked of them is good for all, including their teacher. Because students with mental retardation are easily distracted, class observers should be kept to a minimum or, perhaps best, be included in the class activities.

Praise should be offered generously for the efforts of the youngster. The attempt may not result in successful performance, but the effort that is exerted should be commended by the teacher. Sincere praise can be one of the teacher's most effective motivators and helps to create the kind of learning situation most conducive to progress.

The teacher should exercise firm and consistent discipline without resorting to threats and corporal punishment. The disciplining must take a form that the group is capable of comprehending, such as withholding approval. Those who present a disruptive influence may be temporarily removed from the class and dealt with in a small group or on an individual basis.

Individuals with mental retardation perform best the first few times they do a skill. **Consequently, it is to their advantage to end the practice of any one skill before frustration at inability to master the skill sets in.** After the skills of a game have been mastered over a gradual period of time, they should be reviewed briefly each time before the game is played. These drill periods should be just long enough to refresh the students' memories.

Because many individuals who are mentally retarded have low physical vitality, they fatigue easily. This has important implications for the teaching situation. First, it means that new and complex activities should be planned for the early part of the period while the students are fresh and alert. Then, too, a greater chance of injury exists after fatigue sets in, so it is extremely important for the instructor to watch for signs of fatigue. However, the teacher should

also incorporate fitness activities into each lesson. Research supports that fitness levels can be significantly improved if opportunities and proper training supervision takes place (Lavay & McKenzie, 1991; Pitetti & Tan, 1991).

Special efforts may be required to evoke responses from torpid youngsters. Such students are particularly in need of physical activity but show no interest in play. It may be necessary to use physical assistance and progressions; for example, tossing balloons at the student so that he or she will raise the arms for protection or will attempt to catch or dodge the balloons. From the use of balloons, the instructor may progress to beanbags and large soft balls that would not cause serious hurt if they were not warded off. Eventually the child can be taught catching, throwing, and other simple motor skills.

In some instances, physical education teachers have obtained the assistance of outstanding high school students on a volunteer basis in providing individual attention for youngsters with mental retardation. This has proven to be a worthwhile learning experience for students with and without a disability. Parents of students with mental retardation are often willing to volunteer their services. When this occurs in the school setting it is to the benefit of both parent and child to assign to the parent a child other than the parent's own. Maguire (1985) found that parents can be effective implementors of instruction in physical education if properly trained and provided with periodic feedback. In his approach the parents were asked to supplement through home instruction programs that were conducted at school. The rate at which skills were acquired was faster in this approach than a school-based program alone. To utilize program volunteers effectively, they must be trained and the teacher and parents must provide a daily written program for each student emphasizing the skills to be learned. A concerted effort must be made to monitor the efforts of the volunteers, correcting and reinforcing them when appropriate.

The physical educator also has the opportunity of teaching the student with mental retardation certain health and safety facts and of encouraging the development of habits pertaining to personal care and protection as well as the wise use of leisure time. In the area of health, such personal hygiene matters as showering after activity, care of the feet to prevent athlete's foot, and cleanliness of gym clothes and socks are covered. Good safety practices, such as not throwing the bat, should be clearly and firmly established so that they will be observed not only in supervised play but also in free play. By providing in the physical education curriculum opportunities to learn games that can be played during leisure hours, the wise use of such time can be encouraged. Because of their generally restricted interests and recreational opportunities, individuals with mental retardation often pursue undesirable leisure activities or idle the time away, which has a negative impact from the standpoint of their development. They may become harmful to themselves and to society.

For the low-functioning youngster, the health and safety habits to be taught are simple and more fundamental in nature. Examples are when and where to go to the toilet, how to wash the hands, and being aware that a shoe is untied.

Physical Activities for Students with Mild Mental Retardation

The physical education program must present a variety of activities directed toward the special needs of children with mental retardation. These experiences, depending on the functioning ability of the individual, range from basic motor skills to leisure activities. The discussion that follows applies primarily to the youngster who, although not severely retarded, possesses movement deficiencies serious enough to require modification or adaptations in some or all of the activities of the regular physical education class. For a more complete discussion of the motor skills, games, sports, and other activities discussed within this section, refer to the chapters within this text and CD devoted to those topics. An excellent example of a comprehensive physical education curriculum developed for students with mental retardation is the I CAN materials prepared by Janet Wessel and her associates (1976) as well as the I CAN PRIMARY for children with and without disabilities (Wessel & Zettel, 1998).

Basic Motor Skills

For very young children and those who cannot participate with success in more complex exercises and games, a variety of simple activities that will achieve the goal of desired physical development should be introduced (figure 11.6). Among the very simplest of these activities are the basic motor skills of everyday living: walking, balancing, twisting, turning, bending, and climbing stairs. Slightly more involved are the basic play skills: running, hopping, jumping, skipping, kicking, hanging, catching, and throwing. Perceptual motor skills such as visually tracking a suspended ball and stepping over and under obstacles placed at various heights should also be emphasized.

The skills must be presented to students so that they will take pleasure in performing them. Variety in presentation is also vital to achieving interest in their performance.

Figure 11.6 Teaching students basic motor skills such as walking up and down steps is an important aspect of programs for children with special needs.

The following suggestions are ways in which this may be accomplished:

1. Walking at varied tempos and with different sizes and kinds of steps, such as short, quick steps; slow giant strides; tiptoeing.
2. Running at varied tempos.
3. Jumping on both feet, alternating feet, one foot; attaining various heights.
4. Hopping on one foot and on alternate feet.
5. Skipping at varied tempos.
6. Marching at varied tempos; alternating with running, skipping, and jumping; accompanied by hand clapping.
7. Climbing stairs, alternating the feet.
8. Catching and throwing a large balloon.
9. Catching and bouncing a ball.
10. Throwing the ball for distance and at objects; throwing the ball to a catcher.
11. Kicking, with the leg swinging freely, at a large ball, at a small ball.
12. Hanging from a bar or the rung of a ladder, with both arms, with one arm; climbing the ladder with the hands only.
13. Balancing on a balance beam or log; walking along a chalked line; stepping on the rungs of a ladder placed on the floor.

Springing up and down on a jouncing board,[3] leaping from the board to the ground.

15. Walking on and jumping on and off tires.

16. Crawling through and over barrels or large pipes.

17. Walking on a balance beam while focusing on a fixed point at the end of the beam.

18. Walking on a balance beam while focusing on a fixed point to the side of the beam.

19. Jumping and turning to the right and then the left side.

20. Rolling on a large inflated ball.

The possibilities for emphasizing the basic motor skills through mimetic play are practically limitless. Pretending they are animals, the children can waddle like ducks, hop like bunnies, leap like frogs, and walk softly (on tiptoes) like kittens. Imitating the actions of people, they may vigorously chop wood, march in a band, sweep the floor, or iron clothes. At times the mimetic activities may be done to musical accompaniment, both for the added interest provided by the music and for the introduction it provides to instruction in dance.

Games

Activities such as relays, parachute play, and simple games may be introduced to those who have acquired some basic skill movement and can follow simple directions. The following guide is offered for the selection of simple activities. The more capable the students are of participating in complex activities, the less necessity there will be for the games to meet all of the suggested criteria. A very simple game is one in which

1. All children do the same thing.
2. The space is relatively small.
3. Choices that must be made are few in number.
4. Positions are fixed.
5. Quality of performance brings no penalties or privileges.
6. The possible directions of movement are restricted.
7. Personnel remain the same.
8. Motor skill requirements are limited.

Whenever possible, games that reinforce cognitive concepts such as letter, color, and symbol recognition should be incorporated into activities. In addition to the obvious value of these experiences, they are also highly motivating and are enjoyed by the children. Physical education activities designed to reinforce cognitive concepts also will help the student generalize material taught by the special educator to other settings.

For the higher-functioning adolescent who has successfully participated in activities meeting the previous crite-

[3]A board one inch thick, six to eight inches wide, and six feet long, balanced on two supports.

ria, opportunities to learn lead-up games, such as kickball, keep away, line soccer, twenty-one, and newcomb, should be provided.

Rhythmic Activities

Like most children, individuals who are mentally retarded enjoy music and respond well to dance and rhythmic activities. Such activities are valuable in improving coordination, flexibility, and body carriage (figure 11.7). Improvement in rhythm may also lead to improvement in the smooth performance of skilled movements (Liemohn, 1984). Extensive dance activities, ranging in complexity from simple movements to musical accompaniment to folk dances of complex patterns, should be included in the physical education program. Moreover, they provide a release from tensions and anxieties, which is in itself extremely valuable for these students. The listening experience also heightens auditory perception.

Efforts at teaching rhythmic patterns should initially focus on having children learn to keep time with one hand, then two hands, and finally, for the more advanced, incorporating the feet into the sequence as well. Children unable to master this sequence should be encouraged to let their bodies sway from side to side with the music. Making and utilizing their own instruments to play along with the music is also an activity from which all children, including those with mental retardation, can derive much pleasure.

Physical Fitness Activities

Special Olympics (www.specialolympics.org) began in 1968 to provide sports participation for individuals with mental

Figure 11.7 Emphasis on basic motor skills such as jumping is important for later skill development.

retardation. Special Olympics has grown to an international organization:

> Special Olympics is an unprecedented global movement which, through quality sports training and competition, improves the lives of people with intellectual disabilities and, in turn, the lives of everyone they touch.
> Special Olympics empowers people with intellectual disabilities to realize their full potential and develop their skills through year-round sports training and competition.

The Special Olympics *Healthy Athletes* program, begun in 1996, seeks to improve athletes' ability to train and compete in Special Olympics. Local program development and resource material for training are available online.

Special Olympics' initial competitions were offered for individuals with mental retardation, and in later years the Unified Sports program was added. This program offers opportunities for individuals with mental retardation and those without a disability to participate together in athletic competition: to come together to train and compete. In 2001, a national evaluation of the Special Olympics Unified Sports Program was undertaken to strategize about the future of expanding the program from the state to the national and international arena in a manner comparable to the Special Olympics program.

The Surgeon General's Report from the Conference on Health Disparities and Mental Retardation (2002) reported that the health status of those with mental retardation is lower than those without disabilities, yet their life expectancy has increased along with the general population. The average life expectancy of those with mental retardation is 66.1 years, and younger adults with mental retardation are expected to live as long as their peers. This means that it is important to develop and facilitate physical activity access and the maintenance of a healthy lifestyle.

Individuals with mental retardation, as a group, are deficient in all of the components of physical fitness. To a great extent this poor performance is due to a lack of opportunity to participate in play activity. Therefore, if programs are well designed and administered by an enthusiastic teacher, noticeable improvements in physical fitness can be achieved. The total amount of physical education time devoted to fitness activities for students who are mentally retarded need not be extensive. However, a developmental program of from twenty to thirty minutes that contributes to strength, flexibility, and endurance should be provided daily.

Children with mental retardation enjoy doing exercises with their teacher. The program may include such simple activities as bending, squatting, twisting the trunk, and rotating the arms. Students can achieve considerable skill in the performance of more complicated calisthenics, such as the push-up and jumping jack. Circuit training, in which different exercises are performed at various stations in the room, is highly motivating for the student and has been successfully implemented for this population (Horvat, Croce, & McGhee, 1993; Rimmer & Kelly, 1991). Charts should be provided at each station with pictures depicting the exercises to be performed and the number to be executed. Aerobic activities such as fast walking, jogging, cycling, and swimming are essential if improvements in cardiorespiratory fitness are to be obtained. For all of the physical fitness activities, records simple enough for the students to understand should be maintained to help teacher and student "see" progress.

Moon and Renzaglia (1982), in a comprehensive review of fitness of individuals with mental retardation, suggest that there is little empirical evidence to indicate the activities and instructional techniques best suited for this population. There is every reason to believe that significant gains in fitness levels can be obtained with this population. Future efforts, however, must be directed toward documenting these changes and to ensuring that opportunities to maintain fitness levels are available. **Many of the techniques and strategies that have been developed and successfully utilized with nonretarded youth can be implemented with students with mental retardation.** Careful attention, however, must be directed toward the use of systematic instructional techniques if desirable gains are to be achieved. Instruction in fitness programs, similar to academic and motor skill activities, requires the use of task analysis, daily data keeping, reinforcement, and the use of a prompt hierarchy from verbal through modeling to physical assistance as necessary.

Team Sports

As students with mental retardation achieve success through lead-up games, additional instructional time should be directed toward teaching the various team sport activities. Most of these youngsters will be familiar with sporting events as a result of attending local contests, watching television, or looking at pictures in books describing sport activities. Individuals who are mentally retarded, like most others, thoroughly enjoy these exposures. Teachers of students with mental retardation often marvel at the number of their students who can recall the names of local and national sport heroes. **Because of this high interest level, the physical education program should provide as many of these sports and games as possible.** They provide the vigorous muscular activity essential to improving physical fitness in these youngsters. Besides the physical benefits are the recreational and socializing values, which have already been stressed.

Capable teachers have been able to teach the skill of team play well enough to students who are mentally

TABLE 11.2   Adapted Skill Areas and Recreation Activity

Adaptive Skill Area	Possible Challenge	Recreation-based Interventions
Communication	Difficulty expressing feelings	Use music or art as an avenue of expression.
Home living	Difficulty managing finances	Reinforce money-management by budgeting for recreation. Assist with payment and counting change whenever possible.
Community use	Limited knowledge/use of community resources	Use community reintegration to introduce community resources. Assist in community use with a "leisure buddy."
Health and safety	Poor physical fitness	Teach active recreation skills like bike riding, roller-skating, weightlifting, swimming, etc. Developing a fitness routine and encourage follow-through.
Leisure	Limited leisure repertoire	Assess leisure interests. Teach a variety of age-appropriate leisure skills that students can use individually or in groups.
Self-care	Poor hygiene or difficulty dressing	Reinforce self-care skills, such as changing or showering before and after physical recreation activities like swimming or sports.
Social skills	Inappropriate social skills	Provide structured social skills instruction and reinforce appropriate social skills during recreation activities. Use cooperative games for social skills training.
Self-direction	Difficulty making decisions or setting goals	Provide two to three choices of recreation activities during unstructured time and use a decision-making model to encourage decisions related to leisure.
Functional academics	Difficulty recognizing and using numbers	Make a "friends" book with pictures and telephone numbers of friends. Monitor/count the number of phone calls made in the course of a weekend.
Work	Difficulty staying on task	Provide recreation opportunities as reinforcement during breaks or as positive reinforcement for staying on task.

retarded that they have been able to compete against other teams. Many individuals have been provided extensive opportunities to participate in competitive athletics under the auspices of the Special Olympics program sponsored by the Joseph P. Kennedy, Jr., Foundation. Individuals with mental retardation enjoy competition of this nature and desire it for the personal satisfaction and social approval that it brings them. An in-depth discussion of the organization and structure, including sponsored events of the Special Olympics, may be found in chapter 18.

Competition for some, however, may promote undesirable aggressive behavior on the one hand or cause them to lose interest entirely on the other. The teacher coaching a competitive team should attempt to prevent these reactions through careful development of the best possible attitudes toward competitive play. This is accomplished by emphasizing the competitive opportunities as an outgrowth of well-developed and implemented instructional programs (table 11.2).

Leisure Skills Transition Services in Physical Activity

Transition Services for Youth and Adults with Disabilities

According to IDEA 2004, the education of a youth with a disability includes the formulation of a goal that addresses the student's transition upon leaving the educational system for his/her life in the community, or as the law states "post-school adult living objectives." Besides focusing on work-related skills, the development of leisure activities is also addressed. Goals that address these areas are referred to in IDEA 2004 as Transition Services (Section 1401(34), Sub-Section 141(d)(A)(i)(VIII)). Goals are written into the student's Individualized Education Program (IEP) based on assessment and the resulting evaluations of a number of people.

Various professionals become involved with transition services for developing the student's skills and knowledge in order to engage in post-school physical and leisure activities. Physical educators, recreation therapists, community recreation specialists, or special education teachers may assess leisure skills, interests, and community resources to formulate an appropriate evaluation to submit to the IEP team (Folsom-Meek, Nearing, & Block, 2007). The transition IEP is begun at age 16 according to IDEA 2004, but in some states like Minnesota, it begins as early as age 14.

For the sake of the material in this text, transition IEPs will focus here on the physical educator/special physical educator roles and activities. IDEA 2004 intends that assessment takes into account the student's strengths, preferences, and interests (Section 1401(34)). All members of the IEP team collaborate to achieve meaningful goals. The student and a parent or caregiver must be a member of this IEP team.

Assessment for Transition Services

Fitness

The IEP team will need assessment of a student's skills for leisure with emphasis on life-long physical activity. The Brockport Physical Fitness Test (Winnick & Short, 1999) remains a solid tool for assessing health-related fitness of youth ages 10-17 with disabilities. The test itself is described in chapter 6. Historically, functional, age-appropriate fitness activity that improves muscle strength/endurance and cardio-respiratory capacity has escaped the youth with a disability. For example, some students with cerebral palsy were encouraged not to work with weights. Fortunately, the National Center on Physical Activity and Disability (NCPAD) (www.ncpad.org) began its web-based resource for just such purposes: to provide guidelines for fitness activity. Using this resource, guidelines for safely and successfully engaging in physical activity are found for a multitude of disabilities. One can register online to receive the monthly newsletter and also easily search online for a specific disability as well as resulting activity guidelines and physical activities. NCPAD and the Brockport have helped physical educators create those age-appropriate programs in physical activity for youth with disabilities. They have dispelled the notion that individuals with disabilities should not build muscles and can't be fit.

The firm establishment of the Paralympics Games, following the Olympics, have helped youth with disabilities to develop role models for being physically fit and even motivated some for elite athletic participation. It cannot be denied that broader coverage of athletes with disabilities is a boon to the physical educator trying to motivate youth with disabilities to become physically fit and active. Video footage of Paralympic activity can be found on the Internet and used in the school setting.

Involvement in Special Olympics, and other adapted athletic competitions that are local or state-wide, is appropriate for a transition IEP goal. Some schools hold after-school practices. Teachers, coaches, allied health professionals, and university faculty and students volunteer their time to teach the skills, organize transportation to competitions, and obtain the team shirts and shoes (if appropriate). In most cases, the philosophy of participating in these activities is to be honorable in the pursuit of the activity rather than to win at any cost. Special Olympians take an oath incorporating this philosophy: "Let me win. But if I cannot win, let me be brave in the attempt" (www.specialolympics.org). For the sake of our material in special physical education and transition IEPs, the focus here will be on the physical educator/special physical educator. These individuals will note that IDEA 2004 intends that assessment takes into account the student's strengths, preferences, and interests (Section 1401(34)).

Leisure

Complementary to the creation of the health-related physical fitness goals is a good assessment of the student's leisure interests and abilities. This is an exciting area in which recreation therapists led the way in creating and publishing assessment tools. Yet, as time has passed since the federal educational law of 1975, the school recreation therapists (as a related service in the law) have moved. These specialists are now in community parks, recreation settings, and clinical settings in hospitals and outpatient clinics. So, reviewing assessment areas such as motivation and leisure skills interests have expanded to meet more community and clinical needs where there is time for one person to assess with a needed depth. The commonly referred to "Big Red Book" is the two-inch-thick, red-bound *Assessment Tools for Recreational Therapy and Related Fields*, Third Edition (Burlingame & Blaschko, 2002), where the total *Leisurescope Plus* and *Teen Leisurescope Plus* is described (pp. 276–300; the kit can be obtained from www.IdyllArbor.com). This tool is used with those who do not have cognitive impairment. The authors recommend that physical educators, or those assigned to assess leisure skills, use it with youth who have emotional problems and poor cognitive ability.

A trend observed is that, in addition to more formal tests with reported validity and reliability, physical educators and those who are responsible for the IEP team transition goals in leisure and recreation are creating their own leisure skills inventories. These checklists are administered to the student and also with their parents and caregivers. The inventory is designed with the student's community in mind. Here the critical question addressed is: What is available in our community for physical recreation

TABLE 11.3 Leisure Skills Checklist

Aerobics (land & water)	Diving (SCUBA & board)	Roller skating
Archery	Fishing	Rollerblading
Backpacking	Floor hockey	Rope jumping for conditioning
Badminton	Frisbee	Rope courses
Bicycling (also large tricycling, tandems, & side-by-sides)	Frisbee golf	Sailing
	Gardening (flowers & vegetables)	Shooting baskets
Billards	Golf	Sled ice hockey
Bird watching	Hackey sack	Sledding/tubing
Boating (rowing & boat safety)	Hiking	Snowshoeing
Boccia (bocce)	Horseback riding	Softball/T-ball
Bowling	Horseshoes	Special Olympic programs
Broomball	Ice skating	Swimming
Canoeing	Jai Lai	Table tennis
Climbing (wall & rock)	Kite flying	Throwing & catching
Collecting things	Jogging/running	Tennis
Community clean-up	Lawn games (darts, lawn golf, etc.)	Tobogganing
Croquet	Martial arts	Treadmills & stationary bikes
Cross-country skiing	Miniature golf	Walking (distance, fitness, & collecting)
Curling	Orienteering	Water parks
Darts	Pickle ball	Weight lifting/Training
Dancing (line, square, etc.)	Racquetball	Yoga
Disability—specific sports		

Folsom-Meek, Nearing, and Block, 2007.

activity? A list is drawn up and the physical educator, special education teacher, or paraprofessional can administer the checklist. After the skill content is identified, a task analysis of the skills involved is developed so that instruction can be initiated. In addition, an Ecological Task Analysis (Davis & Burton, 1987) can be outlined that includes the various physical areas where the student will participate and what level of assistance, if any, the student needs. For example, if swimming is a leisure interest, then a task analysis of swim instruction is designed. In addition, the student must learn how to enter the changing room, change, use the locker, shower, and come out to the pool area. These tasks take into account the environment and the education required to be successful.

Where is the validity and reliability with these self-constructed checklists or questionnaires? We argue that there is social validity if parents and caregivers look at the results of the assessment (the final evaluation) and say, "Yes, that is my child!" and students communicate in some form that they are pleased with their choices. Additionally, if the assessments are formed into evaluation reports, and the reported plan of action results in a student who obviously has skills for leisure and knows how to use the associated environment successfully, then the checklist has contributed to additional social validity.

Other Assessment Data and Guidelines

The transition plans in physical activity must mirror the activities of the general physical education program (Folsom-Meek, Nearing, & Bock, 2007). As the student matures to the older ages and grades, the time spent in the school setting should diminish as more and more of the physical education activities take place in the community. This is why community recreation specialists are important members of the transition team. This mirroring of the general physical education program can be seen in a checklist of activities that include the general education activities (e.g., floor hockey, soccer, volleyball) with additional units for an adapted curriculum (e.g., Frisbee, juggling, throwball). A form can easily be created for this use, like the one in table 11.3. The activities reflect the students culture and geography.

Many school districts have curriculum for physical education that includes the social skills associated with being physically active per each grade level. These can be accessed as checklists filled out by parents or physical educators/adapted physical educators. This assessment clearly shows what is needed for a transition activity to be successful.

Tools for perceived competence in physical activity have been developed. Ulrich and Collier's Pictorial Scale of Perceived Physical Competence (1990, in Horvat, Block, & Kelly, 2007) allows the student with mental retardation to look at pictures of children in a physical activity. The student then indicates such competencies as being good at jumping, or can run really fast.

The whole IEP team adds to the transition goals. For example, is it always the physical educator's responsibility to report on social skills, seizures, medications, attention span, techniques for motivation, communication skills, one-step directions versus multi-step directions, what evokes anxiety, what are calming activities that work best, use of the toilet, eating restrictions, dressing oneself, and any danger of running away, hitting, or biting? Many different members of the team (e.g., parents, special education teachers, school psychologists) contribute their expertise to make the transition goals in physical activity successful for all involved! A recent review of a community-based Therapeutic Recreation (TR) Intake Form had everything on it except for the participant's recreation interests (figure 11.8). Of course, one can assume that the TR person automatically evaluates the levels of social/emotional/adaptive skill and directs the individual to appropriate activities. But choice is important for the individual and engaging in a discussion of interests, however adapted that may be, allows for choice and for ownership of one's leisure time.

Physical Activities for Students with Severe Mental Retardation

The range of activities in a physical education program for those who are severely retarded is necessarily limited. These individuals, if not properly stimulated, often sit or lie for hours and appear to be totally unaware of their environment. Until recently, little attention has been devoted to the educational and motor development needs of individuals with severe retardation. Confined to an institution, they were frequently permitted to exist in a vegetable-like state. The lack of suitable programs may be attributed to inadequate staff-resident ratio as well as to the belief of many that the most severely retarded were incapable of learning. Changes in this attitude are evident today, and an increasing number of professionals are focusing on this forgotten population. Because those with severe retardation exhibit numerous motor deficiencies, it is essential that attention be directed toward remedying these problems. Although little research has been conducted to provide evidence to support the choice of program content, physical education experiences for this population have consisted primarily of sensory-motor experiences and the fundamental motor skills of everyday living. In addition, Croce (1990) and Tomporowski and Ellis (1984) have successfully implemented well-structured physical education classes for institutionalized individuals which have resulted in positive physiological and behavioral changes.

Sensory-Motor Experiences

Based on information gathered from the study of infant development, sensory-motor experiences usually consist of activities to increase awareness of stimuli and to improve manipulative activity. Experiences designed to raise the awareness of those severely involved should be developed for all of the senses. Stimulation of the tactile senses may include vigorously rubbing the skin with towels and brushes of various textures to obtain a motor response. Lights and sounds of various intensities may be moved from one side to the other to elicit head turning responses. Providing opportunities to discriminate between various tastes, odors, and temperatures is useful for developing avoidance (turning away) and approach (turning toward) motor responses. Combinations of various sensory stimuli may also be presented. For many individuals who are severely retarded, an extensive time allotment should be provided for sensory awareness activities. Without the ability to attend to relevant stimuli, further educational experiences for this population will be seriously impeded.

The skills of reaching, grasping, holding, and releasing do not develop normally for individuals with severe mental retardation. Therefore, opportunities for these individuals to play with toys of various colors and textures should be provided. Finger, hand, and arm movements may also be obtained through the use of materials such as water, sand, and clay. Efforts also should be directed toward teaching self-help skills that emphasize manipulative activities, such as eating and dressing.

Student's Name _____ DOB _____ Teacher _____

Environment _____ Initiation of Program _____ Assistant _____

Sub-Environment	Steps Person without Disabilities Uses	Level of Assistance (specific to learner)	Possible Adaptations for Learners with Disabilities
Gym: Meeting			
Activity 1	Brings gym bag		Peer assistant may remind learner
Activity 2	Locates gym		Cues on doors/walls
Activity 3	Locates attendance space		Peer assistance
Activity 4	Sits quietly and listens for directions		Peer tutor may simplify instructions
Bus: Transport			
Activity 1	Locates bus loading area		Follows peer assistant
Activity 2	Gets on bus		Follows verbal cues of peer assistant
Activity 3	Finds seat and sits quietly		Follows peer lead
Activity 4	Stands after bus reaches fitness club and is completely stopped		Follows peer assistant lead
Activity 5	Exits bus		Follows peer assistant
Fitness Club (FC)			
Activity 1	Locates FC entrance and waits for instruction		Follows peer lead
Activity 2	Locates locker room		Follows peer lead
FC Locker Room			
Activity 1	Locates locker room		Cues on doors/walls
Activity 2	Enters locker room		None needed
Activity 3	Locates locker		Teach learner to find a locker that is not being used; assistant may help locate and code it so it can be easily found after activity
Activity 4	Takes off clothes		Practice at home
Activity 5	Places clothes in locker		None needed
Activity 6	Changes into appropriate workout clothes and shoes		Use pull-on type clothing and shoes with Velcro fasteners; peer assistance
Activity 7	Locates group exercise room		Follows peer assistant; use cues on walls and doors
FC: Group Exercise Room			
Activity 1	Finds space and waits for directions		None needed
Activity 2	Sets up equipment		Peer assistant helps/checks for safety
FC: Warm-Up			
Activity 1	Marches in place to music		Follows instructor's lead
Activity 2	Follows instructions for general warm-up		Follows instructor's lead with peer assistant providing cues and routine
FC Step Aerobics			
Activity 1	Does 8 basic steps at half-time speed with R lead		Follow instructor; peer assistant provides cues and physical assistance
Activity 2	Performs lead foot change, repeat L		Peer assistant provides cues
Activity 3	Does 8 basic steps R lead; change to L leads at regular time		Instructor lead and cueing; peer assistant provides cues
Activity 4	Adds arm movements		Instructor lead; peer assistant provides visual cues and modifications

Figure 11.8 Ecological task analysis: fitness club

Activity 5	Cuts to 4 basic steps per side		Follow instructor's visual and verbal cues; peer assistant provides cues
Activity 6	Changes arm movements		Follow instructor's visual and verbal cues; peer assistant modifies as needed
Activity 7	Adds linear progressions		Follow instructor's cues; peer assistant provides cues and modifications
FC: Cool Down			
Activity 1	Does basic aerobic dance movements on floor without arm movements		Follows peers and instructor
Activity 2	Walks around room		Follows peers
Activity 3	Does cool down stretches		Follows instructor and peers
Activity 4	Does relaxation exercises		Follows instructor and peer assistant
Activity 5	Thanks instructor, exits exercise room to locate locker roomwalls and doors		Follows peer assistant's lead; use signs on
FC: Locker Room			
Activity 1	Locates locker		Peer assistant provides cues to locate locker
Activity 2	Takes off work-out clothes		Peer assistant provides physical assistance as needed
Activity 3	Places work-out clothes in bag		None needed
Activity 4	Gets towel, soap, and shampoo		Peer assistance
Activity 5	Locates shower		Use visual cues, peer assistance
Activity 6	Turns on water, checks temperature		Practice adjusting temperature from cold to warm, peer assistant monitors
Activity 7	Shampoos hair and washes body		Peer assistant gives cues; wash from top to bottom
Activity 8	Shuts shower off and gathers personal items		Step away from spray, turn hot first, may paint visual cues on shower
Activity 9	Dries hair and body		Dry from top to bottom; peer assistant gives cues
Activity 10	Uses deodorant and personal hygiene items		Peer assistant cues
Activity 11	Puts on street clothes		Peer assistance and cues as needed
Activity 12	Combs hair and performs other grooming tasks		Peer assistance and cues
Activity 13	Collects and places all personal items in bag		Student uses picture list, peer assistance as needed
Activity 14	Leaves locker room and locates FC exit to wait and board bus		Use cues on wall, peer assistance as needed
Bus: Transport to School			
Activity 1	Gets on bus and finds seat		Follows peers
Activity 2	Rides quietly		None needed/follow peers
Activity 3	Stands after bus reaches a complete stop at school		Follow peer assistant
Activity 4	Exits bus and goes to next class		Follow peer and cues on wall

*Levels of assistance code:

I	= independent	P	= physical assistance (Student passive)
M	= modeling	P+	= physical assistance (Student tries to help)
V	= verbal cue	P-	= physical assistance (Student resists)

Bock, R. (2006)

Figure 11.8   *continued*

Fundamental Motor Skills

In addition to the sensory-motor experiences, the physical education curriculum for individuals who are severely mentally retarded should include activities that develop basic everyday skills, such as lifting the feet over objects and up steps. Additional examples of the basic activities that can be included in the program and the techniques most frequently used for teaching them appear in the following list. Because of the individual variation found within this population, the techniques listed are suggestions and do not preclude the use of others.

1. Crawling (arms, chest, belly, legs): demonstration, physical assistance (use crawler, if necessary)
2. Creeping (hands and knees): demonstration, physical assistance
3. Rolling: demonstration, physical assistance
4. Sitting: demonstration, physical assistance (external supports such as straps, if necessary)
5. Standing (with and without assistance): demonstration, physical assistance
6. Walking: demonstration, physical assistance (use parallel bars and weighted cart, if necessary)
7. Bending at the waist to pick up a favorite toy: demonstration, physical assistance
8. Bending at the knees to pick up a favorite toy: demonstration, physical assistance
9. Stair climbing: demonstration, physical assistance
10. Balancing: physical assistance (use wide beam; assist student along beam)
11. Stepping over and into objects: physical assistance (use tires, boxes, beams)
12. Bouncing: physical assistance (use trampoline; start pupil by bouncing on bed; later a jouncing board may be used)
13. Jumping from object: physical assistance (use object or beam no higher than one foot in the beginning; start by pulling student off balance)
14. Climbing: physical assistance (use a ladder or Swedish box)
15. Running: demonstration, physical assistance (pull by the hand or use rope around the waist)
16. Throwing: physical assistance (use eight-inch or larger ball and a tire as a target; have student start by dropping the ball and gradually increase the distance from the tire)
17. Catching: physical assistance (use eight-inch ball; in the beginning use short distances and place the ball into the hand)
18. Kicking: demonstration, physical assistance (use large, soft rubber balls or heavy cardboard boxes)

The way in which these activities are presented by the teacher is extremely important in achieving good results.

As pointed out previously, teaching low-functioning individuals requires a very low teacher-to-pupil ratio—in most cases, one to one.

No more than two or three activities should be presented during any one class period. Anyone who refuses to participate in one kind of activity may take part in another. Participation should be of short duration. After leaving one activity the teacher may return to it in a few minutes or at some time before the period is over. The same activities should be presented every day until learned. After the skills of one activity have been mastered, new activities may be introduced; but the skills already learned should be reviewed briefly from time to time. An obstacle course in which students climb stairs, duck under bars, step over ropes, and step into and out of tires provides a good warm-up and a means of quickly reviewing important activities.

Teaching these students requires great patience and kindness. The teacher should never resort to pressure tactics to achieve improvement. The instructor's attitude must be that improvement may come very slowly, and he or she must work patiently with the student until it comes. All genuine effort by the student should be acknowledged with indications of approval. Heward and Orlansky (1992) recommend that a behavioral approach with the following elements be employed with individuals who are mentally retarded:

1. Require the student to perform the target behavior repeatedly during each session.
2. Provide immediate feedback, usually in the form of positive reinforcement.
3. Use cues and prompts that help the student respond correctly from the very beginning of the lesson and systematically withdraw these as appropriate.
4. Help the student generalize the newly learned skill to different, nontraining environments (1992).

Additional suggestions for developing programs for those with severe disabilities are presented in chapter 14.

Behavior Modification

Verbal praise has its limitations with those who are severely and profoundly retarded because many of these students do not comprehend the spoken word; therefore, other means of rewarding successful behavior have been experimented with. One of the most effective of these is a procedure known as behavior modification.

Behavior modification is defined as the systematic use of selected reinforcers to weaken, maintain, or strengthen behaviors. Although there are several behavior modification techniques, the two most successfully employed with those who are severely mentally retarded are positive reinforcement and modeling. Combining these two techniques provides a system in which a skill is demonstrated and modeled, and the student is reinforced for initiating any movement that resembles or approximates the skill. It may be necessary to shape the behavior of some totally dependent individuals by isolating and reinforcing very basic responses, such as the turning of their heads and eyes toward the demonstration. Reinforcing those who are functioning at a lower level while they are manually guided through the skill may also develop within them a sense of pleasure that over a period of time may gradually be associated with the movement. Several types of reinforcers may be employed. These include manipulatables such as toys, trinkets, and hobby items; visual and auditory stimuli such as films, records, and animations; and social stimuli such as verbal praise and attention (Dunn, 1975). Selection of the appropriate reinforcer must be determined for each person. For some students, praise or knowledge that the attempt was successful is sufficient reinforcement. For others, especially the more severely involved, a reward of food is effective. The time between the reinforcement and the desired behavior must be as short as possible; otherwise the student is not always certain what he or she is being rewarded for. The reward should be given consistently and only for performance at maximum capacity.

A movement that is made up of two or more parts must be broken into its components and each taught separately. For example, the movement pattern of reaching for and picking up a ball may be broken down into these components:

1. a movement in the direction of the ball,
2. touching the ball,
3. placing the fingers around the ball, and
4. lifting the ball up.

The student is first encouraged to reach for the ball; any effort to do so is rewarded with a reinforcer and words of praise. Thereafter, the reward is given when the student reaches the same distance or a greater distance than in the initial effort. Whenever the student reaches a greater distance, bringing the hand closer to the ball, the new distance becomes the point of reinforcement. When the student finally touches the ball, this becomes the point of reinforcement; the same applies when he or she grasps it and when he or she picks it up. After the individual has mastered the skill, the reinforcer is slowly withdrawn by offering it only periodically. Praise and approval continue to be given for successful effort. Often, they can eventually be used entirely as the reinforcer.

Summary

Information concerning individuals with mental retardation was presented in this chapter. An overview of the nature and needs of this population and the classification systems used in mental retardation were described. In discussing the emotional, social, learning, and motor characteristics of these students, emphasis was placed on the significant variability found within this population, including the unique physical and medical needs of the Down syndrome population. Modern views of mental retardation recognize that individuals with cognitive disorders are capable of contributing to society and benefiting from interactions with other individuals without mental retardation. The emphasis today is on deinstitutionalization and normalization. The progressive view of mental retardation is reflected in the definition of mental retardation, which emphasizes that the intelligence quotient is only one factor in determining mental retardation. Adaptive behavior is recognized as essential in determining the presence or absence of mental retardation. This view is also evident in schools, where the traditional segregated class for students with mental retardation has been replaced by resource rooms where students who are mentally retarded obtain assistance as needed. Instructional integration is the norm, with segregated experiences provided for more involved students who need the structure and individualization offered in special classes.

In physical education there is increasing awareness that individuals with mental retardation as a group do not compare favorably with students without mental retardation on measures of physical and motor fitness. These differences to a large extent may be attributed to the lack of activity and structured programs provided for these students. If programs are properly presented, significant gains will occur. This means that motor and fitness skills must be task-analyzed with appropriate cues and consequences utilized. Data must be maintained with positive reinforcement provided when learning occurs. Efforts must also be directed toward ensuring that skills learned are maintained. Parents therefore should be encouraged to reinforce selected skills at home. In addition schools should coordinate with other community agencies to help students make the transition from the gymnasium to other play and recreational settings. The outlook for individuals with mental retardation is very positive. Given properly trained professionals with progressive attitudes it is probable that significant gains will be made in the overall health and physical performance level of individuals with mental retardation.

Enhancing Activities

1. Volunteer to participate as a coach or official for the local Special Olympics organization. Write a paper describing your reaction to this experience.

2. Attend a local meeting of the Association for Retarded Citizens. Compare this meeting, including the agenda, to a meeting of the local Parent Teacher Association.

3. Interview an adolescent who is mentally retarded. Obtain his or her views on physical education and recreation. Is physical activity an important aspect of the individual's life? What recommendations does he or she have for improving the way programs are conducted?

4. Visit a group home or special facility for those who are mentally retarded. Record your impressions and compare those to the living arrangements—meals, activities, routine—found in other homes.

5. Observe a physical education class in which a student with mental retardation enrolled. What adaptations in instruction and/or activity were made for the student? Suggest other adaptations or modifications that might be made.

6. Select one of the tests described in chapter 6 and administer the test to a student who is mentally retarded. Given the test results, recommend a goal and objectives that should be included as part of the student's IEP.

7. Visit a local school and review curricular materials used to teach basic skills to students who are mentally retarded. Identify ways in which the physical education experience for those students could be structured to complement instruction in the classroom. Identify changes that could be made in the classroom that might facilitate learning in the gymnasium.

Selected Readings

American Association on Mental Retardation (AAMR) (2002). Retrieved July 2004 from www.aamr.org

Baer, J. S., Sampson, P. D., Barr, H. M., Connor, P. D., & Streissguth, A. P. (2003). A 21-year longitudinal analysis of the effects of prenatal alcohol exposure on young adult drinking. *Archives of General Psychiatry, 60*, 377–385.

Baroff, G. S. (1982). Predicting the prevalence of mental retardation in individual catchment areas. *Mental Retardation, 20*, 133–135.

Bar-Or, O. (1983). *Pediatric sports medicine for the practitioner: From physiologic principles to clinical applications.* New York: Springer.

Bell, N., Kozav, W., & Martin, A. (1979). *The impact of Special Olympics on participants, parents and the community.* Lubbock, TX: Texas Tech University.

Bergen, A. M. E., & Mosley, J. L. (1994). Attention and attentional shift efficiency and individuals with and without mental retardation. *American Journal on Mental Retardation, 98*, 688–743.

Beuter, A. (1983). Effects of mainstreaming on motor performance of intellectually normal and trainable mentally retarded students. *American Corrective Therapy Journal, 37*, 48–52.

Block, M. E., & Krebs, P. L. (1992). An alternative to least restrictive environments: A continuum of support to regular physical education. *Adapted Physical Activity Quarterly, 9*, 97–113.

Block, M. E., & Vogler, E. W. (1994). Inclusion in regular physical education: The research base. *Journal of Physical Education, Recreation and Dance, 65*, 40–43.

Bruininks, R. (1974). Physical and motor development of retarded persons. In N. R. Ellis (Ed.), *International review of research in mental retardation* (Vol. 7, pp. 209–261). Ellis, NY: Academic Press.

Burger, A. L., Blackman, L. S., & Tan, N. (1980). Maintenance and generalization of a sorting and retrieval strategy by EMR and nonretarded individuals. *American Journal of Mental Deficiency, 84*, 373–380.

Burlingame, J., & Blaschko, T. M. (2002). *Assessment tools for recreational therapy and related fields* (3rd ed.). Ravensdale, WA.: Idyll Arbor, Inc.

Chiu, L. H. (1990). Self-esteem of gifted, normal, and mildly mentally handicapped children. *Psychology in the Schools, 27*, 263–268.

Colarusso, R., & O'Rourke, C. (2003). *Special education for all teachers,* Dubuque, IA: Kendall/Hunt.

Connolly, B. H., & Michael, B. T. (1986). Performance of retarded children, with and without Down syndrome, on the Bruininks Oseretsky Test of Motor Proficiency. *Physical Therapy, 66*, 344–348.

Craft, D. (1994). Inclusion: Physical education for all. *Journal of Physical Education: National status-update.* DeKalb, IL: Northern Illinois University.

Cratty, B. J. (1969). *Motor activity and the education of retardates.* Philadelphia: Lea and Febiger.

Croce, R. V. (1990). Effects of exercise and diet on body composition and cardiovascular fitness in adults with severe mental retardation. *Education and Training in Mental Retardation, 25*, 176–187.

Davis, W. & Burton, A. (1991). Ecological task analysis: Translating movement theory behavior into practice. *Adapted Physical Activity Quarterly, 8,* 154–177.

Del Rey, P., & Stewart, D. (1989). Organizing input for mentally retarded subjects to enhance memory and transfer. *Adapted Physical Activity Quarterly, 6,* 247–254.

DiRocco, P. J., Clark, J. E., & Phillips, S. J. (1987). Jumping coordination patterns of mildly mentally retarded children. *Adapted Physical Activity Quarterly, 4,* 178–191.

Dobbins, D. A., Garron, R., & Rarick, G. L. (1981). The motor performance of educable mentally retarded and intellectually normal boys after covariate control for differences in body size. *Research Quarterly for Exercise and Sport, 52*(1), 1–8.

Dobbins, D. A., & Rarick, G. L. (1976). Separation potential of educable retarded and intellectually normal boys as a function of motor performance. *Research Quarterly, 47*(3), 346–356.

Downs, P., & Williams, T. (1994). Students' attitudes toward integration of people with disabilities in activity settings: A European comparison. *Adapted Physical Activity Quarterly, 11,* 32–43.

Dummer, G. (1988). Teacher training to enhance motor learning by mentally retarded individuals. In C. Sherrill (Ed.), *Leadership training in adapted physical education* (pp. 349–359). Champaign, IL: Human Kinetics Publishers.

Dunn, J. M. (1975). Behavior modification with emotionally disturbed children. *Journal of Physical Education and Recreation, 46,* 46–70.

Dunn, J. M., & French, R. (1982). Operant conditioning: A tool for special physical educators in the 1980s. *Exceptional Education Quarterly, 3,* 42–53.

Dyer, S. M. (1994). Physiological effects of a 13-week physical fitness program on Down syndrome subjects. *Pediatric Exercise Science, 6,* 88–100.

Eberhard, Y., & Eterradossi, J. (1990). Effects of physical exercise in adolescents with Down syndrome. *Adapted Physical Activity Quarterly, 16,* 281–287.

Eichstaedt, C. B., & Lavay, B. W. (1992). *Activity for individuals with mental retardation: Infancy through adulthood.* Champaign, IL: Human Kinetics Publishers.

Ellis, D. N., Cress, P. J., & Spellman, C. R. (1993). Training students with mental retardation to self-pace while exercising. *Adapted Physical Activity Quarterly, 10,* 104–124.

Faison-Hodge, J., & Porretta, D. L. (2004). Physical activity levels of students with mental retardation and students without disabilities. *Adapted Physical Activity Quarterly, 21*(2), 139–152.

Feingold, B. (1975). *Why your child is hyperactive.* New York: Random House.

Folsom-Meek, S. L., Nearing, R. J., & Block, R. E. (2007). Transitioning children, youths and young adults with disabilities. *Journal of Physical Education, Recreation & Dance, 78*(3), 38–51.

Fryers, T. (1993). Epidemiological thinking in mental retardation: Issues in taxonomy and population frequency. In Norma W. Bray (Ed.), *International review of research in mental retardation* (Vol. 19, pp. 97–127). San Diego, CA: Academic.

Gibbons, S. L., & Bushakra, F. B. (1989). Effects of Special Olympic participation on the perceived competence and social acceptance of MR children. *Adapted Physical Activity Quarterly, 6,* 40–51.

Glaze, R. E. (1985). *Height and weight of Down syndrome children as compared to normal children aged ten to eighteen.* Unpublished masters study. Illinois State University, Normal, IL.

Grossman, H. J. (1973). *Manual on terminology and classification in mental retardation.* Washington, DC: American Association on Mental Deficiency.

Haywood, K. M. (1993). *Life span motor development* (2nd ed.). Champaign, IL: Human Kinetics Publishers.

Heward, W. L., & Orlansky, M. D. (1992). *Exceptional children* (4th ed.). Columbus, OH: Charles E. Merrill Publishing Co.

Hoover, J., & Wade, M. (1985). Motor learning theory and mentally retarded individuals: A historic review. *Adapted Physical Activity Quarterly, 2*(3), 228–252.

Horgan, J. S. (1983). Mnemonic strategy instruction in coding, processing and recall of movement related cues by the mentally retarded. *Perceptual and Motor Skills, 57,* 547–557.

Horvat, M., Block, M. E., & Kelly, L. (2007). *Developmental and adapted physical activity assessment.* Champaign, IL: Human Kinetics.

Horvat, M., Croce, R., & McGhee, T. (1993). Effects of a circuit training program on individuals with mental retardation. *Clinical Kinesiology, 47,* 71–77.

Houston-Wilson, C. (1993). The effect of untrained and trained peer tutors on the Opportunity to Respond (OTR) of students with developmental disabilities in integrated physical education classes. Unpublished doctoral dissertation. Oregon State University. Corvallis, Oregon.

Johnson, L., & Londeree, B. (1976). *Motor fitness testing manual for the moderately mentally retarded.* Washington, DC: American Alliance for Health, Physical Education, Recreation, and Dance.

Koop, C. B., Baker, B. L., & Brown, K. W. (1992). Social skills and their correlates: Preschoolers with developmental delays. *American Journal on Mental Retardation, 96,* 357–366.

Larson, S. A., Lakin, K. C., Anderson, L., Kwak, N., Lee, J. H., & Anderson, D. (2001). Prevalence of mental retardation and developmental disabilities: Estimates from the 1994/1995 National Health Interview Survey Disability Supplements. *American Journal of Mental Retardation, 106*(3), 231–252.

Lawson, L. M., Coyle, C. P., & Ashton-Shaeffer, C. (2001). *Therapeutic recreation in special education: An IDEA for the future.* Alexandria, VA: American Therapeutic Recreation Associations.

Lavay, G., & McKenzie, T. (1991). Development and evaluation of a systematic run/walk program for men with mental retardation. *Education and Training in Mental Retardation, 26,* 333–341.

Liemohn, W. (1984). *Rhythmicity and timing in special populations.* Paper presented at the American Alliance for

Health, Physical Education, Recreation, and Dance Annual Convention. Anaheim, CA.

Lindgren, G. W., & Katoda, H. (1993). Maturational rate of Tokyo children with and without mental retardation. *American Journal on Mental Retardation, 98,* 128–134.

Londeree, B., & Johnson, L. (1974). Motor fitness of TMR vs EMR and normal children. *Medicine and Science in Sports,* 247–252.

Luckasson, R., Coulter, D. L., Pollaway, W. A., Reiss, S., Schalock, R. L., Snell, M. E., Spitalnik, D. M., & Stark, J. A. (1992). *Mental retardation: Definition, classification and systems of support* (9th ed.). Washington DC: American Association on Mental Retardation.

Maguire, P. (1985). *The effects of supplemental home instruction by parents utilizing the data based gymnasium instructional model on the performance of selected motor skills with moderately and severely mentally retarded children.* Unpublished doctoral dissertation. Oregon State University, Corvallis, OR.

McCubbin, J., Frey, G., & Lavay, B. (1992). Fitness assessment of persons with disabilities: Past, present, and future. Presentation at the International Federation of Adapted Physical Activity Conference. Miami, FL.

Merrill, E. C. (1990). Attention resource allocation and mental retardation. In Norma W. Bray (Ed.), *International review of research in mental retardation* (Vol. 16, pp. 51–88). San Diego, CA: Academic.

Moon, M. S., & Renzaglia, A. (1982). Physical fitness and the mentally retarded: A critical review of the literature. *Journal of Special Education, 16,* 269–287.

Moss, S. C., & Hogg, J. (1981). The development of hand function in mentally handicapped and nonhandicapped preschool children. In P. Mittler (Ed.), *Frontiers of knowledge in mental retardation* (pp. 35–44). Baltimore, MD: University Park Press.

National Center on Physical Activity and Disability (NCPAD). (2004). Retrieved July 2004 from www.mcpad.org. July 2004.

National Organization on Fetal Alcohol Syndrome (NOFAS). (2004). Retrieved July 2004 from www.nofas.org

Newell, K. M. (1985). Motor skill orientation and mental retardation: Overview of traditional and current orientations. In J. E. Clark & J. H. Humphrey (Eds.), *Motor development: Current selected research* (Vol I). Princeton, NJ: Princeton Book Co.

Pitetti, K. H., Climstein, M., Campbell, K. D., Barrett, P. J., & Jackson, J. A. (1992). The cardiovascular capabilities of adults with Down syndrome: A comparative study. *Medicine and Science in Sports and Exercise, 24,* 13–19.

Pitetti, K. H., & Fernhall, B. (2004). Comparing run performance of adolescents with mental retardation, with and without Down syndrome. *Adapted Physical Activity Quarterly, 21*(3).

Pitetti, K. H., & Tan, D. M. (1991). Effects of minimally supervised exercise program for mentally retarded adults. *Medicine and Science in Sports and Exercise, 23,* 594–601.

Porretta, D. L. (1985). Performance variability of educable mentally retarded and normal boys on a novel kicking task. *Adapted Physical Activity Quarterly, 2*(1), 76–82.

Rarick, G. L. (1971). Evaluation of local Special Olympics programs. Unpublished study. University of California, Berkeley, CA.

Rarick, G. L. (1973). Motor performance of mentally retarded children. In G. L. Rarick (Ed.), *Physical activity: Human growth and development* (pp. 225–256). New York: Academic Press.

Rarick, G. L., Dobbins, P. A., & Broadhead, G. D. (1976). *The motor domain and its correlates in educationally handicapped children.* Englewood Cliffs, NJ: Prentice-Hall, Inc.

Rarick, G. L., & McQuillan, J. P. (1979). *The effects of individualized physical education instruction on selected perceptual motor and cognitive functions of institutionalized and home reared TMR children.* Final Report, U.S. Office of Education, Bureau of Education for the Handicapped (Grant No. G007601432).

Rarick, G. L., McQuillan, J. P., & Beuter, A. C. (1981). *The motor, cognitive, and psychosocial effects of the implementation of Public Law 94–142 on handicapped children in school physical education programs.* Final Report, Department of Education (Grant No. G007901413).

Rarick, G. L., Widdop, J. H., & Broadhead, G. D. (1970). The physical fitness and motor performance of educable mentally retarded children. *Exceptional Children, 36,* 509–519.

Reid, G. (1980). Overt and covert rehearsal in short-term memory of mentally retarded and nonretarded persons. *American Journal of Mental Deficiency, 85,* 69–77.

Reis, S. (1994). Issues in defining mental retardation. *American Journal on Mental Retardation, 99,* 1–7.

Riggen, K., & Ulrich, D. (1993). The effects of sport participation on individuals with mental retardation. *Adapted Physical Activity Quarterly, 10,* 42–51.

Rimmer, J. H., & Kelly, L. E. (1991). Effects of a resistance training program on adults with mental retardation. *Adapted Physical Activity Quarterly, 8,* 146–153.

Roberton, M. A., & DiRocco, P. (1981). Validating a motor skill sequence for mentally retarded children. *American Corrective Therapy Journal, 35,* 148–155.

Savage, M. P., Petratis, M. M., Thomson, W. H., Berg, K., Smith, J. L., & Sady, S. P. (1986). Exercise training effects on serum lipids of prepubescent boys and adult men. *Medicine and Science in Sports and Exercise, 18,* 197–204.

Seefeldt, V., & Vogel, P. (1987). Children and fitness: A public health perspective. *Research Quarterly for Exercise and Sport, 58,* 331–333.

Share, J., & French, R. (1982). *Motor development of Down syndrome children: Birth to six years.* Sherman Oaks, CA: J. B. Share.

Sheppard, R. J. (1990). *Fitness in special populations.* Champaign, IL: Human Kinetics Publishers.

Special Olympics Bulletin. (1983). Participation by individuals with Down syndrome who suffer from the atlantoaxial dislocation. Washington, DC: Joseph P. Kennedy Jr. Foundation.

Streissguth, A. (1997). *Fetal alcohol syndrome: A guide for families and communities.* Baltimore: Brookes.

Sugden, D. A. (1978). Visual motor short-term memory in educationally subnormal boys. *British Journal of Educational Psychology, 48,* 330–339.

Surgeon General (2002). www.surgeongeneral.org. Retrieved May, 2002.

Thase, M. E. (1982). Reversible dementia in Down syndrome. *Journal of Mental Deficiency Research, 26,* 111–113.

Tomporowski, P. D., & Ellis, N. R. (1984). Effects of exercise on the physical fitness, intelligence and adaptive behavior of institutionalized mentally retarded adults. *Applied Research in Mental Retardation, 5,* 329–337.

Tomporowski, P. D., & Hager, L. D. (1992). Sustained attention in mentally retarded individuals. In Norma W. Bray (Ed.), *International review of research in mental retardation* (Vol. 18, pp. 111–136). San Diego, CA: Academic.

Ulrich, D. A., & Collier, D. H. (1990). Perceived physical competence in children with mental retardation: Modification of a pictorial scale. *Adapted Physical Activity Quarterly, 7,* 338–354.

Wehman, P. (1977). *Helping the mentally retarded acquire play skills.* Springfield, IL: Charles C. Thomas.

Wessel, J. A. (1976). *I CAN.* Northbrook, IL: Hubbard Publishing Company.

Wessel, J. A., & Zittel, L. (1998). *I CAN primary skills*: K–3 (2nd ed.). Austin, TX: Pro-Ed.

Winnick, J. P. (1979). *Early movement experiences and development: Habilitation and remediation.* Philadelphia: W. B. Saunders Co.

Winnick, J. P., & Short, F. X. (1999). *The Brockport Physical Fitness Test.* Champaign, IL: Human Kinetics.

Wolfensberger, W. (1991). Reflections on a lifetime in human services and mental retardation. *Mental Retardation, 29,* 1–16.

Wright, J., & Cowden, J. E. (1986). Changes in self-concept and cardiovascular endurance of mentally retarded youths in a Special Olympics swim training program. *Adapted Physical Activity Quarterly, 3,* 177–183.

Zittel, L. L. (1994). Gross motor assessment of preschool children wtih special needs: Instrument selection considerations. *Adapted Physical Activity Quarterly, 11,* 245–260.

CHAPTER 12

Learning Disabilities and Attention Deficit/Hyperactivity Disorder

CHAPTER OBJECTIVES

After studying this chapter, the reader should be able to:

1. Define the expression *learning disabilities* and discuss the areas in which discrepancy between actual and expected levels of achievement normally occur in this population.
2. Identify the common causes of learning disabilities and the relationship of these to educational programs for students with this disorder.
3. Discuss the learning and behavioral characteristics of individuals with learning disabilities and the relationship of these to instruction in physical education.
4. Define and explain the various perceptual disorders and terms associated with learning disabilities including "hyperactivity," "laterality," "directionality," "visual discrimination," and "auditory discrimination."
5. Develop guidelines for the implementation of appropriate physical education programs and experiences for students with learning disabilities using an ecological task analysis and a top-down movement assessment approach.
6. Recognize and appreciate the importance of a multidisciplinary team approach toward the assessment and implementation of effective learning environments for students with learning disabilities.
7. Appreciate what is known and not known about the nature, cause, and treatment of individuals with learning disabilities.
8. Suggest activities and instructional procedures for teaching physical education to students with learning disabilities.
9. Explain what is meant by the expression: *Attention Deficit/Hyperactivity Disorder (ADHD)*.
10. Recognize that there is comorbidity with the diagnosis of attention deficit/hyperactivity disorder and learning disabilities. Some students will be both ADHD and LD, and some will carry only one diagnosis. ADHD and LD are also comorbid with other disorders.

Facilitating the physical activity of individuals with learning disabilities, as well as students with attention deficit disorder (ADD) and attention deficit/hyperactivity disorder (ADHD), is receiving more attention due to recent research on teaching strategies and also because of the debate among educators, families, and medical personnel regarding diagnosis and treatment approaches. This chapter will address the arena of learning disability first, and then discuss ADD and ADHD. **It is understood that the diagnosis of these problems is complex, and a cooperative effort is required among clinical personnel (e.g., developmental pediatricians, school psychologists with special training in these areas), general and special education teachers, and the family of the student**. Information and astute observation is needed on many different levels for a correct diagnosis. The complexity of the situation is compounded by the reality that many of the symptoms associated with each of these areas are exhibited by children for many different reasons. For example, high activity levels could be associated with anxiety in a child with certain life circumstances, and not solely because the child meets all the criteria of the American Psychiatric Association's (APA) *Diagnostic and Statistical Manual IV-R* for ADHD. Similarly, inattention in the classroom could be due to an undiagnosed learning disability, rather than an oppositional defiant behavior disorder.

Physical educators have remained part of the school educational team that contributes information to assist the clinicians in the diagnosis for these disorders. Physical educators have often been very challenged to engage students with learning disabilities, ADD, or ADHD in the physical education curriculum, and have remained great advocates for respecting the difficulties the student may face in physical education. The chapter will outline information and provide suggestions for successfully engaging the student in the curriculum of the physical education program. Again, an ecological model (Davis & Burton, 1991) is stressed: one that acknowledges the uniqueness of the individual. There is no heterogeneous student when the labels of learning disabled, ADD, and ADHD are used. Sometimes students are both learning disabled and have ADD or ADHD. Often the behaviors exhibited overlap. But, again, professionals with expertise are deferred to for diagnostic work.

Physical educators provide valuable information in movement performance that can be utilized by the IEP team in making judgments about placement and supports for student success in physical education classes and in physical activity in general. Many very accomplished individuals have learning disabilities, ADHD, or ADD. One prominent child psychologist in Oregon commented: "I never knew I was ADHD because my mother was. I just thought it was normal!" In this man's case, he was highly successful in his professional life, highly productive, and highly active. He is a good example of the successful life that individuals can lead with a clinical profile of ADHD. Another developmental pediatrician in the same clinic in Oregon commented that he had never been able to determine which was his left hand or which was his right hand. His wedding ring was the cue for him for the left hand. Again, this inability to distinguish right from left-handedness, often attributed to individuals with learning disabilities and ADHD, did not deter him in medical school or in physical activity. Through medical school, he used figure skating as an activity to balance his demanding academic schedule and family life.

Learning Disabilities

Learning disabilities represent a field of special education that has experienced a tremendous amount of growth, interest, and debate since the early 1960s. Attention has been directed toward students with learning disabilities by scientists, educators, allied health personnel, media representatives, and the general public. This interest has helped to foster an environment in which our understanding of the meaning and significance of learning disabilities has improved dramatically. Although much is unknown about the causes of this disorder, as well as the procedures for

identifying and treating students with learning disabilities, there continues to be an intense focus on developing teaching strategies to employ with students who have learning disabilities. The University of Kansas Center for Research on Learning Institute for Effective Instruction has dedicated decades of research to children with learning disabilities (2004). Currently, their *Learning Strategies Curriculum* is a student-focused set of interventions to assist students with learning disabilities acquire knowledge from the printed word, organize and memorize information, solve math problems, and express information in writing; these are the areas where students with learning disabilities are known to struggle.

Dr. Samuel Kirk is generally recognized as the originator of the term "learning disabilities." In 1963, while addressing a group of parents with children who were experiencing serious difficulties in learning to read, who were hyperactive, or who could not solve math problems, Dr. Kirk commented that recently he had been using the term "learning disabilities" to describe children who had learning problems but who were not mentally retarded or emotionally disturbed. Parents and educators quickly adopted this term as an acceptable label and an appropriate alternative to such terms as "brain damaged," "neurologically impaired," "minimal brain dysfunctions," and "perceptually disabled."

Today, most states and communities have formed chapters as part of a national group known as the Learning Disabilities Association of America (LDAA). The LDAA is an advocacy group dedicated to improving educational services for students with learning disabilities. This group, in joint effort with the Council for Exceptional Children's Division for Learning Disabilities (DLD), has been responsible for persuading the federal government to recognize the needs of those with learning disabilities. Learning disabilities are recognized as a handicapping condition identified by IDEA 2004. Students with this disorder are eligible for federally funded special education programs.

Learning Disabilities Defined

There is considerable discussion among professionals and parents concerning the definition of learning disabilities and the students who should be included within this special population. For some, the term "learning disabled" should be applied to any student who experiences a problem with learning. According to proponents of this philosophy, the term would include any student whose learning is disabled by conditions not classified under other special education categories such as mental retardation and blindness.

Some, however, have argued that learning disabilities is a specific disabling condition and that this term should be applied only to those students whose underachievement is directly attributed to a specific learning disability. Kirk (1978) believes that the term "specific learning disabilities" should be used to differentiate the truly learning disabled from the much larger group of students who have various learning problems. Although the discussion as to the precise definition of learning disabilities continues today, a definition has been proposed for nationwide use by the federal government. Under IDEA '97, "specific learning disability" was defined as:

> a disorder *in one or more* of the basic psychological processes involved in understanding or in using language, spoken or written, which may manifest itself in an imperfect ability to listen, think, speak, read, write, spell, or to do mathematical calculations. Such disorders include conditions such as perceptual disabilities, brain injury, minimal brain dysfunction, dyslexia, and developmental aphasia.

The term does not include learning problems that are primarily the result of visual, hearing, or motor disabilities; of mental retardation; of emotional disturbance; or of environmental, cultural, or economic disadvantages (Section 300.7(c)(10) of 34 CFR Parts 300 and 303).

This terminology and definition is a federal educational one. Federal regulations for IDEA 2004 have further defined LD. There are other definitions for learning disability used by the World Health Organization (WHO) and by the American Psychiatric Association (APA). Historically, the educational diagnostic approach has been to establish a label of learning disability based on a discrepancy between the student's achievement and the student's expected level of achievement: the difference between ability and achievement in the classroom. This term is thought to have been developed to differentiate between students who had low ability, and therefore low achievement, compared with those who were not achieving academically but who were seemingly capable of achieving.

Under the guidelines of Public Law IDEA '97, a multidisciplinary team must be used to establish that a severe discrepancy in one or more areas exists between the student's actual and expected levels of achievement based on the individual's age and ability. Areas in which the severe discrepancy between ability and achievement may be found are as follows:

1. oral expression
2. listening comprehension
3. written expression
4. basic reading skill
5. reading comprehension
6. mathematics calculation
7. mathematics reasoning

To certify a student as learning disabled requires that the individual evidences learning difficulties in one or more of these seven areas. Each state has the discretion to determine the eligibility criteria for "severe discrepancy" for a diagnosis of learning disability. Within IDEA 2004 "severe discrepancy" is being debated. When regulations appear in December 2005, the students may not have to show a "severe" discrepancy. Additionally, the evaluation team must determine that the reason for the severe discrepancy between achievement and ability cannot be attributed to other conditions or sociological factors. Hallahan and Kauffman (1988) argue that there is much controversy about the definition of learning disabilities offered by the federal government. Many scholars of learning disabilities note that the scope of potentially affected areas goes beyond academics, including self-esteem, vocation, socialization, and daily living activities. Using the criteria under IDEA '97, it is generally accepted that approximately 6 to 8% of the nation's school-age children meet the criteria to be identified as learning disabled.

Although it is clear that the definition of learning disabilities proposed by the federal government does not specifically address students with motor learning disabilities, such as awkward or clumsy children, many authorities recognize that some students with learning disabilities do evidence motor deficiencies and some do not. There are long lists of "difficulties" posted by such advocates as the Council on Exceptional Children (CEC) Division on learning disabilities (www.teachingld.org) regarding "hints" of a learning disability. **However, the CEC warns that the difficulties or behavioral problems vary with the child's age and the content area. They also caution that these behaviors be assessed in relationship to the student's age and peers.** For example, for preschool-age children, difficulty "walking forward or up and down stairs" may be suggestive of a learning disability. Most physical education teachers would ask for much more information before suspecting a learning disability. For example, how young is the preschooler: (age three or age four)? What opportunity does the child have with stairs? What are the observations made in the playground or classroom with walking? What is the child's vision like? Many physical educators would require much more information if a child in their class had difficulty with "understanding how to play age-appropriate games." As the CEC website warns, many children exhibit these characteristics at different times in their development for many different reasons. But, experts do argue that children with learning disabilities who have problems in the classroom can also have problems in the gymnasium; yet there are also exceptions. For example, Magic Johnson, the famous professional basketball player, is known to have learning disabilities.

Therefore, an overall balanced approach is that specially designed physical education programs may be necessary for some children with learning disabilities.

Causes of Learning Disabilities

The specific cause of learning disabilities is unknown yet is being researched. Research studies have not been conclusive, however, in support of the once widely accepted proposition that all students with learning disbilities are brain damaged (Smith & Robinson, 1986). CEC explains that the causes of learning disability are complex and still are not well understood. Evidence exists for causation by heredity, prenatal exposure to teratogenic agents (e.g., lead), medical problems such as premature birth or meningitis, and environmental causes, such as poor prenatal care or malnutrition. However, the types of problems students have with reading may occur only in early and intermediate reading or at all levels (early, intermediate, and advanced). The same holds for the variation for children who have problems with mathematical computation problems, as well as students who have problems with written expression. The problems may be the result of different causes.

Although the discussion of biochemical factors and their effect on learning has created a great deal of interest, there is little research evidence at this time to suggest that students with learning disabilities experience biochemical deficiencies (Kennedy, Terdal, & Fusetti, 1993; Spring & Sandoval, 1976).

Some professionals have proposed that the combined variables of poor teaching and inadequate curricular offerings contribute to learning problems. These factors lead to frequent absences from school that may be compounded by lack of student motivation attributed to poor parental and professional attitudes toward education in general and the student in particular. Learning problems also may be caused by family strife, social adjustment difficulties, cultural deprivation, and behavioral disorders. Remedial learning programs for these students will not be successful unless those factors that interfere with the learning environment receive attention.

It appears that the perceptual deficit that causes learning problems may also cause problems in motor learning. For example, it seems reasonable that a perceptual problem, such as a deficit in visual figure-ground discrimination, that interferes with the child's ability to identify a specific word from among the other printed words on a page could also hamper the child's ability to distinguish a target at which a ball is to be thrown from other nearby targets. If a connection of this kind does exist, it might be assumed that improvement in one area affects improvement in the other.

(Early theorists, as noted in chapter 3, did make this assumption and developed perceptual-motor programs in efforts to improve academic skills through improvement of motor skills.) However, **the preponderance of research evidence shows the assumption to be unfounded: no direct transfer of learning occurs between the remediation of learning problems and motor skills.** CEC states that:

> Research seeking to base instruction on the cause of an individual's learning disability has not been successful. Apparently, rather than determining the cause of a student's problems, it is more important to determine the individual's unique educational needs and design instruction that has the best chance of helping him or her to meet those needs. (CEC, see p. 531)

The Research Institute on Progress Monitoring (RIPM) (http://ici.edu/ripm/), housed at the University of Minnesota, is conducting extensive research into how to meet the unique educational needs of *all* students, including those with learning disabilities. Progress monitoring is a well-established approach that uses validated, quick, and easy tools for measuring academic learning in the classroom (Deno, 1998, 2002; Deno, Mirkin & Chiang, 1982; Espin & Deno, 1993a, 1993b; Shinn, 1998). The measures are repeated and are focused on a long range goal, so the student is measured against an established functional goal; for example, in a one-minute reading session, how many correct words are read (e.g., Good & Kiminski, 1996; Kiminski & Good, 1996). "Growth" is tracked and if there is not appropriate positive growth, then the students are assessed more closely to make decisions about what further testing might be needed and, hence, what interventions might be used. It is here that a promising new way to identify students with learning disabilities will come forth, because a *careful long-term observation* can be made about students' progress and the progress of their peers. RIPM will be making contributions to both the diagnosis of discrepancy and the ongoing strategies for instruction in the classroom.

The current science of teaching students with learning disabilities is, therefore, not focused on the etiology, but rather on identifying where the student is having difficulty and what strategies can be employed to assist learning. Experts in learning disability in the classroom note that these students drop out of school at a greater rate than students with more obvious, severe disabilities. The overwhelming evidence is that these students are easily identified by their peers and do not succeed socially, and these facts have life-long ramifications for psychological health and well-being.

Additional research is needed to identify more precisely the real cause of learning disabilities. The present evidence is more speculative than factual. Until such time as hard evidence is available as to the cause of learning disabilities, educators will be required to assess many factors in the student's life to provide answers helpful toward the development of an appropriate educational program.

Learning and Behavioral Characteristics

The classic understanding of learning disabilities is that there are problems with symbolization, which affects conceptualization. Symbolization is defined as the ability to communicate or translate visual and auditory images into meaningful symbols. It includes many of the tasks thought to be requisite to successful reading, writing, spelling, arithmetic, and speaking. On the other hand, conceptualization is regarded as the highest form of intellectual activity, referring to the ability to categorize, to abstract, to critically analyze, to generalize, and to create. Thus, this is the area where students with learning disabilities seem to have difficulties.

Again, this classic understanding has not disappeared, but educational experts are not conducting current investigations using this framework. Rather, they are interested in keen observations of the academic area and in determining which of the interventions will be successful. **In the past, physical educators have relied on the classic approach, which translated into a clear emphasis on improving perceptual motor problems for students with learning disabilities. The authors are encouraging physical educators to consider following with the current research in other academic areas for individuals with learning disabilities by using another approach which will be subsequently described. The authors believe it is important to seek a broader supportive role of education across the lifespan by considering the benefits of engaging students with learning disabilities in physical activity with their peers, knowing and enjoying activity that maintains a healthy body, and experience activity that offers a wide variety of exposure so they can learn preferences for physical activity given their skill level, resources, and interests.** This will be detailed later in the chapter.

Receptive and Expressive Language Deficits

Some students with learning disabilities have deficits related to ability in receptive and expressive language. Because effective teaching is based upon adequate communication, it is imperative that physical educators be cognizant of individual differences among children in ability to receive auditory information and to use language to express themselves.

Classroom teachers should be able to expect physical educators to coordinate the physical education program with the teaching strategies they are employing to ensure that students with learning disabilities are learning. Students who seem to ignore or fail to follow directions often have deficits in receptive auditory language.

Receptive language is the ability to comprehend words and to remember sequences. Teachers should not assume that the student is purposely defiant, but rather is unable to understand information shared in an auditory mode. Students with learning disabilities whose condition has not been correctly diagnosed as a receptive language deficit may develop compensatory behaviors that are either defiant or in some way maladjusted, and end up in trouble with family, school, and peers. These students can be successful in physical education settings when instruction is provided using a multimodality approach. Here the teacher provides a visual prompt along with auditory information. For example, the direction, "Go to the corner of the gym with your team," must be given while pointing to the specified corner.

Expressive language, or the ability to communicate, is also considered an auditory deficit. Auditory expressive language deficits, of course, refer to speaking and are sometimes labeled as expressive aphasias. Characteristics that classroom teachers often report are

1. inability to reproduce simple geometric forms;
2. persistent reversals of words, syllables, or letters;
3. rotation or inversion of letters;
4. reversed sequence of letters and syllables;
5. mirror writing, and
6. transposition of numbers.

Physical educators will notice that these students find it difficult to repeat instructions given to them. They may understand, but cannot verbally explain what is required. Or they may struggle to ask a question about a task in the physical education class. Again, this is where the physical education teacher can coordinate with the special education teacher and the speech therapist to understand the strategies that are being employed to develop the student's ability to communicate wants, needs, and academic material.

Perception Issues, Learning Difficulties, and Physical Activity

Sometimes students with learning disabilities have problems with understanding laterality (e.g., the right and left hand; an awareness of two sides of the body) or directionality (e.g., concepts of over, under). Thus, they may have poor body awareness and poor perceptual skills.

The following information on *visual* perception is presented to assist the physical education teacher in

distinguishing between a student who might have a problem from a student exhibiting noncompliant behavior. Visual perception may be due to deficiency in one or more of the following: visual discrimination, figure-ground discrimination, depth perception, object constancy, and object identification (visual agnosia). Children whose visual perception is affected by inadequate visual discrimination have difficulty in determining the size, shape, color, and texture of an object. Students with faulty visual discrimination are not very successful in physical education. They are likely to be unable to distinguish a large ball from a small ball, a square block from a rectangular block, a blue bean bag from a red bean bag, or rough ground from smooth ground. There are very few games and activities that do not require some degree of discrimination in size, form, color, and texture. Consequently, success and pleasure in play are largely denied these children.

The ability to visually differentiate a specific object from a complex background is minimal in young children, and develops slowly to reach its peak during adolescence. In children with faulty visual perception due to poor figure-ground discrimination, this development is delayed. Such children lack the ability to identify and focus attention upon a single object or figure in a cluttered or complex background. They may, for example, become so confused by the various players that form the background for a game of tag that they cannot locate the one who is "it." Inability by some children to follow the aerial path of a thrown ball is another illustration of the figure-ground problem. Obviously, such children will have difficulties in the performance of many activities in the physical education program.

Depth perception is the term given to the ability to judge distances between near and far objects. Those who have problems determining the distance of an object have difficulty placing their bodies in the proper relationship to the object. In catching a ball, for example, they overreach or do not reach far enough and they miss catching the ball. Any activity that requires judgment of distances is difficult, if not impossible, for students with this visual perception deficit.

The ability to identify an object regardless of the direction from which it is viewed is termed "object consistency." Youngsters lacking this ability become lost in a maze of unrecognizable objects as they move about. For example, such children will not be able to recognize an item of play equipment when viewed from any side other than the one from which they learned to identify it. Such a deficit in visual perception obviously creates many difficulties in physical education and in all other areas of endeavor. The normal development of body image entails mastery of the following tasks at *approximately* the ages cited.

Age three years
  Ability to name one's own body parts. Somewhat later the child learns to identify the body parts of dolls, animals, and other human beings. Last in the developmental sequence, the child learns to recognize body parts depicted in pictures and other one-dimensional media.
Ages six to seven years
  Ability to understand right-left concepts as they relate to one's own body.
Ages eight to nine years
  Ability to understand right-left concepts in terms of other persons.
Ages 11 to 12 years
  Ability to understand right-left concepts in terms of inanimate objects.

Children with perceptual-motor disorders may be slow in the acquisition of these abilities and may manifest confusion with respect to right-left concepts throughout life.

Comorbidity: Learning Disability Plus Other Disabilities

Some students with learning disabilities exhibit behavioral characteristics such as distractibility and hyperactivity. It is likely that a student with a learning disability can have other problems such as ADHD. This disorder will be discussed later in this chapter and is related to the notion of comorbidity, which is a term used in clinical settings to describe the occurrence of other disorders or impairments in addition to a primary problem. For example, given the diagnosis of learning disability, a student may also have other disorders such as hyperactivity. Many students with learning disabilities also have ADHD, but the full clinical picture of the comorbidity of this is still to be researched. It does little good to admonish such children to "pay attention"; they would if they could. Their distractibility is of neurological origin. Other strategies discussed under hyperactivity are more helpful for these students.

Some students with learning disabilities also deal with problems of perseveration on a task of a verbal interest. Perseveration is the inability to shift with ease from one activity to another. Often mistaken for stubbornness, perseveration is of neurological origin. The child would like to follow directions, but he simply cannot respond immediately and appropriately to "stop and start" activities. It is interesting that children with learning disabilities may exhibit any of these behavioral characteristics on some days, but not on others.

Physical Activity and Learning Disability

Physical education for students with learning disabilities has the potential to affect the positive development of social and emotional health and to help such students feel good about themselves despite the difficulties they may have in movement. **Experts agree that the classical approach of working with students with learning disabilities has faded into the background. The classical approach focuses more on the perceptual problems that seem to be linked to the inability to read and write. Instead, a much more functional approach is being advocated.**

Consider the young child whose parents sit in IEP meetings over the years and hear repeatedly from the physical educator about their child's perceptual motor difficulties. Instead, the emphasis could be on the child's strengths in the curriculum and in what areas the child needs support. Taken out of the context of perceptual motor problems, the strengths could be translated into "likes soccer" and the weaknesses described in terms of providing more practice time with the skills. Known as ALT-PE, the academic time in which the student is actively engaged in the skill-learning in class is highly correlated with learning the skill. The performance is this student's "personal best" rather than another student's personal best. In other words, given the extra assistance a student with learning disability might have in a physical education setting, he may not have the highest skill performance in the class. However, with increased participation and learning opportunities, the student learns that he can play soccer with his peers.

The approach used in the top-down assessment (Burton & Miller, 1998), which was described in chapter 4, can be used to make observations about the student's performance within the curriculum. Here we begin at the top: What is the functional skill? The performance is observed and then a determination is made on whether the skill needs to be modified for success.

Using this approach, can the student with a learning disability move along with his peers through a large array of physical activity through the school years without being labeled as a less than valued member of the class? Using the strategies for modification and adaptation (e.g., Lieberman & Houston-Wilson, 2000), can the IEP team give the student the opportunity to succeed?

The notion of ecological task analysis (Davis & Burton, 1991) is recommended for students with learning disabilities: Taking into account the unique aspects of the individual, the unique way a task is being presented to the performer, and the unique environment in which the task is performed. Much work must be done to analyze how these aspects—performer, task, and environment—contribute to the movement performance for a student who *may* struggle in physical activity because of a learning disability. In light of the lack of evidence regarding research along the full spectrum of the educational system in physical education, an accepted alternative procedure is to iden-

tify the motor skills in which the youngster is experiencing problems; employ an ecological task analysis approach, when needed; also task-analyze the skill into small units; provide direct instruction and reinforcement; and allow for sufficient repetition and practice. When more complex physical activities/games are part of the curriculum, it is recommended that the physical education teacher use the top-down approach to assess and evaluate what modifications and adaptations are needed for the student to be successful in the physical education class.

Attention to social skills and perceived social competence is important for students with learning disabilities. Shapiro and Ulrich (2001) found no statistical differences in ratings of social competence by students with and without learning disabilities who were receiving physical education in the mainstream class at ages 10 to 14. They reported no IEPs in motor skills at the time of the study for any of the students with learning disabilities. They also cautioned that this can change as a student's age and peer reference become more influential.

It is widely known that students with learning disabilities are at high risk for developing low self-esteem, and also for dropping out of school. In a new journal devoted solely to learning disabilities (*Learning Disabilities, A Contemporary Journal*), Sideridis and Tsorbatzoudis (2003) studied a similar age-group as Shapiro and Ulrich regarding the academic motivation of students with learning disabilities. They reported that the students were in the lower third of their class and that avoidance and lack of motivation were present: "It is concluded that students with learning disabilities may have 'ill' motivational strategies, and they resemble the learned helpless type described by Seligman (Seligman, 1975) due possibly to exposure to repeated failure" (p. 8).

Students with learning disabilities can use inappropriate coping strategies in the physical education class. Foremost among these strategies are:

1. attention-getting,
2. helplessness,
3. destructiveness or antisocial acts,
4. stubbornness.

Attention-getting may take the form of asking many questions, dropping objects on the floor, cute sayings, or picking on others. On the other hand, the child may seek attention by being sweet and cooperative, shadowing the teacher, and assisting with noninstructional chores. Helplessness may be real or professed; the child who says, "I can't" generally elicits the teacher's sympathy, thereby placing the teacher in the student's service. Destructiveness or antisocial acts often serve to build up the ego; the class bully is seldom ignored and often gains a small following of admirers. Stubbornness, or passive resistance, initiates a power struggle between the child and the teacher.

Children with learning disabilities, like their nondisabled peers, have the capacity to understand and show insight into the meaning of their own behavior. It is important that teachers recognize self-defeating strategies for what they are. Students with learning disabilities need assistance in forming meaningful and satisfactory relationships with others.

Disorders of Attention and Hyperactivity

During the reauthorization of the Education for All Handicapped Children Act of 1975 in 1990, many parents, professionals, and members of Congress questioned whether or not the term "Attention Deficit Disorder (ADD)" should be added as a separate disabling condition. This, of course, raised several questions, including the observation that problems focusing or maintaining attention are frequently noted in individuals with learning disabilities. Some also noted that a related disorder, attention deficit/hyperactivity disorder (ADHD), is also frequently observed in individuals with learning disabilities. It was finally concluded that individuals with ADD and ADHD should receive special education services, if qualified. The appropriate classification would vary depending upon the nature of the primary cause, but could include the IDEA category of other health impaired, learning disability, or serious emotional disturbance.

Children who have problems with attention and concentration are not a homogeneous group. More important, not all children with ADD/ADHD are eligible for special education services. Students must meet the federal and state criteria for eligibility, and thus need special education services in order to succeed in school. Interestingly, students who have ADD/ADHD may be eligible for services under another disability category if they meet specified criteria.

The abbreviations ADD and ADHD are often printed with a slash in between the terms. This does not indicate that the individual has both disorders, but rather that they are often discussed together. ADD is noted in individuals as inability to attend; to the extent that they also have difficulties with being highly active, a diagnosis of ADHD may also be made. In reality, the disorder is not a lack of attention, but rather the inability to filter out unnecessary stimuli; hence the person attends to everything (Kline & Silver, 2004). The behavioral result is a presentation of inattention.

Estimates suggest that 3 to 5 % of the school-aged population has an attention deficit disorder (NIHM, 2003). Recent evidence indicates that about one-third of the children identified as having a specific learning disability also have an attention deficit disorder, and that anywhere from 30 to 65 % of children identified as having a serious emotional disturbance also have attention deficit disorder (Council for Exceptional Children, 1992). **It is important to note, however, that the diagnosis of ADHD is made by clinical personnel such as a psychologist or developmental pediatrician, or trained school psychologist, psychiatrist, neurologist, or clinical social worker; with input from the parents, the classroom teacher, and others as deemed necessary.** Many of the primary symptoms of inattention and impulsivity seen in children with ADHD are also symptoms of other problems, such as depression or anxiety. So, it is important to be sure exactly what the diagnosis is. Input from family history, observations by the classroom teacher concurrent with standardized testing(s), and direct observations and interviews with the student are important components of the diagnostic procedure (see Barkley, 2000).

The guidelines in the APA's *Diagnostic and Statistical Manual of Mental Disorders (DSM-IV–TR)* (APA, 2000) are used to diagnose ADHD and caution that the symptoms must appear prior to age seven years, persist for at least six months; and there are a proportion of criteria that must occur at greater frequency than observed among other children at the same mental age. (See table 12.1.)

Many of these characteristics can be summarized as developmentally inappropriate degrees of inattention, impulsiveness, and/or hyperactivity. In other words, the behavior that is exhibited is at a level not typical for the age of the child. For example, very young children can attend only for a short period of time. This is not inattention. It is developmentally expected.

As stated before, the student with ADHD attends to most stimuli. IDEA '97 describes this inattention as "a child's heightened alertness to environmental stimuli that results in limited alertness with respect to the educational environment" (Section 300.7). Impulsiveness is responding to stimuli quickly (e.g., answers questions before the question is finished, cannot wait for a turn, interrupts others). Hyperactivity is both the high level of activity that is excessive for the student's age, as well as fidgeting with hands or feet. The *DSM-IV-TR* refers to these children as "on the go."

ADHD is a relatively new diagnostic category, first appearing in the *DSM-III-R* in 1987 (see Harvey & Reid, 2003), in which very few clinicians were expert until the past decade or so. Dr. Russell Barkley, a psychologist, and Dr. Dennis Cantwell, a child psychiatrist, have contributed an enormous amount to the understanding of diagnosis, medical management, treatment, and educational concerns of individuals with ADHD. Their research is longitudinal, and their expertise has influenced many scholars, practitioners, and parents.

TABLE 12.1 Attention Deficit/Hyperactivity Disorder (ADHD)

BehaveNet® Clinical Capsule™: DSM-IV & DSM-IV-TR:
Diagnostic Criteria for Attention Deficit/Hyperactivity Disorder (cautionary statement)

A. Either (1) or (2):

   (1) *inattention:* six (or more) of the following symptoms of inattention have persisted for at least 6 months to a degree that is maladaptive and inconsistent with developmental level:

      (a) often fails to give close attention to details or makes careless mistakes in schoolwork, work, or other activities

      (b) often has difficulty sustaining attention in tasks or play activities

      (c) often does not seem to listen when spoken to directly

      (d) often does not follow through on instructions and fails to finish schoolwork, chores, or duties in the workplace (not due to oppositional behavior or failure to understand instructions)

      (e) often has difficulty organizing tasks and activities

      (f) often avoids, dislikes, or is reluctant to engage in tasks that require sustained mental effort (such as schoolwork or homework)

      (g) often loses things necessary for tasks or activities (e.g., toys, school assignments, pencils, books, or tools)

      (h) is often easily distracted by extraneous stimuli

      (i) is often forgetful in daily activities

   (2) *hyperactivity-impulsivity:* six (or more) of the following symptoms of hyperactivity-impulsivity have persisted for at least 6 months to a degree that is maladaptive and inconsistent with developmental level:

Hyperactivity

      (a) often fidgets with hands or feet or squirms in seat

      (b) often leaves seat in classroom or in other situations in which remaining seated is expected

      (c) often runs about or climbs excessively in situations in which it is inappropriate (in adolescents or adults, may be limited to subjective feelings of restlessness)

      (d) often has difficulty playing or engaging in leisure activities quietly

      (e) is often "on the go" or often acts as if "driven by a motor"

      (f) often talks excessively

Impulsivity

      (g) often blurts out answers before questions have been completed

      (h) often has difficulty awaiting turn

      (i) often interrupts or intrudes on others (e.g., butts into conversations or games)

B. Some hyperactive-impulsive or inattentive symptoms that caused impairment were present before age 7 years.

C. Some impairment from the symptoms is present in two or more settings (e.g., at school [or work] and at home).

D. There must be clear evidence of clinically significant impairment in social, academic, or occupational functioning.

E. The symptoms do not occur exclusively during the course of a *Pervasive Developmental Disorder, Schizophrenia,* or other Psychotic Disorder and are not better accounted for by another mental disorder (e.g., *Mood Disorder, Anxiety Disorder, Dissociative Disorders,* or a *Personality Disorder*).

Code based on type:

314.01 Attention Deficit/Hyperactivity Disorder, Combined Type: if both Criteria A1 and A2 are met for the past 6 months

314.00 Attention Deficit/Hyperactivity Disorder, Predominantly Inattentive Type: if Criterion A1 is met but Criterion A2 is not met for the past 6 months

314.01 Attention Deficit/Hyperactivity Disorder, Predominantly Hyperactive-Impulsive Type: if Criterion A2 is met but Criterion A1 is not met for the past 6 months

Coding note: For individuals (especially adolescents and adults) who currently have symptoms that no longer meet full criteria, "In Partial Remission" should be specified.

Reprinted with permission from the *Diagnostic and Statistical Manual of Mental Disorders, Fourth Edition.* Copyright 2000 *American Psychiatric Association.* Also: ADD, ADHD, hyperkinetic child syndrome, hyperkinetic reaction of childhood, minimal brain damage, minimal cerebral dysfunction, minor cerebral dysfunction

• *Attention Deficit Disorder Anonymous*

Myths of ADHD have proliferated: the child is lazy; he is just a kid and will get over it; the child should receive medication and get off it as quickly as possible; he can focus on the video games so he doesn't have ADHD; he just got poor parenting (Reiff & Tippins, 2004). The reality is that these are myths and children with ADHD can become very downtrodden because they would like to succeed if they could. They will not outgrow ADHD, although it may "look different" as they grow older. Being able to focus on video games is not as challenging as academic material, and children with ADHD are not necessarily without parents who care.

The goal, of course, is to ensure that students with ADHD are recognized as individuals who may need special assistance and to provide the appropriate intervention, as necessary. Many of the ideas and suggestions presented in this chapter as well as chapter 13 will provide useful information in developing meaningful and positive physical activity programs for students with ADHD. Again, the reason that the teaching strategies employed with children with behavior disorders are useful with students who have ADHD is because the behavior exhibited can be similar, although the etiology can be vastly different.

Medication

Medication has been helpful to some children with ADHD. The mechanisms of the medicine vary and the choice of which to use is best left to parents and physicians. Typically, parents and clinical personnel work together to understand how and what type of medication can best assist the child with ADHD. The American Academy of Pediatrics Treatment Guidelines for ADHD states:

> The pediatrician or other clinician should recommend medication and/or behavior therapy, as appropriate, to improve the target outcomes that have been identified. If the target outcomes are not met, the treatment team should re-evaluate the original diagnosis, treatments used, adherence to the treatment plan, and presence of any co-existing conditions. (p. 47, Reiff & Tippins, 2004)

Medications can help some children focus on the academic tasks, and therefore increase academic success and social and self-acceptance. Medication alone is not considered the "silver bullet" for solving all the difficulties faced by students with ADHD and their families. Instead, a multipronged approach is recommended, including behavioral strategies as well as medicine. In some cases, it is helpful to know if a student is taking medicine, particularly if there are side effects that the teaching staff should be alerted to and report to the family. Sometimes teachers are asked to help assess whether the medicine is helping the student. Caution is recommended when interpreting the behavior of the student. It is important to take into consideration the context of the behavior. Sometimes students with confirmed ADHD are attributed inappropriately to a behavior that is really reasonable given the situation, and not necessarily due to the ADHD diagnosis.

Physical Activity and ADHD

To successfully engage children with ADHD in physical education classes is to understand the difficulty they will have with attention, and that they will be impulsive as well as highly active. Everyone experiences these behaviors at one time or another, but the diagnosis of ADHD requires that the symptoms be inappropriate for the person's age, excessive, long-term, and pervasive (e.g., observed across different settings) (NIMH, 2003). Many authorities consider ADHD a disorder that is part of the child's neurological and genetic makeup (NIMH, 2003; Reiff & Tippins, 2004), but as yet there is no definitive cause.

Some children with ADHD have problems with movement skill performance, and some do not (Harvey & Reid, 2003). The attribution of movement problems with a diagnosis of ADHD is compounded by the prevalence of comorbidity with other disorders. It is difficult to separate out whether the movement problems are caused by developmental coordination disorder (DCD), learning disabilities (LD), or, in some cases, depression and anxiety, as well as other problems (see NIMH, 2003).

Educational and clinical authorities recommend a multimodality approach to the treatment and care of children with ADHD. The following strategies have been found helpful for children with ADHD: behavior management, cognitive-behavior techniques, direct teaching, and pharmacologic management (see Reiff & Tippins, 2004). For the physical educator, this requires attention to the student's full educational program and the interventions that are being employed in the general education settings. These interventions should be followed in the physical education settings.

The follow up descriptions of the primary and secondary features of ADHD <u>and the behaviors in physical education settings</u> are presented by the authors given clinical experience with these children, their teachers, and their parents (table 12.2).

Facilities and Equipment for Physical Activity

The number of lines on the floor and markings on the wall should also be minimized for students with attentional problems. **It is recommended that "floor spots" in the form of simple geometric shapes or other relevant symbols be placed on the floor to assist young children in finding "their own space" and to assure that the distance between students is sufficient to eliminate body contact.**

Figure 12.1 A student draws a picture of his goal in PE and the number of times he will perform a specific positive social skill.

The second requirement in adapting facilities is the reduction of space in the gymnasium through the use of partitions or the identification of small rooms within the school that can be used for physical education purposes. Placing sturdy tumbling mats vertically on end creates an easily designed but effective cubicle instructional setting for students who are easily distracted. When children play outdoors, it is especially important that small areas be roped off and that space boundaries be carefully defined. Ideally the outdoor area should be surrounded by a high wooden fence to exclude irrelevant stimuli.

TABLE 12.2

Primary Feature	Physical Education
A. Inattention	The child processes few, if any, of the instructions or rules for the game. He will be distracted by the equipment and the other children in the class. He may wander off and be a poor team player.
B. Impulsivity	The child will act before thinking and use equipment before it is her turn, find it difficult to wait in line for her turn, and may call out repeatedly in class. She may be unable to stay on task for any length of time.
C. Hyperactivity	The child has difficulty modulating arousal and will become very active and remain active during the class. Physical activity does not reduce the high activity state.

Secondary Feature	
A. Low Self-Esteem	This child has low tolerance for negative feedback, being on the losing team, and facing failure. (This child regularly receives a high degree of negative feedback.)
B. Lack of Age-Appropriate Social Skills	This child does not know how to be positive and give positive feedback to peers. He may want to be a leader, but does not know how.
C. Anger and Temper Control	This child is quick to become upset if she is called "out" during a game, is on the losing team, feels that a rule is unfair, does not perform lwell.

Teaching Strategies for Children with ADHD in Physical Education Class

Inattention	Keep the instructions simple and short in length.
	Visually remove equipment until it is time to use it.
	Do not give equipment to a student and then ask him to listen to directions.
	Keep the class structured and predictable.
	Provide warnings/signals when activities are going to begin and when they are going to transition or end. Allow some time lapse and then follow through with the next activity.
Impulsivity	Create a sense of self-awareness that is positive regarding the student's uniqueness. Use the term "personal best" to describe the difference in performance. Encourage the student(s) to give high-fives to each other for having done their personal best.
	Encourage the student(s) to self-evaluate by setting realistic goals (e.g., "How many laps can you run?"). Younger students will not be realistic in goal setting, but as they get older they will understand the connection between setting a goal and attaining a realistic goal. Once students have performed the task (e.g., run the laps), see how well they were able to. If the goal was unrealistic, then set a new goal and try again.
	Outside of class, have the students draw out a goal and *have them* keep track of it. (See figure 12.1.)
	Break larger tasks into parts, and thus help the student learn sequences. For example, explain what is expected at the station: pick up the bean bags, throw, count, repeat. This can apply throughout the educational experience in physical education.
	Encourage self-control by creating success. Have enough equipment so all students can be active and enough stations so that students are kept active.
Hyperactivity	For younger children, use markers for their arrival into the gymnasium. For older students, have a predictable routine.
	Do not require the student to listen to long directions. Meet with the student outside of class to review how the class is run and what is expected. Explain that you have observed that she is a good mover and you will want her in your class.
	Use warnings to make transitions from activity to activity. High arousal levels will need teacher-mediated structure to decrease the arousal. Once the student is engaged in an activity that is fun and pleasureable, he may find it difficult to transition to another activity.
	Use a system of one or two warnings: "In 15 seconds we will move to the next station. . . . In 10 seconds we will move to the next station." Younger children do not understand the time concepts, but they do catch on to the use of "warnings" that are cues to activity change.
	Provide a cool-down period before ending the physical education activity. This can be a slow loco-motor activity or an actual relaxation activity with music. Whatever it is, provide it to help the student come off a high activity event and move onto the next classroom activity.
Low Self-Esteem	Provide positive regard to the student even if it is not about the physical activity: "You have a bright red shirt on today!" or "I saw you run as fast as you could today. You did your personal best!"
	Sometimes students with ADHD are so accustomed to negative feedback that they will argue with you about the positive feedback. Do not argue about the positive feedback you give. Let it go and let them continue to hear it from you.
	Prioritize the behaviors that you will concentrate on in the physical education class, then let the others go.
	Have the student describe a reward for doing well in your class (see figure 12.2).

Continued.

Teaching Strategies for Children with ADHD in Physical Education Class (*continued*)

Social Skills Development	Teach the social skills associated with games and activities. Keep the concepts simple and give positive feedback. Establish rules for providing positive feedback to others in the class. Even older students need help with social skills. Sometimes they have missed the instruction or have been sent out of previous classes. (Sometimes teachers will punish an inappropriate behavior in another class by taking access to physical education away from the student. This is not appropriate for many reasons.)
Low Frustration Tolerance	Help students understand that sometimes life is not fair, but you understand that they did their best in the game or activity. Catch students when they "could have lost it, but did not." Sometimes this means noticing that a student's behavior is about to escalate and catching her before she loses control.

Developed by C. Leitschuh.

The third requirement in adapting facilities is consistency from day to day in the organization of teaching stations and the placement of equipment. Because these children are often described as "lost in space," it is recommended that the instructional environment be highly structured with as little as possible left to chance.

In addition to the requirements of stimuli control, space reduction, and consistency in placement of equipment, the facilities for students with learning disabilities should include an adequate number of teaching stations and sufficient equipment for individualized instruction. A Learning Resources Center with high tech equipment, including video camcorders, computers, and hypermedia resources, should be established to provide opportunities for students to view themselves and others in the performance of motor skills.

The modification and adaptation that are needed for a student with ADHD is not necessarily with the movement skills, but rather with the instructional delivery and the organization of the activities. Sometimes poor movement skills performance is due to lack of opportunity to respond, lack of ability to understand the instructions due to impulsivity, and a high activity level. Some children with ADHD also have learning disabilities, as has been previously

Figure 12.2 A student draws a picture of his goal of making a basket.

explained. It is important for the physical education teacher to understand whether auditory processing is a problem for the student with ADHD. This difficulty compounds the problems of being highly active as well as other aspects of ADHD.

Teaching Reminders for Physical Activity

Good teaching is based upon careful diagnosis of individual needs. With the growing popularity of the multidisciplinary approach to learning disabilities, several disciplines may share responsibility for the evaluation of the motor and cognitive development of the child. Depending upon the expectations of the other academic disciplines with which the instructor is working, the physical educator may administer standardized specific tests to assist in identifying children in need of special motor training. Some of these tests were discussed in chapters 3 and 6. However, the most important diagnostic technique remains careful, conscientious observation of the student's motor performance over long periods of time. **It cannot be overemphasized that no single test is valid and reliable enough to determine a child's needs. Nor is it possible for someone with ADHD or learning disabilities to be entirely consistent in his or her motor performance.** The student may lack motivation on one day, be affected by medication on the next, and be convalescing from a cold on the next. It is important to remember that children view their motor acts as an extension of themselves and as a measure of their own worth. Therefore, the process of diagnosis and evaluation, like that of instruction, should be so presented that children feel they are succeeding.

Effective diagnostic techniques enable the physical educator to teach to the level of success. For the student with a learning disability, it is essential to determine whether the major learning disability is auditory, visual, or kinesthetic. The accepted practice is to emphasize the use of those senses that are unaffected rather than to attempt to remedy the disability. This implies that some individuals must be taught mainly through the visual and kinesthetic modalities while others must receive instruction chiefly via the auditory and kinesthetic modalities. Overall, this technique is to teach to the student's strength, whatever sensory medium is strongest for the student (figure 12.3).

One of the fundamental principles in adapting instruction is that of *structure,* a form of conditioning used with distractible children to assure appropriate responses to stimuli. Structure in the teaching situation refers to a planned routine or activity, with as little as possible left to chance, so that children can anticipate the sequence of events and know what is expected of them. In a highly structured physical education program, the children

Figure 12.3   Work on a balance beam helps a child become aware of the sensation of losing and regaining balance.

always enter the gymnasium through the same door, go to the same floor spot, participate in warm-up activities, and start individualized instruction at the same teaching station. The direction of rotation between stations is uniform from day to day, as are the stop and start signals employed by the teacher. The structured teaching environment is adult-dominated; children are not asked to make choices and demonstrate competence in self-direction because they lack the readiness to cope with freedom and the exposure to unessential stimuli that freedom brings.

If, or when, the child learns to control his or her distractibility, structure is gradually lessened. The physical educator should discuss the concept of structure with the classroom teacher and ascertain that the amount of structure imposed in the gymnasium is equal to and consistent with that imposed in the classroom.

Many practices in physical education that traditionally have been thought of as desirable are sometimes *contraindicated for children with ADHD* and those with learning disabilities. Some of these follow:

1. Opportunities to develop leadership-followership qualities through membership on many different kinds of teams with different students serving as leaders each time. Frequent changes in group structure often confuse children with ADHD and learning disabilities. They should be allowed to play with the same small group throughout the year with as few changes in leadership as feasible.

2. Opportunities to "let off steam" and to develop fitness through freedom to run, jump, and shout in an optimal amount of space. Despite the fact that this practice may meet the needs of some children with ADHD and learning disabilities, particularly those with hyperactivity, it tends to heighten the hyperactivity of others. Time should be spent on the mastery of neuromuscular skills that have carry-over value and activities designed primarily for cardiovascular development. Rather than rule out certain types of activities for *all* hyperactive students, it is desirable to experiment with variations in speed and distance to determine which kinds of fitness activities are best for each individual. Use of the goal-setting technique often works well in these situations. It is also very important to use "cool down" activities after heightened physical activity (Sherrill & Pyfer, 1985).

3. Emphasis upon the development of speed through awards for track and field events and the association of winning with the fastest team. Many children with ADHD and learning disabilities need assistance in learning how to perform at their best, which may be different from others. Decrease the emphasis on competition with others and develop the notion of "cooperation with your team," and "doing the best that you can."

The key to successful instruction of children with ADHD and learning disabilities is individualization. It is possible that no two children in the gymnasium will ever be doing the same thing simultaneously. To facilitate implementation of this principle, each child, upon entering the gymnasium, may pick up a card on which his or her activities for the day are printed. The nature and sequence of these activities should not change radically from week to week.

Physical Activities

The program of physical education activities varies with age, degree of involvement, and specific type of learning disability. If the students have learning disabilities, the program should be planned cooperatively by the physical educator and classroom teacher to ascertain that needs are met and that teaching methodology is consistent.

In the primary grades, attention must be focused upon the development of basic movement patterns—running, jumping, hopping, throwing, catching, striking, and kicking. Children should explore their capability for movement on different surfaces—wood, cement, sand, pebbles, high and low grass, both wet and dry. Opportunities to experiment with different sizes, shapes, and weights of balls and sports implements should be provided. Ample time should be spent on climbing and hanging activities as well as creeping and crawling activities. Balancing activities are important provided

they are varied and interesting and the child can achieve some measure of success. The gross motor activities that promote basic skill development and physical fitness often can be combined with sensory experiences to promote perceptual-motor learning; some examples may be found at the end of the chapter.

Instruction in individual and dual sports, with appropriately modified equipment, should begin as early as third grade. Competence in such activities as bowling, ballet, and swimming helps to win the admiration of the peer group, many of whom may not yet have had the opportunity to try these activities. Most important, competence in individual and dual activities enhances self-esteem and serves to compensate for any inability to participate successfully in team activities. Early acquaintance with lifetime sports also contributes to family unity and may lead to closer parent-child relationships when, for instance, parents and children can bowl or swim together.

In the primary grades physical education may play a major role in the development of language and the enrichment of vocabulary. When this is a concern, the teacher should plan contrasting activities, such as up and down, over and under, below and above, forward and backward, to enable students to experience kinesthetically the words they must recognize on paper and in life. Likewise, appropriate time should be devoted to learning the names of body parts and the terms for different kinds of movements and positions in space.

In the intermediate and secondary grades, emphasis upon individual and dual activities should continue. Students should be introduced to mechanical principles and given special assistance in problem solving and generalizing with respect to similarities and differences in basic movements, such as, for instance, the overarm throw, the tennis serve, and the badminton smash. Because of their characteristic deficits in attention and self-control, it cannot be assumed that they will learn through incidental exposure.

Perceptual-Motor Activities

The focus in the approach to involving children with learning disabilities in the general education curriculum has been described earlier in this chapter. It is recommended that this approach be pursued. The information herein on perceptual-motor activity is not intended to replace or duplicate instruction in the classroom; rather, the intent is to supplement and reinforce these experiences. There is agreement that instruction in selected concepts with which children with learning disabilities struggle (for example, discriminating between large and small) can be provided in the physical education class. The concept of over and under, for example, can be introduced in the classroom and reinforced in the gymnasium through the use of activities where the body and body parts are placed over or under selected objects—for example, the arm is "over" the head, the body is "under" the rope. In the following section, various activities are suggested to assist teachers in working with youngsters who experience problems in visual and auditory discrimination, balance, and body awareness. These activities can be incorporated into the physical education program for use in the teaching of various basic skills. These activities are typically fun for all children at these young ages.

Activities Focusing on Visual Discrimination (Size)

1. Tossing balls of various sizes into receptacles of appropriate size to hold them. Several receptacles of different sizes and a ball that will fit into each size will be needed. The child selects the ball that is the most appropriate size (neither too large nor too small) for the container and tosses it in.
2. Running around circles of various sizes marked on the floor. Circles of progressively larger size are painted or drawn on the floor inside a large circle. The child runs around the circle that is the size indicated by the teacher.
3. Selecting a particular-size object and running a designated distance. This activity requires an object so large that running with it is difficult, an object so small that it can be easily held in the hand, and an object of a size between these two. The child is then instructed to run to the teacher (or to run some easily defined distance) with the object with which he can run the fastest; with the one that is largest, the one of middle size, and the smallest one.
4. Crawling through circular objects of various sizes. Hoops, tubes, or similar objects of various circumferences will be needed. The child crawls through the object of the size indicated by the teacher.
5. Running zigzag between chairs that are various distances apart. Several chairs are set three and five feet apart, as shown in figure 12.4. The child runs between the chairs that are closer or farther apart as directed by the teacher.

Activities Focusing on Visual Discrimination (Color)

1. Throwing balls or bean bags of different colors into containers of matching color. Balls or bean bags of various colors with receptacles to match will be needed. The child matches the colors and throws the object into the appropriate receptacle.
2. Selecting an object of designated color from among others and running with it to another group of objects to pick the object of matching color. Two objects of each color are needed. In response to the teacher's instructions, the child picks up an object, runs with it to the location of the other objects, and matches it to one of like color.

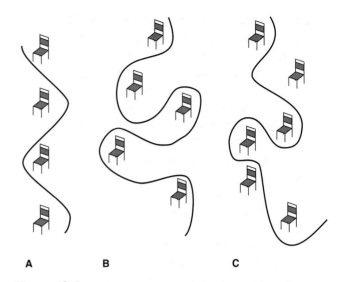

Figure 12.4 Zigzag run uses chairs set various distances apart. The complexity of the task can be determined by changing the distance and spacing of the chairs.

3. Kicking balls into goals of the corresponding color. Several large balls of different colors and goals to match will be needed. (Goals can be improvised from suitably sized paper cartons from which one side is removed to allow the ball to enter.) The child kicks each of the balls into the appropriate goal.
4. Jumping into hoops of different colors after seeing a model of the color. Two hoops of each color will be needed; one set is held by the teacher and the other laid on the floor. The child is shown a hoop of a certain color and must jump into the hoop of the corresponding color. The activity can be varied by placement of other parts of the body in the hoop (figure 12.5).
5. Striking balls with bats of the corresponding color. Several bats and balls of matching color are needed, or the bats may be tied with ribbons in matching colors. The child chooses a bat and then selects a ball of the same color for "batting practice."

Activities Focusing on Visual Discrimination (Shape and Form)

1. Reproducing in movement a specific shape. Several plastic, wood, or cardboard shapes will be needed. The teacher holds up a shape and the child must reproduce it by drawing in the air or walking on the floor.
2. Selecting matching shapes. Two sets of objects of various shapes will be needed. One set is placed in various locations in the room; the other remains with the teacher. When the teacher holds up one of the shapes, the child must find the one like it and run back to the teacher with it.
3. Choosing from among several objects the one best suited to an activity. Several objects such as a large block, large ball, and bean bag are needed. In response

Figure 12.5 Hoops and other objects can be used to create interesting and challenging paths to follow.

to instructions from the teacher, the child must select the object most suitable for sitting, rolling, and throwing, and then use the object in the appropriate activity.

4. Matching paper shapes with objects of similar form. Shapes that resemble several of the items of furniture or equipment in the room should be cut from heavy paper. Upon being handed one of the paper shapes by the teacher, the child must locate the item that has a similar form and carry it to a designated spot. (The items will need to be ones that the child is able to carry.)

5. Reproducing shapes with the body. A child who knows the letters of the alphabet can attempt to form such letters as c, l, and y with his or her body, or several children may work together to reproduce in a lying position on the floor most of the letters of the alphabet.

Activities Focusing on Visual Discrimination (Distance)

1. Throwing at a goal from various distances. The goal may be a box or container for younger children and a basketball hoop for older ones. Three marks are made on the floor at various distances from the goal, and the child is instructed by the teacher to shoot a ball at the goal from the mark nearest the goal, farthest from the goal, and from the mark between the two.

2. Throwing at targets of various heights. Targets are placed or drawn on a wall at three different distances

from the floor. The teacher instructs the child to throw a ball or bean bag at the highest target, the lowest target, and the one at the middle distance.

3. Judging distance of an object from a given point. Several objects are placed around the room at different distances from the point where the child will stand. The student is asked to estimate how many steps away each object is from him or her. Then he or she checks the accuracy of the estimates by stepping off the distance.

4. Rolling a large ball different distances. A large ball, such as a medicine ball, will be needed. Two or more sets of marks, each set placed the same distance from the starting point, but in different directions from it, are drawn or painted on the floor. From the starting point, the child must roll the ball to a set of marks that are the same distance away.

5. Tossing an object into the air at various distances. A ball or bean bag will be needed. The teacher instructs the child to throw the object a long distance into the air, a short distance, and an intermediate distance. For more acute discrimination, the child may be asked to throw the object at distances between the three; for example, to a height higher than the lowest distance but lower than the middle distance.

Activities Focusing on Visual Discrimination (Speed)

1. Running at different speeds. In response to directions from the teacher, the child runs slowly, moderately, and fast.

2. Throwing objects of different kinds to compare speed of movement. The activity requires balls of various sizes, a bean bag, and a balloon. The teacher throws the objects and the child determines which ones move more slowly, which ones move faster, and which is the slowest and which the fastest.

3. Swinging a suspended ball at different rates of speed. A ball of medium size is suspended by a cord from the ceiling. The child puts the ball in motion by hitting it with his or her hand so that it will swing slowly, moderately, or fast in response to the instructions of the teacher.

4. Rolling a ball various distances to judge the speed of movement. Objects that will serve as backstops are placed at various distances from the starting point. The teacher rolls a ball toward each object, and the child judges the speed at which each ball travels.

5. Moving the body in various forms of locomotion to determine the speed of each. The child moves over a designated distance by hopping, crawling, jumping, and so forth, and decides which form of movement is the fastest and which the slowest, and which is faster or slower than some other one.

Activities Focusing on Figure-Ground Phenomenon

1. Catching a ball suspended in front of a distracting background. A brightly colored ball is hung from the ceiling so that it is suspended in front of other objects. When the ball is swung, the child concentrates on following it with his or her eyes in order to catch it.

2. Rolling a ball between objects. A tennis ball or ball of similar size will be needed, as will several objects that cannot be easily knocked over with the ball. The child rolls the ball toward the objects in an attempt to place it between two of them.

3. Locating and kicking a moving ball in a group of stationary balls. Several balls of medium size are placed on the floor a short distance from the child. One is put into motion by the teacher, and the child must move to it in order to kick it.

4. Throwing a ball at a target. A target of any kind is placed against a wall on which there are pictures or other objects. The child concentrates on the specific target and attempts to hit it with a ball thrown from several feet away.

5. Playing tag in a small space. Confining the game to a small space will make it easier for the child to keep his or her attention focused on the person he or she is trying to catch.

Activities Focusing on Auditory Discrimination

1. Responding to different tones and frequencies with a specified motor movement. Various objects that create different tones and frequencies will be needed. The teacher works out the motor movement with the children, such as nodding the head or waving the hand, that will be used to respond when a certain tone or frequency is produced.

2. Identifying the direction of a sound. Two children work together in this activity. One child bounces a ball in various directions; the other child must determine the direction from which the sound is coming. Sight may be used to help locate the right direction.

3. Differentiating the sounds made by a ball. The child bounces a ball and describes the difference between the sound that is made when the ball is struck with the hand and that made when the ball strikes the floor.

4. Differentiating sounds made by striking objects. A short, thin piece of wood or drumstick is used to strike against various objects in the room. The child listens to the sounds and tries to match each sound with its source.

5. Isolating a sound from background noise. This activity requires that there be a number of sounds emitted from various sources in the room, such as from the play activities of several children. The teacher helps the child to isolate some of the sounds and then encourages him or her to try to isolate others. The child may use vision to locate the source and identify the sound.

Activities Focusing on Balance

1. Standing on one foot. While standing, the child lifts one foot and tries to balance. The difficulty of the activity can be increased by moving the raised leg to various positions and by moving one or both arms to various positions.

2. Standing on the balance beam. The child stands with one foot behind the other on the balance beam. The activity can be made more difficult by balancing only on one foot, walking on the beam, reversing direction, squatting, and so forth.

3. Walking the line. Strips several inches wide are applied or painted on the floor. The student walks along the strips, placing one foot in front of the other.

4. Balancing objects. A book or similar object is placed on the head to be balanced while walking or is placed on the feet to be balanced while holding the legs straight up from a supine position. Other parts of the body might also be used in various positions.

5. Walking on a resilient surface. The child walks around the top of a large inner tube, maintaining balance. The trampoline may be substituted in this activity and may be used for other simple balancing stunts.

Activities Focusing on Identity of Body Parts

1. Touching parts of the body (i.e., head, legs, elbow . . .). This activity is like a game of Simon Says, with all the activity consisting of touching parts of the body.

2. Tossing a balloon and allowing it to land on a part of the body. Each child is supplied with an air-filled balloon. The balloons are tossed into the air and the children maneuver so that the balloons land on the part of the body the teacher designates.

3. Moving a part of the body in response to its being named. The teacher or a child chosen as the leader calls out a part of the body, such as foot, arm, head, and the group responds by moving that part.

4. Naming the body part used to produce a movement. The child performs a leap or squat or picks up or throws an object and names the parts of the body involved in the action.

5. Using parts of the body to form a shape. Children are divided into pairs for this activity. One child directs the other to form his or her body into a certain shape by telling the child which parts of the body to move.

Activities Focusing on Body Awareness

1. Observing reflections of movements in the mirror. The child observes in a mirror the movements made with various parts of the body. The child is encouraged to talk about what he or she is doing, such as by saying, "My arm is moving up over my head."

2. Analyzing different kinds of locomotion. The child moves across the floor by crawling, rolling, sliding, hopping, skipping, or running. He or she is asked to describe the movements made in the particular locomotion skill.

3. Describing positions of the body. The child takes a position such as the stork stand. He or she identifies the shape and describes the movements and parts of the body involved.

4. Performing movements of different quality. The child makes a movement that has a certain quality, such as a languid swing of the arm, and then explores other ways of making the movement to achieve other qualities, such as strength, fluidity, tenseness.

5. Performing one part of a movement pattern without engaging the rest of the parts. The child isolates one movement of a total movement pattern and performs it without moving any other part of his body.

Activities Focusing on Laterality

It is important to note that some students never can indicate left and right without some sort of cue that they contrive or learn. But, doing these activities assumes that there is an increased awareness of the reality of a left and a right side, even if the student does not always get it "right."

1. Sliding to right and left. In response to the teacher's direction, the child slides his foot to the left or right. Sometimes ribbons can be attached at the wrist to indicate the right or left side.

2. Walking and retracing steps on the balance beam. The child walks on the balance beam and turns left or right, as indicated by the teacher, and retraces the steps.

3. Following footprints. Footprints are drawn or painted on the floor in such a manner that the child must, in stepping on them, cross one foot over the other (figure 12.6).

4. Crawling on alternate hands and feet. The crawl is made with the hand and the leg of opposite sides extended forward at the same time.

5. Combining arm movements with a zigzag run. The student follows a zigzag pattern and, as he or she turns to the left or right, holds up the arm on that side of the body.

Activities Focusing on Directionality

1. Passing to the left or right. The child walks toward the teacher and passes to the left or right side of the teacher as directed.

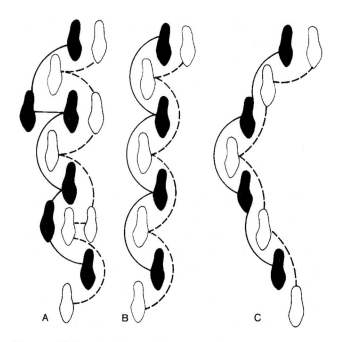

Figure 12.6 Patterns of footprints for an activity to promote laterality. *(A)* Simple, *(B)* moderately complex, *(C)* complex.

2. Matching the movements of another child. Two children work together, facing each other. One child performs a movement, such as lifting the left foot or raising the right arm, and the other child matches the movement with the same side of the body.

3. Identifying the left and right sides of objects. The teacher directs the child to touch one or the other side of an object in the room, such as a chair, and the child runs to it and places his or her hand on the correct side.

4. Walking between objects. Large objects, such as big blocks or chairs, are placed in a row with enough space between them to allow a child to pass through. The child walks to the right or left of each chair in the row in response to the direction given by the teacher.

5. Touching the corresponding hand or foot of another child. The students work in pairs, facing each other. One child touches his or her right or left hand or foot to the corresponding hand or foot of the other child.

Activities Focusing on Rhythm and Tempo:

1. Marching to a cadence. The teacher beats a drum, increasing and decreasing the tempo to enhance the experience.

2. Keeping time with a swinging ball. A ball is suspended from the ceiling by a cord. It is swung at various speeds by the teacher, and the child swings his or her foot, arm, leg, head, or trunk to match the swinging of the ball.

3. Moving various parts of the body to a cadence. The cadence is supplied by a strong beat on the drum or piano. The child responds by keeping time with different parts of the body—fingers, head, arms, legs, and so forth.

4. Jumping in rhythm to a swinging rope. The teacher and a helper swing a jump rope back and forth (not a full turn of the rope). The child jumps over the rope as it passes near his or her feet.

5. Performing various movements to a beat. This activity is like number one except that the difficulty is increased by having the child skip, jump, or hop to the cadence.

Summary

There are more children identified as learning disabled than any other disabling condition in the United States. There is general agreement that a learning disability occurs when there is a major discrepancy between an individual's actual and expected levels of achievement that cannot be attributed to other handicapping conditions or sociological factors. People with learning disabilities are normally bright people who can excel in many areas if provided proper instruction and a positive learning environment. Although there is much that is not known about the reasons for a learning disability, many attribute the condition to one of three primary causes: brain damage, biochemical imbalance, and environmental factors.

Persons with learning disabilities have difficulty translating visual and auditory images into meaningful symbols. In addition to these problems, some students with learning disabilities have motor impairments. There is also evidence, however, that some students with learning disabilities have excelled as athletes. The physical educator is advised to utilize a top-down assessment and to employ an ecological task analysis of skills for informing modifications and adaptations in the physical activity class.

Students with attention deficit/hyperactivity disorder (ADHD) may or may not be learning disabled. Information on these disorders was provided in this chapter because of the prevalence of hyperactivity among children with learning disabilities. It should be understood, however, that students with ADHD may or may not qualify under IDEA '97 and if they do qualify could be classified as other health impaired, learning disabled, or seriously emotionally disturbed.

As is true with all disabling conditions, the physical education program must be based on the individual needs combined with the general practice of creating a successful and positive experience, and should be used in teaching students with ADHD and learning disabilities. Participation should be approached from the top-down assessment strategy and skills should be approached from an ecological task-analysis. Students should be given the opportunity to practice skills with reinforcement provided as learning occurs. Specific perceptual-motor programs, when used, should function as a supplement to the physical education program.

Although much is not known about students with ADHD and learning disabilities, specific gains have been made in the past few years that indicate that those with learning disabilities, if provided with a positive and skill-oriented curriculum, can be successful in schools and make major contributions to society. Where would we be without Albert Einstein, generally recognized as having a learning disability, and his work in helping to understand the nature of the universe?

Enhancing Activities

1. Many famous and distinguished people such as Thomas Edison, Woodrow Wilson, Winston Churchill, and Albert Einstein are believed to have had a learning disability. Develop a list of other well-known figures who have a learning disability.

2. Review the reference list at the end of this chapter and obtain a copy of one of the articles of interest to you. Upon completion of the article develop a list of the major points discussed by the author.

3. Engage in a debate with a person who opposes your views concerning the value of perceptual-motor programs. Upon completion of the debate, identify the major areas of agreement and disagreement.

4. Explore the web page of the Division of Learning Disabilities of the Council for Exceptional Children to obtain general information from it concerning learning disabilities.

5. Develop some activities that could be used in physical education to help students with learning disabilities improve their ability to understand selected concepts such as left and right or over and under. What recommendations could be made for a student who, because of his or her poor visual discrimination, is unable to strike a tennis ball?

6. Develop a list of suggested activities that could be used to encourage students to move "slowly." Example: Who can take the longest time to walk between point *x* and point *y?* In this example the students would have to walk the designated route and not be permitted to come to a complete stop.

7. Observe two or three students with learning disabilities in a physical education class. Explain why these and similar students would benefit from instruction in integrated settings with nonhandicapped youngsters—or why they wouldn't. What other placement options might be recommended?

8. Seek permission to attend an IEP meeting for a student with a learning disability. Observe the various professionals and the interaction that occurs in a multidisciplinary setting. Did you find the session helpful in identifying the type of physical education program to be provided for this student?

Selected Readings

American Psychiatric Association (APA). (2000). *Diagnostic and statistical manual of mental disorders* (4th ed.)–*Text Revision*. Washington, DC: Author.

Amerikaner, M., & Summerlin, M. (1982). Group counseling with learning disabled children: Effects of social skills and relaxation training on self-concept and classroom behavior. *Journal of Learning Disabilities, 15*, 340–343.

Arnheim, D. D., & Sinclair, W. A. (1979). *The clumsy child* (2nd ed.). St. Louis: C. V. Mosby Co.

Barkley, R. A. (2000). *Taking charge of ADHD (Revised)*. New York: Guilford.

Barkley, R. A., McMurray, M. B., Edelbrock, C. S., & Robbins, K. (1990). The side effects of methylphenidate in children with attention hyperactivity disorder: A systemic, placebo-controlled evaluation. *Pediatrics, 86*, 184–192.

Bauer, A. M., & Shea, T. M. (1989). *Teaching exceptional students in your classroom*. Needham Heights, MA: Allyn and Bacon, Inc.

Bruininks, V. L., & Bruininks, R. L. (1977). Motor proficiency and learning disabled and non-disabled students. *Perceptual and Motor Skills, 44*, 1131–1137.

Burton, A. W., & Miller, D. (1998). *Movement skill assessment*. Champaign, IL: Human Kinetics.

Children with ADD: A shared responsibility. (1992). Reston, VA: Council for Exceptional Children.

Churton, M. (1989). Hyperkinesis: A review of literature. *Adapted Physical Activity Quarterly, 6*(4), 313–327.

Cratty, B. J. (1975a). *Physical expressions of intelligence*. Englewood Cliffs, NJ: Prentice-Hall, Inc.

Cratty, B. J. (1975b). *Remedial motor activity for children*. Philadelphia: Lea and Febiger.

Cratty, B. J. (1979). *Perceptual and motor development in infants and children* (2nd ed.). Englewood Cliffs, NJ: Prentice-Hall, Inc.

Cratty, B. J., & Martin, M. (1969). *Perceptual-motor efficiency in children*. Philadelphia: Lea and Febiger.

Cruickshank, W. (1967). *The brain-injured child in home, school, and community*. Syracuse, NY: Syracuse University Press.

Davis, W. E., & Burton, A. W. (1991). Ecological task analysis: Translating movement behavior theory into practice. *Adapted Physical Activity Quarterly, 8*, 154–177.

DeFries, J., Fulker, D., & LaBuda, M. (1987). Evidence for a genetic aetiology in reading disability of twins. *Nature, 329*, 537–539.

Deno, S. L. (1997). Whether thou goest . . . Perspectives on progress monitoring. In J. W. Lloyd, E. J. Kameenui, & D. Chard (Eds.), *Issues in educating students with disabilities* (pp. 77–99). Mahwah, NJ: Lawrence Erlbaum.

Deno, S. L. (2002). Problem solving as "Best Practice." In A. Thomas & J. Grimes (Eds.), *Best practices in school psychology IV* (pp. 37–56). Washington, DC: National Association of School Psychologists.

Deno, S. L., Mirkin, P. K., & Chiang, B. (1982). Identifying valid measures of reading. *Exceptional Children, 49*(1), 36–45.

Deshler, D. D., & Bulgren, J. A. (1997). Redefining instructional directions for gifted students with learning disabilities. *Learning Disabilities, 8*(3), 121–132.

Deshler, D. D. (1998). Grounding interventions for students with learning disabilities in "powerful ideas." *Learning Disabilities Research and Practice, 13*(1), 29–34.

Espin, C. A., & Deno, S. I. (1993a). Content-specific and general reading disabilities of secondary-level students: Identification and educational relevance. *Journal of Special Education, 27*(3), 321–337.

Espin, C. A., & Deno, S. I. (1993b). Performance in reading from content area text as an indicator of achievement. *Remedial & Special Education, 14*(6), 47–59.

Feingold, B. F. (1975). Hyperkinesis and learning disabilities linked to artificial food flavors and colors. *American Journal of Nursing, 75*, 797–803.

Good, R. H., III, & Kiminski, R. A. (1996). Assessment for instructional decisions: Toward a proactive/prevention model of decision-making for early literacy skills. *School Psychologist Quarterly, 11*, 326–336.

Gresham, J. F., & Reschley, D. J. (1986). Social skill defects and low peer acceptance of mainstreamed learning disabled children. *Learning Disability Quarterly, 9*(1), 23–32.

Hallahan, D. P., & Kauffman, J. M. (1988). *Exceptional children* (4th ed.). Englewood Cliffs, NJ: Prentice-Hall, Inc.

Harvey, W. J., & Reid, G. (2003). Attention deficit hyperactivity disorder: A review of research on movement skill performance and physical fitness. *Adapted Physical Activity Quarterly, 20*, 1–25.

Haubenstricker, J. L. (1983). Motor development in children with learning disabilities. *Journal of Physical Education, Recreation, and Dance, 53*, 41–43.

Kavale, K., & Forness, S. (1985). *The science of learning disabilities.* San Diego, CA: College-Hill Press.

Kavale, K., & Mattison, P. D. (1983). One jumped off the balance beam: Meta-analysis of perceptual-motor training program. *Journal of Learning Disabilities, 16*, 165–173.

Kendrick, K. A., & Hanten, W. P. (1980). Differentiation of learning disabled children from normal children using four coordination tasks. *Physical Therapy, 60*, 784–788.

Kennedy, P., Terdal, L., & Fusetti, L. (1993). *The hyperactive childbook.* New York: St. Martin's Press.

Kephart, N. C. (1971). *The slow learner in the classroom* (2nd ed.). Columbus, OH: Charles E. Merrill Publishing Co.

Kerr, R., & Hughes, K. (1987). Movement difficulty and learning disabled children. *Adapted Physical Activity Quarterly, 4*, 72–79.

Kiminski, R. A., & Good, R. H. (1996). Toward a technology for assessing basic early literacy skills. *School Psychology Review, 25*, 215–227.

Kirk, S. A. (1978). An interview with Samuel Kirk. *Academic Therapy, 13*, 617–620.

Kirk, S. A., & Gallagher, J. J. (1989). *Educating exceptional children* (6th ed.). Boston, MA: Houghton Mifflin.

Kline, F. M., & Silver, L. B. (2004). *The educator's guide to mental health issues in the classroom.* Baltimore: Brookes.

Levy, L., & Gottlieb, J. (1984). Learning disabled and non-learning disabled children at play. *Remedial and Special Education, 5*(6), 43–50.

Lieberman, L. J., & Houston-Wilson, (2000). *Strategies for INCLUSION.* Champaign, IL: Human Kinetics.

Martinek, T., & Karper, W. (1982). Entry-level motor performance and self-concepts of handicapped and nonhandicapped children in mainstreamed physical education classes: A preliminary study. *Perceptual and Motor Skills, 55*, 1002.

Morris, P. R., & Whiting, H. T. A. (1971). *Motor impairment and compensatory education.* Philadelphia: Lea and Febiger.

Myers, P. I., & Hammill, D. D. (1982). *Learning disabilities: Basic concepts, assessment practices, and instructional strategies.* Austin, TX: Pro-Ed Publishers.

National Institute of Mental Health. NIMH. (2003). Retrieved from www.mimh.nih.gov/publicat/adhd.cfm.

Parker, H. (1992). *The ADD hyperactivity handbook for schools.* Plantation, FL: Impact.

Reiff, M. E., (Ed.), & Tippins, S. (2004). *ADHD: A complete and authoritative guide.* Elk Grove Village, IL: American Academy of Pediatrics.

Seligman, M. E. P. (1975). *Helplessness: On depression, development and death.* San Francisco: Freeman.

Shapiro, D. R., & Ulrich, D. A. (2001). Social comparisons of children with and without learning disabilities when evaluating physical competence. *Adapted Physical Activity Quarterly, 18*(3), 273.

Shaywitz, S. E., & Shaywitz, B. A. (1987). Attention deficit disorder: Current perspectives. Paper presented at the national conference on Learning Disabilities. Bethesda, MD: National Institutes of Child Health and Human Development (NIH).

Sherrill, C., & Pyfer, J. L. (1985). Learning disabled students in physical education. *Adapted Physical Activity Quarterly, 2*, 283–291.

Shinn, M. R. (Ed.). (1998). *Advanced applications of curriculum-based measurement.* New York: Guilford.

Sideridis, G. D., & Tsorbatzoudis, C. (2003). Intragroup motivational analysis of student with learning disabilities: A goal oriented approach. *Learning Disabilities: A Contemporary Journal, 1*(1), 8–19.

Smith, D. D., & Robinson, S. (1986). Educating the learning disabled. In R. J. Morris & B. Blatt (Eds.), *Special education: Research and trends* (pp. 222–248). New York: Pergamon Press.

Spring, C., & Sandoval, J. (1976). Food additives and hyperkinesis: A critical evaluation of the evidence. *Journal of Learning Disabilities, 9*, 560–569.

Tarver, S., & Hallahan, D. P. (1976). Children with learning disabilities: An overview. In J. M. Kauffman & D. P. Hallahan (Eds.), *Teaching children with learning disabilities: Personal perspectives.* Columbus, OH: Charles E. Merrill Publishing Co.

University of Kansas Center for Research on Learning Institute for Effective Instruction (2004). Retrieved from http://www.ku-crl.org/iei

U.S. Department of Education. (1994). *Sixteenth annual report to Congress on the implementation of the Education of the Handicapped Act.* Washington, DC: Author.

Wallace, G., & Kauffman, J. M. (1978). *Teaching children with learning problems.* Columbus, OH: Charles E. Merrill Publishing Co.

Wallace, G., & McLoughlin, J. A. (1979). *Learning disabilities: Concepts and characteristics* (2nd ed.). Columbus, OH: Charles E. Merrill Publishing Co.

Wiederholdt, J. L. (1974). Historical perspectives on the education of the learning disabled. In L. Mann & D. A. Sabatino (Eds.), *The second review of special education.* Philadelphia: JSE Press, Division of Grune and Stratton.

Emotional/Behavioral Disorders and Pervasive Developmental Disorder

CHAPTER OBJECTIVES

After studying this chapter, the reader should be able to:

1. Define emotional disturbed and pervasive developmental disorder and comprehend the various terms used to describe this population.
2. Recognize the characteristics of students with serious emotional problems and pervasive developmental disorder and the importance of analyzing the frequency, intensity, and duration of behavior in assessing the seriousness of the problem.
3. Appreciate the classification systems used to identify those who have a mental disorder and the important role mental health specialists play in developing appropriate treatment and education programs.
4. Identify characteristics associated with conduct and personality disorders and other behavior disorders that affect children and youth.
5. Suggest activities and physical education program considerations for students with emotional problems and pervasive developmental disorder.
6. Appreciate the important role physical educators must assume in helping students to overcome fears or apprehensions sometimes associated with activities such as swimming, contact sports, and experiences involving height.
7. Recognize the significance of recent research that suggests activity and exercise programs help to reduce behavior problems and contribute to greater academic production.

There is a growing awareness of the need to provide educational programs for students whose conduct at school and home deviates to a marked extent from what is generally accepted as appropriate behavior. These are youngsters whose lives appear to be in constant turmoil. They show their unhappiness in a variety of ways ranging from violent and destructive acts at one extreme to withdrawn and sullen behavior at the other end of the spectrum. Making friends, accepting themselves, and cooperating with teachers and parents are all very difficult for these individuals.

Students with serious behavioral problems are currently referred to as "students with challenging behaviors." In the past these students may have been referred to by a variety of names such as "socially maladjusted," "emotionally handicapped," or "emotionally disturbed." The educational category under IDEA 2004 for students with challenging behaviors is emotionally disturbed (ED), which describes youngsters whose actions and conduct are considered socially unacceptable. Under IDEA '90 the category was *seriously* emotionally disturbed (SED), but intense negative pressure regarding this label for students resulted in the word "serious" being dropped (Colarusso & O'Rouke, 2003). The acceptance of these descriptions is due to the growing awareness among educators that the identification and treatment of behavior problems is an integral part of the educational community's responsibility. Physical educators, too, are becoming more acutely aware of their role and responsibility in providing quality experiences for students with serious behavior challenges. Physical education experiences that incorporate skill development, exercise, and fun through games, dancing, and sport activities are an integral part of the comprehensive program for students with behavior disorders.

Autism was originally considered an emotional disturbance in the Education of All Handicapped Children Act,

PL 94-142 (1975) and categorized under seriously emotionally disturbed (SED), but as understanding of the disability has grown, autism has been removed from this category. In 1981, autism was moved to the category of other health impaired (OHI), and then in 1990 under IDEA, it was moved into its own category. As IDEA 2004 stands, autism remains its own category. Currently, the term "pervasive developmental disorder (PDD)" is a broader term used by the American Psychiatric Association (APA), and autism is considered a classification under PDD. According to Houston-Wilson and Lieberman (2003), students with autism are often included in the general education class and can "baffle even the most seasoned teacher" (p. 40).

Within this chapter, a definition of emotional disturbance will be provided as well as a definition and description of pervasive developmental disorder. Information about the causes and a classification system for these disabilities will also be presented. The last section will focus on teaching considerations and implications for program development. Although educational programs for those with emotional disturbance and with PDD have improved dramatically, much is still unknown about the learning characteristics and instructional methodology most appropriate for these students in physical activity.

Defining Emotional Disturbed

There is not a commonly accepted definition among professionals for the term "emotionally disturbed." Much of the confusion is due to the lack of understanding of what constitutes good mental health. The orientation of the professionals involved—for example, psychologists, psychiatrists, and educators—also adds a new and sometimes different dimension to the definition. Educators, for instance, have generally found the following definition originally proposed by Kauffman (1977) as acceptable: individuals with behavior disorders are "those who chronically and markedly respond to their environment in socially unacceptable and/or personally unsatisfying ways but who can be taught more socially acceptable and personally gratifying behavior" (p. 23).

Unlike other definitions that have been proposed by medical and allied health personnel, this statement indicates clearly that students can be taught to respond and act in more socially acceptable ways. Kauffman's definition also underlines the importance of the student's environment as both a potential cause of conflict and an important variable in the development of a successful instructional program. This realization is in contrast to the belief of some professional personnel in medicine and health who have traditionally viewed behavior problems as inherent within the student's personality composition.

In an effort to provide guidelines for the identification and educational treatment of students with behavior disorders, federal education law stipulates that students have a condition exhibiting one or more of the following characteristics over a long period of time and to a marked degree, which adversely affects educational performance:

1. an inability to learn that cannot be explained by intellectual, sensory, or health factors;
2. an inability to build or maintain satisfactory interpersonal relationships with peers and teachers;
3. inappropriate types of behavior or feelings under normal circumstances;
4. a general, pervasive mood of unhappiness or depression;
5. a tendency to develop physical symptoms or fears associated with personal or school problems.

The term includes children who are schizophrenic and have a serious personality disorder. The term does not include children who are socially maladjusted, unless it is determined that they are seriously emotionally disturbed.

According to special educators Colarusso and O'Rouke (2003), there is debate within special education as to the usefulness of the federal law's definition of emotionally disturbed. An advocacy group has formed in which researchers and authors use the terms "emotional/behavioral disorders (E/BD)." This chapter will use E/BD and behavior disorders.

The definition accepted by the federal government was first proposed by Bower in 1969. A clarification of the characteristics inherent within the definition is necessary to fully comprehend the intent of the definition. First, students classified as emotionally disturbed are individuals with average to above average learning capabilities, and their school-related problems are not the primary result of any intellectual inadequacy. **If learning problems are evident, they are attributed to the student's behavioral patterns rather than to the individual's ability to comprehend information. Additionally, the student's difficulty relates to an inability to interact positively with peers and teachers, and to respond appropriately in various settings. Although most authorities recognize that all children and adults have difficulty responding appropriately at various times, the difference for students with behavior disorders is found in the frequency, duration, and intensity of their behavior patterns.** In essence, the most effective way to describe students with behavior problems is to actually define those behaviors that seem unusual and then to specify the frequency, duration, and intensity of the behavior.

Frequency refers to how often the particular behavior is performed. All children cry, get into fights, and at times respond aggressively. Exhibiting these behaviors, however, does not constitute a behavior problem unless the specific behavior—fighting, for example—occurs frequently. Although the student who is disturbed exhibits inappropriate behaviors similar to those of other children, he or she makes the undesirable responses much more often.

Duration, which is closely related to frequency, is a measure of how long a student engages in an activity. The amount of time students with behavior disorders act unacceptably is different from that of their peers. For example, although all children experience temper tantrums lasting a few seconds to a few minutes, the student with severe behavior problems may have a tantrum for a period of time approaching one hour or longer. Occasionally the problem involves exhibiting a behavior for too short a period of time, such as paying attention or attending to a task.

The third variable that helps to explain behavior disorders relates to the magnitude of a given behavior. Magnitude refers to the intensity of the behavior. Although many people may occasionally respond angrily in a loud voice, individuals with behavior disorders frequently rely on a high-pitched voice as the medium to express all of their demands. There are also students with behavior problems who express themselves too softly to be heard. The concept of magnitude may be applied to many behaviors, such as the intensity with which a youngster fights, slams a door, or picks on others.

Defining behaviors by focusing on their frequency, duration, and magnitude helps in the identification and treatment of students with serious behavior problems. This technique also adds meaning to the definition of emotional disturbance proposed by the federal government.

There continues to be disagreement and confusion as to the "best" definition or term to identify and describe students with behavior disorders. Most authorities agree, however, that having a behavior disorder involves the following:

1. behavior that goes to an extreme—behavior that is not just slightly different from the usual;
2. a problem that is ongoing—one that does not disappear, and
3. behavior that is unacceptable because of social or cultural expectations (Hallahan & Kauffman, 1991).

Prevalence

It is generally acknowledged that the government's estimate of children who are E/BD and the number actually served are very conservative. Some of the confusion relates to the status of students who are juvenile delinquents. While some argue that these students qualify as emotionally disturbed, others counter that most juvenile delinquents are socially maladjusted, not emotionally disturbed.

Although there may be differences as to the actual number of children who are E/BD, there is general agreement that the number is large and that many with emotional problems may not be receiving the special education services they need.

Classification

There are many systems that have been proposed to classify those with mental illness. The American Psychiatric Association relies, for instance, on a collection of categories catalogued in its *Diagnostic and Statistical Manual for Mental Disorders* (DSM-IV-TR). Although this system assists psychiatrists, its application in the educational setting is complicated by many problems, including its emphasis on labels without application to individual treatment. In addition, earlier editions of the system were not very reliable. Even with the more precise language found in the 2000 revision, mental health professionals vary in their use of the categories in classifying individual children. Nevertheless, familiarity with aspects of the system is important so that physical educators will be able to communicate with the various mental health specialists. In addition, there are characteristics of the students that teachers will observe during the school day. These characteristics have been classified by some researchers and provide a framework for the medical terminology used to diagnose E/BD.

Characteristics of the Students

According to Quay (1986, in Colarusso & O'Rouke, 2003), there are two differences in the expression of emotional problems: one is to direct them outwardly (externalizing), and the other is to direct them inwardly (internalizing). Students who are verbally or physically abusive are considered to be *externalizing their emotions,* whereas students who become depressed or have deep fears are said to be *internalizing their emotions.* Students with E/BD can direct their emotions inward, outward, or a combination thereof. The following is a classification from Quay and Peterson (1987, in Colarusso & O'Rouke, 2003) with modified descriptions.

> ### Oppositional Defiant Disorder (ODD) Characteristics
>
> - Losing one's temper
> - Arguing with adults
> - Not complying with adult's roles
> - Deliberately annoying others
> - Exhibiting anger and resentment
> - Showing spite and vindictiveness

1. Conduct disorder (CD): antisocial, acting out, disruptive, temper tantrums, negative, argumentative, bully, blames others, selfish, cruel.
2. Socialized aggression (SA): socialized delinquents, possible gang membership, lies, runs away, steals, admires criminals.
3. Attention problems-immaturity (AP): acts younger than age, difficulty with directions, distractable.
4. Anxiety-withdrawal (AW): anxious, depressed, believes will fail, complains of being sick, difficulty making decisions.
5. Psychotic behavior (PB): difficulty differentiating between reality and fantasy, hallucinates.
6. Motor excess (ME): jumpy, fidgety, nervous, high activity level.

According to a publication on mental health in the classroom edited by Kline and Silver (2004), some of the *DSM-IV-TR* (APA, 2000) diagnostic categories that encompass some of the above classifications are those with oppositional defiant disorder (ODD) and conduct disorder (CD). The student with ODD has a pattern of defiant and hostile behavior directed at others, particularly those in authority positions (Kline & Silver, 2004). According to the *DSM-IV-TR*, the behavior must last for at least six months and be manifested at a higher frequency than seen in other children at similar developmental levels. They must exhibit four of the following characteristics: losing one's temper, arguing with adults, not complying with adults' rules, deliberately doing things that annoy others, exhibiting anger and resentment, and showing spite and vindictiveness.

A student with CD has behaviors that oppose societal rules and violate other's basic rights. The student may be aggressive toward people and animals, destroy property, seriously violate rules, be deceitful, or engage in theft. Regarding aggression, *DSM-IV-TR* indicates that three or more of the following behaviors must be present: bullying, threatening, intimidating; physical fights, where a weapon

Conduct Disorder (CD) Characteristics

- Aggressive toward people and animals
- Destroy property
- Seriously violate rules
- Deceitful
- Stealing

was used and caused harm; physically cruel to people; forceful sexual activity; or theft (mugged, robbed). At least one of these must have occurred within the last six months. Onset of CD can occur in early childhood or in adolescence.

Mood disorders are also found in the classifications of Quay and Peterson (see table 13.1). *DSM-IV-TR* describes depressive and bipolar disorders that can be seen in the school setting. Students with chronic, low grade depression may have what is referred to as dysthymic disorder. This student is sad and withdrawn and may experience lethargy, low self-esteem, poor concentration, feelings of hopelessness, sleep problems, and changes in appetite (over- or under-eat). Students who have major depression exhibit characteristics for at least two weeks with behaviors that include loss of interest and pleasure, or irritability. The expression of this depression is intense and recurs numerous times (Kline & Silver, 2004).

Bipolar disorder includes both a depression and a mania (Kline & Silver, 2004), which is a disturbance to a significant degree where the mood of the student is ". . . disturbed by inflated self-esteem, a decreased need for sleep, pressured speech or increased talkativeness, racing thoughts, distractability, or psychomotor agitation" (p. 198). The mood can last a week or more.

Anxiety disorders are seen in students who exceed normal levels of anxiety and fear. Interestingly, anxiety and depression in children often have similar symptoms, which

TABLE 13.1   Categories of Emotional/Behavioral Disorders According to Quay and Peterson

Behavioral Disorders (externalizing)	Emotional Disorders (internalizing)
Undersocialized Aggressive Conduct Disorder	• Anxiety-Withdrawal
• Conduct Disorder	• Psychotic Behavior
•Attention Problems—Immaturity	
• Motor Excess	
Socialized Aggressive Conduct Disorder	
• Socialized Aggression	

Characteristics of Chronic Depression

- Sad
- Withdrawn
- Lethargic
- Low self-esteem
- Poor concentration
- Feelings of hopelessness
- Sleep problems
- Changes in appetite

makes it difficult for teachers to recognize what is going on. There are many different types of anxiety disorders, but general symptoms include: dread, fear, worry, school avoidance, withdrawal, sweating, nauseated, shake, and tremor. Diagnosis is aided by observing which symptoms are present, and when and where they occur.

Students who are actively psychotic—those with psychotic disorders—cannot distinguish reality from fantasy and may also hallucinate (e.g., schizophrenia). When students are experiencing this type of mental health problem, they usually are not in the general school program. Given appropriate treatment by a clinical team, the student may return to a general educational setting.

Understanding the causes of E/BD is complex and is based on the orientation of the investigation or investigators. Although there is no basis to say with certainty that school and family environments cause emotional problems, it must also be emphasized that these two social institutions have a responsibility to help prevent the development of behavior problems. This means that students should be treated fairly, recognizing and accepting their individual differences. Teacher and parent expectations must be reasonable, not too high or too low. Most importantly, teachers and parents should reward students

Characteristics of Anxiety Disorders

- Dread
- Fearful
- Worried
- School avoidance
- Withdrawal
- Sweating
- Nauseated
- Shaking
- Tremors

for good behavior and withhold reinforcement for inappropriate behavior. The breakthrough in furthering our understanding of the causes of behavior disorders may come from a recognition of ways to prevent the occurrence of emotional problems.

Researchers, educators, mental health experts, and medical personnel all have concern for the well-being of individuals who experience mental health problems. For physical educators, it is important to work with the IEP team to create positive experiences in physical activity for any student in a school program. The interventions utilized by the special educator or behavior specialist, as well as the recommendations made by the clinical personnel, should all be considered for the physical education program. Often individuals with E/BD qualify for special physical education services not because of motor deficiencies, but rather because their behavior prevents them from being successful in a physical education program. Dr. Don Hellison has devoted his physical education expertise to working with students classified at risk for behavior problems, if not actually having engaged in a significant degree of maladaptive behavior (Hellison, 2003). Hellison believes that teaching physical education is not about disciplining students, but rather about using specific skills and strategies. He also believes that being a physical education teacher has a spirit . . . "a moral compass, a sense of purpose, a passion, a vision . . . [and] I want (and kids need) an imaginative, creative teacher who can go beyond connecting the dots to creating the dots."

Hellison's levels of student responsibility developed in the physical education class has five levels of progressions toward developing skills of caring: level zero, irresponsibility; level I, respect; level II, participation; level III, self-direction; and level IV, caring (figure 13.1).

Teaching Guidelines

Those who work with students who have E/BD recognize the value that positive physical education experiences have for the students. Not only do students have an opportunity to learn skills related to health and fitness, they also have the opportunity to "blow off steam" in a day that can be filled with challenges. Again, one of the *inappropriate* "consequences" given to a student who has E/BD is either to hold him back from recess or to not allow him to participate in physical education class. Unless physical harm to self or others is anticipated, this is not an appropriate solution to the student's behavior in educational settings. Physical education is an academic area. Although numerous studies verify that the unstructured nature of recess time can be troublesome for students with behavior problems, it can be accessed given teacher supervision and structure.

Level IV, Caring

Students at Level IV, in addition to respecting others, participating, and being self-directed, are motivated to extend their sense of responsibility beyond themselves by cooperating, giving support, showing concern, and helping.

Level III, Self-direction

Students at Level III not only show respect and participation but also are able to work without direct supervision. They can identify their own needs and begin to plan and carry out their physical education programs.

Level II, Participation

Students at Level II not only show at least minimal respect for others but also willingly play, accept challenges, practice motor skills, and train for fitness under the teacher's supervision.

Level I, Respect

Students at Level I may not participate in daily activities or show much mastery or improvement, but they are able to control their behavior enough that they don't interfere with the other students' right to learn or the teacher's right to teach. They do this without much prompting by the teacher and without constant supervision.

Level Zero, Irresponsibility

Students who operate at Level Zero make excuses, blame others for their behavior, and deny personal responsibility for what they do or fail to do.

Figure 13.1 The levels presented as a cumulative progression. Adapted by permission, from D. Hellison, 1985, *Goals and strategies for teaching physical education* (Champaign, IL: Human Kinetics), 6–7.

A physical education class for students with E/BD must be predictable and structured. For many students, life is often unpredictable. For example, researchers have shown that if parents know where their child is when she is not at home, then the child will most likely be doing well on many different levels. Advertisers have used this research to promote parenting skills needed particularly in the adolescent years. Other researchers have shown that if very young children are not supervised, there is high risk for developing behavior problems.

Predictability in the physical education class offers the student the opportunity to learn the expected skills needed in physical education: social, emotional, and physical. Predictability is related to the manner in which the teacher works with students, is consistent with rules (shaped in a positive form, e.g., what students will do as opposed to what they will not do), divides up the class time, and teaches skills. The structure for the class needs to be predictable. Also, the students need to be informed as to what the content will be for the class and when it will change. For example, when nearing the end of a volleyball unit, it would be important to inform the students that the swim unit will begin next. Some students with E/BD do not have experiences with typical age-appropriate activity. Therefore, it is helpful to inform them of what the swim program will include ahead of time.

It is important to offer structured choices in class; for example "Do you want to practice kick or throw first?"

Also, a teacher can make a list of the games that students know and ask them to pick a game for the end of class. As students develop their knowledge and skill in other games, those games can be added to the list.

The physical education teacher must maintain consistency by using the same consequences and rewards approach that is being used in the special education or general education program for the student with E/BD. Students need to be aware *before a problem ever arises* what the consequences of their actions will be. For example, if anger and temper control are problems for the student in physical education, then the agreement can be that she will remove herself from the game for a time. Or, if the problem becomes full-blown in a class, the teacher can remind the student of the consequence. Some days will be better for compliance than others, and physical education teachers can decide, with the other educational team members, what the priority behaviors are to be. Additional information is provided in this chapter under placement.

Planning the Physical Activity Program

Physical education experiences contribute in many ways to enhance the total well-being of the student who is emotionally disturbed. Obvious benefits of a well-designed program include improvement of the student's motor and physical fitness performance. Some research has indicated that students with behavior problems experience deficiencies in these important areas. These differences have generally been attributed to the lack of appropriate programs rather than to an inherent motor deficiency in those who are emotionally disturbed.

Exercise programs also have been studied to determine their effect on the behavior patterns of children who are emotionally disturbed. Allan (1980) reported a 50 percent decrease in the disruptive behavior of children who participated in a ten-minute daily jogging program. The effect of exercise on boys with autism was found by Watters and Watters (1980) to decrease self-stimulatory behavior, such as rocking back and forth and hand flapping, by 32 percent. Their study also indicated that vigorous activity such as jogging does not interfere with the student's ability to concentrate following an exercise program. Evans and associates (1985) found that jogging and touch football resulted in fewer talkouts and increased academic production in the classroom. Findings such as these help to dispel a common myth that exercise programs tend to excite students with behavioral disorders and in turn inhibit their performance upon returning to the classroom after participating in physical education activities.

The specific physical education objectives for those with behavior disorders should be developed and specified in the student's Individualized Education Program. As with all students with physical education deficiencies, the program should be based on the student's needs as identified through formal and informal assessment techniques. Instructions should be simple but structured.

Group participation in play activities is highly desirable because it makes social contacts possible. Some students may experience considerable strain in social adjustment, so it may be necessary to work gradually toward group activities. For some students it may be necessary to progress from spectatorship to one-to-one instruction and eventually to small group activity. As the youngsters become accustomed to small group play, more peers can be taken into the group to increase the scope of social contacts. Their inclusion in the activity also provides an incentive for approved social conduct, but the instructor should monitor carefully to ensure that certain students do not dominate the game or detract in any way from the successful performance of any of the students.

Basic motor skill games and exercises that do not require fine coordination are usually the most suitable. Individuals who are very regressed or experience motor disturbances due to medication are easily frustrated by activities requiring numerous movement patterns and detailed

directions. Activities of limited responses and simple structure that may be successfully used with the older school-age group are shuffleboard, casting, croquet, horseshoes, ring toss, bowling, weight lifting, bag punching, and the basic sport skills of throwing, catching, dribbling, and striking a ball. A certain element of competition in the games usually is acceptable. For most students, contact sports and highly competitive games that tend to encourage the expression of aggression directly toward others are contraindicated.

For younger children, the elementary activities utilizing the basic skills (running, throwing, catching, jumping, and so forth) are appropriate and are readily taught. More competitive activities often encourage antisocial conduct, either withdrawal or aggression; therefore, their use in the curriculum should be limited. Children who are aggressive may benefit from participation in strenuous games and activities, as vigorous exercise is helpful in reducing aggressive conduct in some persons. Some aggressive students act as they do because of a subconscious desire for attention, and it is possible to modify their behavior by giving them recognition. Making such a child a squad leader or putting him or her in charge of an activity can often reduce the aggressiveness. Special efforts should be made to get students with behavior disorders to interact. Activities must be planned that promote group interaction. Neel (1986) suggests that simply by varying methods used with traditional activities, opportunities for interaction can be created. For example, in the game of musical chairs, when the music stops, the child left without a chair must approach each of the other children in the group and say "hi" or "hello," give his or her name, and shake hands. There is no need to remove a chair as the game continues until each child has had the opportunity to initiate contact.

Shy children need special help in developing self-confidence. The teacher can help by showing confidence in the child's ability and setting goals that realistically can be achieved. Such children should not be forced into any activities they fear. This also holds true for overanxious children. Both kinds of students should be brought to accept an activity that causes them fear and worry by very gradual exposure to parts or elements of the activity until the emotional reaction subsides.

Co-recreational activities in which both genders can mingle socially should be given appropriate attention in the program. Because of the appeal of music to the emotions, one of the most successful co-recreational activities is social dancing. Square and folk dances are usually too complicated in structure for most students who are severely disturbed, although they are greatly enjoyed by some. Those who cannot participate in these forms of dance can be encouraged to perform simple rhythmic activities to music. Modern or interpretive dance has interesting possibilities as a therapeutic aid for persons who are mentally ill whose other means of expression are blocked. Because of the strong emotional involvement in this type of dance expression, it is recommended that this form of dance be approached only with the consultation of a psychologist and a dance therapist. Popular dance is fun for some students with behavior problems, and they may have talent in this area.

Swimming should be included among the activities of the program because of the desirable effects that water produces. It frequently acts as a stimulant to the depressed and encourages movement in the extremely withdrawn. Persons who are hyperactive are often greatly relaxed by the water, particularly if it is warmer than normal.

The instructor must plan for successful participation in the activities by the students. **Success is extremely important to them.** To be successful does not necessitate being a winner, but it does require that the activity be fun and self-satisfying. To ensure success the instructor must consider the special needs and interests of each person; give friendly, patient instruction in the skills; and continually encourage a wider interest in play and in the people who play.

Above all, **the instructor must treat the student with a behavior disorder as an individual who is deserving of respect and consideration.** There is still in our society a great stigma attached to being publicly recognized as mentally ill; those who have a mental illness are regarded by far too many as misfits and failures. Of course, students with behavior disorders are well aware of these attitudes and anticipate being degraded in their dealings with others. This obviously interferes with establishing social relationships. Peers tend to reject students with behavior disorders more than youth without behavior disorders (Sabornie & Kauffman, 1985), and, not surprisingly, youth with behavior disorders report feelings of extreme loneliness (Asher & Wheeler, 1985). Because most students with behavior disorders are not socially adept, having generally spent withdrawn and aloof lives, failure to treat them as deserving of the dignity accorded other human beings is defeating to them and defeating to the success of the physical education program.

In trying to institute programs with such people, it should also be borne in mind that many of them are extremely concerned about their personal problems (some students who are severely disturbed may even be pondering the desirability of death over their present life), so that games of any sort are of little interest to them. Although they may participate, if forced to do so, because of their passivity, they will not enjoy the activity and will probably feel degraded and silly doing it. Such a response is, of course, detrimental to the objectives of the program.

Students with behavior disorders need help and it is the responsibility of all professionals, including physical educators, to create success-oriented programs. The environment must be structured but sensitive to the needs of these at-risk youth. For some students, the physical education teacher and the emphasis on physical activity may make the difference in enhancing their lives.

Instructional Placement

The appropriate instructional placement for the student with behavior disorders will vary according to the nature and severity of the disability. As specified in IDEA 2004, the desired goal is to place students with disabilities in the educational environment which is least restrictive and will allow for the greatest educational gain. Students who have severe behavior disorders may need separate educational experiences, but for some of these students, the IEP team recommends placement, with modification, in the general physical education program. These critical decisions about placement reside with the student's IEP team. One of the primary reasons that it is highly desirable, if possible, to include students with behavior disorders in the general physical education program is based on research demonstrating that the most effective way to teach students behaviors they are lacking is to teach them the appropriate skill and expose them to others who demonstrate the appropriate behaviors. Placement alone does not ensure that the student will necessarily model or emulate the desired behavior. Direct instruction on target behaviors is often required to help students master them. Consultation with other specialists, including the special education teacher, school psychologist, and others may prove helpful in devising an effective strategy. To most effectively address the student's needs in general physical education, as well as ensure a positive experience for other students, the following suggestions were proposed by the Council for Exceptional Children (Lewis, Heflin, & DiGangi, 1991), and continue to guide instruction.

1. Keep an organized classroom learning environment.
2. Provide an abundance of success for all students.
3. Hold high expectations.
4. Devise a structured behavior management program.
5. Maintain a close working relationship with the special education teacher and other staff members.
6. Collect data so that the effects of instruction-based decisions can be evaluated and modified.

As an aid in using data to make instructional decisions, figure 13.2 provides a very simple example of how graphing data will be helpful in assessing the effectiveness of a particular program or strategy. As noted in figure 13.1, the steps involved in developing the graph include:

Step One. Establish baseline data. As an example, the physical education teacher might want to graph the number

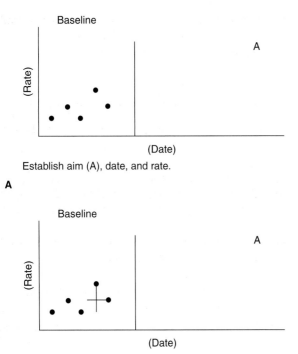

Establish aim (A), date, and rate.

A

Determine mid-date and mid-rate of last three days of baseline.

B

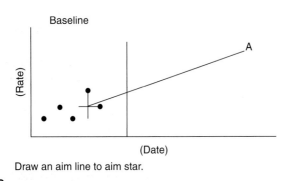

Draw an aim line to aim star.

C

Figure 13.2 Plotting data on a graph helps teachers make wise instructional decisions.

of times the student is verbally rude to other students. It is recommended that the baseline include at least three data points (e.g., number of occurrences per day for three days) (figure 13.2A). In consultation with others, the teacher should determine a target (A) representing the desired reduction in the target behavior (verbally rude to other students). The baseline might include total number of occurrences per the entire period or some time sample. This will depend on the amount of time and instructional support available.

Step Two. Determine the mid-date and mid-rate of the last three days of baseline data points (figure 13.2B). Mid-date and mid-rate are the median or middle-most points. For the mid-date, count left to right. For the mid-rate, count bottom to top.

Step Three. Draw an aim line through the mid-date/mid-rate intersection to the aim star (figure 13.2C).

Step Four. Formulate data decision rules. The goal is to assess how the treatment is working and to know when to consider alternative approaches if the plan is not working (e.g., if the data fall above the aim line for three consecutive days, consult with the others to determine if a change in strategy is needed).

Instructional Approaches to Physical Activity

Although many different educational approaches have been used to teach students with behavior disorders, the two techniques that are widely acclaimed to be effective are the behavioral and ecological approaches.

The behavioral model assumes that the behavior exhibited by students has been learned. Providing appropriate educational experiences requires, therefore, that the teacher use behavior modification techniques to teach appropriate responses and eliminate inappropriate ones.

An ecological approach stresses the importance of the student's interaction with his or her peers, teachers, and parents. Treatment is directed toward teaching the child to function within the home/school setting. This approach requires that all those who relate with the individual respond to his or her behavior in a consistent manner.

The behavioral and ecological approaches can effectively be used together if teachers, parents, and peers are taught to employ some basic reinforcement techniques. Basic concepts that need to be stressed include the following:

1. Reinforcers should be those rewards that are desired and enjoyed by the students. Some teachers identify appropriate reinforcers by observing the students to determine their likes and dislikes. Talking with the student about favorable reinforcers is also possible with some individuals.
2. If possible, the reinforcers should be ones that are most natural and closely associated with the social reinforcers that work with most individuals. Some children who are severely disturbed, however, may not respond to social reinforcers, and it may be necessary to select more primary reinforcers such as toys and food.
3. Rewards should be given immediately following the desired behavior. A delay of longer than a few seconds can create a situation in which the student is reinforced for some unacceptable acts that followed the appropriate response. Many teachers have successfully used a token economy system with students with behavior disorders to facilitate the process of immediate reinforcement. Check marks, stars, and pluses are examples of tokens that may be given in the gymnasium and used later in exchange for a particular reward.

4. Social rewards should always be paired with primary reinforcers, with the ultimate goal of helping the student to eventually respond to the natural reinforcers.

Many of the concepts used in behavior modification systems are simply good commonsense application of the laws of learning. Unfortunately, however, too few physical educators use this approach in their interaction with children who are emotionally disturbed. As indicated in an article by Dunn and French (1982), behavior modification is one of the tools that special physical educators must understand and employ with students with disabilities, particularly those who are emotionally disturbed.

In addition to skills in the application of behavior modification principles, the teacher of students with behavior disorders must have an unusual capacity to witness extreme acts of anger, hate, and aggression from youngsters without in turn responding in a similar manner. This means that the teacher must accept such outbursts as very visible signs of the students' frustration with others and themselves. The teacher's role is not to condone such acts but to accept the behavior in an empathetic manner, stressing to the student that there are more appropriate ways to express feelings of frustration and anger.

Teachers must also realize that they serve as models for the students who are emotionally disturbed. Their actions, therefore, must be consistent, mature, and controlled. Emotional outbursts and angry shouting exchanges with students inhibit rather than create a healthy educational environment.

Specific suggestions that the teacher working with children who are emotionally disturbed can apply are indicated in the following (Fried, 1980):

1. Ignore inappropriate behavior. This technique, frequently referred to as extinction, is used to communicate that the *behavior* is unacceptable, not the child.
2. Catch the student doing something positive. Search for opportunities to reinforce the child by acknowledging good behavior or quality efforts to learn a new skill.
3. Use closeness. Teachers can sometimes avoid a potential problem by moving closer to a student.
4. Tell the student how you feel. Frequently it is best to appeal directly to the child by explaining that a particular behavior is annoying to you and to others in the class.
5. Use physical restraint when necessary. Occasionally a student may lose control so completely that restraint or removal is required to avoid harm being done to the student or to others. The exact restraint procedures to be used should be discussed by the student's IEP team. It is very important to emphasize that when a student is restrained or removed, the teacher should be firm but not punitive. Unfriendly remarks by the teacher and other children should be avoided.
6. Learn to say no. Teachers of students with behavior disorders must establish clearly defined limits and expectations. Students accept a "no" response more easily if they realize that the denial is consistent with the established

---

TABLE 13.2   Tips for Helping Students with Behavior Disorders

1. Provide a carefully structured environment with regard to physical features of the room, scheduling and routines, and rules of conduct. If there are to be unstructured activities, you must clearly distinguish them from structured activities in terms of time, place, and expectations.

2. Let your pupils know the expectations you have, the objectives that have been established for them, and the help you will give them in achieving those objectives. When appropriate, seek input from them about their strengths, weaknesses, and goals.

3. Reinforce appropriate behavior; inappropriate behavior should be ignored or mildly punished. Model appropriate behavior and refrain from behavior you do not wish students to imitate.

4. Do not expect students with behavior disorders to have immediate success; work for improvement on a long-term basis. Reinforce approximations to or attempts at the desired behavior. Continue with the intervention strategy being used when a student is making progress toward an objective; try another way if there is no progress.

5. Be fair, be consistent, but temper your consistency with flexibility.

6. Be sensitive to your students as individuals and as a class; balance individual needs with group requirements.

7. Try to understand the frustrations, hopes, and fears of your students and their parents.

Source: Haring, N., & McCormick, L. (1986). *Exceptional children and youth* (4th ed., p. 199). Columbus: Charles E. Merrill Publishing Co.

guidelines. Therefore, the behavior guidelines, not the teacher, become the object of the students' dislike.

7. Help the student build a positive self-image. Frequently, students who are emotionally disturbed devalue their true worth. Teachers must strive to create positive self-concept builders. Physical educators who employ a problem-solving teaching approach can create many situations in which children can be successful.

8. Encourage students to express themselves verbally. Many youngsters who are emotionally disturbed find talking about their anger an effective means of maintaining their composure. Teachers must be prepared to be good listeners. It is a normal part of life to get angry. **How the student deals with the anger can be maladaptive.** Students must be taught to express their anger in an acceptable manner.

Other suggestions or tips for helping teach the student with behavior disorders are summarized in table 13.2. These tips, developed by Cullinan and Epstein (1986), apply equally to the classroom or gymnasium setting.

Pervasive Developmental Disorder and Autism Spectrum Disorder

The broad term used by the American Psychiatric Association (APA) (2000) for those with autism is "pervasive developmental disorder (PDD)." Other autism-related disorders include Rett's disorder, Childhood Disintegrative Disorder, and Asperger's syndrome. Individuals with only some of the symptoms of PDD are described as PDD-NOS, meaning PDD "not otherwise specified." According to Hagin (2004):

> Individuals with autism and severe pervasive developmental disorders (PDDs) share fundamental impairments in three areas of human activity: social responsiveness and interactions, verbal and nonverbal communication, and behavioral flexibility. . . . Their major personality disturbances are manifested in distortions and delays in their emotional relationships with adults and other children, their comprehension and use of language, their cognitive functioning, their acquisition of self-help skills, and their responses to sensory stimuli. (p. 56)

Autism Spectrum Disorder (ASD)

Children with autism are being identified for special education in very high and increasing numbers across the United States. As such, physical educators are teaching these children with a sometimes slim amount of education what actually works in gymnasiums, swimming pools, tracks, and the community. Resources for teaching these children cannot come out fast enough to serve both the teacher and the child.

A large multi-site project devoted to producing evidence-based interventions, professional development, and other resources and training is ongoing under the National Professional Development Center on Autism Spectrum Disorders at the University of North Carolina Chapel Hill (www.fpg.unc.edu/projects). Begun in 2007, the project is directed by Dr. Sam Odom and funded by the Office of Special Education Programs, United States Department of Education. One resource nearing completion is a list of evidence-based practices: those practices that have been validated in research with children with autism. According to Odom (2008), this list is short despite the long list of contacts. For researchers this is always a cry for more research dollars and larger banks of data to draw on at the national level. Basic science research is looking at neurological differences with the brains of children with autism and their typically developing peers.

However, physical educators must educate here and now.

The teaching strategies considered best practice, hence those that are effective, will be detailed in this section. Programs and their matching teaching strategies vary (e.g., TEACCH TEACCH@unc.edu), from classrooms for children with autism that have an extremely small student to staff ratio and intense behavior modification, to special education classrooms with mixed diagnosis students that receive education with higher student staff ratios where aides for that child are prevalent.

Autism is a neurobehavioral disorder that has an onset in early childhood with apparent deficits in behavioral and cognitive dimensions of language, social skill, and the presence of repetitive and/or restrictive behaviors (e.g., Alaron, Yonan, Gilliam, Cantor, & Geschwind, 2005). For example, this is the child whose processing of stimuli produces a varied response. In the swimming pool, the lights under the water (stimuli) may behold the most fascinating allure, trumping instruction for the flutter kick (desired response). Instead, the swimmer(s) immediately dive down to gaze intently at the lights (response). The child's love of the swimming lesson may have different responses than the instructor's outcomes!

In 1943 the characteristics of autism were first described by Leo Kanner, who considered the disorder to have an emotional cause. As described earlier in this chapter, the understanding of the cause has shifted over the decades. Autism is now considered a neurobiological disorder. Hence, physical educators need to be aware that the differences seen in individuals with autism are influenced heavily by the differences in the neurological makeup of the individual. But, as previously stated in this text, each student with a disability is a unique person with a unique history, experiences, and genetic makeup. Therefore, the individuality of the person with autism must be taken into account when designing the physical education program.

The behavioral characteristics of autism range from mild to severe. The subtype of the disorder also influences its expression. According to special educators Colarusso and O'Rourke (2003), parents, professionals, and advocates of individuals with autism use the term "autism spectrum disorders" to recognize the range of expression of the behaviors as well as the subtypes of the disorder. "Autism" is the term used in the federal educational law, IDEA 2004, as an eligibility category. The diagnostic criteria for autistic disorder used by the APA is seen in figure 13.3. The category of autism used in IDEA '97 is described as follows:

Autism means a developmental delay significantly affecting verbal and non-verbal communication, social interaction, generally evident before the age of 3, that adversely affects educational performance. Other characteristics often associated with autism are engagement in repetitive activities and stereotyped movements, resistance to environmental change or changes in daily routines, and unusual responses to sensory experiences. The term does not apply if a child's educational performance is adversely affected primarily because the child has a serious emotional disturbance. (34 C.F.R., Sec. 300.7 [b][1])

As is apparent, the terminology used in the diagnosis of autism differs by profession. The social and behavioral impairments described by the psychologist differ from the terms used by the neurologist. Language delays are recognized most prominently by speech and language pathologists.

Figure 13.3 Diagnostic criteria for 299.00 Autistic Disorder.

A. A total of six (or more) items from (1), (2), and (3), with at least two from (1), and one each from (2) and (3):
  (1) qualitative impairment in social interaction, as manifested by at least two of the following:
    (a) marked impairment in the use of multiple nonverbal behaviors such as eye-to-eye gaze, facial expression, body postures, and gestures to regulate social interaction
    (b) failure to develop peer relationships appropriate to developmental level
    (c) a lack of spontaneous seeking to share enjoyment, interests, or achievements with other people (e.g., by a lack of showing, bringing, or pointing out objects of interest)
    (d) lack of social or emotional reciprocity
  (2) qualitative impairments in communication as manifested by at least one of the following:
    (a) delay in, or total lack of, the development of spoken language (not accompanied by an attempt to compensate through alternative modes of communication such as gesture or mime)
    (b) in individuals with adequate speech, marked impairment in the ability to initiate or sustain conversation with others
    (c) stereotyped and repetitive use of language or idiosyncratic language
    (d) lack of varied, spontaneous make-believe play or social initiative play appropriate to developmental level
  (3) restricted repetitive and stereotyped patterns of behavior, interests, and activities, as manifested by at least one of the following:
    (a) encompassing preoccupation with one or more stereotyped and restricted patterns of interest that is abnormal either in intensity or focus
    (b) apparently inflexible adherence to specific, nonfunctional routines or rituals
    (c) stereotyped and repetitive motor mannerisms (e.g., hand or finger flapping or twisting, or complex whole-body movements)
    (d) persistent preoccupation with parts of objects
B. Delays or abnormal functioning in at least one of the following areas, with onset prior to age 3 years: (1) social interaction, (2) language as used in social communication, or (3) symbolic or imaginative play.
C. The disturbance is not better accounted for by Rett's Disorder or Childhood Disintegrative Disorder.

Some clinicians believe that rigid categories should be abandoned and that core symptoms be recognized so that reasonable and functional interventions can be utilized.

Many educators have noted the increase in incidence of students with autism. An increase of 200 percent in the incidence of mild autism has been reported between 1991 and 1997. Wing and Potter (2002) analyzed these data and reported that the increased incidence was most likely due to increased awareness of the range of autistic disorders, not necessarily because there was a rise in numbers of individuals with autism (Hagin, 2004). In addition, these researchers also found weak scientific evidence that environmental factors are responsible for the increased incidence of autism; or that diseases such as measles, mumps, and rubella were increasing the incidence.

The following information is shared to assist the physical educator in understanding the complex nature of the diagnosis and the process that families undergo as they deal with the diagnosis of autism for their child. It has been described by clinicians as a very painful time for parents. Parents describe being unevenly dealt with by diagnosticians: Some are better than others and some listen better than others. In the end, the diagnosis is a startling one. It is important that the physical educator work with the family to gain the best knowledge of the child's strengths in physical activity and the interventions that will be helpful to teach the child in the physical education curriculum. Groft and Block (2003) remind physical education teachers that the actions seen in physical education are not due to willful misbehavior by individuals with Asperger's syndrome (a subtype of autism).

According to Hagin (2004), the diagnosis of PDD is made by professionals, including the educator, social worker, psychologist, and medical doctor working with the parents and the child. A history of the child's development is obtained from the parents over the course of time. Due to the difficulty of children with PDD to respond on demand, it is recommended that the approach to assessment be done in a relaxed manner with the child over time. Parents initially are asked about the child's strengths, weaknesses, and progress, and about how behavior is managed at home, school, and in the community. The problems identified in this *initial encounter* then become the cornerstone for the *next step* in the diagnostic procedure, which includes:

- all previous evaluations, family history, and child's medical history
- the parent's first-hand view of the child's typical day
- completion of questionnaires for autism
- if possible, testing of the cognitive, verbal, and nonverbal communication skills
- a play observation in a natural setting
- integration of data from multiple sources, presentation of the material to the family, and planning for the next steps in diagnosis and intervention

The diagnosis is considered a process whereby the examiners of the child must listen to the parental descriptions of the child: These situations can never be replicated in a clinical setting. Examiners are asked to make intelligent selections of test instruments, adapt testing procedures to obtain information from the child (e.g., use gestures and pictures to help the child respond), and use observations of the child in the natural environment.

Core characteristics of individuals with autism include impaired responsiveness, delays in language development, inconsistent sensory awareness, preoccupation with circular movement (e.g., the spinning movement of fans and wheeled toys), uneven cognitive functioning, and a restriction of interests (Hagin, 2004).

Teaching Strategies for Physical Activity

For physical educators to develop successful programs for individuals with autism, it is important to recognize some of the instructional strategies that have shown to help students with autism learn. As in other areas of special education, it is important to work with the educational team.

Klin (1996) believes that children with autism need direct instruction in:

- interpreting the behaviors of others,
- monitoring their own social interactions,
- using eye contact, gaze, and gestures in interpersonal relationships, and
- understanding the practical aspects of language.

Temple Grandin, a professor of agriculture in Wyoming who has autism, has written about her educational experiences, particularly about the difficulties she had with understanding language and verbal expression (1991, 2002). She has recommended the following teaching methods:

- use concrete visual methods to teach numbers
- avoid long verbalizations
- avoid exposing children to loud verbal sounds; whispering is effective

Characteristics of Autism

- Impaired responsiveness
- Language development delays
- Inconsistent sensory awareness
- Preoccupation with circular movement
- Uneven cognitive functioning
- Restriction of interests

- avoid overloading children with perceptual information
- use realistic pictures or photographs, rather than line drawings

Whatever plans have been made within instructional areas, they should be carried out in the physical education program. Groft and Block (2003), as well as Houston-Wilson and Lieberman (2003), have examined the behavioral characteristics of students with autism and offer suggestions for the physical education setting.

- Consistency in behavioral management is imperative. Whatever strategies the team is employing in the other settings in the school should also be employed in the physical education class.
  - Social skill reinforcement. Identify what is being reinforced, ignored, or has a specific consequence.
  - Melt-down. Understand what this outburst looks like for this student and what the quiet, safe place is for the cool-down. Observe what occurred before the melt-down that may have affected the student. If possible, talk with the student and emphasize his positive qualities.
- Attend to the cognitive challenges, and develop strategies to gear instruction to success.
  - Give the student choice within the physical education class, but limit choices to two or three.
  - Keep directions simple.
  - Singing instructions can help some students.
  - For short periods of time, provide a distraction-free opportunity to practice new concepts with a peer.
- Teach social skills.
  - Teach a child how to find a partner (e.g., walk up to a partner, ask).
  - Provide opportunities within the physical education class to practice the skill.
  - Teach how to take turns in an activity.
  - Use "social stories" to teach how a social situation is handled; use the student's name or "I." Or help the child learn how to say "excuse me" or "thanks" by short stories.
- Understand the communication strategies that work for the student.
  - Keep an even tone to your voice. Be calm, predictable, and matter-of-fact.
  - Use part-to-whole verbal approach (e.g., kick the ball; kick the ball to John).
  - Use communication boards that have pictures with hook-and-loop tape attached to the back (sometimes referred to picture boards). The pictures depict the class activities (see figure 13.4).
  - Interpret body language and nonverbal cues for the student if misinterpretation is apparent.

- Motor and fitness activities that are not competitive are better options.
  - Examples: rowing, stationary biking, running, rowing, horseback riding, skating, bowling, swimming, bicycling.
  - Manipulative skills, such as catching and throwing, can be practiced with a peer when the whole class is working as a group.
  - Modify the team sport to accommodate poor motor coordination, if necessary.
  - Present a social story about not winning to develop the individual's social skills with losing.
  - Use some of the preoccupations as motivators in the class (e.g., You're a train and going fast . . . run! You're an airplane, put your arms out and fly around the gym.)
- Organize and structure events to reduce sensory overload
  - Give a predictable beginning, middle, and end to the class.
  - Keep some of the material in class familiar and add new material to the old.
  - Develop routines in class for the skills taught. For example:
    - place ball on tee
    - pick up bat
    - hold bat over shoulder
    - swing bat at ball
    - when ball is off the tee, put bat down
    - run to base.
  - Give meaning to the skills taught (e.g., When the ball is off the tee, run as fast as you can so you don't get tagged out).
  - Forewarn about transitions (e.g., three minutes until you switch with your partner)
  - Provide additional warnings as time draws near to initiate another activity.
  - Allow the student to indicate her preference(s) via a picture board, signed requests, or simple verbal response.
  - Token economy can be employed to increase positive behavior (e.g., reward the student when a targeted behavior is appropriate). A token must be of value to the student. Thus, checks and stars can be accumulated for a special object/event.
    - Students can be encouraged to participate in a less desired activity if the reward is a preferred activity. This increases his skills/interests for physical activity. But caution is important. Do not have more nonpreferred activities than preferred; or only use the preferred activity when the nonpreferred one has been accomplished.
- Explain and organize the physical education space for the student.

Prominent Behaviors	Teaching Strategies	Pictorial Examples
Environmental resistance to change	Identify class location: outdoor field, pool, or gymnasium	
A. Situational resistance to change	A. Identify class structure: predictable start & finish	
B. Situational resistance to change	B. Identify class structure: warm-ups & class activities	
Lack of eye to eye contact	Look & speak directly but softly with the student	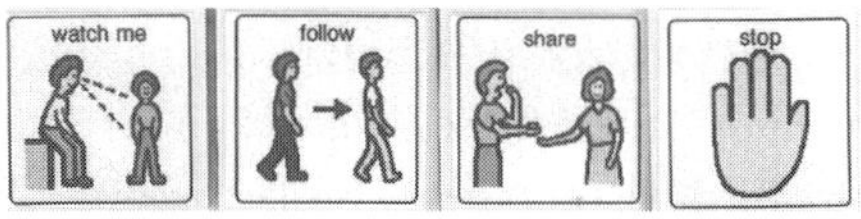
Short attention span	Use of activity stations	
Inappropriate obsessive focus	Behavior limited by counting down minutes left until done	
Activity participation issues	Offer choice of motor activities with time limitations & then count down	
Difficulty with skill generalization	Provide skill opportunities in a variety of motor activities	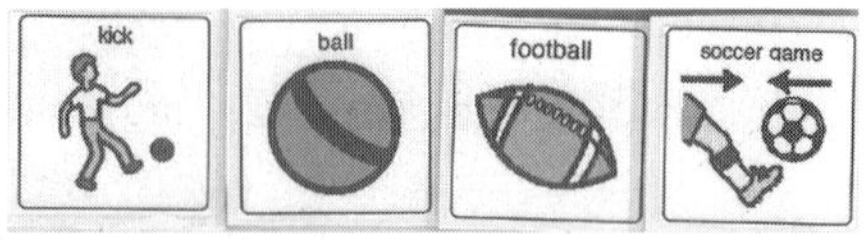
Possible picture comprehension delays	Point to picture when behavior is exhibited	
Difficulty understanding verbal directions and/or inability to verbally communicate	Create pictorial examples	See above

Figure 13.4   Autism picture board. Boardmaker (www.mayer-johnson.com/software/boardmkr.html) for pictures for Velcro cards. Schnizlein, B. (2004). Autism: What physical educators need to know. Unpublished Masters project. University of Minnesota, Minneapolis.

- Explain where activities are performed: gym, track, swimming pool.
- Explain where things are located: balls in the bin, racquets on the hooks.
- Explain how to move from one activity to the other: moving from inside to outside.
- Establish boundaries: If a student needs to stay at a station, place a red cone there.
- Use the picture board for the child to see how the class is structured and what the activities will be for

the student, and a picture for the ending transition of class. See figure 13.4 for pictorial examples tied into the prominent behaviors and teaching strategies.
- Train support personnel, such as educational assistants, to provide additional teaching and practice time in a motor skill, or to be of assistance in use of equipment or routines.

Summary

Information was provided in this chapter concerning emotional disturbed and pervasive developmental disorder. As is true with the other disabilities, specific criteria are applied to differentiate those youngsters who are seriously emotionally disturbed from those whose behavior is within the range of normalcy. For a given behavior problem, the intensity, frequency, and duration of the problem must be considered in differentiating more permanent disorders, such as autism, from temporary problems.

Various classification systems are employed to identify and classify those with mental disorders. The American Psychiatric Association's *Diagnostic and Statistical Manual of Mental Disorders* is widely used by mental health specialists. Why students have behavior disorders is not clearly known. Some have attributed the cause to psychological, sociological, or physiological problems. Psychoanalysts argue, for instance, that children are behaviorally disordered because they have not successfully dealt with problems as they have developed. While behaviorists might concur with this premise, the intervention strategy they promote doesn't emphasize determining the cause but stresses helping the youngster to interact positively with peers, teachers, and parents.

In developing educational programs for students with emotional behavior disorders, there is consensus that certain educational practices should be followed. These include: structure the learning environment; clearly establish student expectations and consequences; provide success-oriented experiences; use behavior modification concepts with an emphasis on positive reinforcement; analyze tasks into small steps and recognize gains even when very small. Teachers must

be patient, sensitive, good listeners, and fair and consistent in their treatment of the student with a behavior disorder.

There is increasing evidence that physical education programs play a significant role in treatment and intervention programs for students with emotional/behavior disorders. Programs that emphasize skill development contribute to a positive self-image. Exercise programs that emphasize cardiorespiratory endurance decrease disruptive behavior and increase academic production. Physical educators recognize, too, that care must be taken to assist students who are fearful of participation in some or all physical education activities. The emphasis must be placed on positive learning experiences with special efforts directed toward avoiding unnecessary emotional stress in the physical education class.

The outlook for students with behavior disorders is very encouraging. Physical education can and should play a significant part in helping these students enhance their quality of life.

Students with PDD such as autism can successfully engage in physical education activities when the prominent features of their disorder are recognized and teaching strategies are matched to the features. The use of picture boards is recommended to detail the structure of class as well as the specific activities in which the student will be participating. Physical educators are encouraged to work closely with the student's other educational specialists, and with the family, to provide consistency in the classroom interventions and to reinforce behaviors across settings. Physical education activities are important to the student's health, and also to develop a broad range of skill and interest for physical activity.

Enhancing Activities

1. Obtain a copy of the American Psychiatric Association's *Diagnostic and Statistical Manual of Mental Disorders* (DSM-IVR) and review the various disorders included in the manual.

2. Review the studies of Allan; Watters and Watters; and Evans, Evans, Schmid, and Pennypacker. Analyze these studies and their positive findings concerning the effects of exercise programs with students with behavior disorders.

3. Observe a physical education class and chart the number of behavior problems or incidences that occur during a specified time frame (one period, several periods, etc.). Note the frequency, intensity, and duration of the problem(s). Develop a baseline and projected target.

4. Interview the parents of a child with a conduct disorder. Obtain their perceptions of this disorder and their views concerning the importance of physical activity programs for youngsters similar to theirs.

5. Discuss the following question with some of your classmates. If you were hired as a physical education teacher, what would your reaction be to knowing that a student with a behavior disorder would be mainstreamed into your regular physical education class?

6. Visit a program for students with behavior disorders. Record your perceptions as to the program, students, teachers, and curriculum. Did you find the program to be structured with rules and consequences clearly established? How was the program similar to or different from that provided for non-behavior-disordered youth?

Selected Readings

Alaron, M., Yonan, A. L., Gilliam, T. C., Cantor, R. M., & Geschwind, D. H. (2005). Quantitative genome scan and ordered-subsets analysis of autism endophenotypes support language QTLs. *Molecular Psychiatry, 10,* 747–757.

Allan, J. I. (1980). Jogging can modify disruptive behaviors. *Teaching Exceptional Children,* 66–70.

American Alliance for Health, Physical Education, and Recreation. (1976). *Physical education, recreation, and related programs for autistic and emotionally disturbed children.* Washington, DC: Author.

American Psychiatric Association. *Diagnostic and Statistical Manual of Mental Disorders (DSM-IV).* (2000). Washington, DC: Author.

Asher, S. R., & Wheeler, V. A. (1985). Children's loneliness: A comparison of rejected and neglected peer status. *Journal of Consulting and Clinical Psychology, 53,* 500–505.

Bandura, A. (1977). *Characteristics of children's behavior disorders.* Columbus, OH: Charles E. Merrill Publishing Co.

Bauer, A. M., & Shea, T. M. (1989). *Teaching exceptional students in your classroom.* Boston: Allyn and Bacon, Inc.

Bower, E. (1969). *Early identification of emotionally handicapped children in school* (2nd ed.). Springfield, IL: Charles C. Thomas.

Campbell, D., Sutcliffe, J., Ebert, P., Militerni, R., Bravaccio, C., Trillo, S., et al. (2006). A genetic variant that disrupts MET transcription is associated with autism. *Proceedings of the National Academy of Sciences, 103* (45), 16834–16839.

Colarusso, R., & O'Rourke, C. (2003). *Special education for all teachers.* Dubuque, IA: Kendall/Hunt.

Connor, F. (1990). Physical education for children with autism. *Teaching Exceptional Children, 23*(1), 30–33.

Cullinan, D., & Epstein, M. H. (1986). Behavior disorders. In N. G. Haring & L. McCormick (Eds.), *Exceptional children and youth* (4th ed., pp. 160–199). Columbus, OH: Charles E. Merrill Publishing Co.

Davis, K. (1990). *Adapted physical education for students with autism.* Springfield, IL: Charles C. Thomas.

Dunn, J. M., & French, R. (1982). Operant conditioning: A tool for special physical educators in the 80s. *Exceptional Education Quarterly, 3,* 42–53.

Edelbrock, C. (1979). Empirical classification of children's behavior disorders: Progress based on parent and teacher ratings. *School Psychology Digest,* 355–369.

Epstein, P. B., Detwiler, C. L., & Reitz, A. L. (1985). Describing the clients in programs for behavior disordered children and youth. *Education and Treatment of Children, 8,* 265–273.

Evans, W. H., Evans, S. S., Schmid, R. E., & Pennypacker, H. S. (1985). The effects of exercise on selected classroom behaviors of behaviorally disordered adolescents. *Behavioral Disorders, 11,* 42–51.

Fried, H. (Ed.). (1980). *Plain talk about dealing with the angry child* (DHHS Publication No. ADM 80–781). Rockville, MD: National Institute of Mental Health, United States Department of Health and Human Services.

Geschwind, D., & Levitt, P. (2007). Autism spectrum disorders: Developmental disconnection syndromes. *Current Opinion in Neurobiology, 17,* 103–111.

Grandin, T. (1991). Overcoming autism: A first-person account. *Harvard Mental Health Newsletter, 3,* 1–4.

Grandin, T. (2002). *Teaching tips for children and adults with autism.* Fort Collins, CO: Center for the Study of Autism.

Groft, M., & Block, M. (2003). Children with Asperger's syndrome: Implications for general physical education and youth sports. *JOPHERD, 74*(3), 38–43.

Hagin, R. A. (2004). Autism and other severe pervasive developmental disorders. In F. M. Kline & L. B. Silver (Eds.), *The educator's guide to mental health issues in the classroom* (pp. 55–73). Baltimore: Brookes.

Hallahan, D. P., & Kauffman, J. M. (1991). *Exceptional children: Introduction to special education* (5th ed.). Englewood Cliffs, NJ: Prentice-Hall, Inc.

Hellison, D. (2003). *Teaching responsibility through physical activity* (2nd ed.). Champaign, IL: Human Kinetics.

Heward, W. L., & Orlansky, M. D. (1992). *Exceptional children* (4th ed.). Columbus, OH: Charles E. Merrill Publishing Co.

Hewett, F. M., & Taylor, R. D. (1980). *The emotionally disturbed child in the classroom: The orchestration of success.* Boston: Allyn and Bacon, Inc.

Houston-Wilson, C., & Lieberman, L. J. (2003). Strategies for teaching students with autism in physical education. *Journal of Physical Education Recreation and Dance, 74*(6), 40–44.

Johnson, C., Myers, S., & the Council on Children with Disabilities. (2007). Identification and evaluation of children with autism spectrum disorders. *American Academy of Pediatrics, 120,* 1183–1215.

Johnson, J. (1988). The challenge of substance abuse. *Teaching Exceptional Children, 20*(4), 29–31.

Juul, K. D. (1986). Epidemiological studies of behavior disorders in children: An international survey. *International Journal of Special Education, 1,* 1–20.

Kanner, L. (1943). Autistic disturbances of affective contact. *Nervous Child, 2,* 217–250.

Kauffman, J. M. (1977). *Characteristics of children's behavioral disorders.* Columbus, OH: Charles E. Merrill Publishing Co.

Kauffman, J. M. (1986). Educating children with behavior disorders. In R. J. Morris & B. Blatt (Eds.), *Special education: Research and trends.* New York: Pergamon Press.

Kazdin, A. E. (1987). *Conduct disorders in childhood and adolescence.* Beverly Hills, CA: Sage Publishing.

Kirk, S. A., & Gallagher, J. J. (1989). *Educating exceptional children* (6th ed.). Boston, MA: Houghton Mifflin.

Klin, A. (1996). *Asperger's syndrome: Guidelines for treatment and intervention.* Pittsburgh: Learning Disabilities Association of America.

Kline, F. M., & Silver, L. B. (Eds.). (2004). *The educator's guide to mental health issues in the classroom.* Baltimore: Brookes.

Kugelmass, N. I. (1974). *The autistic child.* Springfield, IL: Charles C. Thomas.

Lewis, T. J., Heflin, J., & DiGangi, J. A. (1991). *Teaching students with behavioral disorders.* Reston, VA: Council for Exceptional Children.

Mandell, C. J., & Fiscus, E. (1981). *Understanding exceptional people.* St. Paul, MN: West Publishing Co.

Mendelsohn, S. R., & Jennings, K. D. (1986). Characteristics of emotionally disturbed children referred for special education assessment. *Child Psychiatry and Human Development, 16,* 154–170.

Neel, R. S. (1986). Teaching functional social skills to children with autism. *Focus on Autistic Behavior, 1,* 1–8.

Plomin, R. (1986). Behavior genetics and intelligence. In J. Gallagher & C. Ramey (Eds.), *The malleability of children.* Baltimore, MD: Paul H. Brookes Publishing Co.

Quay, H. C. (1972). Patterns of aggression, withdrawal, and immaturity. In H. C. Quay & J. S. Werry (Eds.), *Psychopathological disorders of childhood.* New York: John Wiley and Sons, Inc.

Reid, G., Collier, D., & Morin, B. (1983). Motor performance of autistic individuals. In R. L. Eason, T. L. Smith, & F. Caron (Eds.), *Adapted physical activity: From theory to application* (pp. 201–218). Champaign, IL: Human Kinetics Publishers.

Reinert, H. R. (1976). *Children in conflict.* St. Louis: C. V. Mosby Co.

Ross, A. O. (1974). *Psychological disorders of children: A behavioral approach to theory, research, and therapy.* New York: McGraw-Hill, Inc.

Sabornie, E. J., & Kauffman, J. M. (1985). Regular classroom sociometric status of behaviorally disordered adolescents. *Behavioral Disorders, 10,* 268–274.

Sebat, J., Lakshmi, B., Malhotra, D., Troge, J., Lese-Martin, C., Walsh, T., et al. (2007). Strong association of de novo copy number mutations with autism. *Science, 316,* 445–449.

Swanson, H. L., & Reinert, H. R. (1979). *Teaching strategies for children in conflict.* St. Louis: C. V. Mosby Co.

Thompson, W., Price, C., Goodson, B., Shay, D., Benson, P., Hinrichsen, V., et al. (2007). Early thimerosal exposure and neuropsychological outcomes at 7 to 10 years. *The New England Journal of Medicine, 357*(13), 1281–1292.

Vojdani, A., Campbell, A., Anyanwu, E., Kashanian, A., Bock, K., & Vojdani, E. (2002) Antibodies to neuron-specific antigens in children with autism: Possible cross-reaction with encephalitogenic proteins from milk, chlamydia pneumonia and streptococcus group A. *Journal of Neuroimmunology, 129,* 168–177.

Watters, R. G., & Watters, W. E. (1980). Decreasing self-stimulatory behavior with physical exercise in a group of autistic boys. *Journal of Autism and Developmental Disorders, 10,* 379–387.

Webster, C. D., Konstanteres, M. M., Oxman, J., & Mack, J. E. (1980). *Autism: New directions in research and education.* New York: Pergamon Press.

Wing, L., & Potter, D. (2002). The epidemiology of autistic spectrum disorders: Is prevalence rising? *Mental Retardation and Developmental Disorders, 8*(3), 151–161.

14

Physical Education for the Student with Severe Disabilities

CHAPTER OBJECTIVES

After studying this chapter, the reader should be able to:

1 Appreciate the needs and rights of students with severe disabilities and the important contribution physical activity makes in the lives of these individuals.
2 Recognize the social, cognitive, language, and motor characteristics of individuals with severe disabilities.
3 Identify successful practices that have been used in developing appropriate education programs for individuals with severe disabilities.
4 Recognize that structured learning experiences, including the use of appropriate cues and consequences and task analysis, are essential in developing success-oriented, positive experiences for students with severe disabilities.
5 Apply the principles and suggestions presented in this chapter to the teaching of physical education skills to students with severe disabilities.
6 Appreciate the importance of group instruction to the overall development of students with severe disabilities, including helping them generalize skills and make successful transitions to the community.
7 Understand the need for data-based instruction in assisting the teacher to make informed decisions concerning future instructional and program needs.
8 Serve as an informed advocate for persons with severe disabilities, emphasizing that these individuals can learn if structured learning experiences are provided.

One of the trends in the field of special education over the past 15 years has been the development of appropriate learning experiences for students with severe and profound disabilities. Historically, those who deviated significantly from the accepted societal norm were frequently committed to institutions, where they would reside for their entire lives. Those with severe disabilities were segregated, set apart, and hidden from the mainstream of public life. Unfortunately, the institutions into which individuals with severe disabilities were placed were usually underfunded and understaffed. The conditions in many of these institutions were dehumanizing and without the necessary resources to provide treatment, rehabilitation, and educational programs.

Fortunately, there is a national commitment to accept those who are severely disabled as citizens with the same basic needs and rights as all citizens. Within public schools,

for instance, it is common to find students who have significant impairments, and who require unique educational programs and instructional approaches.

Support for the educational rights of persons with severe disabilities was spearheaded by professional organizations such as the National Association for Retarded Citizens and the American Association on Mental Deficiency. Members from these groups banded together to inform the public that those with severe disabilities could benefit from education and training programs. The federal government, too, through the Office of Special Education and Rehabilitative Services, supported the cause of these individuals by funding projects designed to develop curricular materials and instructional techniques for those with severe disabilities. The formation in 1974 of The Association for Persons with Severe Handicaps (TASH), formerly known as the American Association for the Education of the Severely/Profoundly Handicapped, and its rapid membership enrollment attest to the number of professionals and parents committed to improving the educational opportunities available for individuals with severe disabling conditions. This association is now known solely as TASH (www.tash.org), and continues a strong advocacy. Its mission is to focus on people with disabilities who are:

> ... most at risk for being excluded from the mainstream of society; perceived by traditional service systems as being most challenging; most likely to have their rights abridged; most likely to be at risk for living, working, playing, and/or learning in segregated environments; least likely to have the tools and opportunities necessary to advocate on their own behalf; historically have been labeled as having severe disabilities; and, most likely to need on-going, individualized supports in order to participate in inclusive communities and enjoy a quality of life similar to that available to all citizens. (TASH, 2004)

This statement reflects the difficulties that individuals with disabilities have regarding inclusion in society in general. Physical educators working with these individuals can use this information to guide them over the years of instruction in physical activity. Certainly, over the student's academic lifetime, different supports will be required and different issues regarding exclusion will arise.

The efforts of concerned citizens, parents, and professionals on behalf of the severely disabled was rewarded in 1975 when Public Law 94-142, the Education for All Handicapped Children Act of 1975, was signed into law by President Gerald R. Ford. This law not only mandated that appropriate educational programs must be provided for *all* students with disabilities, but specified that priority consideration should be given to those with severe disabilities and those with unmet needs. Public Law 94-142 also stipulated that special education students are to be educated in the least restrictive environment. This implies that placement of children with severe disabilities in public schools is more desirable than placement in an institution.

Although the future for individuals with severe disabilities is more encouraging than in the past, much work remains in developing educational programs that are responsive to their unique needs. More personnel are needed in the field of physical education who are committed to working with individuals with severe disabilities.

Defining Severely Disabled

In earlier chapters of this book, a variety of disability populations have been discussed. It is possible that within each of these populations a certain segment could be classified as severely disabled—the severely mentally retarded, the deaf-blind, and the multiply disabled. However, in combining the severely disabled segments within these groups it becomes apparent that this population or any population of students labeled severely disabled is very heterogeneous. The only commonality found within this group is that their educational needs are such that, compared with peers of similar disability, they require greater assistance. *In essence, students with severe disabilities are individuals who are divergent in degree, not kind.* Sontag and his associates (1977) explain that individuals who are severely disabled have huge deficits in functional skills. **These severe impairments require the individuals to receive special assistance to help them function at a level consistent with their ability level.** For students who are deaf-blind this may mean special instruction to assist them to develop necessary communication skills. Students with orthopedic disabilities, unable to stand or sit, will require educational techniques that recognize the mobility limitations with which they must deal. Programs must be developed and instruction individualized to assist those with severe disabilities to overcome, to the extent possible, their functional deficits.

If services are not provided, maladaptive behavior is likely to prevail (Snell & Renzaglia, 1986). Recognizing the degree of the disability and the need for specialized services, the United States Office of Special Education has proposed the following definition: "Severely handicapped children are those who because of the intensity of their physical, mental, or emotional problems, or a combination of such problems, need educational, social, psychological, and medical services beyond those which are traditionally offered by regular and special education programs, in order to maximize their potential for useful and meaningful participation in society and for self-fulfillment."

The underlying theme of this definition is that children with severe disabilities can learn if provided with the necessary educational and support services.

TASH suggests that the term "severely disabled" should include "individuals of all ages who require extensive ongoing support in more than one major life activity in order to participate in integrated community settings and to enjoy a quality of life that is available to citizens with fewer or no disabilities" (Meyer, Peck, & Brown, 1991, p. 19). Block (1992) acknowledges that while the TASH definition is useful, it does not adequately address the profoundly disabled. He suggests that there is a difference between those with *profound* as contrasted to *severe* disabilities. Block contends that the phrase "students with profound disabilities" should refer to those with "... very limited skills in terms of awareness, movement, and communication. In addition, these students are prone to health disorders that can lead to medical complications" (Block, 1992, p. 199).

A major challenge in trying to identify or define those whose disability would be classified as severe or profound is directly related to the number of individuals with more than one disability. A few of the more common disabilities that tend to be found in combination include:

Mental Retardation. While the nature of mental retardation in and of itself creates challenges for the person who is mentally retarded and his or her teacher, the challenges become even greater when there is a secondary disability, such as cerebral palsy, hearing impairment, or behavioral problems. The concern, of course, is that the instructional adaptations required for an individual who is mildly mentally retarded may not work and/or need further adaptations when a secondary disability is present. Depending upon the nature of the secondary disability, the individual may require services and treatments more commonly reserved for those who are severely disabled.

Autism. Although there have been significant improvements in the understanding and educational treatment of individuals with autistic disorders (see chapter 13), this population continues to challenge many special and regular educators. Autism is really a combination of disabilities. For some this involves speech and communication delays, inappropriate social behavior, sensory disabilities, and significant learning delays. The syndrome of disorders associated with autism collectively place these youngsters in a high risk situation such that their disability is frequently viewed as severe or profound.

Deaf-Blind. The individual who loses one of the major senses (hearing or vision) is at a major disadvantage for many of life's activities, including the process of acquiring an education. For the individual who is without functional vision and hearing, the loss is devastating and much greater than the summative loss of two senses (i.e., the dual sensory loss is much more like a three or four sensory loss in terms of life and educational impact). It is known, however, that individuals who are deaf and blind (e.g., Helen Keller) are capable of great gains and contributions if needed family and educational support is provided. Due to the nature of the disability and the specialized skills and instruction required (see chapter 9), teachers who work with these students may find some of the suggestions and instructional approaches described in this chapter helpful.

The discussion in this section provides some examples of the type of individual who, because of the severity of a single disability or a combination of disabilities, might be viewed as someone with a severe disability. It must be emphasized, however, that this is not a complete description of all the children who might be viewed as having severe or multiple disabilities (e.g., there are many individuals who might be classified as medically fragile such that their condition would qualify as a severe or profound disability). The important point to remember is that our recent breakthroughs and educational gains with individuals with severe and profound disabilities is encouraging and a tribute to teachers who focus not on the educational challenges presented by these children, but the opportunity to help them learn and live.

Prevalence

Because of the absence of a uniform definition, the number of children with severe disabilities cannot be accurately identified. Over the years, the prevalence has ranged from 0.1 percent to 1 percent of the population. Scholars have estimated that this number has increased due to federally mandated Childfind activities.

Regardless of the number of children with severe disabilities, it is clear that school systems across the United States are now providing programs and services for these students. Given the influence of PL 94-142, PL 101-476, and the emphasis on early intervention stressed by PL 99-457, it appears likely that the number of children with severe disabilities enrolled in the public schools will continue to increase dramatically in the future.

Characteristics of Those with Severe Disabilities

Discussing the characteristics of individuals with severe disabilities is difficult, if not impossible. As indicated previously, those with severe disabilities are a heterogeneous population and the differences among the members of this population are greater than their similarities. What will be presented here, therefore, are those behaviors or conditions that are more commonly found in students with severe disabilities. It must be emphasized, however, that not all students with severe disabilities possess the characteristics described in this section and no two individuals exhibit the same behavior patterns.

Social Development

Many students with severe disabilities have difficulty interacting with others. Frequently, it appears that they are oblivious to the presence of others. Some students with severe disabilities neither initiate interactions with others nor respond when others try to interact with them. This type of behavior is more commonly observed in individuals who are severely mentally retarded and those with extreme behavior disorders.

Deficiency in performing many self-help skills is a characteristic found in some students with severe disabilities.

The ability to perform functions such as dressing, feeding, and grooming oneself may be totally absent, or present in varying degrees. Many students with severe disabilities also are unable to be toilet trained. For some individuals, such as students with spina bifida and meningomyelocele, the neurologic damage they have sustained precludes developing the necessary sphincter control. Other students with severe disabilities, however, are unable to perform self-help skills because they are developmentally delayed and have not yet mastered these essential skills.

Abnormal behaviors are also evident with some individuals with severe disabilities. These include self-abusive acts as well as behaviors that are injurious to others. Examples of self-abusive behaviors include head banging, pinching, biting, scratching, and excessively rubbing the eyes. Fortunately, the prevalence of self-abusive acts is not common, and when they do occur they are more frequent at younger ages and more common to those who are severely mentally retarded and emotionally disturbed (Corbett, 1977).

Stereotyped behaviors are also seen in some students with severe disabilities. These include bizarre acts such as rocking back and forth, waving the hands in front of the eyes, spinning objects, and making strange sounds with the mouth. Students who are deaf-blind and those with serious cognitive dysfunctions are most likely to exhibit these behaviors. Some speculate that stereotyped behaviors are caused by the individual's need for self-stimulation.

Cognitive Development

Students with severe disabilities exhibit a great deal of variation in their cognitive development. If the student's primary disability relates to an orthopedic or health impairment, it is likely that the individual's cognitive development is progressing normally, assuming that his or her education has not been interrupted for surgery and other medical reasons. Although students who are deaf-blind may experience academic problems, the difficulty may be attributed in many cases to communication problems rather than to any inherent cognitive dysfunction.

Students who are severely mentally retarded and seriously emotionally disturbed have obvious problems in cognitive development. Many of these students will be unable to respond to simple commands, identify shapes and colors, or recognize symbols and words. Some may also have difficulty recognizing family pictures and familiar surroundings. The ability to apply generalized skills learned in one setting to a different environment is also very difficult for many students who are severely mentally retarded. This does not mean, however, that essential pre-academic skills are beyond the reach of these students. Given a well-defined curriculum,

qualified instructors, and a well-designed instructional format, many educational gains can be made with any students.

Language Development

Students who are severely disabled frequently experience some problems in language development. Common problems include delays in speech and language, lack of speech clarity, and unusual speech patterns.

One of the greatest frustrations experienced by many students with severe disabilities is their inability to communicate clearly with others. For many of these individuals, speech patterns are not developed to the point that they can be easily understood. This creates a frustrating situation for the student as well as for teachers, parents, and peers. Major strides, however, have been made in technological advances to develop systems enabling those with speech impairments to communicate.

Some students with severe disabilities, particularly those with cognitive deficiencies, understand little of what is said to them. Teachers, therefore, must communicate using simple statements and gestures and observe these children closely to anticipate their needs.

Unusual speech patterns are noted in some individuals with severe disabilities. For example, some will continuously repeat certain phrases or passages that they have memorized. Students with severe mental retardation may also speak out of turn or interject a statement that is inappropriate to the topic of discussion. Some individuals may tend to repeat what is said to them. This phenomenon, which is observed in those who are severely mentally retarded and emotionally disturbed, is called echolalia. As the term implies, students repeat or echo questions or statements directed toward them.

Motor Development

Motor development delays are very common among students who are severely disabled. Specific problems that may be observed include difficulty in walking or sitting without support. Many children are unable to perform such basic tasks as rolling over, grasping objects, or holding their head up. Developmental delays are sometimes so significant that the primitive reflexes discussed in chapter 2 are either nonexistent or persist for an abnormal period of time.

Other motor development problems frequently observed in individuals with severe disabilities include deficiencies to varying degrees in the performance of motor tasks that involve strength, flexibility, agility, coordination, and reactions. With those who are more severely involved, problems in gross motor development are usually attributed to central nervous system damage.

An increasing number of universities with teacher education programs in the area of the severely disabled require courses in the field of motor development. There is also evidence that some departments of physical education recognize that it is necessary to provide coursework in the field of physical education on physical activity for individuals with severe disabilities if quality movement experiences are to be provided for this unique population.

Heward and Orlansky (1992) have summarized the characteristics of children with severe disabilities as follows:

1. Little or no communication
2. Delayed physical and motor development
3. Frequent inappropriate behavior
4. Deficits in self-help skills
5. Infrequent constructive behavior and interaction

While this list may paint a picture of those with severe disabilities as negative, it is important to emphasize that significant gains can be made when appropriate educational services and programs are provided. Given the right educational, medical, and family treatment, the positive attributes of this population become very apparent. **Again, individuals with severe disabilities are not homogeneous. It is important to note that some individuals with severe disabilities do not have intellectual deficits, but rather severe physical disabilities.** An adult example is Professor Stephen Hawking, a brilliant British theoretical physicist with severe disabilities caused by amyotrophic lateral sclerosis (also known as Lou Gehrig's disease). He does not have cognitive deficits but requires extensive support both to care for himself and conduct his professional life, yet his contribution to physics has been dramatic, extensive, and thought-provoking.

Planning the Physical Activity Program

The need to provide appropriate physical education experiences for those who are severely disabled is readily acknowledged by most educators. Desire, concern, and care, however, are not enough to respond to the unique problems evident in this population. Likewise, placing these students in the traditional physical education class and expecting them to respond in an appropriate fashion to the instruction provided is inadequate. What is needed are structured learning experiences to help them benefit from instruction. This means that what is to be taught, how the material is to be presented, why something is taught, and when the skill is to be achieved must be carefully developed and structured by the teacher. Several investigators (Dunn, Morehouse, & Fredericks, 1986; Jansma, 1982; Stainback, Stainback, Wehman, & Spangiers, 1983) have emphasized that those

with severe disabilities can benefit from physical activity programs if instruction is provided in a systematic and consistent manner.

Principles of Program Development

The following are general principles that should be adhered to in the development of quality physical education experiences for students with severe disabilities. Many of these concepts were developed at Oregon State University after extensive field testing with students enrolled in the National Model Program for Severely Handicapped Children conducted by Teaching Research in Monmouth, Oregon (Dunn, Morehouse, & Fredericks, 1986).

1. Every student, regardless of disabling condition, can learn. This is an important principle that must be continually emphasized in educational programs for those with severe disabilities. Occasionally the educational gains may be so small as to appear insignificant, but as long as there is progress the student is benefiting from the program. If the student is not learning, then the teacher must experiment by (a) changing the method used to present material, (b) employing a different technique to reinforce the student, or (c) reducing the task to be learned to smaller steps.

2. Physical education is an integral component of the educational curriculum for students with severe disabling conditions. As an important area, it is essential, therefore, that physical education programs adhere to the same standards expected of other areas. Instructional programs should be sequenced, task-analyzed, and data-based so that performance changes in physical education skills can be determined.

3. Students with severe disabilities learn at a slower rate than other students. This means that they will require more extensive and intensive education to compensate for their slower learning rates. Because it is generally impossible to extend the time of the school day, maximum use of the time available will require that parents and volunteers assume responsibility for conducting part of the instruction.

4. There is no way of determining the extent to which a student with severe disabilities will progress. Therefore, no ceiling is placed on the physical education curriculum. The teacher must be prepared to take the student as far and as rapidly as possible. Physical education curricular materials should extend from very basic skills such as executing various body movements while standing to more advanced game skills such as catching and throwing.

5. Effective instruction for those who are severely disabled frequently requires that programs be conducted in a one-to-one relationship. This is necessary because of

the heterogeneous nature of the population and the behavior problems sometimes evident with this population. The utilization of trained volunteers is necessary, therefore, to provide individualized instruction in the gymnasium.

6. Physical education experiences for students with severe disabilities must be designed to ensure student success. Many students with severe disabilities have found previous educational experiences very frustrating. Teachers must be sensitive to this possibility and the all-too-common attitude of "I can't." This can best be dealt with by structuring educational experiences in such a way that success is guaranteed.

Employing these principles requires that educators, in cooperation with parents and surrogates as part of the IEP process, review carefully a few overriding issues related to the education of the individual who is severely or profoundly involved. Some of these important issues are detailed in the following sections.

Placement

It is generally acknowledged that the educational needs of individuals with severe disabilities are such that a highly structured, specialized program taught by a specialist is required. This may or may not be true. As Block and Krebs (1992) have emphasized, the goal of all educational programs is to make as many adaptations as possible within the general program such that no student, regardless of his/her disability, would be excluded automatically from contact with peers in general physical education. Within this chapter, many of the educational concepts, even one-to-one instructional approaches, have been employed with students who are severely involved and are in the general physical education program. While this approach does not necessarily lead to direct interaction with nondisabled peers and involvement in the activities engaged in by other children, it does ensure that the student is part of the general educational program. Such an approach, as is emphasized later in this chapter, requires that the teacher develop skills as an instructional manager and undertake the training of a cadre of volunteers, including peers, to serve as instructional assistants (Block, 2000; Choi, Meeuwsen, French, Sherrill, & McCabe, 2001; Lieberman & Houston-Wilson, 2002). While these "extras" require teacher time and energy, more and more teachers and schools recognize that direct interaction between students who are severely involved and their peers is beneficial to the entire school and community (Obrusnikova, Valkova, & Block, 2003; Vogler, Koranda, & Romance, 2000).

There are, of course, times when students with severe disabilities will benefit from instruction outside of the general physical education program. For example, the use of specialized instructional or health-related equipment may lead to temporary separate placements. Also, many students with severe disabilities will benefit from supplementary or intensive instruction. Even in these situations, however, it is difficult to justify total isolation from peers for an extended period of time. **As Block (1992) has emphasized, the principle of partial participation suggests that through the use of available technology and creative teachers, all students can enjoy some participation in natural environments.**

Age-Appropriate and Functional Curriculum

One of the challenges of teaching and working with those who are severely and profoundly disabled is to avoid the trap of teaching concepts, games, and activities that are not age appropriate or functionally appropriate. For example, using musical chairs as an activity with fifteen- and sixteen-year-old individuals who are severely mentally retarded would not be an age-appropriate activity.

Proponents of a developmental approach to physical education will need to exercise care in how programs to teach selected concepts are sequenced. For example, some developmentalists will not introduce an activity (e.g., roller skating) unless all of the prerequisite balance skills are demonstrated. For some individuals with severe disabilities, this can be devastating because they may have some success with the activity without having all of the prerequisite skills in place. For additional examples of chronologically age-appropriate activities, please refer to table 14.1.

Functional skills refer to those skills used frequently in natural settings, including the work and play environment (e.g., recreational settings). Unfortunately, many individuals with severe and profound disabilities are frequently taught essential skills using inappropriate settings. For example, it does little good to teach an individual to go up and down fabricated steps if the goal is to use stepping up and down in functional settings (e.g., going up and down the steps in the school, home, or for purposes of boarding a bus). In physical education activities, the goal is to use meaningful activities that are as close to the functional skill as possible. For example, functional activity is having the student who is deaf-blind substitute throwing the ball when "batting" is far less functional for them. A functional curriculum in special education, also referred to as a community-referenced curriculum, is developed from a top-down approach (Brown et al., in Colarusso & O'Rourke, 2003) ". . . where goals and objectives are defined by the skills needed in the settings in which we want the student to function. These settings include home, school, neighborhood shops and services, leisure and work settings" (p. 362). The bottom-up approach is developmental where chronological age determines skills taught.

TABLE 14.1   Chronological Age-Appropriate Activities and Sample Modifications for Elementary-Age Students with Profound Disabilities

Age-Appropriate Activities	Modifications
Manipulative patterns	
Throwing	Pushing a ball down a ramp, grasp and release
Catching	Tracking suspended balls, reaching for balloons
Kicking	Touching balloon taped to floor, pushing ball down ramp with foot
Striking	Hitting ball off tee; hitting suspended ball
Locomotor patterns	
Running	Being pushed quickly in wheelchair while keeping head up
Jumping/hopping	Lifting head up and down while being pushed in wheelchair
Galloping/skipping	Moving arms up and down while being pushed in wheelchair; also, student can use adapted mobility aids such as scooterboards and walkers
Perceptual-motor skills	
Balance skills	Propping up on elbows, balancing prone over wedge
Body awareness	Accepting tactile input, attempting to imitate simple movements
Spatial awareness	Moving arms in when going in between, ducking head under objects
Visual-motor coordination	Tracking suspended objects, attempting to touch switches that activate visually stimulating toys
Physical fitness skills	
Endurance	Tolerate continuous activity, move body parts repeatedly
Strength	Use stretch bands, use isometric exercises
Flexibility	Perform range-of-motion activities as suggested by PT

Note: In all activities, utilize the principle of partial participation to ensure that the student is successful.

Taken from Block, M. E. (1992). What is appropriate physical education for students with profound disabilities? *Adapted Physical Activity Quarterly,* 9(2), p. 201.

Mastery in the skill area allows the student to move onto the next developmental skill. This approach has been applied to physical education by Burton as described in chapter 3 (Burton & Miller, 1998) and is not recommended for persons with severe physical limitations. Figures 14.1*A* and *B* are examples of activities engaged in using a top-down approach rather than bottom-up.

Community-Based

One of the essential goals of any good instructional program for students with severe and profound disabilities is to use the skills learned in natural community-based settings. In earlier years, many thought that this could be accomplished by first teaching the skill in a non-natural setting and then transferring the skill to the real setting (e.g., teaching individuals to bowl in the gymnasium and then expecting them to transfer these skills to the community bowling lane). This approach entailed much relearning and has proved to not be very efficient. The challenge, of course, is developing a strategy that will provide access to community-based settings with minimal cost and interruption in the daily school or instructional schedule. Some have overcome this problem by simulating to the greatest extent possible the community setting in teaching the skill (e.g., roller skating with intermittent trips to the "real" setting when possible). Coordinated planning with parents and surrogates can help to move in the direction of an exciting community-based approach to instruction.

Choice-Making

The concept of choice-making in its simplest terms suggests that everyone should be allowed to make decisions and to have input in the activities planned for him or her. One of the most refreshing advances in the education of students

Figure 14.1 *(A)* and *(B)* Physical activities can be engaged using a top-down approach to instruction.

with severe and profound disabilities addresses the concept of choice-making. And it is now clear that everyone should have some control and choice in daily activities. In the physical education setting, this might mean allowing the individual to choose the ball to be thrown or allowing the individual to indicate whether he or she wishes to continue or to stop an activity. Effective instructional strategy, of course, will structure the choices (e.g., limit the number of balls from which to choose) such that the desired educational goals and objectives can be reached.

Block (1992), in emphasizing many of the previous points, has suggested that the ideal curriculum for the student with a severe or profound disability would be based on a functional, life-skills curricular model. This approach would include age-appropriate and functional activities, taught in natural settings, adhering to the principles of partial participation and choice-making, and using data-based instructional strategies.

Instructional Procedures

Educators generally recognize that students with severe disorders will benefit from instruction designed to improve their physical and motor fitness levels. One could even argue that because the motor needs of those with severe disabilities are so great, they will benefit more than their higher-functioning peers from specially designed movement experiences. However, there is little information available in the physical education literature that focuses on teaching strategies for working with this population. More is known about ineffective educational strategies than about procedures that have been found to be helpful. For example, it is clear that individuals who are severely and profoundly disabled will not be successful in the general physical education

program without needed support and services. Serious motor deficiencies and failure to respond cognitively to basic game and activity structure present challenges that require special instructional techniques and approaches.

The technique most frequently employed to teach those who are severely disabled is known as behavior modification (see chapter 5), also known in special education as behavioral prompting strategies. This approach is based on educational curriculum that is delivered in a direct, systematic, and consistent manner. The instruction clearly identifies for the student the behavior to be performed, as well as the consequences of performing or not performing the behavior. The teacher must identify the skill to be taught, as well as the materials, opportunity, cues, environment, and resulting expected outcome (Colarusso & O'Rourke, 2003). The sequence of *antecedent* (e.g., materials, cues), *behavior* (skill(s)), *consequence* is referred to as A-B-C (see figure 14.2). The essence of this approach is that the instructor makes maximum and efficient use of the environment to assist a student in learning a behavior (defined skill). Physical educators are becoming more aware of this instructional strategy and the positive manner in which behavior modification or reinforcement strategies can be employed to assist the severely disabled learn basic movement skills. Dunn and associates (1986) have successfully utilized a modified behavioral approach to teach physical education to individuals with severe disabilities. In this section, selected components of their approach will be presented.

Physical Activity Considerations

Throughout this chapter it has been emphasized that educational programs for the severely involved must be systematically designed. An important element in achieving this

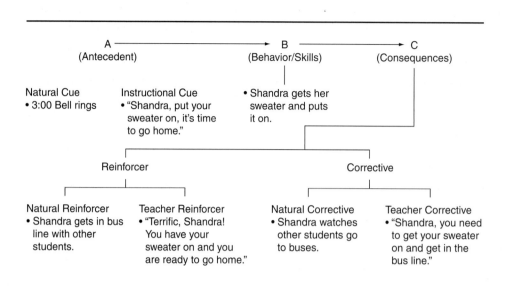

Figure 14.2 A-B-C Analysis of behavior

goal is to develop a curriculum that specifies the individual functional life skills or behaviors considered essential. Each behavior must be presented in a task-analyzed format so that elements of the task from least to most difficult can be identified. For example, in the *Oregon State University Data Based Curriculum for the Severely Handicapped,* skills have been divided into four broad sections.

> **Section 1, Movement Concepts, deals with movement through space in one's immediate personal environment to movement skills in more complex environments.**
> **Section 2 includes skills found in many of our popular elementary games.**
> **Section 3 includes physical fitness skills essential for survival in modern society.**
> **Section 4 focuses on age-appropriate leisure skills, including activities such as those enjoyed by young children, such as tricycle riding and swinging.**

An important preliminary consideration related to curriculum development is the critical decision of what to teach. Obviously, this decision is determined by the educational needs of each individual student. This implies, therefore, that some type of educational assessment be utilized. In choosing an appropriate test to use with those who are severely disabled, Jansma (1982) recommends that the test should be

A. developmentally low with respect to comprehension and performance,
B. observational in nature, and
C. accompanied by curriculum/programming ideas.

Given these guidelines and the heterogeneous nature of this population, criterion-referenced tests are the preferred evaluation method for determining the students' functioning levels. If the curricular materials are sequentially developed, the criterion for each behavior or skill in the curriculum can be used as a means of determining students' abilities. This would necessitate that students be evaluated on selected behaviors within the curriculum to determine areas of strength and weakness and, ultimately, to make decisions about where educational programming should begin (Jansma, 1993).

A qualified teacher is needed to implement the curriculum and to respond to the educational needs of students with severe disabilities. Although the person selected to fulfill this assignment will vary from school to school, the professionals chosen most frequently are either special educators or physical educators. Preferably, the individual selected should also have additional training in the area of working with individuals with disabilities. **The best approach is one in which the special educator and physical educator cooperatively develop the student's motor and physical fitness program.** The special educator can contribute information about the student's behavior patterns and language capabilities. The physical educator would assume responsibility for the design of the physical education program and the instructional procedures to be utilized.

The physical education teacher also must be prepared to serve as an instructional *manager,* making decisions about the student's physical education program but not providing all of the direct teaching. Students with major disabilities require educational settings in which they are instructed individually or in small groups. This requires, therefore, that the teacher be provided time to recruit, train, and supervise volunteers to provide the needed one-to-one instruction.

The utilization of parents is also an essential part of the instructional team. Effective instruction can be carried out by parents at home. Parents can serve to not only maintain skills learned in physical education, but also actually accelerate learning. Maguire (1985) found that parents of children with severe disabilities successfully provided home-based instruction in physical education after training. Children who received instruction from their parents as a supplement to the school physical education program progressed more rapidly than those children who received only the school program.

Thus, coordination with parents is an important element in enhancing the motor and physical fitness of students with severe disabilities.

Educational Approach in Physical Activity

Educators generally agree that the learning and behavior needs of those with severe disabilities are such that structure and careful planning are essential in developing educational programs. Ludlow and Sobsey observe that "Precise behavioral objectives, task analysis, and other individualized instructional techniques combine to form a powerful teaching process" (1984, p. 22) for students with severe learning needs. Heward and Orlansky (1992) believe that the following components must be given careful consideration in the development of instructional programs for students with severe disabilities.

1. The student's current level of performance must be precisely assessed.
2. The skill to be taught must be defined clearly.
3. The skills must be ordered in an appropriate sequence.
4. The teacher must provide a clear cue or instruction to the child.
5. The child must receive feedback and reinforcement from the teacher.
6. The teacher should include strategies to facilitate generalization of learning.
7. The child's performance must be carefully measured and evaluated.

According to Colarusso and O'Rourke (2003), the characteristics of a student with moderate to severe mental retardation should be taken into account: skills will be learned and will require more instructional opportunities (trials). Thus, the teacher should prioritize what is most functionally

important for the student to learn given the time available in a school year. There is an inability to generalize from one situation to the next, therefore, context is important when teaching a skill. To the extent possible, learning should take place in the environment where the skills will be used. Memory may be affected, so skills selected for learning must occur frequently in the student's daily life. Attention is given to both relevant and irrelevant stimuli. Therefore, prompting to gain student attention is important. Synthesizing information is difficult and task analyzing skills into component parts facilitates learning. Skills are taught directly. Systematic instruction in social skills is required and varied practice is needed for application across individuals and settings in the home, school, and community. Finally, a functional behavioral assessment may be conducted to identify a plan to deal with challenging behaviors in the classroom (e.g., head banging, hitting others, rocking/flapping).

The following principles have been applied successfully to physical education programs for students with severe disabilities by Dunn, Morehouse, and Fredericks (1986). The procedures used to implement some of these principles are described in the following section.

The basic learning approach for teaching physical activities requires that careful attention be given to three important variables:

1. the method used to present material,
2. the complexity of the behavior the student is asked to perform, and
3. the procedure used to reinforce or correct the student. Each of these variables will be discussed in the following paragraphs.

Cuing Students with Severe Disabilities

The cue is the sign, signal, request, or information that calls for the occurrence of a behavior. Cues are those things in the environment that "set the occasion" for the student to behave. For instance, "Come to me, Johnny" is a cue for the student to respond to verbal instructions and to move toward the teacher. The presentation of a ball that the student is to throw is a cue. Thus, a cue can take the form of any instructional materials, verbal, printed, or gestural, that are presented to a student. The concept of cue includes all the verbal instructions by the teacher. It includes the gestures of the teacher as well as the way in which objects or materials are presented.

Cues may be ordered according to their level of complexity. Although many students with disabilities respond to verbal cues, this is very difficult for individuals with severe disorders. The cues used by teachers must be specific and easily understood. Cues are often referred to as prompts, and a prompt hierarchy is employed using a sequence. The following sequence has been found to be effective in teaching those with severe disabilities:

1. Verbal cue is given—student is told what to do. If the student does not respond or responds incorrectly, go to step 2.
2. A demonstration of the skill (visual cue) is combined with the verbal cue. If the student does not respond or responds incorrectly, go to step 3.
3. A demonstration of the skill (visual cue) is combined with the verbal cue and the student is given help in the form of manual physical assistance (figure 14.3) (see chapter 5). Gradations in the amount of physical assistance provided (e.g., heavy—manually moving a body part, to light—touching or tapping the body part) are also possible.

Obviously, the intent of this hierarchy is to help students perform physical tasks at the highest cue level possible. While a verbal cue is a higher-level prompt, some students will not move to that level for some time. For these students, a visual and verbal combination is the highest cue possible. Special care must be taken to utilize verbal cues that are sensitive to the age of the individual. With verbal cues, the tone of voice, inflections, and terms should be appropriate to the individual's age. Using the student's name in the verbal cue is recommended, for example, "Mark, throw the ball."

Figure 14.3 Physical assistance is an instructional technique frequently used with students who have special needs.

Analyzing the Behavior to Be Taught

The second variable that must be considered in teaching students with severe disabilities is to analyze carefully the behaviors to be taught. A behavior is anything a person does. It includes lifting a little finger, blinking an eye, kicking a ball, or climbing a rope. In the teaching of students, a behavior is a particular task that the student is to learn. Behavior can be something as simple as having the student extend the arms or as complex as having the student bat a pitched ball.

When teaching a behavior, however, the teacher should constantly keep in mind that most behaviors can be divided into smaller behaviors or pieces of behavior. It is these pieces of behavior that make up the teaching sequence. Take, for instance, riding a tricycle. Riding a tricycle is called a terminal behavior. Yet, it is comprised of a number of small behaviors—mounting the tricycle, placing the feet on the pedals, pushing the pedals, turning the tricycle, stopping, and so on, step by step until the tricycle can be ridden. The smaller or less difficult behaviors are called *enabling* behaviors. The learning of them enables the student to learn the terminal behavior.

This process of breaking down a terminal behavior into the enabling behaviors is called analysis of behavior or task analysis (see chapter 5). Breaking the behaviors or tasks down into smaller steps helps the physical education teacher to create instructional settings geared toward student success. As additional behaviors are learned, these are combined so that ultimately the student performs the terminal behavior. Nietupski, Hamre-Nietupski, and Ayres (1984) report that there is ample evidence to support the use of task-analytic procedures as effective in the instruction of leisure skills, including physical fitness tasks, to those who are moderately and severely disabled.

Consequences

Consequences are the third major variable that must be considered in developing effective instructional programs for students with severe disabilities. Consequences can be likened to a feedback system. After the student performs a particular behavior, feedback or a consequence for that performance is provided. This consequence tells students that what they did was correct or incorrect. In a school setting one might think of the student taking a motor fitness test and having the test score interpreted as a consequence of the way the individual performed. The consequence can either be pleasing or displeasing to the person receiving it. A consequence that is pleasing to a person is called a reinforcer; a consequence that is displeasing used to be referred to as a punisher, but now is referred to as a corrective. The basic concept underlying utilization of consequences is that the reinforcers delivered following a behavior increase the probability of the behavior occurring again; correctives delivered following a behavior decrease that probability.

A reinforcer must be pleasurable to the person experiencing it. Because it is pleasurable and because the person desires that pleasure and associates a particular behavior with the receipt of the reinforcer, a reinforcer by definition increases the probability of a behavior recurring. The student who enjoys social praise may increase the quality or quantity of his or her performance after being told, "You're doing a nice job!" Consequently, reinforcers by definition must be individualized because what is pleasing and, therefore, reinforcing to one person may not be pleasing and reinforcing to another. The principle of individualization also applies to punishers. A verbal reprimand may be severely punishing (displeasing) to one student whereas another student may not perceive that same reprimand as punishing. Therefore, correctives, like reinforcers, must be individualized.

A basic rule in the use of consequences is to rely, if at all possible, on the natural consequences of the environment. Fortunately, in the physical education environment there are many activities and experiences that in themselves are reinforcing, such as watching the movement of a ball after it is rolled. For some, however, the natural consequences of the environment are not sufficient and it may be necessary to identify other types of reinforcers to utilize with the student. This may be accomplished by exchanging ideas with the special education teacher and the student's parents, and subsequently coordinating the use of types of reinforcers decided upon.

Maintaining Data

The effectiveness of the instructional process is determined by reviewing data maintained on each student. For example, in the Oregon State University system, data are initially kept on each instructional trial. Therefore, every time a student is cued, an X indicating the student performed the skill correctly or an O indicating the student did not perform the skill correctly is recorded on the data sheet. A daily review of the data helps the teacher to update the student's program for the next day. If, for example, it is apparent that after ten trials (or another designated number) the student has yet to do the skill correctly, the teacher must review the elements of instruction (cue, behavior, and consequences) and make the appropriate changes. Frequently, the problem relates to a need to further analyze the behavior into smaller steps (task analysis). It is also possible that the cue or method of "consequating" the student should be modified. The ultimate criterion of a successful program is whether the student is learning. Morehouse (1988), in employing the Data

Based Gymnasium Model, reported that using three consecutive executions of physical activity tasks was an effective criterion standard. Using the three consecutive criteria as a rule of thumb provides the physical education teacher with guidance in determining when to advance to the next step in the task analysis. Maintaining data provides the teacher with an excellent opportunity to make informed decisions about student progress. Focusing on the elements in the instructional process—the cue, behavior, and consequences—helps the teacher to make adjustments, when necessary, in a systematic manner.

Managing the Instructional System

The instructional elements described previously must be coordinated into a system that is practical and efficient for the teacher to manage. This requires that information on each student in the program be readily available and in a format that is easy to use. In the Oregon State University system, a clipboard record is developed for each student, on which pertinent information related to instructional procedures is maintained (figure 14.4). In keeping with HIPAA regulations as mentioned in chapter 2, the clipboard may need a cover sheet that literally covers the information so that information is private and can be used only by the teachers and aides for the instructional program. That said, the clipboard describes in detail what to do with each student, where to record the information (data), and how to interact with the student. It is the "communication channel" through which information to volunteers is provided by the teacher. The clipboard also provides a mechanism whereby feedback comes to the teacher so that the student's individualized program can be modified.

Each student's clipboard contains the weekly cover sheet specifying all programs, including the physical education programs in which the student is currently engaged (figure 14.4). A student may be engaged in as many as five to twelve programs, such as physical education (underhand roll), eating (finger foods), and writing (reproduced shapes). The number of programs will be determined by the student's capability and number of volunteers available to conduct each program.

Immediately following the weekly cover sheet on the clipboard is the consequence list and language file (see figure 14.5 on page 321). The consequence list identifies things that are reinforcing to the student. This list provides the teacher and volunteer with information about reinforcers for the student. On the sheet with the consequence list is a section for general comments. Included here are instructional tips that the teacher has found successful in working with the student.

Weekly Cover Sheet

Name   John Q.

Program	M	T	W	Th	F
1. Game Skills Basic—underhand roll					
2. Personal Space—move arms up and down					
3. Self-Help Skills—button coat					
4. Writing—reproduce shapes					
5. Color—recognize primary colors					
6. Language—recognize prepositions					
7.					
8.					
9.					
10.					

Figure 14.4 Weekly cover sheet.

The language section is divided into three parts:

1. receptive language,
2. expressive language, and
3. new vocabulary.

The receptive language section defines the degree of understanding the student has of spoken language. The expressive language section describes the degree of language capability to be expected of the student. The new vocabulary section includes new words or sounds the student has acquired that need to be reinforced. In all programs, including physical education, the consequence and language sheet are used by all teachers and volunteers. Whether in the gymnasium or in the classroom, consistency in behavior treatment and communication procedures is essential for successful programming.

Following the consequence file and language sheet are three sheets (a behavioral sequence sheet, a program cover sheet, and a data sheet) for each program listed on the weekly cover sheet. The behavioral sequence sheet (see figure 14.6 on page 322) contains an example of a task analysis of one skill and the program cover sheet (figure 14.7) describes how a sample program is to be run. The latter enables the volunteer to see what the verbal and nonverbal cues are, materials to be used, the reinforcement ratio, and the criterion level of success. This information helps the volunteer conduct the program as designed by the teacher. The last form is the data sheet (see figure 14.8 on page 323). Taking data assists the teacher in reviewing the student's performance so that an informed decision can be made to update the program appropriately for the following day.

Once criterion for a skill has been reached, it is essential that the skill be used if it is to be retained. The effectiveness of efforts to help students with severe disabilities maintain skills can be monitored by making periodic checks to evaluate the degree to which students perform the skill. In the Oregon State University system, this is accomplished by placing all skills that have been learned by each student into a maintenance file. The student is then asked to demonstrate the skill at scheduled times during the six-month period following the date on which the student reached the desired criterion level.

Group Physical Activity

Students with severe disabilities, as previously discussed, frequently require an instructional setting of one instructor to one student. Insufficient motor and physical fitness levels necessitate an approach in which students with severe disabilities can receive intense instruction to offset their movement deficiencies. **As the basic foundational skills are gained, however, the student should be provided the opportunity to generalize the skills learned to instructional situations involving more students.** When several students share equipment, take turns, and receive group directions, new opportunities are created to allow those who are severely involved to respond to experiences similar to those found in many physical education activities.

Indicated in the following paragraphs are some suggested developmental stages for helping students to progress from individual instruction to group instruction. Not all students

Language File, Consequence File, and General Comments

Child's Name: John Q.

Reinforcement File

    PRIMARY / TANGIBLE:

       Swinging on a rope

       Playing with a ball

       Turning a kaleidoscope

       Rubbing a stuffed animal

SOCIAL: (Examples)

    "Give me five"

    "Nice going"

    "Super job"

    "Right on"

    Smile

Receptive Language

      Be sure John is attending prior to giving cue

      Make eye contact with John

      John responds to two concept commands

Expressive Language

      John will emit one and two word responses

      Require John to respond verbally to questions

      If John wants something have him ask for it

General Comments

      John must keep his hands to himself before delivering a new cue

      John is right handed

      Conduct the behavior treatment program if John strikes someone

Figure 14.5 Language and consequence files.

with severe disabilities will be able to progress to Stage VI. The student should be taken as far as possible consistent with the individual's needs and ability to be successful.

Stage I (Individual)

As described in the previous section, the basic intent of this stage is to ensure that students can learn in a systematic way given that appropriate cues and corrective procedures are used. One teacher or volunteer is necessary for each student.

Stage II (Advanced Individual)

This stage is similar to stage I but two or three students are assigned to each teacher. Again the attempt is to provide systematic instruction, with the teacher conducting programs,

GAME SKILLS, BASIC

A. Underhand Roll

Terminal Objective:	Student, from a standing position, will perform an underhand roll by swinging the arm backward and then forward while stepping forward simultaneously with the opposite foot and releasing the ball at the end of the swing in the direction of the target.
Prerequisite Skills:	Gross Motor, DD; Fine Motor Skills, A and G.
Phase I	Sitting in a chair, swing arm backward and then forward, releasing ball.
Phase II	Standing with knees bent, swing arm backward and then forward, releasing ball.
Phase III	Standing with one foot forward and one foot back, and knees bent, swing arm backward and then forward, releasing ball.
Phase IV	Standing with knees bent, swing arm backward and then forward, releasing ball while simultaneously stepping forward with the opposite foot.
Teaching Notes:	1. For those students in wheelchairs, the underhand roll can be performed with the student sitting in the wheelchair, thus eliminating the need for the above prerequisite body positions.
	2. For nonambulatory students who are not in a wheelchair, ball rolling could be taught from a supported sitting position.
	3. When students have problems with timing the step and throw, the teacher may choose to physically assist, and/or prompt the foot during the throw.

Suggested Materials: A tennis ball and a 3-foot x 3-foot target placed on the floor. Any type or size of ball may be used to facilitate learning.

Figure 14.6 An example of one skill from the Oregon State University *Game, Exercise, and Leisure Sport Curriculum.*

Figure 14.7 Example of a program cover sheet.

PUPIL: John Q. DATE STARTED: October 3, 1996 DATE COMPLETED:	PROGRAM: Game Skills, Basic—A. Underhand Roll
SETTING (NONVERBAL CUE): Establish eye contact with John prior to delivering the cue.	MATERIALS: Clipboard Pencil Chair Ball 3-foot x 3-foot target
INSTRUCTIONAL PROCESS: Verbal Cue — John, roll the ball underhand. Model — Demonstrate if the response to the verbal cue is incorrect. Physical Assistance — Provide assistance if the response to the verbal cue and demonstration is incorrect.	CRITERION: Three consecutive responses before moving to the next phase.

Reinforcer	Phase	Step	Trials											Comments	Date
Social	I		0	0	0	X	X	0	0	0	X	0	Has trouble attending	3/8
Social	I		0	0	X	X	0	(X	X	X)			Seems to have the idea	3/9
Social	II		0	X	0	X	0	0	X	0	X	X	Needs help with backward swing	3/10
Social	II		X	0	(X	X	X)						Good day	3/11
Social	III		0	0	X	0	X	0	(X	X	X)		Has the idea	3/12
Social	IV		0	X	0	0	0	X	0	0	X	0	Has difficulty with step	3/15
Social	IV		X	0	X	0	(X	X	X)					3/16
Maintenance															

Figure 14.8 Example of a program data sheet for the underhand roll.

alternating from student to student. This stage allows for early peer interaction and creates opportunities for students to observe the skill performance of others.

Stage III (Transition)

The ultimate goal of this stage is to advance students from the instructor-directed individual setting in which specific cues are used to a generalized instructional format. The students are given general directions and are then assigned an area within the gymnasium to practice specific skills. Each student is expected to function independently at the assigned station, with the teacher assisted by volunteers providing direct instructional cues when needed.

Stage IV (Skills with Peer Interaction)

Stage IV is an advancement over stage III because at this level students interact with one another through the medium of various skills; in other words, students practice skills together. One student, for instance, may practice rolling a ball while another student practices trapping the ball. The important element in this stage is the emphasis on creating opportunities for peers to interact. If the student can successfully perform at this stage, it is possible that the individual will be able to achieve success and to participate more fully in the regular physical education program.

Stage V (Basic Games)

In this stage, students are provided an opportunity to play basic games using two sequenced skills, such as hitting and running to first. The fielder in this example would field and then throw to first. Many elementary games could be introduced at this level. The primary point to remember is that no more than two skills should be sequenced. Students with severe disabilities need opportunities to learn phases of a game before they are introduced to the complexity of the total activity. Some may never progress beyond learning certain aspects of the game.

Stage VI (Intermediate Games)

This stage is an advancement over stage V because students are now asked to sequence three skills. A student, for example, might be asked to hit a ball, run to first, and then return to home plate. Another example might be to catch a pass, dribble the basketball to the basket, and then shoot the ball. Obviously, sequencing three skills requires not only an advanced skill level but also high receptive and expressive abilities.

The appropriate stage for each student may change from day to day depending upon the skill to be learned and the ability of the student. It must be emphasized, however, that a student who is severely disabled must experience some success at stages I and II before the individual is faced with the challenges inherent in the more advanced stages.

The key to group experiences for students with severe disabilities is to allow for as much independence as possible. For example, some students will respond very well to stage III (transition), where the teacher provides general cues (directions) to the class and then assigns each student to a particular station to practice a specific skill. In this situation, the student is expected to respond to very natural cues. For example, the presence of a bucket of balls means to throw the balls one at a time at a target using an overhand throw. When the teacher notices an error in performance or behavior, a nondirective cue can be used. For example, if the student is not throwing with the correct arm, the teacher might ask, "Mary, which arm do you throw with?" If the response is correct a mild positive social reinforcer should be used, such as saying, "okay." If Mary continues to throw with the wrong arm, then a direct verbal cue is necessary such as, "Mary, throw with the *other* arm." Occasionally, it may be necessary to move to the next cue level, the use of a model, or demonstration. If this is not successful, physical assistance should be used to ensure that the student experiences success and comprehends the verbal information.

The ultimate goal is to use natural cues when possible and move as necessary to teacher-directed cues. An overview of the cue hierarchy system is presented in figure 14.9.

During group programming, data must be maintained to determine the effectiveness of the program. The emphasis on trial-by-trial data found in stages I and II is replaced in the more advanced stages by taking data only on two of the student's trials. For example, in the Group Data Sheet for five students participating at a stage III instructional level (figure 14.10), the students are working on the same motor skill—kicking. It is quite acceptable, however, for the teacher to create situations in which students work on different skills, having the students rotate from station to station. In this situation, the teacher has a separate data sheet with the name of each student listed for each specific skill. For the more advanced stages, V and VI, the data sheet is very similar to that used in stage III except for the name of the program and the identification of the phase. As indicated in figure 14.11 on page 326, the students are at stage V, working on a two-part motor skill sequence, kicking a ball and running to a base. The phases and steps of the skills are not identified. The focus of the instruction and, therefore, the data collection is to ensure that the student can sequence the skill, successfully relying on natural cues. It cannot be emphasized too strongly that each of the stages used in group instruction can be implemented in the general physical education class. In many

Figure 14.9   Cue hierarchy system. (*Source*: Dunn, J. M., & Morehouse, J. W. *Leadership Training*. Corvallis, OR: Oregon State University, Department of Physical Education.)

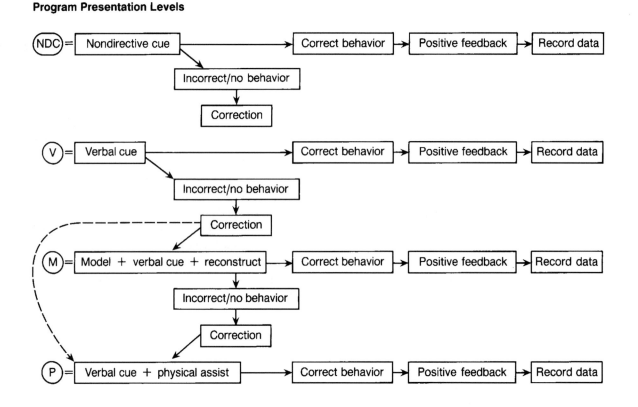

Program Presentation Levels

Group Data Sheet

Skill: ___Kicking___

Stage: ___III___

Names

Sam	**Date**	3/10/96		3/11/96		3/12/96		
	Phase/Step	VI	1	VI	1	VI	1	
	Data	O	X	O	X			
Jenny	**Date**	3/10/96		3/11/96		3/12/96		
	Phase/Step	VI	1	VI	1	VI	2	
	Data	X	O	X	X			
Paul	**Date**	3/10/96		3/11/96		3/12/96		
	Phase/Step	VI	1	VI	1	VI	1	
	Data	O	O	X	O			
Dick	**Date**	3/10/96		3/11/96		3/12/96		
	Phase/Step	VI	1	VI	1	VI	1	
	Data	X	O	O	X			
Ann	**Date**	3/10/96		3/11/96		3/12/96		
	Phase/Step	VI	1	VI	1	VI	2	
	Data	O	X	X	X			
	Date							
	Phase/Step							
	Data							
	Date							
	Phase/Step							
	Data							

Figure 14.10 Group data sheet, stage III. (*Source*: Dunn, J. M., Morehouse, J. W., & Fredericks, H. D. (1986). *Physical Education for the Severely Handicapped*. Austin, TX: Pro-Ed Publishers, p. 122.)

instances, this approach will resemble a side-by-side instructional environment, where the student or students with severe disabilities would occupy an area in the gymnasium along with the students participating in the regular instructional activities. To do this successfully, however, requires the use of volunteers, including appropriately trained peers. These individuals can be assigned by the teacher to assist students with severe learning needs who require systematic instruction, including the use of carefully developed individualized cues and consequences. The goal, of course, is to maximize, to the extent possible, the interaction between individuals with severe disabilities and their nondisabled classmates.

The purpose of developing physical education skills is to use them in game or leisure activities. Higher-functioning students who have received one-to-one programming with sufficient opportunities to practice these skills in small group settings are capable of successfully participating in modified forms of popular games and thus achieving the goal of partial participation. Students who have mastered the skill of hitting should be challenged to sequence this skill into an activity such as hit and run. Only through opportunities like these will students make the transition from successful mastery of an isolated skill to the use of the skill in a meaningful context.

Group Data Sheet

Activity: _Kick ball_

Skill: _Kicking and running to a base_

Stage: _V_

Names

Sandra	Date	5/21/96							
	Data	O	X						
Danny	Date	5/21/96							
	Data								
Peter	Date	5/21/96							
	Data								
Joel	Date	5/21/96							
	Data								
Michael	Date	5/21/96							
	Data								
Jenny	Date	5/21/96							
	Data								
	Date	5/21/96							
	Data								

Figure 14.11 Group data sheet, stage V. (*Source*: Dunn, J. M., Morehouse, J. W., & Fredericks, H. D. (1986). *Physical Education for the Severely Handicapped*. Austin, TX: Pro-Ed Publishers, p. 122.)

Summary

Although there is no universally accepted definition of severely disabled, it is generally recognized that students with severe disabilities need assistance in self-help, motor, cognitive, social, and communication skills. Usually these are students with multiple disabilities who look and act differently than other children. However, there is much individual variation in these children with no two being identical in their needs and/or abilities.

In recent years educators have demonstrated rather convincingly that individuals with severe disabilities can learn if provided an appropriate instructional environment. This means that educational experiences should be structured with the skills to be taught task-analyzed. In addition, the educational approach for students with severe disabilities requires precise teaching techniques with appropriate cues and consequences. A system approach, in which data are taken on individual trials, should also be incorporated so that informed decisions can be made about the individual's educational progress. Dunn, Morehouse, and Fredericks (1986)

have demonstrated that these principles can be effectively utilized to teach physical education skills to those with severe disabilities.

Efforts should be made to include, to the extent possible, students with severe disabilities in group experiences. This will require the assistance of parents and the availability of appropriately trained volunteers and aides. Significant gains can be made in physical education classes with students who are severely disabled if support personnel are available.

Future directions in the education of those with severe disabilities will focus on the need to generalize skills to a variety of settings including community recreational centers. The emphasis will be, as it should be, on the need to develop age-appropriate, functional, leisure, and work-related skills. This will require close articulation and cooperation between physical educators and community recreators. Federal legislation makes it clear that educational programs and services must be provided for those who are severely disabled. The legislative emphasis has helped educators demonstrate what many knew—persons with severe disabilities can learn if given the opportunity. This observation is true whether applied to the classroom or gymnasium. Greater efforts must be directed toward assisting these individuals to realize their full human potential. Physical educators can play a significant role in making this possible. In some instances this will mean teaching a youngster to roll a ball or helping a child to learn to swim or to use playground equipment. Given dedicated and caring professionals, the future for persons with severe and profound disabilities is very promising, with much of the potential in this population yet to be realized.

Enhancing Activities

1. Observe a class where students with severe disabling conditions are engaged in a physical activity. In your observation note the heterogeneity of the students and the instructional techniques used by the teacher.
2. Select a physical skill and task-analyze the skill. Make sure that the steps and progressions are small enough so that the students with severe disabilities can experience success. Search for a website that contains information and examples of a task analysis for physical activity skills. See how your task analysis matches what you have found.
3. Observe various settings (college classes, shopping, sporting events, etc.) and note the variety of cues and consequences employed. Is feedback (consequence) frequently or infrequently used? Is the level of cue appropriate? Contrast the use of cues and consequences you observe with those that might be appropriate for individuals with severe learning difficulties.
4. Review the list of nondirective cues reported in figure 14.9. Identify other nondirective cues that would be appropriate for the physical education class.
5. Select a skill and develop a program cover sheet (see figure 14.7). With the assistance of your teacher and using the principles identified in this chapter, implement the program with a student who is severely disabled.
6. Review the TASH website, their history, and their current political projects. Reflect on how this would impact you as a physical education instructor with individuals with disabilities.

Selected Readings

Bambra, L. M., Dunlap, G., & Schwartz, I. S. (Eds.). (2004). *Positive behavior support: Critical articles on improving practice for individuals with severe disabilities.* Baltimore: ProEd.

Bender, M., & Valletutti, P. J. (1976). *Teaching the moderately and severely handicapped: Vol. I. Behavior, self care, and motor skills.* Baltimore: University Park Press.

Bigge, J. L., & O'Donnell, P. A. (1976). *Teaching individuals with physical and multiple disabilities.* Columbus, OH: Charles E. Merrill Publishing Co.

Block, M. E. (1992). What is appropriate physical education for students with profound disabilities? *Adapted Physical Activity Quarterly, 9*(3), 197–213.

Block, M. E. (2000). *A teacher's guide to including students with disabilities in general physical education.* Baltimore: Brookes.

Block, M. E., Conatser, P., Montgomery, R., Flynn, L., Munson, D., & Dease, R. (2001). Effects of middle school-aged partners on the motor and affective behaviors of students with severe disabilities. *Palaestra, 17*(4), 34–38.

Block, M. E., & Krebs, P. L. (1992). An alternative to least restrictive environments: A continuum of support to regular physical education. *Adapted Physical Activity Quarterly, 9*(2), 97–113.

Browder, D. M. (1987). *Assessment of individuals with severe handicaps.* Baltimore, MD: Paul H. Brookes Publishing Co.

Burton, A. W., & Miller, D. E. (1998). *The assessment of movement skills.* Champaign, IL: Human Kinetics.

Choi, S., Meeuwsen, H. J., French, R., Sherrill, C., & McCabe, R. (2001). Motor skill acquisition, retention, and transfer in adults with profound mental retardation. *Adapted Physical Activity Quarterly, 18*(3), 257.

Cleland, C. C. (1979). *The profoundly mentally retarded child.* Englewood Cliffs, NJ: Prentice-Hall, Inc.

Colarusso, R., & O'Rourke, C. (2003). *Special education for all teachers.* Dubuque, IA: Kendall/Hunt.

Corbett, J. (1977). Aversion for the treatment of self-injurious behavior. *Journal of Mental Deficiency Research, 19,* 79–95.

Croce, R. V. (1990). Effects of exercise and diet on body composition and cardiovascular endurance in adults with severe mental retardation. *Education and Training in Mental Retardation, 25*, 176–187.

Dunn, J. M., Morehouse, J. W., & Dalke, B. (1981). *Game, exercise, and leisure sport for the severely handicapped.* Corvallis, OR: Oregon State University, Department of Physical Education.

Dunn, J. M., Morehouse, J. W., & Fredericks, H. D. (1986). *Physical education for the severely handicapped.* Austin, TX: Pro-Ed Publishers.

Fredericks, H. D. B. (1976). *The teaching research curriculum for moderately and severely handicapped.* Springfield, IL: Charles C. Thomas.

Geddes, D. (1974). *Physical and recreational programming for severely and profoundly mentally retarded individuals.* Washington, DC: American Alliance for Health, Physical Education, Recreation, and Dance.

Heward, W. L., & Orlansky, M. D. (1992). *Exceptional children* (4th ed.). Columbus, OH: Charles E. Merrill Publishing Co.

Jansma, P. (1980). Psychomotor domain tests for the severely and profoundly handicapped. *Journal of the Association for the Severely Handicapped, 5*, 368–381.

Jansma, P. (1982). Physical education for the severely and profoundly handicapped. *Exceptional Education Quarterly, 3*, 35–41.

Jansma, P. (Ed.). (1993). *The psychomotor training and serious disabilities.* Lanham, MD: University Press of America, Inc.

Lieberman, L. J., & Houston-Wilson, C. (2002). *Strategies for inclusion.* Champaign, IL: Human Kinetics.

Ludlow, B. L., & Sobsey, R. (1984). *The school's role in educating severely handicapped students.* Bloomington, IN: Phi Delta Kappa Educational Foundation.

Maguire, P. (1985). *The effects of home instruction by parents utilizing the data based gymnasium instructional model on the performance of selected motor skills with moderately and severely mentally retarded children.* Unpublished doctoral dissertation, Oregon State University, Corvallis, OR.

Meyen, E. L. (1978). *Exceptional children and youth.* Denver, CO: Love Publishing Co.

Meyer, L. H., Peck, C. A., & Brown, L. (Eds.). (1991). *Critical issues in the lives of people with severe disabilities.* Baltimore, MD: Paul H. Brookes Publishing Co.

Morehouse, J. W. (1988). *The effect of trials-to-criterion on the retention of a discrete motor skill by moderately and severely mentally retarded individuals.* Unpublished doctoral dissertation, Oregon State University, Corvallis, OR.

Nietupski, J. A., Hamre-Nietupski, S., & Ayres, B. (1984). Review of task analytic leisure skill training efforts: Practitioner implications and future research needs. *Journal of the Association for Persons with Severe Handicaps, 9*, 88–97.

Obrusnikova, I., Valkova, H., & Block, M. E. (2003). Impact of inclusion in general physical education on students without disabilities. *Adapted Physical Activity Quarterly, 20*(3), 230–245.

Sims-Tucker, B. M., & Jensema, C. K. (1984). Severely and profoundly auditorially/visually impaired students: The deaf-blind population. In P. J. Valletutti & B. M. Sims-Tucker (Eds.), *Severely and profoundly handicapped students.* Baltimore, MD: Paul H. Brookes Publishing Co.

Snell, M. E. (Ed.). (1987). *Systematic instruction of persons with severe handicaps* (3rd ed.). Columbus, OH: Charles E. Merrill Publishing Co.

Snell, M. E., & Renzaglia, A. M. (1986). Moderate, severe, and profound handicaps. In N. G. Haring & L. McCormick (Eds.), *Exceptional children and youth* (4th ed., pp. 271–310). Columbus, OH: Charles E. Merrill Publishing Co.

Sontag, E., Smith, J., & Sailor, W. (1977). The severely/profoundly handicapped: Who are they? Where are we? *Journal of Special Education, 11*, 5–11.

Stainback, S., Stainback, W., Wehman, P., & Spangiers, L. (1983). Acquisition and generalization of physical fitness exercises in three profoundly retarded adults. *Journal of the Association for the Severely Handicapped, 8*, 47–55.

The Association for Persons with Severe Handicaps (TASH). Retrieved 2004 from www.tash.org

Vogler, E. W., Koranda, P., & Romance, T. (2000). Including a child with severe cerebral palsy in physical education: A case study. *Adapted Physical Activity Quarterly, 17*(2), 161–175.

Activities and Programs

The focus of this final section is on activities and programs for students with disabilities. Some of the chapters provide comprehensive descriptions of adaptations for a wide variety of physical education activities to permit participation by students with disabilities. Ideas are included for modifying rules and regulations, adapting playing techniques and equipment, and devising new versions of the activities. Other chapters describe special program offerings that are particularly beneficial to students with disabilities.

OBJECTIVES

This section is designed to help the reader to:
- Modify lifetime activities, individual and dual sports, and dance forms so students with disabilities can successfully and safely participate in activity.
- Appreciate the value of teaching relaxation and posture in the special physical education program and their contribution to the total well-being of persons with disabilities.
- Utilize methods and techniques to teach persons with disabilities to swim effectively and safely.
- Provide competitive sport experiences for students with disabilities consistent with their needs, interests, and abilities.

CHAPTER 15

Activities and Games for Young Children

CHAPTER OBJECTIVES

After studying this chapter, the reader should be able to:

1 Appreciate the contributions of early intervention programs toward the development of individuals with disabilities.
2 Recognize that recent federal legislation (IDEA 2004) addresses the need for motor and physical activity programs for infants, toddlers, and young children.
3 Understand that young children with and without disabilities benefit from the opportunity to participate together in movement experiences.
4 Identify gross motor assessment instruments and procedures commonly used with young children ages three to five.
5 Develop movement and activity programs that can be used to address the locomotor, non-locomotor, and manipulative skill needs of young children with disabilities.
6 Appreciate the significance of games and their contribution to the cognitive, affective, and psychomotor development of children.
7 Select games on the basis of their ability to enhance the basic motor and physical fitness skills.
8 Identify numerous games played by children and be familiar with the structure and strategy of various games.
9 Adapt and modify games so that children with disabilities can participate with their nondisabled peers.
10 Organize the instructional environment so that children can learn to participate in games successfully and safely.
11 Assist children, including those with disabilities, in creating new games and activities.
12 Structure games and play activities so that the experience is enjoyable and beneficial to all children, including those with disabilities.
13 Recognize the need for games that encourage cooperation and maximum participation, as contrasted to those that are competitive and designed to minimize participation.

Over the last two decades a growing number of authorities have concluded that intervention activities and educational services for individuals with disabilities must begin as early as possible following the identification of a disability, developmental delay, or risk of delay. The support and evidence for early intervention services have resulted in federal legislation that stipulates the provision of appropriate services for infants age birth through two years, and young children beginning at age three. The focus of the federal legislation Individuals with Disabilities Education Improvement Act (IDEA 2004) emphasizes clearly that early intervention services will be provided, parents will play an integral part in the delivery of services, schools and others will cooperate in providing programs, and personnel from various disciplines will be involved in delivering appropriate programs. In 1986, Title I of PL 99-457 mandated that states develop a statewide plan that will ensure that all children with special needs, birth through thirty-six months, receive a comprehensive evaluation, Individualized Family Service Plan (IFSP, see chapter 2), and access to procedural safeguards (Eichstaedt & Lavay, 1992). Title II of PL 99-457 makes it clear that children between three and five must receive the same services and protection now provided to school-age children. These services include, in part, full and appropriate education, due process, and the development of an Individualized Education Program (IEP). The Individuals with Disabilities Education Improvement Act (IDEA 2004) reinforces PL 99-457 and reaffirms the commitment to provide educational services for infants, toddlers, and young children.

The position statement of the National Association for Sport and Physical Education (NASPE, 2002) is that "All children birth to age five should engage in daily physical activity that promotes health-related fitness and movement skills" (p. 1). A federal effort to promote regular participation in physical activity across the lifespan was strongly voiced in 1996 (U.S. Department of Health) and has been reinforced in the U.S. Surgeon General's reports. Child development experts recommend that educating toward a healthy lifestyle is best begun early in life. Hence, all children need early access to developmentally appropriate physical activity opportunities. There is much discussion regarding the importance of early developmental opportunities for young children for healthy brain development. Although research is ongoing, experts do agree that if a delay in development is identified, or if a child is at risk for delay, intervention needs to begin as soon as possible (Shonkoff & Phillips, 2002).

Although the physical educator may have limited opportunity to work with infants and toddlers, an understanding of appropriate physical activity programs at these young ages is important because often the physical educator is viewed in the community as the expert. They are the community advocates for physical activity. As special education law has extended to infants, toddlers, and preschool-aged children, the physical educator can be the advocate for developmentally appropriate activity, if not the actual direct service provider. In any case, the need for intervention when delay is apparent or suspected is paramount to the spirit of the law: Early intervention assists development and avoids cumulative developmental risk (e.g., Tronick & Beeghly, 1999).

Motor and physical activity programs are viewed as being essential in the education of infants and young children with disabilities (McCubbin & Zittel, 1991). Cowden and Eason (1991) have reinforced this need, arguing that early motor programs are so critical that a new cadre of specialists with training as pediatric adapted physical educators should be developed. As discussed in chapter 2, infants and toddlers who experience deviations from normal development benefit from early movement experiences, including programs with a sensorimotor emphasis.

Infancy and Toddlerhood

The Individualized Family Service Plan (IFSP) is developed by the parents with the team of professionals to address the delay in development and the means by which intervention will be conducted. According to IDEA 2004, infants and toddlers with a disability are those children who are under three years of age who need early intervention because they have a documented delay in one or more areas of functional development: cognitive, physical, communication, social/emotional, or adaptive skill. Such children may also be considered for early intervention if they have a condition, either mental or physical, that typically results in a developmental delay (e.g., cerebral palsy, visual impairment). Finally, states have discretion to serve infants and toddlers who are at risk for delay if they were not receiving early intervention (e.g., prenatal drug exposure, poverty). Because it can take time to determine the cause of a delay, infants and toddlers can receive services under the general category of developmental delay (DD). Definitions for developmental delay eligibility vary by state. In time, the exact category of disability may become more apparent. Qualifying for early intervention services can be specified by a state using a combination of reports on standardized tests of a functional area (e.g., two standard deviations below the mean in a functional area), or an informed judgment of a team of professionals when a standardized test is not available or appropriate given the child's age or condition. In some states, the delay must be in more than one developmental area before the child is considered eligible.

As with an IEP, when an IFSP is developed, a specification is made as to who will provide services and where. The guiding terminology in early intervention is to provide the services in the child's natural occurring environment. For some families, the services will be delivered in the home, for others the services will be provided at a center, and for some families, the child will receive both in-home and center-based services. There are numerous ways that education districts configure services based on resources (cooperation with other agencies and school districts) and the needs of the family and child. The Infant Health and Development Project (1990) reported that children gain developmentally through programs that have individualized goals and objectives for the child and well-trained personnel. Typically, there is a service coordinator who works with the family and the agencies and personnel involved. The IFSP must also specify transition plans as the toddler moves to preschool or other appropriate services.

Assessment

Children can be screened for suspected delay using tools like the Denver Developmental Screening Test (Denver II) (Frankenburg & Dobbs, 1992) described in chapter 2. Standardized tests commonly used at these early ages to determine eligibility are: the Peabody Developmental Motor Scales (2nd ed.) (Folio & Fewell, 2000); the Bayley Scales of Infant Development-III (3rd ed.) (Bayley, 2005); and the Brigance Inventory of Early Development (Brigance, 1991). Curriculum-based assessments are a preference for many interventionists working with young children because the evaluation items are based in a curriculum area considered appropriate to the child. If the child is delayed in that curriculum area, then it is easy to translate the assessment information into the intervention plan. Curriculum assessments include: the Assessment Evaluation and Programming System for Children Birth to Six Years (AEPS) (Bricker, 2002); the Carolina Curriculum for Infants and Toddlers with Special Needs (Johnson-Martin, Jens, Attermeier, & Hacker 1991); and the Hawaii Early Learning Profile Strands (HELP) (Parks, 1992).

Some agencies use a transdisciplinary play-based assessment (Linder, 1993a) whereby the professionals from the necessary disciplines gather around and observe the child in play with a facilitator in the child's natural environment. Parents are involved in the processing of the observation and contribute data from developmental checklists.

Tools for monitoring development in early childhood have been implemented by the Early Childhood Research Institute on Measuring Growth and Development (1998; McConnell, McEvoy & Priest, 2001). The most rapid rate of development occurs in early childhood (e.g., Gabbard, 2004). The monitoring of development at these young ages is a reasonable method to identify early on those children who may need intervention. These tools are referred to as Individual Growth and Development Indicators (IGDI). Here the notion is to have non-experts in a given domain use tools that are quick, easy, and inexpensive. An Infant-Toddler Movement IGDI has been developed (Leitschuh, 2004). See the coding form used to monitor the growth of infant-toddler movement skill in figure 15.1. The skills represented in this coding form are considered research-based skills found to contribute to positive developmental trajectories (growth in movement) during infancy and toddlerhood. Research conducted on the tool validates a positive correlation ($r = 0.79$, $p = 0.01$) with the Toddler Infant Motor Evaluation (TIME) (Miller & Roid, 1994), which is a standard measure of motor skills in early childhood.

Movement Activity for Infants and Toddlers

Infancy

For young children, to move and explore their environment is to come to know themselves, the people with whom they interact, and the environment in which they live. As Piaget explained, the work of children is to play. NASPE (2002) recommends providing a safe environment for infants to move and play: one that is supervised and has safe objects available for play. The early movement milestones (Burton & Miller, 1998) are object control and locomotor skills that emerge before the onset of bipedal or upright locomotion. These skills emerge before walking. In this time, the primary object control skills are reach, grasp, and release. The primary locomotor skills are rolling over and crawling skills (as defined in chapter 2). The transitioning in and out of these skills is also part of movement skill development (Dunn, 2002) at these young ages. The skill of standing up from another position is often considered preparatory to walking.

At these early ages, there is an assumed "range of normal" by which children perform movement skills: Variation exists in the onset of skills given an age. For example, some children walk at around age 10 months, whereas others walk at around 16 months. This is not outside the range of normal. Children at these early ages have "interests" in movement skill (Dunn, 2002). A child may be fascinated with crawling to a place and sitting, then crawling again. Other children are very content to sit on a blanket for long periods of time, and when they do move, it is not considered very far.

Designing movement programs or encouraging movement activity takes into account the range of the normal development skills and the interests of the child for moving. NASPE (2002) recommends open environments for infants to explore and to develop the skills of rolling over, sitting up, crawling, and standing up. Sometimes young children do not develop their interests or their skills due to lack of opportunity to explore and to play with safe toys. An engaged caregiver who facilitates this exploration by encouraging the infant to play will help the infant develop more confidence and interest (if it is lacking) in movement. Although many people believe that these skills develop naturally, NASPE experts suggest they are influenced by a supportive environment. Environment entails the physical setting as well as those caretakers in the setting.

The notion of scaffolding development promoted by the Russian psychologist Vygostky means that adults are there to encourage the child's play and then assist "just enough" to move them along to the next developmental

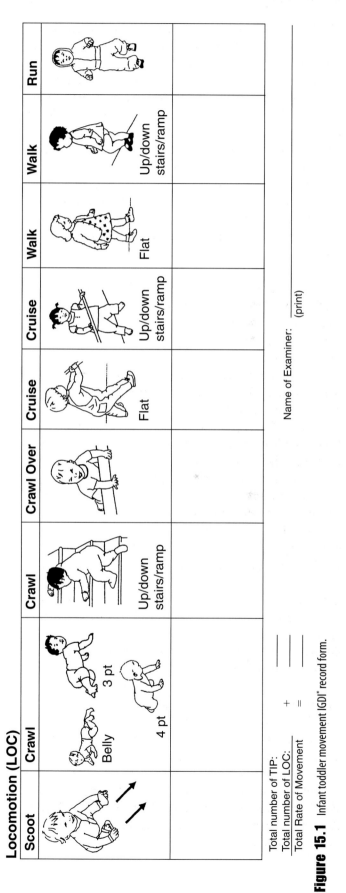

Figure 15.1 Infant toddler movement IGDI* record form.

task. For example, the child who is learning to sit up can be held in the seated position by the caregiver and then released momentarily, so the child gets the sense of sitting independently. Gradually, the child will move to independent sitting.

The notion of instruction in movement at these early ages is one of providing opportunity that is developmentally appropriate and giving time to practice the skills repeatedly. Encouragement is provided by setting up the environment and by having engaged caregivers who respond verbally and also in an emotionally positive manner regarding movement skill acquisition.

Two terms often used in describing movement skill acquisition in infancy and toddlerhood are "emerging" and "mature." Children will demonstrate a skill periodically when it is emerging. For example, a child may intermittently be able to pull her body up to stand holding onto a coffee table. Other times, she may start the pull up and then tip off to the side. Here, the skill of pulling up to stand is still emerging; this is developmentally expected.

Toddlers

Walking affords toddlers the opportunity to explore numerous areas and arenas for movement skill acquisition. The fundamental movement skills that emerge at this point (Burton & Miller, 1998) are object control and locomotor skills. Object control skills include throw, catch, kick, strike, bounce, pull, and push. Locomotor skills include walk, run, jump, slide, skip, gallop, hop, and leap. These skills will emerge through early childhood as toddlers are given opportunity to practice skills that they are developmentally capable of performing.

According to NASPE, toddlers should engage in nonstructured as well as some structured physical activity. Examples of unstructured physical activity are: running around with peers, moving under and over playground

Object Control Skills

- throw   - bounce
- catch   - pull
- kick   - push
- strike

Locomotor Skills

- walk   - skip
- run   - gallop
- jump   - hop
- slide   - leap

structures, playing with large balls, digging in sandboxes, and rolling down a hillside. It is also recommended that a number of objects are available to ride on, push, balance on, climb up, and jump down from safely. NASPE believes this helps develop strength and endurance for the young child.

Structured physical activity is using child-sized equipment (e.g., push carts, plastic tricycles), using follow-along songs with basic movements and rhythms, playing with musical instruments and moving, as well as throwing objects to targets with a caretaker. Children can either play with an adult or with a small group of children under adult supervision.

Physical educators can assist parents and caregivers with creating time and opportunity for these activities either at home or in the community. They can also be advocates for the child's access to these activities by emphasizing to parents and caregivers the importance of physically active children for overall health and well-being as well as for learning movement skills.

Infants and Toddlers with Disabilities

Those children who lag in developmental skill can benefit from engaging in the previous activities given the emphasis indicated by the IFSP team for movement. In other words, where does the child need the assistance? In some cases, the physical and occupational therapists have specific suggestions for helping to develop movement skills that are lagging. These strategies can be built into the child's day care or home program, as well as be applied to learning new movement skills. Too often movement for children with disabilities is immediately assumed to mean therapy. This should not be the case. Children with disabilities are children first and should be engaged in movement activities for the same reasons as their peers developing typically: for fun, play, and learning (figure 15.2). Therefore, broad exposure, structured learning time, and unstructured time is helpful in developing movement skills. It is important to communicate to families that not all the movement time is therapy time.

A technique to use in play situations that allows for indirect teaching is to "follow the child's lead." The teacher, caregiver, or parent watches what the child is doing, describes it, and follows along with the activity. (This is directly opposite of teaching techniques used with older students, which are often direct instruction.) Given a number of toys, the child may choose a ball to kick. The adult would say, "You are kicking the ball." Then the adult would join in the kicking.

In developing the IFSP interventions, the family's identified values and aspirations for their child are critical. It is suggested that the physical educator ask the family members what they would like to see their child doing,

Figure 15.2 Physical activity is essential in the education of very young children with disabilities. An Individualized Family Service Plan (IFSP) identifies intervention strategies to facilitate movement skills.

or what their concerns are about movement. Some parents are not familiar with typical motor development, much less atypical development. Descriptions of what their child currently does well is important, as well as a description of what could be considered for the next skill development. Children with disabilities do not necessarily follow typical developmental patterns. Instead, they may skip a skill completely or, because of lack of interest or ability, may not want to perform the skill. Careful observation of the child's movement skill by professionals and careful listening to descriptions from parents will create more appropriate intervention plans.

Preschool programs for children with disabilities vary in content and length. In some states, the programs are nonexistent and in other states more programs are being developed. Within this chapter, the emphasis will focus on activities and programs for young children three to eight years of age. Under IDEA 2004 the category of developmental delay can be used for children up through nine years of age. Each state has discretion in deciding the upper age range after six years. Some states have elected to maintain the limit only through six years of age which is required by the law.

Assessing Young Children with Disabilities

As described in chapter 6, there are several instruments that can be used to assess the motor performance of young children with disabilities. Zittel (1994) conducted an extensive analysis of tests that have been used with young preschool children, including tests frequently used to assess the gross motor performance of children with disabilities. In assessing the merit of tests to use with young children, Zittel suggests that the following criteria should be employed: test purpose; technical adequacy; nondiscriminatory items; administrative ease; instructional link; and ecological validity (table 15.1). In applying these criteria to tests commonly used with young preschool children, Zittel suggests that the instruments most closely meeting all of the criteria include the Peabody Developmental Motor Scales, Test of Gross Motor Development (TGMD), and the Battelle Developmental Inventory. Summary information about these tests and other instruments rated highly can be found in table 15.2. It should be noted that this information in table 15.2 is still appropriate although some of the tools have been renormed including the TGMD, now referred to as the TGMD-2 (Ulrich, 2000), as well as the Peabody Developmental Motor Scales, 2nd Edition (PDMS-2) (Folio & Fewell, 2000). The Test of Gross Motor Development (TGMD) (Ulrich, 1985), and TGMD-2 (Ulrich, 2000) continue to be widely used in physical education because the test includes locomotor and object control items commonly found in quality movement programs for young children (Ulrich & Sanford, 2002).

It is essential that sound evaluation procedures be used in physical education programs for individuals with disabilities. Eason (1991) has identified assessment as one of the essential components in an effective physical education program for preschool children with disabilities. Federal legislation mandates that special programs be provided for young children, ages three to five, who are "at risk" or with a developmental delay. While it may be difficult at times to find the "best" test to use with preschool children with disabilities, this should not be used as an excuse to avoid evaluating the students and their educational gains. If necessary, physical educators should employ other procedures to determine educational progress, such as task analyses and checklists as described in chapter 6. Baganto and Neisworth (1990) proposed that clinical judgment is a highly representative form of assessment and provides a broad description of behavior. Using this approach, the teacher is asked to use subjective checklists to evaluate the child over time and in various settings. Sherrill (2004) believes that the best way to evaluate young children is to observe them in informal play settings as they engage in movement. Collecting and sharing observational data with other professionals, including special educators and related services personnel, will provide a rich source of information on which to base a determination of the child's developmental status and future progress.

TABLE 15.1 Key Features for Selecting an Appropriate Preschool Gross Motor Assessment Instrument

Criteria	Selection Features
Purpose	Resource materials state:
	What the instrument is designed to provide
	How the measurements can be used
	The type of reference
Technical adequacy	Evidence for validity
	Evidence for reliability
	Standardized population
Nondiscriminatory	Adaptations permitted
	Multisource information permitted
	Standardized sample sensitive to culture and disability
Administrative ease	Scoring more than pass/fail
	Interpretation includes a raw score summary, comments related to performance, or level of mastery indicated
	Administration time clearly stated or flexibility in test component administration allowed
Instructional link	Curriculum-referenced
	Test items sequenced to provide low inference for instructional objectives
	Ability to monitor progress
Ecological validity	Familiar materials
	Familiar setting
	Caregiver present

From: Zittel, L. L. (1994). Gross motor assessment of preschool children with special needs. *APAQ*, *11*(3), p. 247.

TABLE 15.2 Summary of Nine Gross Motor Assessment Instruments

Name	Age (Years)	Type of Reference	Component Areas	No. Items	Publisher
I CAN Preprimary Motor and Play Skills	Preprimary	Criterion	Locomotor Object control Body control Health/fitness Play equipment Play participation	31 total 26 gross motor	Michigan State University Instructional Media Center
OSU Scale of Intra-Gross Motor Assessment	2½–14	Criterion	Gross motor	11	Ohio Motor Assessment Associates
Peabody Developmental Motor Scales	Birth–7	Norm Criterion	Gross motor Fine motor	282 total 170 gross motor	DLM Teaching Resources

Test of Gross Motor Development	3–10	Norm Criterion	Gross motor: locomotor object control	12	Pro-Ed, Inc.
Battelle Development Inventory	Birth–8	Norm Criterion	Personal/social Adaptive Motor Communication Cognitive	341 total 82 motor 44 gross motor	DLM Teaching Resources
Brigance: Inventory of Early Development	Below the developmental age of 7 years	Norm Criterion	Motor Self-help Speech/language General knowledge/ comprehension Early academic skills	98 total 13 gross motor	Curriculum Associates
Denver Development Mental Screening Test-II	Birth–6	Norm	Gross motor Language Fine motor/adaptive Personal/social	125 total 32 gross motor	Denver Development Materials
Developmental Indicators for the Assessment of Learning— Revised	2–6	Norm	Motor Conceptual Language	24 total 8 motor 2 gross motor	Childcraft Education Corp.
Miller Assessment for Preschoolers	2.9–5.8	Norm	Sensory Motor Cognitive	27 total 8 motor 3 gross motor	The Psychological Corp.

From L. L. Zittel, 1994, Gross motor assessment of preschool children with special needs: Instrument selection considerations, *Adapted Physical Activity Quarterly* (vol. 11, No. 3), pp. 252–253, Copyright © 1994 by Human Kinetics Publishers, Inc. Reprinted with permission from Human Kinetics (Champaign, IL).

Planning the Physical Activity Program

The education of young children has received increased attention since the mid-1980s. Much of this concern has been driven by the recognition that an increasing number of young children, ages three to five, are receiving services in day care centers and preschool programs. As more and more young children have been placed together in educational centers and settings, organizations such as the National Association for the Education of Young Children (NAEYC) have developed position papers and statements which describe developmentally appropriate practices for the education of young children. A publication by NAEYC, *Active for Life* (Sanders, 2002), attests to the emphasis educators who are not necessarily trained extensively in physical education are placing on program development in physical activity for children in child-care centers and preschools. The Council on Physical Education for Children (COPEC), an organization within The American Alliance for Health, Physical Education, Recreation, and Dance, also has identified appropriate and inappropriate practices in the education of young children with disabilities. COPEC's (1994) guidelines provide educators and parents a starting point from which to evaluate the quality of movement programs and experiences offered to young children. NASPE and COPEC have continued to develop materials regarding the physical activity for children from birth to five years of age (NASPE, 2000 & 2002). Developmentally appropriate practices for young children are based on a number of important premises, including the value and benefit of interacting with children of various abilities, including those with disabilities (Aufesser, 2003; Block, 2003).

NASPE (2002) recommends a minimum of sixty minutes per day of *structured* physical activity and 60 minutes to several hours of *unstructured* physical activity. These recommendations support the notion that free play within a recess or break time is not considered the only means by which young children learn movement skills (e.g., McCall & Craft, 2000). Young children need instructional time and also time to play and explore movement, as well as repeated practice time in order to build and grow in their movement skill.

NASPE (2000, 2002) emphasizes that developing quality programs for young children ages three to five years is different from program development and instruction for older children. Here, it is imperative that instruction matches developmental maturational level. NASPE offers five guidelines for program development:

1. **Teachers of young children are guides or facilitators.**
   Young children learn through involvement, observation, and modeling, which requires teachers to facilitate children's active involvement in learning. Teachers construct the environment with specific outcomes in mind and then guide the children toward these goals. By carefully observing the children's responses and interests, teachers are able to adapt the learning experiences to best meet each individual child's needs. Children are allowed to make choices and seek creative solutions. They are provided the time and opportunity to explore appropriate responses. Teachers show interest and participate in movement activities, and engage the children in the activity, thereby extending the children's learning.

2. **Children should engage in movement programs designed for their developmental levels.**
   Young children need a variety of experiences that will lead to mature fundamental motor skills. The development of fundamental motor abilities is age related, not age determined. Teachers of three-, four-, and five-year-old children need to fully understand the continuum of motor development from infancy through age five as it differs from that of elementary school–aged children.

3. **Young children learn through interaction with their environment.**
   This well-established concept has been stated in many ways: children learn by doing; children learn through active involvement with people and objects. Developmentally appropriate movement programs for young children are designed so that all children are active participants.

4. **Young children learn and develop in an integrated fashion.**
   Motor, cognitive, emotional, and social development are interrelated. Learning experiences in movement should encompass and interface with other areas of development. Regularly scheduled movement experiences should focus on the development of fundamental motor skills while incorporating these experiences in the child's total development. Movement is a primary medium for learning in young children.

5. **Planned movement experiences enhance play experiences.**
   A combination of play, combined with planned movement experiences specifically designed to help children develop fundamental motor skills, is beneficial in assisting young children in their development. Regularly scheduled and appropriately designed movement experiences are enhanced with regular indoor and outdoor play experiences, giving children an opportunity to freely practice and develop skills.

There is an extensive body of literature to support the value of including young children with disabilities in programs with nondisabled peers. Block (1994, 2003) has articulated the benefits of inclusion for children with and without disabilities (table 15.3). It is important to note that young children with and without disabilities are enriched as a result of the opportunity to engage in programs together. History has revealed time and time again that individuals who do things together at early ages have the best opportunity to develop positive attitudes toward one another. Young children without disabilities will need guidance and direction from teachers and adults to help them understand and appreciate peers who are disabled (Block, 2003). If this is done properly, however, nondisabled peers can be effectively utilized to help or assist learners who have special physical education needs (Houston-Wilson, 1994).

The majority of activities and games that are developmentally appropriate for children nondisabled also are appropriate for young children with disabilities. This would include activities that emphasize health-related fitness as well as movement skills commonly found in well-designed programs for young children. The goal, of course, is to ensure that the educational program is leading to desired changes for students with and without disabilities. For the student with a disability to experience success, it may be necessary, depending on the level of severity, for the teacher to modify the instructional approach. See figure 15.3 on page 340 for an example of modifying an existing physical education curriculum in preschool to include children with disabilities, while also offering enrichment activities for all students.

There are numerous modifications that can be made to ensure that the young child with a disability can be successful in a general setting. Chief among these is the manner in which information is presented. For example, a verbal cue, while appropriate for many young children, will need to be modified for the student with a hearing, visual, or processing disability. Block (1994) has succinctly captured many of the modifications that may need to be made in the instructional approach to working with young children with disabilities (see table 15.4 on page 341). Numerous other examples may

TABLE 15.3	Benefits of Inclusion

To children with disabilities:
- Opportunity to learn social skills in integrated, more natural environments.
- More stimulating, motivating, normalized environment.
- Availability of age-appropriate, nondisabled role models and peer supports.
- Can participate in a variety of in-school and extracurricular activities.
- Potential new friendships with peers who live in same neighborhood.
- Improved self-esteem.

To children without disabilities:
- With guidance from adults, can improve attitudes toward children with disabilities.
- With guidance from adults, can learn how to interact with, be friends to, assist, and advocate for peers with disabilities.
- Availability of special resource personnel, instruction, and equipment that may be beneficial to children without disabilities.
- Perspective—having a hurt knee, acne, or losing a friend suddenly seems somewhat trivial compared to the daily challenges faced by children with disabilities.
- Future parents of children with disabilities, future taxpayers, future teachers, and future business persons have greater personal knowledge of disability and thus are less prejudiced.
- Improved self-esteem.

Source: What is appropriate physical education for students with profound disabilities? by Martin Block, *Adapted Physical Education Quarterly* (vol. 9, no. 3), p. 201, Copyright © 1992 by Human Kinetics Publishers..

be found in earlier chapters devoted specifically to a particular disability.

In employing a physical education curriculum for the young child with a disability, it may be necessary to modify various movement experiences such that the child can experience success. In the section on Adaptations, found later in this chapter, information is provided about various modifications that can be made in conventional games to accommodate the needs of the young child with a disability. Many of these suggestions represent good common sense such as altering or reducing the activity space for individuals unable to move with the same ease as their classmates.

One of the highly desirable features of teaching activities and games to young children with and without disabilities is that the content can be varied to respond to individual needs. Teaching the movement skills found in table 15.5 on page 342 and using a movement concepts approach (table 15.6) creates exciting opportunities to permit all students to learn and to experience success. For example, in teaching static balance using a movement concepts approach, the skill can be varied according to duration (time) of the balance, and the body in relation to an object (i.e., balancing on something, etc.). For a young child with a disability, the nature of the balance task can be varied in numerous ways (e.g., the time to balance reduced, the number of body parts to use in the balance activity

increased, use two or three contact points instead of one, etc.). For students who use assistive devices such as walkers and wheelchairs, movement skills that emphasize dynamic or static balance can be modified in many ways, permitting the young child to experience success by incorporating the assistive device into the balance activity. For example, in a dynamic balance task emphasizing space and the use of pathways (straight, curved, zigzag), the child who walks with the aid of a crutch or uses a wheelchair can participate fully in the activity with minimal modifications and, most importantly, benefit from the unit on balance.

Using Games to Encourage Physical Activity

In addition to the teaching of movement skills and concepts, the familiar games of childhood have a definite place in educational programs for young children with and without disabilities. Participation in game activities contributes in many ways to the growth and development of children. Games promote development of students' motor and physical fitness levels. By virtue of their structure, games provide unique opportunities for learning to share, take turns, and cooperate. Reinforcement of academic skills related to language, mathematics, science, and social studies can be accomplished with appropriate adaptations of games, such as those described by Humphrey (1976), Cratty and associates

Movement Component	Movement Skill	Modification of Activity	Enrichment Activity
Locomotor Skills	Jumping	Assisting a child by holding hands and giving verbal cues, such as "bend knees," "swing arms," and "jump."	Combining different movement components when jumping (i.e., jumping off a high object, jumping and turning, jumping and landing in a hoop).
Object Control Skills	Catching	Providing hand-over-hand assistance to child catching a ball.	Throwing a small ball at wall and catching it on the rebound.
Body Awareness	Identifying Body Parts	Playing "Copy Cat." Adult touches head and says, "This is my head." Child imitates actions.	Using activities/challenges involving body identification, body actions, and cognitive skills, such as: "If you have the color blue on your skirt, shake your arm."
Spatial Concepts	Moving Through an Obstacle Course	Following an adult or peer through an obstacle course.	Designing, demonstrating, and telling other children how to move through an obstacle course.
Body Actions	Imitating Body Movements	Imitating movements repetitively (i.e., bending, stretching).	Demonstrating a sequence of movements such as bending knees, stretching arms, turning around.
Rhythmic Activities	Manipulating Ribbon Sticks	Imitating movements with rhythm sticks.	Designing and demonstrating a sequence of two to four movements with ribbon sticks.
Play Skills	Pedaling a Wheeled Toy	Assisting child by using a push-pull bar attached to wheeled toy.	Pedaling a wheeled toy following commands (i.e., "stop," "ride around the cone.").
Group Games	Playing Parachute Game ("Popcorn")	Providing hand-over-hand assistance while shaking parachute.	Shaking parachute with one hand or both hands. Shaking parachute at fast and slow speeds. Shaking parachute held at various heights.

Figure 15.3 Curriculum components for preschool physical education with examples of movement skill activity, modifications, and enrichment activity. Taken from Minnesota Department of Education, Active Learning (2003). *A resource guide for designing and implementing developmentally appropriate movement experiences, ages 3–5.*

(1970), and Werner (1994). In addition, most games have a folk origin and so offer children a chance to learn about different cultures as well as to expand their understanding of their country's heritage and the importance that game experiences have played in the history of the world.

Young children enjoy moving and learning through music. A list of songs to be used, as well as the artist and the name of the compact disc/cassette/record, is included at the end of this chapter. This reference was compiled by adapted physical education professionals specializing in early childhood special education (Active Learning, 2003).

Significant as these contributions of game activities are, of even greater importance is the role that games play in developing the basic locomotor and manipulative skills discussed in chapter 2. Young children find games to be an exciting environment in which to utilize the basic motor

skills they have acquired, and so they are motivated not only to improve the quality of their skills but also to apply them in new experiences. Observing children in game activities also provides teachers with a unique opportunity to assess the skill level of students and to evaluate their performance.

For example, the teacher closely watches for the performance errors as the child executes the basic skills indigenous to the game during play. When it is observed that the child is making an error in movement, the teacher can provide information and assistance to the individual to correct the error and then offer them opportunities to practice the correct movement by itself and in game situations. In the case of a child with a disability, the limitations and potentiality of movement must be carefully considered in assessing the efficiency of skill performance: The most efficient and effective

TABLE 15.4   Suggested Modifications in Activity for Young Children with Specific Needs

Does the student have limited strength?

THINGS TO CONSIDER

❑ shorten distance to move or project object
❑ use lighter equipment (e.g., balls, bats)
❑ use shorter striking implements
❑ allow student to sit or lie down while playing
❑ use deflated or suspended balls
❑ change requirements (e.g., a few jumps, then run)

Does the student have limited speed?

❑ shorten distance (or lengthen for others)
❑ change locomotor pattern (allow running v. walking)
❑ make safe areas in tag games

Does the student have limited endurance?

❑ shorten distance
❑ shorten playing field
❑ allow "safe" areas in tag games
❑ decrease activity time for student
❑ allow more rest periods for student
❑ allow student to sit while playing

Does the student have limited balance?

❑ provide chair/bar for support
❑ teach balance techniques (e.g., widen base, extend arms)
❑ increase width of beams to be walked
❑ use carpeted rather than slick surfaces
❑ teach students how to fall
❑ allow student to sit during activity
❑ place student near wall for support
❑ allow student to hold peer's hand

Does student have limited coordination and accuracy?

❑ use stationary balls for kicking/striking
❑ decrease distance for throwing, kicking, and shooting
❑ make targets and goals larger
❑ use larger balls for kicking and striking
❑ increase surface of the striking implements
❑ use backstop
❑ use softer, slower balls for striking and catching
❑ in bowling-type games, use lighter, less stable pins

Modified from Block, M. E. (1994). *A teacher's guide to including students with disabilities in regular physical education.* Paul H. Brookes Publishing Co., P. O. Box 10624, Baltimore, MD 21285–0624.

movement for a child with a disability may not be the same as that for a child without a disability. The information acquired through informal evaluation can, if desired, be recorded after class to provide a permanent record to be utilized in reporting progress or for the development of specific lessons to improve deficiencies in the basic skills. To fail to provide children with the opportunities for development engendered by play in the basic skill games is to deny them entrance to one of the best avenues to optimum growth and development.

Organizing for Game Instruction

Because the space required for playing the basic skill games need not be large, the games can be organized for play

TABLE 15.5	Fundamental Movement Skill Themes

Skills

Locomotor ⇒	walking
	running
	jumping
	galloping
	sliding
	hopping
	leaping
	skipping
Stability ⇒	stretching
	curling
	bending
	twisting
	body rolling
	dodging
	balancing
	inverted supports
Manipulative ⇒	dribbling
	throwing
	catching
	kicking
	punting
	trapping
	volleying
	striking

Source: Journal of Physical Education, Recreation, and Dance, Aug. 1994, p. 29. JOPERD is a publication of the American Alliance for Health, Physical Education, Recreation, and Dance, 1900 Association Drive, Reston, VA 22091.

almost anywhere—on the playground, in the classroom, in the gymnasium or all-purpose room, even in hallways. Equipment is relatively simple and inexpensive: balls, beanbags, boxes, batons, and plastic bowling pins. Most of these items are easily obtained or readily improvised. Beanbags, for example, can be made from scrap cloth sewn into a bag and filled with dried beans or rice. Wood scraps of suitable size and free of splinters may be substituted for batons and empty milk cartons or plastic jugs for bowling pins.

The strategies for including the child with a disability into game activities will vary according to the disability, severity level, and the nature of the game (Engstrom & Engstrom, 2003). If the student has sufficient skill, but the nature of the game itself is restrictive (for example, a student in a wheelchair playing dodge ball), the activity should be modified to accommodate the special needs of the student. A discussion of strategies useful in modifying activities to permit the integration of children with disabilities with their nondisabled peers will be presented in the last section

of this chapter. The following list indicates some instructional guidelines teachers should observe when teaching games to children. The following have been modified from Dauer and Pangrazi (1986) and Pangrazi (2004).

1. The teacher should study the game before attempting to teach it. This will require not only knowledge of the game itself (rules and equipment) but also an understanding of how to modify or adapt the game as various situations unfold.

2. When presenting a new game to a class, the teacher should have the youngsters sit or stand in the formation that they are going to use. The directions should be well organized and presented clearly in a concise and succinct manner. Efforts should be made to ensure that students with disabilities understand the directions. For example, the student with a hearing loss may need to be reminded to sit close to the front so that he or she can hear and observe the teacher (figure 15.4).

TABLE 15.6   The Movement Concepts

Effort	Space	Relationships
Force	*Levels*	*Objects/People*
strong	high/medium/low	over/under
light		in/out
	Directions	between/among
Time	forward/backward	in front/behind
fast	diagonally/sideways	above/below
slow	up/down	through/around
sudden		
sustained	*Pathways*	*People*
	straight	mirroring
Flow	curved	shadowing
free	zigzag	in unison
bound		
	Ranges	together/apart
	body shapes	solo
	body spaces	partner/group
	body extensions	

Source: Journal of Physical Education, Recreation, and Dance, Aug. 1994, p. 29. JOPERD is a publication of the American Alliance for Health, Physical Education, Recreation, and Dance, 1900 Association Drive, Reston, VA 22091.

3. Allow students to try the game early before all of the rules and strategies of the game are introduced. Do not keep score during early stages of the game learning. This will generate student interest without requiring the students to listen to a long presentation. This approach is particularly beneficial to many students with disabilities who rely on visual rather than verbal cues.

4. Games provide excellent opportunities for children to learn selected social skills. For example, youngsters may be asked to call infractions or penalties on others as well as themselves. This will help them develop a sense of ethics and fair play as well as learn to accept the judgment or ruling of others. This approach also allows the child with a disability to be a judge as well as to be judged. Some children, too, learn quickly that it is "okay" to modify the rules for some youngsters. For example, a child with a congenital hip dislocation may be allowed to run a shorter distance in a relay game or be permitted a head start.

5. Every effort should be made to ensure that all children play an equal amount of time in games that require the taking of turns. The teacher should make a special note to minimize the use of elimination games so that children, particularly youngsters with disabilities, do not sit out for an extended period of time.

6. Games tend to be most enjoyable when they are novel. A variety of games should be used to stimulate and

Figure 15.4 Language concepts such as "crawl into" can be reinforced through movement activities.

maintain interest. In addition, it is effective to stop games at the height of interest. Children will consequently look forward to playing the game again in the near future.

Choosing Appropriate Games

The selection of games for use in the program for any given class depends upon the objectives being sought; the number and abilities of the children; and the space, time, and equipment available (figure 15.5). An analysis of the nature of a game indicates which of the basic skills of running, throwing, catching, kicking, and so forth, the game may be expected to accomplish. The locomotor and manipulative skills essential to growth and development were discussed in chapter 2. The abilities of the children can be determined both by observation and testing. Procedures for the latter are discussed in chapter 6.

To facilitate the selection of appropriate games for various ages, the games that follow, which are only representative of the vast number of existing games and stunts, have been labeled according to the levels for which they are most suited as determined by the abilities, interests, and needs of young children (Kozub, 2002). It must be remembered, however, that the manner in which a game is presented has a direct bearing on its acceptance by any age group. In the case of individuals who are mentally retarded, the chronological age alone cannot always be relied upon as an effective guide for choosing appropriate games. A guide to game selection with individuals with mental retardation is to teach to the chronological age and design the activities around the developmental age. In other words, select activities based on the age of the individual and what his/her peers would be engaged in, but teach the content based on what the child can be expected to perform from a developmental maturational level. A child who is in the first grade will want to join in the activities of his physical education class, but if his maturation level is low compared to his peers, then he will struggle unless modifications are provided. Games for younger children may be considered too babyish and many individuals with mental retardation will refuse to play them or be so embarrassed while playing them that the potential

value of the game is lost. Care must be exercised in selecting games that these children, particularly the older ones, are willing to accept as fitting for their age. The basic skills each game emphasizes are identified in table 15.7. The games listed here begin in the preschool years and will follow a young student to fifth grade. Other good examples of games for preschoolers are found in *Moving with a Purpose* (McCall & Craft 2000), *I Can Primary Skills* (Wessel & Zittle, 1998), *Smart Start* (Wessel & Zittle, 1995), and movement activities with and without music (Pica, 1999, 2000a, 2000b, 2000c). Another resource for both teachers and parents of young children is found in *Make It, Take It* (Cox & Lubbers, 1999). Here veteran adapted physical educators specializing in early childhood offer information on movement activities for young children and the "how to" for the activity kits/equipment.

Ringmaster (Preprimary–First Grade)
Players form a circle, with one player called the *Ringmaster* in the center. The Ringmaster pretends to snap a whip and calls out the name of an animal. All those in the circle imitate the animal named. This procedure continues with different animals. Finally the Ringmaster calls, "We will all join in the circus parade," and everyone moves around the circle imitating any animal. Ringmaster then picks another player to take his or her place.

Bouncing Ball (Preprimary–First Grade)
Children choose partners, with one becoming a *ball* and the other the *bouncer*. The one who is the bouncer pushes on the partner's head as if bouncing a ball. The partner does a deep knee bend and returns to standing position.

Kitty Wants a Corner (Preprimary–First Grade)
Circles are drawn on the floor for each player. One player, called *Kitty*, walks to different circles saying, "Kitty wants a corner." The player in the circle answers, "Go to my next-door neighbor." Meanwhile, as Kitty is at other circles, the remaining players signal each other and attempt to exchange places. Kitty tries to occupy a circle left by another player. The one left without a circle becomes the new Kitty. A player who continues as Kitty too long may call "All change" and quickly find a vacant circle as everyone changes circles.

Circle Ball (Preprimary–First Grade)
Players form a circle with a leader in the center. The leader tosses the ball to each player in the circle, who then tosses it back. (The teacher may serve as the leader in order to give the children practice in catching the ball at different levels, since most young children cannot throw well enough to control the heights at which the ball is to be received.)

Figure 15.5 Variables to consider in selecting games.

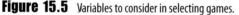

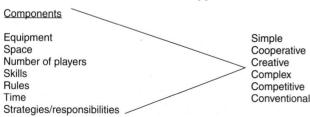

Components

Equipment
Space
Number of players
Skills
Rules
Time
Strategies/responsibilities

Simple
Cooperative
Creative
Complex
Competitive
Conventional

TABLE 15.7   Games to Reinforce/Teach Motor Skills

Game	Crawling	Walking	Running	Jumping	Hopping	Galloping	Skipping	Throwing	Catching	Kicking	Striking
Ringmaster	X	X	X	X	X	X	X				
Bouncing Ball					X						
Kitty Wants a Corner			X								
Circle Ball								X	X		
Spider and Flies		X		X							
Jouncing on Jouncing Board				X							
Circle Relay			X								
Magic Carpet		X					X				
Elephant Walk		X									
Bronco Relay						X					
Midnight			X								
Farmer and the Chickens		X	X								
Jumping Jack				X							
Walking, Balancing Beanbag on Head			X								
Target Toss								X			
Skunk Tag			X								
Eagle and Sparrows			X								
Partner Ball Toss								X	X		
Cats and Mice		X	X								
Call Ball								X	X		
Hop Tag					X						
Red Light			X								
Post Ball								X	X		
Measuring Worm	X										
Fire on the Mountain			X								
Chain Tag			X								
Circle Weave Relay			X								
Cross Tag			X								
Wall Ball								X	X		
Circle Kick Ball										X	
Line Soccer			X							X	
Hot Potatoes						X					
Crows and Cranes			X								
Parachute Play		X	X	X	X	X	X				

Spider and Flies (Preprimary–Second Grade)
Mark off two goal lines forty feet apart. Draw a circle between the goal lines large enough to hold all the players. One player is a *Spider* and squats in the circle while the rest of the players are *Flies* and stand behind the goal lines. All Flies advance toward the circle and walk around to the right. When the Spider jumps up, all Flies run toward a goal while the Spider tags as many Flies as possible before they get back behind either goal line. Those tagged join the Spider in the circle and help catch the remaining Flies. The last Fly caught is the Spider in the next game.

Jouncing on Jouncing Board (Preprimary–Second Grade)

A two- by eight-inch board several feet long is supported by two sturdy uprights. Participant stands in the middle of the board and jounces.

Circle Relay (Preprimary–Second Grade)

Players form circles of six to eight players. Number one in each circle is given a handkerchief. He or she runs counterclockwise around the circle and gives the handkerchief to number two, who repeats the same procedure. The relay continues until each person has had a turn. The first circle finished is the winner.

Magic Carpet (Preprimary–Second Grade)

Large circles called poison spots are drawn in the play area. On signal, eight to twenty players march or skip to the right, stepping in each spot. When "stop" is called, players stop promptly in position. Players attempt to move quickly to avoid being caught on a spot.

Elephant Walk (Preprimary–Second Grade)

Each child stands and bends forward at the waist, clasping the hands together and letting the arms hang in imitation of an elephant's trunk. The arms are swung from side to side as the child walks with back rounded and knees slightly bent.

Bronco Relay (Preprimary–Second Grade)

Players form lines of even numbers of players. Each line divides into partners. The first couple, one behind the other, straddles a broomstick at the starting line. On the signal, they gallop with the broomstick to a specified turning line and back to the starting point, where they give the broomstick to couple number two, who repeat the same action. The line in which all the couples complete the relay first is the winner.

Midnight (Preprimary–Second Grade)

For this game two players are designated as *Mr. Fox* and *Mother Hen* and all the other players are called *Chickens*. The Hen and Chickens have a goal line thirty yards away from the Fox. Mother Hen leads the chickens to Mr. Fox and asks, "What time is it?" Mr. Fox may give any time in reply, but when the answer is "Midnight," the Hen and Chickens run toward their goal with Mr. Fox chasing them. Those tagged become Mr. Fox's helpers.

Farmer and the Chickens (Preprimary–Second Grade)

One player, the *Farmer*, pretends to toss out seed and to lead other players, the *Chickens,* away from their safety area, or *Pen*. When Farmer has taken them far enough from the Pen, he or she calls, "Today is Thanksgiving," and chases the Chickens, who run for the Pen. Chickens caught become Farmer's helpers.

Jumping Jack (Preprimary–Second Grade)

Children squat down and cross arms on chest and then jump to standing position with arms out to the sides.

The movements are repeated to create jumping jacks. Legs may also be spread in the jump to increase the difficulty of the exercise.

Walking, Balancing Beanbag on Head (Preprimary–Second Grade)

Players form even-numbered teams into lines about four feet apart. The first person in each line, balancing a beanbag on the head, walks to a line twenty feet away, touches the marking, walks back to the starting line, and gives the beanbag to the second player, who repeats the same procedure. Players dropping the bag must start over. The first team finished is the winner.

Target Toss (Preprimary–Second Grade)

Players form groups of four to eight players. Each group has a beanbag and a circle drawn on the floor. The children in each group stand in a straight line ten feet from the circle. Each child tosses the beanbag at the target and receives one point for getting it in the circle. The group with the greatest number of points at the end of the playing time wins.

Skunk Tag (Preprimary–Second Grade)

Eight to ten players spread around the playing area. One person who is *It* runs around trying to tag someone. To avoid being tagged, children must hold their nose with their right hand and hold their left foot with their left hand. Anyone tagged before getting into this position becomes the new It.

Eagle and Sparrows (Preprimary–Third Grade)

One player is chosen as the *Eagle*. Other players, six to eight, are *Sparrows*. Sparrows stretch their arms to the sides and circle them up, back, down, and forward. The Eagle chases the Sparrows as they run while rotating arms in the described fashion. Sparrows, when tagged, become Eagles.

Partner Ball Toss (Preprimary–Third Grade)

Players choose partners. Each pair throws the ball back and forth. Each time the ball is caught, the partners move farther apart, attempting to get as far from each other as possible. If the ball is missed, they start over at the original positions.

Wring the Dish Rag (Preprimary–Third Grade)

Partners stand facing each other and join hands. One raises his or her left hand, elevating the right hand of the other. Partners lower the other arms and turn under the raised arms, ending in a back-to-back position. They then raise the other pair of arms, turning under them to face each other again. Repeat several times.

Cats and Mice (Preprimary–Third Grade)

Players divide into two teams called *Cats and Mice*, which stand sixty feet apart on their respective goal lines. Each team chooses a leader. All Cats, except the leader, turn around. The Mice walk up, and when the leader of the Cats thinks they're close enough he calls, "The Mice are coming!" The Cats chase the Mice, attempting to tag them before they reach their goal line. All Mice tagged become Cats. The procedure is reversed for the next game. The team having the largest number at the end of the playing time wins. If leaders are caught, the teams pick new ones.

Call Ball (Preprimary–Third Grade)

Players form a circle of six to ten players. One player who is *It* stands in the center of the circle and, while tossing the ball into the air, calls a player's name. This player must catch the ball before it bounces more than once. If the player succeeds, he or she becomes the new It. If not, the one in the center remains until a player successfully catches the ball.

Hop Tag (Preprimary–Third Grade)

Eight to ten players spread around the playing area. One player who is *It* hops around trying to tag another player who is also hopping. Any player who is tagged becomes the new It.

Simon Says (Preprimary–Fourth Grade)

The leader performs simple activities, such as putting hands on shoulders, which the children imitate if the leader prefaces the activity with the words "Simon says do this." However, if the leader says only the words "Do this," the children must not execute the movement.

Red Light (Preprimary–Third Grade)

Eight to twenty players form a line standing side by side. One player who is *It* stands about twenty yards in front of the line and faces in the opposite direction. The one who is It rapidly counts to ten, during which the line of players runs forward to try to tag It before the count is completed. Upon reaching ten, It calls "Red Light" and all players must stop running before It turns around. Anyone seen moving by It must return to the starting point. The first one to tag It becomes the new It.

Post Ball (First to Fourth Grade)

Two or more teams participate. They form parallel lines with each player about three feet behind the other. A leader stands facing each line twelve feet away. On signal, the leader tosses a ball to the first player in line, who catches it, throws the ball back, and squats in line. The leader repeats the same procedure with each one in the line. The team finishing first and dropping the ball the least number of times wins.

Stork Stand (Second to Fourth Grade)

Child places hands on hips, raises one foot and places it against the inside of the opposite knee. To eliminate the role of the eye in achieving balance, the participant may close the eyes while attempting to maintain balance.

Measuring Worm (Second to Fourth Grade)

Child bends over and places hands on the floor and extends legs to take a front leaning position. With the hands in place, the child walks toward the hands. Keeping the feet in place, the child walks on the hands away from the feet. The elbows and knees remain straight as the actions are repeated several times.

Fire on the Mountain (Second to Fourth Grade)

Players form two circles with one circle, called the *Trees,* standing inside the other circle, called *Children.* In the center is one player who is *It.* The one who is It begins clapping and calls, "Fire on the Mountain. Run, Children, run!" The Trees remain standing while the Children run to the right behind the Trees. When It stops clapping, he or she and the Children run to stand in front of a Tree. The one who does not find a Tree is the new It. In the next game, the Trees and Children change roles.

Chain Tag (Second to Fourth Grade)

One player, who is *It,* tags another player, and the two join hands and run to tag other players. Each player who is tagged joins the chain at the end. Hands must remain joined and only the first and last players in the chain are allowed to tag.

Circle Weave Relay (Second to Fourth Grade)

Players form circles, six to eight players to a circle. One player from each circle starts the relay by running to the outside of the player to the right, to the inside of the next, and continues weaving in this pattern around the circle to the starting position. The player tags the next child on the right, who similarly runs to the right around the circle. The relay continues until everyone in the circle has had a turn. The first circle to complete the relay is the winner.

Cross Tag (Third to Fourth Grade)

Eight to ten players scatter around the playing area. One player who is *It* runs and tries to tag another player. If another player crosses between the chased player and It, It must change and chase the crossing player.

Wall Ball (Third to Fourth Grade)

Players divide into groups of four to six players. Groups form lines about four feet apart, perpendicular to a wall. Distances are marked off every foot, beginning at three feet from the wall and ending at eight. Starting at the three-foot mark, the first player in each line makes three throws and catches of the ball off the wall. Upon successful completion of the three catches, the player may move back to the next mark. Any time the catch is missed, the player must go to the end of the line, and the next player in line takes a turn, beginning at the three-foot mark. Each player in the line does likewise. A player who successfully completes the catches at each mark is through. Others must repeat the throws and catches, beginning at the mark of their previous miss. The team with all of its players completing their catches first is the winner.

Circle Kick Ball (Fourth to Fifth Grade)

The players form two teams. One team stands in one half of a twenty-five-foot circle, the other team in the remaining half. The leader rolls a ball to one team, which kicks the ball toward the opposite team, which kicks it back. One point is scored for each ball kicked out of the circle past the opponents at waist height or below. A ball kicked out above the waist scores for the opposite team. The team having the highest number of points at the end of the playing time wins.

Line Soccer (Fourth to Fifth Grade)

Two even-numbered teams form lines facing each other. Players stand side by side in each line. Teams count off from diagonal ends so that number one of one line faces the last number in the opposite line. A leader places the ball between the lines and calls out a number. The two players with that number rush into the center and attempt to kick the ball through the opposite line. Players in line may stop the ball from going through. A ball kicked through the line scores a point.

Hot Potatoes (Fourth to Fifth Grade)

Players form a circle with six to twenty players in the circle. Players all sit crosslegged and roll or punch balls across the circle. Three or four balls are kept going at once. Players try to knock the ball past other players through the circle. The player permitting the least number of balls to go through the circle wins. An extra player retrieves all the balls going out of the circle. No ball higher than the shoulders counts. Balls may not be bounced or thrown.

Crows and Cranes (Fourth to Fifth Grade)

Players divide into two groups of eight to twenty players. One group is called *Crows* and the other *Cranes*. The playing area is divided with a line in the center and a goal line at each end of the area. Crows and Cranes stand facing each other at the center. The leader calls "Crows" or "Cranes." The group called runs to the goal line behind it with the other group chasing. Players tagged go to the other group. Crows and Cranes return to the center line. The leader gives the call again. The group with the larger number of players at the end of the playing time wins.

Seal Walk (Fourth to Fifth Grade)

Child puts weight on the hands on the floor and extends legs backward. Child walks forward on the hands, dragging legs behind.

Rocker (Fourth to Fifth Grade)

Children lie on their stomachs and arch their backs to grasp the raised legs at the ankles with their hands. In this position, they rock forward and backward.

Crab Walk (Fourth to Fifth Grade)

Children take a squat position. They reach back and place hands flat on the floor without sitting. Distributing the weight equally on all fours, they walk forward in this position.

Stand-Up (Fourth to Fifth Grade)

Partners stand back to back and lock elbows with each other. They push against each other's back and with small steps walk forward and sit on the floor. To stand up, the partners keep arms locked and bend the knees with the feet close to the body. They brace their feet, push against each other's backs, extend legs, and come to a standing position.

Stand-Up Wrestle (Fourth to Fifth Grade)

Partners stand facing opposite directions beside each other. The outsides of the right feet are placed together. Right hands are joined. The two players push and pull until one partner's right foot is lifted from position. The one whose right foot remains in position wins.

Wheelbarrow (Fourth to Fifth Grade)

Partners stand one behind the other facing the same way. The one in front places hands on floor while the one behind lifts the partner's legs at the ankles. The first child walks forward on the hands with the legs supported by the partner in wheelbarrow fashion.

Parachute Play (Fifth to Eighth Grade)

To start parachute play, the chute is spread out on the floor and the students take positions around it, equidistant from each other. Twenty to thirty students can participate when a regulation-size parachute is used. The students kneel on one knee and grasp the chute by its edge with both hands in any one of three ways: palms up, palms down, or one palm up and one palm down. The palms-down grasp is generally the most effective. Some parachutes have handles that make holding the chute easier for the children.

In lifting the chute into the air, height is achieved by everyone simultaneously raising the chute to the maximum of his or her reach. As the parachute fills with air, it rises to form a canopy above the children. A small aperture in the center of the chute permits enough air to escape in order to stabilize the parachute as it slowly descends.

Various actions are possible during the rise and descent of the parachute. Students may move to the right or to the left or in alternate directions. Their movement may be at various tempos: walking, run-

Figure 15.6 The creative possibilities of parachute play are not limited by restrictions on mobility.

ning, galloping, skipping. Musical accompaniment may be used, if desired. Another possibility involves the use of a light ball. The chute is raised with the ball resting on top. The class attempts to bounce the ball or otherwise maneuver it about on the parachute.

Interesting possibilities exist for creative play (see figure 15.6). The parachute can be held at waist height, and different patterns of waves and billows can be created by each child shaking the chute in independent action. Unusual patterns can be created also by small groups working together to achieve a specific motion. To facilitate this activity, the children can be separated into groups of three or four to plan the movement they will contribute to the total pattern.

Adaptations for Young Children's Physical Activity

Games or activities that have been designed by others and taught without modification are usually referred to as conventional games. Many of the games described in the preceding section would be classified as conventional games. While the use of conventional games is widely accepted and encouraged, there is general recognition that many games when modified or adapted create new and exciting challenges and allow for the successful inclusion of children with disabilities. In the following section, general guidelines for the adaptations of the games will be presented. These adaptations can apply to the games previously discussed as well as many other games.

Modify the Rules of the Game

Many games that children play have intricate rules that require a high level of comprehension and reasoning ability. Children who are mentally retarded or those with learning

problems frequently find the structure and rules of some games too complex. For instance, the game of Call Ball requires that a player must respond when his or her name is called by catching a ball that has been thrown into the air before it bounces more than once. This game requires quick reaction, good motor skills, and the ability to process information quickly. For young children with learning problems the game can be modified in several ways. For example, the child who is to throw the ball into the air could call the special child's name *before* the ball is thrown into the air, permitting a longer time to respond to the command. In addition, some students may require two, three, or even four bounces instead of the specified one bounce before they retrieve the ball. A ball of a different size, color, or texture may also be helpful to some children.

Many games emphasize the skill of running. For children with limited mobility, these games can be discouraging unless some provision is made to accommodate their special needs (figure 15.7). In relay races, for instance, the distance the student who is orthopedically impaired has to run can be reduced. It is also helpful to modify running games by structuring experiences to encourage slow rather than fast movements: for example, substituting walking for skipping and running. The size of targets, balls, and other equipment also can be easily adapted to accommodate the special needs of children with disabilities.

Figure 15.7 Students who are orthopedically impaired can be integrated into general physical education experiences if the rules of traditional activities are modified.

Avoid Elimination Games

Many elementary games are designed to eliminate players, such as in tag games. These activities are particularly discouraging to students with disabilities who find that they are frequently eliminated first because of the effects various disabilities have on their movement capabilities. Most activities in physical education can be structured to include rather than exclude children. Even the simple task of asking children to jump over a rope held parallel to the floor can be altered by holding the rope higher at one end than the other. This modification provides children an opportunity to select an appropriate jumping height and avoids the common problem of children eliminating themselves by jumping and missing or avoiding the activity entirely because the rope is too high. Developing activities that include rather than exclude children

only requires a teacher who cares and is sensitive to the needs of children (Auxter, Pyfer, & Huettig, 2005).

Accommodate the Special Needs of Children

Children with orthopedic and sensory impairments will find it impossible to participate with success in some games unless their special needs are considered (figure 15.8). For instance, the game of line soccer will require special adaptations for children who are visually impaired or who are unable to move their lower limbs. Students who are blind could be accommodated in this activity by having their opponent on the opposite team serve as their helper. For example, when the number of the student who is blind is called, the student in the opposite line with the same number could run to the ball and use his or her voice to guide the

Figure 15.8 Examples of simple aids that assist in walking.

Weighted wagons and chairs can be used as walking aids for both typically developing children and some children with cerebral palsy.

Rolling walkers are used for some school-aged children who have difficulty getting around.

nonsighted player from the opposite team to the ball. If the sighted player was successful in helping the student who is visually impaired locate the ball within a designated time period the team could be awarded a point. The nonsighted player's team would earn its points in the usual manner, by having the visually impaired student kick the ball past the opposing team.

In some games it may be necessary to change the skill for students with disabilities. For example, some individuals with orthopedic impairments are unable to use the lower extremities, so a throw will have to be substituted for a kick in games involving the skill of kicking. Similarly, in the game of Bat Ball the students who are visually impaired could hit the ball from a batting tee and run to first base using a rope, an aide, or the sound of a coach's voice. The same youngster could field a ground ball with the verbal assistance of a teammate. A rule modification that a runner going to first is out if the fielder with a visual impairment locates, picks up, and brings the ball to waist level could be made. A throw to first would not be necessary, thus creating a situation in which a student with a disability becomes an asset for a team and not a liability.

Alter the Activity Area

Children with disabilities sometimes experience movement limitations that require the activity area in some activities to be altered. For example, in games in which students with limited mobility serve as goalies or protectors of a certain area, the designated goal should be reduced in size, thereby enhancing the player's success as a goalie. In throwing and kicking activities the distance to the target might be changed, permitting closer action. Enlarging the target likewise will ensure a success-oriented experience for children whose skill level requires this modification. All students find adaptations such as these acceptable if efforts are made to explain the rationale for the alterations in the activity.

Encourage Creativity

Teachers can structure games so that children are asked to respond to challenge questions such as, "Make a bridge with your body," "Balance on five body parts," "Move forward," and "Now show me another way to move forward." Such an approach permits students with various disabilities to respond in ways that allow for success. Students in wheelchairs, for instance, could respond successfully to each of the previous questions by bending forward with their arms or arching their arms to the side to make a bridge; balancing on five body parts by placing their foot or a stick on the floor (four wheels on the chair plus the foot or stick); and successfully moving forward two ways using the conven-

tional manner plus using one arm rather than two arms for the second method.

Games such as Ringmaster are excellent for encouraging students' creativity. The children are asked to move as they think a particular animal moves. All students can be successful in this experience regardless of their physical or mental limitations. One of the authors was pleased to encounter a young child who, although completely paralyzed, participated successfully in this activity by making the sounds of the various animals.

Children, too, can be very effective in creating new games. The extent of their effort can range from a modification of an activity to creating an entirely new activity. Having children create new games can be a particularly effective strategy in helping youngsters with and without disabilities interact. Both groups can learn to accept and appreciate the skills and abilities that are unique to each person.

Graham, Holt-Hale, McEwen, & Parker (1980) has suggested the following guidelines for helping students create their own games:

1. Begin gradually. More structure will be needed at the beginning; however, as students become more adept, the teacher should slowly decrease the structure.
2. Limit your interference. If students are to learn to make significant decisions, they must be responsible for the consequences.
3. Always be aware of safety. Regardless of the level of decision making given the child, a safe environment is the teacher's responsibility. An unsafe situation is one of the few times that the teacher must interfere. When possible, unless the situation calls for an immediate change, make the students aware of the potential hazard and allow them to decide on an alternative.
4. Allow students to enforce their own rules. If students are given the opportunity to make rules, they should enforce them as well. Keep the control in their hands and act only as a facilitator.
5. Remind students of the creative concept—the only rule is that the game can always be changed. Remind them to be flexible; if they are unhappy or can create another aspect, encourage them to make a change!
6. Be patient! The creative process is often time-consuming. The process is as important as the product. Once the general idea of game components and how to manipulate them is mastered, the quality of response will increase.

Emphasize Cooperative Games

Fortunately, greater emphasis today is placed on cooperative play experience. Games like Walking Chairs, for example, impress upon children that success is frequently dependent upon a planned, coordinated group effort. This provides the teacher a unique opportunity to help students understand more about the capabilities and limitations that everyone experiences. Cooperative games also help nondisabled students better understand and accept those with disabilities.

Games in which the student's disability becomes an asset are also excellent opportunities for students to experience cooperative group activities. Blindfolding students and asking them to walk to a designated sound affords the student who is visually impaired a chance to assist sighted classmates. Students in wheelchairs find helping their nondisabled friends move a wheelchair in and out of an obstacle course fun and rewarding. Through cooperative experiences, individuals learn to be considerate of others, to be aware of an individual's feelings, to practice sharing, and to perform with another's interest in mind.

Change the Method of Communication

Students with disabilities sometimes require communication systems that are specific to their needs. For example, verbally explaining a task may not match up well with some children's information processing systems (e.g., Berkeley, Zittel, Pitney, & Nichols, 2001). Information that is more specific might be provided in other ways. The instructor or a peer helper, for example, could demonstrate the game or activity. Also, the teacher could permit a student to "feel" a specific component of a game by encouraging the child to hold onto the teacher's hand as together they explore the equipment used in various games. Some students need not only to hear about or to see a game but also to read a description or a story about the game. This need can be met for poor readers or nonreaders through the use of poster board to which stick figures are attached to show the sequence of a game such as Post Ball.

Summary

In recent years an increasing number of educators, therapists, and allied health personnel have stressed that infants, toddlers, and young children with disabilities should receive early intervention services as soon as the disability becomes apparent. For some individuals the disability might be evident at the time of birth or soon thereafter. The literature offers substantial evidence that early intervention services for young children with disabilities can make a difference in how these individuals develop. Federal legislation requires that early intervention services be provided for individuals "at risk" or those with developmental delays. Because of the important role movement plays in early development, it is obvious that programs for young children with disabilities must include programs that emphasize locomotor, non-locomotor, and manipulative skills.

Within this chapter information is provided about approaches for assessing young children with disabilities as well as ideas for developing appropriate movement-based programs. It is clear that young children with disabilities should be educated, to the extent possible, with their nondisabled peers. Programs based on the concept of inclusion benefit all young children, including those with and without disabilities. Programs that focus on fundamental movement skills (locomotor, non-locomotor, and manipulative) taught using a movement concepts approach provide exciting opportunities for all young children, including those with disabilities, to benefit from positive and enjoyable learning experiences.

Games have long been recognized as an important aspect in the development of young children. Participation in games contributes to growth and development and helps children to learn the essential affective skills of taking turns, sharing, and cooperating. In addition, games can be used to reinforce selected cognitive concepts such as shapes, sizes, and colors and to teach children about their heritage and the culture of other individuals. Most importantly, games can be used to enhance basic motor skills such as running, throwing, jumping, and kicking.

Games can be structured so that they are fun and challenging yet designed to elicit desirable movement patterns. In selecting games to use with young children, attention must be given to the number, age, and ability of the youngsters. Games can be played in any environment, including the classroom and gymnasium. Equipment need not be elaborate, and the necessary items can be made inexpensively.

Within this chapter information is presented about the importance of adapting and modifying activities so that young children with disabilities can participate in games with their nondisabled peers. The integration of children with disabilities can be accomplished if special efforts are made to modify rules as appropriate, encourage inclusion rather than exclusion activities, and emphasize games that promote cooperation. In addition, teachers should be creative in the development of new games and should encourage children to participate in the design and modification of games. There is a growing awareness that young children with special needs can participate with other children in game activities if a proper attitude and creative efforts are employed. The ultimate value is establishing at the earliest of ages that individuals with disabilities can and should enjoy a lifetime of participation in activity with their nondisabled peers.

Enhancing Activities

1. Select one of the activities identified in this chapter and modify the activity so that it would be possible for a youngster with a disability such as a visual or hearing impairment to participate in the activity.

2. Meet with a group of children and have them create a game or activity that is designed to include children of various ability levels, including those with disabilities.

3. Observe a group of young children playing. Do they understand the nature of the game and enforce the rules fairly? Observe to see if the children naturally modify the activity in any way to accommodate the special needs of their peers.

4. Meet with children and have them review a popular game such as kick ball. Have them generate ideas as to how the activity could be modified to become more of an inclusion activity rather than exclusion activity.

5. With a group of young children, organize an activity in which the form of communication must be other than talking. Note the children's responses and discuss with them later their reactions. Observe the creative efforts used to help others understand the rules and strategy.

6. Given a child who is having difficulty kicking a ball with accuracy and distance, select or design a game(s) that could be used as a fun activity to help the child improve his or her performance.

7. Interview a teacher of young children ages three to five as to the importance of movement experiences in the development of young children.

Selected Readings

Active Learning. (2003). Active Learning: A resource guide for designing and implementing developmentally appropriate movement experiences for young children ages 3–5 in home, school and community environments. Minnesota Adapted Physical Education Leadership Committee and the Minnesota Department of Education. Minneapolis: Minnesota Department of Education.

Auxter, D., Pyfer, J. & Huettig. (2005). *Principals and methods of adapted physical education and recreation* (10th ed.). Dubuque, IA: McGraw-Hill.

Avery, M. (1994). Preschool physical education: A practical approach. *Journal of Physical Education, Recreation, and Dance, 65*(6), 37–39.

Baganto, S. J., & Neisworth, J. T. (1990). *SPECS: System to plan early childhood services.* Circle Pines, MN: American Guidance Service.

Bailey, D. B., Bruer, J. T., Symons, F. J., & Lichtman, J. W. (2001). *Critical thinking about critical periods.* Baltimore: Brookes.

Bayley, N. (2005). *Bayley Scales of Infant and Toddler Development-III* (3rd ed.). San Antonio: Psychological Corp.

Berkeley, S. L., Zittel, L. L., Pitney, L. V., & Nichols, S. E. (2001). Locomotor and object control skills of children diagnosed with autism. *Adapted Physical Activity Quarterly, 18*(4), 405.

Block, M. E. (1994a). Including preschool children with disabilities. *Journal of Physical Education, Recreation, and Dance, 62*(6), 45–49, 56.

Block, M. E. (1994b). *A teacher's guide to including students with disabilities in regular physical education.* Baltimore, MD: Paul H. Brookes Publishing Co.

Block, M. E. (2003). Inclusion: Common problems—practical solutions: Introduction. *Teaching Elementary Physical Education, 14*(3), 6.

Bredekamp, S. (1997). *Developmentally appropriate practice in early childhood programs serving children from birth through age 8.* Washington, DC: National Association for the Education of Young Children.

Bricker, D. (2002). *Assessment, evaluation, and programming system for birth to three years and three to six years* (Vol. 2). Baltimore: Brookes.

Brigance, A. H. (1991). *Revised Brigance Diagnostic Inventory of Early Development.* North Billerica, MA: Curriculum Associates.

Burton, A. W., & Miller, D. E. (1998). *Movement skill assessment.* Champaign, IL: Human Kinetics.

Campos, J. J., Anderson, D. I., Barbu-Roth, M. A., Hubbard, E. M., Hertenstein, M. J., & Witherington, D. (2000). Travel broadens the mind. *Infancy, 1,* 149–219.

CEED Center on Early Education and Development. www.cehd.umn.edu/ceed/publications/manuals. Retrieved May 2009.

Clements, R. L. (1993). *Let's move, let's play. Developmentally appropriate movement and classroom activities for preschool children.* Reston, VA: NASPE/AAHPERD.

Clements, R. L. (1995). *My neighborhood movement challenges. Narratives, games and stunts for ages three through eight years.* Reston, VA: NASPE/AAHPERD.

Cowden, J. E., & Eason, R. L. (1991). Pediatric physical education for infants, toddlers, and preschoolers: Meeting IDEA H and IDEA B challenges. *Adapted Physical Activity Quarterly, 8*(4), 263–279.

Cox, L., & Lubbers, T. (1999). *Make it, take it, Creating movement challenge kits for play at home or school.* Teknabooks: www.teknabooks.com.

Cratty, B. J., et al. (1970). *The effects of a program of learning games upon selected academic abilities in children with learning difficulties.* Washington, DC: U.S. Office of Education.

Cratty, B. J. (1973). *Intelligence in action.* Englewood Cliffs, NJ: Prentice-Hall, Inc.

Dauer, V., & Pangrazi, R. (1986). *Dynamic physical education for elementary school children* (8th ed.). Minneapolis: Burgess Publishing Co.

Dunn, J. M. (1979). *Adaptive physical education: A resource guide for teachers, administrators, and parents.* Salem, OR: State of Oregon Mental Health Division.

Dunn, J. M. (Feature Editor). (1991). P L 99–457: Challenges and opportunities for physical education. *Journal of Physical Education, Recreation, and Dance, 62*(6), 233–234, 247.

Dunn, W. (2002). *Best practice occupational therapy.* Thorofare, NJ: SLACK.

Early Childhood Research Institute on Measuring Growth and Development. (1998). *Theoretical foundations of Early Childhood Research Institute on measuring growth and development: An early childhood problem-solving model* (Vol. 6). Minneapolis: University of Minnesota, Center for Early Education and Development.

Eason, R. L. (1991). Adapted physical education delivery model for infants and toddlers with disabilities. *Journal of Physical Education, Recreation and Dance, 62*(6), 41–43, 47–48.

Eichstaedt, C. B., & Lavay, B. (1992). *Physical activity for individuals with mental retardation: Infant to adult.* Champaign, IL: Human Kinetics Publishers.

Engstrom, L. F., & Engstrom, D. (2003). Teaching games that facilitate inclusion. *Teaching Elementary Physical Education, 14*(6), 24.

Folio, M. R., & Fewell, R. R. (2000). *The Peabody Developmental Motor Scales* (2nd ed.). San Antonio: Psychological Corp.

Frankenburg, W. K., & Dobbs, J. (1992). *Denver II.* Denver: Denver Developmental Metrics.

Gabbard, C., LeBlanc, E., & Lowy, S. (1987). *Physical education for children—Building the foundation.* Englewood Cliffs, NJ: Prentice-Hall, Inc.

Gabbard, C. (2003). *Lifelong motor development.* San Francisco: Cummings.

Gallahue, D., & Ozman, J. (2002). *Understanding motor development: Infants, children, adolescents, adults* (5th ed.). New York: McGraw-Hill.

Graham, G., Holt-Hale, S. A., McEwen, T., & Parker, M. (1980). *Children moving: A reflective approach to teaching physical education.* Palo Alto, CA: Mayfield Press.

Hammett, C. T. (1992). *Movement activities for early childhood.* Champaign, IL: Human Kinetics.

Hannaford, C. (1995). *Smart moves: Why learning is not all in your head.* Alexandria, VA: Great Ocean.

Hardin, B. (2002). Content specific pedagogy for children with disabilities. *Teaching Elementary Physical Education, 13*(3), 20–21.

Henderson, H. L., French, R., & Kinnison, L. (2001). Reporting grades for students with disabilities in general physical education. *Journal of Physical Education, Recreation and Dance, 72*(6).

Houston-Wilson, C. (1994). *The effect of untrained and trained peer tutors on the motor performance of students with developmental disabilities in integrated physical education classes.* Unpublished doctoral dissertation, Oregon State University, Corvallis, OR.

Humphrey, J. H. (1976). *Improving learning ability through compensatory physical education.* Springfield, IL: Charles C. Thomas.

Ignico, A. (1994). Early childhood physical education: Providing the foundation. *Journal of Physical Education, Recreation, and Dance, 65*(6), 37–39.

Infant Health and Development Program. (1990). Enhancing the outcomes of low-birth-weight, premature infants: A multisite, randomized trial. *Journal of the American Medical Association, 263*, 3035–3042.

Johnson-Martin, N., Jens, K. G., Attermeier, S. M., & Hacker, B. J. (1991). *The Carolina curriculum for infants and toddlers with special needs.* Balitmore: Brookes.

Kalish, S. (1996). *Your child's fitness: Practical advice for parents.* Champaign, IL: Human Kinetics.

Kozub, F. M. (2002). Using scooters and frisbees to teach invasion games. *Teaching Elementary Physical Education, 13*(5), 28–30.

Kruger, H., & Kruger, J. (1989). *The preschool teacher's guide to movement education.* Baltimore: Gerstung.

Landy, J. M., & Burridge, K. R. (1999). *Fundamental motor skills and movement activities for young children.* The Center for Applied Research in Education. West Nyack, NY: Prentice Hall Direct.

Landy, J. M., & Burridge, K. R. (2000). *Motor skills & movement station lesson plans for young children.* The Center for Applied Research in Education. West Nyack, NY: Prentice Hall Direct.

Leitschuh, C. (2004). Center on Early Education and Development (CEED) at University of Minnesota. http://education.umn.edu/CEED

Lieberman, L., & Cowart, J. F. (1996). *Games for people with sensory impairments: Strategies for including individuals of all ages.* Champaign, IL: Human Kinetics.

Lieberman, L., & Houston-Wilson, C. (2002). *Strategies for inclusion: A handbook for physical educators.* Champaign, IL: Human Kinetics.

Linder, T. W. (1993a). *Transdisciplinary play-based assessment: A functional approach to working with young children* (Rev. ed.). Baltimore: Brookes.

Linder, T. W. (1993b). *Transdisciplinary play-based intervention: Guidelines for developing a meaningful curriculum for young children.* Baltimore: Brookes.

Linder, T. W. (1995). *And you thought they were just playing: Transdisciplinary play-based assessment.* Baltimore: Brookes.

Logsden, B., Allemen, L., Straits, S., Belka, D., & Clark, D. (1997). *Physical education unit plans for pre-school-kindergarten.* Champaign, IL: Human Kinetics.

Marlowe, M. (1980). Games analysis: Designing games for handicapped children. *Teaching Exceptional Children,* 48–51.

McCall, R., & Craft, D. (2000). *Moving with a purpose, developing programs for preschoolers of all abilities.* Champaign, IL: Human Kinetics.

McConnell, S. R. (2000). Assessment in early intervention and early childhood special education: Building on the past to project into the future. *Topics in Early Childhood Special Education, 20,* 43–48.

McConnell, S. R., McEvoy, M. A., & Priest, J. S. (2001). "Growing" measures for monitoring progress in early childhood education: A research and development process for Individual Growth and Development Indicators. *Assessment for Effective Intervention.*

McCubbin, J. A., & Zittel, L. (1991). P. L. 99–457: What the law is all about. *Journal of Physical Education, Recreation, and Dance, 62*(6), 35–37, 47.

Miller J. M., & Roid, G. H. (1994). *The toddler and infant motor evaluation.* San Antonio: Therapy Skill Builders.

Morris, G. S. D. (1980). *How to change the games children play* (2nd ed.). Minneapolis: Burgess Publishing Co.

National Association for Sport and Physical Education. (NASPE). (2000). *Appropriate practices in movement programs for young children ages 3–5.* American Alliance for Health, Physical Education, Recreation, and Dance. [pamphlet]. Reston, VA: NASPE/AAHPERD.

National Association for Sport and Physical Education. (NASPE). (2002). *Active start: A statement of physical activity guidelines for children birth to five.* American Alliance for Health, Physical Education, Recreation and Dance. Reston, VA: NASPE/AAHPERD.

Orlick, T. (1982). *The second cooperative sports and games book.* New York: Pantheon Books.

Pangrazi, R. P. (2004). *Dynamic physical education for elementary school children* (14th ed.). San Francisco: Cummings.

Parks, S. (Ed.). (1992). *HELP strands: Curriculum-based developmental assessment birth to three years.* Palo Alto, CA: VORT.

Phillips, D. A. & Shonkoff, J. P. (2000). *From neurons to neighborhoods: The science of early childhood development.* National Research Council and Institute of Medicine. Washington, DC: National Academy Press.

Pica, R. (1999). *Moving & learning across the curriculum.* Albany, NY: Delmar.

Pica, R. (2000a). *Moving & learning series: Toddlers.* Albany, NY: Delmar.

Pica, R. (2000b). *Moving & learning series: Preschoolers & kindergarten.* Albany, NY: Delmar.

Pica, R. (2000c). *Experiences in movement* (2nd ed.). Albany, NY: Delmar.

Sanders, S. (1994). *Designing preschool movement programs.* Champaign, IL: Human Kinetics.

Sanders, S. (2002). *Active for life: Developmentally appropriate movement programs for young children.* National Association for the Education of Young Children. Champaign, IL: Human Kinetics.

Shonkoff, Jack P. & Phillips, D. (2000). *From neurons to neighborhoods the science of early childhood development.* National Research Council (U.S.) Committee on Integrating the Science of Early Childhood Development (COR). Natl Academy Pr.

Sherrill, C. (1993). *Adapted physical activity, recreation, and sport* (4th ed.). Madison, WI: Brown and Benchmark.

Timiras, P. S. (1972). *Developmental physiology and aging.* New York: Macmillan.

Torbert, M., & Schneider, L. B. (1993). *Follow me too, A handbook of movement activities for 3–5 year olds.* New York: Addison-Wesley.

Tronick, E. Z., & Beeghly, M. (1999). Prenatal cocaine exposure, child development, and the compromising effects of cumulative risk. *Clinics in Perinatology, 26*(1), 151–171.

Ulrich, D. A. (1985). *Test of gross motor development.* Austin, TX: Pro-Ed Publishers.

Ulrich, D. A. (2000). *Test of gross motor development.* Austin, TX: Pro-Ed.

Ulrich, D. A., & Sanford, C. B. (2002). TGMD-2: Evidence of reliability and validity. *Journal of Sport & Exercise Psychology, 22.*

Virgilio, S. (1997). *Fitness education for children: A team approach.* Champaign, IL: Human Kinetics.

Weikart, P. S. (1990). *Movement in a steady beat. Activities for children ages 3–7.* Ypsilanti, MI: High/Scope.

Weikart, P. S. (1997). *Movement plus, rhymes, songs, and singing games. Activities for young children* (2nd ed.). Ypsilanti, MI: High/Scope.

Weikart, P. S., & Carlton, E. B. (1995). *Foundations in elementary education: Movement.* Ypsilanti, MI: High/Scope.

Werner, P. (1994). Whole physical education. *Journal of Physical Education, Recreation, and Dance, 65*(6), 40–44.

Wessel, J. A. (1976). *I CAN program.* Northbrook, IL: Hubbard Scientific Co.

Wessel, J. A., & Zittel, L. L. (1995). *Smart start, Preschool Movement Curriculum, Designed for children of all abilities.* Austin, TX: Pro-Ed.

Wessel, J. A., & Zittel, L. L. (1998). *I Can Primary Skills K–3.* Austin, TX: Pro-Ed.

Zittel, L. L. (1994). Gross motor assessment of preschool children with special needs: Instrument selection considerations. *Adapted Physical Activity Quarterly, 11*(3), 245–260.

Early Childhood Greatest Musical Hits

	Song	Artist	CD/Cassette/Record
1.	In My Backyard	Greg & Steve	Big Fun
2.	Silly Willies	Greg & Steve	Big Fun
3.	The Macken Chicken Dance	Greg & Steve	Big Fun
4.	The Movement Medley	Greg & Steve	Big Fun
5.	I Can Work With One Hammer	Greg & Steve	Fun & Games
6.	Beanie Bag Dance	Greg & Steve	Kids in Action
7.	Beautiful World	Greg & Steve	Kids in Action
8.	Can't Sit Still (warm-up/body actions)	Greg & Steve	Kids in Action
9.	Conga Line	Greg & Steve	Kids in Action
10.	New Beginning	Greg & Steve	Kids in Action
11.	The Way We Do It (warm-up/body actions)	Greg & Steve	Kids in Action
12.	Body Rock (body ID, vocab)	Greg & Steve	Kids in Motion
13	Freeze (body ID)	Greg & Steve	Kids in Motion
14.	Warmin' Up	Greg & Steve	On the Move
15.	(Cool down songs)	Greg & Steve	Quiet Movements with Greg & Steve
16.	Loop D' Loo	Greg & Steve	We All Live Together Vol. 1
17.	Skip to My Loo	Greg & Steve	We All Live Together Vol. 1
18.	Good Morning	Greg & Steve	We All Live Together Vol. 2
19.	Listen & Move (locomotor skills)	Greg & Steve	We All Live Together Vol. 2
20.	Number Rock	Greg & Steve	We All Live Together Vol. 2
21.	Popcorn	Greg & Steve	We All Live Together Vol. 2
22.	Resting (cool down)	Greg & Steve	We All Live Together Vol. 2
23.	The Boogie Walk	Greg & Steve	We All Live Together Vol. 2
24.	The Freeze	Greg & Steve	We All Live Together Vol. 2
25.	The World Is a Rainbow (ribbons)	Greg & Steve	We All Live Together Vol. 2
26.	Rainbow of Colors (ribbons)	Greg & Steve	We All Live Together Vol. 5
27.	A Walking We Will Go (locomotor skills)	Greg & Steve	We All Live Together Vol. 5
28.	Bean Bag Rock	Georgiana Stewart	Beanbag Act's & Coordination Skills
29.	Good Morning	Georgiana Stewart	Good Morning Ex. For Kids
30.	Warm-up Time	Georgiana Stewart	Get a Good Start
31.	Chug-a-long ChooChoo	Georgiana Stewart	Preschool Aerobic Fun
32.	Bean Bag Alphabet Rag	Hap Palmer	Can a Cherry Pie Wave Goodbye?
33.	Let's All Clap Our Hands	Hap Palmer	Can a Cherry Pie Wave Goodbye?
34.	Stepping Out on the Town	Hap Palmer	Can a Cherry Pie Wave Goodbye?
35.	The Bean Bag	Hap Palmer	Easy Does It
36.	Birds in the Circle	Hap Palmer	Easy Does It

	Song	Artist	CD/Cassette/Record
37.	Smoke Drifts to the Sky (cool down)	Hap Palmer	Easy Does It
38.	Move Around the Color	Hap Palmer	Feelin' Free
39.	Rockin' Hula	Hap Palmer	Feelin' Free
40.	Streamers (ribbons)	Hap Palmer	Movin'
41.	Put Your Hands Up in the Air	Hap Palmer	Vol. 1 (black)
42.	Parade of Colors	Hap Palmer	Vol. 2 (red)
43.	Triangle, Circle, Square	Hap Palmer	Vol. 2 (red)
44.	Walter the Waltzing Worm	Hap Palmer	Walter the Waltzing Worm
45.	What a Miracle	Hap Palmer	Walter the Waltzing Worm
46.	Let's Get Started	Mr. Al	"Bop 'til you Drop" (Melody House)
47.	Hello Everybody (warm-up/body actions)	Mr. Al	Mr. Al Sings and Moves (Melody House)
48.	Rock 'N Roll Body Parts (warm-up/body actions)	Mr. Al	Mr. Al Sings and Moves
49.	Moonbeams (ribbons)	Mr. Al	Mr. Al Sings and Moves
50.	Wiggle Your Knees Boogie	Mr. Al	Mr. Al Sings and Moves
51.	Shake Everything (body actions)	Mr. Al	Mr. Al Sings and Moves
52.	The Jumping Song	Mr. Al	Mr. Al Sings and Moves
53.	Galloping Country Style	Mr. Al	Mr. Al Sings and Moves
54.	Move to the Music	Mr. Al	Mr. Al Sings and Moves
55.	Bean Bag Bop	Silly Willy	Sports Workout
56.	Cool	Silly Willy	Sports Workout
57.	Let's Hop	Silly Willy	Sports Workout
58.	Marching	Silly Willy	Sports Workout
59.	Pre-Jump Rope Skills	Silly Willy	Sports Workout
60.	Pony Ride	Silly Willy	Sports Workout
61.	Stretching	Silly Willy	Sports Workout
62.	Workout	Silly Willy	Sports Workout
63.	Gallop	The Learning Station	Physical Ed
64.	Jumpin' Jacks	The Learning Station	Physical Ed
65.	Run & Walk	The Learning Station	Physical Ed
66.	Stretch	The Learning Station	Physical Ed
67.	Stomp & Clap	The Learning Station	Physical Ed
68.	The Marching Game	The Learning Station	Physical Ed

10-minute blank tapes:

World Class Tapes wholesale catalog
670 Airport Blvd., Suite 1
Ann Arbor, MI 48108
(800) 365–0669

Media Express
1402 First Ave. S.
Minneapolis, MN 55403
(612) 872–0369
(They will make tapes to your specifications: two-, three-, five-, ten-minute, whatever you would like.)

CHAPTER
16

Swimming

CHAPTER OBJECTIVES

After studying this chapter, the reader should be able to:

1. Appreciate the importance of swimming and water-related activities for individuals with special needs.
2. Modify instruction in swimming so that individuals with various disabilities learn to float, swim, and enjoy the water.
3. Discuss the appropriate use of various assistive devices, including flotation devices, as aids for helping those with disabilities float and swim.
4. Recognize the importance of modifying the pool and locker room to increase the accessibility of these facilities.
5. Select and organize games and activities that can be used to help students orient to the water.
6. Apply appropriate instructional activities, including task analysis and evaluation procedures, to create effective and efficient swimming experiences for individuals with various disabilities.
7. Recognize when swimming might be contraindicated for some students and the appropriate procedures for helping students with special needs such as epilepsy and incontinence.
8. Analyze the beginning and intermediate strokes used in swimming and modifications that can be made in these strokes for individuals with various orthopedic impairments.

Swimming ranks high among the physical education activities that can be most successfully taught to those who have a disability. The success is due in large part to the buoyancy of the water, which, in providing support for the body, is both helpful and reassuring to the student engaged in learning a new skill. Sustained by the water, an individual with an orthopedic impairment can perform otherwise impossible movements; even those students who are incapable of walking, as is the case with those who have severe cerebral palsy, are frequently able to learn to swim. Students who are mentally retarded find the buoyancy of the water comforting, and this fact is a great help to the teacher in allaying the fears that often prevent successful learning of an activity by individuals with mental retardation.

Swimming is also high among the activities that are most beneficial to individuals with disabilities. Swimming, of course, provides the student with important skills for

safety on, in, or near the water. It also makes possible participation in a recreational activity that is popular with the nondisabled and so opens opportunities for socialization and involvement in water-related family activities. In addition, the swimmer with special needs reaps important physiological benefits.

The beneficial effects upon the body result from the amount and nature of the work performed in swimming. Even mild activity in the water has a good effect upon those whose movements are severely restricted. Improved circulation and increased strength are likely to occur in most participants. Those who have restricted movements in the joints caused by pain and stiffness often benefit greatly from the increased movement of the joints made possible in the water. Likewise, those with cerebral palsy often find that because of the water's buoyancy they are able to make movements in the water that they are not otherwise able to make.

Even children who are denied participation in so many other activities can enjoy the pleasures of swimming. For children who cannot stand erect in the water, the buoyancy of the water reduces the pressure of body weight on the head of the femur. For others, the water buoyancy makes control of the body easier by minimizing the effects of weak muscles and the lack of balance and stability that hinder or restrict movement out of the water. Appliances that must always be worn otherwise can usually be removed for swimming.

Organizing the Instruction

Swimming instruction should be scheduled regularly for students who are to be in the swimming program. Class size will vary with conditions. If the students' disabilities are not severe, the teacher will be able to handle larger numbers in a single period. With few exceptions, those with disabilities usually may be included in a regular swimming class for nondisabled students. When the disabilities of students are more severe, the size of the class for one teacher must be reduced proportionately to retain teaching effectiveness and maintain the safety of the participants. For some students with severe disabilities it may be necessary to provide individual instruction. In the school situation, individual instruction may be provided by student helpers. In a community swimming program, volunteers may be recruited from throughout the community.

Before organization of the class and methods of instruction are developed, the instructor must determine each student's present level of skill, movement capabilities, and attitude toward the disability (see figure 16.1). An example of an evaluation checklist for entering and exiting the water, using a task-analytic format, is presented in figure 16.2. Similar forms should be used to evaluate the individual's performance level. Different kinds of disabilities impose different limitations. The kinds of movements an individual can make will determine the approach used by the instructor. Analysis of movement will provide information for deciding which strokes should be taught and what modifications are necessary. The student's acceptance or lack of acceptance of the disability determines to a considerable extent the way in which the instruction, particularly in its initial phase, is presented.

Consideration must also be given to provisions for those who are incontinent. For example, youngsters with myelomeningocele will have bowel and bladder incontinence. The former is usually managed by appropriate diet and training and, if managed well, is not a problem during activity in water. If the individual has an ileostomy or colostomy and uses an external collection device, the bag should be emptied and cleaned before entering the pool. The bag is not removed for swimming and can be protected from view by the swimming suit to avoid any potential embarrassment. The stoma or opening in the side should be sealed with a watertight bandage. A skimmer should be readily available for dealing with the occasional emergencies when feces are deposited in the pool. Chemicals should be put into the water to prevent such an occurrence from posing a health problem.

As a general rule, swimming is recommended for all individuals with disabilities. There are, however, some

Figure 16.1 This young girl is participating in a water orientation activity and this boy is supported during his swim instruction.

Enter/Exit Checklist   Name_____

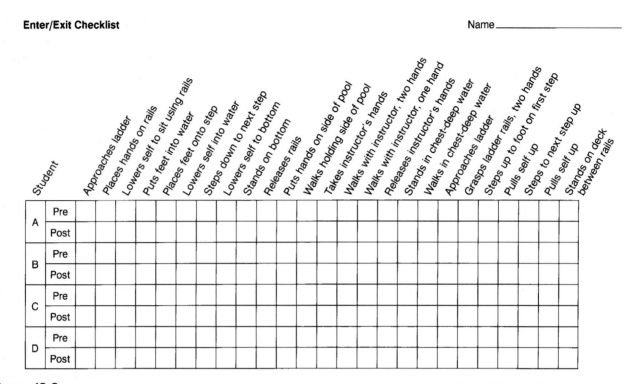

Figure 16.2 Task analysis of entrance into and exit out of the pool. *(Source:* from *Aquatics for Special Populations.* (1987). YMCA, p. 134.)

conditions that require close articulation with physicians to determine the suitability of swimming and its effect on the safety and health of the affected child as well as others. Some of these conditions include infectious diseases in the active stage (such as when the child has an elevated temperature); chronic ear infections; chronic sinusitis; allergies to chlorine or water; open wounds and sores; skin conditions such as eczema; osteomyelitis in the active stage; acute episodes of rheumatoid arthritis; venereal disease; and severe cardiac conditions.

The previous list does not include children with epilepsy. These children should be encouraged to participate in swimming and other water-related activities. The instructor and lifeguard should be aware of those youngsters who have epilepsy. This is best handled by noting and remembering those who have epilepsy rather than requiring the child to wear a special hat or some other symbol which stigmatizes the youngster. In the event that a child experiences a grand mal seizure in the water, the first aid response is similar to that described in chapter 19 on the CD. The procedure would call for the instructor or lifeguard to maintain the head above water with the head tilted back to ensure a clear airway and allow the seizure to happen. If time permits, the child should be moved to shallower water; no forced effort, however, should be made to remove the child from the water. In some instances a blanket can be placed in the water under the person to provide additional support. When the seizure is finished, the individual should

be removed to a dry and warm room. As discussed in chapter 19 on the CD, parents and other appropriate officials should be notified so that an accurate record of the frequency of the seizures may be maintained. If the seizure lasts for an extended period of time or a seizure is followed immediately by a second seizure, medical assistance should be obtained. Some authorities recommend, because of the possibility of shock from the ingestion of water, that anyone who has a seizure in the water should be taken to an emergency room for a medical check-up. The swim staff should be aware of the procedures the parents recommend.

Techniques for Getting into and Out of the Pool

Locker Room Accessibility

An important consideration in providing swimming instruction for the student with special needs is to ensure that the locker room facilities are accessible. This means, for instance, that the lockers are large enough to accommodate braces and other appliances or orthotics. Some of the lockers should also be opened by a key rather than a combination to assist students who are visually impaired. Tables and benches should be available to aid those students who need to dress and undress in a back-lying position. Tables and benches also can be effectively utilized for purposes of transferring to and from a wheelchair. Handrails should be available on some of the walls as well as in the shower and toilet areas. Drinking fountains and showers should be designed to allow the individual with no arms or restricted use of the arms to turn the water on and off.

Priest (1980) suggests that wheelchairs should be permanently stored within the locker room. These chairs could be used to transport nonambulatory students from the locker room to the pool. There are two advantages to this approach: first, the wheelchair would be free of dirt; and second, the individual's primary chair would not be subjected to the water and pool chemicals.

The doors into the pool area should be wide enough to accommodate the wheelchair. The locker room floor including the shower area should have a nonskid surface.

Some students, too, may need the assistance of volunteers or peers. These individuals can be very helpful in assisting with dressing and undressing and providing other support as necessary. Volunteers should be cautioned, however, to encourage as much independence as possible and to avoid being oversolicitous.

Students with limited mobility need to develop effective ways of getting into and out of the pool. Ramps and steps with handrails are helpful to those who need only such support as these provide. The techniques for using the ramps and rails need to be worked out by the teacher and the individual student. If these devices, as well as hydraulic lifts, are not available or if they are insufficient, the student will need to be lifted into and out of the pool. Technically, it should be noted that manual lifting of students is considered a violation of the Americans with Disabilities Act (ADA, 1990). The intent of the ADA is not to discourage schools and community centers from offering swimming to students with disabilities, but rather to emphasize that barrier free environments that encourage independence is the desired goal. The ADA and others recognize, however, that until all of the necessary modifications can be made, reasonable accommodations, including lifting individuals to and from the pool, may be necessary.

The usual procedure for lifting students into and out of the pool requires two people. The person who is being assisted may sit on the deck, if able, or be seated in a wheelchair. In the latter case, a helper stands behind the chair and reaches under the student's arms to grasp the wrists and bring them to the chest. The other helper stands in front of the wheelchair and takes hold around the thighs. Together the helpers lift the person free of the chair for seating on a piece of canvas or on a kickboard that has been placed at the edge of the pool. He or she is seated parallel to the pool and supported by one helper while the other enters the water to take a position in front of the student. The helpers turn the canvas so that the student's legs hang over the edge of the

pool. The helper on the deck then gently pushes forward on the shoulders of the student while the helper in the pool takes hold at the waist to guide the body into the water. For a student who does not need to be lifted to the edge of the pool, only the techniques for lifting into and out of the water are utilized.

In addition to the previous information, Adams and McCubbin (1991) emphasize the following points when doing lifts and transfers:

1. Make certain that the brakes on the wheelchair are locked. If additional people are available, have someone hold the wheelchair in addition to locking the brakes.
2. Lifters should use good body mechanics when lifting. The distance the person is lifted should be as small as possible.
3. Explain to the person prior to lifting him or her the plans for the lift and transfer.
4. Lifters should lift the person in unison, with one person giving directions.
5. The swimmer should be lifted from the chair to the deck, then from the deck to the pool. The deck should be nonabrasive. If the deck is abrasive, use a towel or blanket to pad the surface.
6. Ensure that a helper is available to support the person on the deck if necessary.
7. Always have a helper in the pool to help the swimmer into the water.

Special care also will be required when helping the child with a urinary bag transfer into and out of the pool. As indicated in figure 16.3, the hip on the side of the stoma (opening) must be lifted as the child moves from the deck to the water and vice versa.

A hydraulic lift (figure 16.4) is sometimes available at pools to assist students in wheelchairs into and out of the pool. Although many different systems are available, the goal is to allow the individual to enter and exit the water with as much independence as possible.

If the pool has a ramp, an old wheelchair designated for this purpose is used to wheel the student into the water to chest height. A single helper can then easily transfer the student into the water by placing one arm under the legs and the other behind the back to make the lift. Portable steps into the pool also provide helpful assistance and independence for wheelchair users who are more mobile (figure 16.4)

In all these techniques, the steps for getting students into the pool can be reversed to lift or assist them out. It is assumed, of course, that adjustments are made as required in individual cases.

The choice of techniques used to get someone into and out of the pool is dependent upon the facilities available and the method preferred by the swimmer. For example,

Figure 16.3 Modification of over-the-side pool exit for a spina bifida child with stoma and bag.

although the availability of a hydraulic lift is desirable, some pools may not have this piece of equipment and some swimmers may prefer to be assisted manually.

Pool Accessibility

Generally there are few, if any, modifications that need to be made in the aquatic facility to meet the needs of special students. It is far better to provide swimming instruction for students with disabilities than to argue that the program is not possible because of a poorly designed and somewhat inaccessible pool. Many professionals today realize that creative solutions to problems related to accessibility can be achieved given a proper attitude and a desire to make things better. Consumers with disabilities recognize, too, that an inaccessible pool is a serious problem only if the pool manager and instructor are unresponsive and unwilling to seek alternative solutions to help them.

In some school systems and communities that have more than one pool, it may be possible to identify a pool that may be more desirable for use by students with disabilities.

Figure 16.4 A hydraulic lift is sometimes useful to help the person with a disability get into and out of the water.

The following list indicates some factors that should be considered in checking to determine the appropriateness of the pool.

1. Decks should be wide and slip-resistant. It is also desirable to have a deck that is no more than twelve inches above the water line.
2. The water depth of the pool should be such that a suitable instructional area is available to teach young students with disabilities (see figure 16.9 on page 369). An instructional depth of three and one-half to four and one-half feet is highly desirable. Benches used as resting platforms should be placed in the water to reduce the depth of the pool for paraplegics and double-leg amputees who find a depth of even three feet too deep for them to stand.
3. Higher water temperatures help some individuals, particularly students with cerebral palsy, relax in the water. A water temperature of 80°F to 90°F is generally recommended. Indoor pools also should have an air temperature of 4°F to 6°F higher than the water temperature.
4. Ramps at the shallow end of the pool are helpful in getting students with orthopedic impairments into and out of the pool. As few older pools are designed with ramps, marine plywood may be used to construct a portable ramp when necessary. Special care must be taken to provide a gradual descent from the ramp into the pool.
5. The bottom of the pool should be as slip-resistant as possible with a gradual slope in the shallow end of one inch per each one and one-half feet of horizontal slope.
6. The depth of the pool should be clearly marked on the vertical wall or deck of the pool. The markings should be large and bright so that they may be easily distinguished.
7. Handholds should be provided at depths greater than three and one-half feet and spaced no greater than four feet apart. Rope fastened to the wall, at or slightly above

water level, is an inexpensive adaptation that can be used to assist students with disabilities.

8. Information about accessible dressing rooms, showers, and lockers may be found in appendix VI on the CD.

Overcoming Fear of the Water

Most nonswimmers feel some anxiety about entering the water in the beginning. This is especially true of nonswimmers with disabilities because they lack confidence in their movement capabilities. Consequently, the teacher should strive to make the introductory activities to the water as much fun as possible so that the students will begin to feel secure in the water before they have time to be frightened.

The introductory water activities can be fun if the teacher's manner is sincere and friendly, if the instructions are clearly stated and calmly spoken, if the teacher's attitude conveys understanding and appreciation of each student as an individual, and if the instructor's own enthusiasm for water activities is transmitted to the participants.

The teacher should seek to provide experiences that will lead the students from that to which they are accustomed and readily accept to new experiences that will effect complete acceptance of the water. Sitting on the side of the pool splashing with the feet is one example of an activity that is generally accepted without anxiety and that can be directed toward the objective of complete acceptance of the water. Ambulatory students may progress from dangling the feet to standing in waist-deep water and from this to bobbing up and down to their shoulders and eventually to their chins. The final step would be ducking completely under the water and opening the eyes.

For some young students, water adjustment skills are best taught by using a wading pool. The smaller and familiar environment of the wading pool enables the instructor to initiate contact in a setting comfortable to the student. In subsequent sessions the wading pool can be moved closer to the main pool until such time as the trust between student and instructor reaches a point that a successful transfer to the regular pool can be accomplished.

Those who are not ambulatory or have severe limitations in motor movement may need support in the water. Support may be provided by the instructor if this seems necessary or desirable. There are a number of flotation devices (figure 16.6 on page 365; 16.12 on page 372) such as buoyant belts, inflatable vests, arm supports, and swim suits with built-in flotation support that may be used to support or stabilize the body in the water. The students should be held in such a manner as to relieve all fear and anxiety that may develop. Slowly, as their confidence increases, the amount of support can be reduced and finally withdrawn (figure 16.5).

Figure 16.5 Portable steps are helpful for youngsters using and not using a wheelchair and can be easily removed from poolside after use.

With persistent practice almost all children with disabilities can learn to float, or to move in some manner to stay afloat. However, there will be a few who, because of extreme deformity or movement limitations, will always require flotation devices for support in the water.

For students with cerebral palsy it is an absolute necessity that anxiety be kept at a minimum to allow muscular relaxation. For these students, as well as for others who experience difficulty in relaxing in the water, relaxation exercises such as floating the arms and legs while in a sitting position in shallow water are very helpful. Maintaining the water temperature in the middle eighties, which is somewhat higher than the 78° temperature recommended for normal usage, also aids in muscular relaxation.

Students with visual impairments must be oriented to the pool environment thoroughly to ensure that they have a well-developed mental image of the pool and the surrounding area. The orientation may be accomplished by walking around the pool with the student and explaining concepts such as pool depth and slope. The location of permanent fixtures such as wall ladders, stairs, diving boards, and lifeguard stands also should be identified for the student who is visually impaired. Opportunities to touch and manually explore pool equipment also assists the blind to develop a meaningful picture of the water environment.

Special care must be taken with the visually impaired and hearing-impaired to ensure their appropriate responses to sensory cues. Establishing a meaningful communication system is particularly desirable for fostering a favorable water environment for student and teacher. For the deaf and hard-of-hearing, this usually requires developing some simple hand signals that communicate concepts such as stop, watch, yes, and so on. Demonstrating the skill to be performed is also effective. With students who are visually impaired, the teacher must promote the desired responses to auditory, tactile, and kinesthetic cues.

During the introductory activities, care should be taken to prevent fearful, cautious individuals from being suddenly and unexpectedly splashed by the more adventurous. A good rule to establish firmly in everyone's mind before entering the water is no deliberate splashing of other people. Care must also be taken to prevent accidents caused by lack of concern for personal safety. Children with cerebral palsy have been observed by swimming instructors to sometimes make no effort to surface for air, after they have become familiar enough with being in the water to enjoy submerging themselves. These children must be closely watched to avert possible drowning owing to passivity to immersion; their lack of concern gives a false impression of being fully in control.

Individuals who are mentally retarded can be very successful in water-related activities if the various skills, including the orientation phase, are divided into small tasks and sequenced appropriately (see table 16.1 on page 366 and figure 16.7 on page 368). Swimming instructors also should remember that individuals who are mentally retarded need assistance in generalizing skills. Applied to swimming, this means that some orientation activities will be necessary each time the person is exposed to a new water environment. Instructors must emphasize to the student and parents that additional practice will be necessary to ensure success and safety in other water settings.

Evaluation

As indicated in chapter 6, it is essential that information about student progress be monitored for each instructional unit. In aquatic programs, various types of charts may be used, and skills to be included will vary according to the content of the swimming program. The SUNY Brockport Motor Fitness Clinic Checklist developed by Dr. Cathy Houston-Wilson (Lieberman & Houston-Wilson, 2002) is presented in table 16.1 on pages 366–368. The checklist is hierarchical in that skills build upon one another and are listed in order of complexity. The checklist also indicates the swimmer's level of independence with the skills. Houston-Wilson recommends using the checklist for the initial evaluation of skill as well as for monitoring progress. Measuring progress helps students and instructors appreciate the educational gains that are possible through well-designed instructional programs. A record of the skills achieved should be shared with parents and filed for subsequent use by other instructors.

The I CAN: Aquatics Skills (Wessel, 1976) is an example of a curriculum. Extensive information on various disabilities and aquatics activity modification and adaptation is found in the text by Lepore, Gayle, and Stevens (1998). This resource served as the springboard for one Minnesota school district to fund and promote a full program of aquatics for students with disabilities.

Water Orientation Activities

Students with disabilities frequently require a longer orientation period in the water before they are ready to be taught the basic swimming skills. This longer adjustment time is necessary for several reasons. For some students with disabilities, their previous water experiences have been very limited and they need time to explore the water environment. Some youngsters who are orthopedically impaired find, for instance, that the body movements and positions created by the water buoyancy are exciting, but they need time to explore these new movement sensations (figure 16.8 and figure 16.9). Children who are mentally retarded and neurologically impaired may not have developed the movement concepts, like spatial relationships, that are essential for success in water activities. Regardless of the reason, the time spent in the water in preswimming activities should be structured to create a worthwhile experience for the special student (see figure 16.7 on page 368). Some of the water activities that can be used in the early water orientation sessions follow.

Simple Relays

Games in the shallow end of the pool, in which students are asked to walk to and from designated areas, are fun and encourage students to explore the water.

Basic Skill Games

Many motor experiences that children have previously learned can be reinforced in the pool environment. These

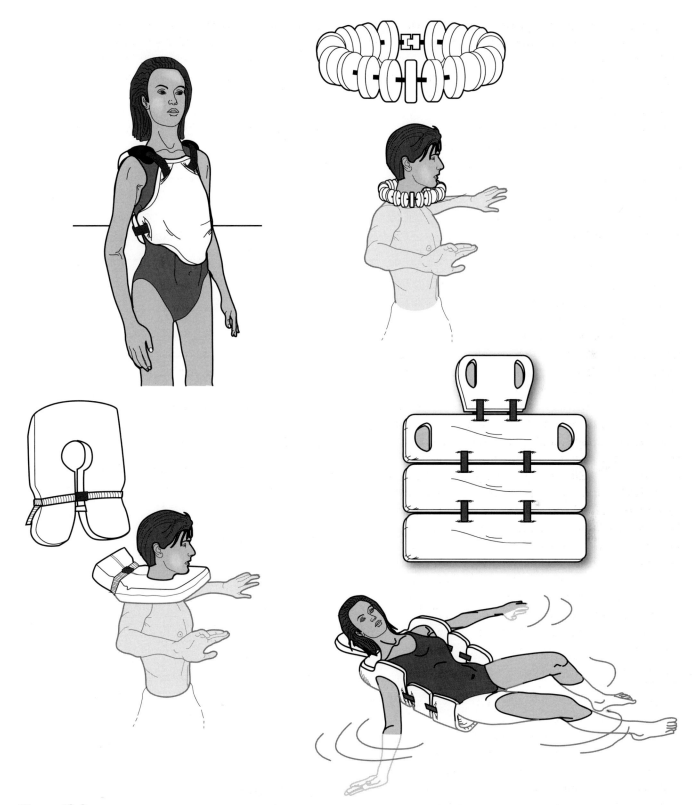

Figure 16.6 Various commercially available flotation devices.

include simple throwing and catching games. Items such as sponges and Frisbees make ideal objects to throw. The transfer of a familiar skill to the pool environment helps many students in their adjustment to the water.

Circuit Pool

An activity in which children are asked to move around the pool stepping over, around, and under items helps students to associate an enjoyable and familiar land

TABLE 16.1   SUNY Brockport Motor Fitness Clinic Aquatic Skills Checklist

By Cathy Houston-Wilson, PhD

Student: _____ Age: _____ Date: _____

Instructor: _____

	Independent	Needs Assistance	Total Assistance
Pool preparation			
Proper behavior en route to the pool			
Takes clothes off			
Hangs clothes in locker			
Puts bathing suit on			
Takes shower			
Awaits directions before entering pool			
Pool entry			
Sits at edge of pool, feet in water			
Puts water on body			
Lowers self into pool			
Climbs down stairs and enters pool			
Adjustment to water			
Splashes water around with no fear			
Holds gutter and kicks legs			
Kicks on front while being towed			
Kicks on back while being towed			
Moves arms and legs in swimming motion while being towed			
Blows bubbles			
Treads water for 30 seconds			
Puts whole face in water for 5 seconds			
Holds breath while submerged for 10 seconds			
Bobs up and down 5 times			
Continuous rhythmic breathing while holding side of pool and turning head to side 10 times			
Continuous rhythmic breathing from prone position while kicking with kickboard for 20 feet			
Floating skills			
Floats on front while holding kickboard with arms fully extended and face submerged			
Front float			
Back float			
Basic propulsion			
Flutter kicks with kickboard while on front for 15 feet			

Glides on front with push-off, holding kickboard with arms extended, and flutter kicks for 15 feet			
Glides on front with push-off and flutter kicks with no kickboard for 15 feet			
Glides on front with push-off and flutter kicks with face submerged and no kickboard for 15 feet			
Glides on back with push-off, holding kickboard with arms extended, and flutter kicks for 15 feet			
Glides on back with push-off and flutter kicks with no kickboard for 15 feet			
Rolls over, front to back, while gliding			
Rolls over, back to front, while gliding			
Swimming strokes			
Does freestyle stroke, arms only, face out of water, for 10 strokes			
Does freestyle stroke, arms only, face submerged, for 10 strokes			
Does freestyle stroke, arms and legs, face submerged, for 10 strokes			
Does freestyle stroke, arms and legs, with rhythmic breathing, for 10 strokes			
Swims under water for 10 feet			
Does side stroke on either side for 10 feet			
Does breast stroke for 10 feet			
Does back crawl stroke, arms only, for 10 strokes			
Does back crawl stroke, arms and legs, for 10 strokes			
Diving skills			
Dives from a sitting position			
Dives from squat or crouched position			
Dives from standing with knees slightly bent			
Dives from standing with spring and arm action			
Performs standing dive from end of low board			
Water safety and deep water skills			
Bobs 15 times			
Treads water for 30 seconds			
Survival floats			
Jumps feet first into water, surfaces, and swims back to side of pool			
Begins freestyle stroke after jumping or diving into pool			
Changes directions while swimming			

(continued)

TABLE 16.1 SUNY Brockport Motor Fitness Clinic Aquatic Skills Checklist (Continued)

	Independent	Needs Assistance	Total Assistance
Changes position while floating and swimming (rolls from front to back)			
Changes from horizontal to vertical position while treading water			
Dives off side and swims under water for 15 feet			

For more information on adapted aquatics see Lepore, M., Gayle, W. G., & Stevens, S. (1998). *Adapted Aquatics Programming.* Champaign, IL: Human Kinetics.

Figure 16.7 Sample task analysis for swimming. (*Source: Aquatics Sports Skills Program Guide.*)

Walk across the pool holding onto the side with one hand 4 out of 5 times.

Task Analysis

a. Enter pool.
b. Stand next to and face pool wall.
c. Place both hands on wall.
d. Side step the width of the pool.
e. Release one hand and sidestep the width of the pool with support of one hand.
f. Stand with back to pool wall.
g. Hold onto pool wall with one hand (outside hand) and walk from corner to corner in the shallow end.

Teaching Suggestions

• Scatter a large quantity of toys (i.e., balloons, plastic bottles, sponges, etc.) in pool requiring the student to move the toys out of his/her way in order to move about the pool with or without assistance.

Walk across the pool alone 4 out of 5 times.

Task Analysis

a. Enter pool.
b. Stand with back to pool wall.
c. Walk from corner to corner in the shallow end.
d. Walk across the pool in shoulder-deep water.

Teaching Suggestions

• Place hula hoop on top of the water and have students go under the hoop. Once this is accomplished lower the hoop into the water so the students have to go under the water to get through the hoop.
• Have student count your fingers or his/her own while he/she is submerged under the water and his/her face is above the water. Once this is accomplished, student should learn how to open eyes under water and then count fingers.
• Have students search for objects under water, such as rings or large washers. Hands must be used to retrieve objects.

Figure 16.8 For teaching swimming, a plastic-coated gymnastics mat can serve as a safe and successful platform.

experience with the water while practicing important orientation skills.

Retrieval Games

Children enjoy opportunities to retrieve items that have been placed into the water and around the pool's edge. At first, it is best to have students focus on retrieving objects that do not require them to place the head under water. Later experiences in retrieval of objects with the face in the water can be incorporated into some games students will learn later as they establish their breathing rhythm.

As the students become more accustomed to the water, special group games can be included in the water orientation sessions. These activities will reinforce many of the same concepts, such as taking turns, sharing, and following directions, that students have previously learned. Some popular group water experiences include the following.

Figure 16.9 A Tot Deck can be placed in the shallow end of the pool for smaller children to gain confidence in the water.

Circle Volleyball

This activity requires that the players keep a beach ball in the air for as long as possible without permitting the ball to touch the water. One student is designated as the server to bat the ball into the air to begin the game. Students are encouraged to count the number of consecutive hits they make before the ball touches the water.

Simon Says

This game, with which most children are familiar, is played by having all the students form a circle with one student designated as the leader. The leader calls out movements to be made, prefacing some with the words "Simon says" and others without. Players try to perform only those movements that "Simon says." Various movements such as stepping forward, backward, stooping, bending, and so on, can be incorporated into this activity.

Garbage Clean-Up

Cork balls, ping-pong balls, and other items such as sponges are placed into the pool. The players are divided into two teams. At a given signal, they pick up all the items and place them into buckets placed along the deck. The team collecting the most items is declared the winner.

Movement Relays

Each team is composed of an equal number of players. One member from each team starts the activity by moving to the other side of the pool and back. Upon returning, the player touches a teammate who moves to the other side and returns. The team that has its last player return first is declared the winner. As the name of this relay implies, various movement patterns should be emphasized, such as walking forward, backward, sideways, stooped walking with the chin touching the water, arms over the head, and so forth. Some relays should also be designed to encourage controlled movements such as walking three steps, stop, turn completely around, and move forward again.

Object Relays

Relays in which students move various objects such as kickboards, ping-pong balls, sponges, and plastic balls around the pool are enjoyable. This activity should be structured so that students have to use various body parts to move the designated objects. Beginners, for instance, might be asked to use their chests to move a beach ball. As the students become better adjusted to the water, this activity can be increased in difficulty by having the students push the ball with the chin. Obviously, this latter experience is an excellent lead-up to placing the face into the water.

Add-Ons

Children enjoy this activity in which one student starts by making a movement that must be repeated by a second student before the latter adds a second movement. The next student performs the first two movements and adds a third. This is an excellent activity because students challenge one another and the instructor is provided an opportunity to observe and assess the quantity and quality of the student's water orientation skills.

One of the concomitant values of the water orientation activities described in this section is that these experiences also reinforce many of the skills taught in the classroom. Specific academic skills that can be supported through water orientation experiences include counting, recognizing letters, and color discrimination. Basic arithmetic and spelling concepts, for example, can be reinforced by having students count the number of plastic letters retrieved from the bottom of the pool and asking them to form words with the letters. The letters could also be sorted by color and size and alphabetized to help students with their color, visual, and language skills. Additionally, children are taught to follow directions, take turns, and develop sequence skills. Although helping the special student orient to the water is in and of itself a worthy objective, other benefits such as reinforcing classroom skills are possible in well-designed water adjustment programs.

Establishing Breathing Rhythm

As soon as the students show sufficient confidence, they may proceed to place their faces in the water while holding their breath. This is done by bending over from a standing position in chest-high water. Students should be encouraged to repeat the action until they are able to hold their face under the water fifteen to twenty seconds.

The next step is to exhale through the mouth while the face is submerged. The final step is to establish a definite rhythmic pattern of breathing. To achieve this the students bob the head up and down in the water, taking air in through the mouth while the head is above the water and exhaling through the mouth while the head is down.

Those who cannot stand may take a sitting position on the bottom of the pool if the water is shallow enough. A steel chair may be used where the water is not sufficiently shallow to permit sitting on the bottom. The seated student performs these activities in the sitting position. If a student must be wholly supported by the instructor or helper, which may be the case in muscular disorders or severe conditions of cerebral palsy, the introduction to the water is made by the instructor holding the student around the waist from the back. If the pool is shallow enough, the teacher sits down in the water while providing support with one hand. In this position the student's arms and legs can be moved alternately by the teacher in the swimming pattern, starting with raising the arms over the head and pulling them to the sides and followed by moving the legs in a kicking fashion. The kinds and amount of movement that can be made by the arms and legs depend, of course, on the limitations of the individual. Later, when progress permits, the student may be held in a prone position to allow lifting the head above and lowering the face into the water at will.

Individuals with cardiac conditions should not be allowed to practice breath holding. For these students, instruction in how to expel air while the face is under water must accompany the instruction in how to place the face in the water. Or, if their conditions are moderate to severe, they may be taught floating and swimming techniques that do not require submersion of the face.

Some children affected by the rubella syndrome appear to have a high sensitivity to certain pool chemicals, even if they have no visual disability. For this reason, a container of clean water should be kept at pool level so that these students can bathe their eyes at regular intervals.

Rhythmic breathing assists students with cerebral palsy to develop their breathing skills as well as improve their breath control and speech pattern. For this reason, some variation of breathing exercises should be incorporated into every lesson for the student with cerebral palsy.

Assistive Devices

There are numerous assistive devices that can be used to help the nonswimmer learn to swim. Swim fins, for example are recommended for children with spastic cerebral palsy. The fins tend to minimize the exaggerated stretch reflex and provide additional power in the kick. Fins are also used to increase the length of a short extremity or serve as a replacement for an extremity. Some students who are quadriplegic, for example, have learned to swim with the assistance of four swim fins serving as the legs and arms. The fins are attached with straps that cross the swimmers' shoulders and lower trunk, simulating the action of the arms and legs. For swimmers with upper extremity amputations, a swimming hand prostheses (figure 16.10) has been suggested as a valuable aid by Radocy (1987).

Goggles, nose clips, and ear plugs can be used to assist some students who experience discomfort in the water. Some physicians will recommend that ear plugs, in particular, be used by certain students. Goggles can be effective in helping the student whose eyes are extremely sensitive to the chemicals used in the water. Generally, swimmers who are blind or visually impaired require few equipment modifications to

Figure 16.10 The tabula swimming hand prosthesis.

swim successfully. Some may prefer to use an audible cue, such as a beeper device, to assist them in maintaining a straight line when swimming laps. Tap-sticks, which are used by coaches to signal when to begin the flip turn or to indicate distance from the edge of the pool, are helpful and used by some swimmers with visual impairments (figure 16.11).

While some have questioned the use of flotation devices in swimming programs, they have been found to be invaluable in programs for students with disabilities. They can be used to equalize the body by adding needed buoyancy to one of the sides. In addition, flotation devices allow swimmers with severe impairments to enjoy the water without being held or holding on to an object or another person. Some flotation devices can be made from discarded items such as plastic milk jugs and soda bottles. Kickboards, plastic doughnut rings, and styrofoam buoys are items that can be used and are normally available in most swimming pools.

Personal flotation devices (formerly known as life jackets) also can be a helpful and useful swimming aid for the individual who is severely involved (figure 16.12). There are five types of personal flotation devices (PFD) graded

according to the amount of buoyancy they provide, with Type I being the most buoyant. Types I, II, and III PFDs are designed to maintain the swimmer in a vertical and slightly backward position in the water. Each swimmer, however, should try the PFD to ensure that the desired fit and action in the water are achieved. Swimmers who are orthopedically impaired, including those with neuromuscular disorders, may find that the PFD does not respond as expected. Bradley, Fuller, Pozcos, and Willmers (1981) caution that PFDs may not give adequate support if used as a life jacket for some individuals with disabilities. They stress that some of the PFDs available on the market may not provide correct positioning in the water and are difficult to put on.

Heckathorn (1980) recommends that flotation devices be used to regulate body positions. When the following conditions exist, she offers these guidelines:

1. Affected Side Floats Lower in Water
   Life preserver (PFD I, II, or III) around waist, hips, or chest.
   Plastic bottles with Velcro strap around waist, hips, or chest.

Figure 16.11 Coaches can use a "tap-stick" to allow swimmers who are blind and visually impaired to know when to begin their flip turns.

Figure 16.12 Combo-head flotation device and sectional raft.

Plastic bottles with strap or flotation collar around affected leg(s) and/or arm(s).
2. Legs Sink
   Plastic bottles with Velcro strap around legs, hips, or waist.
   Life preserver (PFD I, II, or III) around waist or hips.
3. Hips Sink
   Plastic bottles with Velcro strap around hips or waist.
   Life preserver (PFD I, II, or III) around waist or hips.

Adams and McCubbin (1991) believe that the standard Personal Flotation Device works well for those needing support of the head or neck. They caution, however, that the PFD restricts swimming to the supine or backstroke position. The Delta Swim System, developed by Danmark, is a viable alternative and is adaptable to meet various aquatic needs (figure 16.13).

In presenting adaptations that can be made, very brief descriptions of the specific skills are given to enable the reader to make a better comparison of the adaptation with normal performance and so gain a better understanding of the process of adapting skills for those with disabilities. It is not the intent to provide instruction for learning to perform the skills. Those who wish this information are referred to the books in Selected Readings at the end of the chapter.

Beginning Swimming Skills

Teaching a person to float requires an understanding of Archimedes' Principle, which states that a body submerged in a liquid is buoyed up by a force equal to the weight of the

Figure 16.13 The Delta Swim System.

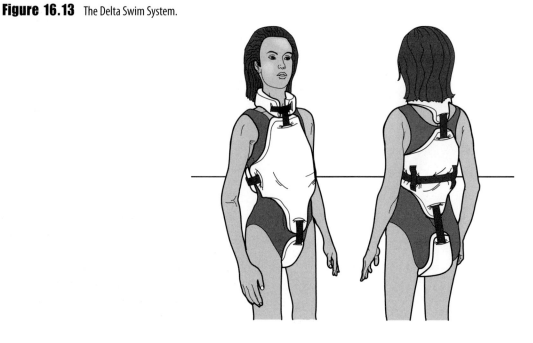

displaced liquid. In applying this to swimming, it means that a person will float if the individual's weight does not exceed that of an equal volume of water. This concept is expressed by the following formula:

$$\text{Specific Gravity} = \frac{\text{Weight of Equal Amount of Water}}{\text{Weight of Body}}$$

The specific gravity (also known as relative density) for most adults, after full inspiration, is slightly less than one. The smaller the specific gravity, the easier it is to float. The relative density of the human body varies with age. Young children float easily because their relative density is, on the average, 0.86. Because muscle weighs more than fat, young athletic individuals, particularly males, experience greater challenges in floating. With age and an increase in adipose tissue, the relative density becomes less, allowing an individual to float with greater ease.

An understanding of the center of buoyancy is also an important concept when teaching a person to float. The center of buoyancy of an individual is that point at which weight is concentrated and serves as a fulcrum about which the body rotates. The center of buoyancy may be thought of as the center of gravity, but applied to the body in water. Only when the center of buoyancy and center of gravity are in the same line can a person float without motion. For some individuals, this will be a position at which the body is parallel to the water. Others, however, will float in almost a vertical position with the legs and feet below the shoulders. Each person must experiment to find that place where the centers of buoyancy and gravity are aligned vertically.

Bloomquist (1992) stresses that the following factors should be considered for all floaters:

1. When any body part is removed from the water, the buoyancy decreases.
2. When the head is lifted during supine floating, the feet sink.
3. When balance is lost, the falling is slowed because of the resistance of the water, allowing for more recovery time.
4. When the head turns to the side, the body tends to follow, causing rotation on the vertical axis.
5. Air held in the lungs increases floating ability.
6. Long, heavy legs lower the center of gravity, causing feet to drop.
7. Bending the knees raises the center of gravity, thereby increasing floating ability.
8. Raising arms over head slowly and underwater raises the center of gravity, thereby increasing floating.
9. People with a greater-than-average amount of fat float more easily.
10. Muscular people and adolescents have more difficulty floating.
11. Children, because of their low density, and the elderly, because of their increased adipose tissue, tend to float more easily.
12. Gripping with hands, holding the breath, or shutting the eyes increases tension and decreases relaxation which is important to successful floating.
13. Fear and cold decrease floating.
14. Because of the need to rotate from prone to supine and return, all swimmers should learn to exhale and blow bubbles as soon as the face enters the water.

In teaching individuals with disabilities to float, the instructor will need to be cognizant of the specific disability and adaptations that may be required. Some examples of factors identified by Bloomquist (1992) to consider when teaching people with disabilities to float include the following:

1. Muscles that are spastic are heavier and tend to decrease floating ability in the affected area.
2. Paralyzed, flaccid muscles are less dense and tend to increase the ability to float in the affected area.
3. A body with a spinal deviation (e.g., scoliosis) will tend to cause body rotation.
4. An individual who is spastic hemiplegic will: (a) have decreased respiration and less buoyancy on the affected side thereby decreasing floating ability and (b) tend to be shorter on the affected side and roll toward that side.
5. Individuals who are blind or visually impaired will have more difficulty floating and following instructions when their main mode of communication (hearing) is lost because of ears being below the water line when floating.
6. A person whose spasticity places elbows, wrists, or knees in flexion may have difficulty keeping body parts in the water, thus reducing buoyancy.

The Tuck Float

Learning to float helps greatly to promote self-confidence in the beginning swimmer. The tuck float is an easy float for the beginner to learn; moreover, in the process of learning it, the student develops the ability to regain the feet in the water. To learn the tuck float, a nonswimmer should stand in water about chest deep. A deep breath is taken and the face is placed in the water; then the knees are pulled up to the chest and gripped with the arms. Holding this position, the body floats to the surface. A return to the standing position is accomplished by releasing the knees and thrusting the feet down. At the same time the head is raised. The hands push down on the water to help regain balance.

The Face Float

The prone face is executed by bending at the hips and placing the face in the water. At the same time the feet are pushed against the bottom of the pool to place the body in a horizontal position face down on the surface of the water. The hands are extended in front. The return to a standing position is made by raising the head and bringing the knees up under the body. The arms are brought forcefully to the sides while at the same time the legs are extended downward into a standing position.

The Back Float

In the back float, a position is taken by extending the head back and pushing slightly with the feet from the bottom. The hips are lifted high and the head is placed back so the ears are under the water. The arms may be held at the sides or extended to the side. A recovery to a standing position is made by bringing the knees toward the chin as the head is brought up and forward. The hands are brought down and past the hips. As the body rights itself, the legs are extended to the bottom.

Adaptations: Tuck and face floats cannot be taught to students who should not hold their breath (for example, those with cardiac disturbances). In these cases the vertical float is used as a substitution.

Some students who are learning disabled also prefer the vertical float position because of the visual field distortion they experience in the back float position.

Students with severe cerebral palsy will often be non-buoyant, and the use of flotation devices may be necessary. These individuals also frequently have difficulty maintaining head control. For this reason it is recommended that the vertical float be emphasized and that each individual be assessed carefully before progressing to a back or front float position. Frequent rest periods are also recommended. Chairs and benches placed in the water can be effectively used as rest stations. The youngster with cerebral palsy who has the spastic hemiplegic condition will have difficulty maintaining the symmetry necessary for effective floating. A technique that can be used to compensate for this is to turn the head away from the side to which the body wants to roll. If this is not sufficient compensation, the affected leg may be crossed over the nonaffected leg, either at the knee or ankle, depending on the amount of roll that requires correcting. In the vertical float, the body is at approximately a seventy-degree angle with the face lifted just enough to clear the water. This will need to be done in water that is chin deep or deeper. A slight movement of the arms may be necessary to keep the chin above water. A helper may support the body until the swimmer gains confidence and skill in using the

arms. To give support, the helper places one hand under the swimmer's chest.

Those who cannot support themselves in the water on their feet should be held by a helper until they have acquired sufficient confidence to use the kickboard or hang on to the gutter for support. A hand placed under the chest in the face float or under the head in the back float will provide sufficient support.

Those who do not have use of the arms will need help at first in regaining their feet from a float position, but they can learn to right themselves by a very forceful extension of the legs while simultaneously lifting the head and shoulders. If the swimmer has the use of only one arm, the arm action used to regain the feet should be executed as near to the center of the body as possible for maximum effectiveness.

Individuals who are visually impaired will have difficulty floating and following instructions when their ears are below the water line. For some this may require the assistance of flotation devices or reliance on the face rather than the back float.

Individuals who are orthopedically impaired will need to experiment with various positions to offset the effect of the displacement of the center of gravity and center of buoyancy. For example, a student who has lost a right leg will tend to roll to the left where the weight of the body is centered.

Where the legs or hands are atrophied due to disease, they are less dense and float easily. Therefore, children with spina bifida and paraplegia will find that their limbs rise to the surface. In the back float position, the swimmer will need to extend the head to depress the feet.

Drownproofing Technique

Regardless of the swimming skill level achieved by students with disabilities, they should eventually be exposed to the water survival skill of drownproofing. This technique, developed during World War II by Fred Lanoue, was used initially to teach servicemen how to remain afloat in water. Today this system of vertical floating is routinely taught as a part of school and community swimming programs. The drownproofing technique can be learned by individuals of various ages and body compositions, including those who are orthopedically impaired.

The basic concept that all good drownproofers must learn is to float face downward in a vertical position. This is the natural position dictated by the buoyant effect of the water. From this position one is taught to breathe about five or six times a minute by lifting the head slightly. Obviously, much energy is conserved by lifting the head only when one wants to breathe. However, the action of lifting the head causes a reaction that tends to send the body downward. This response can be countered by a simple kick of the legs, which assists the body to maintain its relaxed vertical position. People who learn the skill of drownproofing can travel and breathe in the water with only a minimal use of any limbs. This is an important consideration for swimmers with disabilities, particularly those who are orthopedically impaired.

The sequence used in breathing in a vertical float position is as follows:

1. Take a deep breath and assume the vertical face-down position. Relax the entire body with the chin to the chest and the arms hanging freely at the side.
2. Slowly cross the arms in front of the forehead with forearms together.
3. Gently raise the head out of the water to chin level while breathing out at all times.
4. Breathe in normally while gently moving the arms down and out.
5. Let the head descend under water. The arms should assume a relaxed position at the sides of the body. From this vertical rest position, the breathing cycle should be repeated.

Adaptations: Swimmers with paralyzed or amputated limbs will need to modify the drownproofing technique to compensate for their increased buoyancy. For example, a swimmer with only one arm will tend to list to one side in the vertical float position. For this individual a modification will be necessary in the way the head is raised from the water during the breathing cycle. Each adaptation of this nature will have to be individually designed to respond to specific needs.

The student who is ataxic should be watched during attempts to regain the standing position because of a poor sense of balance, particularly when the feet cannot be seen.

The Glide and the Flutter Kick

After beginners have learned the face float, they may be taught how to glide in the prone position. The glide is performed much like the face float except that, instead of lifting the feet off the bottom, the feet push off from the bottom to move the body forward in a prone float position.

The flutter kick is the simplest kick to learn. The student assumes a prone position and thrashes the legs alternately up and down. The kick starts at the hip, followed by extension of the knee. The toes are extended. The feet are spread vertically from fifteen to twenty inches. For younger children, the spread will be less.

Adaptations: If physical abilities permit, the kick may be introduced as a land drill; the student assumes a prone position on a bench with the legs projected beyond the bench. The kick also can be practiced while holding on to the gutter

or a kickboard. After the kick is mastered, it is combined with the prone float to propel the body forward.

Those who cannot put their faces in the water should be assisted by helpers who take the swimmers by their extended hands to tow them while they kick.

Swimmers who have lost the use of one leg must learn to use the remaining leg in the flutter kick. If the leg is paralyzed, it may be helpful to put a small float under the thigh of the affected leg.

The Dog Paddle and the Human Stroke

In the dog paddle the head is held above the water. The arms are alternately extended forward and downward and then pulled backward under the chest. At the same time the feet are moved in the flutter kick. The human stroke is executed much like the dog paddle except that the face is in the water as in the prone float and the arms are fully extended in front of the head before pulling down and back. As in the dog paddle, the hands do not leave the water.

Adaptations: Those who are able may practice the arm stroke with the leg kick on a bench before getting into the water. Following this the arm movement is practiced while standing in chest-deep water.

Land practice of swimming strokes is not effective for swimmers with cerebral palsy because of the increased tension in the muscles when they are out of the water. Consequently, all of their practice should be in the water.

Swimmers who have limited movement of their limbs will need to be supported by a helper who passes a hand under the swimmer's chest. Flotation devices also may be used as supports for these students. Those who have difficulty balancing in the water because of amputation or atrophy of a limb must make the necessary movements of the active limbs close to the center of the body to overcome the imbalance. The best placement of the limbs can be determined by movement analysis and subsequent experimentation.

Some youngsters with disabilities will not be able to learn to swim or float in the prone position. For these, the progression in swimming should be from the back float to the elementary back stroke or, if this is not feasible, any movement that propels the body in any direction while supine.

Intermediate Swimming Strokes

The side stroke, the elementary back stroke, and the crawl are strokes that are frequently taught on the intermediate level.

The Side Stroke

The body is turned on its side with the stronger arm on top. The arm under the water is fully extended at right angles to the body while the other arm rests fully extended along the side of the body. The under arm is brought down to a nearly vertical position and then the elbow is bent. At the same time, the top arm is brought up to enter the water near the head. This arm recovers to the starting position with a downward reaching movement. Meanwhile the other arm is recovering with a pulling movement toward the body.

The kick for the side stroke is called the scissors. The legs are bent slightly at the knees as one leg (usually the top leg) is brought in front of the body and the other leg is moved to the rear. The legs are then extended fully and brought together forcefully in a movement resembling the opening and closing of a scissors.

The movements of the arms and legs are coordinated to begin and recover simultaneously. The body glides momentarily in the water before the next stroke begins.

Adaptations: Those who have weak shoulder joints subject to frequent dislocation will find the side stroke the safest stroke for swimming. It will also be the most effective stroke and the most easily learned by those who have lost one limb. When there is a disabled or missing arm, the side stroke is performed with the functional arm on the bottom.

When one leg is missing or disabled, the functional leg may be on either the top or the bottom, whichever proves better through trial and error. If both legs have been lost, the swimmer will probably have to find a suitable modified position through experimentation; this will usually be a partially prone position rather than wholly on the side of the body.

Many students who are visually impaired or blind feel the side stroke is the ideal stroke for them because one ear is always above water, allowing them to listen for and respond to auditory cues.

The Elementary Back Stroke

The arm movement for the elementary back stroke begins with the arms fully extended at a forty-five-degree angle between the head and shoulders. The arms are brought to the sides of the body in a sweeping arc. In the recovery the hands are brought along the sides of the body to shoulder height. They are then fully extended to begin the next downward stroke.

In the kick, the knees are brought up and out to the sides about shoulder width apart. The kick starts when the heels drop below the water surface, then the feet are brought outward with the ankles flexed and toes pointing outward. Finally the legs are extended and feet brought together.

The straightening of the legs occurs at the same time that the arms are being brought down to the sides. The arms recover along the body to the armpits before the legs start their recovery.

Adaptations: Many students with disabilities find it easier to swim on the back than in any other position. In the back position, almost any kind of movement with the arms or legs will move the body in some direction. If the swimmer does not have use of the arms, the legs may be used in a flutter kick to propel the body; conversely, if the legs cannot be used, the arms may be used as in the back stroke. Finning and sculling movements with the hands may be substituted for the arm stroke if movement of the arms is restricted.

The Crawl

In teaching the crawl, it is necessary only to add the arm movement to the flutter kick and breathing technique introduced in the beginning skills. The arm stroke is made by extending the arm fully in front of the face and pressing downward against the water, with the hand leading the rest of the arm. When the arm is beneath the shoulder, the shoulder is lifted and the elbow is raised until it clears the water. The arm is then brought forward above the water with the fingers near the water, ready for entrance into the water for the next stroke.

The arms stroke alternately, and inhalation should occur as the shoulder is lifted in the recovery. The head may be turned to either side, depending upon which seems more natural for the swimmer. The kick is coordinated with the arms to accomplish a smooth and rhythmical stroke.

Adaptations: The crawl is the most satisfactory stroke for those with loss of movement in the legs. In some cases of leg disability, flexion and extension may be developed to compensate for lack of leg action. Hip impairment may require the swimmer to execute the flutter kick with greater knee bend.

The arm stroke may be modified for those with arm and shoulder limitations by reducing it to less than the full stroke. The crawl should not be swum by those with weak shoulder joints subject to frequent dislocation.

Quad amputees have learned to perform the crawl stroke effectively with the assistance of fins attached to their stumps.

Summary

Swimming is a desirable activity for students with disabilities for many reasons. Instruction and programs in swimming improve physical fitness, develop desirable water-related safety skills, provide fun and wholesome recreation, and serve as one more important outlet for individuals with disabilities to interact with the nondisabled. In addition, the water's buoyancy allows individuals with orthopedic impairments and muscular disorders to make movements they are not otherwise able to make.

Most individuals with disabilities can learn to float and swim. The extent to which the individual becomes proficient as a swimmer will vary depending upon the level of disability. Many swimmers with disabilities have achieved at a high level. These successes are attributed to individual effort and the availability of instructional programs. As was emphasized in earlier chapters, good instruction requires that the swimming tasks be broken down and sequenced according to their level of difficulty. An evaluation system should be utilized to help the instructor keep track of student progress. Swimming instructors should be creative in modifying the various strokes and use, when necessary, selected assistive devices. Flotation devices can be very helpful in assisting the swimmer who has a disability in floating and/or supporting the body so that various strokes can be performed.

An important element in the swimming program for swimmers with disabilities is the availability of an environment that is sensitive to their special needs. Emphasis should be placed on the accessibility of the pool and locker room. In addition, the temperature of the water should be higher to help the swimmer relax and to compensate for the slower movements of some of the swimmers. Assistive devices including fins, goggles, ear plugs, nose clips, and various flotation devices should be available as needed.

One of the primary goals of the swimming program is to keep individuals with disabilities safe in the water. Special emphasis, therefore, should be placed on helping the swimmer to understand buoyancy and its effect in relationship to the individual's disability. This will require some experimentation to determine the best floating and swimming position.

Swimming is an excellent activity for its obvious physiological and psychological benefits. Learning to swim is also important as a means of ensuring that a child with a disability is included in water-related activities with other children. Many of the summer activities for children and their families include being in or close to water. The ability to swim will help students with disabilities to be part of the mainstream in a very popular school, community, and family activity. With the assistance of knowledgeable and creative instructors and the availability of accessible facilities, individuals with disabilities will have the opportunity to enjoy the fun and excitement of being in the water.

Enhancing Activities

1. Using the facility checklist found in appendix VI on the CD, conduct a survey of a neighborhood or school swimming pool and the adjacent locker-room area. Suggest modifications that might be made to increase the facility's accessibility.

2. Float and swim with an inflatable ring attached to your leg. Note how the increased buoyancy on one side requires you to compensate and change your technique for floating and swimming.

3. Swim the length of the pool with your legs tied together. Identify the various ways in which the stroke is changed to compensate for the loss of the legs.

4. With the assistance of helpers, transfer from a wheelchair into and out of the pool.

5. Develop a list of water games and water orientation activities that expand upon those identified in this chapter.

6. Volunteer to assist in a swimming program for those with special needs. Apply your knowledge of task analysis to develop appropriate learning activities.

7. Visit the local offices of the YMCA or Red Cross to obtain information and resources concerning swimming for individuals with disabilities.

Selected Readings

Adams, R. C., & McCubbin, J. A. (1991). *Games, sports, and exercises for the physically handicapped* (4th ed.). Philadelphia: Lea and Febiger.

American National Red Cross. (1975). *Swimming for the handicapped—Instructor's manual* (Rev. ed.). Washington, DC: Author.

American National Red Cross. (1977). *Adapted aquatics*. Garden City, NY: Doubleday and Company, Inc.

Bettsworth, M. (1977). *Drownproofing*. New York: Schocken Books.

Bloomquist, L. C. (1992). *University of Rhode Island adapted aquatics program manual* (3rd ed.). Kingston, RI: Rhode Island Board of Governors of Higher Education.

Bradley, N. J., Fuller, J. L., Pozcos, R. S., & Willmers, L. E. (1981). PFDs, personal flotation devices. A lifejacket is a lifejacket . . . not necessarily so, especially if you're disabled. *Sports 'n Spokes, 23–25.*

Campion, M. R. (1985). *Hydrotherapy in pediatrics*. Rockville, MD: Aspen Systems Corporation.

Cordellos, H. C. (1976). *Aquatic recreation for the blind*. Washington, DC: American Alliance for Health, Physical Education, Recreation, and Dance.

Council for National Cooperation in Aquatics and American Association for Health, Physical Education, and Recreation. (1969). *A practical guide for teaching the mentally retarded to swim*. Washington, DC: AAHPER.

Grosse, S., & McGill, C. (1979). Independent swimming for children with severe physical impairments. In *AAHPERD Practical Pointers* (p. 3). Washington, DC: American Alliance for Health, Physical Education, Recreation, and Dance.

Heckathorn, J. (1980). *Strokes and strokes*. Reston, VA: AAHPERD Publications.

Lieberman, L. J., & Houston-Wilson, C. (2002). *Strategies for INCLUSION*. Champaign, IL: Human Kinetics.

Lepore, M., Gayle, G. W., & Stevens, S. (1998). *Adapted aquatics programming: A professional guide*. Champaign, IL: Human Kinetics.

Newman, J. (1976). *Swimming for children with physical and sensory impairments*. Springfield, IL: Charles C. Thomas.

Paciorek, M. J., & Jones, J. A. (1989). *Sports and recreation for the disabled*. Indianapolis: IN: Benchmark Press, Inc.

Priest, E. L. (1980). *Teaching of adapted aquatics*. Lecture presented at summer workshop, Illinois State University, Normal, IL.

Radocy, B. (1987). Upper extremity prosthetics: Considerations and designs for sports and recreation. *Clinical Prosthetics and Orthotics, 11*(3): 131–153.

Special Olympics Sports Instructional Program. (n. d.). *Swimming and diving*. Washington, DC: Joseph P. Kennedy, Jr., Foundation.

United Cerebral Palsy Associations, Inc. (n. d.). *Swimming for the cerebral palsied*. New York: United Cerebral Palsy Associations, Inc. (321 West 44th Street, New York, NY, 10036).

Wessel, J. A. (1976). *I CAN Fundamental Skills*. Austin, TX: PROED.

YMCA of the United States. (1987). *Aquatics for special populations*.

Physical Fitness

CHAPTER 17

CHAPTER OBJECTIVES

After studying this chapter, the reader should be able to:

1　Define the terms "physical fitness" and "motor fitness" and explain the difference between these concepts.
2　Identify and describe the components of health-related fitness and the importance of these for individuals with disabilities.
3　Describe the various tests of physical fitness including those that have been specifically developed for individuals with disabilities.
4　Develop physical fitness programs for various disability populations utilizing scientific concepts from exercise science.
5　Recognize the need for physical fitness programs that are responsive to the individual needs of special populations.
6　Adapt physical fitness and exercise programs to accommodate the special needs of individuals with various disabilities.
7　Understand that the physical fitness needs of those with disabilities are very similar to those of the nondisabled and that integrated fitness programs should be encouraged.
8　Recognize that for individuals with severe cognitive dysfunction, physical fitness programs must be data based and systematically structured.

Physical education in the United States was founded on the premise that students' health is enhanced through formal exercise. The earliest school programs consisted primarily of group calisthenics designed to exercise the major muscle groups and improve posture and breathing. Early leaders of American physical education included Dr. Edward Hitchcock, Dr. Dudley Sargent, Dr. Edward Hartwell, and Dr. William Anderson, all medical doctors who were convinced of the need for the preservation of health through exercise and knowledge of the laws of hygiene. Though the scope of physical education has expanded beyond that of health maintenance, achievement of healthful levels of physical fitness has remained a major objective of physical education programs in our schools.

Growing public awareness of the relationship of physical fitness to health since the 1950s has produced additional emphasis on physical fitness as a paramount objective of physical education. The focus began with the observations of Hans Kraus and Ruth Hirschland that

American children were less fit than many European youths. President Dwight D. Eisenhower reacted by creating the President's Council on Youth Fitness. Their goal was to promote programs designed to enhance the physical fitness of children. The Council continues today as the President's Council on Physical Fitness and Sports and has been instrumental in promoting school and private physical fitness programs. In 1958 the American Association for Health, Physical Education, and Recreation[1] initiated the Youth Fitness Test, with national norms for school-age children. This test served to foster interest in physical fitness improvement through school physical education programs. A separate Health Related Physical Fitness Test was subsequently developed to emphasize the important distinction between physical fitness and motor fitness. In

[1]The name of the organization has since been changed to the American Alliance for Health, Physical Education, Recreation, and Dance (AAHPERD).

1993, the American Alliance for Health, Physical Education, Recreation and Dance (AAHPERD), in an effort to provide the best possible health-related fitness program, developed a partnership with the Cooper Institute for Aerobic Research (CIAR). Under the agreement with the CIAR, AAHPERD accepted responsibility for developing and producing fitness education materials and CIAR agreed to develop the fitness assessment and supporting material. It was further agreed that the Prudential Fitnessgram, a criterion-referenced instrument, would be used to measure physical fitness. Using the Fitnessgram, performance is judged with regard to standards which reflect a desirable state of health-related physical fitness. Standards exist for the following components: aerobic capacity, body composition, muscular strength and endurance, and flexibility. The most recent tool for evaluating the health-related fitness of individuals with disabilities for physical education/physical activity has been the Brockport Physical Fitness Test (BPFT) (Winnick & Short, 2001). This tool will be discussed later in this chapter.

The rise in the incidence of obesity in America (referenced in chapter 21 on the CD) has direct bearing on the work of physical educators, teachers, and concerned health professionals, as well as parents of children with disabilities. Recently, the Centers for Disease Control and Prevention (CDC) declared that obesity is an epidemic (Wallace, 2003). The federal government, through the Surgeon General's reports, has documented a steady and alarming increase in the incidence of obesity in the United States (U.S. Dept. of Health and Human Services, 1996, 2004b). *Healthy People 2010*, a federal government report, has recently identified "physical activity and obesity issues" among its "leading health indicators" (U.S. Dept. of Health and Human Services, 2004c).

According to Wallace (2003), obesity is excess body fat that causes impairment of health. There is debate in how obesity is measured and reported, but if current height and weight tables are used, then people are obese when they are 20 percent above the desired weight listed in the tables. According to formulas used to determine an individual's Body Mass Index (BMI), the ratio of body fat to height and weight, such individuals can be rated in the mildly obese to morbidly obese range (www.nhlbi.nih.gov). The National Heart, Lung, and Blood Institute reports that athletes and those who are fragile and older can receive inaccurate readings of their BMI. So if a person is in that category, consult the client's medical doctor for accurate understandings of BMI.

Increased concern over the incidence of heart disease, obesity, and high blood pressure has spurred an interest in cardiorespiratory fitness. Under federal educational law, fitness is a component of physical education (e.g., McKechnie, 2002; Seaman, 2001).

Center for Disease Prevention and Control (CDC) Recommendations

The CDC encourages those who are able to exercise at moderate (e.g., brisk walking, table tennis) to vigorous (e.g., jogging, wheelchair tennis) intensity levels to do so, but offers others the recommendation that engaging in an active lifestyle with *some* of their activity at these levels is appropriate for improving or maintaining physical fitness. CDC recommends the following guidelines for exercise:

- Adults should engage in moderate intensity exercise for at least 30 minutes on 5 or more days of the week. This is a joint recommendation of CDC and the American College of Sports Medicine (ACSM).
  OR
- In *Healthy People 2010*, the United States Surgeon General's report (2004b), the recommendation for adults is to engage in vigorous intensity physical activity three or more days per week for 20 or more minutes per session.
- All adolescents should be physically active daily, or nearly every day, as part of play, games, sports, work, transportation, recreation, physical education, or planned exercise, in the context of family, school, and community activities (Sallis et al., 1994).
- Adolescents should engage in three or more sessions per week of activities that last 20 minutes or more at a time and that require moderate to vigorous levels of exertion (Sallis et al., 1994).
- Elementary school–aged children should accumulate for most days of the week at least 30 to 60 minutes of age-appropriate and developmentally appropriate physical activity from a variety of activities, as recommended by the National Association for Sport and Physical Education (NASPE).
- Some of the child's activity each day should be in periods lasting 10 to 15 minutes or more and include moderate to vigorous activity. This activity will typically be intermittent in nature, involving alternating moderate to vigorous activity, with brief periods of rest and recovery, as recommended by NASPE.

Lower Fitness Levels

It is generally recognized that individuals with disabilities have lower levels of fitness than their peers without disabilities. Resources are being developed to address this reality and increase exercise and fitness levels of individuals with disabilities. Recently, the American College of Sports Medicine (2009) issued a full text on exercise management for persons with chronic disease and disability. The authors detail individual disability areas and expected responses to exercise, and recommend exercise testing methods with a special chapter devoted to children. Information on adults and disability covers such areas as cardiovascular diseases, pulmonary diseases, metabolic diseases, immunology disorders, orthopaedic diseases and disabilities, neuromuscular disorders, and cognitive, psychological, and sensory disorders.

Another invaluable resource for facilitating the physical fitness of individuals with disabilities is Dr. Jim Rimmer's National Center on Physical Activity and Disability (www.ncpad.org). According to NCPAD:

> The mission of the National Center on Physical Activity and Disability (NCPAD) is to promote substantial health benefits that can be gained from participating in regular physical activity. The slogan of NCPAD is Exercise is for EVERY body, and every person can gain some health benefit from being more physically active.

The center's website provides information and resources that enable people with disabilities to become physically active. The philosophy of NCPAD is summed up by belief. The presence of a disability does not exclude participation in physical activity and, thus, an active life and healthy lifestyle.

Due to a combination of factors including physical inability, overprotection, self-consciousness, and societal pressures, individuals with disabling conditions often engage in less daily physical activity than do those who are not disabled. This reduced level of daily exercise negatively affects the functional capacity of their neuromuscular and cardiorespiratory systems, producing a generally lower level of physical fitness.

Lieberman and Houston-Wilson (2002) address health and fitness modifications and adaptations for special physical education because they believe that "A basic fitness level is vital to enjoyment of physical activity and sport" (p.167). These authors also promote the use of peer tutors to facilitate the involvement of children with disabilities in physical activity. They also provide lists of modifications and adaptations that can be used for individualizing a person's aerobic workout (figure 17.1). Drawing on an extensive understanding of the use of *trained* peer tutors, the authors describe four types of peer tutoring:

1. Unidirectional: a trained peer teaches throughout and the child with a disability remains with the student.
2. Bi-directional: both the child with and the child without a disability form a dyad where they take turns being the student.
3. Class-wide peer tutoring: the entire class forms dyads. Everyone is given task cards and the tutor fills in the skills the student has accomplished.
4. Cross-age peer tutoring: an older student tutors a younger student.

One special group, individuals with **mental retardation**, have been identified as having significantly poorer scores on some tests of physical fitness and especially on measures of body fatness and cardiorespiratory endurance (Dobbins, Garron, & Rarick, 1981; Fernhall, Tymeson, & Webster, 1988; Moon & Renzaglia, 1982; Rimmer, 1992). Similar findings have been reported for other disability populations including the **visually impaired** (Jankowski & Evans, 1981), **learning disabled** (Rimmer & Rosentsweig, 1982), those with **cerebral palsy** (Short & Winnick, 1986; Winnick & Short, 1991), children with ostomy (Vogler, 1990), and children and adolescents with insulin dependent diabetes mellitus (Kertzer, Croce, Hinkle, & Janson-Sand, 1994). These findings indicate that those with disabilities, as a group, are less physically fit than the nondisabled. Enhanced opportunity for activity and attempts at motivating individuals with disabilities to be more physically active would serve to improve their general physical fitness status.

The rehabilitative value of exercise has been universally accepted as an adjunct in the return of injured persons to normal functioning as well as in retarding the progress of some diseases. Similar exercise techniques can be used to strengthen alternate muscle groups to aid in compensating for ineffective muscle actions in those with disabilities (Broad, 2001; Cotugna & Vickery, 2003).

In addition to the direct health benefits, enhanced physical fitness may produce desirable changes in an individual's appearance, self-concept, social relations, and general improvement in the quality of life (Pitetti & Campbell, 1991). A physically fit body is generally associated with a more desirable physical appearance. The body image of individuals with disabilities is often quite negative due to their specific abnormalities. This negative attitude toward the body is often generalized and dominates their ideas of how they look to others. By enhancing the fitness of an individual with a disability, a positive change in body image can result. As the person becomes more capable physically, his or her concept of self in a physical sense is usually improved and may result in greater self-acceptance as well as in acceptance by others. Improved physical fitness will allow the individual with a disability to participate more fully in the normal activities of life. This enhanced participation is likely to lead to social development and increased social acceptance (figure 17.2).

Most sports and physical games have as a basis some component of physical fitness; that is, some degree of

Potential Modifications and Adaptations

Equipment	Rules	Environment	Instruction
— Lower steps	— Shorter movements	— Flat surface	— Repetition
__ Light weights	— Keep moving	__ Accessible	__ Peer tutor
__ Modify weights	__ Cooperation	__ Least restrictive	__ Partner up
__ Stereo	__ Grades based on	environment	__ Demonstration
__ Lines on floor	effort	__ Inclusive	__ Command
__ Poly spots	__ Go at own pace	__ Space	__ Physical assistance
__ Ribbon	__ Modify movements	__ Bright boundaries	__ Cardio workout
__ Scarves	__ Be creative	__ Spots mark places	__ Visual aids
__ Television	__ Work together	__ Large room	__ Shadowing
__ Stretch bands	__ Four beats	__ Quiet	__ Verbal cues
__ Step on mat	__ Changing complexity	__ Close to instructor	__ Task analyze
__ Matless	__ Slower beat	__ Closed gym	__ Brailling
__ Task cards	__ Low impact	__ Scheduled	__ Feedback
__ Mirrors	__ Number of steps	__ Slower steps	__ One-to-one
__ Lights	__ Time	__ Slower tempo	__ Reinforce
	__ Eight-count beat	__ Smaller group	__ Lesson plan on board
	__ Work side by side	__ Steps by the wall	
	__ Respect classmates	__ Limit distractions	
		__ Indoors or outdoors	
		__ Blinking lights to beat	

Example 1: Basic Aerobic Workout

Tasks	Aerobics: basic workout
Task description	Students will participate in a 30-to-45-minute aerobics class
Scale components	(a) ability to execute the skill that is demonstrated, (b) keeping up a 1/8 beat, (c) duration of continuous exercise
Rubric level & color	**Rubric descriptors**
1-white	Student will be able to execute 3–4 aerobic moves with no music, as demonstrated by the instructor
2-yellow	Student will be able to execute 5–8 aerobic moves with no music, as demonstrated by the instructor
3-orange	Student will be able to execute at least 8 aerobic moves with no music, as demonstrated by the instructor, to a 1/4 count, for 10 minutes continuously
4-green	Student will be able to execute at least 10 aerobic moves with music, as demonstrated by the instructor, to a 1/4 count, for 15 minutes continuously
5-blue	Student will be able to execute at least 10 aerobic moves with music, as demonstrated by the instructor, to a 1/8 count, for 20 minutes continuously
6-brown	Student will be able to execute any number of moves with music, as demonstrated by the instructor, to a 1/8 count, for 20–30 minutes continuously
7-black	Student will be able to execute any number of moves with music, as demonstrated by the instructor, to a 1/8 count, for 30–45 minutes continuously * Optional—student could lead all or part of the workout
Specific adaptations	

Figure 17.1 Aerobic activity

muscular strength, endurance, and flexibility is necessary to perform the skills of the game. Enhancement of the physical fitness components can serve as a means of ensuring sufficient prerequisite physical development to enable mastery of the motor skill. The learning rate of the skill is then accelerated over that of the unfit learner. More rapid learning of the skills has a very positive effect on the motivation of the learner to continue with the activity.

Although it is rare that all forms of exercise are contraindicated for individuals with special needs, often specific activities are inappropriate for an individual and cause aggravation of the condition. In general, these have been noted in

Figure 17.2 Participation in most activities requires some component of physical fitness.

the discussion of the specific conditions identified in section 3. The physical educator should guard against the generalization that exclusion from all forms of exercise is necessary for a person for whom one type of exercise is contraindicated.

Simply increasing the amount of total exercise one experiences daily is not sufficient to produce systematic improvement in physical fitness. Exercise physiologists have concluded that physical fitness is a multifaceted concept made up of a variety of independent components, each of which responds to specific activities and exercises. Thus the design of exercise programs to improve the various aspects of physical fitness must be carefully undertaken. The term "exercise prescription" has been used to denote an individually designed set of exercises specifying frequency, intensity, and duration of each component of the exercise session. This term is used with adults rather than children. Children do not "exercise" like adults. For example, children do not need to maintain continuous activity in the way that adults do to improve and maintain health-related fitness.

To enable effective design of exercise programs for special students, the professional must be knowledgeable about the essential nature of the fitness components, principles governing fitness enhancement, tests of physical fitness, and appropriate exercise programs for improving physical fitness. These concerns are dealt with in the remaining portions of this chapter, and some guidelines will be detailed regarding physical activity.

Common Physical Fitness Components for Individuals

There appears to be no universally accepted definition of the term "physical fitness." Common usage of the term by physical educators, coaches, athletes, and the public varies widely.

Because physical fitness has often been linked with athletic ability, some consider any quality that aids athletic ability as a quality of physical fitness. Because this concept encompasses such a large array of possible components, it is now becoming common to separate those qualities that are primarily related to the learning of skills from those qualities that are physiological capacities of the body. Aspects of skill learning (coordination, balance, speed, agility, and so on) are considered motor fitness components, related to learned neuromuscular control patterns. They do not respond to progressive overloading. Physiological capacities including muscle strength, muscle endurance, flexibility, and cardiorespiratory endurance are considered physical fitness components. Given this separation of qualities, physical fitness can be defined as "the functional capacity of the various systems of the body that support exercise, specifically muscle strength, muscle endurance, flexibility, and cardiorespiratory endurance."

Muscle Strength

Muscle strength is the maximal amount of force that a muscle or functional muscle group can exert. It is usually measured in pounds or kilograms of tension. Total strength may be estimated by sampling several of the large muscle groups throughout the body. However, it is quite possible to be strong in one muscle group and weak in another. Consequently, if knowledge of the strength for a particular action is desired, the muscles involved in the action should be specifically tested. The development of muscle strength is particularly important to individuals with disabilities because of the greater independence, freedom from assistive devices, and increased capacity for a variety of physical tasks, including the learning of sport skills, made possible through sufficient strength.

Muscle Endurance

The capacity to sustain repeated muscular contractions with a load representing some percentage of the strength of the muscle is termed "muscle endurance." Defined in this manner, muscle endurance depends upon the ability of the muscle to get and use oxygen and to rid itself of waste. Muscle endurance is measured by the number of times a given movement can be performed, carrying a load that is a given percentage of the strength of the muscle(s), before fatigue causes cessation.

A person can possess exceptional muscle endurance without being especially strong. The leg muscles of the marathon runner may not be nearly as strong as those of the football player but they possess far greater endurance capacity. As is true of strength, each muscle possesses a degree of endurance and must be tested separately to determine its capacity to sustain repeated contractions. Improving muscle endurance is especially beneficial to individuals with disabilities in achieving efficient performance of numerous repetitive tasks, such as operating a wheelchair or executing various personal care activities.

Flexibility

The capacity to move a joint through a range of motion is termed "flexibility." It is usually measured in degrees of joint rotation, 360 degrees being a full circle. The more flexible person can move through a larger range of motion of the major body joints than can a less flexible person. In those conditions in which total movement potential is restricted, maximal flexibility in each functional joint is a definite asset. Additionally, flexibility exercises may retard the loss of movement potential often accompanying a variety of neuromuscular diseases. It is also important to note that a person can be flexible in some joints, but not others. Differences can also be noted from one side to the other (e.g., more flexible in the left shoulder than the right).

Cardiorespiratory Endurance

This quality of physical fitness is determined by the amount of oxygen that the cardiovascular and respiratory systems can deliver to working muscles. The laboratory measurement of *cardiorespiratory endurance* actually measures the amount of oxygen supplied per minute in maximal exercise. Improved cardiorespiratory endurance enables persistence at physically demanding tasks and decreased recovery time, a definite benefit in performing any activities requiring continued large-muscle exercise. In addition, an efficient cardiovascular system offers substantial health benefits.

Body Composition

Body composition, or body fatness, refers to the percentage of the total body weight that is fat. Although not a functional capacity of the body, total body fatness significantly affects the other qualities previously noted and if in excess may be a serious health liability. Although norms vary with age, males should not exceed about 18 percent of their weight as fat; females should not exceed 28 percent. Due to less than normal activity levels, many individuals with disabilities may have excessive body fat percentages. Some individuals with disabilities may not appear overly fat by casual observation. However, when one realizes that their muscle mass may be quite small and their size mainly attributed to fat content, what appears to be normal size

may in fact be substantial extra fat. For these reasons body fatness will be included in this discussion as an important factor affecting physical fitness.

The components of physical fitness—muscular strength, muscular endurance, flexibility, and cardiorespiratory endurance plus body composition—have a relation to healthful functioning of the body. Muscular strength and endurance allow a wide range of activities to be undertaken with decreased incidents of muscle strains and sprains. Flexibility also reduces the chances of the occurrence of these conditions, especially in the low back and hamstring muscle groups. The health benefit of cardiorespiratory endurance is apparent through improved cardiac function, primarily a reduced heart rate and enhanced stroke volume as well as more efficient respiratory patterns. The relationship between the reduced capacity of the cardiorespiratory system and a variety of cardiovascular degenerative diseases is becoming widely accepted by the medical profession. Body fatness has been implicated in a variety of poor health conditions, including high blood pressure, heart disease, and diabetes.

Health-Related Fitness

The increased awareness of the contribution that these components of physical fitness can make in promoting good health was emphasized dramatically in 1994, when AAHPERD joined forces with the Cooper Institute for Aerobic Research (CIAR) and adopted the Prudential Fitnessgram, a criterion-referenced test, as the instrument to assess health-related fitness. The Fitnessgram assesses aerobic capacity, body composition, muscular strength and endurance, and flexibility. A brief overview of the test and items to assess each of the components is presented in the following text.

Aerobic Capacity: The test items used to represent aerobic capacity in the Prudential Fitnessgram are the one-mile run/walk and the pacer. The specific health fitness zones and standards for aerobic capacity as well as other components appear in tables 17.1*A* and 17.1*B*.

Body Composition: The sum of triceps and subscapular skinfolds are used as measures of body composition. The sum of these two measures range from 12–33 mm for boys and 20–44 mm for girls. Fitnessgram also provides an estimate of the appropriateness of weight relative to height in the form of a Body Mass Index (BMI). The criterion-referenced BMI standards associated with healthy fitness zones are found in tables 17.1*A* and 17.1*B*.

Flexibility: The ability to move muscles and joints through a full range of motion is an indicator of flexibility. On the Fitnessgram, the back saver (see tables 17.1*A* and 17.1*B*)

TABLE 17.1*A*   The Prudential FITNESSGRAM Standards for Healthy Fitness Zone*

	Boys											
	One Mile min:sec		Pacer # laps		$\dot{V}O_{2max}$ ml/kg/min		Percent Fat		Body Mass Index		Curl-up # completed	
5	Completion of		Participate in				25	10	20	14.7	2	10
6	distance. Time		run. Lap count				25	10	20	14.7	2	10
7	standards not		standards not				25	10	20	14.9	4	14
8	recommended.		recommended.				25	10	20	15.1	6	20
9							25	10	20	15.2	9	24
10	11:30	9:00	17	55	42	52	25	10	21	15.3	12	24
11	11:00	8:30	23	61	42	52	25	10	21	15.8	15	28
12	10:30	8:00	29	68	42	52	25	10	22	16.0	18	36
13	10:00	7:30	35	74	42	52	25	10	23	16.6	21	40
14	9:30	7:00	41	80	42	52	25	10	24.5	17.5	24	45
15	9:00	7:00	46	85	42	52	25	10	25	18.1	24	47
16	8:30	7:00	52	90	42	52	25	10	26.5	18.5	24	47
17	8:30	7:00	57	94	42	52	25	10	27	18.8	24	47
17+	8:30	7:00	57	94	42	52	25	10	27.8	19.0	24	47

	Trunk Lift inches		Push-up # completed		Modified Pull-up # completed		Pull-up # completed		Flexed Arm Hang seconds		Back Saver Sit & Reach** inches	Shoulder Stretch
5	6	12	3	8	2	7	1	2	2	8	8	Passing = Touching the fingertips together behind the back.
6	6	12	3	8	2	7	1	2	2	8	8	
7	6	12	4	10	3	9	1	2	3	8	8	
8	6	12	5	13	4	11	1	2	3	10	8	
9	6	12	6	15	5	11	1	2	4	10	8	
10	9	12	7	20	5	15	1	2	4	10	8	
11	9	12	8	20	6	17	1	3	6	13	8	
12	9	12	10	20	7	20	1	3	10	15	8	
13	9	12	12	25	8	22	1	4	12	17	8	
14	9	12	14	30	9	25	2	5	15	20	8	
15	9	12	16	35	10	27	3	7	15	20	8	
16	9	12	18	35	12	30	5	8	15	20	8	
17	9	12	18	35	14	30	5	8	15	20	8	
17+	9	12	18	35	14	30	5	8	15	20	8	

*Number on left is lower end of HFZ; number on right is upper end of HFZ.

**Test scored Pass/Fail; must reach this distance to pass.

is used to measure the flexibility of the hamstrings. A score of eight inches for boys, ages 5–17+, and scores ranging from 9 to 12 inches for girls, ages 5–17+ are considered acceptable. The Fitnessgram also includes a shoulder stretch, scored pass/fail, to measure upper body flexibility and a trunk lift test to measure trunk extensor strength and flexibility (see tables 17.1*A* and 17.1*B*). Standards for the trunk lift test are 6 to 12 inches for boys and girls, ages five to nine, and 9 to 12 inches for boys and girls, ages 10–17+.

Muscular Strength and Endurance: The Fitnessgram has selected the upper body and abdominal/trunk regions as areas for testing muscular strength and endurance because of their perceived relationship to maintaining functional health and correct posture, thus reducing possibilities of future low back

TABLE 17.1B   The Prudential FITNESSGRAM Standards for Healthy Fitness Zone*

Girls

	One Mile min:sec		Pacer # laps		$\dot{V}O_{2max}$ ml/kg/min		Percent Fat		Body Mass Index		Curl-up # completed	
5	Completion of distance. Time standards not recommended.		Participate in run. Lap count standards not recommended.				32	17	21	16.2	2	10
6							32	17	21	16.2	2	10
7							32	17	22	16.2	4	14
8							32	17	22	16.2	6	20
9							32	17	23	16.2	9	22
10	12:30	9:30	7	35	39	47	32	17	23.5	16.6	12	26
11	12:00	9:00	9	37	38	46	32	17	24	16.9	15	29
12	12:00	9:00	13	40	37	45	32	17	24.5	16.9	18	32
13	11:30	9:00	15	42	36	44	32	17	24.5	17.5	18	32
14	11:00	8:30	18	44	35	43	32	17	25	17.5	18	32
15	10:30	8:00	23	50	35	43	32	17	25	17.5	18	35
16	10:00	8:00	28	56	35	43	32	17	25	17.5	18	35
17	10:00	8:00	34	61	35	43	32	17	26	17.5	18	35
17+	10:00	8:00	34	61	35	43	32	17	27.3	18.0	18	35

	Trunk Lift inches		Push-up # completed		Modified Pull-up # completed		Pull-up # completed		Flexed Arm Hang seconds		Back Saver Sit & Reach** inches	Shoulder Stretch
5	6	12	3	8	2	7	1	2	2	8	9	
6	6	12	3	8	2	7	1	2	2	8	9	
7	6	12	4	10	3	9	1	2	3	8	9	
8	6	12	5	13	4	11	1	2	3	10	9	
9	6	12	6	15	4	11	1	2	4	10	9	
10	9	12	7	15	4	13	1	2	4	10	9	Passing = Touching the fingertips together behind the back.
11	9	12	7	15	4	13	1	2	6	12	10	
12	9	12	7	15	4	13	1	2	7	12	10	
13	9	12	7	15	4	13	1	2	8	12	10	
14	9	12	7	15	4	13	1	2	8	12	10	
15	9	12	7	15	4	13	1	2	8	12	12	
16	9	12	7	15	4	13	1	2	8	12	12	
17	9	12	7	15	4	13	1	2	8	12	12	
17+	9	12	7	15	4	13	1	2	8	12	12	

*Number on left is lower end of HFZ; number on right is upper end of HFZ.

**Test scored Pass/Fail; must reach this distance to pass.

pain (Cooper Institute for Aerobics Research, 1992). Selected test items used to assess abdominal/trunk strength include the curl-up and trunk lift test (see tables 17.1A and 17.1B). Upper body strength and endurance is measured by the push-up, modified pull-up, pull-up, and flexed arm hang. Standards for healthy zones for muscular strength and endurance appear in tables 17.1A and 17.1B.

Evaluation

Physical Best

Physical Best, AAHPERD's companion education program to the Prudential Fitness Challenge, provides a highly flexible award system for recognizing the fitness levels of students.

TABLE 17.2	Physical Best Awards
Participation Award	Recognizes individuals for participation in activity outside the education setting
Personal Goal Award	Awarded to individuals who meet personalized fitness goals and objectives
Performance Award	Awarded to individuals who meet pre-established health-related physical fitness standards or goals

Individuals can earn awards for developing and maintaining an active lifestyle, achieving specified goals (e.g., related to the IEP), or for reaching the standards identified in the Fitnessgram's Healthy Fitness Zone. These awards are officially known as the Participation Award, Personal Goal Award, and Performance Award (table 17.2). Because the award program is based on personal goal setting, all children can participate and be recognized through the program. This feature is particularly desirable for youngsters with special needs and can be included in the Individualized Education Program. It is important to note, too, that developers of the Fitnessgram recognize that adaptations of test items would be necessary for some individuals with disabilities. This might entail, for example, developing alternative test items for students with cerebral palsy or using procedures such as task analysis to address the fitness levels of individuals with severe mental retardation. The goal, of course, is to assess, to the extent possible, the individual's fitness level. Equally important is the need to encourage and promote fitness and not adhere to a

specific test item that may be inappropriate for assessing one's fitness level. A team of adapted physical education experts, coordinated by AAHPERD, have developed a manual of useful information on assessing individuals with disabilities (Seaman, 1995). The manual provides extensive discussion and examples of alternative testing ideas and strategies.

Brockport Physical Fitness Test (BPFT)

The BPFT assumes ". . . that youngsters with disabilities typically have the same health-related concerns associated with a lack of physical activity and fitness as their non-disabled peers. However, they also have additional health-related concerns that may relate to fitness. . . . The BPFT recognizes the unique needs of youngsters with disabilities . . ." (Winnick & Short, 2001, p. 6). Health-related fitness is related to the ability to perform daily activities and demonstrate the traits or capacities that are associated with low risk for

Figure 17.3 Relationships among health, physical activity, and health-related physical fitness.

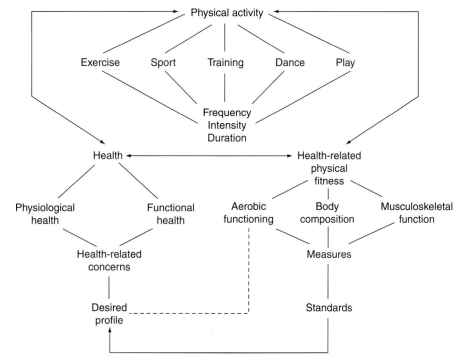

developing diseases. Therefore, the BPFT tests levels of aerobic capacity, body fat, and musculoskeletal function (see figure 17.3), which are known to be related to reduction of risk factors for disease. Using a criterion-referenced approach, the BPFT tests cardiorespiratory endurance and body composition, muscular strength and endurance, and flexibility/range of motion. Modifications and adaptations for testing as well as developing health-related fitness programs in disability areas are included for mental retardation, visual impairments, spinal cord injuries, cerebral palsy, and congenital anomalies or amputations. Software is provided for record keeping, which assists with identifying and tracking specific goals and fitness plans for students. Also, the BPFT generates the test items appropriate for testing by disability area; therefore, contraindicated fitness activities have been addressed within the test. These features are easily linked into creating IEP outcomes.

The BPFT was designed for individuals ten to seventeen years of age with disabilities. It was begun under the direction of Dr. Joe Winnick, State University of New York at Brockport, through an extensive research effort to establish and validate criterion-referenced physical fitness test items and standards for adolescents with selected disabilities. This effort is built on the successes of Prudential Fitnessgram.

Concepts of Fitness Development

Improvement in physical fitness components is accomplished as a result of the body's response to the stresses of exercise. The components of physical fitness are separate qualities, each of which must be attended to if total fitness improvement is desired. This principle of specificity of development states that development will only occur in the specific muscles or organs stressed and that the type of development will be governed by the type of stress experienced. Thus, each exercise causes a very specific developmental response by the body and there is no one exercise or sport that develops all aspects of fitness. Exercises that develop muscular strength in the arms obviously do little for the strength of leg muscles or for the flexibility of those same arm muscles. If both strength and flexibility are desired, both qualities must be provided for in the exercise program. Heavy resistance movements for strength, and movement through a maximal range of motion for flexibility, are required for development of both qualities. Similarly, the development of muscle strength has little effect on cardiorespiratory endurance, yet each can be increased with specific exercises. The following chart identifies the appropriate type of exercises for adults and some high school students for achieving improvement in each component of physical fitness.

Component	Type of Exercise
Muscle strength:	Heavy resistance exercises that produce fatigue within ten repetitions.
Muscle endurance:	Light resistance exercises conducted for a prolonged time, producing fatigue in ten to one hundred repetitions.
Flexibility:	Joint movement held at the extremes of the range of motion for fifteen to thirty seconds.
Cardiorespiratory:	Continuous large-muscle activity producing rates of 70 to 90 percent of maximum heart rate for at least fifteen minutes. (Lower values may be appropriate for very unconditioned individuals.)
Body composition:	Sustained large-muscle activity that causes substantial caloric expenditure. (The total work accomplished as estimated by force × distance will give an approximation of the relative caloric cost of the activity.)

Children improve and maintain fitness through being physically active, rather than through specific exercises to improve fitness. Young children need to be taught physical activity skills and need to be engaged in games and sports. The main thrust on addressing the fitness needs of young children is to engage them in physical activity that is age-appropriate and appropriate to their maturity level. Young children need regular structured and unstructured time to be physically active.

When subjected to the stress of an unaccustomed exercise, the body responds by adapting to enable a higher level of functioning. After repeated exercise bouts using the same intensity, the body will eventually develop to the point where this exercise is easily accommodated. For greater improvement in function to occur, the intensity of the exercise must be further increased. As intensity increases the body will begin to respond, increasing its capacity over the previous level. Thus, continued improvement in any of the fitness components depends upon the exercise program being periodically increased in intensity or duration. This process is commonly known as the principle of progressive overload, or systematically increasing the strenuousness of the exercise program as one's body responds by increasing its capacity for exercise.

The reverse of the progressive overload principle applies when one reduces or ceases to exercise regularly. The body responds to a lack of stress by becoming less capable of performing. This transitory nature is an important aspect of physical fitness. The various components of fitness can be rapidly improved through systematic exercise but are also rapidly lost when habitual exercise is reduced. This is another way in which physical fitness varies from motor fitness. Generally, motor skills, once learned, are retained at a reasonable level with little or no practice. Physical fitness qualities, however, are developed rather than learned and necessitate continued attention to be maintained.

Strength and muscular endurance losses can also be due to disorders that affect the neuromuscular system. Injury to the motor centers or the peripheral nerves and debilitating diseases such as muscular dystrophy, multiple sclerosis, myasthenia gravis, and polymyositis are some of the disorders that cause muscular weakness and lack of muscular endurance. Muscles that are affected by these disorders may not respond to the progressive overload principle in the same manner as normal muscles, and, in some cases, strength and endurance exercises can even affect the muscles adversely and are, therefore, contraindicated. Joint and bone disorders also can affect the development of strength detrimentally; and for individuals with such disorders, strength and muscular endurance exercises involving the affected parts of the body also may be contraindicated. Although there is evidence to support the use of progressive resistance exercises in programs for individuals with spastic cerebral palsy, further study is needed (Horvat, 1987).

Flexibility exercises generally are of value to all persons with neurological and muscular disorders. In some cases of neurological disorders, such as cerebral palsy, the flexibility exercises should be planned in consultation with medical personnel because of the importance that only certain specified muscles be stretched. Specific stretching or flexibility exercises are done in compliance with the medical prescription.

In light of the foregoing discussion about the specificity of development and realizing the unique needs and interests of each individual, it is apparent that developmental fitness programs should be individually tailored for each participant. It is important that approval of the program be obtained from the student's physician in cases of cardiac problems and muscular and neurological disorders.

The basic steps in constructing an individual fitness program include:

1. Establishing a desired goal or outcome,
2. Testing current fitness status and assessing limitations imposed by the disabling conditions,
3. Devising the exercise program and periodic reassessment of status resulting in alteration of the prescription, and
4. Assisting the individual in understanding the nature of the program and the benefit from participating. This is an essential step for success for everyone, but critical for individuals whose mental capacity makes it difficult to internalize the value of good health.

Establishing the goals of the exercise program focuses attention on the specific components of physical fitness to be developed. Although everyone should strive to achieve a modest level of each of the components, unique needs and interests will modify the desired development beyond the minimal healthful level. One student may desire to participate in wheelchair basketball, another to reduce flexibility loss, and a third to learn swimming. The specific fitness components important in each of these cases differs greatly. Testing of the appropriate fitness components will identify the current level of functioning and establish the necessary information for the construction of the exercise program.

The program identifies the actual exercises that will be performed, stating intensity (how much resistance or how fast the activity will be performed), duration (how many times or for how long the exercise will last), and frequency (how many times per day or per week it will be performed). For example, one exercise in the workout program for the student who desires to play wheelchair basketball might be a seated press with a barbell, an exercise that strengthens the triceps and deltoid muscle groups used in shooting the ball. The program might be:

Intensity: 80 percent of maximum press strength
Duration: three sets of eight repetitions
Frequency: three days per week

A portion of the exercise program for the student who is experiencing loss of flexibility might include a seated low back and hamstring stretch with the following prescription:

Intensity: Stretch to limit of forward flexion
Duration: Hold for twenty seconds, relax, repeat five times
Frequency: Every day

Because swimming involves sustained arm work, one appropriate exercise for a student desiring to learn to swim might be on an overhead pulley done to the following prescription:

Intensity: ten pounds
Duration: two sets of fifty repetitions
Frequency: three days per week

In light of the principle of progressive overload, the intensity or duration of each exercise should be increased regularly, normally about every week or two. Periodic retesting of maximal capacity should be conducted to identify gains, establish new goals, and serve as the basis for revision of the exercise program.

General survey tests of physical fitness are valuable in identifying areas of deficiency and can serve as a basis for setting appropriate fitness goals. It may thus be the decision of the physical educator or therapist to begin the process with a general test that samples from all of the fitness qualities. The results of the test can then aid in the selection of appropriate goals and exercises.

Techniques for Improving Physical Fitness

The popularity of exercise programs to improve physical fitness has increased due to wide acceptance of the ability of these programs to aid in altering body proportions, reducing fat, and gaining enhanced strength, flexibility, and endurance. The rehabilitative value of exercise for many injuries and diseases is becoming as well recognized as the value of exercise training in preparation for athletic participation. Even with populations such as those with spina bifida, ostomy, and multiple sclerosis, where historically little information exists regarding health status and response to exercise, researchers (Coutts, McKenzie, Loock, Beauchamp, & Armstrong, 1993; Holland, Bouffard, & Wagner, 1992; Rimmer, 1992; Rowland, 1990; and Vogler, 1990) are providing new insights that will help practitioners develop meaningful programs. While current research suggests that differences exist between the health-fitness status of individuals with disabilities and those without disabilities, the differences may be attributed to many factors, including limited opportunities and expectations that undervalue the potential of many individuals with disabilities. For these reasons, large numbers of boys, girls, men, and women are now exercising regularly to improve their physical fitness. The person with a disability can benefit from these same values as well as specific remediation of some physical conditions.

The section of this chapter dealing with the concepts of fitness development might well be reviewed at this point. The following material will discuss particular means for improving the components of fitness based upon the concepts presented earlier.

Development of Muscle Strength and Endurance

The improvement of muscle strength and endurance is best accomplished through the use of some type of resistive exercise device. The necessary load, or resistance, may be created by springs, elastic cables, friction devices, or, most commonly, by barbell weights. Exercise physiologists recognize resistance training as the most efficient means of enhancing muscle development.

The use of weight training for the improvement of muscular strength and endurance has become a standard practice for all ages and both sexes. Weight training for those with disabilities provides an opportunity for participation with nondisabled peers in a popular activity (figure 17.4). In many instances, individuals with disabilities can engage on an equal basis with nondisabled peers when performing exercises not involving their specific impairment. This offers an opportunity for beneficial social acceptance and self-image development. An individual with an amputation may be quite capable of outperforming nondisabled peers on an arm curl or bench press exercise.

Weight training requires very little space; an area as small as one hundred square feet is adequate. The floor must be able to support considerable weight; therefore, a concrete floor is desirable. However, if the floor is wooden, heavy planks may be placed over it.

Equipment consists primarily of barbells and dumbbells. The barbells are used for exercises with two hands, whereas the dumbbells, which are shorter, are used chiefly for one-arm exercises. Weight-lifting machines eliminate the use of barbells and dumbbells; all lifts that are possible with weights can be done with the machine. In addition, some special pieces of equipment have been devised to expand the exercise possibilities; among these are head straps, iron

Figure 17.4 Those with lower limb involvement perform lifts while seated in the wheelchair.

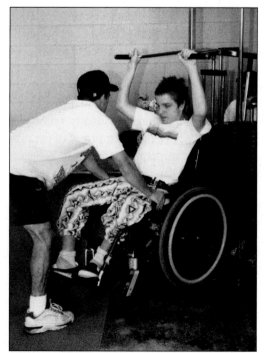

shoes, knee exercisers, wall pulleys, wrist rollers, chest springs, inclined boards, and leg-press apparatus.

Weight training lends itself readily to self-paced programs. After initial instruction in the lifts, students may proceed on their own or in pairs. For those working alone, the use of a personal progress sheet is very helpful; at the end of each class period students should record the amount of weight lifted and the number of repetitions made. This will enable the student to know exactly where to begin at the start of the next class. A sample weight lifting form developed for Special Olympians is found in figure 17.5.

Regardless of the class organization for instruction in weight training, all students, before they begin, should have a clear understanding of the activities they must avoid, the adaptations they must make, and the safety precautions they must observe.

Safety regulations should be stressed emphatically by the teacher. The first one applies when using either the weight-lifting machine or the barbells and dumbbells; the other three apply only to the use of the latter.

1. Warm-up exercises should be performed before attempting a heavy lift. The warm-up may consist of the side-straddle hop exercise or running in place with exaggerated arm movements.

2. In moving a heavy weight from one place to another, the lift should be made with the knees flexed and the back straight. No one, especially those with back difficulties, should ever lift heavy weights by bending at the hips with the legs straight.

3. Collars (the metal pieces that hold the weights to the bar) should be fastened securely. They should be checked before each lift is attempted.

4. A lift should never be made over someone who is sitting, squatting, or lying on the floor.

All exercises that may involve diseased or disabled parts of the body should be reviewed with the student's physician before implementing. Participants with weakened or injured muscles should use light loads as prescribed. When exercising those parts of the body that are not injured, the utmost care must be taken to prevent the injured part from being brought into action inadvertently. Special care must be taken so that the lifter will not slip or allow the load to slip, thereby bringing into action a muscle that was being protected. To be absolutely safe, a lifter with an injury should not make

Figure 17.5 Special olympics weight training chart. (*Source: Total Conditioning for the Special Olympian* (1986), Lincoln, NE: National Strength and Conditioning Association.)

Special Olympics Weight Training Record Chart

Name _____

Starting Date _____

		1				2				3				4			
Exercise	MA	Wt.	R	Wt.	R	Wt.	R	Wt.	R	Wt.	R	Wt.	R	Wt.	R	Wt.	R	Wt.	R	Wt.	R	Wt.	R	Wt.	R
Bench press	C																		
Standing/seated lateral dumbbell raises	S																		
Bent knee sit-up	ST																		
Deadlift	LB																		
Bent-over rowing	UB																		
Bicep curl	FA																		
Tricep press	BA																		
Date																			

Wt. - Weight
R - Repetitions
Numbers (1, 2, 3, 4) represent training weeks
MA - Muscle area most involved

C - Chest
FA - Front of arm
S - Shoulder
UB - Upper back

BA - Back of arm
ST - Stomach
LB - Lower back

an all-out effort even though the injured part is not involved in the effort.

Those for whom lifting weights is contraindicated for the leg area may do their lifting while sitting or lying down, avoiding all lifts involving the legs. Students who use wheelchairs can perform the lifts while seated in their wheelchairs. Some participants with minor back difficulties may be allowed to take arm and leg exercises if the back is protected against undue stress. To protect the back in such exercises as the two-arm curl, lateral raise, front raise, and military press, these lifts can be made sitting down, with the back held firmly against the back of the chair. Exercises that require heavy weight on the shoulders are contraindicated for those with weak backs. Exercise with the leg machine is a possible substitution for the deep knee bends, which require heavy weight on the shoulder to develop the quadriceps of the legs. Exercises from the prone position do not place undue stress upon the back and therefore need not be adapted. In the supine position those exercises that have a tendency to hyperextend the back, such as the leg raises and the supine pullover, are contraindicated for those with any type of back difficulties or with exceptionally weak abdominals.

In lifting heavy weights, a deep breath is taken and held to stabilize the thoracic region. When this is done, there is an extreme elevation of the arterial blood pressure because the increased pressure in the thoracic region prevents blood from returning to the heart. If the effort is prolonged, the blood pressure falls after its initial rise. This is known as the Valsalva phenomenon. Because of the increase in blood pressure caused by lifting of weights, the activity is not usually recommended for those with cardiac or circulatory disorders.

The student with the use of only one arm will perform all the lifts involving the use of an arm with this arm. The weights should be sufficiently light so that lifting them with one arm will not produce twisting of the body or bending of the spine laterally, for such movements may produce muscular development that will cause postural difficulties. Students with functional stumps may find it possible to do the lifts with a prosthesis.

In presenting adaptations that can be made for those with disabilities in weight training, very brief descriptions of the specific lifts are given to enable the reader to make a better comparison of the adaptation with normal performance and so gain a better understanding of the process of adapting the lifts for participants with disabilities. It is not the intent to provide instruction for learning to perform the lifts. Those who wish this information are referred to the books in Selected Readings at the end of the chapter.

Lifting Techniques

There are many different types of lifts. Many of them exercise different muscles; others exercise muscles in different groups or exercise the same set of muscles. The muscles that are primarily involved in any given lift can be determined with some degree of accuracy even by someone who does not have a thorough knowledge of anatomy. It must be remembered that a muscle does not push but always pulls to move a joint and that a contracting muscle is harder than a muscle not being worked. Consequently, by examining the direction of movement of the part of the body involved and by palpating the muscle or muscles while the lift is being executed, the muscles being used can be located. Then, by referring to a chart of the skeletal muscles like the one shown in appendix V on the CD, the muscles can be identified.

The lifts presented here are selected to give a fairly complete workout to the major muscle groups in a minimum number of exercises. All lifts using barbells and dumbbells are made from the standing position unless otherwise indicated. Positions for the lifts on the weight-lifting machine will vary according to the kind of machine. The subsequent lifts are described for the barbells and dumbbells, but most of the lifts can be done on the various machines. (For location of muscles listed for each test, see appendix V on the CD.)

Neck Extension and Neck Curl

Neck extension exercises the posterior muscles of the neck (sacrospinalis, cervical muscles, trapezius). A prone position is taken on a bench or on the floor. If a bench is used, the neck extends over the end of the bench. A plate of the barbells is held with both hands on the back of the head. The head is lifted backward as far as possible while the chest rests on the bench or floor. The neck is then lowered to the starting position.

The neck curl is performed in the supine position, and the weight is held on the forehead. The head is brought up and forward until the chin touches the chest.

Adaptations: The weights held to the head may be eliminated to decrease the strenuousness of the exercise. If there is extreme muscular weakness or cervical vertebrae injury or malfunction, the neck muscles may be exercised by tightening the flexors and extensors at the same time and holding for approximately six seconds, repeating until sufficient work has been given to the muscles, as a substitute for the exercise with weights.

For those who use wheelchairs, a head harness may be attached to a wall pulley. The medical records of individuals with Down syndrome should be checked to ensure that an anomalous defect know as atlantoaxial instability is not present. If this condition exists, exercises that place undue pressure on the neck would be contraindicated.

Bench Press

The muscles involved in this lift are the pectoralis major and minor, triceps brachia, and the anterior and middle deltoid. This lift is made from a back-lying position on a bench with the buttocks, shoulders, and head in contact with the bench. The feet should comfortably straddle the bench and be in contact with the floor. To perform the bench press, an overhand grip with the hands slightly wider than the shoulders is recommended. The bar is lowered to and touches the chest just below the nipple, and then is pushed upward until the elbows are in an extended position.

Adaptations: A spotter should be used when performing the bench press. The spotter is responsible for assisting the lifter in the event that help is needed. In addition, individuals should be cautioned to avoid arching the back by bringing the buttocks off the bench when performing the lift. Arching the back places tremendous stress and pressure on the lower back region. This can be corrected by using lighter weights and emphasizing that the back must maintain contact with the bench.

Military Press or Standing Press

The muscles involved in this lift are the deltoid, pectoralis major, and triceps. To make the lift, a pronated grip is taken on the bar. The bar is lifted and brought to rest against the chest. The bar is then raised straight over the head until the arms are fully extended. The bar is lowered to the chest position and the exercise repeated.

Adaptations: Care must be taken to keep the back straight as the weight is lifted above the head. This is especially necessary if the lifter has lower back difficulties. To avoid the tendency to hyperextend the back, the participant may sit in a chair with a high back, holding his or her back firmly against the chair's back.

Two-Arm Curl

The biceps and the brachialis are the primary muscles used in the two-arm curl. The supinated grip is taken. The bar is brought to the thighs. The bar is raised to the shoulders by bending the elbows. The weight is then lowered until the arms are fully extended. The lift may be done by taking a pronated grip. The extensors of the fingers and wrist can be exercised by hyperextending the wrist while lifting the weight to the shoulders.

Adaptations: Lifters with back disorders must take the utmost care to avoid pushing the hips forward to help start the lift upward. This movement hyperextends the back, thereby placing undue stress upon it. To avoid this possibility, the lifter should keep the weight light enough to be handled easily with the arms. As additional protection against hyperextension the lifter may stand with the back against the wall so that movement of the hips is kept to a minimum during the lift. The use of cuff weights or weighted wristbands may be necessary for those who have limited use of the wrists and hands.

Straight-Arm Pullover

The major work in this lift is performed by the pectoralis major and minor, triceps, latissimus dorsi, and serratus anterior muscles. A supine position is taken. The bar is on the floor at arm's length from the head. A grip is taken with the palms up. The bar is pulled and lifted with the arms held straight to a position above the chest. The bar is returned to the starting position and the exercise repeated.

Adaptations: To decrease the difficulty of the lift for those lacking arm strength, the pullover may be done with the arms bent until the bar is above the head, at which time the arms are extended fully. The bar is lowered in a reverse manner.

Those with weak backs should not perform the straight-arm pullover.

Straight-Leg Dead Lift

In this lift the back muscles and upper posterior leg muscles (erector spinae, gluteus maximus, and hamstrings) are used. The bar is placed near the toes. The body is bent at the hips and the upper back held straight. An alternate grip is taken on the bar (one hand pronated and the other supinated), and the bar is lifted by straightening the back. The knees are locked and the arms are kept straight. The bar is then lowered to its original position.

Adaptations: Those with back injuries should modify the lift to reduce the strain on the back muscles and yet exercise the extensors of the back, as follows: A sitting position is taken on a bench, with a light dumbbell in each hand. The shoulders are hunched forward, and the chin rests on the chest. The head is lifted, the shoulders thrown wide, and the back straightened. Return to the original position and repeat the exercise.

Sit-Ups

The major muscles involved in the sit-ups are the abdominals and the iliopsoas. A supine position is taken, with the knees bent to approximately a ninety-degree angle and the toes hooked under the bar. A weight is held to the back of the head with both hands. The head is brought forward until it is approximately thirty degrees off the floor. Movement beyond this range uses the hip flexor muscles and provides little value to the abdominal muscles.

Adaptations: No weight is placed behind the head. The head is brought forward until the chin touches the chest. Then the shoulders start to raise from the floor. The small of the back remains in contact with the floor throughout the lift. The return is made to the supine position.

Knee Bend and Heel Raise

In the knee bend the gastrocnemius, soleus, quadriceps, and gluteus maximus are used extensively. The bar is held across the back of the neck and shoulders, and the body is lowered to a squat position with the upper legs parallel to the floor. The return is made to the original position.

In the heel raise, the gastrocnemius, soleus, and plantar flexor of the feet are developed. The bar is carried on the shoulders as in the deep knee bend. The bar is lifted by raising the heels off the ground until the weight is resting on the balls of the feet. The heels are then lowered.

Adaptations: Some authorities feel that deep knee bends affect the ligaments of the knee to their disadvantage and therefore recommend that only a three-quarter squat be taken.

Those suffering from injured knees should substitute a knee exerciser for the knee bends. Students with back difficulties should not perform the lift with heavy weights on the shoulders. Those with arch problems in the feet should not do the heel raise.

Lateral, Forward, and Backward Lifts

The muscles involved in each of these lifts are: lateral lift—deltoid, supraspinatus, trapezius, serratus anterior; forward lift—deltoid, pectoralis major, coraco-brachialis, serratus anterior, trapezius; backward lift—deltoid, teres major, rhomboids, trapezius.

Dumbbells are grasped in each hand with the hands at the sides of the body. In the lateral raise, the arms are lifted directly sideways to the horizontal level. For the forward raise, they are lifted forward. In the backward raise, the arms are raised backward and upward as far as possible without bending the trunk.

Adaptations: In the lateral and forward lifts, a sitting position may be taken to avoid hyperextending the back. Those with weak shoulder joints subject to dislocation should never raise the arms higher than shoulder level. As an additional safety precaution, the exercise should be performed with one arm at a time. The opposite arm is brought across the chest and the hand grasps the shoulder to pull it in toward the body during the lift. In this way it becomes impossible to raise the arm inadvertently above the desired level.

The backward lift is contraindicated for those suffering from weak shoulder joints subject to dislocation.

Prone Lateral Raise

The deltoid, pectoralis major, infraspinatus, teres minor, and trapezius muscles are brought into play in this exercise. A prone position is taken on a bench, and the hands grasp dumbbells on the floor to each side of the body. The weights

are lifted toward the ceiling as far as possible, keeping the arms straight. The dumbbells are then lowered slowly to the floor.

Adaptations: No modification is required except for individuals with missing limbs and those with heart disorders.

Supine Horizontal Arm Lift

The following muscles are used in this lift: deltoid, pectoralis major, coracobrachialis, and serratus anterior. A supine position is taken with the arms extended out from the shoulders. The dumbbells are grasped with the palms facing up. The arms are raised over the chest with the elbows locked and then returned to the original position.

Adaptations: The lift usually will not require adaptation except for individuals with heart disorders and amputations.

Prone Arch Back

The performer lies face down on a bench, with the upper half of the body extended over the end of the bench; the ankles are held securely by a partner. Holding a dumbbell behind the head, the performer arches the back and holds this position for eight to ten seconds.

Adaptations: To reduce the strain on weak extensor muscles of the back, the amount of the weight is decreased. Also a small stool may be placed beneath the lifter's chest to prevent going all the way to the floor. This exercise should not be used for individuals with lower back pain unless specifically prescribed by the student's physician.

Most of the typical exercises used in weight training can be simulated as isometric contractions, thereby making them adaptable for use by those who are unable to engage in isotonic weight training. Isometrics require exerting a muscle against some immovable object. Pushing against a door frame or against stall bars or using ropes or towels to restrict the ability to move can provide isometric contractions. Other body parts can be used as resistance also; for example, one can use the hand to resist head movements or flex one arm while resisting with the other. Isometrics have been criticized for their inability to improve muscle endurance. If repeated contractions are performed, as would be the case in using barbells for muscular endurance, this limitation can be eliminated. One significant advantage of isometrics is that they allow a specific weak point in a movement to be exercised without necessitating the use of the entire range of motion. This advantage may be of special value to a person with a condition for whom stress in one part of the range of motion is contraindicated.

In addition to the typical resistance training exercises, a variety of other games, stunts, and sports can be utilized for the purpose of increasing muscle strength and endurance. Many gymnastics skills performed on the parallel or uneven bars, rings, and side horse will develop significant upper body strength. Floor stunts, hand balancing, and shot putting are also good strength developers. Various types of relay races such as wheelbarrow races, seal walks, one-leg hopping, and medicine-ball passing can provide novelty while stimulating muscular development. Performing calisthenic movements in a swimming pool provides another alternative form of resistance exercise. The force necessary to move the limbs through the water is much greater than that in air. These aquatic exercises also effectively allow for differences in fitness levels. The stronger individual is instructed to move faster, the water providing increased resistance.

Equipment other than free weights or weight machines can be used to develop muscular strength. For instance, young children will enjoy the use of weighted stuffed animals. Various exercises can be performed with the stuffed animals to encourage the development of appropriate levels of strength. Some have found the use of flexible (surgical) tubing effective for providing resistance through a range of motion. Flexible tubing can be particularly effective when used with individuals who are recovering from serious injury or those who have limited musculature. Tubing or rope also can be held and pulled by two individuals to create a challenging form of resistance.

Circuit training or the use of exercises performed at various stations can also be an effective method for enhancing muscle strength and endurance. Using this approach, students are challenged to perform a certain number of lifts or exercises at a station before moving to the next station. The activity can be individualized for each participant by specifying the number of repetitions at each station and/or the number of times to go through the circuit. The stations should be varied so that different muscle groups are used in adjacent stations. Circuit training can be very effective in motivating students because of the individualized approach used in this system. The individual with a disability will be able to participate with nondisabled peers in the circuit training program.

Exercise Considerations for Children with Disabilities

Basically, it is a child's nature to be physically active. The American College of Sports Medicine (ACSM) has outlined considerations for exercise for children and youth with disabilities (Riner & Sabath, 2003). Exercise restriction during growth in childhood is viewed as detrimental to overall development and health.

- There are differences in the way that children respond to exercise and the way adults respond.
  - For example, the maximum and submaximum heart rate of children and adolescents is higher than in

adults; therefore, exercising at the "target heart rate" must be altered.
- Compared with adults who exercise in hot weather, children sweat less, acclimatize to exercise less, and their core temperature rises at greater rates. Therefore, it is recommended that children be exposed to warm weather exercising gradually and be encouraged to drink liquids.
- Muscle mass and strength increases significantly for males during adolescence. Resistance training for both genders can be encouraged after the onset of puberty.
- For children, exercise has been shown to reduce stress and the symptoms of depression. Obviously, children who live stressful lives can benefit from access to physical activity.

Testing children and youth for exercise is different than testing adults, and the following guidelines are important to build into the testing:

- If children are tested in a lab, the lab should be attractive to children.
- Enthusiastic and compassionate staff are needed.
- Age-appropriate language about the equipment should be used and desired outcomes explained.
- Pictures of children performing the exercises are displayed.
- Appropriate-sized equipment is required.
- Children rate themselves lower on perceived exertion charts than adults and adolescents. Therefore, they may be exerting more than they are able to report.
- An exercise program that is recommended ". . . should be enjoyable and relatively non-specific, with increased movement as the initial goal . . ." (p. 18). (Riner & Sabath, 2003)

Concerns for children with disabilities in exercise include the following:

- Children with disabilities are assessed for exercise using the *same measures* (e.g. body composition) as their nondisabled peers.
- The therapeutic benefit of exercise for children with disease or disability is enormous if the child can come close to living a normal life where exercise improves the quality of life in the social, psychological, and physical realms.
- Intensity of activity, environmental conditions (e.g., temperature), and risk for injury due to physical contact should be reviewed; each may need to be altered (e.g., lower intensity, moderate temperature, individual assessment of risk given a specific disability).
- Children without a disability respond and adapt to exercise differently than do adults, and children with a disability may have even greater variation. Individualized

observation and coordination with parents and medical personnel are recommended. (See Riner & Sabath, 2003, for specific considerations for heart defects, diabetes, neuromuscular disorders, and pulmonary disorders.)

In conclusion, ACSM is clear that exercise for children and youth with disabilities is reported to improve the quality of life and to mitigate long-term consequences of disease and disability. Guidelines set for testing children and youth with and without disabilities and engaging them in physical activity is drawn from the most current research; hence, for the physical educator, evidence-based practice can result in developing programs in physical activity for these children.

Special Considerations for Individuals who are Mentally Retarded

Recent attention has been focused on those with mental retardation and their low levels of physical fitness. Several investigators have concluded that this population tends to have low levels of physical fitness. Although there may be in some instances of mental retardation a physiologic reason for this, the low levels of physical fitness are probably due to the lack of opportunity and appropriate programs for this population. There is growing evidence to suggest that significant improvements in fitness can be made with those who are mentally retarded, including those severely involved, if programs are systematically developed and implemented. Some suggested guidelines are indicated in the following list:

1. Communicate the importance of physical fitness. Many individuals who are mentally retarded have difficulty understanding the "why" of physical fitness—why should someone jog? Halle, Silverman, and Regan (1983) found that a puppet could be used to help children who are mentally retarded focus and listen to information about health and fitness. A valuable communication device for emphasizing the importance of fitness is to perform the exercises with the class. Seeing the teacher "work out" helps the adolescent who is mentally retarded recognize that running and flexibility exercises are not just activities for children.

2. Task analyze the exercise. Many of the fitness activities will require that the activity be broken down into smaller steps and taught to the participants. The amount of instruction required will depend upon the level of retardation and past experience of the individuals. Participants who are mentally retarded will require extended practice to ensure that the exercises are familiar and understood.

3. Establish goals and criteria for success. During the first week of the program it is essential that baseline measures be taken on the performance capability of the students. For example, the number of sit-ups an individual can perform in sixty seconds should be recorded as well as other indicators such as distance walked/jogged in twelve minutes. Given this information, individual goals and objectives can be developed.

4. Design a motivational system. Because the gains experienced by people who are mentally retarded can sometimes be small, it is essential that a recording system be developed so that the participants can "see" change. This can be accomplished in several ways. For example, a poster with the name of all the students can be displayed and stickers applied for each day that the individual meets or exceeds the prescribed goal. Group or class support can be developed by allowing the class to do something special, such as having a party when all of the participants reach their individual goals. A graphic display of the total number of minutes spent in physical activity can be effective in helping some recognize that it is not necessary to be the fastest or the strongest to be successful.

5. Use peers as tutors to provide for direct and continuous motivation for the students. Rintala, Dunn, McCubbin, & Quinn (1992) found peers very helpful in encouraging young adult males to walk long distances at a rapid rate. Peers provide constant feedback and help to make the exercise session enjoyable and natural. Peer-tutoring is advocated by Lieberman and Houston-Wilson (2003) to increase the physical activity level of individuals in physical education classes.

6. Probe for change in performance. To determine whether the participants are improving, formal measures of the fitness test items should be conducted at regular intervals of time, such as every two weeks. The level of performance should be compared to the initial score and a graph developed to illustrate change. If the expected gains are not evident, then an effort should be made to determine if the goal or program should be modified. Occasionally the problem may be that the specific exercise has not been learned, resulting in little practice. Frequent testing helps to emphasize that physical fitness is important and that gains will occur when the program is followed.

7. Incorporate the exercise program into the home. Maintenance and generalization of physical fitness and the exercise program will require the support of parents. Individuals with mental retardation require additional time to learn and incorporate selected concepts. Parents can be very effective in helping children to appreciate the importance of fitness and the value of exercise. Teachers should provide frequent feedback to parents

about the fitness levels of their children and encourage parents to exercise with their children.

The fitness levels of individuals who are mentally retarded can be improved, but gains will not occur without a systematic training program. In addition, efforts should be made to incorporate fitness and physical activity into the regular daily life patterns of these individuals. Improvements in physical fitness will be maintained if individuals are consistent in their exercise practices.

Individualized Fitness Programs: An Example

In most cases, the program of physical fitness will need to be individualized for the student with a disability. When setting up such a program, consideration must be given to the characteristics, attitudes, and interests of the individual as they relate to the assessment of needs and the selection of activities for the program (figure 17.6). The following is a hypothetical example of the fitness evaluation and prescription process.

Description of Subject

Marcia Cox, 152 pounds, fourteen-year-old female, has required the use of a wheelchair since she was hit by an automobile while riding her bike at age ten. Marcia is an above-average junior high school student. Previously, she received no more activity than that required to achieve her mobility from class to class and around her house. Marcia's parents have requested that an assessment be conducted and that

Figure 17.6 Professionals today can help the individual with a disability monitor personal health and fitness.

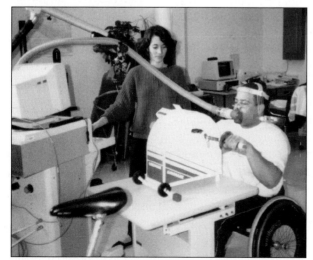

fitness be incorporated into Marcia's Individualized Education Program (IEP) in physical education.

Evaluation of Needs

In discussions with Marcia it was clear that she had a rather low self-concept. She indicated a concern over her tendency to be overweight and expressed a desire to be more active. When asked, Marcia responded that she did know how to swim before her accident and had enjoyed it. She commented that she would like to lose some body weight and learn to swim again.

Fitness Testing

Marcia's general fitness was observed to be poor. It was determined that several tests would be appropriate for a fitness evaluation—the results of which would be shared with the IEP team and used as a basis for construction of a specific exercise program. The tests selected were handgrip strength, arm extensor strength, shoulder and neck flexibility, skinfold body fat test, and a modified cardiorespiratory test. This test involved five minutes of a speed-controlled shuttle of fifty feet using her wheelchair with a count of her pulse rate for fifteen seconds immediately following the exercise.

The results of the testing were as follows:

1. Grip Strength: right—18 kilograms, left—16 kilograms
2. Seated Barbell Press: 35 pounds
3. Shoulder Flexibility (flexion-extension): 185°
4. Neck Flexibility (rotation): 130°
5. Skinfold Fat: triceps—27 millimeters, subscapular—29 millimeters
6. Cardiorespiratory Endurance: 15 second pulse count = 47 = 188 per-minute; resting rate = 78

Marcia's grip strength was interpreted as being below that desired. Her barbell press strength was adequate but could be enhanced as an aid to swimming, especially because all her stroke power must come from her arms. Her flexibility was deemed to be adequate but would be increased for the extra value it has for swimming. The measure of her body fat, though it should not be compared to norms, appeared to be rather elevated. The cardiorespiratory endurance task will be used for future comparisons. Subjective observation was that she had rather poor cardiorespiratory endurance.

Prescription Program

The following was designed as a beginning exercise program for Marcia with reevaluation to take place in three months. Workouts were scheduled three times per week.

She was encouraged to also add some other activity such as accompanying her parents on walks. She was also counseled to follow a moderate diet. Marcia's parents, as members of the IEP team, agreed to help their daughter follow the program.

1. A generalized warm-up consisting of five minutes of continuous laps around the gym in her wheelchair. Moderate speed was suggested and her pulse checked to achieve approximately 125 beats per minute.
2. Stretching exercises for the neck, shoulder, and spine. A variety of exercises were used, each held for fifteen seconds and repeated four times.
3. Weight Training Exercises: (a) barbell press: 20 pounds, 8 to 10 repetitions, 3 sets (b) dumbbell curl: 5 pounds, 10 to 12 repetitions, 3 sets.
4. Swimming—total pool time twenty minutes. Combination of various strokes.

Heart rate checked every five minutes—attempting to keep it at approximately 145 beats per minute, working up to 155 beats per minute by the end of the first month.

$$
\begin{array}{ll}
220 & 60\% \ (206 - 78) + 78 = 154.8 \ \text{target heart rate} \\
-14 & (\text{age of subject}) \\
\hline
206 & (\text{max. heart rate}) \\
78 & = \text{resting heart rate} \}
\end{array}
$$

The exercise prescription was modified to increase the work intensity periodically as Marcia appeared to be making progress. Marcia enjoyed the workouts. Both the social contact with the physical educator and the activities were enjoyable. She especially liked the swimming and by the second month was feeling quite at home in the water. She expressed that she felt she would be able to enjoy swimming with some friends by summer.

At the end of three months Marcia had improved in all areas of fitness tested. Her second set of test scores was then recorded alongside her initial test results.

This program was deemed a success. Marcia was pleased with her progress and a new set of goals was established with a slightly altered exercise prescription to concentrate more on the first phase of weight reduction with increased physical activity in the community pool.

Summary

There is increasing awareness of the importance of physical fitness and its contribution toward a healthy lifestyle. The relationship between inactivity and heart disease, obesity, and high blood pressure are well documented. Many have argued that physical fitness reduces selected health risk factors and contributes toward an overall feeling of well-being. Recognition has also grown in recent years of the importance of the health benefits of enhanced physical fitness to the typically less active, including those with disabilities. Due to a combination of factors including the lack of opportunities, overprotection, and self-consciousness, individuals with disabilities often engage in less daily physical activity than do those who are not disabled. Fortunately, significant efforts are underway to improve the physical fitness of those with disabilities and in turn enhance their overall quality of life.

Within this chapter information was presented on the distinction between physical fitness and motor fitness. Motor fitness has to do with selected factors that lead to the learning of selected motor skills and includes such variables as balance, coordination, and speed. Physical fitness, also known as health-related fitness, consists of five components: cardiorespiratory endurance, muscular strength, muscular endurance, flexibility, and body composition. Each of these components is important in contributing to a healthy and active life. Procedures and tests have been developed to assess physical fitness. Some tests have been specifically developed for special populations with norms that allow for comparisons by disability. Although much work remains to be done in this area, the tests that have been developed have provided needed standards and norms for individuals with disabilities.

Programs to improve the physical fitness of individuals with disabilities follow many of the same guidelines as those for the nondisabled. For example, the principle of progressive overload can be applied, with few exceptions, to individuals both with and without disabilities. Exceptions may be necessary for those with progressive neuromuscular conditions. The endurance of individuals with disabilities can be improved by following a program based on target heart rate and standardized according to the frequency, intensity, and duration of the exercise. Modifications, of course, will be necessary to accommodate those with sensory, neuromuscular, and orthopedic impairments. Users of wheelchairs, for instance, will need to modify their program to ensure that the cardiovascular system experiences sufficient stress to achieve a training effect. Those who are quadriplegic may find the duration of the activity a better guide than heart rate for assessing the intensity of the workout. Fortunately, there are several organizations that are providing leadership and training in this area. The message is very clear. Children and adults with disabilities should be encouraged to lead active lives with an emphasis on maintaining an appropriate level of physical fitness; to do otherwise may place greater emphasis on disability as opposed to ability.

Enhancing Activities

1. Select one of the tests referenced in this chapter and give the test to a youngster with a disability. Write up the results of the test with suggestions for program development.
2. Debate with one of your friends the similarities and differences between physical fitness and motor fitness. This activity might be enlarged to include the entire class, utilizing a formal debate approach.
3. Simulate a disability and take one of the physical fitness tests. This could entail wearing a blindfold or using a wheelchair. Write a short paper describing your feelings regarding your performance on the fitness test.
4. Undertake a study of the physiologic response of individuals with paraplegia and quadriplegia to exercise.

Describe the similarities and differences in these populations compared with those who are not disabled.
5. Implement a fitness program with an individual with a disability. Establish a baseline that describes the student's initial level of fitness, implement the program, and conduct periodic assessments to determine the amount of progress.
6. Develop a list of strategies that might be employed to motivate students with disabilities to develop and maintain an appropriate level of fitness. Explain how the list might differ depending on the level of disability (severe to mild) and type of disability (such as mental retardation contrasted to paraplegia).

Selected Readings

AAHPERD Fitness and Educational Program. (1987). *ARAPCS Physical Fitness Council Newsletter* (Spring 1988 ed., p. 1). Reston, VA: American Alliance for Health, Physical Education, Recreation, and Dance.

American Alliance for Health, Physical Education, Recreation, and Dance. (1975a). *Testing for impaired, disabled and handicapped individuals.* Washington, DC: Author.

American Alliance for Health, Physical Education, Recreation, and Dance. (1975b). *Youth fitness test manual.* Washington, DC: Author.

American Alliance for Health, Physical Education, Recreation, and Dance. (1976). *Special fitness test manual for mildly mentally retarded persons.* Washington, DC: Author.

American Alliance for Health, Physical Education, Recreation, and Dance. (1980). *Health related physical fitness test manual.* Washington, DC, Author.

American College of Sports Medicine. 2009. www.acsm.org retrieved April 24, 2009.

Baumgartner, T., & Horvat, M. (1991). Reliability of field based cardiovascular fitness running tests for individuals with mental retardation. *Adapted Physical Activity Quarterly, 8,* 107–114.

Bloomquist, C. E. C. (2003). Deaf and hard of hearing. In J. L. Durstine & G. E. Moore (Eds.), *ACMS's exercise management for persons with chronic diseases and disabilities* (2nd ed., pp. 320–324). Champaign, IL: Human Kinetics.

Buell, C. (1980). *Physical education and recreation for the visually handicapped.* Washington, DC: American Alliance for Health, Physical Education, Recreation, and Dance.

Broad, E. (2001). Sports nutrition for athletes with disabilities. *International SportsMed Journal, 2*(1).

Centers for Disease Control and Prevention. (CDC). (1996). www.cdc.gov

Cooper, K. H. (1970). *Aerobics.* New York: Bantam Books, Inc.

Cotugna, N., & Vickery, C. E. (2003). Community health and nutrition screening for Special Olympics' athletes. *Journal of Community Health, 28*(6), 451–457.

Coutts, K., McKenzie, D., Loock, C., Beauchamp, R., & Armstrong, R. (1993). Upper body exercise capacity in youth with spina bifida. *Adapted Physical Activity Quarterly, 10,* 22–28.

Davis, G. M., Tupling, S. J., & Shephard, R. J. (1986). Dynamic strength and physical activity in wheelchair users. In C. Sherrill (Ed.), *Sport and disabled athletes* (pp. 139–146). Champaign, IL: Human Kinetics Publishers.

Dobbins, D. A., Garron, R., & Rarick, G. L. (1981). The motor performance of educable mentally retarded and intellectually normal boys after covariate control for differences in body size. *Research Quarterly for Exercise and Sports, 52*(1), 1–8.

Dreisinger, T. E., & Londeree, B. R. (1982). Wheelchair exercise: A review. *Paraplegia, 20,* 20–34.

Fait, H. F., & Kupferer, H. (1956). A study of two motor achievement tests and its implications in planning physical education activities for the mentally retarded. *American Journal of Mental Deficiency, 60,* 728–732.

Fernhall, B. (2003). Mental retardation. In J. L. Durstine & G. E. Moore (Eds.), *ACMS's exercise management for persons with chronic diseases and disabilities* (2nd ed., pp. 304–309). Champaign, IL: Human Kinetics.

Fernhall, B., McCubbin, J. A., Pitetti, K. H., Rintala, P., Rimmier, J. H., Millar, A. L., et al. (2001). Prediction of maximal heart rate in individuals with mental retardation. *Medicine and Science in Sports and Exercise, 33*(10), 1655–1661.

Fernhall, B., Tymeson, G. T., & Webster, G. E. (1988). Cardiovascular fitness of mentally retarded individuals. *Adapted Physical Activity Quarterly, 5,* 12–28.

Halle, J. W., Silverman, N. A., & Regan, L. (1983). The effects of a data-based exercise program on physical fitness of retarded children. *Education and Training of the Mentally Retarded,* 221–225.

Holland, L. J., Bouffard, M., & Wagner, D. (1992). Rating of perceived exertion, heart rate, and oxygen consumption in adults with multiple sclerosis. *Adapted Physical Activity Quarterly, 9,* 64–73.

Horvat, M. (1987). Effects of a progressive resistance training program on an individual with spastic cerebral palsy. *American Corrective Therapy Journal, 41*(1), 7–11.

Jankowski, L. W., & Evans, J. K. (1981). The exercise capacity of blind children. *Journal of Visual Impairment and Blindness,* 248–251.

Johnson, L., & Londeree, B. (1976). *Motor fitness testing manual for the moderately mentally retarded.* Washington, DC: American Alliance for Health, Physical Education, Recreation, and Dance.

Kertzer, R., Croce, R., Hinkle, R., & Janson-Sand, C. (1994). Selected fitness and motor behavior parameters of children and adolescents with insulin-dependent diabetes mellitus. *Adapted Physical Activity Quarterly, 11,* 284–296.

Kraus, H., & Hirschland, R. (1954a). Minimum muscular fitness tests in school children. *Research Quarterly, 25*(2), 178.

Kraus, H., & Hirschland, R. P. (1954b). Muscular fitness and orthopedic disability. *New York State Journal of Medicine, 54,* 212–215.

Lessare, B. (1986). Fitness is for everyone. *Sports 'n Spokes, 11*(6), 35–36.

Lieberman, L. J., Houston-Wilson, C. (2002). *Strategies for INCLUSION: A handbook for physical educators.* Champaign, IL: Human Kinetics.

Maksud, M., & Hamilton, L. (1974). Physiological responses of EMR children to strenuous exercise. *American Journal of Mental Deficiency, 79,* 32–38.

McKechnie, S. (2002). Fitness meets special needs. *IDEA Health and Fitness Source, 20*(8), 32.

Moon, S. M., & Renzaglia, A. (1982). Physical fitness and the mentally retarded: A critical review of the literature. *The Journal of Special Education, 16,* 269–287.

Moore, G. E., Durstine, J. L., & Marsh, A. P. (2003). Framework. In J. L. Durstine & G. E. Moore (Eds.), *ACMS's exercise management for persons with chronic diseases and disabilities* (2nd ed., pp. 5–15). Champaign, IL: Human Kinetics.

National Association for Sport and Physical Education (NASPE). (2002). *Active start: A statement of physical activity guidelines for children birth to five. American Alliance for Health, Physical Education, Recreation and Dance.* Reston, VA: NASPE/AAHPERD.

National Strength and Conditioning Association. (1986). *Total conditioning for the Special Olympian.* Lincoln, NE: Author.

Pitetti, K. H., & Campbell, K. D. (1991). Mentally retarded individuals—A population at risk? *Medicine and Science in Sports and Exercise, 23,* 586–593.

Pizzaro, D. C. (1990). Reliability of the health related fitness test for mainstreamed educable and trainable mentally handicapped adolescents. *Adapted Physical Activity Quarterly, 7,* 240–248.

Rarick, L., & Francis, R. J. (1960). Motor characteristics of the mentally retarded. In *Competitive Research Monograph.* Vol. 1. U.S. Office of Education.

Rasch, P. J. (1982). *Weight training* (4th ed.). Dubuque, IA: Wm. C. Brown Publishers.

Rimmer, J. H. (1992). Cardiovascular fitness programming for adults with mental retardation: Translating research into practice. *Adapted Physical Activity Quarterly, 9,* 237–248.

Rimmer, J. H. (1994). *Fitness and rehabilitation programs for special populations.* Dubuque, IA: Brown and Benchmark.

Rimmer, J., & Rosentsweig, J. (1982). The physical working capacity of learning disabled children. *American Corrective Therapy Journal, 36,* 133–134.

Riner, W. R., & Sabath, R. J. (2003). Considerations regarding physical activity for children and youth. In J. L. Durstine & G. E. Moore (Eds.), *ACMS's exercise management for persons with chronic diseases and disabilities* (2nd ed., pp. 16–22). Champaign, IL: Human Kinetics.

Rintala, P., Dunn, J. M., McCubbin, J. A., & Quinn, C. (1992). Validity of a cardiorespiratory fitness test for men with mental retardation. *Medicine and Science in Sports and Exercise, 24,* 941–945.

Roswal, G. M., Roswal, P. M., & Dunleavy, A. O. (1986). Normative health-related fitness data for Special Olympians. In C. Sherrill (Ed.), *Sport and disabled athletes* (pp. 231–238). Champaign, IL: Human Kinetics Publishers.

Rowland, T. P. (1990). *Exercise and children's health.* Champaign, IL: Human Kinetics Publishers.

Seaman, J. (1994). AALF and the alliance: Partners in fitness education. *American Association for Active Lifestyles and Fitness Newsletter.* Reston, VA: AAHPERD.

Seaman, J. A. (Ed.). (1995). *Physical best and individuals with disabilities.* Reston, VA: AAHPERD.

Seaman, J. A. (2001). Physical activity and fitness for persons with disabilities. *IDEA Personal Trainer, 12,* 33–41.

Short, F. X., & Winnick, J. P. (1986). The performance of adolescents with cerebral palsy on measures of physical fitness. In C. Sherrill (Ed.), *Sport and disabled athletes* (pp. 239–244). Champaign, IL: Human Kinetics Publishers.

Simmons, R. (1986). *Reach for fitness: A special book of exercises for the physically challenged.* New York: Warner Books.

Skuldt, A. (1984). Exercise limitations for quadriplegics. *Sports 'n Spokes, 10*(1), 19–20.

Stainback, S., Stainback, W., Wehman, P., & Spangiers, L. (1983). Acquisition and generalization of physical fitness exercises in three profoundly retarded adults. *The Journal of the Association for the Severely Handicapped, 8*(2), 47–55.

Steadward, R., & Walsh, C. (1986). Training and fitness programs for disabled athletes: Past, present, and future. In C. Sherrill, (Ed.), *Sport and disabled athletes* (pp. 3–20). Champaign, IL: Human Kinetics Publishers.

Stopka, C., Morley, K., Siders, R., Schuette, J., Houck, A., & Gilmet, Y. (2002). Stretching techniques to improve flexibility in Special Olympics' athletes and their coaches. *Journal of Sports Rehabilitation*, 11(1), 22–34.

U.S. Department of Health and Human Services. (1996). *Physical activity and health: A report of the Surgeon General.* Atlanta, GA: U.S. Department of Health and Human Services, Centers for Disease Control and Prevention, National Center for Chronic Disease Prevention and Health Promotion.

U.S. Department of Health and Human Services. (2004a). *Healthy people 2010: The cornerstone for prevention.* Retrieved July 2004 from www.cdc.gov

U.S. Department of Health and Human Services. (2004b). *The Surgeon General's Call to action to prevent and decrease overweight and obesity: Overweight in children and adolescents.* Retrieved July 2004 from www .surgeongeneral.gov/topics/obesity/calltoaction/fact_ adolescents.htm

U.S. Department of Health and Human Services. (2004c). *Healthy People* 2010. Promoting healthy eating and physical activity for a healthier nation (full text: www.health.gov/healthypeople)

Vogler, E. W. (1990). Fitness data of children with ostomy: A pilot study. *Adapted Physical Activity Quarterly*, 7, 259–264.

Wallace, J. (2003). Obesity. In J. L. Durstine & G. E. Moore (Eds.), *ACMS's exercise management for persons with chronic diseases and disabilities* (2nd ed., pp. 149–156). Champaign, IL: Human Kinetics.

Winnick, J. P. (1994). Personal correspondence.

Winnick, J. P., & Short, F. X. (1985). *Physical fitness testing of the disabled.* Champaign, IL: Human Kinetics Publishers.

Winnick, J. P., & Short, F. X. (1991). A comparison of the physical fitness of nonretarded and mildy mentally retarded adolescents with cerebal palsy. *Adapted Physical Activity Quarterly*, 8(1), 43–56.

Winnick, J. P., & Short, F. X. (2001). *The Brockport Physical Fitness Test.* Champaign, IL: Human Kinetics.

Competitive Sport for Athletes with Disabilities

CHAPTER OBJECTIVES

After studying this chapter, the reader should be able to:

1 Recognize important events in the historical development of competitive sport experiences for individuals with disabilities.
2 Understand that federal legislation (PL 108-446, Individuals with Disabilities Education Improvement Act of 2004; PL 101-476, Individuals with Disabilities Education Act; PL 94-142, The Education for All Handicapped Children Act; PL 93-112, Rehabilitation Act of 1973; and PL 95-606, The Amateur Sports Act) emphasizes the importance of sport and its contribution to the lives of individuals with disabilities.
3 Describe the value of sport for individuals with disabilities and its evolution from a primarily therapeutic experience to a recognized sport for novice as well as highly skilled athletes.
4 Identify and discuss the various sport associations that promote and govern national and international competition for athletes with disabilities.

Society's awareness, understanding, and acceptance of individuals with disabilities have improved in very significant ways during the past twenty years. Perhaps this evolution is best demonstrated by analyzing the provisions of sport for those with disabilities. For too many years, educators have ignored the potential value of sport opportunities for special education students. This was due to the once common philosophy that education for students with disabilities should focus on the basic educational skills. Little attention, therefore, was given to extracurricular activities such as sport experiences. Some, too, may have felt that students with disabilities would not benefit from sport experiences. An unfortunate but common assumption of the past was that students with orthopedic and sensory impairments would not be able to successfully participate in sport activities. Enlightened school officials recognize today that education for any student is more than the basics, and taking a student's needs or desires for granted is indeed dangerous.

Legislation has reinforced the individual with a disability's right to participate in sport activities. Public Law 94-142, the Education for All Handicapped Children Act of 1975 (now named IDEA, 2004) and Section 504 of the Rehabilitation Act of 1973, Public Law 93-112, specify that physical education experiences, including intramural activities and sports, must be available to students with disabilities to the same extent these opportunities are available to nondisabled students (Dougherty et al., 1994). The law indicates that students with disabilities should not be denied equal opportunity to participate on school teams or comparable special teams.

The following pages will provide information about the origins and purposes of sport for people with disabling conditions. Sport organizations and suggestions for developing sport programs for individuals with disabling conditions will also be discussed.

Historical Development

Prior to World War II there is little evidence of organized efforts to develop or promote sport for people with disabilities. Some individuals, due to their own initiative, did achieve success prior to this time. Karoly Tacaczs, a Hungarian marksman who lost his right arm in 1938 after an accident, transferred his skill by intensive training to his left arm, which he had never used previously. He later became a two-time Olympic champion. There are certainly other examples of individuals who overcame many obstacles to achieve success with little, if any, support.

One of the earliest sport organizations for people with disabilities was the Sports Club for the Deaf, founded in 1888 in Berlin, Germany. In 1924, national sport organizations for the deaf were merged into a world organization, *Comite International des Sports Silencieux*. The British Society of One-Armed Golfers is another early sports organization. This group, founded in 1932, holds its annual championships on leading courses throughout England. Today there is also the Association of Disabled American Golfers for golfers with various disabling conditions. Although they represent modest beginnings, these early pre-World War II efforts did illustrate that those with disabilities, too, could grow and benefit from opportunities to participate in sport.

The Effects of World War II

The large number of soldiers injured in World War II posed a great challenge to medical authorities. Traditional methods of rehabilitation did not satisfactorily respond to the medical and psychological needs of the war injured. For instance, those with spinal paraplegia were considered to be hopeless cripples with a short life span of two to three years. Early deaths were attributed to infection of the paralyzed bladder resulting in the destruction of the kidneys.

Recognizing this problem, the British government in 1944 opened the Spinal Injuries Center at Stoke Mandeville Hospital in Aylesbury. The opening of this center under the direction of Dr. Ludwig Guttmann is, perhaps, the most significant event in the history of sport for people with spinal paralysis. Dr. Guttmann recognized from the outset that previous efforts at rehabilitation had failed due to the fragmentation of medical services. Treatment of patients with spinal cord injuries, in Dr. Guttmann's opinion, required a team oriented to all aspects of the injured person's needs. To alleviate boredom and enhance the neuromuscular system, Dr. Guttmann and his staff introduced sport to their patients as a form of recreation.

Early sport forms used at the Stoke Mandeville Center included punch ball exercises, rope-climbing, and wheelchair polo, the first competitive team sport for individuals with paraplegia (Guttmann, 1976). Wheelchair basketball was introduced in 1945 and quickly became the most popular team sport for people with paralysis.

These early attempts to incorporate sport into the medical rehabilitation of people with paralysis soon spread from Great Britain to other countries, including the United States.

Early Efforts in the United States

As in Great Britain, medical personnel in the United States found themselves developing new modes of comprehensive treatment to assist those injured in the war. Veterans' Administration hospitals throughout the United States encouraged those with disabilities to become active as sport participants. This effort was assisted in 1946 by the United States tour of the Flying Wheels Team of Van Nuys, California. The Flying Wheels Team, an extraordinarily talented group, assisted all people, disabled and nondisabled, to comprehend the value and enjoyment sport holds for athletes with disabilities. Several other wheelchair basketball teams were organized in 1947 and 1948. These included the Brooklyn Whirlaways, Queen's Charioteers, New York Spokesmen, and the Pioneers of Kansas City, Missouri (Adams & McCubbin, 1991).

The interest of the United States in sport for the wheelchair athlete was enhanced when Dr. Guttmann traveled to New York in the early 1950s to meet with Benjamin H. Lipton, Director of the Joseph Bulova School of Watchmaking. Lipton, along with Dr. Timothy Nugent of the University of Illinois, was responsible for spearheading the growth of sport for individuals with disabilities in the United States. As an outgrowth of the meeting between Guttmann and Lipton, the first National Wheelchair Games in the United States were held in 1958. Although these games were patterned after the Stoke Mandeville Games, new events such as the 60-, 100-, and 220-yard dashes were introduced. These games, which are still a popular annual event, provided a format to train, compete, and eventually select the best athletes to represent the United States in international competition.

Influence of Amateur Sports Act

In 1975 President Gerald Ford formed the President's Commission on Olympic Sports to review the status of Olympic sports and related topics. The commission's findings, published in 1977, formed the basis for the Amateur Sports Act of 1978, PL 95-606. This legislation resulted in the reorganization of the United States Olympic Committee (USOC) and reaffirmed the commitment to amateur athletes in the United States. Given the emphasis on physical education and sport found in PL 93-112, Rehabilitation Act of 1973, and PL 94-142, Education for All Handicapped Children Act of 1975, advocates of sport for people with disabilities were successful in ensuring that the Amateur Sports Act included those with disabilities. Specifically the Act led to the inclusion of the following in the Objects and Purposes Section of the USOC Constitution:

> To encourage and provide assistance to amateur athletic programs and competition for handicapped

individuals, including, where feasible, the expansion of opportunities for meaningful participation by handicapped individuals in programs of athletic competition for able-bodied individuals.[1]

To achieve this objective, a special committee, Committee on Sports for the Disabled (COSD), was established by the USOC. The COSD meets semiannually to promote sport for individuals with disabilities. These activities include: coordinating programs and national and international competition for athletes with disabilities, encouraging research and the dissemination of information, and seeking funds and support from the USOC. Several disability sports organizations are affiliated directly with the United States Olympic Committee: USA Deaf Sport, United States Association for Blind Athletes, Special Olympics, Wheelchair Sports USA, United States Cerebral Palsy Athletic Association, and Disabled Sports USA.

The influence of the Committee on Sports for the Disabled (COSD) has been significant in promoting sport activities for special populations. Through the efforts of the COSD, the 1984 Olympic Games in Los Angeles featured a wheelchair demonstration (800-meter race for women and 1,500-meter race for men); this was the first time athletes with disabilities received recognition in the summer Olympic games. Also for the first time, an athlete in a wheelchair, Neroll Fairhall from New Zealand, qualified to compete in the Olympics. Her success in archery has opened new doors of understanding concerning people with disabilites and their potential as athletes.

Purpose of Sport for Individuals with Disabilities

Society's treatment of those with disabilities has undergone radical changes since the early 1900s. No longer, for instance, is it universally believed that institutionalization is the accepted environment for individuals with disabilities. Efforts have been made to recognize, value, and accept those who deviate from the norm. The ultimate goal is to create an environment in which those with disabilities can achieve a sense of self-realization, a charting of their own course (Dunn & Sherrill, 1996).

Athletes with disabilities and their sport advocates have made great strides in their acceptance of the true meaning of sport. Sport for people with disabilities was initially conceived in a very narrow way as primarily a clinical experience designed to assist the rehabilitative process. Today, athletes with disabilities recognize that sport is broader than this and that sport can contribute to their lives in several ways.

[1]USOC Constitution, Article II(13), p. 2.

Health and Fitness

Participation in sport makes an important contribution to the health and fitness of individuals with disabilities. Although the amount of information is limited, studies suggest that the fitness levels of youth who have disabling conditions are lower than those of their nondisabled peers. Some of the factors that interfere with the health and fitness of individuals with disabilities are discussed in the following paragraphs.

Nutrition

The nutritional status of some youth with disabilities is affected by several factors including specific disability, medication required, and behavioral influences. The majority of children with developmental disabilities exhibit nutritional disorders.

Sedentary Lifestyles

Young persons with disabilities frequently find opportunities to participate in activity outside of their homes or residential settings to be more restricted than for the nondisabled. For many children, youth, and adults, access to mainstream or specialized programs is restricted due to lack of private or public transportation. This results in greater reliance on television and other forms of sedentary entertainment.

Lack of Understanding of the Concept of Fitness

Some youth with cognitive deficits, particularly those with mental impairments, fail to understand the important relationship between health and fitness.

Hereditary Factors

The nature of some disabilities is such that associated health problems can lead to further deterioration in the individual's physical fitness. For example, 40 percent of people with Down syndrome have a congenital heart disorder.

Fear of Failure

For individuals with disabilities, particularly those who are mentally retarded, orthopedically impaired, and sensory impaired, the performance of "routine" exercises can be very difficult. The inability to grasp the technique of the exercise or to possess the coordination to perform the exercise can create a vicious cycle of failure, followed by avoidance.

Program and Facility Accessibility

Unfortunately, the health fitness level of many individuals with disabilities is lower than expected because of the lack of appropriate programs, or programs conducted in accessible facilities.

Young people with disabilities need as many opportunities as possible to improve their health and fitness levels. Sport can play a significant role in developing the desired levels of fitness. Studies indicate that persons with disabling conditions, including those with severe mental retardation, can be taught sport skills, thereby improving important variables such as health and physical fitness.

Psychological Value

Physical activity is an integral part of the function of daily life. Daily tasks such as rising from bed, eating breakfast, and preparing for work all require different forms of movement. For those with disabilities, some of these activities, considered routine by many nondisabled people, require preliminary planning and intensive effort to perform. The ability to undertake the activities of daily living and having the stamina to perform part-time or full-time work may be the deciding factor between earning one's own income or being dependent on others for financial resources. Some individuals with disabilities become disheartened when they struggle with basic activities that seem so easy for others. Frequently, this feeling is reinforced by family members and friends who treat the individual with a disability as though he or she is helpless. Some who are disabled begin to develop an inferiority complex, characterized by anxiety with a loss of self-confidence and self-esteem. The result is self-pity, self-centered isolationism, and antisocial attitudes.

Participating in sport often can restore psychological equilibrium, counteract feelings of inferiority, and become a motivating force in the enjoyment of life, which is so necessary to people with disabilities in coming to terms with their ability and disability levels. Sport provides an opportunity for an individual with a disability to express in a very visible way that having an impairment is not synonymous with being helpless or an invalid. Following extensive interviews with more than 300 athletes with disabilities, Sherrill (1986) reported that almost all of the athletes saw sport as a means of affirming their competence, thereby seeking to focus attention on their abilities rather than disabilities. The psychological contribution coupled with the physiological value assists many individuals with disabilities to use sport as a means of enhancing their concept of self.

Normalization

Sport has been recognized by several authorities as an important institution within society. Individuals with disabilities, therefore, striving to be part of society, recognize that participation in sport will help them to integrate more fully into family and community activities. For instance, students with visual impairments who master the art of swimming can use this proficiency not only to compete but,

perhaps more importantly, be a welcomed addition to all water activities enjoyed by their families.

Individuals with disabilities also use sport to assure others that, although they have impairments, they are not ill. There is a general tendency for the public, educators, and even some medical personnel to equate the term "disability" with "sickness." This misconception is quickly destroyed when individuals with disabilities are observed strenuously participating in sport forms common to the general public.

The ultimate form of integration for individuals with disabilities is to participate with nondisabled people in activities in which their disabilities do not interfere with their own or the team's performance. Many examples are found in sport where people with disabilities have successfully participated or competed with the nondisabled. Harold Connoly, one of the United States' great Olympians, won a gold medal in the hammer throw although he performed with a disabled left arm. Jim Abbott, a professional baseball player and former Big Ten baseball pitcher, received the Sullivan Award as the United States' top amateur athlete, even though he was born without a right hand. Many other examples could be included here to illustrate that some individuals with disabilities have overcome obstacles to participate successfully with their nondisabled peers.

Sport for Sport's Sake

Although many benefits—both physiological and psychological—accrue to the individual with a disability through sport activities, the primary motivation for many who participate is the need for recognition. This is a common motivation of most participants in sport activities. Athletes with disabilities have become more adamant in recent years in urging others to recognize that they enjoy sport for the same reasons nondisabled individuals do. They stress that sport for them is a "sport" experience, as it is for everyone, and not a therapeutic or rehabilitative program. Similar to the nondisabled, some athletes with disabilities have become very serious in their training programs, emphasizing quality efforts and maximum performance. For these athletes, the ultimate goal is to someday be recognized as an athlete capable of outstanding sport performance. This is an evolutionary goal that builds upon the therapeutic, psychological, and normalizing value of sport to an acceptance of people with disabilities and their right to achieve self-realization through the medium of sport.

Recognition of the last purpose of sport for those with disabilities, sport for sport's sake, suggests, too, that sport participation for all athletes, with and without disabilities, is subject to potentially negative features. Overzealous athletes and coaches can lead to situations in which the desire to win is greater than the desire to compete or cooperate fairly.

Some athletes with disabilities are not immune from the plague of winning at all costs, as are some nondisabled athletes. Professionals with strong and ethical value systems are needed to assure that sport for people with disabilities is conducted according to the highest ethical standards. Fortunately, the leaders of sport for athletes with disabilities have made some positive rule changes that differ from the traditional perception of sport. For instance, classification systems that rate athletes according to ability categories are very common in sport for people with disabilities. Examples of this excellent idea that should be incorporated into sport for *all* people will be presented later in this chapter.

Those who have been trained in physical education, or who have competed successfully in sport, have a tendency to believe that all individuals should respond in a positive way to sport competition. **It must be recognized, however, that many individuals respond negatively to the direct competition of sport that requires a loser before a winner is produced. Others who enjoy direct competition in other areas of life often shun competition that requires physical strength, speed, and prowess. The variance in responses to sport competition among individuals with disabilities will be no less than in the population as a whole. The educator working with special students in physical education should keep in mind that they need to develop their physical and motor abilities to the optimum but that the process does not necessarily require direct competition with others.** It is also essential not to create an atmosphere that encourages an attitude that those who do not wish to participate in sport competition are inferior to those who do and that participation in competitive sports is the most important activity in the program. However, for a large number, *successful* sport competition provides an opportunity to develop an optimum level of physical performance and, additionally, offers the satisfaction of gaining personal recognition and participating with peers. All persons, with and without disabilities, must not be deprived of this experience.

Sport Associations for Individuals with Disabilities

Throughout this chapter references have been made to athletes with paralysis, amputations, and other orthopedic impairments. Although it is true that among special populations those with physical impairments, particularly athletes who use wheelchairs, were the first to benefit from organized sport, there also have been great strides made in recent years to promote sport for other disability populations. Some of these highlights will be discussed in this section. Organizations have been formed that promote sport for a particular disability group using various sport events. It is interesting to note that several of the sport organizations for the disabled recognized by the U.S. Olympic Committee offer swimming to the athletes in their group. Each group has a slight variation on the events offered for swimming and slightly different rules; however, the majority of the rules that govern swimming for nondisabled athletes hold true for athletes with disabilities. So in order to conduct a swim meet for athletes with disabilities it is necessary to know the rules of the national governing body, *U.S. Swimming,* as well as the rules for the particular sport organization. This is true for track, field (Track and Field USA), skiing (U.S. Ski Association), and all other sports recognized by the U.S. Olympic Committee. Primary emphasis will be given to those groups that are actively promoting national and international games for athletes with disabilities and recognized by the United States Olympic Committee. A selected list of organizations is found in Appendix II on the CD.

USA Deaf Sports Federation (formerly American Athletic Association of the Deaf (AAAD))

This association, organized in Akron, Ohio, in 1945, is composed of approximately 160 member clubs with 20,000 members. The purpose of AAAD is to foster and regulate competition, develop uniform rules, and promote interclub competition. A primary function of this organization is to select a team to participate in the World Summer and Winter Games for the Deaf and the Pan American Games for the Deaf. In 1985, the Summer Games were held for the first time in the United States. The games were very successful with over 2,500 athletes from forty-two nations competing. Team sports consist of soccer, water polo, handball, volleyball, and basketball. The individual sports offered in the Summer Games include cycling, wrestling, swimming, track and field, tennis, table tennis, badminton, and shooting. Annual national tournaments are also held in basketball and softball. Participation in AAAD-sponsored events requires that the individual have a hearing loss of fifty-five decibels or greater in the better ear. There is only one classification, with all athletes with hearing impairments competing together. The organization of the AAAD is somewhat unique among sport organizations for athletes with disabilities because all of the management personnel are hearing impaired. In 2000 AAAD was renamed: USA Deaf Sports Federation.

National Disability Sport Alliance (formerly United States Cerebral Palsy Athletic Association (USCPAA))

Recognizing that athletes with cerebral palsy have movement characteristics different from other athletes with disabilities, the National Association of Sports for Cerebral Palsy was formed in the mid-1970s. The name of this organization was changed in 1987 to the United States Cerebral Palsy Athletic Association (USCPAA). USCPAA's purpose is to promote competitive sport programs and recreational opportunities for persons disabled from cerebral palsy, head trauma, and other conditions resulting from damage to the brain (J. McCole, personal communication, December 26, 1993). Outstanding athletes from local, state, and regional levels are selected for the national team that represents the United States in international competition. International meets, currently involving more than a dozen nations, are held every two years in such places as Scotland, Holland, and Denmark. The United States was the host for the 1984 International Championships.

USCPAA events include a few team sports such as soccer, but the majority of activities involve dual competition. Currently sponsored events under USCPAA auspices include the following: ambulatory soccer team handball (formerly wheelchair soccer), boccie, archery, bowling, cycle racing, horseback riding, rifle shooting, swimming, table tennis, track and field, and weight lifting. Because of the unique needs of the athlete with cerebral palsy, special field events have been designed to be included with the track and field competition. Some of the events, such as the soft shot distance, precision soft shot, and distance soft shot, use a lighter implement such as a five-ounce bean bag to encourage athletes to compete while recognizing their strength limitations. Athletes who have limited use of their arms, Class 2 Lower, compete in two kicking events, distance kick and thrust kick. In the distance kick a thirteen-inch playground ball is used. For the thrust kick, a six-pound medicine ball is used.

The USCPAA has implemented an eight-category classification system that is sensitive to the participant's type of cerebral palsy, degree of involvement, and mode of ambulation (table 18.1). This system, which requires each athlete to complete a series of functional movement tasks, is used to equate for competition, thus allowing, in the USCPAA's opinion, *sport by ability—not by disability.* The USCPAA offers clinics to advise professionals in coaching techniques, classification of athletes, conduct of meets, and program finances. USCPAA is now known as National Disability Sport Alliance (NDSA) (www.ndsaonline.org).

Wheelchair Sports USA (formerly NWAA)

Wheelchair sports was founded in 1959 as the National Wheelchair Athletic Association (NWAA) and is the primary organization that promotes competitive sport experiences for amputees and individuals with spinal cord injuries. Wheelchair Sports, USA is the umbrella term for various wheelchair sports organizations including the national governing bodies for: American Wheelchair Archers, American Wheelchair Table Tennis, National Wheelchair Basketball Association, National Wheelchair Shooting Association (air weapons), U.S. Quad Rugby, U.S. Wheelchair Swimming, U.S. Wheelchair Weightlifting, and Wheelchair Athletics (track and field). The addition of the National Wheelchair Basketball Association and the name change from National Wheelchair Athletic Association to Wheelchair Sports, USA will enhance the recognition of accomplishments of athletes who use wheelchairs in the general public.

Due to the variety of sport offerings, each association classifies athletes according to the demands of the sport, medical evaluation, and in many cases how well the athlete performs the skill. For example, weight lifters are classified by age, gender, and body weight. Basketball has a three point system with class one athletes having the least physical function. Each basketball player is assigned a point value of either one, two, or three; however, the team may only use players whose combined point values do not exceed twelve points at one time. Similarly in quad rugby, seven classifications are possible starting with 0.5 and ending with 3.5, but the number of players actively participating may not exceed eight points for four players. Recent changes in classification have resulted in a separation of track (five levels) and field (nine levels) and the expansion of swimming classifications to twenty categories. Physical educators and coaches are encouraged to contact the national governing body for complete details about classification systems. Becoming involved in coaching, officiating, or sponsoring meets is an excellent way to learn more about classification systems.

Quad Rugby is a fairly recent addition to the growing family of wheelchair sports. The game was designed specifically for athletes with cervical injuries and was formerly known as murderball. Rugby is played on a regulation basketball court, with four players on each side. The object is to score points by carrying the ball over the opponent's goal area on the endline. Players may advance the ball (regulation volleyball) by passing in any direction. Quick play is encouraged by a ten second rule that demands a pass or bouncing the ball within that time limit. The number of Quad Rugby teams and players more than tripled in the early 1990s, indicating this team sport responded to a previously unfulfilled need (B. Mikkelson, personal communication, December 23, 1993).

Track has expanded the number of racing events to include every Olympic distance from 100 meters to 10,000 meters. While slalom is no longer an official event for adults, many junior meets offer this obstacle course event to display the unique skills of athletes who use wheelchairs. Weight lifting has two events, the bench press (chest,

| TABLE 18.1 | Sport Classifications for Persons with Cerebral Palsy |

Class	Description
1	Uses motorized wheelchair because almost no functional use of upper extremities. Severe involvement in all four limbs, limited trunk control, has only 25% range of motion. Unable to grasp softball.
2	Propels chair with feet and/or very slowly with arms. Severe to moderate involvement in all four limbs. Uneven functional profile necessitating subclassifications as 2 Upper (2U) or 2 Lower (2L), with adjective denoting limbs having greater functional ability. Has approximately 40% range of motion. Severe control problems in accuracy tasks, generally more athetosis than spasticity.
3	Propels chair with short, choppy arm pushes but generates fairly good speed. Moderate involvement in three or four limbs and trunk. Has approximately 60% range of motion. Can take a few steps with assistive devices, but is not functionally ambulatory.
4	Propels chair with forceful, continuous arm pushes, demonstrating excellent functional ability for wheelchair sports. Involvement of lower limbs only. Good strength in trunk and upper extremities. Has approximately 70% range of motion. Minimal control problems.
5	Ambulates without wheelchair but typically uses assistive devices (crutches, canes, walkers). Moderate to severe spasticity of either (a) arm and leg on same side (hemi-plegia) or (b) both lower limbs (paraplegia). Has approximately 80% range of motion.
6	Ambulates without assistive devices, but has obvious balance and coordination difficulties. Has more control problems and less range of motion in upper extremities than Classes 4 and 5. Moderate to severe involvement of three or four limbs, with approximately 70% range of motion in dominant arm.
7	Ambulates well, but with slight limp. Moderate to mild spasticity in (a) arm and leg on same side or (b) all four limbs with 90% of normal range of motion for quadriplegia and 90 to 100% of normal range of motion for dominant arm for hemiplegia.
8	Runs and jumps freely without noticeable limp. Demonstrates good balance and symmetric form in performance, but has obvious (although minimal) coordination problems. Has normal range of motion.

Adapted from: Sherrill, C. (1993). *Adapted physical education and recreation* (4th ed.). Dubuque, IA:William C. Brown Publishers.

extended arms, chest) and the powerlifting press (extended arms, chest, extended arms). Each lifter is scored for the bench press, the powerlifting press, and the total of the two presses. Team scoring is now possible in weight lifting, and lifters of unequal body weights may be compared by using the Schwartz index.

Archery, table tennis, and shooting (air weapons) have fewer participants than the well-publicized wheelchair sports. Because many wheelchair athletes are fully integrated into schools and there are a number of athletes, grouping may not be easy. It may be necessary to practice alone, or in sports clubs with able-bodied participants, to get ready for competition. For children, novice athletes, and those self-coached, a training camp or technique workshop is highly recommended. Kevin Hansen, who has coached many national and international record holders in wheelchair track and road racing, communicates to skilled athletes such as Craig Blanchette and Eric Neitzel long distance via phone, fax machine, and electronic mail.

United States Association for Blind Athletes (USABA)

In 1976 the USABA was formed to promote opportunities for athletes with visual impairments to participate in regional, national, and eventually international competition. The impetus for forming the USABA began in 1975 when the International Sports Organization for the Disabled

(ISOD) announced that the 1976 Olympics for the Physically Disabled would for the first time include athletes with visual impairments. Plans were initiated for American participation through the formation of the United States Olympic Committee for the Blind. Through a process of trials and selections, twenty-seven athletes were sent to the 1976 event, the first time that men and women with visual limitations from the United States participated in international competition.

Annual national championships have been held for athletes with visual impairments since 1977, when the first competition was conducted at Western Illinois University in Macomb, Illinois. In 1980, more than 500 athletes participated in the annual meet. Two downhill skiers went to the 1994 winter Paralympics at Lillehammer. Sanctioned sports include power and weight lifting, swimming, track and field, wrestling, goal ball, women's gymnastics, downhill and cross-country skiing, tandem cycling, and speed skating. Three classification categories have been established to permit equal competition of participants with similar visual disorders (table 18.2). There are no age limits for USABA participants.

The USABA, in an effort to reach as many athletes with visual impairments as possible, sponsors demonstration teams in sports activities in addition to its eleven fully sanctioned sports. The Carol Center in Massachusetts offers a full spectrum of water sports, including sailing. USABA web address: http//www.usaba.org.

Special Olympics

In 1968, the Joseph P. Kennedy, Jr., Foundation, with the guidance of Eunice Kennedy Shriver, founded the Special Olympics. This organization is designed to promote and conduct local, regional, national, and international sport experiences for athletes with mental retardation. Individuals eight years of age or older, with an intelligence quotient of less than seventy-five, are eligible to participate. Competition divisions adjusted for age and ability have been established. The official Special Olympics sports include aquatics, track and field, basketball, bowling, gymnastics, floor and poly hockey, figure and speed skating, alpine and cross country skiing, soccer, softball, and volleyball. The Special Olympics also offers clinics on demonstration sports including canoeing, cycling, equestrian sports, racquet sports, roller skating, and weight training. In an effort to reach individuals with mental retardation who are severe and profound, Special Olympics has established a Developmental Sports Skills program to train individuals with mental retardation with low motor abilities in sensorimotor and basic motor skills.

The Special Olympics has conducted international games since 1968. The movement has experienced tremendous growth. In 1968, one thousand participants from the United States were involved. Today, the Special Olympics programs encompass millions of athletes from the United States and sixty other countries, and hundreds of thousands of volunteers and coaches worldwide (www.specialolympics.org).

The philosophy of Special Olympics supports the belief that striving is more important than success, and determination is more important than winning. The spirit that brings participants to the starting line is more important to the Joseph P. Kennedy, Jr., Foundation than the skill that carries Special Olympic athletes across the finish line.

United States Amputee Athletic Association (USAAA)

A small group of athletes with amputations founded the USAAA in 1981. This organization sponsored national competition annually for athletes with amputations in a variety of events including air pistol, archery, standing basketball, track and field events, sit-down and standing volleyball, swimming, table tennis, and weight lifting. International competition is available through the International Games for the Disabled and other sport-specific competition. The USAAA filed for bankruptcy in 1989, and the athletes are currently being served by Disabled Sports USA (DePauw & Gavron, 1995).

TABLE 18.2	Sport Classifications for USABA and IBSA
Classification	**Description**
B1	No light perception in either eye up to light perception and inability to recognize the shape of a hand in any direction and at any distance
B2	Ability to recognize the shape of a hand up to a visual acuity of 2/60 and/or a limitation of field of vision of 5°
B3	2/60 to 6/60 (20/200) vision and/or field of vision between 5° and 20°

Athletes with amputations are classified according to their level and site of amputation (table 18.3). In swimming, competitions are offered for athletes in each of the classifications. In some sports such as track and field, the classifications are combined. In the field events, those who have bilateral amputations compete together in one class whether the amputation is above or below the elbow, and single-arm amputees comprise one class. In volleyball, a point system, similar in concept to that used by the National Wheelchair Basketball Association, is enforced. Players are assigned one, two, three, or four points based on their A1 to A9 classification and their muscle strength as determined by certified testers. In competition, the players on the floor must total thirteen or more points.

The USAAA and now National Handicapped Sports have done an excellent job of responding to the needs and ability levels of the athletes. For many sports, athletes with lower limb amputations are permitted the option of using a wheelchair or competing from an ambulatory position. Some sports, such as volleyball, have both standing and sitting competitions. Athletes also may use prostheses and orthoses, depending upon the sport and their classification level.

Disabled Sports USA (DS/USA)

The Disabled Sports USA, founded in 1968, originally was known as the Amputee Skiers Association. As the organization grew and began to serve athletes with disabilities in addition to those with amputations, the name was changed to National Handicapped Sports and later Disabled Sports USA. DS/USA is different than other organizations that promote sport for athletes with disabilities in that it is sport-specific and not disability-specific. Although DS/USA's chapters promote year-round recreational activities and competitive sports, including water skiing and swimming, the organization's primary expertise is in conducting national competition in winter sport programs. For example, DS/USA is responsible for conducting the winter games for athletes with amputations. In addition, the association sponsors a traveling physical fitness team that gives presentations and demonstrations on health and physical fitness for individuals with disabilities. DS/USA now offers clinics and personal fitness trainer certifications for individuals who wish to coach or provide fitness training for athletes with disabling conditions (K. Bauer, Personal Communication, December, 23, 1993) (www.dsusa.org).

Dwarf Athletic Association of America

The Dwarf Athletic Association of America (DAAA) was formed in 1985 and is now officially recognized by the United States Olympic Committee. The purpose of the DAAA is to develop, promote, and provide quality amateur athletic opportunities for dwarf athletes (less than 4'9 10") in the United States. The DAAA sponsors events in track and field, basketball, boccie, powerlifting, swimming, skiing, table tennis, and volleyball. The National Dwarf Games in which athletes compete by age, gender, and functional ability are sponsored by the DAAA. Dwarf athletes can participate in the Paralympics and other international events.

TABLE 18.3	**Nine General Sport Classifications for Persons with Amputations**

Class A1 = Double AK

Class A2 = Single AK

Class A3 = Double BK

Class A4 = Single BK

Class A5 = Double AE

Class A6 = Single AE

Class A7 = Double BE

Class A8 = Single BE

Class A9 = Combined lower plus upper limb amputations

Please note:
AK = Above or through the knee joint
BK = Below the knee, but through or above the ankle joint
AE = Above or through the elbow joint
BE = Below the elbow, but through or above the wrist joint

Clinics, developmental events, and formal competitions at local and regional levels are offered by the DAAA. Athletes as young as seven participate in activities which are used to encourage the enhancement of one's personal best. For children under seven, the DAAA offers wholesome programs that are non-competitive. DAAA programs are also available in youth sports (www.daaa.org).

Although the organizations discussed previously are the major promoters of sport for people with disabilities, several other associations concerned with sport for people with disabilities exist. No attempt will be made here to discuss all of these groups. Some, however, will be identified to illustrate the magnitude of interest now evident concerning sport opportunities for athletes with disabilities. It is hoped that this information will assist teachers to familiarize themselves, and in turn their students, with these associations.

Additional Sport Associations for Athletes with Disabling Conditions

In recent years, several new organizations promoting specific sport activities for athletes who use wheelchairs have been initiated. For instance, there is now a National Foundation for Wheelchair Tennis (NFWT). This organization sponsors programs for young as well as for older players. Wheelchair tennis is played like regular tennis, with the exception that the ball is permitted to bounce twice.

In response to a strong interest in marathon racing expressed by wheelchair athletes, an association known as the International Wheelchair Road Racers Club, Inc. (213/967–2231) was formed. The general public has been intrigued by the speed at which wheelchair athletes can cover a distance of 26.2 miles, surpassing the times the best marathoners have been able to run this distance. Outstanding performances have been achieved on flat courses as well as courses with hills and rough terrain. It is not unusual for marathon champions such as Jim Knaub to finish a marathon distance in an hour and twenty minutes to an hour and thirty minutes, depending on the course. These efforts have dispelled many of the myths about the frail person who sits in a wheelchair.

The reader desiring more information on wheelchair sports is referred to *Sports 'n Spokes*, a very informative periodical found in most university libraries.

Those people with visual impairments interested in bowling should be aware of the American Blind Bowling Association (ABBA). This organization was formed in 1951 in New York and Philadelphia by a group of bowlers with visual limitations who believed that a national organization was necessary to help other persons with limited vision benefit from this sport. Today the ABBA is the official sanctioning organization for ten-pin bowlers and bowling leagues for athletes with visual impairments in the United States and Canada.

A very exciting sport for students with visual impairments is beep baseball. This program is sponsored by the National Beep Baseball Association (NBBA). As the game's name implies, the ball, a regulation 16^1/$_2$-inch-circumference softball, has been equipped with a beeping device. Although the NBBA is a relatively new organization, more than 100 teams from the United States and Canada participate in association-sanctioned regional and national tournaments (www.nbba.org).

The United States Les Autres Athletic Association (USLAAA) has emerged to serve athletes with disabling conditions who have not previously had opportunities to participate and compete. USLAAA serves people with any of 50 or more disabling conditions associated with deficits in locomotion. Many of the athletes have been affected by muscular dystrophy, multiple sclerosis, or dysmelia and frequently use power wheelchairs. Athletes with Les Autres conditions compete in the full spectrum of summer Olympic events and use an integrated classification system which includes both seated and standing classifications, and takes factors such as strength, range of motion, and spasticity into account. This organization is governed by the International Sport Organization for the Disabled.

Teachers also may find organizations within their states that promote or sponsor competition for children with various disabilities. In Oregon, for example, the Oregon Games for the Physically Limited are held annually. In addition to traditional track and field events, the Oregon Games incorporate creative events such as body bowling, obstacle courses, and Velcro darts to ensure that all participants, regardless of disability, have the opportunity to compete and strive to perform at the highest level possible (Dunn, 1987).

Classification Issues

Classification systems have long been used in sports for the nondisabled to promote fairness and equal competition. Boxing has weight classifications matching competitors by body size. Race directors for the ever-popular ten-kilometer road races divide the prize categories by gender, and then further by age. By comparing the age group statistics, each participant can estimate his or her race performance in relation to others of similar age and gender. In the interest of fair competition, it would seem appropriate for sports for people with disabilities to attempt to group competitors by performance similarities. There is little agreement, however, on the mode that should be used to classify participants. Some of the issues surrounding this controversy will be discussed in this section.

Medical Classifications

Medical models have long been used to determine which competitors will vie for medals within a certain class. It was thought that competitors with similar diagnoses would perform athletically in a comparable manner. Early attempts to classify athletes with disabilities were based on medical diagnosis. In sports for athletes with visual impairments, an unusually clear system has been used because the system for diagnosis can be quantified by objective measures. However, with classifications depending on subtle measurements such as muscle testing, dividing the competitors into equitable groups has been extremely difficult. Weiss and Curtis (1986) found that the winners of swimming events and track and field events did not reflect the membership of the Wheelchair Sports, USA (formerly NWAA). They found that certain disability groups were overrepresented compared to their respective percentage of the total membership. Ongoing research must be conducted to determine if classification systems are working as they are intended.

Functional Classifications

More recently organized sport groups such as the National Foundation for Wheelchair Tennis and Special Olympics have taken an approach that is modeled after sport organizations for the nondisabled. Competitors in wheelchair tennis and Special Olympics are grouped by gender, age, and previous performances. The value of the functional model is not only its consistency with sport for the nondisabled but also its matching of competitors by sport performance rather than medical diagnosis.

Wheelchair basketball has recently expanded its classification systems to include functional tests and observations of the athlete during competition. Because the NWBA requires that teams be comprised of players of different medical diagnoses to ensure that players with more severe disabilities receive equitable playing time, the traditional medical classification system has been retained and is used in conjunction with the new functional and observation system.

Integrated Classifications

In the past, national governing bodies for each special sports group held autonomous sporting events. This has resulted in some races and events in which the number of competitors is extremely small. Some have suggested that promotion of sport for individuals with disabilities might be best served by combining the games into sports festivities serving more than one disability group. Advocates of integrated sport suggest that athletes, regardless of disability, be selected for heats and events based on previous performances. Therefore, one might see 100-meter races for athletes with visual impairments, developmental disabilities, and orthopedic impairments all competing in the same race. This approach may be welcomed in accuracy sports such as pistol, rifle, and archery, but rejected in sports with locomotor emphasis such as swimming and road racing. Close observation is needed to determine which approach best serves the needs of the athletes and is consistent with the wishes of the participants.

It should be noted that athletes may retain their sport specific classification at local and regional competitions but may be reclassified at national and international competitions. This reclassification may result in a different class within a familiar classification system or a completely unfamiliar classification in an integrated system. Event outcomes may change significantly because of athlete reclassification. Athletes accustomed to finishing near the top of their class may now finish near the bottom of their event. Adults can understand and accept this phenomenon, even though they are not happy about the results; however, the effect on children is devastating. Wise coaches will counsel their athletes, particularly the ones new to national and international competition, that classification systems have their limitations and that further revisions are necessary.

Models to Engender Novice and Junior Athletes

Remaining an amateur athlete and earning a living pose numerous obstacles for all athletes, with and without disabilities. There seems to be an increasing discrepancy between entry-level athletes and elite (national and international contenders) in many sports for athletes with disabilities. While participation has increased among highly competitive athletes, there has been a decrease in the number of novice and recreational athletes. Because accumulating enough athletes to host a competition requires extensive travel, many events have been limited to wealthy or sponsored athletes. In addition, some events require specialized equipment that is expensive. It is not uncommon for elite track and field wheelchair athletes to own one racing wheelchair that meets the requirements for international events and one to meet the rules for events held in this country, as well as a wheelchair for everyday use. While some athletes can meet the demands for the latest equipment, many find their daily financial obligations prevent them from investing in sports equipment and meeting the associated costs of travel to national and international meets. Young athletes with disabilities and their families may find the costs prohibitive. Brookes and Cooper (1987) suggested divisions for novice athletes and increased local and regional competitions to foster greater participation. Some sports organizations have responded by offering novice and masters classes within each event. The result for recreational and entry-level athletes has increased the opportunity to participate.

The issue of sport classification systems is particularly critical for young athletes with disabilities. Many times it is necessary to travel a long distance or have a person qualified to classify athletes come to the school in order to determine a youngster's classification. School-sponsored sport programs for athletes with disabilities are few. Some have argued that full inclusion has resulted in students being dispersed among several schools, thus making it difficult, if not impossible, to organize a team of athletes with a specific disability. The numerous and often confusing classification systems have compounded the problem. School administrators recognize, however, that children with disabilities and their parents will press for a solution to this problem. One answer, of course, is cooperative planning among school districts and the fielding of teams that represent a large geographic area, such as a county. This may also require a rethinking of the present systems used to classify students with disabilities. The pooling of students and resources should lead to the formation of leagues and the development of a cadre of coaches, volunteers, and parents committed to serving the sport needs of children with disabilities.

Organizing Sport for the Participant with Disabilities

Extracurricular activities, including sport experiences, have long been recognized as an integral part of the educational process. Most public and private schools sponsor teams for boys and girls in a variety of sport activities. These same opportunities must be provided for students with disabilities. This right is guaranteed under the provisions of PL 94-142, the Education for All Handicapped Children Act of 1975, and IDEA '97, IDEA 2004, Section 504 of the Rehabilitation Act of 1973. Although both of these acts require generally the same action on the part of schools, Section 504 of the Rehabilitation Act is broader in coverage and includes not only education provisions but also employment, health, welfare, and other social service programs. Concerning the provisions for sport experiences, Section 504 states:

1. In providing physical education courses and athletics and similar programs and activities to any of its students a recipient to which this subpart applies may not discriminate on the basis of handicap. A recipient that offers physical education courses or that operates or sponsors interscholastic, club, or intramural athletics shall provide to qualified handicapped students an equal opportunity for participation in these activities.

2. A recipient may offer to handicapped students physical education and athletic activities that are separate or different from those offered to nonhandicapped students only if separation or differentiation is consistent with the requirements of 84.34 and only if no qualified handicapped student is denied the opportunity to compete for teams or to participate in courses that are not separate or different.

The task of complying with this mandate causes confusion for many public schools. Therefore, in this section, information will be presented to help school personnel to respond to the sport needs of the student-athletes with disabling conditions.

Preparing the School and Community

The first, and perhaps most important, step in promoting sport for students with disabilities is to meet with school officials, parents, and students with disabilities to enlist their support. This is best accomplished by meeting initially with the Section 504 compliance officer, appointed by the school as required by law. During this meeting the school official can provide information about what has been accomplished and future plans concerning sport opportunities. Appointing a committee comprised of parents, persons with disabilities, students, teachers, and administrators to address future plans related to the issue of sport experiences for students with disabilities is an excellent approach used by some schools. The responsibility of this group is to establish a foundation upon which a strong program can be built. Suggested ideas include the following:

1. Prepare a state-of-the-art paper that discusses the importance of sport for all and documents the existence of local school programs, if any, for individuals with disabilities.

2. Identify, with the assistance of the special education coordinator, the number of students with disabilities within the school system. A chart indicating the number of students, their ages, and their disabilities will be valuable in future planning.

3. Contact the state school athletic association and other school officials to determine if state efforts are now being made to address the sport needs of special students.

4. Communicate with community youth agencies such as the YMCA and YWCA to determine what, if any, programs are available for participants with disabilities.

5. Meet with the school board and key administrators to share the results of all information gathered and to encourage their assistance in promoting equal opportunities.

6. Promote a public awareness program for the community. Activities such as sponsoring a wheelchair basketball game between halves of the local high school game, inviting a well-known athlete to address a school assembly, and staging an event in which public officials play their

sport with an imposed disability (playing golf blindfolded, for example) help to generate public support.

7. Contact national associations that promote sport for individuals with disabilities (table 18.1) and ask for films, materials, brochures, and suggestions for helping local schools to promote athletics for students with disabilities.

8. Encourage pay for qualified coaches of youth who provide their services to public school sport programs for youngsters with disabilities. If a physical educator or other qualified individual receives pay for coaching after-school sports for nondisabled children, those who coach children with disabilities should receive a comparable stipend. While the coach who works with athletes who have disabilities may not have as many athletes or events as those who coach the nondisabled, they must individualize coaching techniques for each student, learn about special equipment and classification systems, raise money for equipment and travel, and perhaps learn specialized medical procedures. Coaching youth sports has never been for individuals seeking money, but those who coach athletes with disabilities provide no less valuable a human service than those who coach the nondisabled.

9. At school sports banquets or assemblies, recognize athletes with disabilities by showing a slide or two, or a brief video, of the athlete in action and a summary of the youngster's accomplishments. If ribbons, medals, and trophies are awarded, insist that all athletes receive comparable recognition.

The primary objective of the committee is to objectively document the sport experiences presently available for individuals with disabilities, recommend improvements where necessary, and communicate this information effectively to the community, thus building a broad base of support for future programs.

Responding to Individual Needs

The educational needs of students with disabilities are so diverse that programs must be individually developed for each student. As discussed in chapter 24 on the CD, responding to unique learning needs requires the development of Individualized Education Programs (IEPs). The process used to develop the IEP also should be employed to respond to the student with a disability's right to participate in extracurricular activities, including sport experiences. Using the IEP mechanism ensures that this important aspect of the student's educational program will not be overlooked. In addition, the involvement of parents and school personnel on the IEP team, as required by law, plus other invited individuals such as therapists and physicians, enhances the probability of identifying sport programs and placement options appropriate for the student.

The IEP team is charged with the responsibility of insisting that the unique needs of students with disabilities are recognized. Achieving this objective as it relates to equal sport experiences requires team members who are willing to challenge some old assumptions about the nature of sport and its relevance for all students. Some of the more frequently discussed issues will be presented here.

Separate or Integrated Sport

The first consideration in identifying appropriate sport activities for the student with a disabling condition is to analyze the regular sport program. In athletics, for instance, it is not at all unusual for individuals with disabilities to participate fully in regular competition. Therefore, the first consideration is the student's possible participation in the regular program. If after careful study, this placement seems inappropriate, even after minor adjustments have been suggested in equipment, rules, facilities, or some other area, efforts should then be directed toward identifying a special sport program. How this may be accomplished for the small school that has a limited special education population will be discussed later.

Academic Standing

Participation in interscholastic athletics normally requires that a student maintain a minimum grade point average. Although it is certainly desirable to encourage athletes to maintain high academic standards, this rule, if administered inflexibly, discriminates against some students with disabilities. For instance, is it realistic to expect the student with mental retardation, who may possess excellent sport skills, to achieve the desired grade point average? A more equitable basis for determining eligibility might be to monitor the student's progress toward meeting the goals and objectives identified in the student's Individualized Education Program (IEP).

This example reinforces the principle that the law mandates equal opportunity, not equal treatment. Requiring that students with disabilities meet the same grade point average required of nondisabled students may be equal treatment, but it obviously denies equal opportunity. Examples of this same principle also will be seen in the next two sections, which discuss medical and age restrictions.

Medical Implications

A student may not be eliminated from participation in an interscholastic team due solely to a medical disability. To exclude a student on the basis of a disability violates the student's basic constitutional guarantee of due process under Section 504. For example, in the past many students who have lost one of a paired organ, such as an eye or a kidney, have been automatically denied eligibility. Although in some cases this may be a wise and prudent decision, this example illustrates that categorical decisions do not allow for the recognition of individual needs. Important decisions such as these can best be made by the combined wisdom and expertise of the student's IEP team.

Fortunately, the National Federation of State High School Association already has proposed a number of rule changes to facilitate the participation of students with disabilities. In football, for example, rules were changed to allow athletes with prosthetic devices, such as artificial arms, hands, and legs, to compete. This is a significant change that will lead to further rule examinations and the elimination of rules restrictive to the student with special needs.

Age Restrictions

State athletic associations usually impose age restrictions on participants. This rule is designed to protect athletes from unfair competition as well as from potential danger due to size and weight inequities. Although this is certainly a logical rule, it does discriminate against students who have been developmentally delayed due to illness, injury, or congenital birth defects. In such cases it would be more appropriate to consider the individual's developmental level rather than chronological age. Any decision of this nature is, of course, best made by the student's IEP team.

Definitive answers to the various issues that arise concerning the student's participation in sport are not possible. Each athlete with a disability is a unique individual with needs that may not be easily accommodated within the existing state, league, and school athletic codes. Policies, however, that categorically discriminate against individuals with disabilities are no longer acceptable. The student's IEP team is an effective mechanism that can be employed to resolve issues concerning the student's eligibility for athletic participation.

Identifying Special Sport Programs

Educational programs, including extracurricular activities such as athletics, must be provided for students with disabilities in the least restrictive environment. Separate or special programs can be offered only if the student's needs require such a program. Although the primary attempt should be to accommodate the need of an athlete with a disability in regular sport activities, this is not always possible. For instance, some students have such severe disabilities that efforts to participate in the regular athletic program could be detrimental to their physical and mental health. In situations where a special sport program is necessary, the school must respond to this need.

Schools in which few students with disabilities are found can offer special sport programs through a variety of options. Some schools have elected to sponsor regional sport teams. For example, few schools have sufficient populations to field a wheelchair basketball team. Other educational units, however, such as county or district programs, could be used for purposes of designating a regional team. Competition would, therefore, be scheduled in the traditional manner, with cooperating schools sharing program expenses. Several states have recently formed athletic associations to coordinate activities such as this.

Schools also may coordinate special sport programs through community agencies. In some cities, recreation departments have developed comprehensive programs for individuals with disabilities, including competitive sport activities. Other organizations such as YMCAs and YWCAs also can be contacted to assess their present offerings and future plans concerning organized sport for individuals with disabilities. Identifying other agencies to provide special sport experiences does not absolve the school of its responsibility for monitoring the program and evaluating the effectiveness of the services provided. Schools also must be willing to financially assist community organizations when they provide services to public school students.

Selecting and Training Coaches

The selection and training of coaches is certainly one of the most important aspects of a good sport program. In addition to the skills required of all good coach-educators—knowledge of the activity, basic understanding of child development and motor development principles, and recognition of good health and safety practices—the coach of the special athlete should possess some additional expertise. Some of these specialized skills will be discussed in the following sections.

Knowledge of Disabilities

Essentially, all that is required here is that the coach have a basic understanding of the nature of the disability, including some practical information about possible causes and characteristics, and the implications of these for the student's health. For instance, it is important that coaches working with children with Down syndrome realize that congenital heart problems are quite frequent with this population. Discussion with the parents and family physician can lead to the development of a program that is safe yet challenging.

Regardless of the student's disability, the focus of the program should be centered on developing the student's ability, not analyzing the disability. A very practical exercise for the novice coach is to have the individual list all of the ways in which a student with a disability is like a nondisabled student. Completion of this task will help the coach to quickly realize that the special student has many strengths and that the athlete with a disability needs empathy, not sympathy.

Appreciation of Skill Level

Nondisabled individuals frequently have difficulty appreciating the skill with which athletes with disabilities perform various sport skills. Prospective coaches of athletes with disabilities should take time to experience sport in ways as similar as possible to those with disabling conditions. For instance, many individuals are surprised to learn that shooting a basketball from a wheelchair is quite different from the procedure to which they are most accustomed, or playing volleyball with cotton in their ears is an experience unlike the noisy environment in which they usually have performed. In a contest between nondisabled javelin throwers and those who had spinal paralysis, Guttmann (1976) determined that the nondisabled throwers could not project the javelin as far from a seated position as could the trained javelin throwers who had paralysis.

This study illustrates two major points:

1. training for sport performance is specific (one becomes good at tasks one practices), and
2. athletes with disabilities develop through training some musculature and skill proficiency that is unique to them.

Some performers with disabilities may never equal the records of their nondisabled peers. This, however, does not negate the relative merit of their effort. Coaches of the athletes with disabilities should recognize and reinforce good performance and help others to appreciate the quality of the athlete's achievement.

Develop Specialized Skills

Coaches who work with athletes who have disabling conditions may also need to learn some special skills. Those coaching the deaf, for instance, should master some of the basic signs used in communicating with people who have hearing losses. Fortunately, many of the signs necessary for communication in the sport setting can be quickly learned because the signed gesture is frequently a demonstration of the sport skill. Examples of some of the signs unique to sport may be found in chapter 9.

Athletes with visual impairments will require a coach who is sensitive to their special needs. For instance, students with visual impairments will require some assistance when they are first introduced to a new environment. The coach also must remember and remind others not to carelessly leave equipment lying around, creating a potentially harmful situation for the student with limited vision. Printed materials such as player handbooks should be available in Braille or audio tape for students who need this assistance. Many of these suggestions are common-sense principles that the enthusiastic coach can easily learn. Specialists, too, such as special educators, speech therapists, and mobility instructors, are available in many schools to help fellow educators respond to the needs of students with disabilities.

Knowledge of Sport Adaptation

Sport for individuals with disabilities requires coaches who are knowledgeable about sport activities and who have the talent to modify these activities, enabling athletes with disabilities to compete successfully. For example, the athlete with cerebral palsy who wants to participate in team soccer, a sport recognized by the United States Cerebral Palsy Athletic Association, must be taught the basics of soccer and the adaptations necessary so that these movement skills can be used efficiently. A thorough understanding of anatomy, physiology, biomechanics, and motor learning is necessary for all coaches, particularly those who work with students who have orthopedic and neurologic impairments. Guttmann's textbook of *Sport for the Disabled* is an excellent reference for the coach who needs additional information about scientifically oriented sport adaptations. A review of chapter 15 in the text and chapters 25, 26, and 27 on the CD will provide the reader with many examples of methods used to adapt sport for individuals with disabilities.

In addition to knowledge regarding the adaptation of sport activities, the coach also should be thoroughly familiar with the various classifications used in sport for individuals with disabilities. Each of the various sport associations discussed in this chapter has systems. The associations may be contacted regarding their classification systems.

Facility Accessibility

Many of the challenges associated with physical disabilities are not due to an individual's specific impairment but are more accurately attributed to the poorly designed and inaccessible environment in which people with disabilities must work, live, and play. Developing sport skills to high levels of proficiency is less frustrating for some athletes with disabling conditions than attempting to find an accessible building in which the skills may be practiced. Fortunately, federal legislation now requires public agencies, including schools, to survey their facilities and modify buildings that contain programs that cannot be moved to sites more available to students with disabilities. Faced with the reality that transferring athletic programs to alternate sites is difficult and the building of new facilities too expensive to be practical, school officials recognize the necessity of renovating gymnasiums, locker rooms, and training areas. An undertaking of this magnitude requires close cooperation among school administrators, consumers, advocates for persons with disabilities, and architects. Individuals with disabilities should be consulted throughout the remodeling period and asked to try out certain design features to assess their usefulness.

It is beyond the scope of this discussion to cover the kinds of designs, construction, or alteration of facilities that must be accomplished to conform with federal statute. Indicated in appendix VI on the CD, however, are some of the items that schools must consider when making athletic facilities accessible. This same survey can be used as a guide for analyzing the accessibility of schools that athletes with disabilities will visit. Complete information containing technical specifications may be obtained from the American National Standards Institute (www.ansi.org).

Financial Considerations

One of the major problems facing educators today is the task of having sufficient funds to cover the many school programs necessary. This is particularly true in athletics, where the impact of Title IX has increased the number of female participants without substantially increasing the funds allocated for athletic programs. Responding to the rights of students with disabilities for equitable sport opportunities also will add to the challenges of an already drained athletic budget. Students with disabilities, however, should not be expected or asked to accept services less than those provided to their nondisabled classmates. The explanation that there are no funds is not a sufficient response. A more acceptable solution, and one that is consistent with the recommendation of Section 504, is to reallocate funds so that *all* students share equally in publicly supported programs. This means that in all budget areas, such as travel, coaching salaries, and equipment, sports for students with disabilities will share equally in the funds budgeted for athletics. This does not mean that athletes with disabilities will receive everything they request or that they should be exempt from participating in special fund-raising drives. All that the athlete with a disability expects is an equal opportunity.

What follows are some suggestions school administrators may want to explore to generate additional funds for use in support of sport programs for students with disabilities.

1. Individuals with Disabilities Education Act '97 provides funds to local school systems to assist in the education of students with special needs. These are discretionary funds that can be used by local schools to provide for the educational needs of students with disabilities. Because IDEA '97 recognizes sport programs as services that should be available, federal funds could be earmarked for programs for athletes with disabilities. This may also be true for IDEA 2004.

2. Many private foundations allocate funds annually to public agencies who serve individuals with disabilities. Due to the recent emphasis on "full" services to those with disabilities, the area of sport programs would appear to be worthy of funding. A school's written plan on sports for students with disabilities could lead to fruitful negotiations with a foundation interested in sponsoring a model program.

3. Local business and industrial leaders may find a request to contribute to athletic programs for students with disabilities a new and innovative approach worthy of a contribution. Some company employees with technical backgrounds may desire to volunteer their skills in the design of special equipment.

4. Sponsorship of a basketball game between two experienced wheelchair teams is a good way to generate funds and educate the public about sport programs for students with disabilities.

5. Local organizations that advocate for people with disabilities (e.g., the ARC) might contribute money to a special fund-raising drive for the expansion of sport experiences for those who are disabled.

These suggestions offer some viable solutions for funding a sport program for students with disabilities. Attempts to secure appropriate funds will be a challenge, but if an effort is made to develop a program that emphasizes the fun in participating and competing and deemphasizes expensive uniforms, equipment, and excessive travel expenses, the overall costs can be managed. A healthy attitude by administrators and teachers toward students with disabilities and their sport opportunities is the most important ingredient in a sport program for those with disabilities. Given this variable, a means of funding the program will be found.

Summary

Opportunities for young people with disabilities to participate in sport programs have increased dramatically in recent years. Parents, professionals, and individuals with disabilities all have become more cognizant of the numerous benefits that can be gained through competitive sport. Sport is good therapy; it promotes health and fitness; and most importantly it provides athletes with disabling conditions an opportunity to demonstrate in a visible way that they are capable of training and participating in vigorous activity. Participation in sport helps the athlete and others to recognize that disability is not synonymous with "no ability." Sport also encourages normalization. Children with disabilities understand that sport is an integral part of the fabric of American society.

It is impossible for some athletes with disabilities to integrate by participating with nondisabled players on a "regular" team. Others, however, will find it more reinforcing to compete against children with similar disabilities. Fortunately, there are a number of sport organizations that conduct local, regional, and national meets and help to promote sport opportunities for people with disabilities.

Although the sport movement for people with disabilities has made significant strides, questions have been raised regarding the procedures used to classify athletes. Some organizations rely primarily on a medical form of classification, while others have adopted a philosophy of classifying athletes on the basis of their performance. Some have extended this philosophy to argue that athletes should not be classified by disability but rather by their performance level. Proponents of this system would have individuals with various disabilities competing in the same race or event. This sensitive issue will continue to receive considerable attention. Federal legislation emphasizes the right of students with disabilities to participate in sport programs. Unfortunately, most school districts have not taken this mandate seriously. Some have argued that because their school has too few children with disabilities it is not possible nor financially feasible for them to field a team. Efforts must be undertaken to educate community and school leaders about their responsibility to provide equitable sport programs for individuals with disabilities and to help them identify alternative ways of providing the programs. Creative administrators and empathetic teachers can do much to ensure that children and youth with disabilities are not deprived of the opportunity to participate in sport programs. Given the success of adult athletes with disabilities, such as George Murray's sub-four-minute mile (1985) in a wheelchair, Craig Blanchette's 1993 world record of 3:31, and the notoriety associated with their performances, it is logical that more and more children and youth with disabilities will be inspired to participate in sport (Ball, 1993). As the number of athletes with disabilities increases, individuals with and without disabilities will recognize that "It's ability, not disability, that counts."

Enhancing Activities

1. Organize a group of nondisabled peers and challenge a group of wheelchair athletes to a wheelchair basketball game.
2. Volunteer to participate as a coach or manager of a youth sport team for individuals with disabilities.
3. Review the athletic program offered by a local high school. Document the number of students with disabilities participating in the program. Recommend strategies for increasing the sport opportunities for students with disabilities, such as types of sports to be offered, integrated and segregated considerations, and possibilities for coordinating with other school districts.
4. Interview an athlete with a disability. Obtain information regarding the athlete's reason for participating in sport and his or her perceptions concerning the importance of sport in the athlete's life.
5. Observe an athletic event sponsored by one of the sport organizations for athletes with disabilities. Write a summary of your impressions of the event. How was the event similar and/or different than that provided for nondisabled athletes?
6. Review the classification systems used by the various sport organizations for athletes with disabilities. Engage in a debate with your peers as to which system seems to be best and why.

Selected Readings

Adams, R. C., & McCubbin, J. A. (1991). *Games, sports, and exercises for the physically disabled* (4th ed.). Philadelphia: Lea and Febiger.

Anderson, L. (Ed.). (1987). *Handbook for adapted competitive swimming.* Colorado Springs, CO: United States Swimming Association.

Brookes, P., & Cooper, R. (1987). Plan for equalizing track competition. *Sports 'n Spokes, 13*(3), 13–14.

Bundschuh, E. L. (1979). *Interpreting Public Law 94–142 and Section 504 of the Rehabilitation Act as it relates to athletic participation.* Paper presented at the annual meeting of the National Council of Secondary School Athletic Directors.

Cooper, R. A. (1990). Wheelchair racing sports science: A review. *Journal of Rehabilitation Research and Development, 27*(3), 295–312.

Cooper, R. A., & Bedi, J. F. (1992). An analysis of classification for top 10 finishers in prominent wheelchair road races. *Palaestra, 8*(4), 36–41.

Coutts, K. D., & Schutz, R. W. (1988). Analysis of wheelchair track performances. *Medicine and Science in Sports and Exercise, 20* (2), 188–194.

Curtis, K. (1989). International functional classification systems. *National Wheelchair Athletic Association Newsletter,* Fall, 7–8.

DePauw, K. P., & Clarke, K. S. (1986). Sports for disabled U.S. citizens: Influence of amateur sports act. In C. Sherrill (Ed.), *Sport and disabled athletes* (pp. 41–50). Champaign, IL: Human Kinetics Publishers.

DePauw, K. P., & Gavron, S. J. (1995). *Disability and sport.* Champaign, IL: Human Kinetics Publishers.

Dunn, J. M. (1981). History of sport for the disabled. In *Proceedings: National Association for Physical Education in Higher Education* (pp. 158–167). Champaign, IL: Human Kinetics Publisher.

Dunn, J. M. (1987). Sports for disabled children. In V. Seefeldt (Ed.), *Handbook for youth sports coaches* (pp. 311–335). Reston, VA: American Alliance for Health, Physical Education, Recreation, and Dance.

Dunn, J. M., & Sherrill, C. (1996). Movement for individuals with disabilities. *Quest.*

Guttmann, L. (1976). *Textbook of sport for the disabled.* Bucks, England: HM & M Publishers.

Guttmann, L. (1979). The importance of sport and recreation for the physically disabled. In A. S. Leon & G. Amundson (Eds.), *First international conference on lifestyles and health* (pp. 45–52). Minneapolis: University of Minnesota.

Hansen, K., & Fuller, L. (2003). Varsity wheelers. *Sports 'N Spokes, 29*(1), 34–38.

Higgs, C., Babstock, P., Buck, J., Parsons, C., & Brewer, J. (1990). Wheelchair classifications for track and field events: A performance approach. *Adapted Physical Activity Quarterly, 7*(1), 22–40.

Howell, R. (1978). History of physical education and sport and the disabled. In J. Hall & J. Stiehl (Eds.), *National Infuse Symposium proceedings* (pp. 37–46). Boulder, CO: University of Colorado.

Jones, J. A. (Ed.). (1988). *Training guide to cerebral palsy sports* (3rd ed.). Champaign, IL: Human Kinetics Publishers.

Lai, A. M., Stanish, W. D., & Stanish, H. I. (2000). The young athlete with physical challenges. *Clinics in Sports Medicine, 19*(4), 793–819.

Lindstrom, H. (1986). Sports classification for locomotor disabilities: Integrated versus diagnostic systems. In C. Sherrill (Ed.), *Sport and disabled athletes* (pp. 131–136). Champaign, IL: Human Kinetics Publishers.

Lively, M. W. (2003). Making sure young athletes are fit to compete in Special Olympics. *Contemporary Pediatrics, 20*(1), 101–105.

Mastro, J. V., & Pearson, S. K. (2002). US blind judo team: A brief history. *Palarstra, 18*(3), 22–26.

Sherrill, C. (1986). Social and psychological dimensions of sports for disabled athletes. In C. Sherrill (Ed.), *Sport and disabled athletes* (pp. 21–33). Champaign, IL: Human Kinetics Publishers.

Sherrill, C., Adams-Mushett, C., & Jones, J. (1986). Classification and other issues in sports for blind, cerebral palsied, les autres, and amputee athletes. In C. Sherill (Ed.), *Sport and disabled athletes* (pp. 113–130). Champaign, IL: Human Kinetics Publishers.

Songster, T. B. (1986). The Special Olympics sport program: An international sport program for mentally retarded athletes. In C. Sherrill (Ed.), *Sport and disabled athletes* (pp. 73–79). Champaign, IL: Human Kinetics Publishers.

Squires, J. (1987). Classification—Can the best means to the fairest end be found? *Palaestra, 3*(4), 45–46, 48.

Stohkendl, H. (1986). The new classification system for wheelchair basketball. In C. Sherrill (Ed.), *Sport and disabled athletes* (pp. 101–112). Champaign, IL: Human Kinetics Publishers.

United States Association for Blind Athletes. (1981). *Athletic handbook.* Beach Haven Park, NJ: Author.

Weiss, M., & Curtis, K. A. (1986). Controversies in medical classification of wheelchair athletes. In C. Sherrill (Ed.), *Sport and disabled athletes* (pp. 93–100). Champaign, IL: Human Kinetics Publishers.

Winnick, J. P., & Short, F. X. (Eds.). (1981). *Special athletic opportunities for individuals with handicapping conditions.* Brockport, NY: State University College of New York at Brockport.

Glossary

abduction withdrawal of a part from the axis of the body; the act of turning outward.

acetabulum large cup-shaped cavity on the lateral surface of the os coxae in which the head of the femur articulates.

achondroplasia those individuals with predominantly short limbs.

acuity clearness of vision.

Adapted Physical Activity Council the organization within AAHPERD responsible for providing services to professionals working with the disabled.

adapted physical education refers to those programs that have the same objectives as the regular physical education program but in which adjustments are made in the regular offerings to meet the needs and abilities of exceptional students.

adduct to draw toward the median line of the body or toward a neighboring part.

adventitious acquired after birth through accident or illness; opposite of congenital.

affective pertaining to an individual's feelings, emotions, moods, temperaments. Used in special education to refer to objectives that deal with attitudes and feelings.

afferent nerves nerves that convey impulses from the sensory endings toward the nerve centers or central nervous system.

agnosia inability to recognize persons or objects. May be restricted to a particular sense modality, as in the following:

auditory agnosia inability to recognize speech sounds.

spatial agnosia inability to find one's way about familiar places.

tactile agnosia inability to recognize objects by touch.

visual agnosia inability to recognize objects that are seen, or color.

agonistic muscle a muscle opposed in action by another muscle.

AIDS acronym for acquired immunodeficiency syndrome. Also referred to as HIV.

allergen any substance that causes an allergic reaction when it comes in contact with the body.

amblyopia the inability to focus or coordinate both eyes simultaneously on the same object; commonly referred to as the lazy eye syndrome.

ambulatory walking or able to walk.

amelia a condition in which all four limbs are absent.

amelioration improvement, as of the condition of a patient.

ament term referring to intellectual subnormality.

Ameslan slang expression for American sign language. This communication system, used by deaf persons, employs the arms, hands, and parts of the body to represent concepts.

amniocentesis a medical procedure used to draw amniotic fluid from the uterus to determine certain aspects of fetal development.

amphetamine a drug with stimulant properties frequently used to treat conditions such as depression, narcolepsy, and obesity; commonly called "uppers."

anemia a condition of the blood in which the quantity of the hemoglobin or the number of red blood cells is deficient.

angina spasmodic, choking, or suffocative pain.

ankylosis abnormal immobility and consolidation of a joint.

anomaly anything unusual, irregular, or contrary to general rule.

anorexia a condition that causes a partial or complete loss of appetite; usually related to a psychological disorder.

anoxia reduction of oxygen content of the blood to a level insufficient to maintain adequate functioning of the tissue.

antagonistic muscle muscle that acts in opposition to the action of another muscle.

antigen a substance that stimulates production of antibodies when introduced into the body.

antigravity muscles muscles that serve to keep the body in an upright position.

aphasia impaired ability to understand or use language meaningfully.

apraxia difficulty in carrying out a specific, purposeful movement; a condition in which movements are awkward and slow; inability to determine what the movement shall be and to recognize the movements necessary for the act.

aquaphobia fear of water.

aqueous humor fluid occupying the space between the lens and the cornea of the eye.

arteriosclerosis hardening of the arteries.

arthrodesis surgical fixation of a joint by fusion of the joint surfaces.

arthrogryposis a congenital severe crippling disease of children in which the joints become fixed or bend only partially.

asthenis lack or loss of strength and energy.

ataxia failure of muscle coordination.

athetoid a type of cerebral palsy involving involuntary occurrence of slow, sinuous, writhing movements, especially severe in the hands.

atonia lack of muscle tone; may be due to nervous system disease, as in infantile paralysis, or to muscle disease, as in muscular dystrophy. May also be due to prolonged bed rest or illness.

atrophy a general wasting away or shrinking due to destruction of the tissue; may be said of any organ, but often used in reference to muscles.

audiogram a graph of the minimal level of sound a person can hear at least 50 percent of the time measured at several frequencies for each ear.

aura a subjective sensation that precedes and marks the onset of a paroxysmal intensification seizure, such as an epileptic seizure.

axillary area hollow formed where arm joins the body at the shoulder; the armpit.

Babinski reflex extension of the toes when the sole of the foot is touched. This reflex is considered normal in infants but may be a sign of nervous disorder in adults.

barbiturates a group of drugs that are used medically for relieving tension, anxiety, and pain and as an anticonvulsant in treating epilepsy.

baseline observational data recorded prior to the beginning of a treatment effect or intervention program.

behavior modification systematic use of the theories of learning to weaken, strengthen, or maintain a behavior.

bilateral having two sides.

blindism mannerism of the blind; purposeless movement.

body image awareness of the position of the body in space and how the body moves.

bulimia a self-induced process used to rid the body of food before it is digested.

bursa a sac or pouch containing fluid useful in reducing friction, such as that found within joints.

calcaneus heel bone.

cataract an eye abnormality caused by opacity of the lens, resulting in a visual impairment or blindness.

catatonic a form of schizophrenia characterized by negative reactions, phase of stupor or excitement, and impulsive or stereotyped behavior.

catheter a narrow tube that can be inserted into the body to empty the bladder or kidneys.

central deafness hearing impairment due to damage to the auditory nerve or in the centers of hearing in the brain cortex.

cephalocaudal used to describe development of the individual that proceeds from the head to the feet.

cerebellum the lower rear area of the brain responsible for fine motor coordination.

cerebral palsy a condition resulting from brain damage that is manifested by various types of neuromuscular disabilities.

cerebrospinal fluid the fluid that surrounds the brain and spinal cord.

cervical pertaining to the neck.

chemotherapy treatment of disease by chemical agents.

chorea minor also called St. Vitus dance or Sydenham's chorea. Acute disease occurring chiefly in children; no specific treatment. Disease of nervous system that causes aimless, wandering movements, especially of the hands and fingers.

choroid thin, dark brown, vascular coat of the posterior of the eyeball.

chromosome a chainlike structure found in the nucleus of cells, composed of many genes, responsible for hereditary factors.

cleft palate a congenital condition that results in an opening in the roof of the mouth (palate), which may extend through the upper lip.

cochlea the organ of hearing located in the inner ear; shaped like a snail.

cognitive refers to the mental process of reasoning, memory, comprehension, and judgment.

coma a state of profound and prolonged unconsciousness usually caused by a disease, such as diabetes.

compensation an attempt to offset some shortcoming or limitation by developing some special talent or ability.

congenital condition present at birth.

conjunctiva the delicate membrane that covers the exposed surface of the eyeball.

continence the ability to retain urine.

contracture shortening of a muscle in distortion; a permanent condition.

cornea the outer coating of the eyeball responsible for the refraction of light rays.

coxa plana inflammation of the hip joint.

craniosynostosis premature closures of the sutures in the skull.

cretinism a form of severe failure of the function of the thyroid gland.

cyanosis a bluish color of the skin and mucous membranes resulting from insufficient oxygen in the blood.

cybernetics self-guidance and control of one's behavior.

decibel a unit of measurement used to record the loudness (intensity) of sound.

delusion an untrue belief held by an individual that cannot be changed by reasoning or explanation of the true facts.

dementia deterioration of emotional or psychological functioning.

dermis innermost layer of skin (beneath the epidermis), consisting of a dense bed of vascular connective tissue.

diabetes a disease in which the body exhibits an inability to properly use the starches and sugars it ingests.

Dilantin an anticonvulsant drug frequently prescribed to control convulsive types of disorders such as epileptic seizures.

diplegia bilateral paralysis; paralysis affecting like parts on both sides of body.

directionality a perception of direction.

distal remote; farther from any point of reference.

distractibility a behavioral characteristic in which the individual is unable to refrain from responding to unnecessary stimuli.

dorsal pertaining to the back.

dorsiflexion the act of bending a part backward.

Down syndrome a specific type of mental retardation resulting from a chromosomal defect or abnormality.

dynamometer instrument that measures muscular strength.

dysmenorrhea painful menstruation.

dyspnea difficult or labored breathing.

echolalia repetition of words, sounds, or sentences spoken by another person.

ectomorph a fragile, thin person having a large surface area and thin muscles and subcutaneous tissue.

edema excessive fluid in the tissue, causing swelling.

educable term used to suggest that one is capable of learning, of being educated, as in the educable mentally retarded.

efferent nerves nerves that convey impulses outward from the nerve centers or central nervous system.

electrocardiogram (EKG) record of electrical impulses produced by contraction of the heart muscle.

electroencephalogram (EEG) record of brain waves.

electromyogram (EMG) record of the changes in electric potential of muscle.

embolus a clot that obstructs a blood vessel.

encephalitis inflammation of the brain.

encopresis inability to control one's bowels.

endogenous describes a condition that occurs from internal rather than external factors, such as hereditary conditions.

endomorph a person with a soft, round body; large trunk and thighs; and tapering extremities.

enuresis involuntary discharge of urine, usually during sleep.

epidermis outermost and nonvascular layer of the skin.

epilepsy a disturbance in the electrochemical activity of the brain that causes seizures and convulsions.

epinephrine a hormone secreted by the adrenal medulla; increases blood pressure and cardiac output; accelerates heart rate and stimulates heart muscle.

epiphysis the growing end of a bone.

etiology the cause of a condition or disease.

euphoria an emotional or psychological sense of well-being and optimism; usually describes a temporary mood.

eversion turning outward, as of the feet (can apply to any part).

exogenous describes a condition that occurs from external rather than internal factors, such as cultural deprivation.

extinction a behavior modification technique used to eliminate an undesirable behavior by the removal of reinforcers.

fetus the developing organism from approximately six weeks after conception to birth.

fibrosis formation of fibrous tissue; usually in a tumor called a fibroma.

finger spelling a communication method used by the deaf in which words are spelled out by different combinations of hand and finger motions.

flaccid flabby.

foramen a natural opening or passage; especially one into or through a bone.

forced expired volume the amount of air which can be forcibly expired in one minute.

fovea the small, central area of the retina in which vision is the most distinct.

genetic refers to hereditary features transmitted by chromosomes from parents to children.

geriatrics branch of medicine that clinically treats problems of the aged, including senility.

gerontology scientific study of the problems of the aged.

gestation the period of pregnancy; time in which the fetus is developing within the uterus.

glaucoma a condition of the eye in which there is excessive internal pressure on the eye; if untreated, will impair vision.

glenoid fossa (of scapula) socket of the shoulder.

grand mal major form of epilepsy; characterized by loss of consciousness and convulsions.

handedness the preference of either the right or the left hand to perform tasks requiring the use of only one hand.

haptic pertains to the sense of touch as determined by tactile and kinesthetic awareness.

hematoma a swelling containing blood.

hemiplegia paralysis of one side of the body.

hemoglobin the oxygen-carrying transporters found in red blood cells.

hemophilia a condition, usually hereditary, associated with the inability of the blood to clot following an injury.

hernia protrusion of an organ or tissue through an abnormal opening of a body part.

hertz a unit of measurement to determine the frequency of sound.

Hodgkin's disease a disease of the blood. Pseudoleukemia.

hydrocephalus abnormal accumulation of fluid in the cranial vault (water on the brain); causes mental weakness, convulsions, and enlargement of head.

hyperactivity abnormally increased activity.

hyperextend extreme extension of a limb or part.

hyperglycemia condition in which there is excessive sugar in the blood.

hyperkinetic excessive movement.

hyperopia farsightedness; a condition in which people have difficulty seeing near objects because the image focuses behind the retina instead of on it.

hyperplasia refers to the number of fat cells.

hypertension a condition characterized by abnormally high blood pressure.

hypertrophia refers to the size of fat cells.

hypertrophy enlargement of an organ or part.

hypoglycemia an abnormally low level of blood sugar caused by an increase in metabolism.

hypokinetic showing abnormally decreased mobility or motor function.

hypoplasia cerebral; defective development of the brain.

idiopathic of unknown cause.

ileostomy a surgical procedure for diverting the feces from the normal passage through an opening in the abdomen.

incontinence inability to control bowel or bladder function.

inguinal hernia hernia of the groin.

institutionalization the placement of individuals with disabilities within residential settings.

insulin a hormone produced by the pancreas used in the treatment of diabetes.

integration describes a setting in special education in which youngsters with and without disabilities are educated together.

intelligence quotient an index of intelligence as determined by standardized intelligence tests. The IQ is computed by dividing the mental age by the chronological age and multiplying by 100.

inversion a turning inward, inside out, upside down, or other reversal of the normal relation to a part.

iris the colored portion of the eye; contracts or expands involuntarily depending upon the amount of light entering it.

isometric (exercise) pertaining to a contracture of a muscle when it is under constant tension.

isotonic (exercise) pertaining to a contracture of a muscle when it is not under constant tension.

jaundice a yellow coloring of the eyes and skin caused by excess bile pigments in the blood and body tissues.

kernicterus a condition resulting from blood incompatibility between the mother and developing fetus.

kinesthesia (kinesthesis) the sense by which muscular motion, weight, position, and so on are perceived.

kinesthesis (method of teaching) involves the adjustment of the body segments to achieve successful performance of a skill.

kyphosis condition characterized by an abnormally increased convexity in the curvature of thoracic spine as viewed from the side.

labeling used in special education to refer to the attachment of a generalized name, such as "mental retardation," to a group of children.

larynx structure located in the upper part of the trachea that contains the vocal cords and essential musculature for the production of speech.

lateral flexion to stretch out to the side of the midline of the body.

laterality internal awareness of the two sides of the body.

least restrictive environment an expression used to emphasize the fact that individuals with disabilities should be educated in the environment that provides for them the greatest opportunity to be successful, including the regular educational setting when possible and desirable.

les autres French term for "the others."

lesion any pathological or traumatic discontinuity of tissue or loss of function of a part.

lip reading speech reading; a skill taught to the deaf and hard of hearing that enables them to understand spoken words by observing the context of the situation and the visual cues of speech, such as lip movement and facial expressions.

little people the term used to describe those individuals who are short or small in stature.

lordosis abnormally increased concavity in the curvature of the lumbar spine as viewed from the side.

low-incidence disability those disabilities that are few in number in comparison to other disability populations; for example, deaf-blind.

lumbar pertaining to the lower back.

luxation dislocation.

macrocephaly a condition in which the head is unusually large.

macula the part of the retina that provides the clearest vision.

mainstreaming placement of students with disabilities into regular educational programs with assistance, when necessary, of appropriate support personnel.

malignant virulent; tending to go from bad to worse.

malleolus a rounded process, such as the protuberance on either side of the ankle joint.

manuometer an apparatus for measuring the strength of the grip of the hand.

maturation physical and behavioral changes attributed primarily to the innate process of growth rather than the influence of the environment.

meninges membrane that surrounds the spinal cord and brain.

meningocele a saclike pouch that protrudes from the vertebral column that contains cerebrospinal fluid but no spinal nerves.

meningomyelocele a meningocele pouch protruding from the vertebral column that contains cerebrospinal fluid and spinal nerves.

menorrhagia excessive uterine bleeding during menstruation; the duration of the flow is also greater than usual.

mesomorphic a body with a relative preponderance of muscle, bone, and connective tissue.

MET metabolic rate at work divided by resting metabolic rate.

metabolic pertaining to the nature of all the physical and chemical processes by which a living organism is maintained.

metastasis transfer of disease from one organ to another.

microcephalus a condition resulting in an unusually small head and reduced brain size.

mitral valve left atrioventricular valve in the heart.

mobility training techniques used with blind individuals to help them to move about in their environment safely and with assurance.

modality employment of a therapeutic agent; limited usually to physical agents.

modeling a technique in which the teacher or another student demonstrates a skill or an appropriate behavior.

monoplegia paralysis of but a single part; as facial, central brachial.

Moro reflex a startle reflex associated with infants caused by a loud sharp noise or by being dropped gently on their backs; characterized by fanning out of the arms and crying.

motor aphasia inability to speak because of a lack of muscle coordination to form words.

motor fitness refers to those components of motor skill learning (coordination, balance, speed, agility, and so on) that are related to neuromuscular control patterns and do not respond to progressive overloading.

multidisabled possessing two or more disabling conditions at the same time.

multiple sclerosis a progressive disease in which the myelin sheath surrounding the nerves degenerates and causes failures in the body's neurological system.

muscular dystrophy a degenerative, noncontagious disease of the muscular system, characterized by weakness and atrophy of the muscles.

mute unable to speak.

myelin a white, fatty-like substance that forms a protective sheath around certain nerve fibers.

myopia near-sightedness; the eyeball is too long from front to back and images are brought to focus in front of the retina.

myositis inflammation of a muscle.

narcolepsy a condition in which an individual has uncontrollable episodes of deep sleep at irregular times.

natal pertaining to birth.

necrosis local death of tissue.

neonatal refers to the first month of life of a newborn.

neoplasia formation of a tumor; a new or abnormal growth.

nephritis inflammation of the kidney.

nerve plexuses a network or tangle of nerves.

neuron structural unit of the nervous system; a nerve cell.

noncategorical refers to special education programs that do not differentiate between or label the various exceptionalities requiring special services.

normalization the principle of educating and treating individuals with disabilities in the "normal" environment of the nondisabled to the greatest extent possible.

nystagmus an involuntary movement of the eyeballs; usually affects both eyes and is associated with impaired vision.

ocular term that refers to the eye.

olfactory pertaining to or relating to the sense of smell.

ophthalmia severe inflammation of the eye or of the conjunctiva.

optacon an instrument used to convert print into tactile images enabling the blind to "read" print.

optic nerve a cranial nerve that transmits nerve impulses to the brain, making sight possible.

organic term used to refer to known structural or neurological abnormality; inherent as contrasted to functional.

orifice a natural external opening of the body, such as the mouth and nose.

orthopedic pertaining to the correction of deformities.

orthotics the field of knowledge relating to orthopedic appliances and their use.

orthotist an individual skilled in making orthopedic appliances.

Osgood-Schlatter disease osteochondrosis of the tuberosity of the tibia.

ossification the formation of bone or of a bony substance.

osteochondrosis a disease of one or more of the growth or ossification centers in children.

osteogenesis imperfecta a hereditary condition in which the bones do not grow normally and break easily.

osteomyelitis inflammation of the bone marrow.

osteoporosis abnormal diminution of bone density and weight due to failure of osteoblasts to lay down bone matrix.

other health impaired One of the categories of disability recognized under PL 101-476. The term refers to limited strength, vitality, or alertness due to chronic or acute health problems which adversely affect a child's education performance.

otitis media an inflammation or infection of the middle ear that can result in a conductive hearing loss.

overt an action or behavior that can be observed directly.

pancreas a gland situated behind the stomach that produces digestive enzymes and insulin.

paralysis refers to loss or impairment of voluntary motion and sensation.

paraplegia paralysis of the legs and lower part of the body, motion and sensation being affected.

paroxysm a sudden recurrence or intensification of symptoms.

patella knee cap.

pathogenic giving origin to disease or morbid symptoms.

pathological pertaining to the branch of medicine that treats disease.

pathology the branch of medicine that deals with the essential nature of disease, especially of the structural and functional changes in tissues and organs of the body that cause or are caused by disease.

perceptual disability inability to consciously and mentally register a sensory stimulus.

perinatal refers to the period of time shortly before, during, or immediately after birth.

peripheral nerve a nerve situated near an outward part of the surface.

perseverate continuous purposeless repetition of an act or behavior.

petit mal a form of epilepsy characterized by a brief blackout with only minor rhythmic movements.

phobia a persistent and unreasonable fear.

physical fitness the functional capacity of the various systems of the body that support exercise, specifically muscle strength, muscle endurance, flexibility, cardiorespiratory endurance, and body composition.

plantar pertaining to the sole of the foot.

plexus a network or tangle.

pneumothorax an accumulation of air or gas in the pleural cavity.

postnatal occurring after birth.

prenatal existing or occurring before birth.

prognosis prediction of probable result of attack of disease.

pronation act of assuming the prone position.

prone lying face down.

prophylaxis the prevention of disease.

proprioceptors sense receptors located in the muscles, joints, and tendons that provide information about the location of the body and its parts and whether or not they are in motion.

prosthesis artificial appliances, such as arms or legs.

proximal nearest.

proximodistal term describing the control of body parts developmentally proceeding from the center to the periphery.

psychogenic deafness deafness having an emotional or psychological origin as opposed to an organic basis.

psychomotor the interaction of motor behavior and psychological processes, primarily perception.

psychomotor seizure a type of epileptic seizure in which the individual goes through a period of inappropriate activity of which he or she is not aware.

psychosomatic illness induced by mental or emotional pressures.

puberty refers to that period in life when an individual's sex organs become functional and the secondary sexual characteristics appear.

quadriplegia paralysis of all four limbs.

rationalization a defense mechanism in which one substitutes a socially acceptable, but not real, reason for some behavior.

regression returning to an earlier and more immature stage of development in response to frustration.

reinforcement an event or reward that increases the probability of a behavior it follows.

renal pertaining to the kidneys or kidney function.

repression the unconscious inhibition of unpleasant memories.

residual paralysis paralysis left behind after therapy has remedied as much of the paralysis as possible.

resource room used in special education to refer to a setting in a school where students with disabilities can go for special assistance with academic or motor skills.

retina inner layer of the eye that is sensitive to light.

rheumatic fever a disease, usually following a streptococcal infection, that is characterized by inflammation of the joints, fever, chorea, and abdominal pain.

rigidity tenseness of movement; inflexibility.

rubella German measles. A communicable disease transmitted by a virus; particularly dangerous to pregnant women during the first trimester.

sacral situate near the sacrum.

sacrum the triangular-shaped bone formed usually by five fused vertebrae that are wedged dorsally between the two hip bones.

schizophrenia a severe mental disorder in which a person is unable to separate self from reality.

sclera the tough, protective covering of the eye.

scoliosis a lateral deviation in the straight vertical line of the spine.

screening in the context of special education, an attempt to locate or identify children who appear to be in need of special help.

seizure a sudden change of consciousness caused by an abnormal brain discharge; associated with epilepsy.

semicircular canal small circular tubes of the inner ear, concerned with balance.

severely disabled a general term used to describe individuals who are experiencing severe physical, emotional, or mental problems, or a combination of these, requiring prolonged and intense treatment.

shaping the gradual molding of desired behavior.

shunt a device used to drain, or provide a bypass, for excess cerebrospinal fluid.

sign language a form of communication, frequently used by the hearing impaired, that involves a systematic use of gestures.

slow learner refers to a student whose academic progress is less than expected for the individual's chronological age.

somatotype a particular category of body build based on physical characteristics.

spasm involuntary muscle contraction.

spastic characterized by sudden, violent, involuntary contraction of a muscle or group of muscles; producing involuntary movement and distortion.

special education specially designed instruction, at no cost to the parent, to meet the unique needs of a disabled child, including classroom instruction, instruction in physical education, home instruction, and instruction in hospitals and institutions.

special physical education refers to programs designed to enhance the physical and motor fitness of individuals with disabilities through modified and developmentally sequenced sport, game, and movement experiences individualized for each participant.

specific gravity weight of body divided by weight of equal amount of water.

spinous process pertaining to the spine or to a spinelike process.

spirometer an apparatus that can be used to measure the flow of air into and out of the lungs.

sprain tearing or stretching of ligaments and tendons.

standard error of measurement the standard deviation of the error distribution around a true score.

static balance   balance while at rest or not in motion.

stenosis   incomplete opening of a valve that restricts blood from flowing.

sternum   breast bone.

stoma   an external opening of the body created by surgery.

strabismus   a condition in which the eyes cross due to a weakness of the eye muscles.

strain   tearing of muscles.

stretch reflex   the tendency of a muscle to contract as a reflex when it is extended suddenly.

sublimation   the replacement of a desire or impulse that cannot be satisfied with one that can.

subluxation   partial dislocation of a joint.

supination   act of assuming the supine position.

supine   lying on the back, face upward.

syndactylism   describes a condition in which an individual is born with webbed fingers or toes, or both.

syndrome   a set of symptoms that occur together.

tactile   refers to the sense of touch.

talus   the highest of the tarsal bones and the one that articulates with the tibia and fibula to form the ankle joint.

task analysis   the breaking down of a skill into smaller, sequentially ordered phases and steps.

tensiometer   an apparatus by which the tensile strength of materials can be determined; adapted to measure strength of muscles.

thermal injuries   burns caused by several things including fires, chemicals, and scalding from extremely hot water.

thoracic   pertaining to the chest.

thrombophlebitis   condition in which inflammation of the vein wall has preceded the formation of the thrombus (blood clot).

thrombosis   the formation, development, or presence of a thrombus (blood clot) in a blood vessel or heart.

tibia   the inner and larger bone of the leg below the knee.

tic   an involuntary twitching and contraction of a small group of muscles; frequently occurs in the facial area.

timeout   refers to a behavior modification procedure in which a student is removed from a setting for a designated period of time following inappropriate behavior.

token   an object given to a student as a secondary reinforcer to be traded later for a primary reinforcer.

torticollis   a spasmodic contraction of neck muscles resulting in drawing the head to one side; wryneck.

total communication   a communication system used by the deaf or severely hearing impaired that combines the oral (speech reading) and manual (finger spelling and sign language) approaches.

trailing   a mobility technique used by the blind with which they trace lightly over a straight surface, such as a wall or table top, with the back of the fingers.

tranquilizer   a drug designed to quiet and calm without producing a hypnotic effect.

transverse arch   arch in the area of the ball of the foot; the five metatarsals form the arch.

trauma   wound or injury.

tremor   involuntary trembling or quivering.

triplegia   paralysis of three extremities.

tunnel vision   a condition in which a person's visual field is severely restricted, producing an effect similar to that of looking through a tunnel.

tympanic membrane   the eardrum; a thin membrane between the outer and inner ear.

unilateral   affecting but one side.

valgus   away from the median line.

varus   bent inward; usually referring to a deformity.

vertigo   a disorder of the sense of balance that causes dizziness.

vital capacity   the change in pulmonary volume between a maximal inspiratory effort followed by a maximal expiratory effort.

vitreous humor   the fluid in the back chamber of the eye that fills the space between the retina and the lens.

Credits

Figure 1.1	Michael Beets.
Figure 1.2	Michael Beets.
Figure 1.3	Defense Visual Information Center
Figure 2.1	Michael Beets.
Figure 2.2	Jill Campbell.
Figure 2.3	Jill Campbell.
Figure 2.4	Jill Campbell.
Figure 2.5	Jill Campbell.
Figure 2.6	Jill Campbell.
Figure 2.7a, b	Jill Campbell.
Figure 2.8	Jill Campbell.
Figure 2.12	Michael Beets.
Figure 2.13	Jill Campbell.
Figure 2.14	Jill Campbell.
Figure 2.16	Courtesy of Oregon State University IMPACT.
Figure 3.7	Courtesy of Oregon State University IMPACT.
Figure 3.9	Courtesy of Oregon State University IMPACT.
Figure 4.1a	© 2010 R. Gino Santa Maria. Used under license from Shutterstock, Inc.
Figure 4.1b	© 2010 Myron Pronyshynk. Used under license from Shutterstock, Inc.
Figure 4.2	Courtesy of Oregon State University IMPACT.
Figure 4.3	Michael Beets.
Figure 5.3	Courtesy of Oregon State University IMPACT.
Figure 5.4	Michael Beets.
Figure 5.8	Michael Beets.
Figure 5.10	Courtesy of Oregon State University Special Physical and Motor Fitness Clinic.
Figure 6.6	*Source*: Adapted from *The Learner Outcomes Guide for Physical Education K-10*, pp. 1–35 by Minneapolis Public Schools, 1991, Minneapolis: Minneapolis Public Schools.
Figure 6.8	*Source*: *Physical Activity for Individuals with Mental Retardation: Infancy through Adulthood* by Carl B. Eichstaedt and Barry W. Lavay, Human Kinetics Books, 1992.
Figure 6.9	*Source*: *Strategies for Inclusion: A Handbook for Physical Educators* by Lauren Lieberman and Cathy Houston-Wilson, Human Kinetics, 2002.
Figure 6.13	From *Denver Developmental Screening Test* by W.K. Frankenburg and J.B. Dodds. Copyright © 1990 by Denver Developmental Materials, Inc. Reprinted by permission.
Figure 6.14	*Source*: From *Assessment in Adapted Physical Education* by Werder and Kalakian, 1985, Macmillian Publishing Co.
Figure 7.6	Michael Beets.
Figure 7.9	Courtesy of Oregon State University IMPACT.
Figure 7.16	Jill Campbell.
Figure 8.1	Jill Campbell.
Figure 8.2	Jill Campbell.
Figure 8.5	Courtesy of Oregon State University IMPACT.
Figure 9.2a	Photo courtesy of www.nei.nih.gov
Figure 9.2b	Photo courtesy of www.nei.nih.gov
Figure 9.11	© 2006 JupiterImages Corporation
Figure 11.4	Michael Beets.
Figure 11.5	Courtesy of Oregon State University IMPACT.
Figure 11.6	Courtesy of Oregon State University IMPACT.
Figure 12.3	Courtesy of Oregon State University IMPACT.
Figure 12.5	Courtesy of Oregon State University IMPACT.
Figure 14.1a	Courtesy of Galina Pianykh.
Figure 14.1b	Courtesy of Mary Hadsall.
Figure 14.3	Michael Beets.
Figure 15.1	Copyright © by CEED: Center for Early Education and Development, University of Minnesota. Reprinted by permission.
Figure 15.2	Michael Beets.
Figure 15.4	Courtesy of Oregon State University IMPACT.
Figure 15.6	Courtesy of Oregon State University IMPACT.
Figure 15.7	Courtesy of Oregon State University IMPACT.
Figure 15.8	Jill Campbell.
Figure 16.1	Michael Beets.
Figure 16.4	© 2006 JupiterImages Corporation
Figure 16.5	Courtesy of Oregon State University IMPACT.

Figure 16.8	Courtesy of The Children's Physical Development Clinic, Bridgewater State College, Bridgewater, MA.
Figure 17.2	Copyright © National Center on Physical Activity and Disability (NCPAD). Reprinted by permission. All rights reserved.
Figure 17.4	Courtesy of Oregon State University IMPACT.
Figure 17.6	Courtesy of Oregon State University IMPACT.
Figure 19.2	Courtesy of Oregon State University IMPACT.
Figure 22.2	Jill Campbell.
Figure 22.4	Courtesy of Oregon State University IMPACT.
Figure 23.1	Photos courtesy of Sammons Preston Rolyan.
Figure 23.2	Photo courtesy of Sammons Preston Rolyan.
Figure 23.3c	Photo courtesy of Sammons Preston Rolyan.
Figure 23.5a, b	Photo courtesy of Sammons Preston Rolyan.
Figure 23.5c	Photo © Rifton Equipment. Used by permission.
Figure 23.7	Photo courtesy of S & S Worldwide.
Figure 23.8	Photo © Rifton Equipment. Used by permission.
Figure 23.9	Photo courtesy of Sunrise Medical Inc.
Figure 23.10	Photo courtesy of Sammons Preston Rolyan.
Figure 23.13	Photo courtesy of Sammons Preston Rolyan.
Figure 23.17 a, b, d, f	Photo courtesy of Sunrise Medical Inc.
Figure 23.18	Photo courtesy of Ossur.
Figure 23.21	Photo courtesy of Sammons Preston Rolyan.
Figure 24.14	Courtesy of Oregon State University IMPACT.
Figure 25.1	Axis Dance Company. Photo by Andy Mogg.
Hokey Pokey (page CD 122):	Words and music by Charles P. Macak, Tafft Baker, and Larry LaPrise. Copyright © 1950 Sony/ATV Songs LLC. Copyright renewed. All rights administered by Sony/ATV Music Publishing, 8 Music Square West, Nashville, TN 37203. International Copyright Secured. All rights reserved.
Figure 26.1a	Courtesy of Jeremiah Burke.
Figure 26.1b	Courtesy of Rossmiller Photography.
Figure 26.4	Courtesy of Access to Recreation, Inc. 1-800-634-4351, www.AccessTR.com
Figure 26.5a	Courtesy of Maddak, Inc.
Figure 26.5b	Courtesy of Access to Recreation, Inc. 1-800-634-4351, www.AccessTR.com
Figure 26.7	Photo courtesy of Sunrise Medical Inc.
Figure 26.9	Courtesy of TRS, Inc.
Figure 26.12	Photo courtesy of Ossur.
Figure 27.6	Courtesy of The Children's Physical Development Clinic, Bridgewater State College, Bridgewater, MA.
Figure 28.1	Courtesy of John Joseph, Shoot-A-Way, Inc.
Figure 28.2	Courtesy of Curt Beamer, Paralyzed Veterans of America, with permission of Sports 'N Spokes.
Figure 28.3	Courtesy of Curt Beamer, Paralyzed Veterans of America, with permission of Sports 'N Spokes.
Figure 28.7	Courtesy of The Children's Physical Development Clinic, Bridgewater State College, Bridgewater, MA.
Figure 28.9	Courtesy of Delfina Colby, Paralyzed Veterans of America, with permission of Sports 'N Spokes.

Author Index

Subject Index